INTRODUC

DRAGON AGE INQUISITION

FOREWORD

Three and a half years ago, *Dragon Age's* executive producer, my boss and friend Mark Darrah, said to me: "I want the next *Dragon Age* to be somewhere between 20 and 200 hours. Get on that." What he meant was that he wanted a game that would scale, that you could play the way you wanted to.

A challenge to be sure, but a few months later I was standing in front of the team pitching the idea of a shift to activity-driven gameplay. Rather than major story moments leading directly to more story moments, our mission became giving the player a goal to achieve and letting him or her decide how to achieve it.

In doing so, we would present a wide variety of activities available in a vast world that encouraged true discovery. After achieving that goal, the player could dive back into rich story content, with the hope that different players would be able to share stories of how they got there, and have each be different.

Add to all this a shift to a spectacular new graphics engine, the next generation of console hardware and online exploration, cooperative adventuring for the first time in the series, and it would be understated to declare *Inquisition* "ambitious."

The team rose to every challenge: the art and animation team's attention to detail, programmers building an intricate tapestry of systems, designers assembling all the pieces, producers scheduling thousand-hour projects, and the testers who have hammered on this massive game day after day. I could go on, but all that needs be said is that it was an honor and a privilege to work with them on an undertaking so grand as this.

Here we are, at the end of a very long road. I have been playing the game for months and I still find something new on each pass. You'll have an edge on me, though. You hold in your hands an exhaustively researched guide to *Inquisition's* story, characters, and massive regions. Caves to explore, ancient mysteries to uncover, loot and gearing, and perspectives from the developers—I hope you enjoy it as much as we have truly enjoyed crafting the game.

— Mike Laidlaw, Creative Director

INQUISITION

TIMELINE OF THE WORLD

-186 ANCIENT

> ANDRASTE INTRODUCES THE MAKER

Andraste preaches of a new creator, whom she calls the Maker. The more she says, the more her following grows. Maferath uses her teachings to unite the Alamarri clans under his authority.

-130 ANCIENT

> CHANT OF LIGHT

Andraste's disciples create the Chant of Light, collecting her teachings into hymns.

-100 ANCIENT

> THE FIRST INQUISITION

The Inquisition is founded around this time. The loose association of Andrastian hard-liners hunt heretics and mages in the name of the Maker.

8:98 BLESSED

> HOUSE TETHRAS IS EXILED

House Tethras is exiled to the surface for denying the Voice of the Ancestors and willfully manipulating the sacred Provings.

8:96 BLESSED

> QUEEN MOIRA IS ASSASSINATED

Queen Moira is assassinated. Orlesian forces leverage her death to tighten their grip on Ferelden. Her son Maric escapes.

2:30 GLORY

> WINTER PALACE RETREAT

The Winter Palace, by far the most prominent structure in Halamshiral, becomes a regular seasonal retreat for the empress and selected Orlesian nobility.

8:99 BLESSED

> DRAGONS RETURN

Believed hunted to extinction, dragons emerge first in Antiva, then devastate rural Orlais and Nevarra. Repeated attempts to cull their numbers end in heavy casualties.

9:22 DRAGON

> CASSANDRA PENTAGHAST NAMED A HAND OF THE DIVINE

The Grand Cathedral is set upon by dragons during a 10-year gathering of Chantry faithful. A young Seeker named Cassandra Pentaghast foils what is revealed to be a conspiracy to kill Divine Beatrix III. She is named a hand of the Divine.

-186 -130 -100 2:30 -3 1:1 1:20 2:46

-3 ANCIENT

> CHANTRY IS CREATED

Drakon formalizes the Cult of the Maker, creating the Chantry.

1:1 DIVINE

> FIRST DIVINE

Divine Justinia I is named the first Divine of the new Chantry.

1:20 DIVINE

> NEVARRAN ACCORD

The Chantry and the Inquisition sign the Nevarran Accord. Senior members of the Inquisition form the Seekers of Truth.

1:20 DIVINE

> CIRCLE OF MAGI IS CREATED

The Circle of Magi is created as part of the Nevarran Accord. Mages are now formally permitted to practice magic under the close watch of the Chantry.

1:20 DIVINE

> TEMPLAR ORDER IS FORMED

With the creation of the Circle, the Templar Order is formed to police magic use.

2:46 GLORY

> PENTAGHAST SEIZES NEVARRA

Caspar Pentaghast of Hunter Fell seizes control of the city-state Nevarra.

9:01 DRAGON

> THE DRAGON AGE BEGINS

The Dragon Age begins. It is predicted to be an age of violence and upheaval.

9:10 DRAGON

> GREY WARDENS RETURN TO FERELDEN

King Maric allows the Grey Wardens to return to Ferelden after two ages of exile for their failed coup attempt.

9:20 DRAGON

> CELENE BECOMES EMPRESS

Empress Celene I ascends to the throne in Orlais.

9:20 DRAGON

> FERELDEN AND ORLAIS MAKE PEACE

Soon after Celene I assumes the Orlesian throne, Ferelden and Orlais officially make peace.

9:31 Dragon

> THE FIFTH BLIGHT ENDS

A united Ferelden, led by the Hero of Ferelden, slays Urthemiel at the Battle of Denerim, ending the Fifth Blight.

9:31 Dragon

> QUNARI SHIPWRECK NEAR KIRKWALL

A Qunari dreadnought is shipwrecked near Kirkwall, stranding their Arishok and hundreds of soldiers in the city. They refuse to leave until they recover the stolen Tome of Koslun.

9:31 Dragon

> DEEP ROADS EXPEDITION

The eldest Hawke, released from servitude, helps fund an expedition into the Deep Roads with dwarven brothers Bartrand and Varric Tethras.

9:31 Dragon

> LYRIUM IDOL RECOVERED

The Deep Roads Expedition at Kirkwall discovers an ancient thaig that predates the First Blight. Inside is lyrium that glows red. An idol made of the strange lyrium is recovered.

9:31 Dragon

> HAWKE ATTEMPTS TO DESTROY CORYPHEUS

Hawke enters the Warden prison in the Vimmark Mountains and attempts to destroy Corypheus. History is vague on when exactly this occurs.

9:40 Dragon

> CIRCLE OF MAGI DISBANDED

Empress Celene is called out of Val Royeaux after news of an elven rebellion in Halamshiral. The move is thought to have been orchestrated by Gaspard. Celene's absence fuels rumors of her death or capture. While she is gone, a violent uprising at the White Spire—a Circle Tower in Val Royeaux—leaves many senior mages dead. The uprising is apparently supported by the Divine through her agents, including the bard Leliana. In response, Lord Seeker Lambert declares the Circle of Magi no more, leaving the future of mages in Thedas uncertain.

Following the conflict at the White Spire, Lambert cancels the Nevarran Accord, severing ties between the Seekers and the Chantry. Allegiances between Seekers and templars are split. Some still support the Divine. Lambert goes missing soon after and is presumed dead.

9:40 Dragon

> CASSANDRA PENTAGHAST ARRIVES IN KIRKWALL

Seeker Cassandra Pentaghast, acting under the authority of the Divine, arrives in Kirkwall and interrogates Varric Tethras about Hawke.

9:40
9:31
9:22
8:99
8:98
8:96
9:01
9:10
9:20
9:30
9:34
9:37
9:38

9:30 Dragon

> THE FIFTH BLIGHT BEGINS

It had been a long time since the Fourth Blight, and few thought the sudden appearance of more darkspawn in Ferelden during the Dragon Age to be anything more than an anomaly. The Ferelden Grey Wardens, few in number, knew better. Ferelden's Warden-Commander, Duncan, rushed to bolster his Order's numbers as the darkspawn amassed under the stirring Old God Urthemiel. The darkspawn first exposed their true numbers in 9:30 Dragon during the devastating Battle of Ostagar. King Cailan's trusted advisor, Loghain Mac Tir, quit the field in the heat of battle, leaving the king and the assembled Wardens trapped behind darkspawn lines without support. The Wardens, with the exception of the latest pair to join the Order, were slaughtered along with the king. As the darkspawn marched north to Lothering to destroy the city, the surviving Wardens journeyed the length of Ferelden in search of support, earning the respect of disparate peoples and uniting them against the darkspawn threat. Together, the armies of Ferelden met Urthemiel at the capital, Denerim. The Archdemon was slain in the final bloody battle against the Wardens, ending the Blight and earning the last Warden recruited by Duncan the title "Hero of Ferelden."

9:30 Dragon

> THE HAWKE FAMILY FLEES

The Hawke family flees the destruction of Lothering and travels to Kirkwall, where they begin indentured servitude in order to obtain entry to the city.

9:34 Dragon

> DIVINE BEATRIX III DIES

Divine Beatrix III, long suffering from dementia, succumbs to old age.

9:34 Dragon

> MOTHER DOROTHEA NAMED DIVINE

Revered Mother Dorothea is named Divine Justinia V.

9:34 Dragon

> FIRST BATTLE OF KIRKWALL

Hawke successfully drives the Qunari out in the First Battle of Kirkwall and is named Champion by Kirkwall's Knight-Commander Meredith Stannard.

9:38 Dragon

> DISSENT IN ORLAIS

Unrest brews in Orlais as Grand Duke Gaspard de Chalons stirs dissent against reigning Empress Celene I.

9:37 Dragon

> THE MAGE-TEMPLAR WAR BEGINS

Anders, an apostate and friend of Hawke, destroys the Kirkwall chantry with the grand cleric still inside, inciting the mage-templar war that spreads throughout Thedas.

9:37 Dragon

> CLASH AT KIRKWALL

Hawke leads the push to stop the mages and templars as they clash in Kirkwall. The city's First Enchanter Orsino and Knight-Commander Meredith are both killed.

GETTING STARTED

Ever since the Breach opened following the tragic events at the Temple of Sacred Ashes, southern Thedas has fallen into an even greater state of instability. The templar/mage conflict in Ferelden rages on, as does the civil war in Orlais. And now demons are pouring from Fade rifts scattered across the continent. Are you ready to enter this dangerous and chaotic world? If you're new to *Dragon Age*, take a few minutes to familiarize yourself with some of the core gameplay concepts. Even if you're a grizzled *Dragon Age* veteran, you may find some useful information here.

DRAGON AGE KEEP

Before you even start your adventure in *Dragon Age: Inquisition*, pay a visit to *Dragon Age Keep* (dragonagekeep.com) to customize your world state. Whether you've played previous *Dragon Age* installments or not, *Dragon Age Keep* gives you the opportunity to make some key decisions that influence your own personal world state. If you'd like, stay true to your previous gameplay sessions of *Dragon Age: Origins* and *Dragon Age II*, making the same decisions to continue your story line. Or make different decisions than you did in previous games to adjust the world state in any way you like. *Dragon Age Keep* offers an incredible amount of depth, but you don't have to make every minute adjustment. Simply make the adjustments you feel are important, then move on. Your decisions in *Dragon Age Keep* carry over into *Dragon Age: Inquisition*, impacting the story in subtle (and some not so subtle) ways. As you start your adventure, your decisions in *Dragon Age: Inquisition* are automatically synced to *Dragon Age Keep*, preserving your personalized world state for future adventures.

NOTE You must have an Origin account to access *Dragon Age Keep*. You can set up a free account directly from dragonagekeep.com—all you need is an e-mail address.

CHARACTER GENERATION

Once you've established your game's world state with *Dragon Age Keep*, put some careful thought into selecting your character's race, gender, and class. There are a few important factors to note about race. In terms of attributes, humans gain no bonus while dwarves get a 25 percent bonus to magic defense, elves get a 25 percent bonus to ranged defense, and Qunari benefit from a 25 percent bonus to melee defense. Race also impacts certain conversations and determines how certain characters respond to you. Both race and gender have an impact on what romances are available to your character. For example, Cullen will only show interest if you're playing as a female elf or human—see the Party Members and War Council chapters for more details on character romances. Following selections of race and gender, choose your class to determine what kind of skills, abilities, and equipment your character can use. Before choosing a class, consider referencing the Classes and Abilities chapter to better understand the differences between the rogue, warrior, and mage.

During the opening cinematic you're prompted to choose your character's appearance. There are five heads to choose from, and each can be further customized. Here you can alter your character's head, hair, voice, ears, eyes, nose, mouth, jaw, scars, tattoos, and makeup. These options are largely aesthetic and have no impact on gameplay.

DEVELOPER TIP

Putting just the right amount of stubble on the female dwarf Inquisitor can increase the chances of romance by 10,000,000 percent.

— Shane Hawco, Lead Character Artist

CONVERSATION HUB

Like previous titles, *Dragon Age: Inquisition* requires you to make some tough decisions. These are handled through the conversation hub. Here you have the option of selecting a reply. Some of these choices have consequences, and others don't. Each dialogue option is accompanied by an icon, indicating how your character will respond.

Dialogue Options

Icon	Description	Icon	Description
General Dialogue		**Perk-Based**	
	General		Underworld
	Investigate		Politics
	Attack		History
	Payment		Human
	Romance	**Class and Race**	
	End Romance		Warrior
Special			Rogue
	Special		Mage
	Stoic		Elf
	Sad		Dwarf
	Pleased		Qunari
	Mad		
	Confused		
	Surprised		
	Fear		

NOTE The perk-based dialogue options are only available if you've purchased the associated Inquisition perk. For more details on perks, reference the War Council chapter.

APPROVAL

Choose your words and actions carefully—your followers are paying close attention to everything you say and do. Saying or doing the right/wrong thing can lead to a gain or loss of approval among your party members. Approval is basically your likability among the party members, and it's a key component of initiating romances. While minor approval swings are common during conversations, major approval swings occur when making critical decisions—reference the Decision Point sidebars in the walkthrough. Once you've made a decision, there's no turning back. And unless you're using the walkthrough, you'll be making these decisions blindly, not knowing how your approval with each character will be affected. So it's strongly advised to review these decision points beforehand. Otherwise you may unintentionally sabotage a budding romance.

Character Approvals in Walkthrough

Approval	Icon	Approval	Icon
Strongly Approves	⬆⬆⬆	Strongly Disapproves	⬇⬇⬇
Approves	⬆⬆	Disapproves	⬇⬇
Slightly Approves	⬆	Slightly Disapproves	⬇
		No Change	—

Romance

During some conversations with your followers and advisors, a romance dialogue option appears—take this opportunity to flirt, often gaining approval. But this is just the beginning. Continue flirting and building approval with a particular character to advance the relationship. However, consummating a relationship takes a lot more than staying out of the doghouse and delivering clever one-liners. Take the romance to the next level by completing inner circle quests for your romantic interest—some of these involve acquiring gifts you can use to the help seal the deal. When it comes to romance, persistence pays off, so keep chatting up your love interest on a regular basis—and do as little as possible to piss them off. Also, remember that race and gender make a difference, so don't set your sights on a character you're not compatible with. Reference the Party Members and War Council chapters for more information on pursuing romances with each character.

NOTE Even if you've impressed them, Cole, Varric, Vivienne, and Leliana cannot be romanced. But they'd love to be your friend.

HERO MENU

Whether you need to purchase new abilities, adjust tactics and behaviors, equip new gear, or review codexes and quest information, the radial Hero menu has you covered. The game is paused while the Hero menu is open, giving you ample time to sort through your gear and consider your next move.

> CHARACTER RECORD

The Character Record menu is where you can manage your party's abilities, tactics, and behaviors as well as view their current attributes. This menu cannot be accessed during combat, so make sure you make these adjustments when your character and party aren't under attack.

Abilities

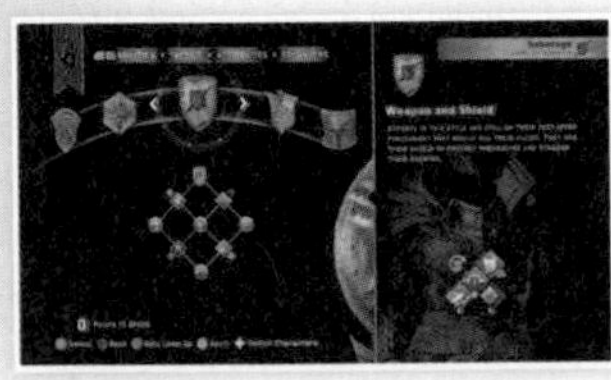

Here's where you select and map a character's abilities, accessible from a variety of ability trees. Each ability tree contains active abilities, upgrades, and passive abilities. Active abilities have diamond-shaped icons—you can map up to eight active abilities for quick deployment during combat. Most active abilities can be upgraded, making them stronger and more effective. Upgrades appear as smaller diamond-shaped icons adjacent to a active ability. Passive abilities are represented by circular icons on each tree. When a passive ability is learned, it's always in play and does not need to be mapped or activated. Some passive abilities also offer permanent bonus attributes when unlocked.

Characters earn one ability point each time they level up. Browse through the available trees and select an ability to learn—it takes one ability point to unlock each ability. You can only learn abilities connected to the root of the ability tree or connected to an ability you've already learned. Active abilities are automatically mapped to an empty hot key or button when learned, but you can customize where each ability is mapped through the Apply function—select a learned ability from the tree followed by the Apply function, then press the desired key or button to map it. Since you can only map up to eight abilities at a time, later in the game you may need to revise your mapped abilities, replacing older, weaker abilities with newer, more powerful ones. Reference the Classes and Abilities chapter for a complete rundown of all abilities, including specializations.

Tactics

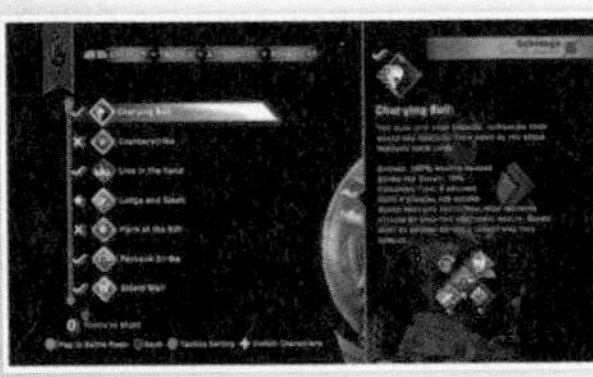

In the Tactics screen you can adjust which abilities your party members use when you're not in control of them. The interface consists of a list of learned abilities, and mapped abilities have a check mark next to them. When an ability is selected you have the opportunity to enable it, disable it, or prefer it. Preferred abilities are used more frequently and are more favored over enabled abilities when both can be used. So if there's a particular ability you'd like a character to use with greater frequency, set it to preferred.

Attributes

The Attributes screen displays a character's current stats as well as any offensive and defensive bonuses. These bonuses are often applied by equipping different weapons, armor, and accessories. Here's a rundown of how each attribute is defined.

Attributes

Strength: The character's physical strength and ability. Each point increases attack (warriors only) and guard damage bonus.

Dexterity: The character's agility, reflexes, and coordination. Each point increases attack (rogues only) and critical damage bonus.

Magic: The character's connection to the Fade and ability to manipulate it. Each point increases attack (mages only) and barrier damage bonus.

Cunning: The character's intelligence and deviousness. Each point increases critical chance and ranged defense.

Willpower: The character's strength of mind and personality. Each point increases attack and magic defense for all classes.

Constitution: The character's physical robustness and endurance. Each point increases health and melee defense.

Offensive

Attack: The attack stat increases all damage that a character does.

Guard Damage Bonus: Increases the damage against enemies under the effect of guard.

Armor Penetration: Each point of armor penetration ignores one point of the target's armor when inflicting damage.

Barrier Damage Bonus: Increases the damage against enemies that are under the effect of Barrier.

Critical Damage Bonus: Increases the extra damage inflicted with a critical hit.

Critical Chance: The chance to score a critical hit for each attack.

Main-Hand Damage: How much damage the weapon in the character's main hand inflicts with each hit.

Off-Hand Damage: How much damage is inflicted by the character's off-hand weapon.

Bleed on Hit: The chance per hit to inflict a bleed effect on the target. The effect lasts a few seconds.

Stagger on Hit: The chance per hit to stun the target. The effect lasts a few seconds.

Heal on Kill: Amount of damage to be healed by each killing blow.

Flanking Damage Bonus: The damage bonus, as a percentage, when attacking a target from the side or behind.

Defensive

Magic Defense: The percentage of damage resistance to all magical or elemental attacks.

Melee Defense: The percentage of damage resistance to all melee physical attacks.

Ranged Defense: The percentage of damage resistance to all ranged physical attacks.

Cold Resistance: The percentage of damage resistance to cold damage attacks.

Electrical Resistance: The percentage of damage resistance to electrical damage attacks.

Fire Resistance: The percentage of damage resistance to fire damage attacks.

Spirit Resistance: The percentage of damage resistance to spirit damage attacks.

Guard: Enemies must first damage the character's guard, if any, before they can damage health.

Armor Rating: Physical damage is reduced by a character's armor rating.

Armor Rating Front: Physical damage inflicted on the character from the front is reduced by armor rating before being applied.

Health: A character whose health drops to 0 falls unconscious and is unable to attack.

Maximum Health: The maximum amount of health a character can regain from healing.

Bleed on Being Hit: The chance per enemy attack on the character that the attack inflicts a bleed effect on the enemy. The effect lasts a few seconds.

Stagger on Being Hit: The chance per enemy attack on the character that the attack stuns the enemy. The effect lasts a few seconds.

Other

Focus: Focus is a resource that you gain each time someone in your party deals damage. Each party member has a personal focus meter, but all party members gain focus when a single member deals damage.

Maximum Focus: The maximum amount of focus this character can generate.

Focus Gain Bonus: Focus gained from all sources is increased by this percentage amount.

Mana/Stamina: The current amount of mana/stamina a character has. Use mana/stamina to trigger special abilities.

Maximum Mana/Stamina: The maximum amount of mana/stamina a character can have.

Combat Experience Points: The character's current experience points.

Level: A character's current combat level.

Cooldown Modifier: Reduces the cooldown on all of the character's abilities.

Behaviors

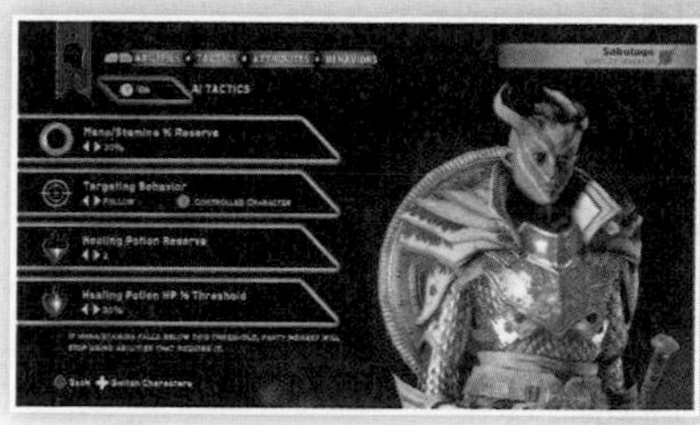

The Behaviors screen allows you to provide instructions to your party on how they should fight, cooperate, and defend themselves in combat. While you can directly control and switch between party members at any time, they will follow these rules when you're not controlling them. Four AI behaviors can be adjusted:

Mana/Stamina % Reserve: If mana/stamina falls below this threshold, the party member will stop using abilities that require it.

Targeting Behavior: Choose targets by following another party member's target or by prioritizing threats to another party member—use this to make the selected character follow or defend a party member of your choice.

Healing Potion Reserve: Party member will not use healing potions if this many or fewer remain.

Healing Potion % Threshold: When the party member's health falls below this threshold, they will attempt to use a healing potion.

> INVENTORY

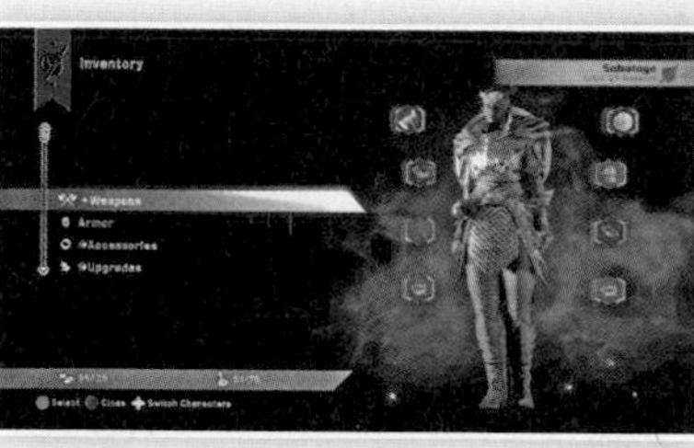

When you acquire new gear, access the Inventory menu to inspect and equip these new items. You can equip weapons, armor, and accessories, applying them to your character or party members. Most equipment is restricted by class and level. So if a character doesn't meet these requirements, the item cannot be equipped. But think twice before selling or destroying this equipment—a party member may benefit from it. The Inventory menu also details all upgrades, crafting materials, valuables, and schematics carried by your party. Crafting materials and schematics do not occupy space in your inventory, but everything else does. So make a habit of selling off excess equipment whenever you're near a merchant. Unless related to a quest or research item, valuables can be sold for gold they serve no other purpose.

When sorting through your items, pay close attention to the rarity. Items with a gray background are common and frequently found in loot drops. Common items aren't particularly noteworthy and fetch little gold when sold to merchants. Items with blue backgrounds are rare. When possible, equip rare items on your characters, because they're often enchanted with runes, giving them stat buffs. Rare items also are worth more when sold to merchants. Unique items have a purple background and are one-of-a-kind—these are usually found on bosses. While you can earn quite a bit of gold by selling unique items, it's better to equip your party members with them. Unique items are often crafted from the best materials and enchanted by runes, giving them a variety of bonuses. Consider holding onto unique items until they're rendered obsolete by newer, better equipment.

NOTE With very few exceptions, loot drops are randomized. So when you open a chest or retrieve loot from a fallen foe, you never know what you're going to get. But loot always closely matches the level of your characters, so you're never going to get high-level loot drops when starting out.

> CODEX

Throughout your adventure you're likely to uncover codex entries providing detailed information on different subjects. Codex entries can be retrieved manually by interacting with notes or other documents. They can also be retrieved automatically when a topic arises in conversation or whenever you encounter an enemy or character for the first time. All of these entries are collected in the Codex section of the Hero menu. Unlocking a codex entry also unlocks the art associated with its card.

> JOURNAL

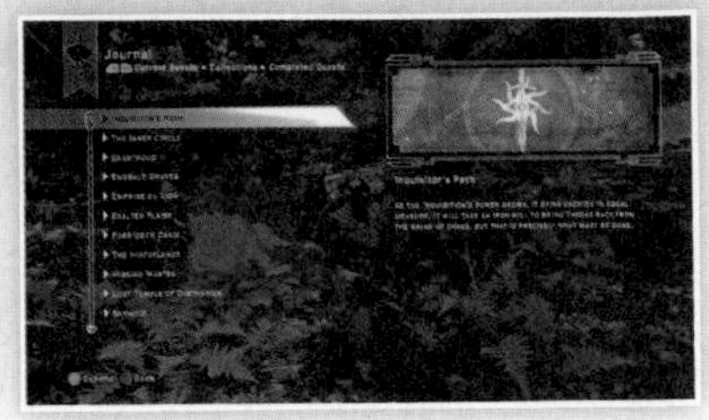

The Journal menu keeps track of all quests you've been assigned as well as those you have completed. Each quest entry provides a brief description and lists objectives. Quests are sorted by Inquisitor's Path (critical path quests), inner circle quests, and locales. When you select a quest from the journal it becomes active, updating icons on the in-game compass and helping you determine where to go next. The Collections tab within the journal keeps track of all the collectibles you've found, including items like bottles, mosaics, and song lyrics. For more information on collections, reference the Exploration chapter.

COMBAT PRIMER

Your journey through southern Thedas isn't without peril. Demons, creatures, and hostile forces attack with minimal provocation, calling on you to defend yourself and your allies. There are two different ways to approach combat in *Dragon Age: Inquisition*. You can either play the game third-person, like an action RPG, or you can take a more tactical approach through the use of the tactical camera. There is no right or wrong way to do this—it all comes down to personal preference.

When playing in the third-person perspective, face your intended target and then press and hold the attack button or key. Alternatively, you can lock on to a target to keep it centered in the camera view. Initiating basic attacks causes your character to unleash a series of slashes, arrows, or elemental projectiles, using an equipped weapon. While basic attacks are effective, they aren't the most powerful—rely on your character's offensive active abilities to pour on even more damage. But not all abilities are offensive. Abilities like Barrier, Leaping Shot, and Evade are defensive, preventing your character (and sometimes the entire party) from taking damage. Abilities consume stamina, mana, or focus, and as such cannot be activated frequently—and each ability has a cooldown period, too. So save your abilities for those critical moments when you need an extra boost in offense or defense to turn the tide.

> TACTICAL CAMERA

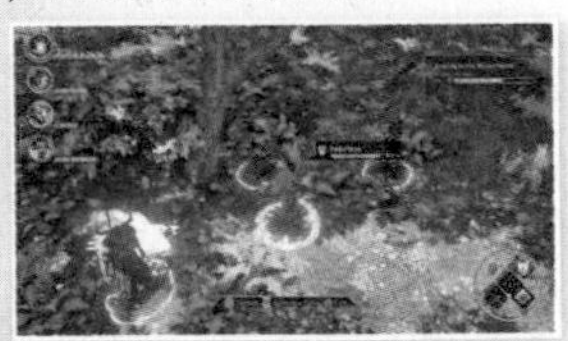

The tactical camera pauses the action, allowing you to view the battlefield from a top-down perspective. While the game is paused, you can issue orders to all your party members, instructing them to move, defend, attack, or use one of their mapped active abilities. Once orders are issued, you can either return to the third-person perspective or stay within the tactical camera to advance time, watching from above as your orders are carried out. Using the tactical camera's reticle, highlight enemies to view details within their information box. Here you can see the enemy's name, health, and armor, as well as any resistances, vulnerabilities, and immunities. This information alone tells you exactly what kind of weapons/abilities will be effective. For example, if an enemy is resistant to cold-based damage but vulnerable to fire-based damage, consider changing your weapons and abilities to compensate.

> POTIONS AND GRENADES

No matter how defensive you are, damage is going to happen and you'll need a way to heal. Fortunately, your party is equipped with eight health potions. (This number can be increased to 12 by purchasing the More Healing Potions Inquisition perk.) Individually, your party members can be equipped with secondary potions that can benefit them in various ways, such as providing temporary resistances to elemental damage. You can unlock more potions by finding or purchasing potion recipes and crafting them from herbs. Potions can be consumed from the in-game radial menu. This menu also allows you to deploy grenades—deployment works similar to that of an area-of-effect (AoE) ability. Grenades aren't readily available but can be crafted, much like potions. Before adventuring into new areas, make sure party members are well equipped with potions and grenades.

> PARTY COMPOSITION

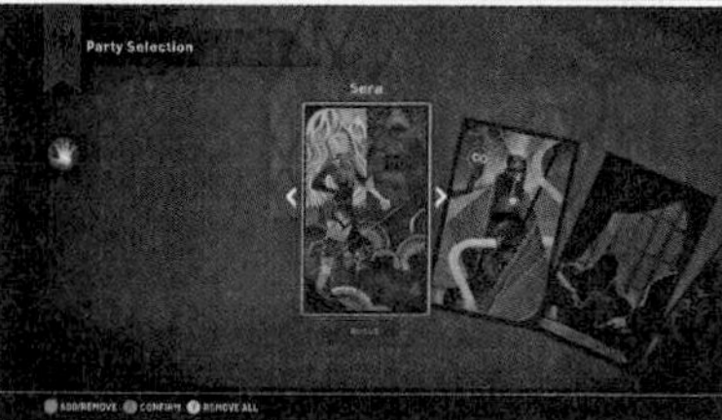

Before you venture out into the wilderness you're prompted to select your party members. As a general rule, it's wise to travel with a balanced party, with at least one warrior, one rogue, and one mage present. In addition to having unique skills (like wall bashing, lock picking, and veilfire), each class has tactical strengths and abilities. Mages and rogue archers specialize in ranged combat, while warriors and dual-wield rogues rely on melee attacks to dish out damage. Having a mix of melee and ranged fighters should serve your party well. Consider making two warriors, a rogue archer, and a mage as your default lineup. While this may not be the best combination for your style of play, it's merely a sample of a well-balanced party. Experiment with your own lineups, paying close attention to the strengths and weaknesses of each class. For an in-depth analysis on each class, including a discussion of all abilities, reference the Classes and Abilities chapter.

MOUNTS

For the first time, mounts are available in *Dragon Age*. But before you can fill your stables with horses, dracolisks, and harts, you must find Horsemaster Dennet in the Hinterlands—he gives you a Fereldan Forder and the opportunity to purchase more mounts at your stable. Mounts offer a quick way to traverse the vast landscapes of Ferelden and Orlais. And while mounts are fast, they aren't capable of outrunning attacks. If your mount takes damage, you'll be thrown off. So it's best to dismount before approaching hostile units. If you use mounts frequently, consider choosing the Rider's Posture and Antivan-Stitched Saddle Inquisition perks to decrease your chances of being unseated. With these perks unlocked, your mount can absorb more damage before throwing you off. For more information on mounts, reference the Skyhold section in the Exploration chapter.

BEGINNER TIPS

- Go out of your way to talk to everyone. All interactive characters have something interesting to say. Some may have quests for you, and others could possibly be recruited as agents.
- When visiting a new locale, try to establish as many camps as possible. Inquisition camps serve as fast-travel points, allowing you to get around the map with ease. Settlements and keeps also serve as fast-travel points.
- As you and your party members gain XP, you'll level up. Look for the arrow icon on each character portrait to identify who has leveled up. Take this as your cue to enter the Character Record menu and select new abilities.
- Some enemies drop research items. Take these items to the Inquisition's researcher to gain bonuses against associated enemy types.
- Weapons and armor sold by merchants are usually inferior to the equipment you can find in loot drops. Save your gold to buy schematics and crafting materials, then craft your own custom equipment. You can't craft runes until the Inquisition acquires Dagna, in Skyhold.
- Collect crafting materials to create your own weapons, armor, upgrades, potions, and grenades. Gather herbs, minerals, cloth, and animal hides during your adventures across southern Thedas, then use schematics to craft new items.
- Before selling any weapons or armor, consider removing any upgrades you'd like to keep. Upgrades can be removed and applied to other equipment. However, runes cannot be removed from equipment. So think twice before attaching runes.
- Before leaving an Inquisition camp, ensure your party is fully stocked on potions. Healing potions are automatically restocked when you establish, rest, or fast travel to a camp. But you may need to craft secondary potions (and grenades) for each individual party member.
- Use the Search function to highlight interactive items, including loot and crafting materials. This is an easy way to find objects that you'd otherwise miss.
- Consider keeping at least one fire-based, one cold-based, and one electrical-based staff in your inventory. These will come in handy for eliminating magical barriers. While any staff can bring down a magical barrier, staves using an opposing elemental magic drop these barriers faster. For example, use a fire staff against a cold barrier, a cold staff against a fire barrier, or an electrical staff against a spirit barrier. Of course, maintaining a mage in your party is essential for equipping these staves and defeating these barriers.
- Before engaging in combat, use the tactical camera to scout the battlefield. Inspect every enemy to determine resistances, vulnerabilities, and immunities.
- Speak to your followers regularly while in Haven or Skyhold, particularly following key events. New dialogue options are opened following the conclusion of most critical path quests.
- You must gain power to scout and unlock new locales. Closing Fade rifts and establishing Inquisition camps are the easiest ways to gain power. Some side quests also reward power.
- Most quests reward influence. Think of this as XP for the Inquisition. As the Inquisition acquires more influence and levels up you can purchase Inquisition perks, benefiting the organization in various ways. See the War Council chapter for more information on Inquisition ranks and perks.

THE INQUISITOR'S PATH

THE INQUISITOR'S PATH

In *Dragon Age: Inquisition,* Thedas faces yet another cataclysmic threat as demons pour through rifts in the Fade. It's up to you, the Inquisitor, and your Inquisition to seal these rifts and restore order. This chapter covers the game's critical path story arc, called the Inquisitor's Path. This is a streamlined walkthrough detailing the bare minimum you must do to complete the game. But there's far more to *Dragon Age: Inquisition* than the Inquisitor's Path. So during your play-through, be sure to reference other chapters in the guide as new opportunities arise. In particular, keep the Exploration chapter bookmarked so you're ready to tackle side quests and other activities in each of the game's sprawling locales. This is your Inquisition. How will you lead it?

THE WRATH OF HEAVEN

The Temple of Sacred Ashes was at the heart of the blast that tore open the sky. Reach the temple and see what can be done.

FROSTBACK MOUNTAINS

PROLOGUE

Something terrible has happened... and you're the prime suspect. Held in a cell beneath the chantry in Haven, your character is questioned by Seeker Cassandra Pentaghast and Leliana about the events leading up to the explosion at the Temple of Sacred Ashes. The temple was the site of a Conclave attended by many from across Thedas. Almost all attendees were killed in a massive explosion that completely leveled the temple. Among the deceased was none other than Divine Justinia V, leader of the Andrastian Chantry. But there was one survivor—you. Unfortunately, your character has no clear recollection of what happened—this only fuels Cassandra's suspicions. In an effort to refresh your character's memory, Cassandra decides to escort you to a rift while Leliana travels to a forward camp.

Outside the chantry a massive hole in the sky is visible, located just above the ruins of the temple. What could have caused such devastation? Cassandra says they're calling the hole in the sky the Breach. It's a massive rift into the Fade. And apparently this Breach is growing. Cassandra fears it will expand until it swallows the world. There seems to be a direct link between the Breach and the green, glowing mark on your character's hand—a sudden pulse from the Breach causes the mark to emit a painful surge through your character's body. Cassandra feels this mark may be the key to closing the Breach. Are you really responsible for all of this? The inhabitants of Haven seem to think so, casting accusatory glances in your direction as you and Cassandra begin your journey to the Breach.

JOURNEY TO THE RIFT

Following the opening cinematic, you gain control of your character. Accompanied by Cassandra, you're on a stone bridge, not far from Haven. Take a moment to familiarize yourself with the movement and camera controls before approaching the gate at the end of the bridge. As you move forward, Cassandra orders a pair of soldiers to open the gate on the north side, allowing you to access the path to the valley. A new Inquisition icon appears on the compass, indicating the location of your current objective.

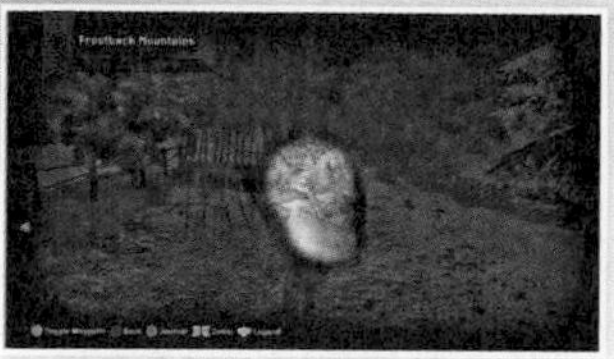

Soon after passing through the gate you can access the quest map to gain a greater perspective of the Frostback Mountains. Only the area you've explored appears on the quest map. The rest of the map is shrouded in darkness, representing areas you haven't explored. The more you travel around the locale, the more the map is uncovered. Pan the map to the left to see the Inquisition icon—this is the location of the rift, your current destination. Close the quest map and continue along the path beyond the bridge.

Codex Entries

Sometimes conversations or object interactions unlock a codex entry—the entry for Divine Justinia V is unlocked when Cassandra mentions her soon after passing through the gate at the bridge. These entries offer more background on particular subjects. Whenever a codex entry is unlocked, a notification appears on the left side of the screen—press the accompanying button/key to open the entry and read up on the topic. All unlocked codex entries can also be accessed from the Hero menu—choose the Codex option. There are hundreds of codex entries waiting to be unlocked during your journey, so make an effort to interact with as many objects as possible.

While moving along the path your character's left hand emits a green glow, accompanied by a sharp jab of pain. Cassandra helps your character to their feet and initiates a conversation. Speaking to Cassandra gives you the opportunity get some background information on the current situation. After the conversation continue along the path.

While crossing the next bridge, green bolts of energy fall from the sky, impacting the surrounding landscape. Suddenly, the bridge itself is rocked, causing it to crumble beneath your feet. As your character recovers on the frozen river below, two demon-like creatures, called shades, appear nearby. As Cassandra charges ahead to confront these demons, your character recovers a weapon from the debris of the bridge. The type of weapon you recover depends on what class of character you're playing. But regardless of what kind of weapon your character is wielding, you can help Cassandra fight off the shades.

Combat Primer

Follow the on-screen instructions to perform a basic attack. Hold down the basic attack button/key to continuously strike one of the shades—for best results, focus on Cassandra's target. These enemies are persistent and continue lashing out with savage melee attacks. Keep hitting back with basic attacks until both shades are defeated. Following the battle convince Cassandra that you need a weapon to defend yourself. Regardless of what dialogue options you choose, Cassandra eventually stands down and allows your character to remain armed. Before moving on, consider healing by opening the tactical wheel and consuming a potion—follow the on-screen prompts. You can also loot one of the corpses lying near the ice. This usually yields a helmet you can equip through the inventory screen in the Hero menu.

TIP

Sometimes enemies drop loot, too. Search the remains of the shades to obtain shadow essence, a research item. Later, research items can be turned over to the Inquisition's researcher, Minaeve. Studying these items can reveal an enemy's weaknesses, giving you combat bonuses during future engagements.

Using the compass as your guide, continue following the path to the rift, engaging two more shades along the way. The on-screen tutorials walk you through the basics of combat, including how to lock the camera onto a target and how to trigger class-specific abilities. Using a mix of basic attacks and abilities, defeat the next two shades.

A shade and wraith block the path ahead. Try to engage and defeat the shade first without drawing the attention of the green, glowing wraith. Unlike shades, wraiths rely solely on ranged attacks, often striking from a distance by firing green orbs of energy. They're best defeated with ranged attacks of your own. However, if your character isn't equipped with a staff or bow, you'll need to rely on basic melee attacks to defeat this demon. Once the wraith and shade are defeated, search the west side of the frozen river to obtain some loot from a corpse.

DEVELOPER TIP

It pays to venture off the path in Frostback Mountains. I've discovered additional loot tucked away in secluded areas.

— Charlene Czirfusz, Test Ops QA

Wraiths and shades loiter along the path ahead. Try to isolate and engage these enemies in small groups to avoid setting off a large, challenging battle. If possible, draw the first set toward you with ranged attacks, defeating the wraith before attacking the shade. Once the first set is dispatched, approach the next group of demons, consisting of a shade and two wraiths. Once the area is clear, move to the north side of the frozen river to loot another corpse. Backtrack to the steps to the west and continue your journey to the rift.

Fade Rift

Just ahead, the green glow of the rift comes into view. Friendly forces are engaged in combat with several shades. Rush forward and join the fight, helping defeat the shades. After the battle, a cinematic is triggered, introducing Solas and Varric. Solas urges your character to use the mark on your hand to close the rift before more demons come through. This mark has the ability to close Fade rifts. Cassandra theorizes the mark could also be used to close the Breach above the nearby temple. Following proper introductions, Solas and Varric join your party. Jump over the nearby barrier and lead your new party down the adjoining slope. You must regroup with allies at a forward camp before proceeding to the temple.

> REACH THE FORWARD CAMP

More shades and wraiths appear on the frozen river ahead. Here you're prompted to use the tactical camera. This feature allows you to pause the game and issue specific orders to each party member. If using a ranged weapon, like a staff or bow, stay on the southern banks of the frozen river and help Solas and Varric rain down fire while Cassandra charges ahead. But if you're carrying a melee weapon, join Cassandra on the icy surface to defeat the demons at close range. After the battle, head to cabin on the east side of the riverbank. Feel free to loot the chest inside—you may find something you or your party members could use.

TIP

Before moving out toward the forward camp, take a detour up the hillside to the southwest, beyond the frozen waterfall. This path leads to small alcove occupied by three shades. Work with your party to dispatch these demons, then loot the corpse found here. Afterward, return to the frozen river and continue your journey to the forward camp.

Climb the slope west of the river and engage more demons along the way. The gate outside the forward camp is blocked by another Fade rift guarded by wraiths and shades. Fade rifts are caused by weaknesses in the Veil. Rifts spawn demons, and can only be sealed once all nearby demons are killed. The mark can disrupt the rift and cause damage to enemies. When you're not being attacked, interact with the rift to damage all of the demons. Once all the demons are dead, interact with the Fade rift to close it, using your mark.

Leveling Up

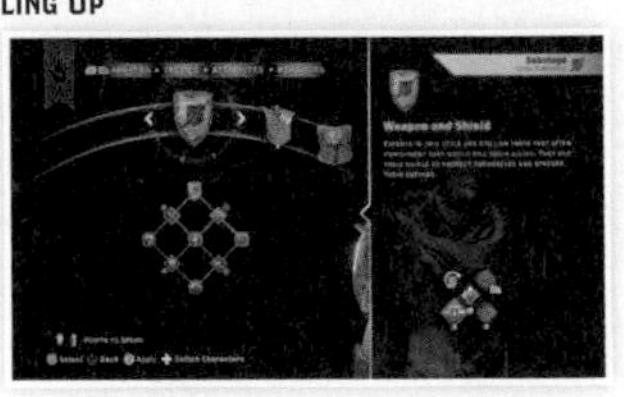

Closing the rift outside the camp awards your character (and party) enough XP to level up. Each time you level up you get one ability point to spend. From the Hero menu, choose Character Record and select a new ability. Each class has a variety of abilities to choose from. Take your time browsing through the options and determining the best long-term path for your character. The diamond-shaped icons represent active abilities. When selected, active abilities are automatically mapped to a button or key for quick access during combat. Passive abilities, indicated by the circular icons, are not mapped to buttons or keys. Instead, your character automatically benefits from passive abilities—you don't have to do anything. In addition to your character leveling up, your party members have leveled up too. Take a moment to choose new abilities for Cassandra, Varric, and Solas.

After closing the rift, open the gate and enter the forward camp. Interact with the supply cache here to refill your potions. Beyond the supply cache, speak with Leliana, standing near the tent with Chancellor Roderick. The ensuing conversation is rife with accusations, panic, and indecision as Leliana, Roderick, and Cassandra argue over which path to take to the temple. Meanwhile your character is brought to their knees, writhing in pain as the mark is once again illuminated. When Cassandra asks which path you suggest, you have the opportunity to make your first key decision.

DECISION POINT

There are no win-win decisions in *Dragon Age: Inquisition*. As in all BioWare games, major decisions have consequences you'll have to live with. Furthermore, your decisions may have an impact on relationships, either gaining or losing approval with your party members. This can positively or negatively affect your ability to pursue successfully a romance with certain characters. So reference these Decision Point sidebars to understand the consequences of these major decisions before you make them. If you take the mountain path, as Leliana suggested, you can attempt to find a lost squad of soldiers—but more demons will come through the breach and kill innocent people. If you choose Cassandra's option and charge with the soldiers, you'll reach the temple faster, but more soldiers will die in the process. As the following table shows, you'll gain approval with Varric if you choose the mountain path—but you'll lose approval from Cassandra. The opposite is true if you choose to charge with the soldiers—Solas remains neutral during this decision.

Approval: Path to the Temple

Party Member	Mountain Path	Charge with Soldiers
Cassandra	↓	↑↑
Solas	—	—
Varric	↑↑	—

NOTE While you can flirt with nearly every major character in the Inquisition, you can pursue a romance with only one of them. Before you set your sights on anyone in particular, make sure your potential love interest is compatible with your race and gender. For more information on romancing specific characters, reference the Party Members and War Council chapters.

> THE MOUNTAIN PATH

The mountain path is steep, requiring your party to traverse a series of three ladders before gaining access to an old mining tunnel. Fight through the shades and wraiths in the tunnel. Try leading with Cassandra, using her Challenge ability to taunt the enemies, causing them to attack her instead of the others. You can also play as Solas or Varric. At the tunnel's exit you find the remains of three soldiers—but this isn't all of them. Continue along the snowy path until you spot another Fade rift, where the surviving soldiers are fighting off several demons. Rush forward and join the fight, defeating the first wave of demons.

After eliminating the first wave of enemies, prepare for a second wave emerging from the Fade, consisting of one terror. These tall, creepy demons are extremely dangerous, and deserving of your entire party's attention. Terrors inflict heavy damage with their melee and area-of-effect attacks. Taunt the terror using Cassandra while the rest of your party members (and the soldiers) assist. Little by little the terror's health is depleted until it is dead. Take this moment to close the Fade rift. The soldiers are grateful for your decision to take the mountain path—surely they would've perished if you didn't come this way. After speaking with the soldiers, descend a couple of ladders nearby and proceed to the temple.

> CHARGE WITH THE SOLDIERS

This path leads directly into the temple's main entrance, where another Fade rift has spawned more demons. Commander Cullen and his men are busy fighting off more demons, so give them a hand. Upon approaching the rift, engage the tactical camera. Move the circular targeting reticle around the battlefield to highlight different enemies. This reveals the enemy's name, level, and health. In some cases it may show vulnerabilities and applied status effects. The usual mix of shades and wraiths surrounds the rift. Send Cassandra into close range to battle these enemies while Solas and Varric attack from a distance—preferably from the ledge to the east. If your character has a ranged weapon, stay put with Varric and Solas. Otherwise, charge into the heat of the battle with Cassandra. The idea is to keep Varric and Solas out of harm's way. Using Cassandra's Challenge taunt ability draws enemies toward her, an ideal tactic for keeping enemies away from Varric and Solas.

Following the first wave of enemies, prepare for a single terror, emerging from the rift. These tall, creepy demons are extremely dangerous, and deserving of your entire party's attention. Terrors inflict heavy damage with their melee and area-of-effect attacks. Taunt the terror using Cassandra while the rest of your party members (and Cullen's men) assist. Keep hitting the terror over and over until it's down for good. Now, close the Fade rift using your character's mark. After a brief conversation with Cullen and Cassandra, proceed into the temple... or what's left of it.

> THE BREACH

Here your party meets up with Leliana as the Breach looms high above. Just below the Breach is another rift. Solas suggests that sealing this rift may be the key to closing the Breach. Follow the path on the west side of the temple to reach the rift. Along the way Varric is unsettled by the presence of red lyrium—after what transpired in Kirkwall, his uneasiness is understandable. The perimeter path leads to a shallow ledge leading down to the rift. Before stepping off the ledge, consider healing your party with potions and equipping new weapons. Fire-based weapons and spells will come in handy for the fight ahead.

When you reach the floor of the temple, voices can be heard emanating from the rift. A transparent vision above the temple floor replays the events leading up to the explosion during the Conclave. Apparently some malicious entity was holding Divine Justinia V captive when your character intervened. Cassandra seems surprised and confused by this revelation, but there are other matters to attend to. Solas reports that the rift is closed but not sealed. He suggests using the mark to open it. But that will likely draw more demons. As your character reaches out with the mark, the rift is opened, drawing forth a massive pride demon.

Pride Demon Battle

Immediately following the cinematic, begin attacking the pride demon. Make note of the gray bars covering the pride demon's health meter. These armor-like icons represent the pride demon's guard. When an enemy (or ally) builds up its guard, it can't be injured. In a sense, this guard serves as a secondary health meter. Before you can inflict damage on an enemy's health, you must first eliminate the guard. Fortunately, disrupting the Fade rift with the mark can temporarily eliminate the pride demon's guard. So approach the rift and interact with it to cause a disruption. This stuns the pride demon, making it vulnerable to attacks. While the pride demon attempts to recover, hit it with everything you have, slowly depleting its exposed health meter. But watch out for more demons pouring out of the rift—use Cassandra's Challenge to draw their attention. Eliminate the shades swarming your party and then resume your attack on the pride demon. When the pride demon has restored its guard, disrupt the Fade rift again. Keep disrupting the Fade rift and attacking the pride demon while it's vulnerable until its health is fully depleted. Once the pride demon and all shades are eliminated, close the Fade rift. This triggers a massive surge of energy to shoot skyward. Yet the Breach in the sky remains.

THE THREAT REMAINS

A chantry cleric named Mother Giselle is tending to refugees in the Ferelden Hinterlands near Redcliffe. Leliana believes she may be sympathetic to the Inquisition's cause.

HAVEN

Following the events at the Temple of Sacred Ashes, your character regains consciousness in a cozy cabin back in Haven. An elf servant informs you that three days have past since you closed the rift at the temple. And while the Breach is still present, it has stopped growing, just like the mark on your hand. The servant then mentions that Cassandra would like to see you in the chantry. Before heading for the chantry, take a moment to get your bearings. There's a small box on the floor you can loot as well as a note on the desk you can read, unlocking another codex entry.

THE INQUISITION REBORN

The chantry is located on the south side of Haven. Open the doors to the chantry and proceed to the room at the back of the structure—this is the war room, where the Inquisition's war council meets. As soon as you pass through the door, Chancellor Roderick demands that you be chained and prepared for trial. But Cassandra comes to your immediate defense—she feels you've been sent by the Maker. You can choose to go along with Cassandra's assumptions or dismiss the notion. In any case, Cassandra is convinced you have been sent here for a reason. Despite Roderick's protests Cassandra reinstates the Inquisition of old, vowing to close the Breach and restore order, with or without the support of the Chantry. After Roderick storms off you have the opportunity to question Cassandra and Leliana about the origins of the Inquisition. Agree to help to conclude the conversation and initiate the game's opening cinematic, showing word of the Inquisition spreading across Thedas.

Following the opening cinematic, Cassandra introduces you to the Inquisition's advisors: Josephine, Cullen, and Leliana. While all the advisors are unified behind the cause of the Inquisition, there is some disagreement over which faction can offer the most support. Leliana suggests courting the rebel mages, while Cullen feels the templars are the better option. But Josephine is quick to point out that neither faction has a favorable view of the Inquisition—that must change if you wish to gain their support. Meanwhile, the Chantry has declared you a heretic. Still, Mother Giselle, a Chantry cleric, has requested to speak to you. She can be found in the Hinterlands, near Redcliffe. Cullen and Josephine suggest expanding the Inquisition's influence while you're there.

THE WAR TABLE

Before you can travel to the Hinterlands, you must first perform a scouting operation on the war table. Completing scouting operations unlocks new areas to explore. The war table allows you to apply the power of the Inquisition throughout Orlais and Ferelden. Power is obtained by completing critical path plots, establishing camps, closing Fade rifts, capturing keeps, finding all landmarks in a locale, or by defeating high dragons. You currently have one power, just enough to scout the Hinterlands. Select Ferelden on the war table and then choose the Scout the Hinterlands option. Next, choose the advisor you wish to conduct the scouting operation—Leliana is the only advisor available for this particular one. This triggers a cinematic showing Harding, a scout, establishing a foothold for the Inquisition in the Hinterlands.

Missions

After the scouting operation, the war table is now open for missions. These operations take time and bring the Inquisition resources and rewards. Missions can only be conducted by Josephine, Cullen, or Leliana. Take time to read the details of each available mission and determine the best advisor for the job. Josephine is a diplomat and relies on connections and influence to complete her tasks. Leliana is a spy master and utilizes her network of agents to collect information. Cullen, a former templar, leads the Inquisition's army and relies on displays of force. Each mission shows how much time it takes for an advisor to complete the task. Generally, the advisor who can complete the operation quickest is usually the best choice for the job. However, rewards differ based on the advisor you select. For now, assign the advisors to the following missions:

Initial Missions

Advisor	Mission	Completion Time	Reward
Josephine	Gather Coin	0:48:00	Gold
Leliana	Hard in Hightown 3: Varric's Revenge	0:12:00	Sturdy Bianca Grip
Cullen	The Teyrn of Highever	0:12:00	Topaz

These particular missions only take a few minutes of game time to complete. After 12 minutes you can come back to the war table and issue new missions for Leliana and Cullen—Josephine's mission will take a bit longer to complete. A message appears on-screen when each mission is complete. Make frequent visits to the war table to keep your advisors busy.

NOTE When it comes to missions, sometimes the fastest advisor isn't always the best. Read the mission details carefully before determining which advisor is best suited for the outcome you desire, regardless of completion time.

> EXPLORING HAVEN

After completing the scouting operation on the war table, you can travel directly to the Hinterlands with your party and seek out Mother Giselle. However, it's highly recommended to spend some time exploring Haven and completing a few side quests. These quests serve as tutorials, familiarizing you with some basic gameplay concepts. So take a few minutes to complete the following optional side quests before leaving Haven.

Haven's Best and Brightest

Quest Giver: N/A

Description: Even in these trying times, good help is not so hard to find. Explore Haven and meet some of the Inquisition's crafting masters.

Requirements: Available after meeting the war council

Reward: 50 XP

Recommended Level: 2

Objectives:

- Speak with the smith.
- Speak with the quartermaster.
- Speak with the apothecary.

This quest is available immediately after the game's opening cinematic ends.

Start by speaking to the blacksmith, Harritt. He's located outside Haven's main gate. Harritt is the one who crafted the new armor you're currently wearing. Here you can craft new weapons and armor as well as modify existing equipment. Question Harritt about different aspects of his job to unlock two more quests: The Right Armor and Piece by Piece. These two quests can be completed here.

Adan, the apothecary, is on the west side of Haven, not far from Solas. He had a hand in your recovery following the incident at the temple. Adan is responsible for supplying the Inquisition with potions. You can come here to craft new potions using recipes and herbs. You can get the Passing Notes and Mixing Potions quests by speaking to Adan.

Next, speak to Threnn, the quartermaster, near the tent outside the chantry. She's responsible for fulfilling requisitions. She has prepared a list of items the Inquisition needs—find some iron and a logging site to complete the Requisition for Weapons quest. Return to the table next to Threnn to complete requisitions.

The Right Armor

Quest Giver: Harritt in Haven

Description: With the right materials, Haven's blacksmith can craft some pretty decent armor.

Requirements: Available after completing Haven's Best and Brightest

Reward: New armor

Recommended Level: 2

Objectives:

- Have some armor made.

Before you can craft some armor, you need to gather raw materials. Usually these items can be found in the wild during your journey. Fortunately, Harritt has a stash of materials nearby. Loot the crate next to the Craft Armor table—this will give you enough material to create some armor. Next, interact with the Craft Armor table. Armor is crafted using a schematic and raw materials. The schematic determines the appearance and potential power of the crafted armor, while the materials determine the specific stats and powers of the armor. Using the provided schematic and materials, craft a new piece of armor to complete the quest. Don't forget to equip the new armor.

PIECE BY PIECE

Quest Giver: Harritt in Haven
Description: The blacksmith can also improve existing armor.
Requirements: Available after completing Haven's Best and Brightest
Reward: Modified armor
Recommended Level: 2
Objectives:

- Modify some armor.

While you're still at the blacksmith's, take a moment to complete this simple quest. Start by looting the crate next to the Craft Weapons table. Inside is an armor upgrade. Next, go to the Modify Armor table. Upgrading armor adds the upgrade's stats to the armor's stats while also altering the armor's appearance. Choose the armor you wish to upgrade, preferably the armor you just crafted. Each piece of armor has two upgrade slots: arms and legs. Apply the upgrade you just retrieved from the crate, then select Confirm Changes to complete the process. Upgrades aren't permanent. They can be removed and applied to other armor. So before selling armor (or weapons), make sure you've removed any upgrades you wish to keep.

PASSING NOTES

Quest Giver: Adan in Haven
Description: Some technical notes were found while exploring Haven. They look like someone named Taigen put a lot of work into them.
Requirements: Available after scouting the Hinterlands
Reward: 100 XP, Regeneration Potion Recipe
Recommended Level: 2
Objectives:

- Find Taigen's notes.
- Return the notes to Adan.

This quest is available after choosing the "Need any help?" conversation option while speaking to Adan—you can do this while completing the Haven's Best and Brightest quest. Adan needs some help finding Master Taigen's notes. Apparently Taigen was working on something special before he died at the Conclave. After speaking with Adan and selecting the quest, go to the purple mark on the quest map. As you near this area, a pulsing blue ring appears around the compass, indicating the presence of a hidden object. Press the button/key shown on-screen to begin searching. Once you initiate a search, a gold ring-like radius emanates from your character's feet. But the ring isn't uniform—it glows brighter along one edge, indicating the direction of the hidden object. Continue searching, using this indicator to move closer and closer to the hidden object. When you initiate a search next to the object, it finally appears on the ground, allowing you to retrieve it. Take Taigen's notes to Adan. In return he gives you access to a new potion recipe. You can now complete the Mixing Potions quest.

TIP In addition to revealing hidden objects, conducting searches also causes nearby interactive objects to glow for a short time. This is a great way to quickly locate herbs, minerals, and loot stashes.

MIXING POTIONS

Quest Giver: Adan in Haven
Description: A recovered recipe can be used to mix a potion at a loadout station. There, the potion can also be equipped or replenished. Potion loadout stations are found in the Inquisition's base of operations or at any claimed camp.
Requirements: Available after completing Passing Notes
Reward: 44 XP, 40 Influence
Recommended Level: 2
Objectives:

- Visit a potion loadout station.

Immediately after completing the Passing Notes quest, interact with the Equip Potions table next to Adan. This gives you access to your Potion Belt menu. Here you can assign or replenish potions for different party members. Healing potions, at the top of the radial, are replenished for free automatically. But all other potions require herbs to replenish them. Select the empty potion slot on the radial and assign the regeneration potion to it. It requires one elfroot to create each regeneration potion—replenish this potion to craft it from existing elfroot. If you don't have any elfroot, it can be acquired outside of Haven—it's by far the most common herb in the game and easy to find in multiple locales. Exit the Potion Belt menu to complete the quest.

KNOW THY ENEMY

Quest Giver: N/A
Description: Some items recovered in battle may later be worth studying.
Requirements: Available after scouting the Hinterlands
Reward: 44 XP, 40 Influence
Recommended Level: 2
Objectives:

- Give Minaeve an item to research.

Minaeve is the Inquisition's researcher. You'll find her in Josephine's chamber within the chantry. Interact with the table next to Minaeve to deposit a research item. Research items can be looted from some fallen enemies following a battle. If you didn't retrieve any research items during your advance to the Temple of Sacred Ashes, you'll need to come back later and complete this quest.

REQUISITION FOR WEAPONS

Quest Giver: Threnn in Haven
Description: With the right materials found, weapons for the Inquisition can be requisitioned through the quartermaster.
Requirements: Available after scouting the Hinterlands
Reward: 1 Power
Recommended Level: 2
Objectives:

- Locate weapon materials (five iron deposits and one logging stand).
- Fill the requisition.

After you speak to Threnn during Haven's Best and Brightest, this quest is automatically added to your list. As the quartermaster, Threnn is responsible for supplying the Inquisition with the materials necessary to outfit soldiers. Right now, she needs iron and wood, acquired from a logging stand.

Exit Haven and head north, searching along the eastern banks of the frozen lake. Deposits of iron can be retrieved from the large boulders here—conduct a search to make nearby iron deposits glow. From the lake, head east, into the forest, to locate three piles of wood—this will make a fine spot for a logging stand. Interact with the spot amidst these piles of wood to plant a flag, claiming the logging stand for the Inquisition.

Once you've found five iron deposits and claimed the logging stand, return to the Requisition table back in Haven. Interact with the table to fill the requisition for weapons. This functions similarly to crafting weapons or armor, utilizing a schematic. Select the Requisition Weapons schematic, then assign the iron and logging stand to the proper slots to complete the requisition. Requisitions are common in all locales, requiring you to find a variety of materials. Completing a requisition grants the Inquisition one power, which can be spent on the war table.

TIP Before leaving for the Hinterlands, consider returning to the war room and assigning Cullen, Leliana, and Josephine to new missions. They've likely completed their previous assignments. Make frequent visits to the war room to keep your advisors busy.

THE HINTERLANDS

When you've completed all the side quests in Haven, travel to the Hinterlands using the quest map. Upon arrival, the Inquisition scout, Harding, greets you and your party while filling you in on the current situation in the Hinterlands. The conflict between the templars and rebel mages has spread to the Crossroads, where Mother Giselle is tending to the refugees—Harding suggests getting there soon. Corporal Vale and his soldiers are defending the area, but they won't hold out for long.

INQUISITION CAMPS

After you perform a scouting operation on the war table, an Inquisition camp is automatically established, serving as your entry point into the locale. At camps you can rest, fill requisitions, equip potions, and change companions. Camps also serve as fast travel points. Establish more camps throughout the Hinterlands and other locales. One power is rewarded for each new camp you establish—this is by far the easiest method to gain power. Camps can only be established at predetermined locations. View the quest map to see these campsites—you can establish five additional camps in the Hinterlands.

NOTE Speak to the lead scout at the Inquisition camp to unlock a requisition quest. Requisition quests are available in every locale, each requiring you to collect a set number of raw materials. The requisition quest you get in each locale is randomized. So there's a chance you may get the same quest more than once. For more information on the requisition quests available in each locale, reference the Exploration chapter.

> SECURE THE CROSSROADS

Lead your party to the Crossroads, moving along the trail to the north. As you approach the Crossroads, Corporal Vale and his Inquisition soldiers are under attack by a group of three templar knights. Immediately engage the tactical camera and take a moment to plan your attack. Templar knights perform similar to shades, relying solely on melee attacks to dish out damage. But unlike shades, they have the ability to block incoming melee attacks. Use Cassandra's Challenge to taunt them, then attack from a distance with Solas and Varric.

After you defeat the templars, rebel mages approach from the east. The group consists of two sellswords and two rebel spellbinders. Target and eliminate the charging sellswords first, using Cassandra to taunt them. The rebel spellbinders are a bit more dangerous, casting spells from a distance. These enemies are vulnerable to cold-based attacks but resistant to fire. Therefore, focus on using cold-based attacks to inflict bonus damage. Also, watch out for the fiery circular glyphs the rebel spellbinders cast on the ground. Think of these fiery glyphs as landmines—if any friendly character steps on one, the glyph explodes and deals heavy fire damage. Rebel spellbinders also have the ability to teleport in an effort to avoid incoming melee attacks. Your party members with ranged attacks have the best chance of taking these guys down.

CAUTION Beware of flames during the fight at the Crossroads. Walking through or standing in flames will cause your party members to take damage.

The third and final wave consists of three templar knights and one templar defender. Focus on the templar knights first, picking them off one by one. The templar defender is the most durable enemy you've faced yet. Equipped with a massive shield, the templar defender can block all frontal attacks. You need to find a way to flank him. Try to draw his attention with Cassandra's Challenge, initiating it while she's standing behind him—otherwise it will be blocked. Once Cassandra has taunted the templar defender, position the rest of your party so they can strike him from the back or sides, preferably forming a circular formation around him. While Cassandra's attacks may cause no damage, any hits from the side or rear get through and inflict damage. Occasionally the templar defender will charge forward, knocking down anyone in his path. Don't let these aggressive displays deter you. Keep taunting him and repositioning your party as necessary so they can score flanking strikes. Knockdown attacks are particularly effective, as the templar knight cannot deploy his shield while on the ground—hammer away at him from all angles as he struggles to get back on his feet.

TIP If you're playing as a mage or rogue archer, consider equipping Varric with a pair of daggers in an attempt to better balance your party—daggers can either be found as loot or purchased from a merchant. Giving Varric daggers allows him to charge forward with Cassandra and perform melee attacks while you and Solas hang back and cast spells or fire arrows. If Cassandra is the only melee member of your party, battles like the one at the Crossroads can be a bit more challenging than they need to be.

> MOTHER GISELLE

After defeating the templars and rebel mages at the Crossroads, your character strikes up a conversation with Mother Giselle. Despite her position as a Chantry cleric, Mother Giselle does not agree with the Chantry's denouncement of you. She suggests seeking an audience with the remaining clerics and convincing them that you're not a threat. In the meantime, Mother Giselle will go to Haven and supply Leliana with the names of Chantry clerics who will agree to meet with you.

Landmarks

After speaking to Mother Giselle, claim the landmark (Saga of Tyrdda Bright-Axe, Avvar-Mother) nearby by planting an Inquisition banner. There are 17 landmarks in the Hinterlands. Each landmark unlocks a codex entry, providing more information on each area. Claiming all landmarks in a locale gives the Inquisition power.

CORPORAL VALE

Next, seek out Corporal Vale—his position is marked on the compass and quest map. Corporal Vale is overseeing the Inquisition's efforts in the Hinterlands. He's grateful for your assistance at the Crossroads, but there's more work to be done. The templars and rebel mages aren't the only threat. Bandits have blocked the nearby road, making it difficult to deliver aid to the refugees.

GAINING POWER

In an effort to stabilize the Hinterlands, you must acquire power and expand the reach of the Inquisition. A total of four power must be earned before you can address the chantry in Val Royeaux. How you gain power is entirely up to you. Establishing camps is the easiest way to gain power, earning you one power for each camp. There are also Fade rifts scattered throughout the Hinterlands—closing each rift earns you power. You can also complete quests to gain power. Once you've acquired at least four power, return to Haven.

Recommended Quests

Quest/Activity	Locale	Power
Requisition for Weapons	Haven	1
Rifts on the Outskirts	The Hinterlands	2
Establish Upper Lake Camp	The Hinterlands	1

NOTE For details on completing each quest in the Hinterlands, reference the Exploration chapter.

HAVEN

Now that you have enough power to address the clerics in Val Royeaux, head for the war council room in the chantry. Outside the chantry an angry crowd has gathered—templars accuse mages of being involved in the Divine's death. Cullen does his best to defuse the situation, but it's clear there's still friction between the few templars and mages who have joined the Inquisition. Chancellor Roderick's pessimism doesn't help matters. Speak to Cullen and do your best to ease Roderick's concerns regarding the Chantry's support of the Inquisition.

Inside the chantry take a moment to speak to Mother Giselle—as promised, she has come to Haven. To unlock a new requisition quest, Lotus and Root, ask her if you can help with anything. Her healers need more supplies (five blood lotuses and five elfroots) to aid the wounded. After speaking to Mother Giselle, turn in any research items you've collected in the Hinterlands to Minaeve—if you haven't already, this completes the Know Thy Enemy side quest, netting you 50 XP. Make a habit of turning in research items each time you come back to Haven. Researching items looted from particular enemies can give you a bonus in combat when facing the same enemies in the future.

INQUISITION PERKS

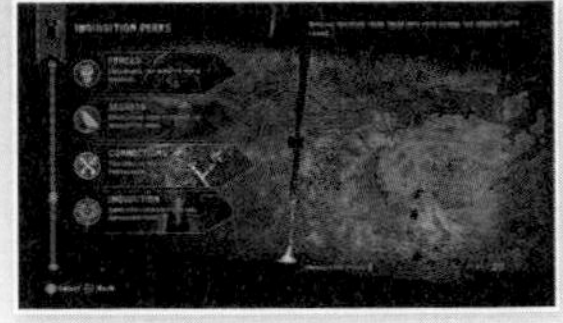

Finally, enter the war room. By now the Inquisition has gained some influence, earning one Inquisition perk. These perks are special training provided by those who have joined the Inquisition. There are four different categories of perks: Forces, Secrets, Connections, and Inquisition. Browse through all four categories to view the available perks. Not all perks are immediately available—most are locked. As you obtain perks in a single category, more perks within that same category are unlocked. So think long term and determine which locked perks will benefit your Inquisition in the future. For more information on Inquisition perks, reference the War Council chapter.

TIP Look for opportunities to recruit agents for the Inquisition. Most agents unlock a unique perk. Reference the War Council and Exploration chapters for more information on Inquisition agents.

THE CHANTRY REMAINS

After selecting a perk, choose new operation assignments for the advisors. Next, choose Orlais on the war table. A pulsing green rift icon appears over Val Royeaux, indicating the critical path. Select The Chantry Remains operation, spending the four power you've acquired. There's some disagreement among the war council regarding this approach. But Cassandra convinces them that it's the Inquisition's only move. Confirm the operation and prepare for immediate departure to Val Royeaux.

VAL ROYEAUX

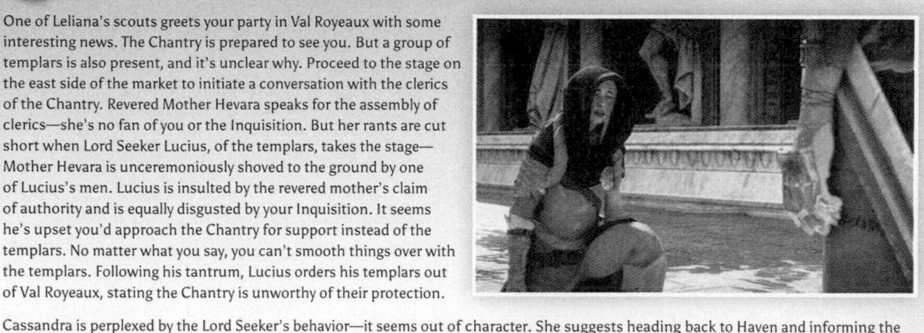

One of Leliana's scouts greets your party in Val Royeaux with some interesting news. The Chantry is prepared to see you. But a group of templars is also present, and it's unclear why. Proceed to the stage on the east side of the market to initiate a conversation with the clerics of the Chantry. Revered Mother Hevara speaks for the assembly of clerics—she's no fan of you or the Inquisition. But her rants are cut short when Lord Seeker Lucius, of the templars, takes the stage—Mother Hevara is unceremoniously shoved to the ground by one of Lucius's men. Lucius is insulted by the revered mother's claim of authority and is equally disgusted by your Inquisition. It seems he's upset you'd approach the Chantry for support instead of the templars. No matter what you say, you can't smooth things over with the templars. Following his tantrum, Lucius orders his templars out of Val Royeaux, stating the Chantry is unworthy of their protection.

Cassandra is perplexed by the Lord Seeker's behavior—it seems out of character. She suggests heading back to Haven and informing the others. But before doing so, take some time to explore Val Royeaux. There are several merchants here as well as some interesting people to talk to.

Agents of the Inquisition

Locate Belle, a merchant, on the east side of the market. Belle is happy the Inquisition is doing something about restoring order, and she wants to do her part. Accept Belle's offer to join the Inquisition to gain one power. As an agent, Belle unlocks the Barter Belle perk, reducing the amount of time it takes Josephine to complete her missions by 5 percent. During your journeys look for more opportunities to recruit agents into the Inquisition. Reference the War Council and Exploration chapters for more information on agents.

As you prepare to leave Val Royeaux, you're approached by Grand Enchanter Fiona, leader of the rebel mages. She extends an invitation to Redcliffe in the Hinterlands, suggesting an alliance with the mages could be mutually beneficial. It's time to head back to Haven and discuss this option with the war council.

> NEW RECRUITS: SERA AND VIVIENNE

Before leaving Val Royeaux, complete the following side quests to recruit Sera and Vivienne.

A Friend of Red Jenny

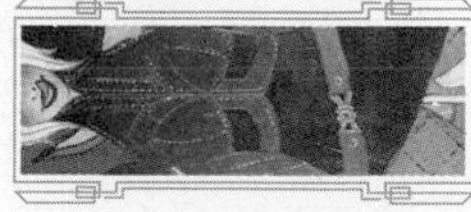

Quest Giver: Arrow in the market

Description: The strange message, delivered via arrow, said there is an enemy of the Inquisition waiting to strike Val Royeaux. It said to search the market, cafe, and docks for things that are red.

Requirements: Available after addressing the clerics

Reward: Sera

Recommended Level: 4-6

Objectives:

- Examine the message.
- Search by the dock.
- Search in the cafe.
- Search the upper market.
- Fend off the guards.

Immediately following the conversation with Mother Hevara and the templars, a mysterious arrow lands nearby. This is the start of a small quest, requiring you to search for red satchels by the dock, cafe, and upper market. Go to each location marked on the compass and conduct searches to find and retrieve the three red satchels. To reach the upper market, enter the blue doors on the southwest side of the market—this gives you access to the balcony above.

Once you have found all three red satchels, a secluded courtyard appears on the world map—travel there. This takes you to small courtyard occupied by hostile reach guards and freeman spotters. Eliminate the first group of enemies, then open the door to the west. Here you encounter a noble, unfriendly to the Inquisition. But he's soon killed by a potential ally, Sera, an elven rogue archer. Sera is the one who led you here. Help Sera fend off the remaining guards before resuming your conversation. Sera is part of a band of mercenaries called the Friends of Red Jenny—accept her offer to join the Inquisition.

Getting Started
Walkthrough
Classes and Abilities
Party Members
The War Council
Crafting
Exploration
Bestiary
Multiplayer
Compendium
The Wrath of Heaven
The Threat Remains
In Hushed Whispers (Mage Path)
Champions of the Just (Templar Path)
In Your Heart Shall Burn
From the Ashes
Here Lies the Abyss
Wicked Eyes and Wicked Hearts
What Pride Had Wrought
The Final Piece
Doom Upon All the World
Dragon Age Inquisition

THE IMPERIAL ENCHANTER

Quest Giver: Circle mage messenger in the market

Description: Vivienne de Fer, the First Enchanter of Montsimmard, has extended an invitation to her salon at the chateau of Duke Bastien de Ghyslain.

Requirements: Available after addressing the clerics

Reward: Vivienne

Recommended Level: 4-6

Objectives:

- Attend the salon.

Speak to the messenger in Val Royeaux's market to receive an invitation from Vivienne de Fer, a well-connected mage in Orlais. The invitation adds the Ghyslain Estate to the world map—travel there. Upon entering the chateau, you're rudely greeted by a marquis who has nothing kind to say about the Inquisition. But he's soon set straight by Vivienne—she even allows you to choose the marquis's fate. After introducing herself, Vivienne gets to the point. As the leader of the last loyal mages of Thedas, she feels compelled to join the Inquisition. Feel free to ask Vivienne more questions, but at the end of the conversation, welcome her aboard—she is a powerful ally, both on and off the battlefield.

HAVEN

Head directly to the chantry to initiate a conversation with members of the war council. The Inquisition has come to a crossroads and a decision must be made soon—will the Inquisition side with the rebel mages or templars? But this decision can't be made just yet. You must acquire more power. Following the conversation, Leliana approaches you and tells you of a Grey Warden sighting in the Hinterlands. His name is Blackwall, and he may know more about the sudden disappearance of the Grey Wardens. Leliana feels the timing of their disappearance is suspicious given the tragic events at the Conclave. After speaking to Leliana, wrap up anything else you need to do in Haven and then travel to the Hinterlands. This time you can choose to bring Sera and Vivienne along with you.

NEW RECRUIT: THE IRON BULL

Before leaving Haven, speak with Krem, standing outside the chantry. He informs you that Tevinter mercenaries have arrived in the Storm Coast. Krem invites you to meet with his commander, Iron Bull, in the Storm Coast. If you don't have enough power to scout the Storm Coast, consider doing so later. Iron Bull can be recruited at any point during your adventure after this.

THE CAPTAIN OF THE CHARGERS

Quest Giver: Krem in Haven

Description: A Qunari warrior known as the Iron Bull is offering aid for the Inquisition from his mercenary company, the Bull's Chargers.

Requirements: Available after returning from Val Royeaux

Reward: Iron Bull

Recommended Level: 4-6

Objectives:

- Meet Iron Bull at the Storm Coast.

Before you can go to the Storm Coast, you must first scout it on the war table, costing five power. When arriving at the Storm Coast head northwest to find Iron Bull and his Chargers engaged in battle against several Tevinter zealots. Once your party arrives, the enemies are outnumbered—help Iron Bull and the Chargers mop up the rest. Following the battle, Iron Bull strikes up a conversation, offering his group's services to the Inquisition. But he also reveals he's working for the Ben-Hassrath, the Qunari secret police. As an agent of the Ben-Hassrath, Iron Bull is tasked with keeping an eye on the Inquisition—the Qunari have a vested interest in closing the Breach. In return, he offers to share Ben-Hassrath information with the Inquisition. If you agree with Iron Bull's terms, ask him to join the Inquisition.

NOTE If you chose to go to the Storm Coast to recruit the Iron Bull, take some time exploring the locale and completing quests, like Cleaning House. It doesn't take long to earn back the five power it cost you to scout the locale. Reference the Exploration chapter for a complete rundown of all activities available in the Storm Coast.

THE HINTERLANDS

GAINING POWER

Upon your return to the Hinterlands, focus on building up power. Whether you choose to side with the rebel mages or templars, you'll need a whopping 15 power to initiate an alliance. Fortunately, there's more than enough to do in the Hinterlands to acquire the power you need. Establish more camps, close Fade rifts, and complete side quests to gain power. Also, if you're interested in gaining access to horses (and other mounts), visit Dennet, the horsemaster, at Redcliffe Farms. He'll have some tasks for you to complete before he decides to help the Inquisition, but it's well worth the effort. Once you have at least 15 power, begin working on the In Hushed Whispers or Champions of the Just quest.

Recommended Quests

Quest/Activity	Locale	Power
Lotus and Root	Haven	1
Requisition in the Hinterlands	The Hinterlands	1
Establish Redcliffe Farms Camp	The Hinterlands	1
Rifts on the Farm	The Hinterlands	2
Master of Horses	The Hinterlands	1
Rifts at the Foothold	The Hinterlands	2
Strange Bedfellows	The Hinterlands	1
Establish Dwarfson's Pass Camp	The Hinterlands	1
Praise the Herald of Andraste	The Hinterlands	1
Love Waits	The Hinterlands	1
Rifts at Dwarfson's Pass	The Hinterlands	3

TIP Even if you don't intend to side with the mages, you can still go to Redcliffe Village and acquire power by closing Fade rifts. There is one Fade rift outside Redcliffe Village and another inside Redcliffe's chantry, available only after completing the meeting in the Gull & Lantern tavern.

DEVELOPER TIP

To make questing easier in the Hinterlands, clear out the templar and mage encampments.

—Jason Baxter, QA Tester

NEW RECRUIT: BLACKWALL

While you're in the Hinterlands, complete the following side quest to recruit Blackwall, the Grey Warden.

The Lone Warden

Quest Giver: Leliana in Haven

Description: One of Leliana's agents reported a man, calling himself Blackwall, dressed in full Grey Warden regalia and last seen traveling through the Ferelden Hinterlands. With so many Wardens disappearing in the wake of the Divine's death, this Blackwall should be questioned.

Requirements: Available after returning from Val Royeaux

Reward: Blackwall

Recommended Level: 4-6

Objectives:

- Search for Blackwall in the Hinterlands.

Blackwall's camp can be found on the western shore of Lake Luthias. He's busy training some recruits when you arrive. But just as you begin talking to Blackwall, his camp is attacked by a group of bandits. Help Blackwall and his recruits defeat the bandits. After the battle, question Blackwall about the disappearance of the Grey Wardens. Blackwall insists the Wardens had nothing to do with the death of the Divine and doesn't know why Wardens have disappeared—he works alone and rarely has contact with other Grey Wardens. As you're about to leave, Blackwall offers to join the Inquisition. Accept his offer and consider adding him to your current party.

DEVELOPER TIP

For some fun banter I like to have Sera and Iron Bull together in my party.

—John Boos, Art QA

CAUTION Blackwall must be recruited before going to Adamant. If you haven't recruited Blackwall by then, you can never get him.

IN HUSHED WHISPERS

Grand Enchanter Fiona, leader of the mage rebellion, has offered an alliance with the rebel mages at Redcliffe.

THE HINTERLANDS

At this point, you don't need to make a final decision on whether to ally yourself with the templars or mages. As some in the war council have suggested, it might be wise to meet with the rebel mages before making a decision. Back in Val Royeaux, Grand Enchanter Fiona invited you to Redcliffe, and it's time to take her up on her offer. Travel to the Crossroads, then head north along the Redcliffe Road to reach Redcliffe Village.

> REDCLIFFE VILLAGE

As you near the gate leading into Redcliffe, a soldier comes running toward your party, warning of a nearby rift. Battle the demons at the rift blocking the village gate. After eliminating the second wave, close the rift, gaining one power for your troubles. The soldier you encountered earlier returns to her post and orders that the gates be opened, allowing you to enter Redcliffe Village.

Just inside the gate, you're greeted by one of Leliana's scouts. Despite Fiona's invitation, it appears your arrival was unexpected. A nervous rebel mage rushes to greet you, apologizing for the confusion. He says Magister Alexius is in charge now, but is delayed. Instead, he offers you the chance to meet with the former grand enchanter. It's unclear exactly what's going on here. But head for the tavern marked on the compass to begin negotiations. On the way to the tavern, feel free to speak with the inhabitants of Redcliffe Village—some of them offer side quests.

The Gull & Lantern

When you're finished exploring Redcliffe Village, enter the Gull & Lantern tavern. Inside you're greeted by Grand Enchanter Fiona—but she claims this is the first time you've met. She hasn't been to Val Royeaux since before the Conclave. Fiona has more unsettling news. The rebel mages have pledged themselves to the Tevinter Imperium, led by Magister Alexius. As a result, Fiona no longer has the power to negotiate with the Inquisition—you must deal with Alexius. As if on cue, Alexius and his son, Felix, arrive to begin negotiations. But the meeting is cut short when Felix pretends to faint, slyly dropping a note during his ruse. Alexius agrees to continue this meeting later before heading back to Redcliffe Castle with Felix and Fiona. The note dropped by Felix warns of danger and urges your party to go to the village's chantry.

Agents of the Inquisition

Before leaving the tavern, speak with Clemence, an alchemist. Question him about Alexius and recent events in Redcliffe. During the conversation, Clemence asks if he can join the Inquisition. At this point he becomes an agent and will appear back in Haven. Some other characters you encounter also have the opportunity to become an Inquisition agent. Agents unlock a unique Inquisition perk. For instance, the Clemence, the Tranquil perk reduces the amount of time it takes for Cullen to complete a operation by 5 percent. As part of the Unfinished Business quest, you can also recruit Tanner outside Redcliffe's chantry. For a listing of all available agents in each locale, reference the Exploration chapter.

Redcliffe Village Chantry

From the Gull & Lantern, head north to Redcliffe's chantry. Inside, a mage named Dorian is busy battling demons emerging from a rift—he asks for your assistance. The chantry's interior is rather cramped for such a large battle. Focus on eliminating the shades before targeting the wraiths and terrors. After eliminating two waves of demons, close the rift. Dorian strikes up a conversation after the battle, revealing that he's a former apprentice of Alexius. But he fears something is terribly wrong with his mentor, citing Alexius's ability to distort time. Felix joins the conversation, admitting his father has joined a Tevinter cult called the Venatori. Both Felix and Dorian feel Alexius must be stopped, suggesting the Venatori may have something to do with the breach. If you choose to take on Alexius, Dorian offers to help. Following the conversation, feel free to explore the rest of the chantry and Redcliffe Village before returning to Haven.

HAVEN

Now is the time to make your decision. Will you attempt to form an alliance with the templars? Or will you take on Alexius in an effort to gain control of the rebel mages? Go to the war room and convene the war council. If you choose to confront Alexius, select the In Hushed Whispers operation on the war table, costing 10 power. Cullen and Josephine feel this is a risky move, realizing you'll be walking into a trap. Despite the reservations of the council, insist on accepting Alexius's invitation to Redcliffe Castle. Leliana devises a plan to sneak her agents into the castle, with Dorian's assistance. Together they'll disarm any traps while you meet with Alexius. Once you settle on this plan, select your companions for this risky mission. Dorian is automatically a party member, leaving only two vacant slots. If you're not playing as a rogue, consider bringing along Varric or Sera—their lock-picking skills will come in handy. Cassandra or Blackwall is a good choice for rounding out your party.

REDCLIFFE CASTLE

When you arrive at Redcliffe Castle, Dorian sneaks around in the shadows while you meet with Alexius. But instead of negotiating with Alexius, let him know that his trap has been exposed. Alexius denies nothing. Instead, he rambles on about the mark on your hand. Felix and Dorian join the intervention, trying to convince Alexius to stand down. But Alexius continues his diatribe, stating that he serves a mysterious figure called the Elder One. When Alexius realizes his guards have been eliminated by Leliana's agents, he uses an amulet to open a rift.

Redcliffe Castle

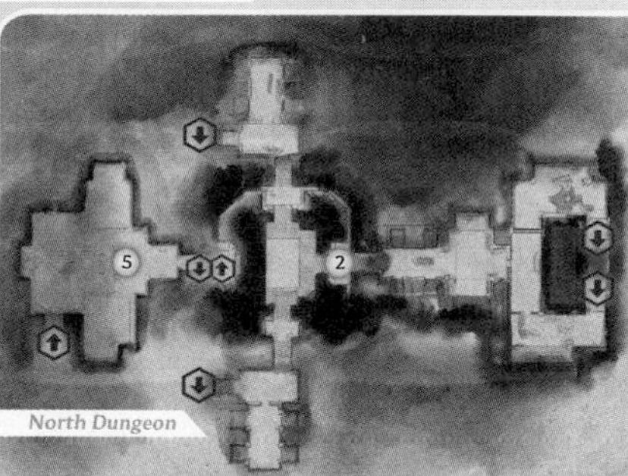

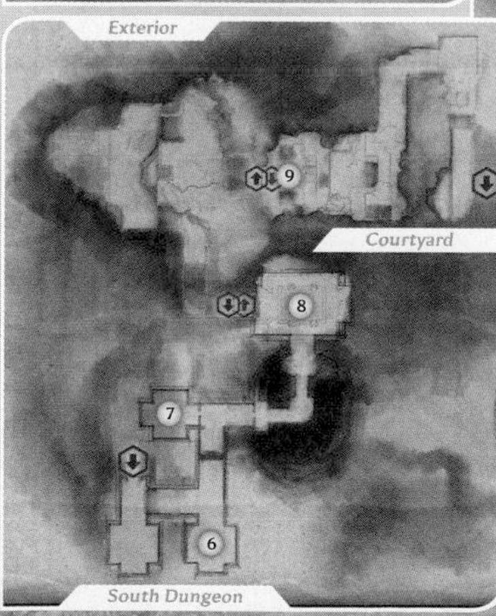

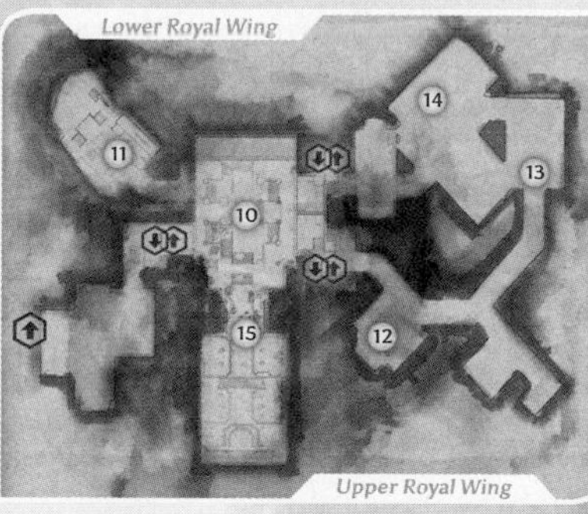

Legend

Level Up
Level Down

> DUNGEON

1. Suddenly, you and Dorian find yourselves in a flooded dungeon beneath the castle. But you don't have time to talk—surprised by your appearance, two Venatori zealots attack you. Eliminate the enemies, then resume your conversation. Dorian theorizes that Alexius's spell has moved you through time—he knows where you are but not *when* you are. Explore the lower cells and upper cells of this wing, looting chests along the way. There seems to be a disturbing amount of red lyrium growing out of the castle's walls.

2. Make your way to the junction linking the three cell blocks. Here you're confronted by two more Venatori zealots—try to knock them off the platform for easy kills. But be careful to mind your own step during this battle, too.

3. After eliminating the enemies at the junction, pass through the door to the south to enter the southern cell block. Search the individual rooms in the upper and lower cells for loot. One room in the lower cells features a particularly large growth of red lyrium. Search the cell in the southeast corner to find Grand Enchanter Fiona, partially encased in red lyrium. Fiona can't be saved, but she's coherent enough to reveal that a full year has passed since you confronted Alexius. Dorian feels he can restore time if he can gain access to Alexius's amulet. Fiona says that Leliana is being held somewhere in the castle. She suggests finding her before the Elder One knows you're here. After talking to Fiona, backtrack to the junction.

4. Before you can find Leliana, you need to find the rest of your party. At the junction pass through the door to the north to enter the northern cell block. Proceed to the lower cells and search for your party members. There are seven possible cells where your party members may reside. Reference the map to locate which cell your party members are in. Regardless of who you brought along, their fate is only mildly better than Fiona's. Languishing in their cell for a year has left them infected with red lyrium. However, they still have the strength to help you confront Alexius.

5. Return to the junction and engage more enemies, including a couple of Venatori marksmen and a Venatori spellbinder. With your party restored, this battle shouldn't be a problem. As before, look for opportunities to knock the enemies off the platform. When the path is clear, cross the bridge to the west and proceed up the stairs to enter the guard barracks. There's plenty of loot here. Take your time to clean out the area, then proceed to the torture chambers.

> TORTURE CHAMBERS

6. In this chamber, a pair of Venatori zealots and a powerful Venatori spellbinder, named Hanley, stand over the body of Mother Giselle. It's not necessary to enter this chamber or complete this fight, but defeating Hanley may yield some rare loot.

7. Leliana is being held in this chamber. As you enter, Leliana's interrogator is distracted, giving her the opportunity to strangle the enemy with her legs. Dorian fills in Leliana on recent events, but she seems more interested in taking out her anger on Alexius. Grab the key on the table in the center of the room and then exit the chamber, heading east. At this point Leliana joins your party, but you cannot take direct control of her. Instead, she will follow and engage enemies on her own.

8. Here you encounter a Fade rift. Battle the shades, wraiths, and terrors, then close the rift—this is the first of several Fade rifts you'll encounter during your approach to the throne room. After the battle, approach the iron gate to the west side of the room. Open the gate by interacting with the wheel to the left side. Once the gate is open, head upstairs to discover the docks—and prepare to confront more demons.

9. Two Fade rifts open in this courtyard. Take on one Fade rift at a time, focusing on the one to the west first. After closing both Fade rifts, head east to enter the castle's royal wing.

> ROYAL WING

10. In this large room within the lower royal wing, you encounter more demons and a Fade rift. There are also several Venatori marksmen and spellbinders in this fight. Try to focus on the demons first, then engage the marksmen and spellbinders. After closing the rift, search the ground for loot. One of the creatures has dropped a red lyrium shard—you'll need five of these shards to enter Alexius's throne room. The remaining four red lyrium shards are scattered throughout the royal wing, each held by a Venatori spellbinder—reference the map for their locations. Collect all five shards and bring them back to this room.

11. This chapel-like room is occupied by more Venatori enemies, including two Venatori gladiators. The enemies are distracted when you enter, giving you the chance to strike first. Ignore the gladiators at the start of the battle and go after the spellbinder and marksmen. Once the ranged threat is eliminated, focus on the gladiators, working to score flanking strikes. When the battle is over, grab the loot where the spellbinder fell to obtain the second red lyrium shard. You'll need to head back upstairs, to the upper royal wing, to obtain the remaining three shards.

12. When you first enter this room, in the upper royal wing, try to take out the Venatori spellbinder first. Next, utilize the staircases in this room as choke points when engaging the numerous Venatori zealots. Block staircases with your warriors or wall spells and then use area-of-effect attacks to inflict heavy damage on the clusters of enemies. Following the battle, gather the loot from the spellbinder to obtain the third red lyrium shard.

13. Climb the ladder to the east of the dining room's entrance to gain a height advantage—your ranged party members are very effective when attacking from this wooden scaffolding while your melee fighters stay on the ground. Take out the spellbinder and marksmen first, then mop up the zealots to finish the battle. The fourth red lyrium shard is left behind by the Venatori spellbinder.

14. This small room is occupied by a single Venatori spellbinder. Make quick work of him, then retrieve the fifth and final red lyrium shard from his remains. The eastern and western walls of this room are weak—use a warrior to bash through them. Alternatively, use a rogue to unlock the doors from the main hall.

15. Now that you have all five red lyrium shards you can access Alexius's throne room. Interact with this door to enter.

TIP Before entering the throne room, seek out a supply cache to replenish your potions. Reference the map for supply cache locations.

CONFRONTING ALEXIUS

Alexius's mood has changed considerably since your last encounter—he finally realizes the calamity his actions have caused. His son Felix cowers by his side, clearly afflicted with some sort of enchantment. But Leliana is in no mood to take pity, drawing a dagger and placing it to Felix's throat. Alexius pleads for Felix's life. But no matter what conversation option you choose, Leliana gets her revenge, killing Felix and initiating a battle with Alexius.

Alexius is likely the most durable foe you've faced thus far. He has no resistances or vulnerabilities, so any attacks and spells are effective. However, Alexius does have a lot of health, so it will take some time to defeat him. As a Tevinter mage, Alexius has the ability to teleport from one spot to another. As a result, ranged attacks are most effective—your melee fighters will need to constantly chase him down. When Alexius's health drops below 50 percent, he opens a Fade rift, causing demons to spill out. During this sequence, Alexius cannot be attacked—he takes shelter behind an impenetrable barrier near the throne. Defeat the demons and close the rift to resume your battle with Alexius. A second Fade rift is opened when Alexius's health drops to 25 percent—once again, defeat the demons and close the rift. After closing the second Fade rift, continue attacking Alexius until he's down for good.

Dorian retrieves the amulet from Alexius's body. But there isn't much time to figure out how the amulet works—the Elder One is coming. Leliana and the two red lyrium–infected members of your party offer to stay back and serve as a deterrent while you and Dorian travel back through time. While Leliana and the others fight off the attackers, Dorian and the Inquisitor escape through a portal, taking them back to the present. Back in the present throne room, Alexius concedes and is taken prisoner by Inquisition troops. Depending on your imported world state, King Alistair or Queen Anora (or both) enter the throne room, ordering Fiona and her rebel mages to leave Ferelden. With nowhere to go, you have the chance to decide the fate of Fiona and her mages. Following the decision, you are automatically transported back to Haven.

DECISION POINT

You can either decide to take the mages as prisoners and conscript them or form an alliance with them. Like any major decision, this will affect your approval with various party members.

APPROVAL: FATE OF THE REBEL MAGES

FOLLOWER	MAGES AS CONSCRIPTS	MAGES AS ALLIES
Blackwall	⬇⬇	⬆⬆
Cassandra	⬆⬆	⬇⬇⬇
The Iron Bull	⬆⬆⬆	⬇⬇
Sera	⬆⬆⬆	⬇⬇
Solas	⬇⬇⬇	⬆⬆⬆
Varric	⬆⬆ (if Hawke sided with templars in DA2) ⬇⬇ (if Hawke sided with mages)	⬆⬆ (if Hawke sided with mages in DA2) ⬇⬇ (if Hawke sided with templars)
Vivienne	⬆⬆⬆	⬇⬇⬇
Dorian	⬇⬇	⬆⬆⬆
Cole	⬇⬇⬇	⬆⬆⬆

HAVEN

Back at the chantry in Haven, some council members are at odds over your decision. Despite the misgivings of some, Cassandra is supportive of your decision—closing the Breach is her main concern. But there are other matters of concern too, including a plot to kill Empress Celine of Orlais. Cullen suggests reconvening in the war room.

NEW RECRUIT: DORIAN

After a brief discussion with the council, Dorian offers to stick around and assist the Inquisition. Accept Dorian's offer to gain access to him as a future party member—it never hurts to have another mage at your disposal.

NOTE Upon completion of In Hushed Whispers, jump ahead to In Your Heart Shall Burn. The next section, Champions of the Just, applies only if you chose to seek aid from the templars.

CHAMPIONS OF THE JUST

The templars have left Val Royeaux and refuse to negotiate with anyone. Gather enough power, then work with the advisors to make contact with the templars.

HAVEN

Once you've made the decision to form an alliance with the templars, go to the war room. Here you have one last chance to choose between the mages and templars. If you want to ally with the mages, choose In Hushed Whispers—reference the previous section for that walkthrough. But if you want to ally with the templars, choose Champions of the Just on the war table. This operation costs a whopping 15 power. So if you don't have enough power yet, head back to the Hinterlands and complete more quests. The Storm Coast and Fallow Mire also offer plenty of power-building opportunities.

As part of the plan to gain favor with the templars and Lord Seeker Lucius, Josephine suggests allying with a number of noble houses in Orlais. These nobles will accompany you to Therinfal Redoubt, strengthening the Inquisition's hand. When choosing your party for this operation, consider taking two warriors, a mage, and a rogue. If you're not playing as a rogue, be sure to take Varric or Sera along with you—there are plenty of locked doors in Therinfal Redoubt that can only be unlocked by a rogue.

THERINFAL REDOUBT

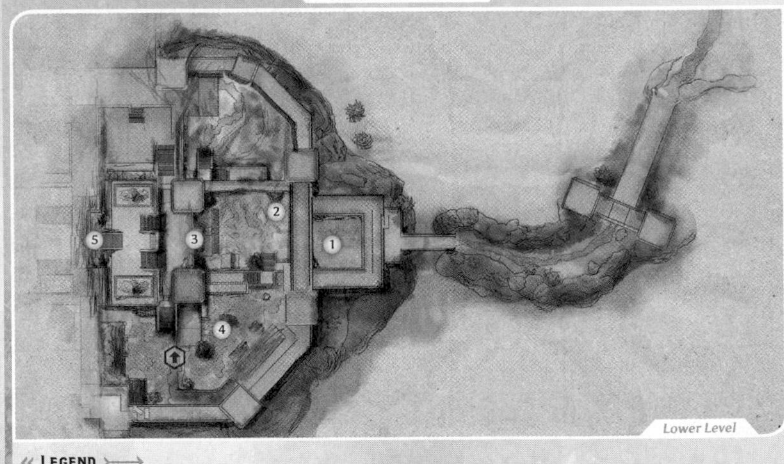

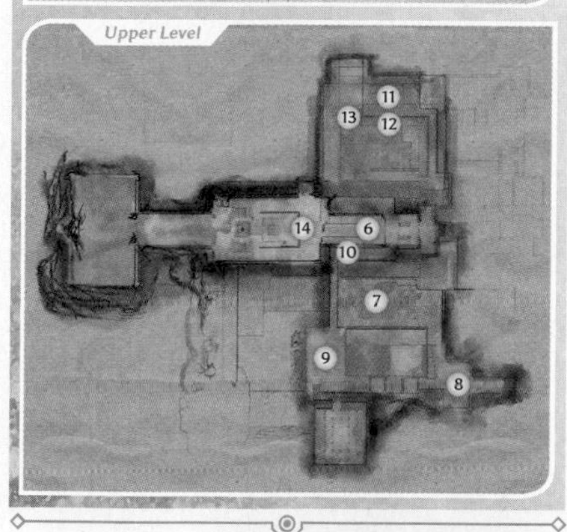

I. Upon arrival at Therinfal Redoubt, you're greeted by Lord Abernache, head of one of the noble Orlesian houses—he'll be pleased if Vivienne is in your party. Abernache states that the Lord Seeker will not meet any of the nobility until he's met the Inquisition in person. After speaking to Lord Abernache, advance across the bridge into the gatehouse and talk to Knight-Templar Barris. Barris seems somewhat confused by the actions of Lord Seeker Lucius, but he remains loyal nonetheless.

2. Before you meet with the Lord Seeker, Barris asks that you complete a ritual in the courtyard, requiring you to raise three flags representing Andraste, the people, and the Templar Order. You can either complete this ritual or refuse to. Lord Abernache is annoyed if you "waste time" doing these rituals, which impacts what happens to him in the following scene. If you choose to complete the ritual, interact with the wheels to raise the corresponding flags in any order you wish—there is no correct answer. In the ritual, the highest flag signifies the faction of greatest importance to you. Once the flags are arranged in the order you see fit, speak to Barris and explain your choices. Afterward, enter the door next to Barris.

3. Inside, Knight-Captain Denam approaches your delegation with some troubling news. Apparently you have somehow ruined the Lord Seeker's plans by arriving "with purpose." If you completed the flag ritual earlier, an irritated Lord Abernache attempts to butter up the templars on his own, and is shot by an arrow when Captain Denam and his men turn on you. If you skipped the rituals, Abernache stays safely by your side and lives through this battle. Knight-Templar Barris is shocked by Captain Denam's betrayal, and joins your party in the fight against Denam and his men. Focus on taking out the red templar marksmen first, followed by the red templars. Engage Knight-Captain Denam last, preferably scoring flanking strikes that he can't block with his shield. After the fight Denam is unconscious but alive. Later on in the game, you can judge him for his betrayal of the Order.

4. Fight your way through a couple of more red templars on your way to this courtyard. Here you're attacked by more enemies, including several red templar marksmen firing from elevated positions. Eliminate these archers as quickly as possible. Otherwise they'll quickly deplete the health of your party. On the east side of the courtyard is a building whose door is locked until you kill enough red templars. Once the door is open, rush through to help an uncorrupted templar who's fighting the red ones. If you get to him quickly enough, he'll survive the battle and follow you, helping out in combat. This staircase gives you access to an upper level walkway. Prepare to engage more red templars up here while proceeding north. There is a door to the west, with a templar banner above it, in this area. It leads to Captain Denam's office. You'll need a rogue to pick the lock. Inside is the body of a templar officer. Barris is shocked—talk to him for more information on the murder. Discovering this room will open up a new option when judging Captain Denam later on in the game.

5. You encounter Lord Seeker Lucius at the door leading to the great hall. But something isn't right. As you approach, the Lord Seeker grabs you and pulls you into a nightmare-like dream world.

> NIGHTMARE CHANTRY

The Lord Seeker has pulled you into a surreal environment obscured by fog. Walk past the flaming corpses to speak with visages of Josephine, Leliana, and Cullen. It becomes apparent you're dealing with an envy demon that has been masquerading as the Lord Seeker, preparing the templars for someone it calls "The Elder One." This nightmare world is a vision being woven inside your mind. Question the envy demon to learn more about what it wants: It wants to take your place, the same way it took the place of Lord Seeker Lucius. Following the conversation, continue through the doorways to the west.

The fountains in this room spew green flames. Don't make contact with the flames or else you'll die. Instead, monitor the rotations of the fountains in the center of the room and look for openings to sneak by. Zigzag through this room to avoid taking damage from the green flames. In the last "safe" alcove, there is a pile of boxes and barrels you have to jump over to get past the rotating fountains. At the west end of the room, enter the side room on the north. Here you encounter an entity named Cole. It's unclear who or what Cole really is, but he offers you help. He helps you extinguish the last set of flames blocking the exit. Pass through the door to enter the prison.

TIP Across from where you meet Cole is a blocked-off room. Mages must take down a barrier, warriors have to bash through the wall, and rogues can lockpick the door. Inside the room is an inscription on a statue. Click on it to gain the first part of a codex entry for Demonic Dogma, a three-part collection quest within the nightmare. It also gives you a one-point boost to your Cunning stat.

> NIGHTMARE PRISON

Advance through the prison. Note the side chambers, where you can see what the envy demon intends to do to "dissidents" when it takes your place. Keep going east until you come to this room. Here you encounter Cole once again. He offers some hints on escaping the prison. Cross the hall to the cell to the north and light a torch from the veilfire brazier. With torch in hand, seek out three unlit braziers in the cells lining the main corridor. Return to the east side of the cell block to light the fourth and final brazier. This reveals the exit. Before you leave, note the locked door opposite the exit. Go west, back to where you started in the prison. Inspect the cell to the south; the veilfire will reveal a prison key on a table hanging from the wall. Pick it up and return east, to the locked door across from the exit. Unlock the door and light the brazier inside the room. Go back into the main corridor—there is now a new brazier on the east wall. Light it to reveal a secret chamber with another inscription for the second Demonic Dogma codex. It will also add two points to your Constitution. Follow the path to a door and ascend the stairs to enter the forest.

> NIGHTMARE FOREST

Violent imagery awaits as you advance through the dense fog of the forest. Stay on the stone path to avoid getting lost. Cole is waiting for you near this gate. Interact with the nearby switch to open the gate and proceed deeper into the courtyard. This is a recreation of the Therinfal Redoubt courtyard. Retrace the same steps you took earlier while advancing toward the doors of the great hall. Enemies may attack you along the way, but they pose no real threat—they can be defeated with a single hit. When you enter a building with stairs that lead you to an exit to the west, look around on the second level of the building for the last Demonic Dogma inscription. Select it to finish the quest and gain three points of Willpower. Head out of the building's western exit and up the stairs. This will lead you back to a dream version of the doors to the great hall. You'll be confronted by the envy demon, who is trying to cling on to your form even though you've almost broken free of its nightmare. Complete the conversation with the envy demon to return to reality.

> GREAT HALL

6. You rejoin your party in the great hall. Knight-Templar Barris has rounded up a small group of templars who haven't been poisoned by red lyrium. Barris and his templars agree to fight together with the Inquisition to stop the envy demon, who has retreated and blocked off part of the fortress with a magic barrier. But Barris will need the support of his lieutenants. He needs your party to find three templar veterans and locate the uncorrupted lyrium stores. Start your search by heading south.

NOTE After you speak to Barris, a status bar appears on the right side of the screen, indicating the status of the great hall. As you exit the great hall to find the veterans and lyrium, this status bar slowly depletes. You must return to the great hall to help Barris and his templars fight off demons. Once the demons have been defeated, the status bar is replenished. If the great hall status bar is completely depleted, the game is over and you must restart from your last save. If the great hall status bar dips below 30 percent, Ser Barris is critically wounded during one of the fights that happen when you return to the great hall, and will die later on.

7. You're ambushed by several enemies here, including red templars and red templar horrors. The red templar horrors are vulnerable to cold-based attacks, so make sure your mage(s) have the proper staves equipped. Focus on freezing, chilling, and defeating the red templar horrors before dealing with the red templars. But don't linger long—while you're fighting, the status bar of the great hall ticks down. There is an entrance to a secret room hidden in the south wall, west of a closed door. Have a warrior wall-bash the entrance open, loot the room, then turn east as soon as you exit the room. To your right will be a closed door. Open it, and continue pushing south to proceed.

8. Here you encounter the first templar veteran busy fighting off some red templar horrors and a red templar marksman. After the enemies here are defeated, the templar veteran agrees to rendezvous with Barris in the great hall. Before heading back to the great hall yourself, advance along the narrow corridor to the west to find the second veteran.

9. If time allows, make an effort to rescue the second veteran here before returning to the great hall. This veteran has also come under attack by red templar horrors and a red templar marksman. Help the veteran fight off his attackers, then immediately head north to enter the great hall.

CAUTION Avoid backtracking through the northern and southern courtyards flanking the great hall. Enemies respawn in these courtyards each time you enter them.

10. You arrive back in the great hall on the second floor. Lower the ladders here and climb down, helping Barris and his templars defeat several red templars. When the great hall is secure, climb the ladders back up to the upper level and proceed through the exit to the north.

11. Fight past the red templars on the upper level walkway to reach the third templar veteran. Pay particular attention to the red templar marksman on the scaffolding to the north. Have your ranged party members deal with this archer while your melee specialists help the templar veteran fight off the rest of the enemies. Now that you've rescued all three templar veterans, it's time to find that cache of uncorrupted lyrium. Head east and descend the stairs to the ground floor.

12. Clear out the adjoining courtyard before entering this room in the northwest corner. Grab the Lord Seeker's key at the back of the room.

13. Using the Lord Seeker's key, open the door to this room and collect the lyrium cache. Immediately return to the great hall.

14. Upon your return to the great hall, assist in clearing out the red templars. Afterward, speak with Knight-Templar Barris. He asks your party to hold off the attackers while he and his small group of templars perform a ritual in an effort to bring down a magic barrier. During this sequence, you must simply survive as red templars, red templar horrors, and red templar marksmen emerge, wave after wave, from the magic barrier to the west. The enemies funnel in along the north and south sides of the central altar, making these narrow choke points ideal locations for devastating area-of-effect attacks. If you have two warriors, place one on the north side and and one on the south side while your ranged party members assist from a distance. Little by little the magic barrier strength is diminished. Keep fighting until Barris and his templars can destroy the magic barrier. If Barris was grievously wounded earlier because the great hall status bar went below 30 percent, he collapses and dies here. Finish off the remaining enemies, then head west to confront the envy demon.

Envy Demon Battle

The envy demon reveals itself in the courtyard west of the great hall. Your party is joined by Cole, who wastes no time attacking the envy demon. The envy demon has attacks similar to a terror, including a powerful area-of-effect attack that can knock your party off their feet. Look for opportunities to disrupt these attacks. While the envy demon has no vulnerabilities or immunities, cold-based attacks work well—two mages casting back-to-back Winter's Grasp spells can keep the envy demon chilled and frozen for much of the fight. When the envy demon's health is reduced to 75 percent, it hides behind a barrier to the west while summoning red templars. After you've eliminated the red templars, the envy demon takes the form of your character. Don't get discouraged by the envy demon's latest trick. Keep hammering away with everything you've got, pouring on as many status effects as possible to hinder the envy demon's performance. While the envy demon is durable, it won't stand up to repeated attacks by your party and Cole. Once the envy demon has been killed, be sure to grab the loot it drops.

DECISION POINT

Following the battle with the envy demon, approach the templars. You have a big decision to make regarding the future of the Order. You have another big decision to make regarding the future of the templars. Will you have them disband and join the Inquisition? Or will you help them rebuild as allies? Your decision is not without consequences. Some of your party members will support your decision, and others will oppose it. Choose carefully.

Approval: Fate of the Templars

Follower	Disband Templars	Ally with Templars
Blackwall	↓↓	↑↑
Cassandra	↓↓	↑↑↑
The Iron Bull	↓↓	↑↑↑
Sera	↑↑↑	↓↓
Solas	↑↑↑	↑↑↑
Varric	—	↑
Vivienne	↓↓	↑↑
Dorian	↓↓	↓↓
Cole	↑↑↑	↓↓↓

HAVEN/NEW RECRUIT: COLE

Your decision regarding the templars reverberates among the council in the war room. But more startling is Cole's sudden appearance on the war table. Cole is here to help. If you accept his help, you calm the fears of your advisors, and gain Cole as a party member. If you refuse and try to kill him, Cole leaves and does not become a follower. Regardless of what you decide to do with Cole, the council is now focused on closing the Breach.

IN YOUR HEART SHALL BURN

With the Inquisition's hard-won allies, it is time to march on the Breach and close it.

HAVEN

Following the conclusion of In Hushed Whispers or Champions of the Just, the Inquisition now has the support it needs to attempt closing the Breach. It only takes one power to gather your forces and make a move on the Breach. Chances are you have enough power simply by completing previous quests. Whether you have the power or not, now is the perfect time to fully explore locales like the Hinterlands, Storm Coast, Fallow Mire, and Forbidden Oasis. These locales not only give you more power-building opportunities, but also provide your character and party members with the XP required to level up—try to reach level eight before attempting to close the Breach. This is also a great time to check in with your party members to see what they have to say—some may even provide inner circle quests. Once you've gathered enough power and XP, return to the war room and select the In Your Heart Shall Burn operation on the war table. After selecting the operation, choose your party. Party selection here determines who joins you at the Breach, as well as who fights with you for the duration of this quest. As usual, a balanced approach is best. A party consisting of two warriors, a rogue, and a mage should give you the balance you need to survive the upcoming encounters.

CAUTION If you're a completionist, don't select the In Your Heart Shall Burn operation until you've completed all quests and requisitions in Haven. This is a major turning point in the game—there is no turning back.

SEALING THE BREACH

With the support of your party, loyal soldiers, and the templars or mages you acquired in the previous quest, the Inquisition returns to the Temple of Sacred Ashes. The Breach still lingers ominously above the ruins of the temple. Your character slowly approaches the Breach and uses the mark to reach out and seal it once and for all. As it closes, the Breach emits a powerful blast of energy, knocking everyone off their feet. But the task is complete—the Breach has been sealed, yet a scar remains in the skies above the Frostback Mountains.

UNDER SIEGE

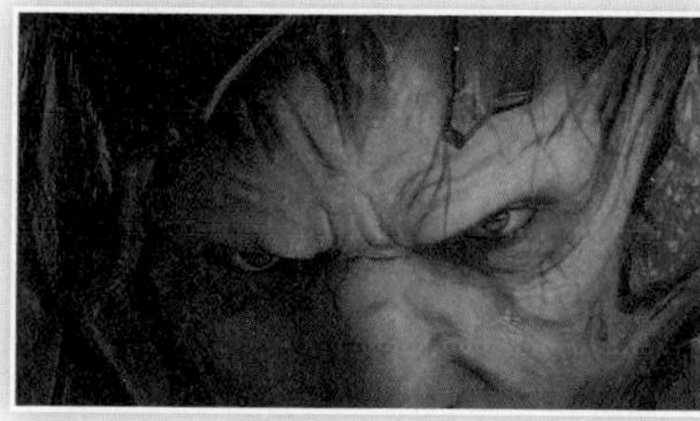

Back in Haven, a festive mood has spread across the camp. Cassandra confirms that the Breach is sealed but reports that several Fade rifts linger. While many questions still remain, Cassandra is comfortable declaring this a victory for the Inquisition. But the celebration is cut short when Cullen reports that an unidentified enemy is marching on Haven. Head for the gates on Haven's north side. This is also a good time to update your party's inventory. At the gate you're introduced to Cole or Dorian. If you completed In Hushed Whispers, Cole arrives to warn you of the incoming red templar threat. If you completed Champions of the Just, Dorian identifies the incoming attackers as the Venatori. Whatever the case, Haven is in great danger as a figure known only as the Elder One looks on from a distant mountain peak.

> NORTH TREBUCHET

As Cullen prepares his soldiers for Haven's defense, lead your party to the northern trebuchet. When you arrive, the trebuchet is surrounded by enemies—you must fend off the attackers while Inquisition soldiers prep the trebuchet. The enemies you face during this battle differ based on whether you chose the rebel mages or templars as allies. If you chose to ally with the rebel mages, you'll face a mix of red templar swordsmen and archers. If you chose to ally with the templars, the enemies consist of Venatori swordsmen, archers, and mages. Make an effort to deal with the ranged threats first, eliminating archers and mages while taunting the swordsmen with your warriors. You will also face red templar guards or Venatori gladiators. Taunt these shielded enemies with your warriors while your ranged party members move to flank. Hold back wave after wave of attackers until the trebuchet can fire. The low, narrow areas of terrain on the east and west sides of the trebuchet serve as natural choke points, ideal for launching devastating area-of-effect attacks. After the trebuchet fires, head for the south trebuchet.

TIP The Venatori spellbinders are vulnerable to cold-based attacks. Adjust your inventory and abilities to best counter this threat. If facing templars, fire-based attacks are most effective against the intimidating red templar knights.

> SOUTH TREBUCHET

The south trebuchet has been overrun by enemies. Eliminate all the hostiles, then approach the trebuchet. The crew has been killed, so it's up to you to fire it. Interact with the wheel-like crank on the trebuchet's east side to prepare the weapon for firing. For best results, position your party members around the eastern platform so they can defend you—the faster you fire the trebuchet, the sooner this battle is over. A status bar in the upper right corner of the screen indicates how much progress is needed before the trebuchet is ready to fire. While your party defends you, keep turning the crank until the trebuchet fires. The trebuchet seems to misfire, hitting the slope instead of the enemy, triggering an avalanche and burying many enemy soldiers in thick, heavy snow. This proves unexpectedly effective and could be a winning tactic that changes the course of the battle. But there's little time to celebrate. A dragon swoops in from above, spewing a fireball that reduces the trebuchet to charred splinters. The dragon's arrival changes everything, and it's obvious to all in the Inquisition. It's time to retreat. Return to Haven's gates immediately—you'll need to take shelter in the chantry.

TIP Interact with the supply caches in Haven to replenish your healing potions. There's one next to Adan's workshop and another near the final trebuchet. You can only use each supply cache once, so make sure you're completely out of potions before topping off.

! EVACUATE HAVEN

Quest Giver: N/A

Description: On your way to the chantry, help evacuate the inhabitants of Haven.

Requirements: Available after firing the south trebuchet

Reward: 128 XP, 80 Influence

Recommended Level: 6-8

Objectives:

- Help Harritt.
- Rescue Lysette.
- Rescue Seggrit.
- Rescue Flissa.
- Rescue Adan.
- Rescue Minaeve.
- Rescue Threnn.

Before reaching Haven's gate, stop at the structure adjacent to the blacksmith—Harritt needs help breaking down the door. Use a warrior in your party to smash the wooden crate blocking the door, allowing Harritt to gain entry and gather some supplies.

After passing through the gate, turn west to find Lysette fighting off several enemies. Help her finish off the attackers to give Lysette a clear path to the chantry.

Climb the central stairs and eliminate more enemies. Afterward, turn to the burning building to the east—Seggrit, the merchant, is trapped inside. Climb the ladder on the north side of the building and drop in through a hole in the roof to rescue Seggrit. Bust down the blocked door to escape.

Cross to the west and head toward the tavern. Eliminate the enemies surrounding the tavern, then enter the structure to save Flissa, trapped beneath a fallen beam.

West of the tavern, Adan and Minaeve have been injured. You must act quickly to help them to their feet before the approaching flames trigger an explosion, detonating the flammable trebuchet pots. If you hesitate, they'll both die.

Before entering the chantry, fight off the enemies on the east side—they've trapped Threnn. Eliminate all the attackers to save Threnn, then enter the chantry—there is nobody else left to assist.

> THE CHANTRY

Having retreated to the chantry, there isn't anywhere else to go. Cullen is inspired by your shot with the trebuchet—another shot could bury Haven, the attackers... and the Inquisition. Although Cullen is willing to sacrifice himself and the Inquisition, Chancellor Roderick, severely wounded during the attack, mentions a little-known path that could serve as an escape route. But if this plan is going to work, your party will need to stay behind and distract the dragon while the survivors of Haven escape.

> HAVEN FINALE

With your party in tow, fight your way back north to the lone trebuchet within Haven's wall. Expect heavy resistance along the way, so take your time. Despite the sense of urgency, there is no need to rush through these skirmishes. Prepare for an even larger battle at the trebuchet. This trebuchet must be rotated and aimed at the mountain behind the chantry. Upon your arrival, immediately interact with the wheel-like crank on the trebuchet's south side. Once again, position your party members around you so they can fend off attackers while you manually turn the crank. Rotating the trebuchet takes a while, and you may need to stop interacting with the crank to help your party members. But as soon as there's a lull in the fighting, return to the crank. This is most likely the toughest battle you've faced thus far, so constantly monitor the flow of the battle, occasionally using the tactical camera to reposition your party members. Among the standard enemies is one of two possible mini-bosses. If you sided with the mages, you'll face corrupted Knight-Templar Denam. If you allied with the templars, you'll encounter a brainwashed Grand Enchanter Fiona.

Knight-Captain Denam

Red lyrium has transformed Knight-Templar Denam into a grotesque behemoth. When he appears, turn your party's full focus to defeating him. Cold-based attacks are the most effective, so try to keep him chilled and frozen for the duration of the fight. Knight-Templar Denam is capable of dishing out heavy melee attacks. He can also create walls of red lyrium, potentially separating your party from one another. If a wall of red lyrium is deployed, make sure your ranged party members still have line of sight on Knight-Templar Denam. The red lyrium wall can be destroyed, but it's much better to focus your firepower on Knight-Templar Denam.

TIP You can end the battles with Knight-Captain Denam and Grand Enchanter Fiona by fully turning the crank on the trebuchet.

Grand Enchanter Fiona

As the leader of the rebel mages, and brainwashed by the Venatori, Fiona is a formidable threat, capable of casting a variety of offensive and defensive spells. She's most vulnerable to physical attacks, so waste no time tanking her with your warriors. Fiona is also resistant to electrical attacks, so consider hitting her with cold- or fire-based spells. Freezing her in place with Winter's Grasp works well, allowing your warriors to move to close range and land some heavy blows.

The Elder One

Once you've aimed the trebuchet, the dragon swoops down and performs a fiery attack, knocking you off your feet and separating you from your party. The dragon's master, the Elder One, approaches through the flames and begins a conversation. It turns out the Elder One is actually Corypheus, thought to have been killed by Hawke, the Champion of Kirkwall. But somehow Corypheus has returned and is very interested in the mark upon your character's hand, calling it the Anchor. Holding a mysterious orb in his hand, Corypheus tries to remove the mark. But despite his best efforts, Corypheus cannot remove the Anchor. Before Corypheus and his dragon can kill you, your character fires the trebuchet, triggering another avalanche. Corypheus and his dragon manage to escape the incoming wall of snow and ice as your character flees into the wilderness, dropping into an icy subterranean passage.

> MARK OF THE RIFT

You find yourself in a tunnel somewhere beneath Haven. Walk toward the objective marker on the compass to find the exit. Along the way you come across a group of four despair demons. Since your encounter with Corypheus you've attained a new ability—Mark of the Rift. This is a powerful area-of-effect (AoE) attack, creating a rift and sucking all nearby enemies into the Fade. Activate the Mark of the Rift ability and place the AoE marker in the middle of the despair demons. If you manage to open the rift close enough to all four enemies, they'll be eliminated, clearing a path to the tunnel's exit. Mark of the Rift is the single most devastating ability in your arsenal. But before you can use it again, you must build focus. Focus is gained every time you and party members inflict damage on enemies. Once enough focus is gained, Mark of the Rift (and other focus abilities) can be activated. Outside the tunnel, head east through a blinding blizzard until you find Cullen, Cassandra, and some Inquisition troops—they've come back to find you.

> THE DAWN WILL COME

Your intervention back in Haven bought the survivors enough time to escape before the avalanche buried the chantry. With nowhere to go, the Inquisition has established a temporary camp in the Frostback Mountains. As your character recovers, members of the war council argue about the next course of action. But Mother Giselle manages to rally the faithful with an old chantry hymn. Solas requests a private audience with you, revealing that the orb Corypheus was holding is of elven origin. He doesn't know how Corypheus could have found such a thing, but he's worried that the Inquisition will think elves are involved—he's especially concerned if your character is an elf. Despite these concerns, Solas offers to help the Inquisition find a new home, urging you to head north.

As Solas advised, your character leads the Inquisition through the Frostback Mountains to an abandoned fortress on the rocky terrain. This is Skyhold—the Inquisition's new home.

FROM THE ASHES

With a new base of operations, the Inquisition is ready to make its mark on the world.

SKYHOLD

As the survivors of Haven and refugees from other regions file in through the gates of Skyhold, Cassandra engages you in a serious conversation. Both Cassandra and Leliana are convinced you should step up as the leader of the Inquisition. How will you respond to this honor?

DECISION POINT

During the conversation with Cassandra and Leliana, you're given the opportunity to declare what kind of leader you'll be. You're given several dialogue options, including some special options depending on your race and class. For instance, if playing as a non-human, you can make state how you'll stand for all, reinforcing the Inquisition's stance as an inclusive organization. Or if playing as a mage, you can choose to set an example for all mages. Pay close attention, because your choice can have a big impact on the approval of your party members. During an impromptu ceremony, Leliana hands over an ornate ceremonial sword while Cassandra, Cullen, and Josephine whip up support among the faithful in the courtyard. Cullen grants you the title of Inquisitor, drawing cheers from the crowd.

Approval: Inquisitor's Resolve

Dialogue Option	Blackwall	Cassandra	Cole	Dorian	The Iron Bull	Sera	Solas	Varric	Vivienne
Servant of Faith	—	↑↑↑	—	↓	—	↓↓	↓↓	—	↑↑
Fight for Order, not Faith	—	↑↑	—	—	—	↑↑	—	↑	—
Because it's Right	↑↑	—	—	—	↑	↑↑	↑	↑	—
Corypheus Must Be Stopped	↑	—	—	↑↑↑	↑	↑↑	—	—	
Do it for my own power	↓↓↓	↓↓↓	—	↓↓	—	↓↓	↓↓↓	↓↓↓	—
Lead them to vengeance	—	↓	—	—	↓	↑↑	↓	↓↓	—
Special Dialogue Options									
A Dwarf Will Stand for Us All	—	—	—	—	—	↑↑	—	—	—
An Elf Will Stand for Us All	—	—	—	—	—	↓↓	↑	—	—
A Qunari Will Stand for Us All	—	—	—	—	↑↑	↑↑	—	—	—
Set An Example as a Mage	—	—	—	↑↑	—	↑	—	—	↑↑↑

DEVELOPER TIP

After getting to Skyhold, your followers will now have an additional skill tree unlocked! Go take a look!

— Barbara Klimek, QA Lead

Dragon Age Inquisition

THRONE ROOM

But there isn't much time to celebrate. As Cullen, Leliana, and Josephine join you in Skyhold's throne room, it's clear this fortress must undergo major repairs before it can become a fitting headquarters for the Inquisition. While Cullen is doubtful Corypheus will attempt a direct attack on Skyhold, the Inquisition must be ready for anything. Leliana is concerned about the plot you uncovered to kill Empress Celene. The death of Celene could cause the chaos Corypheus needs to conquer southern Thedas. Varric joins the conversation, offering some help. He has an old friend who has crossed paths with Corypheus before. Agree to meet with Varric's friend—he can be found on the battlements to the west. But before seeking out Varric's friend, visit Josephine's new workspace.

JOSEPHINE'S CONCERNS

Josephine has set up her office in the antechamber, just north of the throne room. She is deeply concerned about the threat to Empress Celene and feels this is a pressing matter for the Inquisition. If Empress Celene were to be assassinated, Josephine fears it would be a tipping point, causing all of Thedas to fall to Corypheus. Celene will be holding peace talks at Halamshiral under the guise of a grand masquerade ball. Josephine fears if there is an attempt on Celene's life, it will occur at this event. But at the moment, the Inquisition isn't influential enough to warn Empress Celene or acquire an invitation to the ball. Take this as your cue to gain more power. It will take 30 power to attend the ball, unlocking the Wicked Eyes and Wicked Hearts operation on the war table. In the meantime, turn your attention to meeting Varric's friend.

DEVELOPER TIP

After you get settled in Skyhold, you'll get an operation on the war table that allows you to invite three class-specific specialists to teach you their ways. This will unlock one additional skill tree for your character should you complete their quest.

— Barbara Klimek, QA Lead

THE CHAMPION OF KIRKWALL

Climb the western staircase to reach the top of the battlements, then begin a conversation with Varric. Here he introduces you to Hawke, the Champion of Kirkwall—and the hero of *Dragon Age II*. Hawke believes Corypheus is using his connection to the darkspawn to influence the Grey Wardens once more—this may explain the sudden disappearance of the Wardens. Hawke has a Warden friend in Crestwood. The identity of Hawke's Warden ally differs depending on your customized world state imported from Dragon Age Keep. In the default game state the Warden ally is Stroud. But Loghain and Alistair are possibilities if you imported a world state. Whoever Hawke's Warden friend is, they're concerned about corruption within the ranks and have taken refuge in an old smuggler's cave in Crestwood. Hawke suggests meeting him and his Warden friend in Crestwood to learn more about the status of the Grey Wardens. After talking to Hawke, the From the Ashes quest is complete.

Speak to Cassandra after the conversation with Hawke and prepare to intervene (or watch) as she goes after Varric. Cassandra's explosive temper is on full display as she chases Varric, outraged he's been hiding Hawke from her all this time. Try to smooth things over with both Cassandra and Varric—they both have good points. Whom will you support? Take some time exploring Skyhold before heading to the war room to plan the Inquisition's next move.

NOTE For the purpose of this walkthrough the default character of Stroud is used when referencing Hawke's Warden friend.

NOTE If you imported a world state from *Dragon Age Keep*, you can customize Hawke's gender, appearance, and key decisions to match your gameplay experience from *Dragon Age II*.

GAINING POWER

After speaking to Hawke and exploring Skyhold, take stock of the Inquisition's power—you need eight power to unlock the Find the Warden operation on the war table, giving you access to Crestwood. If you've been completing side quests during your adventure, chances are you have enough power to make the next move. Otherwise, you'll need to head out into the wilderness and obtain more power. You can obtain enough power by heading back to the Hinterlands and completing more quests. But there are also plenty of power-building opportunities in the Fallow Mire and Storm Coast. There are new locales now available on the war table, but as with the Fallow Mire and Storm Coast, it will cost you power to scout the Exalted Plains, Emerald Graves, Western Approach, and Emprise du Lion. So if you're set on reaching Crestwood as soon as possible, stick to the Hinterlands when gathering power.

Recommended Quests

Quest/Activity	Locale	Power
Apostates in the Witchwood	The Hinterlands	2
Trouble with Wolves	The Hinterlands	1
Establish Forest Camp	The Hinterlands	1
Establish Dusklight Camp	The Hinterlands	1
The Ballad of Lord Woolsey	The Hinterlands	1
Rifts in the Woods	The Hinterlands	2

EXPLORING SKYHOLD

Before taking off for Crestwood, or any other locale, consider taking some time to get familiar with your new home. In its current state, only part of Skyhold can be explored—rubble and debris block certain passages and doorways. But there are still plenty of places to explore. Also, take a moment to speak to all of your party members. A few side quests introduce you to new areas in Skyhold.

Welcome to Skyhold

Quest Giver: N/A

Description: This new home for the Inquisition has a lot to offer. Take a look around.

Requirements: Available after entering Skyhold

Reward: 50 XP

Recommended Level: 6-8

Objectives:

- Find the war room.
- Find the blacksmith.

The new war room is down the hall from Josephine's office in the antechamber. If you haven't already, visit the war room and assign advisors to new missions. Remember to collect rewards from any completed missions.

Harritt has set up shop in the undercroft—enter the door directly south of the throne. This area contains all the blacksmith stations you became familiar with in Haven. It also contains tables where you can equip and craft potions. Use this opportunity to craft new armor, weapons, and upgrades.

Inquisition Trappings

Quest Giver: N/A

Description: Skyhold can be customized in a variety of ways to best reflect the style and priorities of the Inquisition.

Requirements: Available after entering Skyhold

Reward: None

Recommended Level: 6-8

Objectives:

- Go to the undercroft.

While you're in the undercroft, approach the Skyhold customization bench to plan out the design of the castle. From this menu you can select custom banners, beds, drapery, heraldry, decor, thrones, and windows. Some of these customization options are locked. You'll need to acquire new items through exploration, and some objects can be purchased from merchants in Val Royeaux. These options affect merely the aesthetics of Skyhold and do not impact gameplay.

NEW RECRUIT: COLE

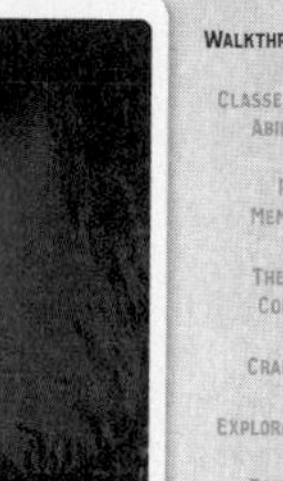

Whether you completed In Hushed Whispers or Champions of the Just, you must speak with Cole to keep him in the Inquisition. Look for Cole in the courtyard, as part of The Forgotten Boy side quest. Cassandra, Solas, and Vivienne discuss what to make of Cole—Vivienne wants him gone while Solas feels he could be helpful. Speak with Cole before making your decision—he's busy tending to the wounded in the courtyard. If you extend an invitation to Cole, you gain immediate retroactive approval for any quests where you helped people, such as those for the refugees at the Crossroads in the Hinterlands. Unlike other party members, Cole doesn't have to be present for you to gain or lose approval from him. As a member of the Inquisition Cole is available to join your party.

NEW RECRUIT: DORIAN

If you completed Champions of the Just, you haven't had many opportunities to speak to Dorian since he showed up at Haven's main gate prior to the Venatori attack. Dorian has followed you here and resides in the library south of the throne room. Head upstairs and have a word with him. At this point you have the opportunity to thank Dorian for assisting the Inquisition back in Haven. You can also ask him to join the Inquisition. Like other companions, Dorian can then be selected as a party member during your future adventures.

NOTE After speaking to Dorian, introduce yourself to Helisma, also in the library. She has replaced Minaeve as the Inquisition's new researcher—even if Minaeve survived Haven, she is now serving the Inquisition in other ways. From now on, drop off any research items on the table next to Helisma.

The Arcanist

At the war table, select the Acquire the Arcanist mission, located in north Ferelden. This mission requires no power and takes no time to complete. Afterward, visit the undercroft to meet Dagna. She allows you to craft your own runes. Using rune schematics and blank runes, you can now add runes to your weapons, improving their stats in various ways. Simply meeting Dagna grants you access to the Corrupting Rune schematic. For more information on crafting runes, reference the Crafting chapter.

HERE LIES THE ABYSS

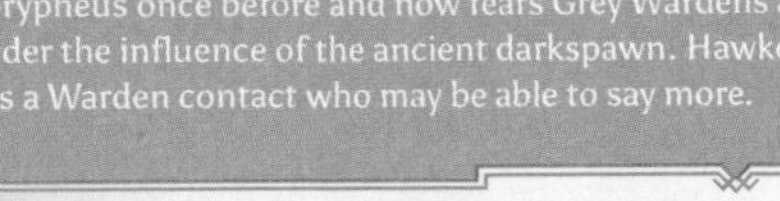

Varric has a friend named Hawke, who fought Corypheus once before and now fears Grey Wardens are under the influence of the ancient darkspawn. Hawke has a Warden contact who may be able to say more.

SKYHOLD

When you've acquired a minimum of eight power, return to the war room in Skyhold. Take a moment to add any perks, then make sure your advisors each have a mission assigned. In Ferelden, locate the Find the Warden marker on the map and select it to access Crestwood—this is where Hawke's Warden friend, Stroud, is hiding out. Crestwood has not been visited since the Breach, so the situation on the ground is unknown. After confirming the scouting operation, Scout Harding reports Hawke's friend is indeed somewhere in Crestwood—along with plenty of undead. Next, select your party and proceed to Crestwood.

JUDGMENTS

Eventually you can interact with the throne in Skyhold to conduct judgments. This is where you decide the fate of criminals within the custody of the Inquisition. Any time you can interact with the throne, a new judgment is available. For more information on judgments (and their consequences), reference the Skyhold section in the Exploration chapter.

NOTE At this point you can choose to complete Here Lies the Abyss or Wicked Eyes and Wicked Hearts; these two quests can be completed in any order. The XP and loot earned from Wicked Eyes and Wicked Hearts can make the combat easier in Here Lies the Abyss.

CRESTWOOD

Scout Harding greets you at the North Gate Camp in Crestwood, filling you in on a few details about the locale. Apparently there was a flood 10 years ago during the Blight, forming a large lake. When a rift appeared in the middle of the lake, corpses began emerging from the water and attacking the living. Stroud has been tracked to a cave to the east—Harding warns you'll likely encounter heavy resistance from the undead along the way. After speaking to Harding, talk to the requisition officer to get a new requisition quest. There is a lot of work to be done in Crestwood. How you proceed is up to you, but for starters, seek out Stroud.

NOTE In the game's default world state, Stroud is the Warden you must find in Crestwood, but if you're importing a world state from *Dragon Age Keep*, you can select Loghain or Alistair as Hawke's Warden ally.

> STROUD: A WANTED WARDEN

On the road east of the camp, you encounter two Grey Wardens battling some corpse archers. Help finish off the undead enemies, then initiate a conversation with the lead Grey Warden. He's grateful for your party's assistance and reveals that he's here to find Stroud—apparently Stroud has gone rogue and is wanted by the Wardens for questioning. The Inquisitor is careful not to reveal any details about Stroud during the conversation. But a greater sense of urgency is now apparent—you need to find Stroud before the Wardens do.

AGENTS OF THE INQUISITION

After speaking to the Warden, enter the house along the road to the north. Inside, a young woman, Jana, is enthused about witnessing the Grey Wardens in action—they saved her from those corpse archers. Persuade her not to join the Grey Wardens—if Hawke's theory is correct, the Wardens have been compromised. If Solas is in your party, he can convince Jana to join the Inquisition instead.

Stroud's Hideout

Head for Stroud's cave to the southeast, passing the village of Crestwood and Caer Bronach along the way. There is a heavy undead presence outside the village's gates. After eliminating the enemies, consider making a quick detour to visit the village's mayor to start the Still Waters side quest. If you want, you can also liberate Caer Bronach to give the Inquisition access to a keep. Continue east and set up an Inquisition camp at Three Trout Pond before meeting with Stroud.

Hawke is waiting for you outside the cave where Stroud has taken refuge. Speak with Hawke, then enter the cave. Stroud reveals that all of the Grey Wardens are hearing the Calling, giving them the false belief that they're dying. Wardens who have heard the Calling head to the Deep Roads to meet their fate against the darkspawn. Stroud feels Corypheus is behind this bluff in an attempt to eliminate the Grey Wardens. With the Grey Wardens gone, there will be nobody left to stop the next Blight. Stroud was forced to run when he protested against Warden-Commander Clarel's plan to perform a blood magic ritual thought to prevent all future Blights. Clarel and the Grey Wardens are gathering near an ancient Tevinter ritual tower in the Western Approach. Stroud wants you to meet him there—perhaps you can find more answers.

> GAINING POWER

You'll need to acquire eight more power before you can join Stroud in the Western Approach. Fortunately, there's plenty to do in Crestwood to obtain the power you need—simply closing a Fade rift earns you two power here. Start by completing the Still Waters quest—it's easy to do Burdens of Command and Homecoming while doing this main quest. Also, Capturing Caer Bronach nets the Inquisition two power and a keep. When you have at least eight power, return to Skyhold.

RECOMMENDED QUESTS

QUEST/ACTIVITY	LOCALE	POWER
Establish Three Trout Pond Camp	Crestwood	1
Rift Near the North Gate	Crestwood	2
Capturing Caer Bronach	Crestwood	2
Rift at Caer Bronach	Crestwood	2
Still Waters	Crestwood	5
Burdens of Command	Crestwood	2
Homecoming	Crestwood	2
Rifts at Three Trout Farm	Crestwood	4

NOTE For details on completing Still Waters and other quests in Crestwood, reference the Exploration chapter.

DEVELOPER TIP

Don't be afraid to head back to your base camp to sell your extra inventory. If you're in the middle of a mission and run out of room, you don't want to leave something behind if you don't have to.

—Arone Le Bray, QA Narrative Analyst

SKYHOLD

Upon your return to Skyhold, head for the war room. Little by little, Skyhold is undergoing repairs, evident by scaffolding and noticeable improvements. Each time you return, more progress will be made. At the war table, update assignments for your advisors—there should be plenty of missions to keep them busy. Next, choose the Investigate the Western Approach operation in western Orlais, costing eight power. Once the operation is complete, Inquisition scouts confirm that a large force of Grey Wardens has arrived in the Western Approach—it appears Stroud's information was correct. It's time to meet up with Stroud in the Western Approach and see what the Wardens are up to. Select your party members and move out.

Inquisitor Trainers

When selecting missions on the war table, don't overlook the Specializations for the Inquisitor mission located in northern Ferelden. This particular mission costs no power and takes no time to complete, so there's no reason to skip it. Upon the operation's completion, three trainers enter Skyhold, each with a specialization quest. Study the requirements for each quest and choose the specialization that best fits your character and style of play. While you can gather components for all three quests, you can only complete one, unlocking only one of the specialization trees. So make your decision carefully. Reference the Classes and Abilities chapter for a complete rundown of all abilities found within each specialization.

Trainer Quests

Trainer	Class	Quest	Trainer Location
Lord Chancellor de Lion	Warrior	Way of the Champion	Battlements
Breaker Thram	Warrior	Way of the Reaver	Battlements
Ser	Warrior	Way of the Templar	Battlements
Heir	Rogue	Way of the Assassin	Near Stables
Kihm	Rogue	Way of the Tempest	Near Stables
Three-Eyes	Rogue	Way of the Artificer	Near Stables
Commander Helaine	Mage	Way of the Knight-Enchanter	Lower Courtyard
Viuus Anaxas	Mage	Way of the Necromancer	Lower Courtyard
Your Trainer	Mage	Way of the Rift Mage	Lower Courtyard

THE WESTERN APPROACH

Upon your arrival in the Western Approach, Harding confirms Grey Warden activity in the area. But her scouts have not been able to get close enough to see what the Wardens are doing—sandstorms and the hostile wildlife have been a challenge. Despite the harsh conditions, Harding's scouts have intercepted a message from a Venatori courier. The message can be found on a table to the east, by the requisition table—it appears the Venatori are searching for something in a nearby mine. After speaking to Harding, talk to the requisition officer to receive a requisition quest for the Western Approach. Next, begin your long journey to the Tevinter tower where Hawke and Stroud are waiting. Close the Fade rift along the road to the west as you exit the Lost Spring Canyon camp—closing Fade rifts here nets you two power each.

NOTE While traveling to the Tevinter ritual tower, complete some side quests along the way, including the closing of more Fade rifts and establishment of camps—you'll need the power later. You can complete the Tevinter side quest by entering the Forgotten Mine in the canyons and reading another note. The mines here also contain red lyrium deposits you can destroy for Varric's Seeing Red quest. Also, look for raiders who have stolen research supplies from Frederic's team to complete the Draconology quest.

Tevinter Ritual Tower

Hawke and Stroud greet you at the entrance of this ancient Tevinter ruin. Stroud fears the Wardens have already begun the blood magic ritual. As you approach, a Grey Warden is killed by one of his brothers as part of the ritual, summoning a rage demon. Magister Erimond, a Tevinter mage, is attempting to teach the Wardens how to bind and control demons—along with the rage demon, they've also taken a few shades under their control. Stroud is outraged by this, but he is incapable of getting through to his fellow Wardens—Corypheus has already claimed their minds. Erimond reveals this was all part of Corypheus's sinister plan—raise a demon army for Corypheus and slay the Wardens in the Deep Roads.

When Erimond attempts to control you through magical manipulation of the Anchor, the Inquisitor fights back, sending a surge of energy back in Erimond's direction. Panicked by the Inquisitor's counter, Erimond flees while ordering the demons and compromised Wardens to attack. Deal with the rage demon first, preferably using cold-based attacks to chill and freeze it while methodically chipping away at its health. There are also a couple of Warden spellbinders among the group—they're vulnerable to fire-based attacks. But watch for the icy glyphs they place around themselves—these are ice mines. Watch your step, or simply eliminate these enemies with ranged attacks.

Following the battle, Stroud notes the direction Erimond fled. There's an abandoned Warden fortress in that direction called Adamant. Hawke and Stroud will scout Adamant to confirm the other Wardens are there and then meet you back in Skyhold.

TIP Don't forget your Mark of the Rift ability. If you've acquired enough focus, opening a rift at the tower is the quickest way to end this fight, pulling your foes into the Fade.

GAINING POWER

Before returning to Skyhold, take some time exploring the Western Approach. Staging an attack on Adamant won't be easy, and you'll need to accumulate 20 power to unlock the operation on the war table. Closing Fade rifts is a worthwhile activity, since each sealed rift earns you two power. There is also a Venatori-held keep to the east—capturing it nets you two power. When you've acquired at least 20 power, return to Skyhold to plan your attack on Adamant.

NOTE The sulfur pits in the Dust Plains prevent you from exploring all of the Western Approach. After capturing Griffon Wing Keep, plant a flag here to unlock the Source of the Darkspawn operation. Complete this operation on the war table (costing two power) to have Cullen's men construct a bridge over the pits. The bridge allows you access to the rest of the Western Approach.

RECOMMENDED QUESTS

QUEST/ACTIVITY	LOCALE	POWER
Rifts in the Canyons	The Western Approach	4
Establish Nazaire's Pass Camp	The Western Approach	1
Rifts off the Pass	The Western Approach	4
Establish Craggy Ridge Camp	The Western Approach	1
Rifts in Sand and Dust	The Western Approach	4
Assault on Griffon Wing Keep	The Western Approach	2
Frederic's Livelihood	The Western Approach	2
Fortress Squatters	The Western Approach	2
How to Lure a Dragon	The Western Approach	2

SKYHOLD

On your return to Skyhold, Hawke is talking to Varric in the hallway leading to the war room. Hawke informs you that the war council is devising a plan to attack Adamant. Continue into the war room to join the conversation. On the war table, select the Here Lies the Abyss operation to begin the assault on Adamant. Cullen is confident the Inquisition's siege engines will make quick work of the old fortress's walls. But Leliana fears Erimond is already raising a demon army within Adamant. Josephine suggests trying to sway the Wardens to join the Inquisition in the fight against Erimond and Warden-Commander Clarel. While convincing the warriors may work, Leliana feels the Warden mages are completely under the control of Corypheus. When you're ready to begin the attack, confirm the operation and select your party. It's a good idea to bring along Blackwall for this mission—he can make a speech to the Wardens at a pivotal moment, making your job much easier. If you haven't already, recruit Blackwall (in the Hinterlands) now. You can't recruit him after Adamant.

DEVELOPER TIP

I enjoy bringing Iron Bull, Sera, and Cole to Adamant Fortress. No one is happy to be there and it results in some phenomenal banter.

—Aron Bend, QA

ADAMANT

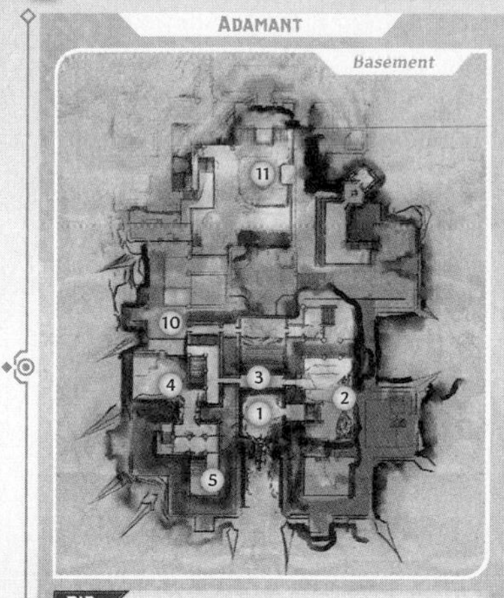

TIP If you prefer, Adamant can be completed after Wicked Eyes and Wicked Hearts. The XP and loot gained from the Winter Palace may make the combat at Adamant a little easier.

The full power of the Inquisition's army is on display during the attack on Adamant. Trebuchets pound the walls of this old Warden fortress, while a battering ram knocks open the main gate. Stroud accompanies your party into the fortress and will fight alongside you during the assault.

LOWER BAILEY

1. In the lower bailey your party faces off against a few shades and a Warden spellbinder. Use your ranged party members to target the Warden spellbinder with fire-based attacks while your warriors deal with the shades. Stroud and a few Inquisition soldiers aid your party in this fight, making it a bit easier. When the enemies are down, Cullen warns that there's too much resistance along the walls, preventing Inquisition soldiers from gaining a foothold. He needs you to help clear out the enemies on the battlements. Start by heading east.

2. Expect more resistance here from a senior Warden and a few of his subordinates. Eliminate the archers first, then focus on the senior Warden and his sword-wielding lackeys. The senior Warden's shield makes frontal attacks useless, so tank him with a warrior while the rest of your party members perform flanking attacks.

3. Eliminate the shades on this bridge, then open the door to the west to access the main bailey.

MAIN BAILEY

4. In the main bailey, there appears to be some resistance among a few Warden warriors. But before you can address the warriors, you must first eliminate the Warden spellbinders and shades. Remember; fire-based attacks are most effective against these corrupted mages. Following the battle, you have an opportunity to address the Warden warriors. Instead of ordering them to surrender, tell them to "Just fall back to safety." Otherwise you'll have another fight on your hands. Next, head through the door to the south.

5. Engage some shades and a Warden archer here, then climb the wooden stairs to reach the battlements.

BATTLEMENTS

6. Fight your way past demons and Wardens to reach the first of three siege points. Securing these points will allow Inquisition soldiers to get a foothold within Adamant. This particular siege point is guarded by a rage demon. Hit the demon with cold-based attacks in an attempt to chill and freeze it. Once the rage demon is down, eliminate all remaining enemies to secure this siege point.

NOTE Clearing the siege points on the battlements is purely optional, but completing this task earns you a generous amount of XP, 150 influence, and two power—well worth the detour.

7. Hawke and a few Inquisition soldiers are busy fighting off a few Warden spellbinders and a massive pride demon at this siege point. Take out the spellbinders first, then focus on the pride demon. After the fight, Hawke offers his assistance. If you tell him to "Keep them off me," Hawke will join you. If you tell him to "Protect my troops," he will stay behind and help hold the battlements. Next, head south to secure the third and final siege point.

8. Several shades and a massive pride demon defend this siege point. If you have enough focus, this is a great time to deploy your Mark of the Rift ability. Otherwise, eliminate the shades first, then turn your full party's attention to the pride demon. By now, your party should be strong enough to handle the pride demon with minor difficulty. For best results, use a mage to freeze the pride demon with Winter's Grasp while your warriors hack away on him. Following the fight here, the battlements are secure, netting your party some bonus XP, influence, and power.

9. Backtrack to these stairs and open the three doors ahead (traveling west) to return to the main bailey.

10. Expect stiff resistance from some shades and a rage demon here—help the Inquisition soldiers finish them off. After the fight, stock up on potions from the supply cache. Heal everyone first, then use the supply cache—you can only use it once. Expect a tough fight ahead.

MAIN COURTYARD

11. You've finally tracked down Erimond and Warden-Commander Clarel. Your party arrives just in time to interrupt the ritual. Do your best to appeal to Warden-Commander Clarel—she seems unaware that Erimond serves Corypheus. Before Clarel summons a demon from the Fade, you have the chance to interrupt. If you have Blackwall in your party, he can address the Wardens, convincing the Warden warriors to join you. Likewise, if you spared the Wardens back in the main bailey, you can get the Warden warriors to fight by your side. But Erimond has a card up his sleeve as well—Corypheus's dragon. Realizing she's been betrayed, Clarel attacks Erimond and the dragon. As Clarel chases down Erimond, she urges her loyal Wardens to assist the Inquisition. Following the cinematic, engage a pride demon and the Warden spellbinders—despite Clarel's orders, the Warden mages are now loyal to Corypheus. However, the Warden warriors will fight by your side. Once again, this a good area to use your Mark of the Rift ability—it can really chew up the pride demon's guard and health. After the battle, head west to pursue Clarel and Erimond along the battlements.

12. Continue along the battlements, battling demons along the way. When you reach this spot, Clarel and Erimond are engaged in a duel. When it appears the Warden-Commander has the upper hand, Corypheus's dragon swoops down and attacks Clarel, biting down on her body and spitting her out. The dragon then stalks your party, pushing you closer and closer to a ledge. Before the dragon can attack, Clarel casts one last spell, striking the dragon's underbelly, causing it to collapse. The dragon tumbles and crashes through the stone walkway, causing it to crumble beneath your party's feet. As your party plummets through the air, the Inquisitor opens a Fade rift, sending you, your followers, Hawke, and Stroud into the Fade.

THE FADE

While you've managed to save yourself, Stroud, Hawke, and your party, you're all now trapped in the surreal world of the Fade—you need to find a way out. On the plus side, you gain 150 influence and two power for your work at Adamant. There's a supply cache just east of the starting position. Take this opportunity to replenish your party's potions.

> THE RAW FADE

1. Climb the stairs to the east to trigger a conversation with none other than Divine Justinia V... or is it? If Cassandra is in your party, even she isn't sure if this is the real Divine or not. Stroud feels this visage is most likely a spirit or a demon. Despite the suspicions of your party, the entity knows what really happened at the Temple of Sacred Ashes. She compels you to recover your memories by slaying demons in the Fade. Help your party eliminate the wraiths that appear. Each wraith leaves behind a green, glowing memory you must pick up, like loot—gather all four memories following the fight. When the final memory is retrieved, a cinematic shows the events leading up to the explosion at the Temple of Sacred Ashes: In an attempt to save the Divine, you interrupted Corypheus's ritual and touched the mysterious orb, causing the Anchor to appear on your hand. It's also revealed that it was the Wardens who were working with Corypheus at the temple, a fact that enrages Hawke.

2. After meeting with the Divine, head here and eliminate a few more wraiths. Interact with the table to begin the Fears of the Dreamers side quest. Use the search function to find a candle east of the table. Retrieve the candle and place it on the table. You can now interact with the nearby chair to gain one point of magic. Look for more Fears of the Dreamers objects during your journey through the Fade—there are five riddles you must solve to complete this quest.

FEARS OF THE DREAMERS

Quest Giver: Interact with the table.

Description: Fears torment the dreamers. Find the answers that may calm their fears, so that they may find peace.

Requirements: Enter the Fade.

Reward: Varied stat boosts, 242 XP, 80 Influence

Recommended Level: 10-12

Objectives:

- Find and solve five riddles.

Five riddles spread throughout the Fade must be solved. Use the accompanying map to locate the objects associated with each riddle. Each time you solve a riddle, you'll obtain a stat boost. This quest is purely optional, but it's easy to complete and well worth the minimal effort.

TIP Interact with the deposits of shadowed viridian crystals to retrieve different types of essence, useful for crafting runes.

3. Fight your way through the shades and wraiths here, then interact with the large mirror-like object to the east—these are called eluvians. Interacting with them boosts a different stat by one point. This one boosts Magic.

4. Return to the area where you spoke to the Divine and descend these stairs—watch out for a couple of shades.

5. When you reach this clearing, the voice of the Nightmare can be heard, taunting you. Ignore the taunts and turn your attention to the large group of wraiths and shades. After defeating the demons, complete the second Fears of the Dreamers riddle. Search for the flowers next to the skeleton in the south and place them in the vase to the north to gain a one-point Constitution stat boost.

6. Examining the eluvian here gives you a Dexterity boost.

7. You come under attack by several giant spider-like creatures called fearlings. But they have different names, like The Blight, Mages, and The Harrowing—are these the fears of the Inquisitor? Don't get lost in the Nightmare's mind games. Eliminate the fearlings with the aid of your party. The tight quarters make AoE attacks very effective, but wait until the creatures bunch up.

8. The Divine is waiting for you here. Feel free to ask her more questions, but she needs you to defeat more demons to recover your memories. Consider replenishing your potions at the nearby supply cache before beginning the attack. Retrieve the memories left behind by the wraiths to trigger another cinematic showing your escape from the Fade after the events at the temple. It was the Divine, not Andraste, who reached out to you. As you escaped, the Divine died. This entity you're speaking to isn't the Divine at all, but a spirit taking the Divine's form. But it isn't a malevolent spirit, as it's helping you escape from the Fade. Hawke and Stroud get in an argument over the Wardens' involvement in all of this—convince them to put their differences aside for now and defeat the next round of fearlings.

9. Complete the third Fears of the Dreamers riddle here. Search for the tarot card next to the skeleton and place it in the cauldron to the west. You earn a one-point Strength increase for solving this riddle.

10. Battle more fearlings and a terror here, then examine the nearby eluvian to increase your Willpower by one point.

11. Defeating the fearlings here allows the spirit to open another barrier, giving you access to a large clearing.

12. Climb the stairs to the north to confront two pride demons. Wait until both pride demons are next to each other, then use Mark of the Rift to eat away their health. Your ability might not be enough to kill both pride demons, but it will weaken them significantly. After the fight, search up here to locate a stuffed animal—the solution to the fourth Fear of the Dreamers riddle. Place the stuffed animal on the bed to the east to gain one point of Willpower.

13. Descend the steps to this lower area to find the fifth and final Fears of the Dreamers riddle—you may have to eliminate a few demons nearby. The solution to the riddle is in the graveyard to the east; notice how each tombstone is inscribed with the name of a Inquisition member, followed by their fear. Search the tombstone in the center of the graveyard to retrieve a vial of darkspawn blood. Take the vial back to the table to earn a one-point Cunning stat boost.

14. If you're up to the challenge, eliminate the gibbering horrors here to gain access to the eluvian. Examining the eluvian gives you a one-point Strength boost.

15. Help the spirit remove another barrier by defeating another round of fearlings. Watch out for the arrival of some shades, wraiths, and despair demons as well. Once these demons are defeated, turn your attention to the pride demon marching down the steps to the north. Try to block him on the staircase, then use AoE attacks to dish out some heavy damage—avoid using Mark of the Rift here; you'll want to use it later. When all the demons are dead, the barrier is removed, giving you access to a rift at the end of a long cave.

16. If you completed all five riddles in the Fears of the Dreamers quest, your reward awaits here. Gather the loot to complete the quest, netting you some bonus XP and influence, as well as some gear. The cave also holds a supply cache. Heal all your party members before interacting with the supply cache—you face a tough fight ahead.

> NIGHTMARE'S LAIR

A rift leading back to Adamant is just ahead, at the cave's exit, but a massive spider-like demon is blocking your path. The friendly spirit charges ahead, sacrificing itself and causing the massive demon to vanish—for now. Turn your attention to the Aspect of the Nightmare—this is a fear demon. This creepy-looking boss is accompanied by several fearlings. Immediately engage the tactical camera and use Mark of the Rift to kill off the fearlings and deplete the fear demon's barrier. The fear demon has the ability to disappear and reappear in a new location, so try to hit it with this AoE ability early on, before it can dematerialize.

This boss is resistant to spirit-based attacks, but all other spells and status effects are effective. Use your party's abilities to pour on as many damaging status effects as possible in an effort to quickly deplete the fear demon's health. Throughout the battle more fearlings (and a few wraiths) will appear, so keep an eye on the compass to identify the appearance of new enemies. Make sure your ranged party members aren't swarmed by these pesky creatures—taunt them with your warriors. The fear demon will also deploy a new barrier from time to time—your party will need to cut through the barrier to resume dealing damage to the fear demon's health.

DECISION POINT

Following the defeat of the fear demon, the massive spider-like demon reappears. Hawke volunteers to stay behind and distract the demon while the rest of you escape through the rift. But Stroud feels it's his responsibility as a Warden to stay behind. You must make the decision, choosing whether Hawke or Stroud remains in the Fade. Your decision has no positive or negative consequences on the approval of your party members, so simply make the decision you feel is right. Once the decision is made, your party rushes through the rift while Hawke or Stroud stays behind and battles the demon.

ADAMANT

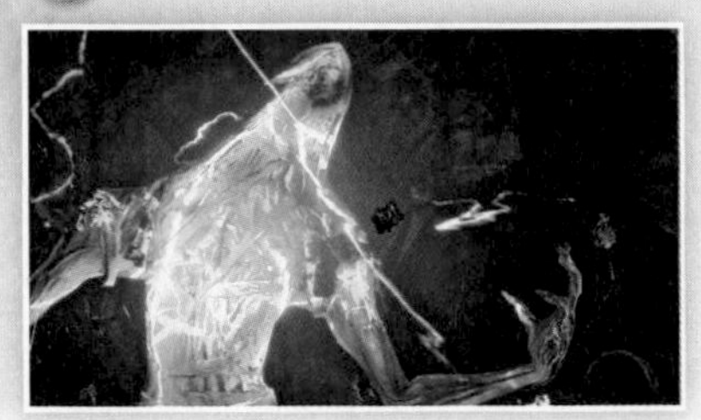

Your party reemerges in Adamant's main courtyard, spilling out of the rift opened by Erimond and Clarel. The Inquisitor uses the Anchor to close the rift, causing all remaining demons to perish—Adamant is now secure and under the control of the Inquisition. An Inquisition scout reports that Corypheus's dragon managed to escape but Erimond has been taken alive. The absence of Stroud or Hawke has not gone unnoticed. Respond how you see fit to explain their selfless sacrifice. Next, you must decide the future of the Grey Wardens. Afterward, you're automatically returned to Skyhold—now that the Warden situation has been resolved it's time to address the threat to Empress Celene.

DECISION POINT

Upon your return to Adamant you must decide what will happen to the Grey Wardens. Now that your memories have been restored, it is now clear that the Wardens have been serving Corypheus and are culpable in the tragedy at the Temple of Sacred Ashes. While the Wardens weren't acting under their own free will at the time, they are prone to corruption by Corypheus. Is this a risk you can afford? Your options are to exile the Wardens from Orlais or to welcome them into the Inquisition. Your party members have strong feelings on this matter, and your decision will have both negative and positive impacts on approval. Make your decision carefully. If you choose to banish the Wardens from Orlais and Blackwall is in your party, you can choose whether he stays with the Inquisition or is exiled with the rest of the Wardens.

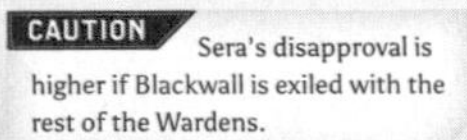

CAUTION Sera's disapproval is higher if Blackwall is exiled with the rest of the Wardens.

Approval: Fate of the Wardens

Follower	Join Inquisition	Exiled
Blackwall	↑↑↑	↓↓↓
Cassandra	↓↓	↑↑
Cole	↓↓↓	↑↑↑
Dorian	↑↑	↓↓
The Iron Bull	↑↑↑	↓↓
Sera	↑↑↑	↓↓
Solas	↓↓↓	↑↑↑
Varric	↑↑↑ (if Warden Ally is left in the Fade) ↓↓↓ (if Hawke is left in the Fade)	↑↑↑ (if Hawke is left in the Fade) ↓↓↓ (if Warden ally is left in the Fade)
Vivienne	↓	↑

WICKED EYES AND WICKED HEARTS

The fate of Empress Celene and, in turn, all of Orlais has been threatened. The Inquisition must intervene.

NOTE Wicked Eyes and Wicked Hearts can be completed before Here Lies the Abyss. These quests can be completed in any order. But both must be complete before advancing to What Pride Had Wrought.

SKYHOLD

Back in Skyhold, the Inquisitor has a conversation with Leliana. She's pleased with the Inquisition's victory at Adamant but stresses the importance of preventing the assassination attempt on Empress Celene. Arrangements have been made for you to attend the masquerade ball being held at the Winter Palace in Halamshiral. Once there, you must uncover and disrupt the Venatori plot against the Imperial Court. Leliana suggests Corypheus may also be behind the conflict between the empress and her cousin, Grand Duke Gaspard. If Celene can be saved, she'll be a powerful ally against Corypheus. If you haven't spoken to Josephine since arriving in Skyhold, do so now. This will unlock the Wicked Eyes and Wicked Hearts operation on the war table, allowing you to attend the ball in Halamshiral.

> GAINING POWER

Before you can attend the ball in Halamshiral, you must acquire a minimum of 30 power. If you've been completing side quests throughout your adventure, there's a good chance you're close to meeting this requirement—simply completing Here Lies the Abyss earns you six power. But if you still need to accumulate some power, put the masquerade ball aside for now and resume exploring the wildernesses you've unlocked thus far. Clearing out Crestwood and the Western Approach should give you enough power to attend the ball. Don't forget revisiting the Hinterlands. If you haven't already, the Fallow Mire and Storm Coast are worth scouting and exploring. Or if you've recovered at least one shard by using an ocularum, pay a visit to the Forbidden Oasis. But you'll get the most power out of completing quests (and closing Fade rifts) in the Exalted Plains, Emerald Graves, and Emprise du Lion. Scouting these locales may cost power, but you'll quickly earn back whatever you spent. Going forward, you'll need more and more power to complete critical path operations on the war table, so now's a good time to expand the Inquisition's influence into locales you haven't visited.

NOTE If you want to explore and gain power in the Forbidden Oasis, you must discover and retrieve at least one shard by interacting with an ocularum.

RECOMMENDED QUESTS

QUEST/ACTIVITY	LOCALE	POWER
Holding the Oasis	The Forbidden Oasis	1
Rifts in the Oasis	The Forbidden Oasis	4
Rifts High and Low	The Forbidden Oasis	4
The Temple of Pride	The Forbidden Oasis	2
Holding the Mire	The Fallow Mire	1
Rifts in the Mire	The Fallow Mire	2
Beacons in the Dark	The Fallow Mire	2
Beneath the Mire	The Fallow Mire	2
Lost Souls	The Fallow Mire	3
These Demons Are Clever	The Fallow Mire	2
The Captain of the Chargers	The Storm Coast	1
Cleaning House	The Storm Coast	1
Rifts on the Coast	The Storm Coast	2
Rift at the Falls	The Storm Coast	1
Holding the Storm Coast	The Storm Coast	2
Wardens of the Coast	The Storm Coast	1

> THE WAR ROOM

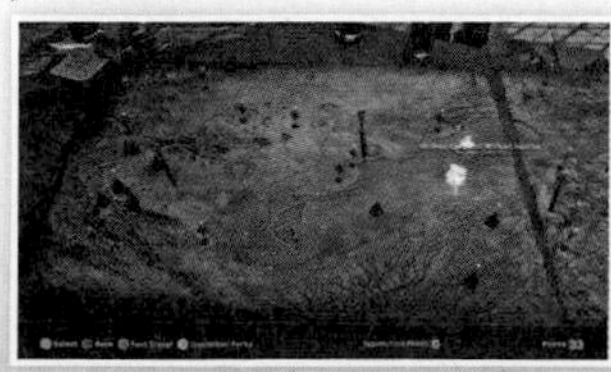

When you have at least 30 power, go to the war table and select the Wicked Eyes and Wicked Hearts operation, costing 30 power. Apparently, Empress Celene will be conducting peace talks at the ball, meeting with Grand Duke Gaspard and Ambassador Briala. Josephine feels the assassin must be hiding among one of these factions. It's believed Corypheus is behind the assassination attempt. Killing Empress Celene will certainly have a destabilizing effect on Orlais, giving Corypheus and the Venatori the opening they've been waiting for. You must get the bottom of this plot and prevent Empress Celene from falling victim to this devious scheme. Select your party, then prepare yourself to delve deep into cutthroat Game of Orlesian politics.

The Winter Palace

Legend

- Entrance/Exit
- Locked Door
- Weak Wall
- Scandalous Secret
- Halla Statue
- Caprice Coin

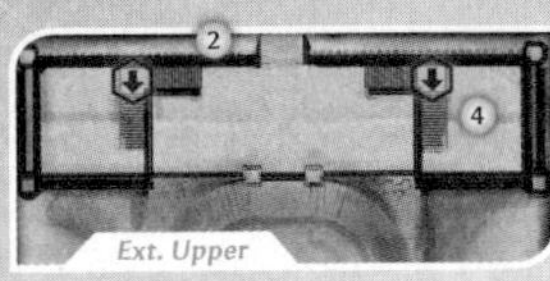

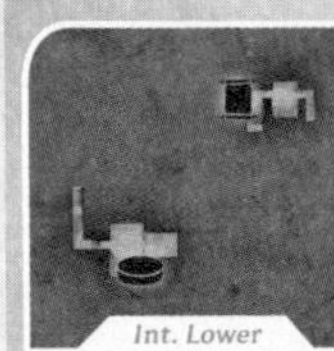

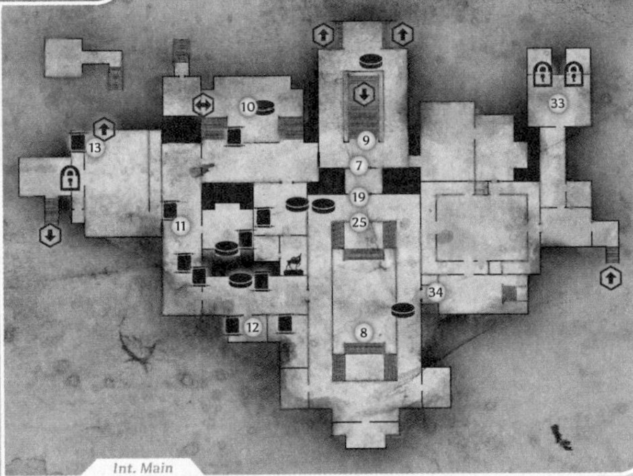

> THE EMERALD CROWN

Sporting formal attire, the Inquisition's delegation arrives at the Winter Palace in Halamshiral and is greeted by Grand Duke Gaspard, cousin and political rival of Empress Celene—it was the duke who extended an invitation to the ball. Gaspard's ambition is no secret, and he promises to be a strong ally of the Inquisition once he becomes the ruler of Orlais. But he's concerned Ambassador Briala will disrupt the peace talks.

1. Following the conversation with Gaspard, search this corner to recover a ring—it belongs to the noblewoman nearby. Return the ring to the noblewoman to gain court approval. The court approval meter, visible in the upper right corner of the screen, indicates how favorably the Inquisition is seen by the Imperial Court—you start with 50 court approval. Approval can be lost by saying the wrong thing or exploring restricted areas of the palace. If the approval meter is depleted, you'll be asked to leave the ball and the mission is a failure. Look for opportunities to gain approval with the court—being agreeable and nonconfrontational during conversations is a good start.

2. Don't enter the palace just yet. Search a planter on this upstairs balcony to uncover the storage key. This opens the door downstairs.

3. Use the storage key to open this door. Search the table next to the door to find a scandalous secret. This is the first of 30 scandalous secrets scattered across the palace. Collect all 30 scandalous secrets, shown on the map, and give them to Leliana to complete The Great Blackmail Hunt quest, gaining a huge boost in court approval. A second scandalous secret is on the table to the west. Search the pot along the north wall to uncover a caprice coin—find all 15 and toss them in the fountain in the garden to complete the Throwing Away Money quest. The locations of all caprice coins are marked on the map.

4. Search this balcony for a halla statue. These statues unlock doors throughout the palace. There are 10 statues—find them all to complete the Herd of Stone Halla quest. This statue can be used to unlock the eastern storage room downstairs.

5. Use the halla statue you found upstairs to unlock this door, giving you access to two loot stashes.

6. Interact with the gate to enter the palace. Josephine has a few words of advice—she stresses the importance choosing your words carefully. Every word you say will be scrutinized by the court, potentially leading to a loss or gain of court approval.

TIP Simply finding scandalous secrets, stone halla, and caprice coins earns you some court approval. You don't have to find them all. But you'll gain more court approval if you complete these collections.

NOTE Who will be the best leader for Orlais? This is a decision you must make before the ball is over. If you're not certain, make an effort to seek out Empress Celene, Grand Duke Gaspard, and Ambassador Briala. You can speak to each of them individually in the palace's grand ballroom after making your entrance. Explore the three adjoining balconies on the south side of the ballroom to speak with them in private. Each prospective leader has a unique vision for Orlais. Use this information to help make your decision.

! THE GREAT BLACKMAIL HUNT

Quest Giver: N/A

Description: Scandalous secrets are everywhere at the grand masquerade. Listen in on conversations to gather gossip and scour the palace for incriminating items and notes. The secrets learned could be used to gain power for the Inquisition and the upper hand in the Grand Game of Orlesian society.

Requirements: Available after finding the first secret

Reward: 128 XP, 80 Influence, 50 Court Approval

Recommended Level: 10-12

Objectives:

- Gather 30 scandalous secrets.
- Deliver secrets to Leliana.

Scour the palace for scandalous secrets, in the form of either notes or gossip. When interacting with some nobles, they will rudely walk away from you. Take this as a cue to listen for gossip. Watch where the nobles relocate, then position yourself within the red circle on the floor to eavesdrop. Sometimes gossip is just that, and reveals no useful information. But sometimes you might gather some juicy details. Keep an eye on the compass too. When it pulses, commence a search to locate scandalous notes. You need a total of 30 scandalous secrets to complete this quest—reference the map to find them all. Talk to Leliana once you've found them all—she can put them to good use, gaining 50 court approval. But you don't have to find them all. Turn in what you have to Leliana to get a boost in court approval. You only have to find all the secrets if you want to complete the quest.

THROWING MONEY AWAY

Quest Giver: N/A

Description: Orlesian nobles have been known to toss caprice coins into fountains as a symbol of status. Doing this may strengthen one's social standing

Requirements: Available after finding the first coins

Reward: 15 Court Approval

Recommended Level: 10-12

Objectives:

- Find 15 caprice coins.

Reference the map for the locations of all 15 caprice coins—you'll need to perform a search at each location to reveal the hidden coin. Tossing each coin in the fountain in the guest garden nets you one court approval—collect and toss all 15 coins in the fountain for a gain of 15 court approval.

HERD OF STONE HALLA

Quest Giver: N/A

Description: There's a veritable herd of halla statuettes scattered around the Winter Palace. They stand out a little too much to be simply decorative.

Requirements: Available after finding the first halla statue

Reward: 242 XP, 80 Influence

Recommended Level: 10-12

Objectives:

- Find 10 halla statuettes.

Halla statues are used to unlock special doors in the palace. Some doors require multiple statues to be unlocked. Reference the map for the location of all 10 halla statues. Note that you can't open all the locked doors in the Winter Palace with just 10 statues. You must carefully choose which doors to open and which ones to leave locked.

VESTIBULE

7. At the moment, there isn't much to do in the vestibule. The perimeter doors here are all locked and cannot be picked—they must be opened from the other side. Feel free to speak to your party members and eavesdrop on a conversation to uncover a secret. After you're finished exploring this area, interact with the door on the south side to enter the grand ballroom.

GRAND BALLROOM

8. It's time to make your entrance. Follow Grand Duke Gaspard across the ballroom to greet Empress Celene and Grand Duchess Florianne. You have the opportunity to warn Celene of the danger to her life, but it won't do any good. It's better to play it cool and conduct a thorough investigation of the palace before making any allegations. Following the conversation with Celene, Leliana asks to have a word with you in private.

VESTIBULE

9. Back in the vestibule, Leliana engages you in a conversation. She reveals Celene has a fascination with mysticism and consults with an occult advisor. In addition to investigating Gaspard and Briala, Leliana suggests looking into this mage who gained favor within the Imperial Court. She suggests starting your search in the guest wing.

HALL OF HEROES

10. This part of the guest wing is a restricted area. While you're in this room, you'll lose court approval at a slow but steady pace, so limit your time here. You can find a caprice coin in the lower level and eavesdrop on a conversation between two elf servants on the west side—they mention something about a package in the upper guest wing. Also, make note of the servants' quarters doorway—you'll be coming back here.

GUEST WING

11. There are a couple of nobles you can speak to in the guest wing—saying the right things will lead to a gain in court approval. Duke Germain likes being asked questions. And when speaking to the Council of Heralds' vassal, agree that Phillipe is a jerk. While exploring this area, don't forget to listen for gossip and conduct searches for more scandalous secrets.

12. Make your way to this balcony, off the guest wing, and conduct a search to recover a cylinder seal. This is a message from one of Briala's agents. Apparently something is happening in the servants' quarters. Finding this clue nets you 60 influence. But before heading for the servants' quarters, you need to find some more clues. Head for the guest garden.

GUEST GARDEN

13. Upon entering the garden, you're greeted by three of Celene's ladies-in-waiting. They report that Empress Celene will pledge her full support to the Inquisition as soon as Gaspard is defeated. After the conversation, explore the garden. There's a fountain on the north end—toss in any caprice coins you've found to gain approval. Next to the fountain is a trellis—climb it to the balcony above.

14. This upper garden walkway is off-limits, and you'll lose approval by being up here. So move quickly to complete the following tasks. Collect the halla statue, then search for a nearby scandalous secret.

15. Using the halla statue, enter this room to discover a ghastly crime; several bloody bodies line the floor. Retrieve the negotiations document lying next to the bodies. The document is signed by Gaspard and addressed to Empress Celene. Apparently Gaspard wants to work together with Celene to stop Briala.

GRAND LIBRARY

16. Search the shelf in the northwest corner of this room and interact with the book to open a secret chamber. Make note of the six urns in the center of the room—these can be lit with veilfire to reveal another secret chamber. You can acquire veilfire in the secret room to the north.

17. Enter this small room and retrieve the letter from the desk. It is a letter from Celene to her occult advisor. In the letter, Celene requests the accompaniment of her occult advisor during the ball—Celene fears that Gaspard may persuade others to use magic against her. Ignite a veilfire torch and return to the previous room to light the six urns.

VALMONT URNS

The six urns in the grand library have markings that represent the Valmont emperors. A plaque hints that chronological order is important: "The arrow of time flies in only one direction. Its path lights our way forward." Scattered through the palace are six unique paintings dedicated to the Valmont emperors, which also note the years they ruled—interact with the plaque beneath each painting to see this information. Using veilfire, acquired in the office of Celene's occult advisor, light the urns in the following order to reveal a secret room containing some loot:

1. Etienne I
2. Reville
3. Etienne II
4. Judicael I
5. Judicael II
6. Florian

18. Search this wing of the grand library for loot and more scandalous secrets. When you're finished searching, exit through one of the doors to the north to return to the vestibule.

VESTIBULE

19. Interact with the door leading into the grand ballroom to trigger a conversation with Celene's occult advisor, Morrigan. She seems to be well aware of your activities in the palace. It turns out Morrigan has the same concerns as the Inquisition. She recently discovered and eliminated an agent from Tevinter and retrieved a key from the body. Morrigan cannot leave Celene unattended this evening, so she asks you to investigate, handing over the key. Following the conversation, return to the Hall of Heroes and use the key to access the servants' quarters.

SERVANTS' QUARTERS

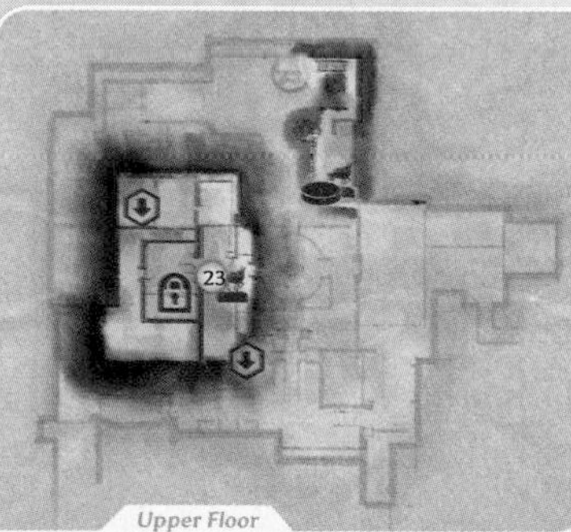

CAUTION The servants' quarters are off-limits. As a result, you'll lose court approval while you're here. Move through this area as quickly as possible to minimize depletion of court approval.

20. You're joined by your party in the servants' quarters, and it's immediately clear something dastardly is afoot. The bodies of two servants lie at your feet upon entry. Before you engage in any combat, take a moment to equip your armor—it offers much better protection than the formal attire. A halla statue can be found in the adjoining kitchen—you'll have to stand on the table to reach it.

Gardens

21. Here you encounter the body of a noble—with a dagger bearing Gaspard's crest protruding from his back. Suddenly a harlequin appears in the distance, cutting down a servant before retreating to a balcony above. Following the cinematic, engage a trio of Venatori zealots. Next, travel north and then west. Fight your way into the grand apartments, eliminating more Venatori zealots and Venatori mages along the way.

Grand Apartments

22. More Venatori agents occupy the first floor of the grand apartments. Move room by room, eliminating resistance while gathering loot. Once the ground floor is clear, use these stairs in the dining hall to reach the second floor.

23. Fight through more Venatori agents upstairs until you reach this hallway. Here you encounter the harlequin responsible for murdering the servant outside. The harlequin is accompanied by several Venatori zealots and a Venatori marksman—this is a good opportunity to use Mark of the Rift. But if you don't have enough focus, rely on other AoE attacks to take advantage of the cramped quarters. The harlequin is highly mobile, so pile on status effects that restrict his movement. After the fight, Ambassador Briala makes an appearance. She's pleased with your work—she came here to avenge the deaths of her agents, but you beat her to it. Given the evidence, Briala feels these Venatori agents are working for Gaspard. Following the conversation with Briala, collect the halla statue nearby.

Gardens

24. Return to the ground floor and exit through the south side of the grand apartments. You come under attack by more Venatori enemies in this alley. Eliminate them, then proceed to the gate to the east to return to the palace. Briala's elven agents will stay behind and secure the rest of the servants' quarters.

NOTE Before leaving the servants' quarters, collect another halla statue on the high balcony to the east of the gardens. Reference the map for its exact location.

GRAND BALLROOM

25. Upon your return from the servants' quarters, head straight for the grand ballroom—you have the chance to dance with Grand Duchess Florianne. Here's your chance to regain some of the court approval you lost while conducting your investigation in the servants' quarters. Florianne urges you to search the royal wing garden for the leader of Gaspard's mercenaries. After the dance, you have a quick meeting with the war council. Leliana suggests letting Celene die during the assassination attempt and choosing from Gaspard or Briala as the next ruler of Orlais. Josephine is not supportive of this plan, but you don't need to make a decision just yet. Return to the vestibule and then enter the royal wing.

TIP Select the following responses during the conversation/dance with Florianne to gain maximum court approval:

- May I help you?
- Let's dance.
- Why don't you educate me?
- Is that what we both want?
- Which am I to you?
- Who do you trust?
- Isn't everyone?

ROYAL WING

CAUTION Like the servants' quarters, the royal wing is a restricted area. You'll lose court approval while exploring this area, so conduct a speedy investigation, then return to the grand ballroom.

Royal Quarters

26. Enter this room to stop an attack on one of Briala's spies—the Inquisitor kicks the attacking harlequin out a window. The spy is convinced Briala set a trap for her and is willing to spill some dark secrets to get her revenge; ask her to testify. You can use this information to blackmail Briala. After talking to the spy, grab the halla statue near the window.

27. Another halla statue can be found in this room, sitting on the table next to the chair. Search for a scandalous secret while you're here.

28. Climb through the open window to enter this room. Inside is another halla statue. You must conduct a search to retrieve this halla statue, located in the southwest corner. Stock up on potions from the supply cache in this room.

29. Conduct a search near the bookshelf here to retrieve another halla statue.

Empress's Private Quarters

30. It takes five halla statues to open the door to Celene's private quarters—reference the map for their locations. Inside, one of Gaspard's agents is stripped naked and tied to Celene's bed. He was tricked into giving Celene details of Gaspard's plans—Celene is prepared to arrest Gaspard as soon as he strikes. Ask the agent to testify in an effort to gain some leverage over Celene. After freeing the agent, search the room for loot, a scandalous secret, and a caprice coin.

Jardin de Rêverie

31. If you haven't already, equip your armor before entering this area. Grand Duchess Florianne has caught you in her trap. She's been working with Corypheus and is the one behind the plot to kill Empress Celene. Her intent is to keep you busy here while she returns to the grand ballroom to assassinate Celene. After Florianne leaves, work with your party to close a Fade rift, defeating demons and Venatori marksmen. Once the rift is closed, your party frees Gaspard's mercenary captain. The captain is convinced Gaspard is the mastermind behind all of this. Ask the captain to testify to gain some leverage against Gaspard. Now that you have evidence against Celene, Gaspard, Briala, and Florianne, head back to the grand ballroom to make your decision.

Le Requiem

32. Defeat the Venatori zealots and Venatori marksmen in this chapel-like room. The pews restrict mobility, making AoE attacks very effective. Once the room is calm, gather loot and exit to the west.

La Serrure

33. Fight your way past more Venatori agents to access this room. One door is marked with a warrior icon, the other with a mage icon. Each door requires five halla statues to open. There aren't enough halla statues to open both doors—and if you opened the door to Celene's private quarters, you don't have enough halla statues to open either door. But if you have enough statues to open a door, expect some nice loot on the other side.

34. Enter this hallway, then interact with the door to the west to return to the grand ballroom.

> GRAND BALLROOM

DECISION POINT

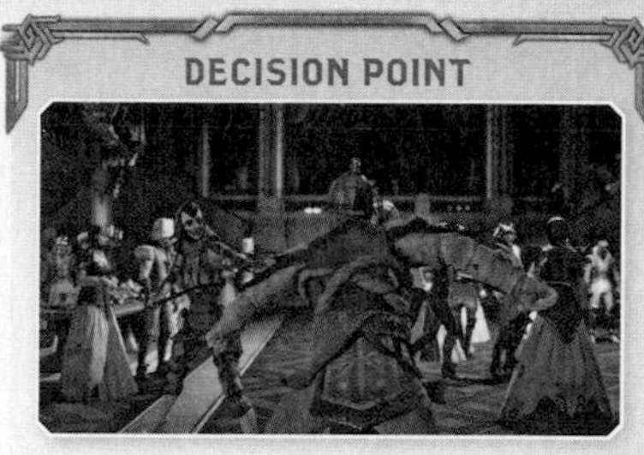

Upon your return from the royal wing, Cullen approaches you—Empress Celene is about to give her speech. Your decision here will determine who will rule Orlais. There are three possible options:

- I'll talk with Florianne: If your court approval is high enough (85+), you can choose to expose Florianne's plan to the court, leading to her immediate arrest. This saves Celene and prevents you from engaging Florianne in combat. You gain approval from Solas, Dorian, and Blackwall for taking this approach. After Florianne is apprehended you have the option to kill her or have her sent to jail. Solas, Blackwall, Dorian, Sera, and Cole approve of taking her captive.
- Wait for Florianne to attack: If this option is chosen, Empress Celene is assassinated before the Inquisition acts, leading to a fight with Florianne. Afterward, you must choose whether Gaspard or Briala rules Orlais. Cassandra and Dorian approve of this option, while Blackwall, Sera, and Cole disapprove.
- Detain the duchess: This option allows the Inquisition to prevent the assassination of Empress Celene before engaging Florianne in combat. Empress Celene remains the ruler of Orlais. You gain approval from Blackwall, Sera, and Cole for taking this action.

NOTE As expected, there are some far-reaching consequences when deciding the ruler of Orlais. Celene will work for peace, and Orlais's prominence as a superpower will diminish. Gaspard will reignite the war between Orlais and Ferelden. Briala will push for more rights for the elves, potentially causing an uprising.

> GRAND DUCHESS FLORIANNE BATTLE

If you were unable to expose Florianne's plan before the court, you must defeat her in combat as she escapes to the Emerald Crown courtyard outside the palace, ditching her dress for attire more appropriate for combat. Florianne is a highly mobile archer. As a result, your ranged party members will have an easier time engaging her as she jumps and flips around the courtyard. Florianne is joined by several Venatori zealots. Wait until she is positioned near a group of her allies, then initiate Mark of the Rift, killing the zealots and inflicting heavy damage on Florianne. Also, utilize abilities that restrict or slow Florianne's movement—cold-based attacks work well. This will allow your melee party members to close in and land some heavy hits. The warrior's Grappling Chain ability is particularly helpful during this battle, ideal for pulling Florianne to melee range.

As Florianne's health drops, she retreats to the walls on the east and west sides of the courtyard. At this point, only your ranged party members can engage her. But there are plenty of her allies on the ground for your warriors to hack and slash. Turn your attention to defeating these lesser enemies before resuming your attacks on Florianne. In addition to firing arrows, Florianne can temporarily put your party to sleep, making them vulnerable to attacks. She also has the ability to build a guard, significantly prolonging her life. But as long as your party keeps on the pressure, you'll eventually whittle down her health until she's dead—be sure to loot her body afterward to score some rare loot. Once you've defeated all the enemies, return to the grand ballroom by opening the gate to the north.

> AFTERMATH

DECISION POINT

After dealing with Florianne, you're engaged in a heated conversation between Briala, Gaspard, and Empress Celene—assuming she survived. If Empress Celene is alive and you've collected blackmail evidence, you have the option of implicating Briala or Gaspard—the traitor will be executed unless you intervene. Or you can forget the blackmail and suggest that all three work together. You even have the chance to patch things over with Celene and Briala, urging them to reconcile. But if Empress Celene died, you must choose the next ruler of Orlais.

Approval: New Orlesian Leadership

Follower	Support Gaspard	Support Briala	Support Celene	Celene/Briala Reunited	Everyone Lives	Florianne Arrested	Save Celene	Celene Dies
Blackwall	↓↓↓	↓↓	—	—	↑	↑↑	↑↑	↓↓↓
Cassandra	↑↑↑	↓↓↓	—	↑↑	↓	—	—	↑↑
Cole	↓↓↓	↑↑↑	—	↑↑↑	↑↑↑	—	↑↑↑	↓↓
Dorian	↓↓	↑	—	↑↑↑	—	↑↑↑	—	↑↑
The Iron Bull	↑↑↑	—	↑↑	—	—	↑↑	—	↑↑
Sera	↑	↓↓	—	—	↑↑	—	↑↑	↓↓↓
Solas	—	↑	—	—	—	↑↑↑	—	—
Varric	—	—	—	—	—	—	—	—
Vivienne	↓	↓↓↓	—	—	—	—	—	—

Next, the Inquisitor joins the leader during a speech to the court, confirming Orlais's alliance with the Inquisition. Following the speech, you're approached by Morrigan. She has been assigned as liaison to the Inquisition and will be joining you in Skyhold. If you've been romancing a character, you have the chance to dance with your romantic interest after speaking to Morrigan. Following the dance, you're automatically transported back to Skyhold.

WHAT PRIDE HAD WROUGHT

The Inquisition's efforts have weakened Corypheus's attempts to stir unrest in Thedas. Now is the ideal time to strike. Consult the advisors in the war room.

SKYHOLD

Upon your return from the Winter Palace, Josephine is engaged in a conversation with Mother Giselle. Giselle feels it's time to select a new Divine, suggesting Cassandra and Leliana are the leading candidates. But Josephine insists that the Inquisition cannot spare Cassandra or Leliana at this time. After turning away Mother Giselle, Josephine urges the Inquisitor to stay focused—the Inquisition's next move is being planned in the war room. Before heading for the war room, consider making the rounds in Skyhold, talking to your followers—new conversation options are available. Both Cassandra and Leliana are conflicted about their opportunity to become the next Divine. This is also a good moment to get acquainted with the Inquisition's new member, Morrigan. She can be found in Skyhold's garden.

WAR ROOM

Your successes at Adamant and Halamshiral have bolstered the Inquisition's hand. Corypheus's army has been forced to retreat and is currently headed toward the Arbor Wilds. But it remains unclear why Corypheus is in such a remote location. Leliana theorizes he's looking for more elven artifacts. Morrigan joins the war council to offer some insight. Instead of explaining what Corypheus is looking for, she offers to show you.

THE ELUVIAN

Morrigan leads you to a mirror-like object called an eluvian—you encountered several broken eluvians in the Fade. Morrigan has restored this eluvian, and another like it is located in the Arbor Wilds. Morrigan fears Corypheus is looking for it. The eluvian Corypheus seeks is located in an elven temple, deep in the Arbor Wilds. As Morrigan demonstrates, the eluvian functions like a portal, leading to a place she calls the Crossroads. The ancient elves used these mirrors to travel between their far-flung ruins. All eluvians connect to this surreal world, and Morrigan suggests Corypheus could use his power to enter the Fade from the Crossroads, as he originally planned to do with the Anchor.

NOTE Here Lies the Abyss and Wicked Eyes and Wicked Hearts can be completed in any order. But they both must be complete before starting What Pride Had Wrought.

GAINING POWER

Before you can march on the Arbor Wilds you must acquire 50 power. If you've been completing side quests during your adventure, chances are you already have enough power to proceed. Otherwise, it's time to take a detour and acquire power from other locales. By now all locales on the war table map can be scouted, including Emerald Graves and the Exalted Plains. Closing Fade rifts and establishing camps in these locales is the quickest way to accumulate power—closing each Fade rift nets you two power. Some side quests also reward power. Keep accumulating power until you have enough to take the fight to Corypheus in the Arbor Wilds.

Recommended Quests

Quest/Activity	Locale	Power
Holding the Emerald Graves	Emerald Graves	3
Rifts at the Cove	Emerald Graves	4
A Vicious Thug	Emerald Graves	2
A Corrupt General	Emerald Graves	2
A Fallen Sister	Emerald Graves	2
A Deluded Chevalier	Emerald Graves	2
Rifts at the Pavilion	Emerald Graves	8
Rifts at the Reach	Emerald Graves	4
Rifts near the Sighs	Emerald Graves	6
Chateau d'Onterre	Emerald Graves	2
Lay Rest the Western Ramparts	Exalted Plains	2
Rifts in the Old Plains	Exalted Plains	8
Rifts on the Battlefield	Exalted Plains	8
Holding the Exalted Plains	Exalted Plains	2
Another Side, Another Story	Exalted Plains	2
Lay Rest the Eastern Ramparts	Exalted Plains	2
Calming Victory Rise	Exalted Plains	2
Rifts in the Fens	Exalted Plains	6

NOTE Now is also a good time to complete your nemesis side quest, Before the Dawn or Under Her Skin—see Cullen for Before the Dawn or Leliana for Under Her Skin. If you complete this quest, your encounter with Samson or Calpernia at the Temple of Mythal may go much more smoothly.

THE WAR ROOM

When you have enough power, return to the war room and select the What Pride Had Wrought operation on the war table. If Corypheus gains control of the eluvian in the Arbor Wilds, Morrigan fears he could access the Fade and obtain the power of a god... or unleash more demons into the world. As Cullen, Leliana, and Josephine argue about the best course of action, advise them to work together. Following the meeting, select your party; given Solas's knowledge of elven artifacts, it's wise to bring him along. Morrigan will join your party in the Arbor Wilds, but she isn't a controllable party member.

CAUTION Before venturing into the Arbor Wilds, make sure your party is up to the task. Most of the enemies you face in the Arbor Wilds are level 16 or higher. So make sure your Inquisitor and party members are at least level 15. Otherwise, grind in other locales until you're ready for high-level combat.

THE ARBOR WILDS

The Inquisition's invasion of the Arbor Wilds is well underway by the time you and your party arrive. A scout reports that Corypheus has been spotted moving to an elven ruin to the north. Morrigan feels Corypheus is headed for the Temple of Mythal—the eluvian is probably contained within. You must reach this elven temple before Corypheus can secure the eluvian. Proceed to the first blockade, where Corypheus's troops are making a stand. Fight your way past several red templars and red templar horrors along the way. You'll be assisted by a few Orlesian troops.

FIRST BLOCKADE

Red templars are defending the ruins of a stone bridge at the Great Waterfall. Initiate the fight with a powerful AoE attack—Mark of the Rift can wipe out almost every enemy here, assuming you ambush them early on. Be mindful of the archers posted on the bridge and surrounding ruins. Position your ranged party members on the bridge so they can rain down arrows and spells on the enemies in the shallow stream below. Once you've cleared out the western span of the bridge, watch out for more enemies positioned near the eastern span. There are some corrupted Grey Wardens in this second group.

TIP The Arbor Wilds is a good source for stormheart and silverite, so keep your eyes peeled for these minerals. You can't return to the Arbor Wilds once this mission is over.

SECOND BLOCKADE

The red templars' forward camp blocks your path to the second blockade. Once again, you have the chance to take these enemies by surprise. If possible, initiate the assault with a few overlapping AoE attacks—or send in a stealthy rogue to assassinate an enemy. But don't neglect the archers posted around the camp's perimeter; eliminate the archers and then claim their perches for your own ranged party members. Try to locate and identify the Sentinel shadow among this group—this highly mobile enemy is deadly when sneaking up on your party members. Gang up on the Sentinel shadow before eliminating the rest of the enemies.

CAUTION Beware of more Sentinel shadows during your journey to the Temple of Mythal. When they're encountered, turn your whole party's focus against them. These elven Sentinels are not affiliated with Corypheus's forces. Instead, they're responsible for guarding the Temple of Mythal from outsiders.

The second blockade is at the ruined archways. Here you encounter more red templars as well as two red templar behemoths—don't let their size intimidate you. Despite their ability to generate guard, your party should have no problem whittling down their health. Attack primarily with your ranged party members, using the elevated positions along the nearby ruins to rain down arrows and spells.

> FINAL BLOCKADE

Expect heavy red templar resistance during your approach to the final blockade. When you reach the temple gates, position your ranged party members on the ruins, next to the Inquisition archers. This allows them to fire down on the senior Wardens and red templar horrors below with minimal fear of reprisal. Send your melee party members down into the shallow riverbed to engage the enemies at close range—Cullen and his men are already engaging them. If available, use Mark of the Rift to wipe out most of these enemies early on. Following the battle, travel north to enter the temple grounds. Heal and use the supply cache on your way in.

> THE TEMPLE OF MYTHAL

Your party looks on as Corypheus and your nemesis (Calpernia or Samson) attempt to cross a bridge leading to the Temple of Mythal. Corypheus is looking for something called the Well of Sorrows. Then something unexpected happens—Corypheus explodes after passing through a magic barrier placed at the bridge's entrance. But he soon reemerges from the body of an unlucky Warden. With the magical barrier disrupted, the Inquisitor sees an opportunity and urges the rest of the party to cross the bridge and enter the temple's courtyard—they manage to seal the doors to the courtyard just as Corypheus's dragon attacks.

NOTE The nemesis you encounter at the Temple of Mythal is determined by which faction you allied yourself with: the mages or the templars. If you chose to side with the rebel mages, your nemesis is Samson. Calpernia, a Tevinter mage, is your nemesis if you chose to side with the templars. Reference the Inner Circle Quests section in the Exploration chapter for more information on Samson and Calpernia.

Outer Courtyard

Morrigan is uncertain what this Well of Sorrows is—perhaps Corypheus isn't looking for the eluvian as she once thought. But it's clear Corypheus's life force can pass to any blighted creature, darkspawn, or Grey Warden. Approach the door to the temple. It can't be opened yet, though—you must complete a ritual.

Temple Ritual

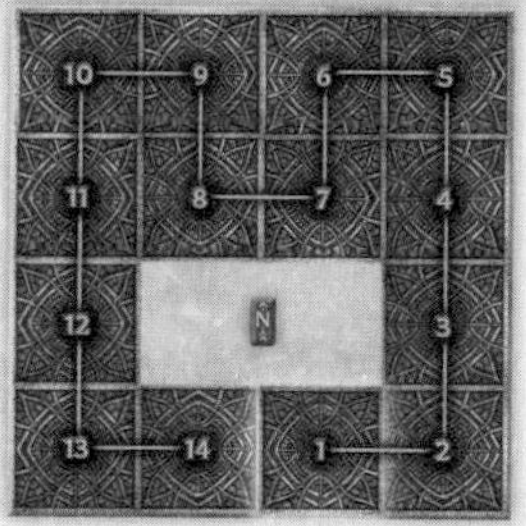

Approach the altar north of the temple's entrance—the large tiles illuminate as you walk across them. You must illuminate all of the tiles surrounding the altar. But you can't step on the same tile twice—yes, it's a puzzle. Reference the accompanying diagram to solve it. Once all tiles are lighted, the door to the Hall of Shrines is unlocked.

NOTE There are numerous ways to solve this ritual and the others in the temple. The provided diagrams are just one possible solution to these puzzles. Feel free to discover your own solutions.

Hall of Shrines

After passing through the door, prepare to engage more enemies on the other side. These are the minions of Calpernia or Samson, your nemesis. This group shouldn't be a match for your party. Before chasing after Calpernia or Samson, Morrigan suggests entering the temple by performing a set of rituals. She feels this may be the key to reaching the Well of Sorrows before Corypheus does. Back at the altar, Morrigan deciphered some elven writing revealing more about the Well of Sorrows—it promises great power, but at a terrible price. At this point you have the option of following your nemesis through the hole in the floor or performing three rituals to gain access to the temple. Solas and Dorian will approve if you do all of the rituals, but everyone else prefers you take a shortcut to the inner sanctum via the hole in the floor. Solving the rituals, however, will make a confrontation with the temple's guardians in the next section go more smoothly for you. Completing the rituals gives you access to the temple's inner sanctum.

NOTE If you don't want to complete the rituals, follow your nemesis down the hole to the north, skipping the inner sanctum entirely. Ignoring the rituals means bypassing an alliance with Abelas and his elven Sentinels, meaning you must fight them as well as Corypheus's army. You gain approval from Iron Bull if you skip the rituals; Solas disapproves.

Western Ritual

Start with this large ritual to the west. This puzzle is divided into a northern section and southern section, but both puzzles must be solved to complete the ritual. Start by working on the northern section first, completing it near the divider on the south side, at tile 28. Once the northern side is complete, jump onto the divider and proceed to the southern section of the puzzle. The second half of the puzzle is solved using a movement pattern similar to the first one—reference the diagram to avoid making a misstep. After completing this puzzle, return to the central courtyard (where you fought the enemies) and cross to the east side.

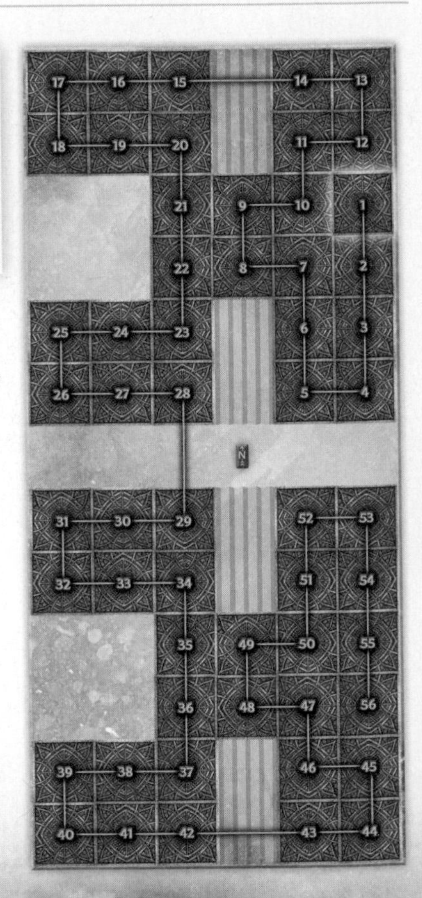

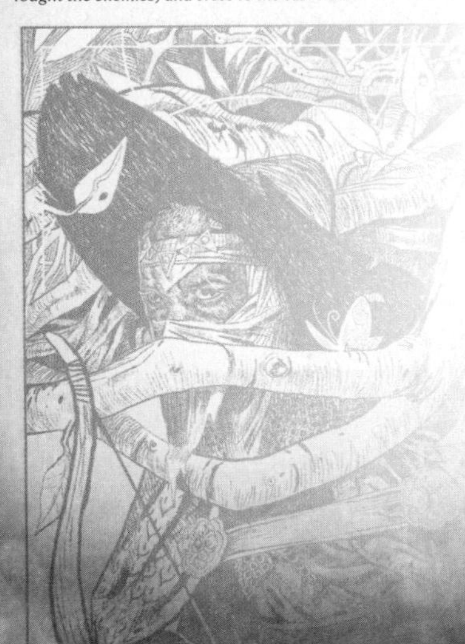

Eastern Ritual

Although smaller, this puzzle is a bit trickier. Sections of this puzzle must be lowered and raised using a switch in the middle. Start by looping around the north side, then cross to the neutral platform after stepping on tile 10. On the platform, interact with the switch—this lowers tiles to the west and raises tiles to the east, allowing you to proceed. Step onto tile 11, to the north, and complete the eastern half of the ritual, as seen in the diagram. When you reach tile 30, step back onto the central platform and interact with the switch again, raising the tiles to the west. From the platform, step onto tile 31, to the west, and complete the ritual. Only one more to go.

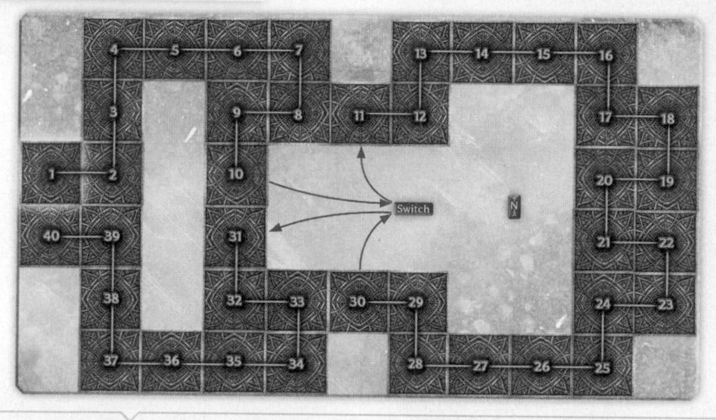

Northeastern Ritual

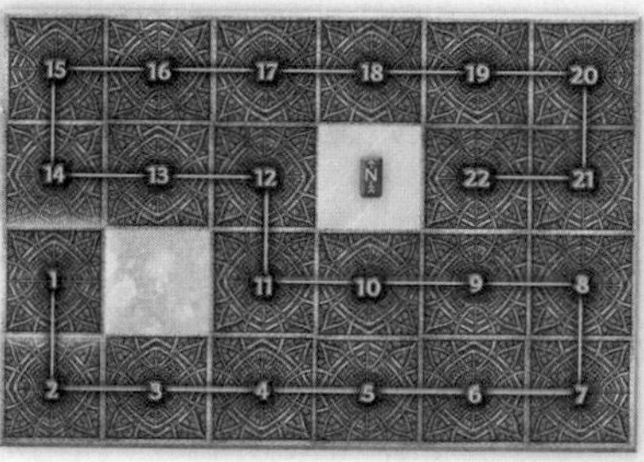

Don't let the small size of this ritual fool you—it can be tricky. As long as you follow the zigzag path shown on the diagram, you'll have no problem conquering this ritual. Like all the rituals, this puzzle can be solved in many ways. The three rituals can be completed in any order. Once all three are solved, the door to the inner sanctum unlocks. Time to go see what's inside.

Inner Sanctum

Your party is halted inside this chamber, surrounded by elven archers. But you don't come under attack—at least not yet. Abelas, leader of this elven contingent, is responsible for guarding the temple from outsiders. Abelas is curious about your party's intentions, but he's unwilling to give you access to the Well of Sorrows, an object he calls the Vir'abelasan. Question Abelas about the Well of Sorrows and any other topics that interest you, but no matter how diplomatic your approach, you can't convince Abelas to give you access to the well. If you did the rituals, Abelas at least agrees to help you drive Corypheus's forces from the temple. If you took the shortcut, these Sentinel elves will turn hostile and attack.

DECISION POINT

Abelas cannot be swayed to give you access to the Well of Sorrows, yet his offer to help you eliminate Corypheus's army is too good to pass up. Morrigan realizes the weight of this predicament but stresses the importance of reaching the well. You can get everything here, assuming you did the rituals earlier and choose the proper reply—agree to ally with Abelas and you'll eventually gain access to the well. If you refuse Abelas's offer, or if you took the shortcut earlier, you'll be forced to engage him and his elven Sentinels in combat through the rest of the temple, in addition to Corypheus's forces.

Approval: Abelas's Offer

Follower	Accept Alliance	Decline Alliance
Blackwall	—	⬇⬇
Cassandra	—	—
Cole	⬆⬆⬆	⬇⬇⬇
Dorian	⬆⬆⬆	⬇⬇⬇
The Iron Bull	⬆	⬇
Sera	⬇⬇	⬆⬆
Solas	⬆⬆⬆	⬇⬇⬇
Varric	—	—
Vivienne	—	—

Temple Path

Following your decision, Abelas exits, vowing to destroy the Well of Sorrows before it can be desecrated by outsiders. Morrigan responds by transforming herself into a bird and chasing after Abelas. If you chose to ally with Abelas, you are prompted to follow an elven guide through the temple—she will lead you to the Well of Sorrows. The guide knows many shortcuts through the maze-like temple, revealing hidden doorways and passages. Keep up with the guide, but don't miss the chance to search for loot along the way. At the end of the path, the guide even opens a secret loot chamber for you.

CAUTION If you didn't ally with Abelas, you must fight your way through the temple, eliminating both Sentinels and Corypheus's army along the way. The same secret passages accessed by the guide cannot be used by your party—you must find your own way through the temple. Pass through doorways and search for switches to find your way out.

Soon after the guide stops, you can hear fighting nearby. Open the door to the east and join the fight as several Sentinels engage a group of Corypheus's minions. If you allied with the Sentinels, this fight shouldn't be a problem. If you haven't, you'll be fighting them and Corypheus's forces in this area. Following the battle, exit through the doors to the south to reach the Well of Sorrows.

Well of Sorrows

Before you can reach the Well of Sorrows, you must first confront your nemesis. If you allied with the rebel mages, you'll face Samson. Calpernia is your nemesis if you sided with the templars.

Samson Finale

Upon exiting the temple, you discover Samson and his red templars have already reached the Well of Sorrows. Samson is eager to serve as a vessel, absorbing the wisdom offered by the well before turning it over to Corypheus. If you completed the Before the Dawn nemesis quest you have a chance in the conversation to make the next fight easier: When it appears, choose the option to use the rune Dagna prepared for you to break Samson's armor. Samson is horrified as his armor is "depowered" and attacks, but he is now a weakened target in combat.

If you didn't complete Before the Dawn, or if you ignore the choice to weaken Samson's armor, you must defeat a fully charged Samson.

If you didn't complete Before the Dawn, you must defeat Samson and his red templars in combat. During this battle, focus on eliminating the red templar horrors before going after Samson—consider casting Mark of the Rift while all of the enemies are clustered together to deal some heavy damage. When all other enemies have been defeated, focus on taking down Samson. Samson is equipped with heavy armor and can build guard. So utilize warrior abilities, like Shield Bash and Break Their Spirit (War Horn), which can help deplete Samson's guard. Carrying a two-handed sword, Samson can perform some devastating attacks, including 360-degree spins, knocking down all enemies in his path. Keep your distance during these attacks to prevent getting knocked down. For best results, taunt Samson with your warriors while your ranged party members pour on attacks from a safe distance. Little by little, Samson's guard and health will drop. Once he falls, Samson is taken into custody and can later be judged at Skyhold.

Calpernia Finale

Descend the steps to trigger a conversation with your nemesis, Calpernia. Loyal to Corypheus, Calpernia is committed to keeping the Inquisition away from the Well of Sorrows. As feared, Calpernia reveals that Corypheus is planning to use the well to enter the Fade. If you completed the Under Her Skin nemesis quest, you can convince Calpernia that she's being played—that Corypheus actually plans to bind her. When you hand over the scroll with Corypheus's binding ritual, Calpernia stands down, realizing you're telling the truth. To avoid a fight with Calpernia, convince her to return to Tevinter.

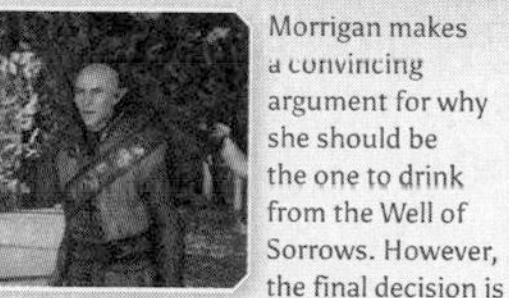

If you haven't completed Under Her Skin or simply want to eliminate Calpernia, be prepared to fight her bodyguards, consisting of Venatori zealots and a Venatori mage. As soon as combat begins, enter the tactical camera and use Mark of the Rift on Calpernia and the nearby Venatori zealots—this is the best way to dish out some heavy damage, while eliminating most of Calpernia's security detail. Calpernia is resistant to fire but vulnerable to cold-based attacks. She can also cast a barrier, significantly prolonging her lifespan. Freeze or chill Calpernia with spells, then focus on eliminating any surviving Venatori zealots and the Venatori mage. Once Calpernia's barrier is weakened, she won't last long. When the battle is over, Calpernia throws herself off a nearby cliff to avoid being killed by the Inquisition.

The Vir'abelasan

After you confront your nemesis, Abelas is seen racing to the Well of Sorrows. But Morrigan reaches the well first and blocks his path. Abelas reveals that the well contains the knowledge of all previous servants of Mythal. He fears this knowledge will be lost if an outsider touches the well. If you allied with him earlier, you can convince Abelas to relent and let you use the well, though he offers a warning before leaving—whoever drinks from the well will be bound forever to the will of Mythal. If you didn't ally with Abelas, he attempts to destroy the well. Morrigan kills him before he can bring the temple down on you.

After Abelas is gone, Morrigan makes note of the intact eluvian near the well. She feels the well is the key necessary to access the eluvian. If the key is taken, the eluvian will no longer function. Morrigan is clearly attracted to the power of the Well of Sorrows, and she makes no secret of her desire to drink from it. Others in your party (notably Cassandra) are resistant to the idea of Morrigan drinking from the well—can Morrigan be trusted with this unknown power? Yet Morrigan persists, stating she is the most qualified to drink from the well.

DECISION POINT

Morrigan makes a convincing argument for why she should be the one to drink from the Well of Sorrows. However, the final decision is up to you. As expected, your decision will have an impact on approval among your party members. Vivienne is outraged if you allow Morrigan to access the well's power. But Sera is equally disgusted if you drink from the well. However, if the Inquisitor drinks from the well, you'll have to tame an ancient dragon later, at the Altar of Mythal. If Morrigan drinks from the well, you won't have to tame the ancient dragon later.

Approval: Well of Sorrows

Follower	Inquisitor Drinks	Morrigan Drinks
Blackwall	↑↑ (if not in a romance with Blackwall)	↑↑ (if in a romance with Blackwall)
Cassandra	↑↑	↓↓
Cole	—	—
Dorian	↓ (or ↓↓ if in romance)	↑↑ (or ↑↑↑ if in romance)
The Iron Bull	↑↑	↓↓
Sera	↓↓↓	↑↑
Solas	↓↓	↑↑
Varric	—	—
Vivienne	↑↑↑	↓↓↓

Whoever wades into the Well of Sorrows experiences strange visions. As the power of the well surges through their body, they collapse, losing consciousness. The party members rush to the aid of their unconscious comrade. But there isn't much time to ask questions. Corypheus can be seen exiting the inner sanctum; he takes to the sky and rushes toward your party at the well. Morrigan urges everyone to race through the eluvian. While your party retreats, a mysterious figure arises from the water of the well, blocking Corypheus's pursuit. This buys the Inquisitor enough time to escape through the eluvian. Once you've passed through the mirror it shatters, preventing Corypheus from chasing your party back to Skyhold.

THE FINAL PIECE

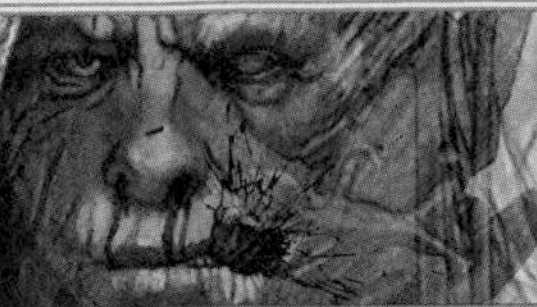

The Well of Sorrows whispered of a power in the Arbor Wilds strong enough to end Corypheus.

SKYHOLD

Your party emerges from Morrigan's eluvian back in Skyhold. Back in the war room, Cullen reports that Corypheus retreated from the Temple of Mythal when you escaped through the eluvian. The council is uncertain what Corypheus's next move will be. If the Inquisitor drank from the Well of Sorrows, vague whispers can be heard—Morrigan is annoyed by the Inquisitor's inability to interpret these vocalizations from the well. Nevertheless, the Inquisitor is able to glean some helpful information regarding Corypheus's weakness—his dragon. If the dragon is killed, Corypheus's ability to leap into other bodies will be temporarily disrupted, leaving him vulnerable. Guided by whispers from the well, the Inquisitor identifies a remote location on the war table—this is where the Inquisition must travel next. Upon exiting the war room, access the world map and travel to the Altar of Mythal. When selecting party members, consider bringing along a couple of mages with ice staves and Winter abilities.

NOTE If Morrigan drank from the Well of Sorrows and had a child from the dark ritual in your custom world state, look for Morrigan in Skyhold's garden. You'll find she's chased Kieran into an eluvian. Follow them through the eluvian to proceed.

ALTAR OF MYTHAL

The Altar of Mythal is in a large clearing within the Arbor Wilds. Lead your party to the objective marker to locate the altar on the south side of the clearing. Interact with the altar to summon Mythal. Soon after the summoning, a mysterious woman comes walking across the clearing—Morrigan clearly recognizes her as Flemeth. Morrigan is confused, yet the voices from the well say Flemeth speaks the truth. Flemeth warns that the altar's guardian will come soon. If you defeat it, the guardian will serve you in the battle against Corypheus. Flemeth then turns around and walks off into the clearing, leaving you to face the guardian of Mythal.

The dragon battle is necessary only if the Inquisitor drank from the Well of Sorrows. If Morrigan drank from the well, she becomes the dragon—see the table to clarify what happens based on your custom world state. Return to Skyhold following the conversation with Flemeth.

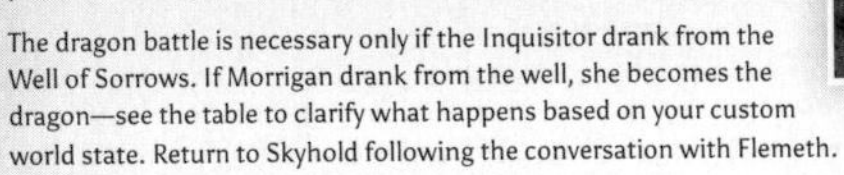

Altar Outcomes

Who Drank?	Dark Ritual Child?	Flemeth Encounter?	Tame Ancient Dragon?
Inquisitor	Yes	In the Fade	Yes, fight to tame ancient dragon
Inquisitor	No	At the altar	Yes, fight to tame ancient dragon
Morrigan	Yes	In the Fade	No, Morrigan becomes a dragon
Morrigan	No	At the altar	No, Morrigan becomes a dragon

> GUARDIAN OF MYTHAL

Immediately following the conversation with Flemeth, prepare yourself for a dragon battle. You must tame the ancient dragon by defeating it in battle in order to gain its allegiance. This fire-breathing dragon is vulnerable to cold-based attacks, so waste no time hitting it with Winter-based abilities like Winter's Grasp, Ice Mine, and Blizzard or Ice Storm. Target the dragon's front two legs first to hinder its mobility. Once the front two legs have been disabled, target the dragon's head.

Area-of-effect attacks are very effective against this dragon, including grenades like a jar of bees. Before initiating an AoE attack, wait until the dragon hops to a new location. This will ensure the dragon takes the brunt of your AoE attack. Also, try to position the AoE attack directly under the dragon's head and front legs. This way the attack damages all three targets. Wait until the dragon's guard is diminished, then unleash Mark of the Rift to dish out some heavy damage—this is a good way to finish the battle.

It takes time and persistence, but eventually the dragon's health will be depleted. However, it's not dead. Instead, the dragon yields to the Inquisitor's commands before flying away. The Inquisitor reports that the dragon will return when summoned. Now, exit the clearing to the west to return to Skyhold.

DOOM UPON ALL THE WORLD

It's time to prepare for the final confrontation with Corypheus.

SKYHOLD

Back in Skyhold, take a moment to visit with all your followers and tie up any loose ends before going after Corypheus. This is a good time to complete inner circle quests and romance plots you may have skipped; these quests are not available after the finale. But don't feel you need to do everything—you can still complete most quests and activities following the final confrontation with Corypheus. Once you're ready to face Corypheus, go to the war room and summon the council. Select the Doom Upon All the World operation on the war table. While the council plans their attack against Corypheus, a bright flash illuminates the war room, accompanied by a sharp pain in the Inquisitor's hand. Corypheus has reopened the Breach. Action must be taken now to stop Corypheus before the Breach expands and swallows the world.

CAUTION Inner circle quests, including follower personal plots and romances, are not available after the finale. Complete them (if you want) before selecting the Doom Upon All the World operation.

TEMPLE OF SACRED ASHES

Corypheus makes a stand beneath the Breach, at the ruins of the Temple of Sacred Ashes. Clutching his orb, Corypheus causes the ruins of the temple to rise into the sky, leaving you no route of escape. As Corypheus's dragon is about to attack your party, your dragon, tamed at the Altar of Mythal, serves as a life-saving distraction. The two dragons engage in aerial combat, leaving your party to confront Corypheus.

> CORYPHEUS BATTLE

Engage the tactical camera and plan your attack against Corypheus. A quick inspection of Corypheus reveals no immunities and no vulnerabilities, meaning any types of attacks are effective. For best results, chill him with cold-based attacks so your melee party members can move to close range and begin hacking away. Pummel Corypheus with your party's most powerful abilities and status effects until he retreats, teleporting to the balcony above.

As the dragons continue fighting overhead, pursue Corypheus onto the balcony, climbing the steps to the west—stay clear of his fiery AoE attack following his retreat. Corypheus can raise walls of red lyrium, potentially cutting off your party members from one another. When possible, step around these walls instead of hacking through them. Also, make sure your ranged party members maintain a clear line of sight on Corypheus—these walls can block their shots.

When Corypheus retreats again, climb a series of stairs to the east and resume the attack. When Corypheus's health drops to 50 percent, a cinematic shows the culmination of the dragon battle in the sky. Your dragon has fallen, and now you must defeat Corypheus's archdemon, a red lyrium dragon. Start by attacking the dragon's front legs, utilizing a mix of AoE and standard attacks. The dragon's fiery attacks are extremely dangerous, so be ready to move out of the way when the dragon rears up on its hind legs to begin this attack. Stand by with health potions and be prepared to revive fallen comrades. Better yet, cast Barrier just before the dragon attacks to prevent allies within the fiery area of effect from being injured.

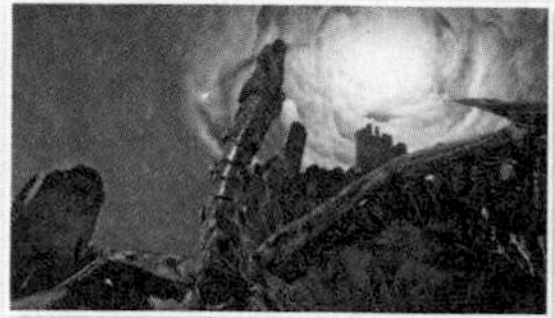

Once you've disabled two of the dragon's legs, it's far less mobile and more vulnerable to AoE attacks. Take this opportunity to focus your attacks on the dragon's head. In the concluding cinematic, the Inquisitor lands a fatal blow to the dragon's neck, causing it to bleed out. Now that the dragon is dead, Corypheus can't jump to other bodies. Defeat him now.

CAUTION Move your characters behind cover to avoid taking damage from Corypheus's AoE pattern attacks. At higher difficulties these attacks are extremely deadly.

Climb the stairs to the east and reengage Corypheus. Pour on the offense, hitting Corypheus with everything your party has. If available, use Mark of the Rift to bring an end to this battle. When Corypheus's health reaches zero, he attempts to expand the Breach, using his orb. But the Inquisitor reaches out with the Anchor, striking Corypheus with a green bolt of energy while snatching the orb from his hands.

As Corypheus crumples to the ground, bleeding from a lethal neck wound, the Inquisitor reaches skyward with the orb and closes the Breach. Finally, the Inquisitor uses the Anchor to vaporize Corypheus. With the Breach closed, massive stones from the ruins of the temple descend from the sky—one lands dangerously close, rendering the Inquisitor unconscious. When the Inquisitor regains consciousness, the dust has settled and Solas is studying the remains of Corypheus's orb—it has been destroyed. After regrouping with the others, the Inquisitor makes the decision to return to Skyhold.

SKYHOLD

To celebrate a hard-fought victory, Josephine has organized a party and feast in Skyhold's throne room. Here you have the chance to speak with all of your followers and thank them for their role. Afterward, retreat to your quarters by entering the door north of the throne. Your romantic interest greets you. Together, you discuss the future and enjoy a view of the picturesque Frostback Mountains.

EPILOGUE

In the concluding cinematic, Morrigan summarizes the events following the Inquisition's victory over Corypheus. The decisions you've made along the way, concerning the Orlesian court, the Grey Wardens, and the next Divine, determine the way this cinematic plays out. Are you satisfied with the results? If not, try again and make different decisions during your next attempt. The decisions you've made here are automatically synced with the *Dragon Age Keep*, determining the state of your world. These decisions will impact the world in future *Dragon Age* adventures.

NOTE After defeating Corypheus you're free to continue your adventure. Chances are there are plenty of locales you haven't fully explored. Take this opportunity to expand the Inquisition's influence into every corner of Orlais and Ferelden.

CLASSES AND ABILITIES

Dragon Age: Inquisition requires you to make some tough decisions. And perhaps the most critical of these decisions is choosing your character's class and abilities. Whether selecting a rogue, warrior, or mage, your class determines what types of weapons and armor your character can equip. To a greater extent, class also dictates which abilities your character can select when leveling up. Before making these decisions, reference this chapter to determine which class and abilities best fit your style of play.

ROGUE

Rogues rely on speed and agility rather than heavy armor, using skill and advantageous position on the battlefield to deal incredible damage. They may get up close and personal with daggers or strike from a distance with arrows.

- Unique Class Ability: Lock-picking

Dual-Wield Starting Abilities

Ability	Name	Description
	Stealth	You step into the shadows, all but invisible to your enemies. Attacking from stealth gives you a damage bonus and brings you back to the enemy's attention. Dealing damage to enemies reduces the ability's cooldown.
	Twin Fangs	You lash out with both daggers, striking deep, with bonus damage if you flank your foe.

Archer Starting Abilities

Ability	Name	Description
	Stealth	You step into the shadows, all but invisible to your enemies. Attacking from stealth gives you a damage bonus and brings you back to the enemy's attention. Dealing damage to enemies reduces the ability's cooldown.
	Long Shot	You fire a powerful single shot that delivers more damage the farther you are from the target.

DEVELOPER TIP

Utilize the tactical camera for setting up visually stunning combos. Lightning Bolt and Long Shot make spectacular explosions.

— Gavin Vankosky, QA Tester

Understanding Status Effects

Shocked: Reduces resistance to fire, cold, and electricity by 20 percent.

Chilled: Creature's movement speed is reduced by 25 percent.

Snared: Creature's movement speed is reduced by 25 percent.

Burning: Creature takes fire damage over time.

Poison: Creature takes nature damage over time.

Weakened: Creature's damage reduced by 15 percent.

Sundered: Creature's armor reduced by 20 percent.

Paralyzed/Stunned/Frozen: Creature is disabled.

Sleep: Creature sleeps in place. Any direct damage will break the effect.

Panic/Fear: Creature runs away in a panic. After 1.5 seconds any direct damage will break the effect.

Taunted: Creature is forced to target the caster for the duration. At the end of the forced taunt the caster is moved to the top of the threat table.

Rogue Starting Stats

Stats	Dual Wield	Archer
Attributes		
Strength	10	10
Dexterity	11	11
Magic	10	10
Cunning	10	10
Willpower	10	10
Constitution	10	10
Offensive		
Attack	0%	0%
Guard Damage Bonus	0%	0%
Armor Penetration	0%	0%
Barrier Damage Bonus	0%	0%
Critical Damage Bonus	53%	41%
Critical Chance	5%	5%
Main-Hand Damage	32	36
Off-Hand Damage	32	36
Bleed on Hit	0%	0%
Stagger on Hit	0%	0%
Heal on Kill	0%	0%
Flanking Damage Bonus	25%	36%
Defensive		
Magic Defense*	0%	0%
Melee Defense*	0%	0%
Ranged Defense*	6%	6%
Cold Resistance	0%	0%
Electrical Resistance	0%	0%
Fire Resistance	0%	0%
Guard	0	0
Armor Rating	43	43
Armor Rating: Front	43	43
Maximum Health	509	509
Bleed on Being Hit	0%	0%
Stagger on Being Hit	0%	0%
Other		
Maximum Focus	100	100
Focus Gain Bonus	0%	0%
Maximum Mana/ Stamina	100	100
Cooldown Modifier	0%	0%

* Base stats listed. Elves get a 25 percent bonus to ranged defense, dwarves get a 25 percent bonus to magic defense, and Qunari get a 25 percent bonus to melee defense.

Rogue Specializations

Specialization	Name	Details
	Artificer	Complete Way of the Artificer offered by Three-Eyes in Skyhold.
	Assassin	Complete Way of the Assassin offered by Heir in Skyhold.
	Tempest	Complete Way of the Tempest offered by Kihm in Skyhold.

> Tactical Considerations

Rogues are masters of stealth and subterfuge, outsmarting and outmaneuvering their opponents to gain a tactical advantage. As a result, this can be a tricky yet rewarding class to play, requiring a heightened sense of tactical awareness, constantly scanning the battlefield for new opportunities. Unlike warriors, rogues do not gain guard and must put an emphasis on evading incoming strikes. In addition to Stealth, rely on abilities like Evade (Subterfuge), Leaping Shot (Archery), and Flank Attack (Double Daggers) to get out of trouble. Have at least one of these abilities mapped and ready to activate whenever you see a large enemy winding up for a major attack.

Armed with daggers, dual-wield rogues are capable of inflicting enormous amounts of damage, particularly when flanking their foes—daggers are some of the highest damage-per-second (DPS) weapons available, and this rogue carries two of them. While these rogues excel in melee combat, they are not designed to go toe-to-toe with heavily armored enemies. Instead, use the Stealth ability to flank and then strike from the shadows with abilities like Twin Fangs. For best results, attack an enemy from behind while they're distracted by one of your party's warriors. If your rogue draws the attention of enemies, use Stealth again to slip back into the shadows before resuming your attack. By utilizing a stick-and-move approach, dual-wield rogues can extend their lifespan while still dishing out more than their fair share of damage.

Archers fill a very different role than their dual-wield counterparts, utilizing bows to strike their foes from long range. Initially, archers are equipped with the Stealth ability, allowing for threat-free deployment at any point on the battlefield. Stealth also comes in handy when it's time to flee—activate Stealth as melee enemies approach and relocate to a safer location before firing more arrows. By investing in the Archery discipline, archers can benefit from powerful abilities like Explosive Shot and Full Draw, turning their bow into a formidable instrument of death. The default Long Shot ability is particularly useful, dealing up to 600 percent bonus damage when engaging targets at 15 meters or more.

NOTE Either rogue can invest in both the Archery and Double Daggers abilities, but they cannot switch between daggers and bows mid-combat, and they cannot use active abilities from the Archery tree while using daggers. Stealth and Subterfuge work equally well with daggers and bows.

> Lock-Picking

Did you find a locked door? Chances are a rogue can open it. The rogue's lock-picking skill is indispensable when scouring dungeons and other hostile locations—always make sure you have a rogue in your party. It's hard to say what you'll find behind each locked door, but there's usually something of value waiting on the other side. After all, somebody locked that door for a reason. However, some doors even a rogue can't unlock. To open these doors you must acquire the Deft Hands, Fine Tools perk. Once this perk is acquired, no lock in Thedas can withstand your rogue's lock-picking prowess.

> ROGUE ABILITIES

Double Daggers

Description: Experts in this style are fast and deadly, their blades slicing through enemies' defenses—and throats—before they have time to react.

Dual-wield rogues are extremely formidable combatants, and these abilities only make them deadlier. But rogues should never stand toe-to-toe and trade blows—stick and move instead. Abilities like Flank Attack, Twin Fangs, and Sneak Attack reward damage bonuses for flanking enemies. The Double Daggers abilities are more effective when combined with those from the Subterfuge discipline, allowing your rogue to deal heavy damage while remaining stealthy and highly mobile, avoiding retaliatory strikes.

Flank Attack

You leap through shadows to attack your foes with deadly strikes that hit them from behind.

Number of Hits: 2

Damage per Hit: 200% weapon damage

Cooldown Time: 8 seconds

Cost: 35 stamina

Skirmisher

Before your target turns to face your blow, you move to stealth, impossible to find.

Ripping Fangs

If flanking, your Twin Fangs attack will keep your target's armor sundered from the blow.

Damage Bonus: 100%

Duration: 8 seconds

Twin Fangs

You lash out with both daggers, striking deep, with bonus damage if you flank your foe.

Number of Hits: 2

Damage per Hit: 200% weapon damage

Damage Bonus: 200%

Cooldown Time: 8 seconds

Cost: 50 stamina

Precision Detonator Ability: Use on incapacitated foes for a combo.

Bloodied Prey

Your strikes cut deeper into any foe whose health is lower than your own.

Damage Bonus: 10%

Cunning on Unlock: +3

Dance of Death

You regain stamina with every kill, the better to continue your assault.

Stamina Restored: 50

Dexterity on Unlock: +3

Unforgiving Chain

Your daggers blur, a dance of deadly pain. Each strike adds to your critical-hit chance. After a critical attack, your chain resets as you begin another dance.

Critical Hit Chance: 1%

Dexterity on Unlock: +3

Sneak Attack

Attacks upon a target's back or flank have double the chance to result in a critical hit.

Critical Hit Chance: 2X base critical hit chance

Cunning on Unlock: +3

Neverending Spin

The number of your deadly slashes grows when you connect with earlier attacks.

Additional Hits: 4

Thrill of Victory

Your strike bites deeper, and if it should kill your target, there's no cooldown on Deathblow.

Damage Bonus: 100%

Spinning Blades

You lash out with a set of slashing blows that bring you in and drive your target back.

Number of Hits: 5

Damage per Hit: 75% weapon damage

Cooldown Time: 16 seconds

Cost: 65 stamina

Parry

You quickly block a strike made by your foe, then counter as their own defenses fall.

Damage: 100% weapon damage

Cost: 10 stamina

Effortless Riposte

If you succeed in countering a blow, your parry costs no stamina at all.

Deathblow

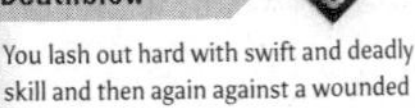

You lash out hard with swift and deadly skill and then again against a wounded foe.

Damage: 200% weapon damage

Damage Bonus: 3% increased damage per 1% missing HP on the target

Health Threshold: 50%

Cooldown Time: 8 seconds

Cost: 50 stamina

Precision Detonator Ability: Use on incapacitated foes for a combo.

Archery

Description: Experts in this style are masters of ranged combat. They can avoid enemies that attempt to close, put arrows or bolts through multiple foes, and even unleash explosive shots to devastating effect.

Any rogue carrying a bow should invest heavily in this discipline, which provides a good mix of offensive and defensive abilities. In an effort to keep your distance from melee attacks, utilize Leaping Shot and Strafing Shots to escape incoming strikes and remain mobile while firing. Explosive Shot comes in handy when targeting clusters of enemies crowded near choke points. But the pinnacle of this discipline is Full Draw. This sniper-like shot deals devastating damage, particularly to uninjured enemies—use this as your opening shot when starting a battle.

Death from Above

You do more damage when firing from elevation.

Maximum Bonus Damage: 25%

Maximum Height: 2 meters

Cunning on Unlock: +3

Archer's Lance

Long Shot now rips through every enemy along its path, doing bonus damage for each extra target it hits.

First Blood

You've learned to pick apart enemies that are still unwounded and unwary. You do more damage to enemies that are only lightly injured.

Damage Bonus: 15%

Health Threshold: 80%

Dexterity on Unlock: +3

Long Shot

You fire a powerful single shot that delivers more damage the farther you are from the target.

Damage: 200% weapon damage

Damage Bonus: 600% at 15 meters

Cooldown Time: 8 seconds

Cost: 50 stamina

Precision Detonator Ability: Use on incapacitated foes for a combo.

Leaping Shot

You dive out of trouble and fire a hail of arrows at the enemies that were trying to close with you.

Projectiles: 12

Damage per Hit: 50% weapon damage

Cooldown Time: 12 seconds

Cost: 35 stamina

Explosive Shot

You fire a powerful shot that explodes on impact, damaging enemies around your target.

Number of Hits: 2

Damage: 100% weapon damage

Impact Radius: 4 meters

Cooldown Time: 12 seconds

Cost: 35 stamina

Rolling Draw

If Leaping Shot hits, you can use the momentum of your leap to do a stronger draw as you come back to your feet. Your next attack, whenever you make it, will knock down its target.

Damage Bonus: 200%

Chain Reaction

Shrapnel from Explosive Shot fills the air and sets off deadly reactions that do more damage the more enemies there are nearby.

Damage Bonus per Target: 25%

Maximum Bonus Damage: 100%

Strafing Shots

You can move faster while firing without sacrificing accuracy.

Speed Bonus: 100%

Dexterity on Unlock: +3

Full Draw

It takes a moment to line up the perfect shot, but it pays off with a devastating hit that bites even deeper against enemies who aren't injured yet.

Damage: 800% weapon damage

Damage Bonus: 800% at full health

Cooldown Time: 24 seconds

Cost: 65 stamina

Stunning Shot

Enemies hit by Full Draw are briefly knocked unconscious by the power of your shot.

Sleep Duration: 20 seconds

Pincushion

If the first arrow doesn't kill them, the 10th might. Each consecutive hit with a bow attack does progressively more damage to the target.

Damage Bonus: 5%

Bonus Duration: 10 seconds

Dexterity on Unlock: +3

DEVELOPER TIP

When playing as an archer, pairing poison with an upgraded Long Shot applies poison to everyone it hits.

—Nathan Kozlowski, QA

Sabotage

Description: Experts in these talents specialize in poisons and traps. Their dirty tricks leave enemies sick and limping, easy pickings for a sharp blade or a barbed arrow.

The abilities in this discipline allow any rogue to become an absolute menace on the battlefield. The poison-based abilities are particularly deadly, slowly draining the health of all affected enemies. Archers utilizing the Poisoned Weapons ability can poison multiple targets within a matter of seconds, making any battle a little easier as enemies succumb to toxins. Caltrops are effective for staging ambushes—place them in choke points and lure enemies into the trap. Both Cheap Shot and Throwing Blades are useful for sundering enemy armor, making targets vulnerable for a short period of time.

Poisoned Weapons

You coat your weapons in a deadly toxin, making every attack poison enemies for a short time.

Duration: 10 seconds
Damage: 25% weapon damage per second
Damage Duration: 8 seconds
Cooldown Time: 24 seconds
Cost: 20 stamina

Infected Wounds

Your poison helps your blades and arrows bite deeper. You do more damage with your weapons while Poisoned Weapons is active.

Damage Bonus: 25%

Tread Lightly

The spikes from Caltrops cover a wider area and impede enemies even more.

Radius: 5 meters
Speed Reduction Bonus: 25%

Caltrops

You scatter spikes behind you, hurting and slowing down enemies who come after you. This ability is considered a trap for any abilities that enhance or affect traps.

Duration: 30 seconds
Radius: 3 meters
Damage: 10% weapon damage per second
Speed Reduction: 25%
Cooldown Time: 16 seconds
Cost: 35 stamina

Fighting Dirty

All of your sunder and poison effects last longer as you make more potent toxins and uglier wounds.

Duration Bonus: 25%
Dexterity on Unlock: +3

Looked Like It Hurt

The worst mistake your enemies can make is to let you see them flinch. Whenever you score a critical hit, you regenerate stamina.

Stamina Restored: 10
Cunning on Unlock: +3

Explosive Toxin

Your poisons curdle the blood of your targets. Enemies that die while poisoned explode in a shower of toxic mist.

Duration: 8 seconds
Radius: 3 meters
Damage: 50% weapon damage per second
Dexterity on Unlock: +3

Cheap Shot

Your critical hits tear through enemy armor, leaving it sundered for a short time.

Duration: 6 seconds
Cunning on Unlock: +3

Toxic Cloud

You unleash a cloud of toxic dust that damages all enemies that remain in the area.

Duration: 8 seconds
Radius: 3 meters
Damage: 15% weapon damage per second
Cooldown Time: 32 seconds
Cost: 50 stamina

Throwing Blades

You hurl a group of knives at all nearby targets, ripping through their armor and leaving it sundered.

Number of Hits: 4
Damage per Hit: 100% weapon damage
Duration: 8 seconds
Cooldown Time: 12 seconds
Cost: 50 stamina

It Beats Walking

You can use Hook and Tackle with no stamina cost or cooldown time.

Contact Poison

Toxic Cloud has a shorter cooldown time and now also poisons enemies in the area.

Cooldown Reduction: 5 seconds
Damage: 25% weapon damage per second
Duration: 8 seconds

Hook and Tackle

You hurl a light grappling hook at a target, then yank hard as you leap to pull yourself to it.

Cooldown Time: 12 seconds
Cost: 20 stamina

Precision Targeting

When facing fewer targets, you group your knives so that the more blades that hit a single target, the more damage they inflict.

Damage Bonus: 25% (Stacks)

Subterfuge

Description: Experts in these talents are masters of misdirection. Whether leaping to safety, disappearing into shadows, or tricking enemies into slashing at empty air, they are never where anyone expects them to be.

Whether carrying a bow or daggers, the abilities offered here play a huge role in keeping your rogue out of danger. Stealth is the cornerstone ability of this tree, giving your rogue the ability to vanish. This makes it easy to sneak up on enemies and attack without drawing their attention, often yielding bonus damage, particularly if you flank using an ability from the Dual Daggers tree. Seek out other abilities, like Ambush and Shadow Strike, that offer bonuses for using Stealth. Abilities like Evasion and Knockout Powder can be an absolute life saver, giving your rogue the chance to escape and regroup before returning to combat.

Stealth

You step into the shadows, all but invisible to your enemies. Attacking from stealth gives you a damage bonus and brings you back to the enemy's attention. Dealing damage to enemies reduces the ability's cooldown.

Damage Bonus: 50%

Duration: 30 seconds

Cooldown Time: 24 seconds

Cost: 20 stamina

Lost in the Shadows

You live in the darkness. Entering stealth is now instant and removes all debilitating effects on you. While in stealth, you can even pass through enemies without being detected.

Easy to Miss

Enemies are likely to overlook you in combat, much to their regret. This is especially true if you're flanking them.

Threat Reduction: 25%

Flanking Threat Reduction: 100%

Cunning on Unlock: +3

Deep Sleep

Enemies affected by Knockout Powder sleep longer and are slow to wake up after being damaged.

Duration Bonus: 10 seconds

Damaged Sleep Duration: 3 seconds

Knockout Powder

You throw a handful of dosed dust into an enemy's face, putting them to sleep for a short time.

Duration: 10 seconds

Area of Effect: 6 meters

Cooldown Time: 20 seconds

Cost: 35 stamina

Evasion

They can't hit what they can't see. Your deceptive fighting style gives you a chance to dodge enemy attacks, taking no damage.

Chance to Activate: 5%

Dexterity on Unlock: +3

Mercy Killing

When their hearts aren't in the fight, it's almost too easy. Your attacks on panicked or sleeping enemies are automatically critical hits.

Cunning on Unlock: +3

Hidden Step

Enemies will swear you're still there, attacking empty air and hurting nobody but themselves as you leap away.

Duration: 3 seconds

Damage: 300% weapon damage

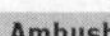

Quick Blade

Shadow Strike costs less stamina, and when you use it while flanking an opponent, you reduce all your activity cooldown times.

Cost Reduction: 10 stamina

Cooldown Reduction: 4 seconds

Evade

You leap away from incoming attack, putting yourself where you need to be to win this fight.

Cooldown Time: 2 seconds

Cost: 20 stamina

Ambush

While you're in Stealth and shortly after leaving it, your attacks ignore some of your target's armor.

Armor Penetration: 50%

Duration: 6 seconds

Dexterity on Unlock: +3

Shadow Strike

You take your enemies by surprise with an attack they never see coming. If you are in Stealth or have not taken damage recently, this attack hits even harder.

Damage: 400% weapon damage

Stealth Bonus Damage: 200%

Not Damaged Recently Threshold: 5 seconds

Cooldown Time: 16 seconds

Cost: 50 stamina

Precision Detonator Ability: Use on incapacitated foes for a combo.

Artificer (Specialization)

Description: These specialists control the battlefield with deadly traps. Neither they nor their explosive mines are ever where the enemy expects them to be.

The Artificer specialization emphasizes the use of traps and other devices to gain a tactical edge on the battlefield. Abilities like Spike Trap, Hail of Arrows, and Elemental Mines add to your rogue's offensive repertoire. If you're looking for a more defensive ability, consider Fallback Plan, allowing your rogue to retreat to a predetermined location and instantly heal in the process. Before settling on Artificer as your specialization, review all of the abilities and determine if they fit your rogue's preferred tactics.

Set Them Up

You've mastered the proper placement of spikes and levers. When you spring any kind of trap, your enemies feel it.

Damage Bonus: 25%

Willpower on Unlock: +3

Spike Trap

You set a trap that, when an enemy approaches, detonates and flings enemies into the air.

Damage: 300% weapons damage

Cooldown Time: 16 seconds

Cost: 35 stamina

Watch Your Step

You can remain in stealth while using Spike Trap, and enemies are flung even farther into the air.

Opportunity Knocks

When an ally critically hits, you take advantage of their success faster with reduced cooldown times.

Cooldown Reduction: 0.5 second

Cunning on Unlock: +3

Elemental Mines

You throw out an assortment of different traps in front of you, applying different elemental effects to enemies that come into range.

Damage: 50% weapon damage

Chill Duration: 8 seconds

Fire Damage: 50% weapon damage per second

Fire Damage Duration: 8 seconds

Shocked Duration: 8 seconds

Cooldown Time: 24 seconds

Cost: 50 stamina

Hail of Arrows

You fire so quickly that enemies will swear there are at least two of you putting arrows into their ranks. While this ability is active, any archery ability you use is duplicated. This ability consumes and is powered by focus.

Tier 1 Duration: 12 seconds

Tier 2 Duration: 25 seconds

Tier 3 Duration: 40 seconds

Throw Everything

It's now or never. You use every ounce of stamina you've got to litter the battlefield with traps. The more stamina you use, the more traps you throw.

Additional Traps: 1 for every 5 stamina

Fallback Plan

You place a thieves' lantern to mark a fallback location before heading into battle. When the fight gets ugly, you leap back to safety, as healthy as you were when you placed the marker.

Duration: 15 seconds

Cooldown Time: 32 seconds

Cost: 35 stamina

And Take Them Down

Your experience with finding and pointing out enemy vulnerabilities gives the entire party a better chance to land critical hits.

Critical Hit Chance Bonus: 5%

Dexterity on Unlock: +3

Tricks of the Trade

You help the team make the most of its abilities, increasing the damage and duration of all status effects anyone in the party applies.

Damage Bonus: 10%

Duration Bonus: 10%

Willpower on Unlock: +3

Bait and Switch

You can fight for a longer time before leaping back, and you pull your closest enemy back with you.

Duration Bonus: 5 seconds

Assassin (Specialization)

Description: Any rogue can kill a target, but assassins make death into an art form. They specialize in quick, deadly kills that let them slide back into shadows undetected, or indirect kills that eliminate targets while the assassin is safely away.

Any dual-wield rogue should strongly consider making Assassin their specialization. Abilities like Hidden Blades make your daggers even deadlier, allowing you to strike multiple times, dealing enormous damage. Abilities like I Was Never Here and Knife in the Shadows make the Stealth ability (from Subterfuge) even more effective. Acquire Mark of Death to boost your party's damage output when engaging single targets—ideal for boss fights. The Cloak of Shadows focus ability allows your rogue (and the entire party) to remain undetected for a short period of time, ideal for staging deadly ambushes or sneaking past enemies.

Hidden Blades

They'll swear you leapt from the shadows like a thrown blade and hit your target with a flurry of strikes from every angle... but it's obvious that you were nowhere near them at the time.

Number of Hits: 3

Damage per Hit: 300% weapon damage

Cooldown Time: 32 seconds

Cost: 65 stamina

Overkill

You use Hidden Blades faster and more easily, launching even more strikes on your victim.

Cooldown Reduction: 4 seconds

Additional Hits: 3

Throatcutter

A wounded enemy is the perfect target. Your attacks are even deadlier against targets that are close to death already.

Damage Bonus: 2% for each 10% missing health

Dexterity on Unlock: +3

Knockout Bomb

You hurl a grenade containing a powerful concoction that puts nearby enemies to sleep. Sleeping enemies awaken after taking damage.

Duration: 10 seconds

Cooldown Time: 20 seconds

Cost: 35 stamina

Comatose

Enemies affected by Knockout Bomb sleep more deeply, allowing your allies to hit them even harder with flanking damage.

I Was Never Here

You have learned to use the distraction of an enemy's death to slip silently into the shadows. Killing a target removes any cooldown on Stealth.

Dexterity on Unlock: +3

Cloak of Shadows

You go into stealth, and your allies follow your lead. The entire party remains undetected for the duration of the effect, even while attacking. This ability consumes and is powered by focus.

Tier 1 Duration: 3 seconds

Tier 2 Duration: 6 seconds

Tier 3 Duration: 9 seconds

Knife in the Shadows

You are a deadly threat to any enemy that can't see you coming. When you attack from stealth, you automatically critically hit.

Dexterity on Unlock: +3

Mark of Death

You mark your enemy, and every hit adds part of its power to the mark's damage. Trigger your mark when you are ready, and watch your foe fall from injuries that were never even noticed. You can manually trigger the mark early for bonus damage.

Stored Damage: 100%

Duration: 8 seconds

Cooldown Time: 32 seconds

Cost: 10 stamina

Mark of Doom

While it is active, Mark of Death leaves the target vulnerable to even more injury.

Armor Reduction: 20%

Gaps in the Armor

Your attacks slip past armor to find a target's hidden vulnerabilities.

Armor Penetration: 25%

Dexterity on Unlock: +3

Tempest (Specialization)

Description: These unpredictable experts specialize in using alchemical mixtures that wreathe them in frost or flame. Fast, chaotic, and possibly mad, they wade into the fight and dare enemies to face the storm.

Tempest emphasizes elixir-based abilities to give your rogue a tactical advantage during combat. Flask of Frost, Flask of Fire, and Flask of Lightning all provide unique benefits, but they can't be used simultaneously—you must wait for the effects of one elixir to expire before activating a new one. The Thousand Cuts focus ability allows your rogue to dash across the battlefield, slashing multiple foes before sinking daggers into the primary target's back, dealing heavy damage.

Flask of Frost

This flask coats you in an icy skin that increases your armor and freezes enemies that strike you in melee range. You can't use this ability while another elixir is active.

Damage Resistance: 85%
Duration: 5 seconds
Freeze Duration: 1 seconds
Cooldown Time: 32 seconds
Cost: 20 stamina

Bitter Chill

Activating Flask of Frost also taunts all nearby foes to attack you.

Radius: 5 meters

Unquenchable Flames

While Flask of Fire is active, all your abilities have no cooldown.

Flask of Fire

This flask coats you in flames that spur you to frenzied action. For a short time, your abilities cost no stamina, and enemies who attack you are knocked backward. You can't use this ability while another elixir is active.

Duration: 5 seconds
Cooldown Time: 32 seconds
Cost: 20 stamina

Flaskmaster

Your experience with elixirs has made you better equipped to handle potions and other consumables, letting you carry more of them at a time and giving you the chance not to use an elixir when you activate an elixir ability. This ability does not apply to healing potions.

Maximum Potions Bonus: 1
Chance to Activate: 25%
Dexterity on Unlock: +3

Fury of the Storm

When your stamina is exhausted, you fight even harder, lashing out with fury to win the fight.

Damage Bonus: 10%
Low Stamina Threshold: 50%
Constitution on Unlock: +3

Thousand Cuts

You choose a target, then dash to and fro—a shadow leaving blood with every leap. After you slice through other nearby foes, you land behind your target, striking deep. This ability consumes and is powered by focus.

Damage per Hit: 300% weapon damage
Tier 1 Number of Hits: 12
Tier 2 Number of Hits: 25
Tier 3 Number of Hits: 38

Ride the Storm

The effect of your elixir lasts longer if you activate one immediately after another expires.

Bonus Duration: 3 seconds
Dexterity on Unlock: +3

Flask of Lightning

This flask sends you into a heightened state of incredible speed. Everyone on the battlefield except you moves much more slowly for a short time. You can't use this ability while another elixir is active.

Duration: 5 seconds
Speed Reduction: 60%
Cooldown Time: 32 seconds
Cost: 20 stamina

Quicksilver

Your Flask of Lightning is more concentrated. Time almost seems to stand still around you.

Speed Reduction Bonus: 39%
Bonus Duration: 2 seconds

Killer's Alchemy

You can use more concentrated elixirs that give you an uncanny edge in battle. You do bonus damage with all attacks for a short time whenever you use an elixir or potion. The effect stacks.

Damage Bonus: 15%
Duration: 10 seconds
Constitution on Unlock: +3

WARRIOR

Warriors are frontline combatants, able to withstand incredible punishment in heavy armor. They are proficient in the use of two-handed weapons like mauls and greatswords but may combine a smaller weapon with a shield for added defense.

Unique Class Skill: Wall Bash

Two-Handed Starting Abilities

Ability	Name	Description
	Mighty Blow	You deliver a powerful attack that crumples foes, leaving them knocked down for a short time. You do more damage to targets that are already knocked down.
	War Cry	You taunt all nearby enemies with a shouted challenge, gaining extra guard for each enemy affected.

Weapon and Shield Starting Abilities

Ability	Name	Description
	Payback Strike	You recover from any disabled condition and lash out with a great blow against nearby enemies. If you've recently taken damage, you hit that much harder and stagger your foes.
	War Cry	You taunt all nearby enemies with a shouted challenge, gaining extra guard for each enemy affected.

Warrior Starting Stats

Stats	Two-Handed	Weapon and Shield
Attributes		
Strength	11	11
Dexterity	10	10
Magic	10	10
Cunning	10	10
Willpower	10	10
Constitution	10	10
Offensive		
Attack	0%	4%
Guard Damage Bonus	1%	1%
Armor Penetration	11%	0%
Barrier Damage Bonus	0%	0%
Critical Damage Bonus	40%	40%
Critical Chance	5%	5%
Main-Hand Damage	60	43
Off-Hand Damage	60	5
Bleed on Hit	0%	0%
Stagger on Hit	0%	0%
Heal on Kill	0%	0%
Flanking Damage Bonus	25%	25%

Stats	Two-Handed	Weapon and Shield
Defensive		
Magic Defense*	0%	0%
Melee Defense*	6%	9%
Ranged Defense*	0%	0%
Cold Resistance	0%	0%
Electrical Resistance	0%	0%
Fire Resistance	0%	0%
Guard	59	40
Armor Rating	46	44
Armor Rating: Front	46	49
Maximum Health	562	562
Bleed on Being Hit	0%	0%
Stagger on Being Hit	0%	0%
Other		
Maximum Focus	100	100
Focus Gain Bonus	0%	0%
Maximum Mana/Stamina	100	100
Cooldown Modifier	0%	0%

* Base stats listed. Elves get a 25 percent bonus to ranged defense, dwarves get a 25 percent bonus to magic defense, and Qunari get a 25 percent bonus to melee defense.

Warrior Specializations

Specialization	Name	Details
	Champion	Complete Way of the Champion offered by Lord Chancellor de Lion in Skyhold.
	Reaver	Complete Way of the Reaver offered by Breaker Thram in Skyhold.
	Templar	Complete Way of the Templar offered by Ser in Skyhold.

> TACTICAL CONSIDERATIONS

Combining taunts, special moves, blocks, counters, and guard-generating abilities, warriors are far more than just tanks. Their presence is essential to your party's survival. Warriors are responsible for doing the heavy lifting, absorbing large amounts of damage while drawing the attention of hostile forces with taunts. Many abilities allow a warrior to build guard. Think of this as a secondary health bar, represented by small armor icons covering the warrior's health bar—a warrior's guard must be completely eliminated before they take damage to their health. By equipping heavy armor and deploying guard-building abilities, warriors can withstand extreme punishment while lashing out at the enemy with their own devastating arsenal of weapons.

When it comes to offense, few classes can match the raw damage output of the two-handed warrior. Capable of equipping massive two-handed weapons, this warrior swings the weapon in wide arcs, striking all enemies nearby. As a result, the two-handed warrior thrives in the heat of battle, surrounded by hostile forces. But close proximity to multiple threats can wear down this warrior fast. As a result, deploy guard-building abilities like War Cry and Charging Bull to reinforce the two-handed warrior's health. Seek out more defensive-oriented abilities and the heaviest armor you can find to further extend your two-handed warrior's lifespan.

Weapon-and-shield warriors take a more balanced approach to combat, utilizing a shield to absorb (and even turn away) most attacks. Their one-handed weapons are significantly weaker than those carried by their two-handed counterparts, but their ability to withstand greater punishment makes them better suited for tanking enemies. Taunt abilities like War Cry and Challenge come in handy for luring enemies while increasing the warrior's guard. Consider selecting the Shield Wall ability early on to enhance your warrior's guard. Likewise, constantly seek out better weapons and armor to maintain an edge in each engagement.

NOTE You can play as a warrior who has abilities in both Weapon and Shield and Two-Handed Weapon, but most players will choose one to specialize in. Battlemaster and Vanguard work equally well with a two-handed weapon or a weapon and shield.

DEVELOPER TIP

As a warrior I like to spec into Charging Bull as quickly as I can. Not only does it help to move around faster but it also can bash doors down as you run into them.

— Leo Potvin, QA Tester, Testing and QA II

> WALL BASH

Sometimes warriors don't need a door—they can make their own by thrusting their boot through a weak wall. Like the rogue's lock-picking skill, this skill allows warriors to gain access to areas that are otherwise off-limits. These secret chambers are often filled with loot and other items beneficial to your party. Look for the bash icon to determine the location of these weak walls—conducting searches also highlights these walls. Using a warrior, interact with these weak walls to knock them down.

> WARRIOR ABILITIES

Weapon and Shield

Description: Experts in this style are still on their feet after punishment that would kill their allies. They use their shield to protect themselves and stagger their enemies.

Any warrior carrying a shield into battle should invest heavily in this discipline to acquire a good mix of offensive and defensive abilities. Rookie warriors can significantly expand their lifespan with Shield Wall, allowing them to block attacks and build guard. While the offensive abilities are beneficial, focus on abilities that improve your warrior's defense, like Bear Mauls the Wolves, Turn the Bolt, and Turn the Blade—these abilities are ideal for tanking, making your warrior a damage sponge.

Shield Wall

You stand firm and block incoming attacks at the cost of stamina. Each block adds to your guard. You move much more slowly while sustaining this ability.

Chevalier's Step

When you use Shield Wall, your movement is not slowed as much. You can also protect nearby allies by giving them improved armor.

Range: 4 meters

Armor Bonus: 30%

Sweet Revenge

You do more damage with Payback Strike, and if you've recently taken damage, you also stun taunted enemies.

Damage Bonus: 200%

Stun Duration: 2 seconds

Payback Strike

You recover from any disabled condition and lash out with a great blow against nearby enemies. If you've recently taken damage, you hit that much harder and stagger your foes.

Damage: 200% weapon damage

Recently Damaged Threshold: 5 seconds

Damage Bonus: 200%

Cooldown Time: 8 seconds

Cost: 35 stamina

Bear Mauls the Wolves

Using techniques perfected by Orlesian chevaliers, you can't be flanked by enemies, and you're less likely to be staggered when hit from the front.

Constitution on Unlock: +3

Warrior's Resolve

You fight all the harder when you're hurting, gaining stamina when you lose health.

Stamina Restored: 10% for every 10% health lost

Constitution on Unlock: +3

Turn the Bolt

Your expertise with the shield protects you against ranged attacks from the front.

Damage Reduction: 50%

Constitution on Unlock: +3

Great Lunge

The farther you lunge before striking your target, the more damage you do to them.

Damage Bonus: 75% at 5 meters

Damage Bonus: 250% at 10 meters

Shield Bash

Many foes think a shield is just for defense. You correct that mistake with a brutal slam that does bonus damage to an enemy's guard.

Damage: 300% weapon damage

Bonus Damage vs. Guard: 800%

Cooldown Time: 8 seconds

Cost: 35 stamina

Ring the Bell

You now lunge forward with Shield Bash, and you do even greater damage to an enemy's guard.

Bonus Damage vs. Guard: 400%

Turn the Blade

Any blow you can see, you can turn aside. All damage coming from the front is reduced.

Damage Resistance: 20%

Constitution on Unlock: +3

Lunge and Slash

You lunge forward, then spin with a slashing strike if your first blow connects. You can use this attack to close with opponents.

Damage: 175% weapon damage

Cooldown Time: 8 seconds

Cost: 35 stamina

Impact Detonator Ability: Use on incapacitated foes for a combo.

Two-Handed Weapon

Description: Experts in this style crush their enemies with massive blows that can break any guard, shatter any armor, and destroy any opponent.

Two-handed warriors seeking greater offensive prowess should consider investing in this style. Take advantage of devastating area-of-effect attacks like Whirlwind and Earthshaking Strike to make your mark on the battlefield. Or knock your foes off their feet with Mighty Blow. But don't overlook Block and Slash and Flawless Defense. These abilities allow you to minimize incoming damage and build guard—something any two-handed warrior will need to stay alive.

Block and Slash

You stand ready to deflect the next incoming attack and deliver a punishing counter to your attacker.

Damage: 150% weapon damage

Cost: 10 stamina (+5 stamina per second)

Flawless Defense

Countering an enemy's attack now does bonus damage and adds to your guard.

Damage Bonus: 50%

Guard Amount: 15%

Easy Target

Might Blow costs less stamina and deals increased damage against targets that have been knocked down.

Cost Reduction: 15 stamina

Damage Bonus: 300%

Mighty Blow

You deliver a powerful attack that crumples foes, leaving them knocked down for a short time.

Damage: 200% weapon damage

Damage Bonus: 200%

Cooldown Time: 16 seconds

Cost: 50 stamina

Impact Detonator Ability: Use on incapacitated foes for a combo.

Flow of Battle

Every critical hit reduces the cooldown times on your abilities, giving you the edge to finish off your enemy.

Cooldown Reduction: 1 second

Strength on Unlock: +3

Shield Breaker

Your critical hits crack armor and rend shields, sundering your enemy's armor for a short time.

Armor Reduction: 20%

Duration: 6 seconds

Strength on Unlock: +3

Lightning Jab

Pommel Strike hits harder and faster.

Cooldown Reduction: 4 seconds

Stun Duration Bonus: 1 second

Rising Winds

Whirlwind becomes more effective the longer you sustain it.

Damage Bonus per Rotation: 15%

Pommel Strike

You lash out with a fast strike that briefly stuns your target.

Damage: 300% weapon damage

Stun Duration: 3 seconds

Cooldown time: 20 seconds

Cost: 35 stamina

Whirlwind

You spin with your weapon outstretched, cutting through any enemies in your path.

Damage per Hit: 70% weapon damage

Cooldown Time: 24 seconds

Cost: 10 stamina

Impact Detonator Ability: Use on incapacitated foes for a combo.

Guard-Smasher

You've learned how to batter through your enemy's defenses, doing more damage to their guard with every hit.

Bonus Damage vs. Guard: 100%

Strength on Unlock: +3

Earthshaking Strike

Your great blow tears open the ground with a shockwave that batters enemies caught in its path.

Number of Hits: 2

Damage per Hit: 150% weapon damage

Area of Effect: 12 meters

Cooldown Time: 20 seconds

Cost: 50 stamina

Shattered Ground

Flames erupt from the fissure left by Earthshaking Strike, damaging enemies that cross it.

Duration: 8 seconds

Burning: 20% weapon damage per second

Burning Duration: 8 seconds

Clear a Path

Hitting multiple targets with a single swing of your weapon restores your stamina for each extra target.

Stamina Restored: 10%

Strength on Unlock: +3

Battlemaster

Description: These cunning warriors control the battlefield and everyone on it. They bolster their allies, hamper their enemies, and take advantage of any sign of weaknesses.

Any warrior can benefit from the abilities in this style, starting off with Grappling Chain—this is great for yanking pesky archers and mages into melee range. If you're looking to gain a serious advantage for your party, invest in the horn-based abilities at the bottom of the tree. Use Horn of Valor to bolster your party members or War Horn to strike fear into the hearts of your enemies. Also, many abilities in this discipline provide a permanent boost to your warrior's Strength.

Grappling Chain

With a hooked chain and a lot of muscle, you drag your target into arm's reach.

Damage: 100% weapon damage
Cooldown Time: 12 seconds
Cost: 20 stamina

Give Them the Boot

After Grappling Chain drags an opponent to you, you stun them with a hard kick.

Damage: 200% weapon damage
Stun Duration: 3 seconds

Hamstring

When you attack a target from behind, you leave them slowed.

Speed Reduction: 50%
Duration: 3 seconds
Strength on Unlock: +3

Combat Roll

You dive and roll to where the battle needs you to be, whether it's escaping from a group or moving to flank an opponent.

Cooldown Time: 2 seconds
Cost: 20 stamina

Crippling Blows

You know how to take the fight out of foes. Your critical hits leave enemies weakened. The effect stacks.

Damage Reduction: 15%
Duration: 10 seconds
Strength on Unlock: +3

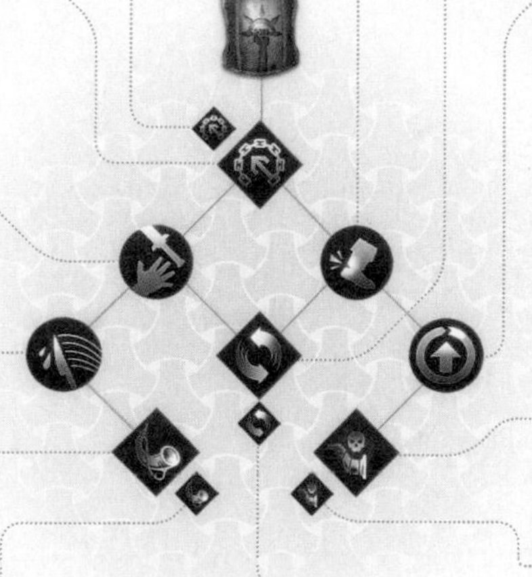

Deep Reserves

You get your breath back faster than most. When your stamina is very low, it regenerates more quickly.

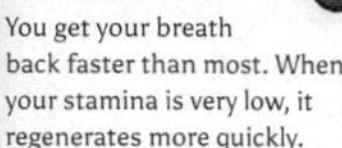

Low Stamina Threshold: 50%
Stamina Generation Rate Bonus: 50%
Strength on Unlock: +3

Coup de Grace

You deal more damage against enemies that are stunned or knocked down. Better them than you.

Damage Bonus: 30%
Strength on Unlock: +3

War Horn

Your war horn's blast puts fear into the hearts of your foes, leaving them panicked.

Area of Effect: 8 meters
Fear Duration: 6 seconds
Cooldown Time: 24 seconds
Cost: 35 stamina

Horn of Valor

Your war horn's blast rings across the battlefield, giving allies the strength to fight harder.

Damage Bonus: 15%
Armor Bonus: 15%
Duration: 10 seconds
Cooldown Time: 18 seconds
Cost: 35 stamina

Break Their Spirit

War Horn now shatters your enemy's guard, and panicked enemies are too shaken to defend themselves, leaving their armor sundered.

Armor Reduction: 20%
Bonus Damage vs. Guard: 1,200%

That's the Spirit

Your horn's blast calls your allies to even greater glory.

Damage Bonus: 35%

Roll with It

You can now use Combat Roll to recover from most disabling conditions.

Vanguard

Description: These stalwart warriors protect their allies by making themselves the biggest target on the battlefield. When enemies take the bait, vanguards pick them apart with brutal precision.

Warriors eager to draw attention away from their more vulnerable party members can find plenty of beneficial abilities within this discipline. Use War Cry and Challenge to lure enemies toward you, making them ignore your other party members—these abilities also build guard. Once you've acquired an enemy's attention, look for opportunities to increase your guard even more with abilities like Charging Bull, Trust the Steel, and Unbowed.

War Cry

You taunt all nearby enemies with a shouted challenge, gaining extra guard for each enemy affected.

Duration: 4 seconds
Guard per Enemy: 20%
Cooldown Time: 24 seconds
Cost: 35 stamina

Call to Arms

You draw strength from your War Cry, improving your armor for the coming fight.

Armor Bonus: 200%
Duration: 10 seconds

Throw the Gauntlet

Successfully hitting a target with Challenge gets your blood pumping, temporarily increasing your stamina regeneration.

Bonus Regeneration: 15 stamina per second

Challenge

Your powerful shout carries across the battlefield, taunting a targeted enemy and improving your guard.

Duration: 8 seconds
Guard Amount: 10%
Cooldown Time: 16 seconds
Cost: 20 stamina

Untouchable Defense

They can't kill what they can't hit. You get a bonus to your maximum guard.

Maximum Guard Bonus: 25%
Constitution on Unlock: +3

Charging Bull

You slam into enemies, increasing your guard and knocking them down as you break through their lines.

Damage: 150% weapon damage
Guard per Enemy: 10%
Cooldown Time: 8 seconds
Cost: 5 stamina per second

It'll Cost You

Any foe that attacks you in melee is going to bleed for it, taking a portion of the damage they inflict.

Damage Returned: 15%
Strength on Unlock: +3

Trust the Steel

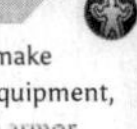

You know how to make the most of your equipment, gaining a bonus to armor when you have active guard.

Armor Bonus: 20%
Constitution on Unlock: +3

Still Standing

Unbowed further improves your guard for each nearby enemy, giving you the strength to stay on your feet.

Guard Generation Bonus: 100%

Not Today

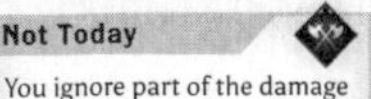

You ignore part of the damage transferred from party members.

Damage Resistance: 50%

Unbowed

You focus on your defensive training, gaining guard for each nearby enemy.

Guard per Enemy: 10%
Cooldown Time: 32 seconds

Gore and Trample

After you finish your charge, your next ability costs no stamina

Duration: 6 seconds

Cutting Words

Your party does more damage to taunted targets as you rattle your enemies' nerves and goad them into mistakes that leave them open.

Damage Bonus: 20%
Strength on Unlock: +3

Bodyguard

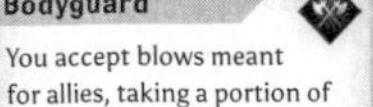

You accept blows meant for allies, taking a portion of the damage.

Damage Transfer: 50%
Duration: 15 seconds
Cooldown Time: 24 seconds
Cost: 35 stamina

Champion (Specialization)

Description: These powerful defenders protect their allies from harm, standing strong against devastating blows with expert training and fierce determination. Enemies can't kill them—and usually can't survive them.

If you're playing as a weapon-and-shield warrior, the Champion specialization is definitely worth considering. The abilities in this emphasize defense and guard, ideal for tanking. Line in the Sand is a good example—use this ability to dominate narrow passages such as doorways and staircases, preventing enemies from passing. Abilities like Counterstrike and Walking Fortress come in handy during those desperate moments when your warrior needs a temporary defensive boost to withstand incoming attacks. Or if you've built plenty of guard, and feel confident, consider activating To the Death, boosting the damage output of both you and your foe. The passive abilities in this tree are all beneficial too, increasing your warrior's durability.

Line in the Sand

You call upon the legacy of the greatest champions in history, defying enemies as you hold your position. This stops enemies from moving past you and enables you to block choke points.

Size: 6 meters
Duration: 12 seconds
Cooldown Time: 20 seconds
Cost: 35 stamina

And No Further

Your protected area increases, making it even harder for enemies to pass by.

Size Bonus: 3 meters

Resilience

You don't flinch, don't blink, and don't back down. Enemies that hit you with melee attacks are staggered by recoil.

Stun Chance: 5%
Stun Duration: 2 seconds
Constitution on Unlock: +3

Counterstrike

You push yourself to the limit, gaining full guard and taunting all nearby enemies. While the ability is active, you automatically counter all melee attacks. This ability consumes and is powered by focus.

Tier 1 Duration: 6 seconds
Tier 2 Duration: 12 seconds
Tier 3 Duration: 20 seconds

Bulwark

You stand all the stronger to finish the fight, gaining a bonus to your maximum guard.

Maximum Guard Bonus: 25%
Constitution on Unlock: +3

Unyielding

An attack that would bring you down instead leaves you with a small amount of health, and you are immune to all damage for a short time.

Invulnerability Duration: 5 seconds
Health Threshold: 5%
Cooldown Time: 60 seconds
Constitution on Unlock: +3

Adamant

You've trained hard, and you know how to make the most of whatever armor you're wearing.

Armor Bonus: 20%
Constitution on Unlock: +3

Walking Fortress

You may not be able to hold them off forever, but right now, nothing can touch you. You have complete immunity to damage for a short time.

Duration: 8 seconds
Cooldown Time: 32 seconds

To the Death

You taunt an enemy into a frenzy. Their damage output increases over time, but so does the amount of damage they take. The effect ends if you get out of range of the enemy.

Range: 15 meters
Enemy Damage Output: 5% increase per second
Enemy Damage Taken: 5% increase per second
Cooldown Time: 32 seconds
Cost: 35 stamina

En Garde

While To the Death is active, your guard improves as your target takes damage and you correct weaknesses of your own.

Guard Amount: 25%

Siege-Breaker

Every attack that strikes you reduces your cooldown time and increases your guard.

Cooldown Reduction: 1 second
Guard Amount: 10%

Reaver (Specialization)

Description: As the battle gets bloodier, these vicious and deadly warriors get even more brutal. Hurting them just makes them mad, a mistake most enemies don't live to repeat.

With the Reaver specialization, your warrior turns the chaos (and pain) of battle to their advantage with a series of powerful (and potentially dangerous) offensive-oriented abilities. This is a high-risk/high-reward discipline, since most of the abilities benefit the warrior when their health is low. When possible, activate Ring of Pain before triggering Devour or Dragon-Rage for some truly devastating bonuses. Rampage, a focus ability, sends your warrior into a brief frenzy, boosting attack speed and damage while stealing health from enemies. The passive abilities only add to your warrior's prowess on the battlefield, making Reaver the definitive offensive specialization for warriors.

Ring of Pain

You mark part of the battlefield as yours. Enemies inside the ring take spirit damage while your own attacks inside the ring hit harder. The more you are hurt, the stronger both effects are. Can be toggled on and off.

- **Area of Effect:** 15 meters
- **Damage:** 15% weapon damage per second
- **Damage Bonus:** 1% for each 1% missing health
- **Cost:** 10 stamina

Torrent of Pain

While Ring of Pain is active, Devour costs less stamina and has a shorter cooldown time, and Dragon-Rage costs less of your own health.

- **Cooldown Reduction:** 4 seconds
- **Cost Reduction:** 20%

Fervor

When an enemy dies near you, the thrill of death spurs you to hit that much harder.

- **Damage Bonus:** 30%
- **Duration:** 5 seconds
- **Range:** 10 meters
- **Cunning on Unlock:** +3

Rampage

You're an unstoppable fury of physical force while this ability is active. Your attacks are harder and faster, and you gain health with each strike. This ability consumes and is powered by focus.

- **Duration:** 10 seconds
- **Tier 1:** 10% attack speed, life steal, and damage
- **Tier 2:** 20% attack speed, life steal, and damage
- **Tier 3:** 30% attack speed, life steal, and damage

Blood Frenzy

They thought you'd get weaker once they'd wounded you. They were very wrong.

- **Damage Bonus:** 5% for each 10% missing health
- **Strength on Unlock:** +3

Scenting Blood

Being near a badly wounded enemy spurs you into a frenzy, driving you to move faster and giving you a better chance of striking deadly blows.

- **Range:** 10 meters
- **Health Threshold:** 35%
- **Speed Bonus:** 50%
- **Critical Hit Chance Bonus:** 10%
- **Constitution on Unlock:** +3

Terrifying Fury

Your critical strikes have a chance to cause a gory mess and send nearby enemies fleeing in panic.

- **Fear Chance:** 25%
- **Area of Effect:** 10 meters
- **Fear Duration:** 6 seconds
- **Cunning on Unlock:** +3

Ravage

For some, Dragon-Rage is a dangerous ability. For you, it's the only way to fight. You now hit harder and reduce the cooldown time for Devour with every attack.

- **Damage Bonus:** 50%
- **Cooldown Reduction:** 2 seconds

Devour

Blood is life. You rip into your enemy, doing damage based on how badly you're wounded and healing yourself. Ring of Pain significantly increases the effect.

- **Damage:** 100% weapon damage
- **Health Restored:** 0.2% for every 1% health lost
- **Damage Bonus:** 2% for each 1% missing health
- **Cooldown Time:** 12 seconds
- **Cost:** 65 stamina
- **Ring of Pain Bonus Health Restored:** 0.4% for every 1% health lost

Consume

After you attack with Devour, your next use of Dragon-Rage has a better chance of ripping deeply into your target for a critical strike.

- **Critical Hit Chance Bonus:** 25%

Dragon-Rage

You launch an attack fueled by your fury, ripping into foes for damage that increases as your own wounds deepen. Ring of Pain significantly increases the effect. You take damage with each swing.

- **Damage:** 150% weapon damage
- **Damage Bonus:** 1% for each 1% missing health
- **Cost:** 2% health
- **Ring of Pain Damage Bonus:** 50%

Templar (Specialization)

Description: These unrelenting warriors specialize in fighting mages and demons. No enemy's magic can withstand them, and they inspire and protect their allies with their righteous power.

Warriors who specializes in the Templar discipline empower not only themselves, but those around them, making every battle a little easier. Whether dispelling hostile magic with Spell Purge or inspiring your comrades with Blessed Blades or Rally, this discipline puts an emphasis on supporting the party—even most of the passive abilities improve the entire party's performance. The pinnacle of this tree is the Wrath of Heaven AoE ability, stunning enemies and damaging demons—this is very effective when attempting to seal Fade rifts.

Spell Purge

Through faith and will, you dispel all hostile magic from the area around you.

Area of Effect: 5 meters
Cooldown Time: 24 seconds
Cost: 35 stamina
Eldritch Detonator Ability: Use on incapacitated foes for a combo.

Spell Shatter

Spell Purge now deals massive area damage when dispelling barriers and other beneficial effects on enemies.

Damage: 600% weapon damage

Lights in the Shadow

Attacking enemies while you're affected by Blessed Blades reduces the cooldown times of Spell Purge and Wrath of Heaven.

Cooldown Reduction: 0.5 seconds

Blessed Blades

You rally all of your nearby allies to fight with greater strength, especially when facing demons.

Damage Bonus: 15%
Duration: 24 seconds
Cooldown Time: 24 seconds
Cost: 10 stamina

Champions of the Just

Your righteous fervor inspires the entire party to fight harder against demons.

Damage Bonus: 10%
Strength on Unlock: +3

Maker's Will

Your party's attacks have a chance to weaken their targets.

Weaken Chance: 5%
Weakened Duration: 6 seconds
Willpower on Unlock: +3

Rally

You inspire your allies to fight harder. Your party's guard, stamina, and mana build over time, and all party members gain damage resistance against incoming attacks. This ability consumes and is powered by focus.

Duration: 15 seconds
Tier 1: 10% guard generation and stamina/ mana regeneration per second, 10% damage resistance
Tier 2: 20% guard generation and stamina/ mana regeneration per second, 20% damage resistance
Tier 3: 30% guard generation and stamina/ mana regeneration per second, 30% damage resistance

There Is No Darkness

Your faith is your protection against the elements, and not for you alone. The entire party gains increased resistance to fire, ice, electric, and spirit damage.

Damage Resistance: 10%
Willpower on Unlock: +3

Wrath of Heaven

You summon a blinding pillar of light that stuns nearby enemies and damages demons.

Damage: 400% weapon damage
Area of Effect: 4 meters
Stun Duration: 4 seconds
Cooldown Time: 24 seconds
Cost: 65 stamina

The Last Sacrifice

Even should you fall, you give your allies strength to fight harder in your name.

Health Amount: 100%
Damage Bonus: 50%
Duration: 10 seconds
Cooldown Time: 60 seconds
Constitution Unlock: +3

Embrace the Light

Wrath of Heaven does even more damage to demons and leaves enemies stunned longer.

Damage Bonus: 300%
Stun Duration Bonus: 2 seconds

 MAGE

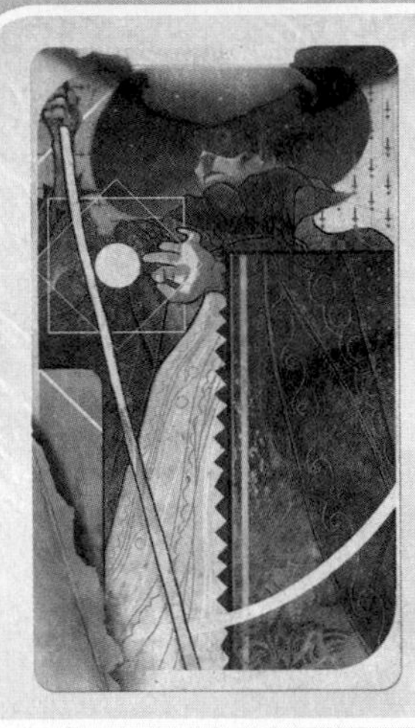

Mages channel magical power into spells capable of a wide range of effects, from debilitating opponents to protecting allies to unleashing devastating elemental energy. Those who wield magic are widely feared for their abilities, and their rebellion against Chantry control has left the land in chaos.

- Unique Class Skills: Veilfire, Energize, Destroy Magical Barriers

Mage Starting Abilities

Ability	Name	Description
	Chain Lightning	You unleash a blast of lightning that shocks one target and arcs to nearby enemies.
	Flashfire	You ignite an enemy with searing pain and send them fleeing in panic.

Mage Specializations

Specialization	Name	Details
	Knight-Enchanter	Complete Way of the Knight-Enchanter offered by Commander Helaine in Skyhold.
	Necromancer	Complete Way of the Necromancer offered by Viuus Anaxas in Skyhold.
	Rift Mage	Complete Way of the Rift Mage offered by your trainer in Skyhold.

Mage Starting Stats

Stats	Mage
Attributes	
Strength	10
Dexterity	10
Magic	11
Cunning	10
Willpower	10
Constitution	10
Offensive	
Attack	0%
Guard Damage Bonus	0%
Armor Penetration	0%
Barrier Damage Bonus	12%
Critical Damage Bonus	40%

Stats	Mage
Critical Chance	5%
Main-Hand Damage	17
Off-Hand Damage	17
Bleed on Hit	0%
Stagger on Hit	0%
Heal on Kill	0%
Flanking Damage Bonus	25%
Defensive	
Magic Defense	6%
Melee Defense*	0%
Ranged Defense*	0%
Cold Resistance	0%
Electrical Resistance	0%

Stats	Mage
Fire Resistance	0%
Guard	0
Armor Rating	38
Armor Rating: Front	38
Maximum Health	456
Bleed on Being Hit	0%
Stagger on Being Hit	0%
Other	
Maximum Focus	100
Focus Gain Bonus	0%
Maximum Mana/ Stamina	100
Cooldown Modifier	0%

* Base stats listed. Elves get a 25 percent bonus to ranged defense and Qunari get a 25 percent bonus to melee defense. Dwarves cannot be mages.

TACTICAL CONSIDERATIONS

Mages remain a formidable threat in *Dragon Age: Inquisition*, capable of casting a variety of elemental spells. But without the support of a balanced party, mages won't last long in battle. So make sure your mage is accompanied by at least one warrior—warriors are needed to taunt enemies, preventing your mage from getting overwhelmed by hostile forces.

Armed with elementally charged staves, mages fill a very specialized role on the battlefield, with an emphasis on ranged combat. As with a rogue archer, keep your mage out of harm's way, picking apart enemies from a safe distance. Of all the classes, mages are the most vulnerable to physical attacks, suffering from low health and minimal armor protection. As a result, take steps to bolster your defensive stats and consider investing in evasive abilities like Fade Step. Barrier is another wise choice, extending a protective barrier around your mage (and allies) for a short time. But before spending your ability points, take into consideration what kind of mage you want to create. A mage with awesome offensive abilities? Or one that fills a more supportive role, protecting, healing, and reviving allies? Study the available abilities and formulate a gameplan early on. Creating a jack-of-all-trades mage can be effective but may prevent you from accessing the more powerful abilities in each discipline's tree.

VEILFIRE

During your journeys you're likely to encounter some unique braziers that can only be lit by a mage. Use a mage to interact with these braziers to create veilfire. Once lit, these blue flames can be toted around on torches (by any class) to reveal ancient runic writing. If there's a veilfire brazier nearby, chances are there's some hidden writing on one of the nearby walls. This is one way to acquire rune schematics. Use these to create new runes, enhancing your party's equipment.

ENERGIZE

Mages can also use their magic to energize debris, creating makeshift bridges and ramps necessary to access areas that are otherwise off-limits. An energize icon will appear wherever these repairs can be made. Perform an interaction at these points to energize nearby objects, rearranging them to open a new path.

DEVELOPER TIP

A cool and highly effective combat combo is using Mark of the Rift in combination with Static Cage.

— Jason Baxter, QA Tester

MAGICAL BARRIERS

Some passages are walled off by magical barriers powered by elemental magic. Only mages can destroy these barriers, giving the party access to restricted areas, often containing loot. There are three types of magical barriers: fire (red), ice (blue), and spirit (purple). While any mage staff can defeat a magical barrier, use a staff of an opposite elemental magic to drop a barrier faster. For instance, use a fire staff to quickly eliminate an ice barrier, an ice staff to dispel a fire barrier, and an electrical staff to drop a spirit barrier. No other weapons will work against these barriers.

> MAGE ABILITIES

Spirit

Description: Masters of this school of magic call upon spirits for protection, as well as the essence of the Fade itself. Their spells disrupt hostile magic, create defensive barriers, and even heal injuries.

Investing in Spirit is a wise move for mages looking to fill a more supportive and defensive role within their party. Barrier, a spell that extends a magical shield around allies, is the cornerstone of this school of magic. This functions much like guard for warriors, serving as a temporary health bar. While all abilities in this tree are beneficial, focus on those that improve Barrier, like Elegant Defense, Transmute Magic, Fortifying Blast, and Strength of Spirits. Dedicated students of this discipline should strive to unlock Revival, capable of raising fallen allies on the battlefield. Also, don't overlook Dispel. If you cast Dispel on a green-glowing spot near a rift before a demon arrives (usually between the first and second waves of a rift fight), Dispel will prevent a demon from being summoned, essentially taking one enemy out of the rift fight early. This makes Dispel incredibly useful while closing rifts.

Barrier

You create a shimmering protective barrier that acts as temporary additional health. The barrier decays naturally over time.

Barrier: 5,500% weapon damage
Area of Effect: 4 meters
Cooldown Time: 24 seconds
Cost: 50 mana

Elegant Defense

You have learned to cast Barrier with a more stable magical pattern. Each time a barrier you have cast expires, the ability's cooldown is reduced.

Cooldown Reduction: 4 seconds

Guardian Spirit

A protective barrier springs into place around you automatically when you are badly injured.

Barrier: 100%
Cooldown Time: 60 seconds
Constitution on Unlock: +3

Peaceful Aura

Your aura of tranquility makes enemies less likely to attack you in battle, even when you damage them.

Threat Reduction: 50%
Willpower on Unlock: +3

Transmute Magic

Dispelling magic and status effects increases your own spells' damage and barrier generation for a brief duration.

Barrier: 50%
Damage Bonus: 25%
Duration: 10 seconds

Fortifying Blast

Each enemy you strike with Mind Blast increases your protective barrier as you turn their pain into your power.

Barrier: 10%

Dispel

You remove hostile magic and status effects from allies while stripping beneficial effects from enemies.

Size: 5 meters
Cooldown Time: 8 seconds
Cost: 35 mana
Eldritch Detonator Ability: Use on incapacitated foes for a combo.

Mind Blast

You send enemies staggering with an explosion of willpower that drives them back and makes them less likely to target you again.

Area of Effect: 5 meters
Cooldown Time: 8 seconds
Cost: 20 mana
Eldritch Detonator Ability: Use on incapacitated foes for a combo.

Strength of Spirits

Your barriers draw on the magic of the Fade to absorb more energy before depleting.

Barrier Bonus: 50%

Rejuvenating Barrier

When you or your allies have an active barrier, the beneficial energy invigorates them and helps them recover mana or stamina more quickly.

Mana Regeneration: 35%
Constitution on Unlock: +3

Life Ward

Spirits now protect your allies for a short time, reducing incoming damage and reviving them if they fall unconscious.

Damage Resistance: 25%
Duration: 15 seconds

Revival

You summon spirits to heal fallen allies in the area, getting them back on their feet and fighting again.

Area of Effect: 2 meters
Cooldown Time: 60 seconds
Cost: 85 mana

Storm

Description: Masters of this school of magic call forth the power of thunder and lightning. Their spells paralyze foes and arc from one enemy to another.

The abilities in this school allow a mage to harness the devastating properties of electricity to shock and paralyze their foes. When shocked, an enemy takes more damage from magic-based attacks. Paralysis simply renders a foe immobile and defenseless for a short time. If you're looking to dabble in this discipline, Chain Lightning is a good starting point. With continued investment in this tree, work your way to learning Static Cage and Lightning Cage for the ultimate display of Storm's awesome power.

Chain Lightning

You unleash a blast of lightning that shocks one target and arcs to nearby enemies.

Distance: 5 meters

Number of Hits: 4

Electric Damage: 250% weapon damage

Shocked Duration: 8 seconds

Cooldown Time: 8 seconds

Cost: 50 mana

Arcing Surge

Chain Lightning arcs farther and hits more targets.

Distance Bonus: 4 meters

Additional Hits: 2

Energy Bombardment

Each hit from Energy Barrage lowers the target's resistance to your staff's magic type for a short time.

Magic Resistance: -2%

Energy Barrage

You launch a salvo of elemental blasts from your staff that homes in on targets ahead of you.

Projectiles: 12

Damage per Hit: 66% weapon damage

Cooldown Time: 16 seconds

Cost: 50 mana

Eldritch Detonator Combo: Use on incapacitated foes for a combo.

Stormbringer

The storm comes to your aid even without your calling it. When you are in combat, lightning will periodically strike a random nearby enemy.

Electric Damage: 300% weapon damage

Radius: 25 meters

Cooldown Time: 15 seconds

Magic on Unlock: +3

Conductive Current

The more magical energy you expend, the more damage your spells do.

Damage Bonus: 5% for every 10% missing mana

Magic on Unlock: +3

Gathering Storm

You use your staff's energy to fill the area with sympathetic magic. Each basic attack shortens your active cooldown time.

Cooldown Reduction: 0.5 second

Willpower on Unlock: +3

Lightning Bolt

You summon a bolt of lightning that blasts and paralyzes a single target. If other nearby enemies are nearby, the bolt will paralyze the target for longer.

Electric Damage: 200% weapon damage

Paralyzed Duration: 2 seconds per nearby enemy

Cooldown Time: 24 seconds

Cost: 65 mana

Static Cage

You trap enemies inside an electricity field that paralyzes those that try to leave.

Duration: 8 seconds

Area of Effect: 9 meters

Paralyzed Duration: 2 seconds

Cooldown Time: 32 seconds

Cost: 65 mana

Exploding Bolt

Lightning Bolt does more damage if there are other enemies nearby, and if there are enough close to the striking point, a wave of force will knock back all enemies except for the paralyzed primary target.

Damage Bonus: 200% for every creature within 4 meters

Lightning Cage

Static Cage is now powerful enough to hurt or even kill enemies who leave its boundaries. Whenever an enemy in the cage takes damage, a lightning bolt strikes them, dealing bonus electricity damage.

Electric Damage: 50% weapon damage

Static Charge

You sheathe yourself in lightning while casting spells. Enemies that attempt to interrupt your casting with attacks are struck by arcs that leave them paralyzed.

Electric Damage: 100% weapon damage

Shocked Duration: 6 seconds

Constitution on Unlock: +3

DEVELOPER TIP

The projectiles launched by the mage ability Energy Barrage slide along walls, floors, and ceilings. So don't hesitate to use it in a tight area like a corridor.

– Thomas Roy, Software Developer

Inferno

Description: Masters of this school of magic dominate the battlefield with unrelenting fire. Enemies who survive the initial blast are driven mad with terror or burn to death in unquenchable flames.

The allure of conjuring fire and using it as a weapon makes Inferno a very appealing discipline. Beyond the expected burning status effect, which slowly drains an enemy's health for a time, some of these spells also imbue panic, causing foes to disengage from combat. Even if your mage isn't intending to become a master of this discipline, having a few of these spells in your arsenal never hurts—Immolate is a great entry-level AoE spell.

Flashfire

You ignite an enemy with searing pain and send them fleeing in panic.

Fire Damage: 300% weapon damage

Fear Duration: 8 seconds

Cooldown Time: 20 seconds

Cost: 65 mana

Blistering Pain

Flashfire burns brighter and hotter, intensifying the panic that your enemy suffers.

Fear Duration Bonus: 8 seconds

Wildfire

Fireball burns hotter and has a shorter cooldown time, allowing you to rain fire upon your enemies more often.

Fire Damage Bonus: 100% weapon damage

Burning: 75% weapon damage per second

Cooldown Reduction: 4 seconds

Immolate

You unleash a massive explosion, leaving enemies in the area burning in agony.

Fire Damage: 300% weapon damage

Burning: 75% weapon damage per second

Burning Duration: 8 seconds

Area of Effect: 3 meters

Cooldown Time: 16 seconds

Cost: 35 mana

Eldritch Detonator Ability: Use on incapacitated foes for a combo.

Flashpoint

After you land a critical hit, your next spell cast doesn't trigger a cooldown period.

Cooldown Duration: 10 seconds

Magic on Unlock: +3

Clean Burn

Your spells burn away ambient magic that would otherwise slow down your casting. Every spell you cast shortens your active cooldown times.

Cooldown Reduction: 1 second

Willpower on Unlock: +3

Pyromancer

You have mastered the summoning of fire, increasing your effectiveness when panicking or burning enemies.

Burning Duration Bonus: 25%

Fear Duration Bonus: 25%

Willpower on Unlock: +3

Lasting Flames

Wall of Fire creates a larger wall, and its flames burn longer on enemies that pass through it.

Size Bonus: 3 meters

Damage Duration Bonus: 4 seconds

Searing Glyph

Targets hit by Fire Mine are launched into the air and set aflame, leaving them burning.

Burning: 200% weapon damage per second

Burning Duration: 8 seconds

Fire Mine

You mark the ground with a glyph that takes a short time to prime. Once it is ready, it will erupt into flame when an enemy crosses it, damaging and staggering the target.

Fire Damage: 1,600% weapon damage

Activation Delay: 3 seconds

Cooldown Time: 24 seconds

Cost: 35 mana

Chaotic Focus

When you cast a fire spell, the spell consumes half of your current barrier to empower it. The larger the barrier consumed, the greater the bonus to the spell's damage.

Barrier Bonus: 50%

Magic on Unlock: +3

Wall of Fire

You conjure a flaming barrier that burns and panics enemies that pass through it.

Size: 6 meters

Duration: 20 seconds

Burning: 200% weapon damage per second

Burning Duration: 8 seconds

Fear Duration: 4 seconds

Cooldown Time: 32 seconds

Cost: 35 mana

Winter

Description: Masters of this school of magic summon cold that bites deeper than the cruelest winter. Their icy spells slow and weaken enemies.

The active abilities within this tree are extremely versatile, with an emphasis on applying frozen and chilled status effects on enemies. When enemies are frozen, they're encased in ice and unable to defend themselves or attack for a short period of time. Chilled enemies move slower and, thus, attack less frequently. But don't overlook the passive abilities here too—Winter Stillness, Frost Mastery, and Ice Armor grant permanent stat bonuses when unlocked.

Winter's Grasp

You lock a target in a sheet of ice, freezing it in place.

Ice Damage: 200% weapon damage
Freeze Duration: 4 seconds
Chill Duration: 8 seconds
Cooldown Time: 16 seconds
Cost: 65 mana

Winter's Chill

Winter's Grasp now damages and chills nearby enemies as well. However, only the primary target is frozen.

Area of Effect: 3 meters

Fade Step

You let invisible waves of magic carry you forward, blurring ahead a short distance.

Duration: 2 seconds
Cooldown Time: 12 seconds

Frost Step

Passing through enemies hurts them and leaves them chilled.

Ice Damage: 300% weapon damage
Chill Duration: 8 seconds

Frost Mastery

You have mastered the calling of cold, increasing your effectiveness when chilling or freezing targets.

Freeze Duration Bonus: 25%
Chill Duration Bonus: 25%
Magic on Unlock: +3

Mana Surge

Your barrier explodes into wild magic when enemies destroy it. The blast freezes all nearby enemies and allows you to cast your next spell without consuming mana.

Area of Effect: 3 meters
Freeze Duration: 2 seconds
Magic on Unlock: +3

Brittle Glyph

While frozen, the victim of Ice Mine loses all armor protection.

Armor Reduction: 100%

Winter Stillness

By standing still, you enter into a meditative state that restores your mana at an enhanced rate and reduces all cooldown times.

Meditation Idle Threshold: 3 seconds
Mana Regeneration Rate Bonus: 50%
Willpower on Unlock: +3

Ice Mine

You mark the ground with a glyph that takes a short time to prime. Once it is ready, it will freeze the first target to step on it.

Freeze Duration: 6 seconds
Activation Delay: 3 seconds
Cooldown time: 18 seconds
Cost: 35 mana

Glacial Strength

Wall of Ice creates a larger wall, and you can cast it more often.

Size Bonus: 3 meters
Cooldown Reduction: 8 seconds

Blizzard

You summon a freezing blizzard to chill and damage enemies caught in the area.

Ice Damage: 75% weapon damage per second
Chill Duration: 8 seconds
Area of Effect: 8 meters
Cooldown Time: 24 seconds
Cost: 5 mana per second

Ice Storm

Blizzard now chills enemies, progressively slowing them until they are frozen.

Damage Bonus: 75%
Freeze Duration: 4 seconds

Ice Armor

You draw on cold magic near you to protect you from all attacks. Standing near a frozen enemy or a persistent cold spell reduces all damage you take.

Damage Reduction: 50%
Willpower on Unlock: +3

Wall of Ice

You raise a wall of ice to keep enemies at bay.

Size: 6 meters
Duration: 20 seconds
Cooldown Time: 24 seconds
Cost: 50 mana

Knight-Enchanter (Specialization)

Description: These rare mages received special dispensation from the Chantry to serve in battle. They summon blades from the Fade and are experts in protection and defense.

Mages seeking greater defensive and supportive abilities should consider choosing Knight-Enchanter as their specialization. Start with Spirit Blade, using it to keep encroaching enemies at bay. Fade Cloak offers the perfect escape, making yourself invulnerable for a brief time. The Resurgence focus ability is the best revival and healing spell available, bringing all party members (including fallen ones) back to full health—this will come in handy during those challenging battles. Or use Disruption Field to slow your enemies, allowing you to retreat to a safe distance.

Spirit Blade

You create a blade of solid magic to make melee attacks against nearby enemies, bypassing their guard and barriers.

Spirit Damage: 300% weapon damage

Bonus: 200% bonus damage vs. Barrier and 400% bonus damage vs. guard.

Cost: 10 mana

Eldritch detonator ability: use on incapacitated foes for a combo

Defending Blade

You deflect incoming projectiles with Spirit Blade, sending a shockwave of energy back at the attacker.

Decloaking Blast

If you rematerialize inside an enemy, the foe is blasted back with massive force.

Spirit Damage: 1,000% weapon damage

Fade Cloak

You surround yourself with the magic of the Veil itself. You are briefly invulnerable and can pass through enemies unharmed.

Duration: 2 seconds

Cooldown Time: 12 seconds

Cost: 20 mana

Combat Clarity

The chaos of combat frightens some, but for you, it's a comfortable rhythm. Your mana regenerates faster when you're near hostile enemies.

Distance: 5 meters

Mana Regeneration Rate: 50%

Constitution on Unlock: +3

Resurgence

You call on benign spirits to restore you and your allies for continuing the fight. All party members are healed to full health, including those who have fallen unconscious, and a glyph around you provides ongoing healing to the party for the spell's duration.
This ability consumes and is powered by focus.

Radius: 5 meters

Duration: 10 seconds

Tier 1: Glyph heals 2% per second.

Tier 2: Glyph heals 10% per second.

Tier 3: Glyph heals 25% per second.

Fade Shield

You draw back the energy released by your enemies in your attacks against them. Any successful attack strengthens your barrier. The more damage you do, the more powerful your barrier grows.

Barrier: 30% of damage dealt

Magic on Unlock: +3

Veiled Riposte

Whenever you have a barrier active, enemies who attack you will take damage in return.

Damage Returned: 20%

Magic on Unlock: +3

Disruption Field

You fill an area with magical energy that slows and weakens your enemies. Enemies larger than the field are immune.

Speed Reduction: 50%

Radius: 3 meters

Duration: 10 seconds

Cooldown Time: 24 seconds

Cost: 65 mana

Stasis Lock

Enemies caught in Disruption Field are slowed to a stop over the course of several seconds. Striking them ends the effect.

Speed Reduction: 99%

Duration: 5 seconds

Knight-Protector

You're adept with defensive magic. Barriers you create take longer to naturally decay.

Barrier Decay Reduction: 35%

Constitution on Unlock: +3

Necromancer (Specialization)

Description: These mages specialize in binding the spirits that are drawn to death. They can put the fear of death into enemies, bring spirits to fight on their behalf, and even cause devastating explosions when their enemies die.

The Necromancer specialization offers some truly powerful abilities, allowing a mage to coerce Fade spirits into doing their bidding while spreading panic and fear across the battlefield. The Haste focus ability is particularly useful, increasing the speed of the whole party for a short time. If enemies are killed with Spirit Mark, they'll fight for you for a short time before finally dying. Or curse a foe with Walking Bomb to trigger a powerful explosion. If dabbling with Fade spirits doesn't creep you out, then Necromancer may be the right choice for you.

Horror

You unleash spirits of fear that terrify enemies within the area.

Panic Duration: 6 seconds
Area of Effect: 3 meters
Cooldown Time: 24 seconds
Cost: 50 mana

Despair

Horror inflicts even deeper terror upon targets and reduces their armor while they are under its effects.

Spirit Damage: 50% weapon damage per second
Armor Reduction: 20%

Blinding Terror

You have learned to leave enemies vulnerable in their terror. Enemies that are panicked take increased damage from all attacks.

Damage Bonus vs. Panicked: 15%
Magic on Unlock: +3

Haste

You increase the speed of the entire party. While this ability is active, all enemies move and attack more slowly by comparison. This ability consumes and is powered by focus.

Tier 1: Enemies slow by 85% for 6 seconds.
Tier 2: Enemies slow by 85% for 12 seconds.
Tier 3: Enemies slow by 85% for 20 seconds.

Death Siphon

Every time an enemy dies nearby, you regain both health and mana.

Mana Amount: 20
Health Amount: 10%
Constitution on Unlock: +3

Simulacrum

If you are knocked unconscious, a spirit you control takes on your likeness and fights on your behalf for a short time. The spirit draws magic directly from the Fade, casting spells without cost. You cannot be revived by any means until the spirit leaves.

Duration: 10 seconds
Willpower on Unlock: +3

Power of the Dead

Killing enemies attracts spirits that increase the power of your spells for a short time.

Damage Bonus: 20%
Duration: 10 seconds
Willpower on Unlock: +3

Walking Bomb

You curse an enemy, inflicting ongoing spirit damage, and then trigger the curse in a devastating explosion.

Spirit Damage: 200% weapon damage per second
Duration: 10 seconds
Explosion Damage: 600% of weapon damage
Area of Effect: 5 meters
Cooldown Time: 20 seconds
Cost: 65 mana

Spirit Mark

You mark a target with an attacking spirit, inflicting ongoing damage. If the target dies while marked, the spirit mimics the victim's body briefly to fight on your behalf. Can be toggled on and off.

Duration: 12 seconds
Spirit Damage: 75% weapon damage per second
Charm Duration: 15 seconds
Cooldown Time: 20 seconds
Cost: 50 mana

Lingering Mark

Targets you kill with Spirit Mark now fight for you longer and harder.

Damage Bonus: 75%
Charm Duration: 45 seconds

Virulent

If Walking Bomb kills your target, the effect spreads to nearby enemies, causing secondary explosions.

Rift Mage (Specialization)

Description: These mages draw upon the force of the Fade, either pulling matter from the Fade to attack or twisting the Veil itself into a weapon to stagger or crush their enemies.

Take your mastery of the Fade to the next level with the powerful abilities in the Rift Mage discipline. Both Veilstrike and Stonefist are powerful offensive abilities, perfect for keeping melee enemies away from you. Or rain down fiery meteors from the sky with the awesome Firestorm focus ability. Consider using Pull of the Abyss to draw multiple enemies to a central location before unleashing Firestorm on their heads. The passive abilities are also effective, applying bonuses when engaging weakened enemies.

Veilstrike

You recreate your own fist from the essence of the Fade and smash nearby foes to the ground.

Area of Effect: 5 meters

Cooldown Time: 24 seconds

Cost: 35 mana

Punching Down

You cast Veilstrike more easily, and the blow weakens your enemies, causing them to do less damage.

Cost Reduction: 15 mana

Weakened Duration: 10 seconds

Shatterstone

The boulder summoned by Stonefist now explodes on impact, weakening and staggering nearby enemies.

Area of Effect: 4 meters

Weakened Duration: 10 seconds

Stonefist

You summon a boulder from the Fade and smash it into your target, sending it flying.

Spirit Damage: 500% weapon damage

Cooldown Time: 8 seconds

Cost: 50 mana

Impact Detonator Ability: Use on incapacitated foes for a combo.

Restorative Veil

You pull stray magic from around weakened enemies to regain mana based on the damage you do to them.

Mana Recovery: 10%

Magic on Unlock: +3

Encircling Veil

You use stray magic around weakened enemies to increase the power of status effects on them.

Duration Bonus vs. Weakened: 25%

Magic on Unlock: +3

Smothering Veil

Weakened enemies have the damage they inflict reduced even further.

Damage Reduction: 30%

Willpower on Unlock: +3

Firestorm

You summon flaming meteors, raining fire down upon enemies all over the area for the next several seconds. This ability consumes and is powered by focus.

Radius: 6 meters

Fire Damage: 150% weapon damage

Duration: 15 seconds

Tier 1: You summon 15 meteors.

Tier 2: You summon 30 meteors.

Tier 3: You summon 55 meteors.

Pull of the Abyss

You create a tiny rift that pulls enemies toward a central point.

Area of Effect: 6 meters

Duration: 12 seconds

Cooldown Time: 32 seconds

Cost: 65 mana

Shaken

You can cast Pull of the Abyss more often, and enemies caught in its effect are weakened.

Cooldown Reduction: 8 seconds

Weakened Duration: 10 seconds

Twisting Veil

You catch stray magic around weakened enemies and use it to increase the damage of your own attacks.

Damage Bonus vs. Weakened: 15%

Magic on Unlock: +3

SPECIALIZATION QUESTS

After arriving at Skyhold, complete the Specializations for the Inquisitor operation on the war table to summon three trainers. Each trainer offers a unique quest, requiring you to collect a number of items. Upon the completion of a quest you have the opportunity to choose the associated specialization. You can only choose one specialization, even if you've completed all three quests. So be sure to review the abilities associated with each discipline before you settle on a specialization.

WAY OF THE ARTIFICER

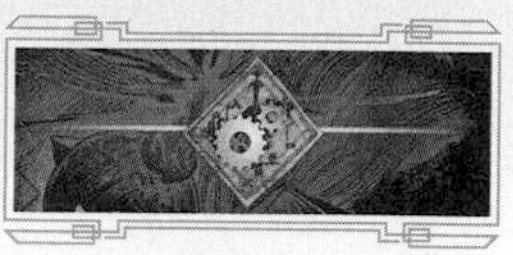

Class: Rogue

Quest Giver: Three-Eyes

Description: Construct the proper tools, study the methods to use them, and Three-Eyes will reveal the secret of the trap-laying Artificer specialization. Alpha quillback spines may be found at Nazaire's Pass, The Canyons, and near Old Prison Road in the Western Approach. Readings can be found among the belongings of Varric or, if those are unavailable, among the wares of the book merchant in Val Royeaux.

Requirements: Complete Specializations for the Inquisitor operation on the war table in Skyhold.

Reward: Artificer specialization

Objectives:

- Acquire writing on artificer methods.
- Acquire three alpha quillback spines.
- Acquire 20 obsidian.
- Gather materials to construct tools.

Western Approach: Alpha Quillback Spines

WAY OF THE ASSASSIN

Class: Rogue

Quest Giver: Heir

Description: Craft a proper knife, study the methods required to wield it, and Heir will reveal the secrets of the Assassin specialization. Guild leader tokens may be found at the East Side Hills, The Flats, and the Black Fens in Crestwood. Readings can be found among the belongings of Cole or, if those are unavailable, among the wares of the book merchant in Val Royeaux.

Requirements: Complete Specializations for the Inquisitor operation on the war table in Skyhold.

Reward: Assassin specialization

Objectives:

- Acquire writing on assassin methods.
- Acquire three assassin guild leader tokens.
- Acquire 20 deathroot.
- Gather knife materials.

Crestwood: Assassin Guild Leader Tokens

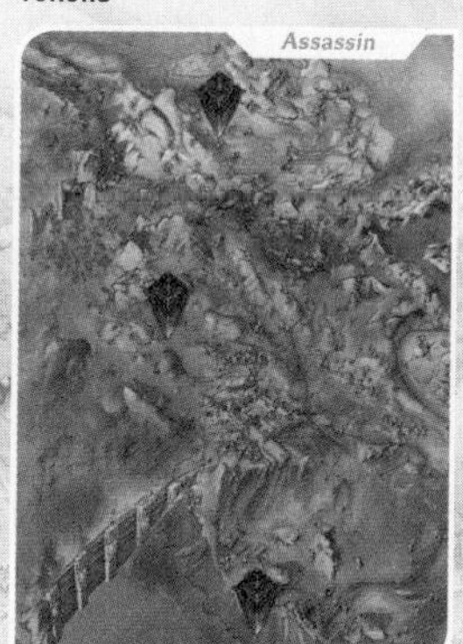

WAY OF THE TEMPEST

Class: Rogue

Quest Giver: Kihm

Description: Fill a bottle of smoke, study the methods required to use it, and Kihm will reveal the secrets of the Tempest specialization. Essence containment apparatuses may be found at Apostate's Landing, Long River, and Storm's Solitude in the Storm Coast. Readings can be found among the belongings of Sera or, if those are unavailable, among the wares of the book merchant in Val Royeaux.

Requirements: Complete Specializations for the Inquisitor operation on the war table in Skyhold.

Reward: Tempest specialization

Objectives:

- Acquire writing on tempest methods.
- Acquire three essence containment apparatuses.
- Acquire one rune of lightning essence.
- Acquire one rune of ice essence.
- Gather materials for a bottle of smoke.

The Storm Coast: Essence Containment Apparatuses

> WAY OF THE CHAMPION

Class: Warrior

Quest Giver: Lord Chancer

Description: Construct a proper standard, study the Champion's code, and Lord Chancer will reveal the secrets of this proud and noble specialization. Fight champions for their heraldic symbols at Ghilan'nain's Grove, Halin'sulahn, and the Desolate Bank of the Exalted Plains. Readings can be found among the belongings of Blackwall or, if those are unavailable, among the wares of the book merchant in Val Royeaux.

Requirements: Complete Specializations for the Inquisitor operation on the war table in Skyhold.

Reward: Champion specialization

Objectives:

- Acquire writing on champion methods.
- Duel three champions for heraldry.
- Acquire 20 veridium.
- Gather standard materials.

Exalted Plains: Champions

> WAY OF THE REAVER

Class: Warrior

Quest Giver: Breaker Thram

Description: Gather the materials to infuse a dragon's blood, study the methods to prepare it properly, and Breaker Thram will reveal the secrets of the punishing Reaver specialization. Kill rivals to claim infusion primers at the East Side Hills, the Flats, and the Black Fens in Crestwood. Readings can be found among the belongings of Iron Bull or, if those are unavailable, among the wares of the book merchant in Val Royeaux.

Requirements: Complete Specializations for the Inquisitor operation on the war table in Skyhold.

Reward: Reaver specialization

Objectives:

- Acquire writing on reaver methods.
- Acquire three infusion primers.
- Acquire 50 rashvines.
- Gather materials to infuse blood.

Crestwood: Infusion Primers

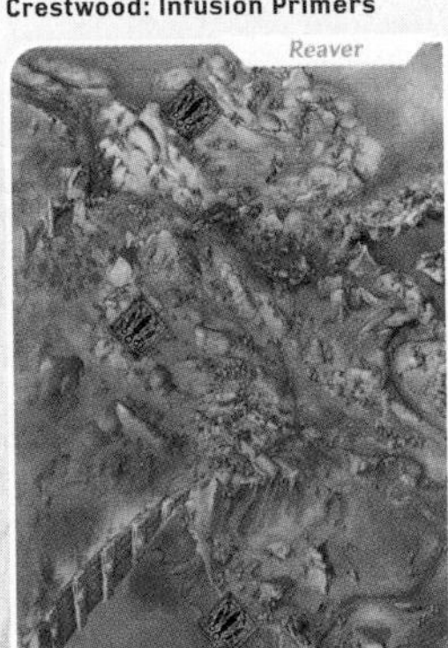

> WAY OF THE TEMPLAR

Class: Warrior

Quest Giver: Ser

Description: Construct a philter, study the methods of the templars, and Ser will reveal the secrets of this legendary specialization. Reclaim the philters of fallen templars from demons at Witchwood, West Road, and Lady Shayna's Valley in the Hinterlands. Readings can be found among the belongings of Cassandra or, if those are unavailable, among the wares of the book merchant in Val Royeaux.

Requirements: Complete Specializations for the Inquisitor operation on the war table in Skyhold.

Reward: Templar specialization

Objectives:

- Acquire writing on templar methods.
- Acquire three broken philters.
- Acquire 50 embrium.
- Gather philter materials.

The Hinterlands: Broken Philters

WAY OF THE KNIGHT-ENCHANTER

Class: Mage

Quest Giver: Commander Helaine

Description: Craft a hilt to hold a spirit blade, study the methods required to wield the blade, and Commander Helaine will reveal the secrets of the Knight-Enchanter specialization. Take the essence from wisps at the Old Thoroughfare, the Weeping Spires, and Granite Point in the Fallow Mire. Readings can be found among the belongings of Vivienne or, if those are unavailable, among the wares of the book merchant in Val Royeaux.

Requirements: Complete Specializations for the Inquisitor operation on the war table in Skyhold.

Reward: Knight-Enchanter specialization

Objectives:

- Acquire writing on knight-enchanter methods.
- Acquire three wisp essences.
- Acquire 10 lazurite.
- Gather materials for a spirit blade.

Fallow Mire: Wisp Essences

WAY OF THE NECROMANCER

Class: Mage

Quest Giver: Viuus Anaxas

Description: Adorn a skull in jewels, study the art of necromancy, and Viuus Anaxas will reveal the secrets of the Nevarran death mages. Destroy undead to gain Nevarran ceremonial skulls at Apostate's Landing, Small Grove, and Storm's Solitude in the Storm Coast. Readings can be found among the belongings of Dorian or, if those are unavailable, the wares of the book merchant in Val Royeaux.

Requirements: Complete Specializations for the Inquisitor operation on the war table in Skyhold.

Reward: Necromancer specialization

Objectives:

- Acquire writing on necromancy.
- Acquire three Nevarran skulls.
- Acquire 20 bloodstones.
- Gather jeweled skull materials.

The Storm Coast: Nevarran Skulls

WAY OF THE RIFT MAGE

Class: Mage

Quest Giver: Your Trainer

Description: Assemble a tome of rifts, study rift magic, and Your Trainer will reveal the secrets of the Rift Mage specialization. Collect tomes from the Venatori at Ghilan'nain's Grove, Halin'sulahn, and the Desolate Bank in the Exalted Plains. Readings can be found among the belongings of Solas or, if those are unavailable, among the wares of the book merchant in Val Royeaux.

Requirements: Complete Specializations for the Inquisitor operation on the war table in Skyhold.

Reward: Rift Mage specialization

Objectives:

- Acquire writing on rift magic.
- Acquire three Venatori tomes.
- Acquire 20 ring velvet.
- Gather materials for a tome of rifts.

Exalted Plains: Venatori Tomes

ADVANCED COMBAT TACTICS

Now that you have a better understanding of the classes and their various abilities, put that knowledge to use in combat. Here we take a deeper look at how you can use abilities, status effects, and combos to gain a significant advantage on the battlefield.

> TACTICAL CAMERA: OBSERVE, PLAN, EXECUTE

While using the tactical camera isn't essential, ignoring its benefits puts you and your party at a serious disadvantage. So before engaging in combat, make a habit of activating the tactical camera to plan your attack. This allows you to scout your opponents, probing for weaknesses and tactical opportunities. First, move the camera around so you can inspect all hostile units in the area. How many enemies are present? Are there archers, mages, spellbinders, or other ranged threats? If so, consider targeting them first. Next, take into account the terrain of the battlefield. Are there any elevated perches where you can position your ranged units? Are there narrow hallways, stairways, doorways, or other choke points you can take advantage of? Once you've scouted the terrain, consider redeploying your party members to establish a dominant position on the battlefield before initiating combat. A little bit of preparation can make each engagement a little easier to manage.

If you encounter an enemy you're unfamiliar with, place the camera's reticle over it to open its information box. This reveals the unit's name, health, level, resistances, vulnerabilities, and immunities—all the information you need to make solid tactical decisions. For instance, if an enemy is resistant to cold-based attacks and vulnerable to fire-based attacks, consider altering your party's equipped weapons and mapped abilities to take advantage of this vulnerability to fire—equipment cannot be swapped during combat.

Once combat has begun, continue using the tactical camera or switch to the third-person view. But if you choose to play from the third-person perspective, remember that the tactical camera is still available if things get a little too hectic. Consider switching back to the tactical camera periodically to reposition your party members or to set up some combos. For instance, use a warrior ability like Mighty Blow to knock an enemy down, then follow up with a rogue ability like Twin Fangs to inflict heavy damage on the downed opponent. Since the tactical camera pauses the action, it makes it much easier to set up combos like this.

> FOCUS

Focus is a replenishable resource like stamina or mana. All characters have their own personal focus meter. But unlike with stamina or mana, all party members gain focus when a single party member deals damage. Focus is used to initiate powerful focus abilities, like the Inquisitor's Mark of the Rift. These powerful abilities aren't available until after the Inquisition evacuates Haven. The Inquisitor gains Mark of the Rift immediately following the escape from Haven. The other focus abilities are tied to class specializations. Each party member unlocks a specialization upon reaching Skyhold, and the Inquisitor can choose a specialization by completing trainer quests.

All focus abilities have three tiers. By default, only tier 1 of each focus ability is available. But through the acquisition of Inquisition perks you can access tier 2 and tier 3 focus abilities. Choose Cullen's Advanced Focus and Master Focus perks to unlock these tier 2 and tier 3 abilities. Higher-tiered focus abilities usually deal more damage or last longer, making them more effective.

During combat, look for opportunities to maximize the use of your focus abilities. Since focus abilities can't be triggered often, consider saving your focus for tough fights, such as those against bosses, dragons, or high-level Fade rifts. If each party member has a focus ability ready to go, even the toughest battles are survivable. Area-of-effect attacks like Mark of the Rift and Firestorm are particularly devastating—trigger these early in a fight to wipe out weaker enemies.

Focus Abilities

Ability	Name	Specialization	Description
Inquisitor			
	Mark of the Rift	Inquisitor	Mark of the Rift causes massive damage and can even kill some enemies instantly.
Rogue			
	Hail of Arrows	Artificer	You fire so quickly that enemies will swear there are at least two of you putting arrows into their ranks. While this ability is active, any archery ability you use is duplicated.
	Thousand Cuts	Assassin	You choose a target, then dash to and fro—a shadow leaving blood with every leap. After you slice through other nearby foes, you land behind your target, striking deep.
	Cloak of Shadows	Tempest	You go into stealth, and your allies follow your lead. The entire party remains undetected for the duration of the effect, even while attacking.

Focus Abilities continued

Ability	Name	Specialization	Description
Warrior			
	Counterstrike	Champion	You push yourself to the limit, gaining full guard and taunting all nearby enemies. While the ability is active, you automatically counter all melee attacks.
	Rampage	Reaver	You're an unstoppable fury of physical force while this ability is active. Your attacks are harder and faster, and you gain health with each strike.
	Rally	Templar	You inspire your allies to fight harder. Your party's guard, stamina, and mana build over time, and all party members gain damage resistance against incoming attacks.
Mage			
	Resurgence	Knight-Enchanter	You call on benign spirits to restore you and your allies for continuing the fight. All party members are healed to full health, including those who have fallen unconscious, and a glyph around you provides ongoing healing to the party for the spell's duration.
	Haste	Necromancer	You increase the speed of the entire party. While this ability is active, all enemies move and attack more slowly by comparison.
	Firestorm	Rift Mage	You summon flaming meteors, raining fire down upon enemies all over the area for the next several seconds.

TIP To build focus faster, equip focus-boosting accessories like the Belt of Focus on all your party members. This allows you to use focus abilities more frequently.

STACKING STATUS EFFECTS

In addition to inflicting damage, many abilities also apply a status effect. There are numerous status effects, and they affect their victims in various ways for a limited time. Many status effects stack, too, allowing you to apply multiple status effects to a single target. Pour on as many status effects as possible to greatly decrease an enemy's performance while whittling away at their health. For example, use the rogue's Poisoned Weapons ability to apply the poison status effect while a mage strikes with Winter's Grasp to apply the frozen status effect. In this instance, the target is encased in ice while suffering continual damage from poison. In this sense, status effects are a true force multiplier and should be applied as frequently as possible to give your party an advantage in each engagement.

Status Effects

Status Effect	Name	Description
	Berserk	Increases damage and movement speed. Additionally adds a layer of either barrier or guard, depending on the creature, and grants additional immunities to controlling effects.
	Burning	Creature takes fire damage over time.
	Chilled	Creature's movement speed is reduced by 25%.
	Disruption Field	Mage Knight-Enchanter ability: Creatures within the disruption field are slowed and weakened.
	Fear	Creature runs away in a panic. After 1.5 seconds any direct damage will break the effect.
	Frozen	Creature is disabled.
	Panic	Creature runs away in a panic. After 1.5 seconds any direct damage will break the effect.
	Paralyzed	Creature is disabled.
	Perceptive	After a duration the player is removed from Stealth when near a perceptive creature. The duration is relative to the strength of the creature—usually 5-15 seconds.
	Poisoned	Creature takes nature damage over time.
	Shocked	Reduces resistance to fire, cold, and electricity by 20%.
	Sleep	Creature sleeps in place. Any direct damage will break the effect.
	Snared	Creature's movement speed is reduced by 25%.
	Stealth	Creature is untargetable unless the player is within 5 meters. Creatures in Stealth are still visible but harder to spot due to transparency.
	Stunned	Creature is disabled.
	Taunted	Creature is forced to target the caster for the duration. At the end of the forced targeting the caster is moved to the top of the threat table.
	Sundered	Creature's armor reduced by 20%.
	Weakened	Creature's damage reduced by 15%.

GUARD AND BARRIER

When selecting abilities for your warriors and mages, choose ones that enhance barriers and guard. Guard and barriers cover your characters' health bars, preventing them from taking damage. Guard is generated by warriors in numerous ways and only degrades when you're being attacked. Barrier is cast by mages as an AoE spell on party members and only lasts a few seconds. Together, guard and the Barrier ability make your party more durable and cut down on the number of healing potions they consume, which is essential during boss fights and dragon battles.

DEVELOPER TIP

Cross-Class Combos

Dan Kading, Lead Combat Design

Cross-class combos require that an enemy be set up with a disabling status effect by one class (Stun for warriors, Sleep for rogues, Freeze or Paralyze for mages), then hit with a different class's detonator ability (Impact for warriors, Precision for rogues, Eldritch for mages). However, each class has one specialization tree that grants a setup or detonator from a different class.

My favorite Inquisitor build is a dual-wielding rogue with the Tempest specialization. Flask of Frost will freeze enemies, normally only possible if you're a mage. I can then circle and hit with Twin Fangs, dealing 4x damage for striking their flank and causing the Shatter cross-class combo for even further damage. I can then transition into an upgraded Flask of Fire, making all my abilities free for a few seconds, and use multiple Deathblows or Shadow Strikes depending on circumstance.

Rupture: Heavy damage over time, ignoring armor
Shatter: Heavy cold damage
Discharge: Strong electric damage to all nearby enemies
Nightmare: Strong damage and causes panicked status
Weakness: Strong damage and causes weakness status
Basic combo: Moderate bonus damage

Cross-Class Combos

Setups	Impact Detonator (Warrior)	Precision Detonator (Rogue)	Eldritch Detonator (Mage)
Warrior: Stun	Basic Combo	Rupture	Weakness
Rogue: Sleep	Rupture	Basic Combo	Nightmare
Mage: Freeze	Shatter	Shatter	Basic Combo
Mage: Paralyze	Discharge	Discharge	Basic Combo

CLASS BUILDS: OUR FAVORITES

During our time with the game we have come across a few different ways to spec the different classes. These aren't necessarily the best way to build out your characters, but merely a starting point. With so many abilities to choose from, the combinations are mind-boggling. Still, concentrate on selecting abilities that complement one another. Define what your character's role is on the battlefield and stay true to that vision through thoughtful ability selection.

SKIRMISHER

Recommended Abilities

Ability	Name	Discipline
	Poisoned Weapons/Infected Wounds	Sabotage
	Parry/Effortless Riposte	Double Daggers
	Evasion	Subterfuge
	Evade/Hidden Step	Subterfuge
	Flank Attack/Skirmisher	Double Daggers
	Bloodied Prey	Double Daggers
	Unforgiving Chain	Double Daggers
	Spinning Blades/Neverending Spin	Double Daggers

Daggers are some of the highest DPS (damage per second) weapons in the game, and the dual-wield rogue has two of them. Therefore, seek out abilities that make these daggers even deadlier, like Poisoned Weapons, Flank Attack, and Spinning Blades. While rogues can dish out some heavy damage, they can't take much in return. Therefore, rely on the default Stealth ability to sneak into close range and attack from the shadows. After striking, use Evade to jump out of the way or Parry to block the retaliating strike. Don't get greedy—going toe-to-toe with heavily armored enemies won't end well. So stick and move to stay alive.

TOXIC ARCHER

Recommended Abilities

Ability	Name	Discipline
	Poisoned Weapons/Infected Wounds	Sabotage
	Explosive Shot/Chain Reaction	Archery
	Death from Above	Archery
	Leaping Shot/Rolling Draw	Archery
	Fighting Dirty	Sabotage
	Explosive Toxin	Sabotage
	Pincushion	Archery
	Full Draw/Stunning Shot	Archery

When equipped with Poisoned Weapons, a rogue archer can spread poison across the battlefield with ease, poisoning every opponent within a matter of seconds. This is why we always start with Poisoned Weapons when playing as a rogue archer. The damage inflicted by poison isn't much, but it adds up over time, particularly once you increase the poison's potency with Infected Wounds and its duration with Fighting Dirty. Add Explosive Toxin to make infected enemies explode, releasing a toxic cloud when they die, poisoning nearby opponents.

TANK

Recommended Abilities

Ability	Name	Discipline
	Shield Wall/Chevalier's Step	Weapon and Shield
	Challenge/Throw the Gauntlet	Vanguard
	Bear Mauls the Wolves	Weapon and Shield
	Turn the Bolt	Weapon and Shield
	Shield Bash/Ring the Bell	Weapon and Shield
	Turn the Blade	Weapon and Shield
	Untouchable Defense	Vanguard
	It'll Cost You	Vanguard

The weapon-and-shield warrior is perfect for tanking, particularly when equipped with abilities that help build guard and deflect damage. Shield Wall is always our first stop, giving our warrior the ability to build guard. While the default War Cry is great for taunting nearby enemies, Challenge comes in handy for taunting those distant enemies who are likely harassing your more vulnerable party members. Passive abilities like Turn the Bolt, Turn the Blade, and Untouchable Defense all reduce incoming damage, ensuring your warrior is around longer to defend allies.

TIP When playing as a warrior, pay attention to your team, as it is more important for them to stay alive than it is for you to avoid taking a beating.

DEVELOPER TIP

I make sure to have one party member with the Revival ability. I let the AI control that party member and make his/her survival a top priority—give them more potions and set a higher "low health" value in the Behavior menu.

— David Doucet, programmer

BERSERKER

Recommended Abilities

Ability	Name	Discipline
	Block and Slash/Flawless Defense	Two-Handed Weapon
	Charging Bull/Gore and Trample	Vanguard
	Shield Breaker	Two-Handed Weapon
	Grappling Chain/Give Them the Boot	Battlemaster
	Whirlwind/Rising Winds	Two-Handed Weapon
	Clear a Path	Two-Handed Weapon
	Earthshaking Strike/Shattered Ground	Two-Handed Weapon
	Guard-Smasher	Two-Handed Weapon

Clearly, the emphasis of this two-handed warrior build is damage output. But even these warriors need some defense, so rely on abilities like Block and Slash/Flawless Defense and Charging Bull/Gore and Trample to build guard—without substantial guard, this warrior won't last long in close contact with multiple enemies. When it comes to offense, place this warrior in the thick of battle, surrounded by enemies, before initiating Whirlwind or Earthshaking Strike. Consider taking this warrior's offense to the next level by mastering the Reaver specialization.

SUPPORT MAGE

Recommended Abilities

Ability	Name	Discipline
	Barrier/Elegant Defense	Spirit
	Peaceful Aura	Spirit
	Immolate/Wildfire	Inferno
	Dispel/Transmute Magic	Spirit
	Winter's Grasp/Winter's Chill	Winter
	Revival/Life Ward	Spirit
	Rejuvenating Barrier	Spirit
	Fade Step/Frost Step	Winter

Our mages tend to fill a supporting role on the battlefield, with an emphasis on preventing damage to themselves and their allies. Barrier is the first line of defense, prioritizing the protection of non-warrior allies who can't generate guard. But a mage needs some offense too, which is why we utilize Immolate and Winter's Grasp to balance out our elemental magics. Revival can be an absolute game-changer in tough battles, instantly raising fallen allies so they can continue the fight. To discourage or escape incoming attacks, we rely on Peaceful Aura and Fade Step.

PARTY MEMBERS

It may be your Inquisition, but you're never alone. As Inquisitor, you're constantly surrounded by a group of loyal followers, all with a vested interest in restoring order. But while these party members are loyal to the cause, they don't always agree with you or with other members of the Inquisition. Each character has a rich and unique background that greatly influences their world view. As leader of the Inquisition, you must choose your words and actions carefully to maintain the approval of your party members. But you can't please everyone. Even the most diplomatic approaches will irk some and impress others.

Reference this chapter to get a better understanding of each character, learning more of their motivations and how to gain their approval. Some followers are even open to romantic gestures. But before you set your eye on someone, make sure they're open to your advances—your character's race and gender may have an impact, not to mention overall approval.

CAUTION This chapter is packed with spoilers, revealing critical plot points. Consider yourself warned.

VARRIC TETHRAS

Inner Circle Quests:

- Seeing Red (Approval)
- Well, Shit (Personal Plot)

Romance: Not available.

Varric Tethras is one part adventurous rogue, one part dashing storyteller, and three parts trouble. Born on the surface, Varric has little love for his underground brethren—all his contacts lie with the dwarves of the merchants guild, though he has little taste for their schemes. Still, he has found a place as an outsider, rubbing shoulders with both the wealthy elite as well as the worst of scoundrels. To hear him tell of it, that's all he truly cares about, though anyone who truly knows him claims differently. They say that, try as he might, Varric has been drawn more and more into conflicts that shake the world—ones that he can't get himself out of with a quick tale.

Starting Abilities

Ability	Name	Description
	Caltrops	You scatter spikes behind you, hurting and slowing down enemies who come after you. This ability is considered a trap for any abilities that enhance or affect traps.
	Long Shot	You fire a powerful single shot that delivers more damage the farther you are from the target.

SPECIALIZATION

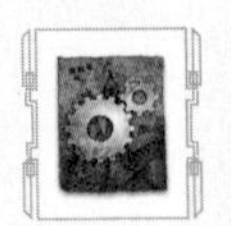

Artificer: After years of experience with the Merchants Guild and the publishing world, Varric has become an expert at handling deadly traps and convoluted devices.

FIRST ENCOUNTER

Armed with Bianca, his beloved crossbow, Varric is busy fighting off demons with Solas at the first Fade rift outside Haven when you first encounter him. This rogue automatically joins your party (along with Solas) when the Fade rift is closed. Bianca gives Varric the ability to engage enemies at range. But if you already have too many ranged party members, consider equipping Varric with a pair of daggers. Varric's lock-picking skill will come in handy as your party continues its adventure into the Hinterlands and beyond.

APPROVAL

Varric is skeptical of just about everything, including the Inquisition. Despite his vocal misgivings about the situation, Varric is loyal to the cause and eager to see a return to normality. While Varric can't be romanced, you can still gain and lose approval with him. Generally, Varric appreciates a good sense of humor, even in the darkest of times. Clever wisecracks and not taking yourself too seriously will gain approval with Varric. Some of Varric's approvals are also tied to events in *Dragon Age II*, depending on whether Hawke sided with the mages or templars.

Approval Gained

- Take the mountain path in the Frostback Mountains during the prologue.
- At Redcliffe Castle, accept the mages as allies (only if Hawke sided with the mages in *Dragon Age II*).
- At Redcliffe Castle, accept the mages as conscripts (only if Hawke sided with the templars in *Dragon Age II*).
- Allow the Wardens to join the Inquisition in Adamant (only if Hawke's Warden ally is left in the Fade).
- Exile the Wardens at Adamant (only if Hawke is left in the Fade).

Approval Lost

- At Redcliffe Castle, accept the mages as allies (only if Hawke sided with the templars in *Dragon Age II*).
- At Redcliffe Castle, accept the mages as conscripts (only if Hawke sided with the mages in *Dragon Age II*).
- Say you'll "do it for my own power" when made Inquisitor.
- Say "lead them to vengeance" when made Inquisitor.
- Allow the Wardens to join the Inquisition in Adamant (only if Hawke is left in the Fade).
- Exile the Wardens at Adamant (only if Hawke's Warden ally is left in the Fade).

CASSANDRA PENTAGHAST

Inner Circle Quests:

- Unfinished Business (Approval)
- Promise of Destruction (Personal Plot)
- Guilty Pleasures (Gift Plot)
- The Ideal Romance (Romance Plot)

Romance: Inquisitor must be male of any race.

Though of noble birth, Cassandra Pentaghast turned her back on a life of wealth and privilege to join the Seekers of Truth. The ancient order serves as a watchful eye over corruption and magical threats, granted ultimate authority in its investigations by the Chantry—or it did, prior to abandoning their duty in response to the mage rebellion. Cassandra did not join her brothers in this, instead remaining loyal to Divine Justinia and her efforts to restore order in the face of chaos. She is both pious and driven, the sword in the right hand of the Divine, seeking justice above all else.

Starting Abilities

Ability	Name	Description
	Challenge	Your powerful shout carries across the battlefield, taunting a targeted enemy and improving your guard.
	Payback Strike	You recover from any disabled condition and lash out with a great blow against nearby enemies. If you've recently taken damage, you hit that much harder and stagger your foes.
	Shield Wall	You stand firm and block incoming attacks at the cost of stamina. Each block adds to your guard. You move much more slowly while sustaining this ability.

SPECIALIZATION

Templar: Long ago, the Seekers of Truth founded the Templar Order and taught them how to deal with hostile mages and their spells. Cassandra thus possesses all of a templar's abilities without the risk of lyrium addiction.

FIRST ENCOUNTER

Initially, you are Cassandra's prisoner following the events at the Temple of Sacred Ashes. As a result, she is the first party member you encounter, joining you during the journey to the first Fade rift, where you meet Varric and Solas. Even at this early stage, Cassandra is a formidable warrior capable of taunting enemies while absorbing and dealing heavy damage. If you're not playing as a warrior yourself, Cassandra is an indispensable member of your party during your early adventures in the Frostback Mountains and the Hinterlands.

APPROVAL

Cassandra isn't the most approachable character in your party, but there are a few things you can say to gain her approval. Generally, embrace your role as the Chosen of Andraste and say favorable things about the Chantry while prioritizing the Inquisition over personal fame and power. Completing Unfinished Business will also grant you some approval. To prevent a loss of approval, avoid making disparaging comments about the Maker or the Chantry.

Approval Gained

- Charge with the soldiers in the Frostback Mountains during the prologue.
- Go to Redcliffe Castle and accept mages as conscripts.
- Go to Therinfal Redoubt and ally with the templars.
- Say you'll be a "servant of faith" when made Inquisitor.
- Exile the Wardens after securing Adamant.
- Support Gaspard at the Winter Palace.
- Empress Celene dies at the Winter Palace.
- Drink from the Well of Sorrows.

Approval Lost

- Take the mountain path in the Frostback Mountains during the prologue.
- Go to Redcliffe Castle and ally with the mages.
- Go to Therinfal Redoubt and disband the Templar Order.
- Say you'll "do it for my own power" when made Inquisitor.
- Allow the Wardens to join the Inquisition after Adamant.
- Support Briala at the Winter Palace.
- Allow Morrigan to drink from the Well of Sorrows.

ROMANCE

Seeker Pentaghast is a very determined and focused woman, seemingly too busy for and uninterested in a romantic relationship. However, if you're playing as a male character (of any race) it's possible to eventually win Cassandra's affection. Start out by building approval and flirting with her at every opportunity. Complete Cassandra's inner circle quests (Unfinished Business and Promise of Destruction) to continue building approval. Also, be sure to complete her gift quest (Guilty Pleasures), convincing Varric to write a new volume of *Swords & Shields* for Cassandra.

During a conversation in Skyhold, Cassandra informs you that your flirts haven't gone unnoticed. But she remains conflicted. She wants an ideal storybook romance. As the Herald of Andraste, she feels you simply can't be that man. The romance can end at this point, but it doesn't have to. Insist that you can be the man she wants to unlock her romance quest, The Ideal Romance.

Once all of Cassandra's inner circle quests are complete, and you've maintained warm approval, you can ask her to meet you somewhere in private, culminating the romance. Following the culmination, you have the option of breaking up with Cassandra or continuing the relationship. If you continue your relationship with Cassandra, no other romances can be started.

SOLAS

Inner Circle Quests:

- Measuring the Veil (Approval)
- All New, Faded for Her (Personal Plot)
- What Lies Dormant (Personal Plot)

Romance: Inquisitor must be female elf.

Solas has spent his life as an apostate, living in the wilderness well away from the civilized world and those who would shackle him for what he is. He mastered his magic without the help of tutors, spending years exploring the spirit realm of the Fade and coming to an understanding of its denizens that few others could claim. He would be happiest left alone to sleep in ancient ruins, searching for memories and knowledge that has been lost for ages, but the Breach in the sky threatens all worlds.

At a time when other mages flee into hiding, Solas has put his freedom at risk by emerging from the shadows to assist those who would combat the chaos. He will not stand idly by when his knowledge of the arcane could mean the difference between salvation and utter destruction.

NOTE Reference the Inner Circle Quests section of the Exploration chapter for more details on each party member's personal plot, gift, and romance quests.

Starting Abilities

Ability	Name	Description
	Barrier	You create a shimmering protective barrier that acts as temporary additional health. The barrier decays naturally over time.
	Winter's Grasp	You lock a target in a sheet of ice, freezing it in place.

Specialization

Rift Mage: Years spent studying the Fade have given Solas the ability to manipulate its energies in unpredictable ways. He can pull matter from the Fade and even twist the Veil into a weapon to hammer his opponents.

First Encounter

During the prologue, you run into Solas and Varric at the first Fade rift—Solas shows you how to use the mark on your hand to close the rift. As the first mage you encounter, Solas offers a welcome mix of skills and abilities, including Barrier. As you continue your adventure in the Hinterlands, use Solas's staff to defeat elemental barriers and his veilfire skill to reveal ancient runic writings—this unlocks different rune schematics.

Approval

The key to winning approval with Solas is to show that you are thoughtful and inclined to see shades of gray in the world. Declaring things to be simple black-and-white matters will earn Solas's disapproval quickly, but asking many questions and looking for more information will impress him. He prefers the thoughtful approach in most situations, and does not approve of you claiming to be sent by Andraste in order to win alliances. You can improve Solas's opinion of you by finding elven artifacts and activating them in order to get a more accurate measurement of the strength of the Veil. These are scattered around the world, but Solas will point them out when you are near one.

Approval Gained

- Go to Redcliffe Castle and ally with the mages.
- At Therinfal Redoubt, accept the templars as conscripts or allies.
- Exile the Wardens after securing Adamant.
- Gain enough court approval (85+) to have Florianne arrested at the Winter Palace.
- Perform the rituals at the Temple of Mythal.
- Accept alliance with Abelas at the Temple of Mythal.
- Allow Morrigan to drink from the Well of Sorrows at the Temple of Mythal.

Approval Lost

- Go to Redcliffe Castle and conscript the mages.
- Say you're a "servant of faith" when made Inquisitor.
- Say you'll "do it for my own power" when made Inquisitor.
- Allow the Wardens to join the Inquisition after securing Adamant.
- Support Briala at the Winter Palace.
- Ignore the rituals at the Temple of Mythal.
- Refuse an alliance with Abelas at the Temple of Mythal.
- Drink from the Well of Sorrows at the Temple of Mythal.

Romance

Once you have asked Solas all about himself and impressed him, you can go with him from Skyhold to Haven for a talk about your first meeting. If you have flirted with him before and are a female elf, you can choose to kiss him here, which opens up the possibility of romance.

After the talk at Haven, Solas will give his plot—a spirit friend has been summoned by mages against its will, and Solas wishes to go free it. If you can free the spirit from its imprisonment without killing it in combat, Solas will approve strongly. Failing to even try to free the spirit will cause Solas to disapprove strongly, and if you are not appropriately apologetic later, you will cut off any chance of romance.

Once his plot is complete and his approval is high enough, Solas will ask you about yourself, confessing himself surprised by your intelligence and thoughtful nature. You can choose to officially begin the romance here. After completing the Temple of Mythal, Solas will talk with you about the future and then ask to spend time together in a scene that marks the culmination of your romance.

VIVIENNE

Inner Circle Quests:

- The Imperial Enchanter (Acquisition)
- Favors the First Enchanter (Approval)
- Bring Me the Heart of Snow White (Personal Plot)

Romance: Not available.

Referred to as Madame de Fer, "the Lady of Iron," Vivienne lives up to her title. A leader among the mages and official enchanter to the Imperial court, she is renowned as a fearsome woman who achieved her position through guile and deft political maneuvering. Vivienne allows nothing to stand in the way of what she desires—not those who claim she is a social climber, not those who seek to restrict her power, not even her fellow mages who would conscript her into a rebellion with which she disagrees. Vivienne fights to restore order in a world gone mad...so long as that leaves her among those left standing, once all is said and done.

> SPECIALIZATION

Knight-Enchanter: Whether it's high fashion or the battlefield, Vivienne prefers to be at the forefront and in control of everything around her. She will personally see order restored—by the blade, if necessary.

> FIRST ENCOUNTER

During your first visit to Val Royeaux, seek out a Circle mage messenger to receive an invitation, unlocking the quest The Imperial Enchanter. This invite allows your party to travel to the chateau of Duke Bastien de Ghyslain, where you meet Vivienne. As the leader of the last loyal mages of Thedas, she feels compelled to join the Inquisition—accept her request to add Vivienne as a party member.

> APPROVAL

Vivienne cannot be romanced, but she holds strong opinions, which can lead to major swings in approval depending on your conversation options and actions. She has a strong need for order and discipline. As such, instability caused by the Breach is a major concern. In addition to sealing the Breach, she wants the mage rebellion crushed and the Circle restored to power. Nothing more, nothing less. She is also very skeptical of Cole and Morrigan's true intentions.

Approval Gained

- At Redcliffe Castle, conscript the mages.
- At Therinfal Redoubt, ally with the templars.
- Say you'll be a "servant of faith" when made Inquisitor.
- Say you'll "set an example as a mage" when made Inquisitor.
- Exile the Wardens after securing Adamant.
- Drink from the Well of Sorrows at the Temple of Mythal.

Approval Lost

- At Redcliffe Castle, ally with the mages.
- At Therinfal Redoubt, disband the templars.
- Allow the Wardens to join the Inquisition after securing Adamant.
- Support Gaspard or Briala at the Winter Palace.
- Allow Morrigan to drink from the Well of Sorrows at the Temple of Mythal.

Inner Circle Quests:

- A Friend of Red Jenny (Acquisition)
- The Verchiel March (Personal Plot)
- A Woman Who Wants for Nothing (Gift Plot)

Romance: Inquisitor must be female of any race.

Sera is impulsive and revels in the moment. For her, it's not about what's right, it's about what's right now. In the Friends of Red Jenny, she humbled the authorities and had fun doing it. But now the nobility are being not just selfish but blind. War, demons, a torn sky: These are more than troubling—they're terrifying. Fortunately, Sera and her "friends" can be frightening, too, and if she needs to put an arrow through some baddies so regular people can sleep at night, so be it. Sera fights for those caught in the middle, but she also needs order restored. The world has to be normal so she can play.

SPECIALIZATION

Tempest: With a satchel of dirty tricks, Sera takes the fight to her opponents before they know they're in it, committing fast and hard—and if covered in alchemical fire, all the better.

FIRST ENCOUNTER

Sera can be recruited during the first visit to Val Royeaux in the quest A Friend of Red Jenny. Search the market for the clues left by "friends" of Red Jenny. The clues lead to a secluded courtyard accessed from the world map and sudden combat with enemies who are very surprised you found them. After the combat, Sera wants to join the Inquisition. The Friends of Red Jenny provide a thread of chaos to the Inquisition, providing resources and contacts in unexpected places. Her network is a rumor mill, drawing from disgruntled servants across Thedas. She wants to get things back to normal so people are safe and she can go back to her fun.

APPROVAL

Sera likes helping people who deserve help, and mouthing off to people who don't—she's immediately suspicious of nobles and titles. Stealing is fine if the target is rich. Taking from the weak pisses her off. She hates people who presume they talk for groups, especially when it is assumed that she is a member of that group. Make choices that mess with nobles, because she thinks they are entitled and abusive. Sera supports liberty, but she fears and distrusts magic and demons. So that liberty doesn't apply to mages without some hefty caveats attached. Individual mages are fine, though. Appeals to tradition fall flat with her. Acting "elfy" annoys her—letting Solas talk or asking his opinion annoys her. Sera likes profit and finding caches left for Red Jenny.

Approval Gained

- At Redcliffe Castle, conscript the mages.
- At Therinfal Redoubt, disband the Templar Order.
- Say you'll "fight for order not faith" when made Inquisitor.
- Say "because it's right" when made Inquisitor.
- Say "Corypheus must be stopped" when made Inquisitor.
- Say "lead them to vengeance" when made Inquisitor.
- Say "a dwarf (or Qunari) will stand for us all" when made Inquisitor.
- Allow the Grey Wardens to join the Inquisition after securing Adamant.
- Everyone lives at the Winter Palace.
- Gain enough court approval (85+) to have Florianne arrested at the Winter Palace.
- Refuse alliance with Abelas at the Temple of Mythal.
- Allow Morrigan to drink from the Well of Sorrows at the Temple of Mythal.
- Agree that events at the Temple of Mythal are nonsense.
- Full agreement after Sera's personal plot.
- Complete romance culmination.

Approval Lost

- At Redcliffe Castle, ally with the mages.
- At Therinfal Redoubt, ally with the templars.
- Say you'll be "a servant of faith" when made Inquisitor.
- Say "an elf will stand for us all" when made Inquisitor.
- Exile the Grey Wardens after securing Adamant (major loss of approval if Blackwall is exiled with Wardens).
- Support Briala at the Winter Palace.
- Allow Empress Celene to be assassinated at the Winter Palace.
- Accept an alliance with Abelas at the Temple of Mythal.
- Drink from the Well of Sorrows at the Temple of Mythal.
- Argue with Sera after the Temple of Mythal.
- Blame Sera after completing her personal plot.
- Break up with Sera in the romance culmination scene.

> FRIENDSHIP

If approval is warm, Sera warms up by taking you down to her level, playing pranks on the advisors of the Inquisition so the leadership seems more human. She wants you to play along but is genuinely surprised and pleased if that happens.

After approval is warm, and once you exhaust Sera's hub topics and reach friend approval, Sera realizes she's got a chance at a home with the Inquisition, and she invites you to try to make new good memories to replace old ones. With cookies. On a roof. This can result in a shouting match but still positive approval, because friendship/romance with Sera can involve passionate fighting. So be honest if it seems foolish, but also be willing to accept that this is just how Sera is, and maybe that's the fun part.

> ROMANCE

Sera's romance is silly, sweet, and sometimes confusing. The basic structure is to flirt when the romance option appears and chat her up by going through her hub topics. Qunari Inquisitors will find approval rises quickly on the flirts. Dwarven and human players won't have it as easy as the Qunari (2x minor gains), but they still fare better than elves (minor gain). Sera is cautious about the expectations of an elf-elf pairing.

If approval is positive, a romance option will open up. You can ask about romance and she'll say maybe. Her personal plot (The Verchiel March) and warm conversation have to be complete before the romance can start. If you're in a romance with anyone else, she'll say you have to talk to them first—she's nobody's second and she doesn't share. When approval is warm, the romance starts from the dialogue hub, so go back and check again after major decisions. If hub topics are continually exhausted as you chat her up, the gift plot (A Woman Who Wants for Nothing) will start—be sure to bring Vivienne and respond positively to her unorthodox suggestion to get bonus content with Sera.

The culmination is only after the friendship conversation and friend hub topics, so keep up that approval. The culmination means you're accepting Sera on her terms, while challenging her to accept her feelings about you as well. Sera doesn't come up—you have to join her on her level.

CAUTION Sera cannot accept what goes on in Mythal. If your character is determined to believe what went on there, it spells the end for the romance.

Nicknames

Sera initially gives her lover the nickname "Inky" when the romance starts. You get one chance to randomly change it in the romance-start conversation, but random means random, and Sera may just decide to keep it the same. You get one other chance in her hub that will change it, but which one is selected is randomly determined.

- Inky (default)
- Shiny
- Tadwinks
- Teetness
- Buckles

If you complete the romance culmination scene, and if you're at a loss for words and just flat out say "Love is the best," Sera gives you a new nickname. If you like a particular nickname, keep Sera away from Cole—they have a banter that will "ruin" the current one, and Sera will randomly change it to one of the others.

The Bad Breakup

You can break up with Sera at a number of points, including off her hub. Most have no lasting animosity, like it was a fling. But there is a special check for "the bad breakup" that locks out a couple of friend hub topics and changes her "can we be friends" response. The Inquisitor and Sera have a bad breakup:

- If you break up with her in the hostile confrontation (only possible pre-culmination with extremely low approval). The romance can't be saved, but she can be convinced to stay. If you drive her down to hostile again, however, she's just leaving. This conversation sets approval to cold.
- If you break up with her during the culmination scene.
- If you break up with her at Mythal (or she breaks up with the player).
- If you break up with her after having romanced her through both her friend conversation and the Mythal conversation. This assumes you have arbitrarily chosen to break up a relationship that has been going for some time.

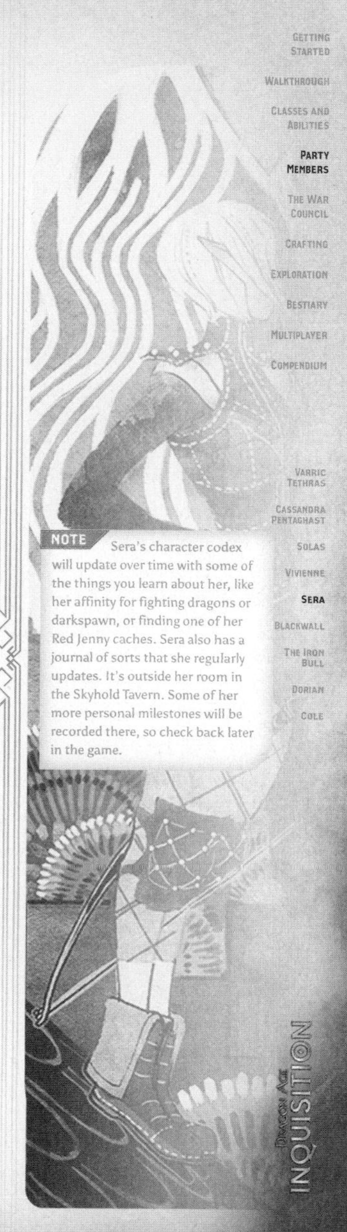

NOTE Sera's character codex will update over time with some of the things you learn about her, like her affinity for fighting dragons or darkspawn, or finding one of her Red Jenny caches. Sera also has a journal of sorts that she regularly updates. It's outside her room in the Skyhold Tavern. Some of her more personal milestones will be recorded there, so check back later in the game.

Inner Circle Quests:

- The Lone Warden (Acquisition)
- Memories of the Grey (Approval)
- Explanations (Gift Plot)
- Revelations (Personal Plot)

Romance: Inquisitor must be female of any race.

The Grey Wardens hold a lonely vigil, enduring lives of hardship and sacrifice to protect the world from an evil that can never truly be conquered. Few would volunteer for this: the suffering, isolation, and promise of a violent death. But the path of a Warden is also one of valor, and those who give themselves to the cause are rewarded with the knowledge that they have become something more than they were. Blackwall is one of the rare few Wardens who choose, of their own accord, to pick up the shield. He believes so wholeheartedly in the noble ideal of the Grey Wardens that he would rather have this life than any other.

SPECIALIZATION

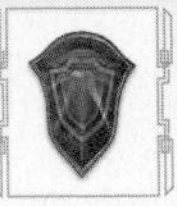

Champion: Blackwall has sworn to give his life to protect his friends and allies. He puts himself between them and danger, and his experience and resolve let him stand against attacks that would fell weaker warriors.

FIRST ENCOUNTER

You first learn of Blackwall from Leliana, following your return from Val Royeaux—this unlocks the quest The Lone Warden. Follow Leliana's lead to find Blackwall training Warden recruits by Lake Luthias in the Hinterlands. After you help him and his recruits drive off an attacking band of mercenaries, Blackwall offers to join the Inquisition. Take him up on his offer and consider adding him to your party immediately. You must recruit Blackwall before Adamant. Otherwise he won't be available.

APPROVAL

Blackwall approves of helping others, whenever possible. He believes the Inquisition has a responsibility to make the world a better place. While huge troubles like war and the Breach are a concern, he doesn't want to see the Inquisitor shutting eyes to the suffering of the average person either. Blackwall also likes to see the Inquisitor give people a second chance, even if they have done terrible things in the past. Summary executions of those the Inquisitor considers enemies may cause him to disapprove.

Approval Gained

- Ally with the mages or the templars.
- Say "because it's right" when made Inquisitor.
- Allow the Grey Wardens to join the Inquisition after securing Adamant.
- Support Gaspard at the Winter Palace.
- Gain enough court approval (85+) to have Florianne arrested at the Winter Palace.
- Save Empress Celene's life at the Winter Palace.
- Drink from the Well of Sorrows at the Temple of Mythal (if Blackwall is not in a romance with Inquisitor).
- Morrigan drinks from the Well of Sorrows at the Temple of Mythal (if Blackwall is in a romance with Inquisitor).

Approval Lost

- Force either the mages or the templars to surrender and serve the Inquisition.
- Say you'll "do it for my own power" when made Inquisitor.
- Exile the Grey Wardens after securing Adamant.
- Support Briala at the Winter Palace.
- Refuse an alliance with Abelas at the Temple of Mythal.
- Allow Empress Celene to be assassinated at the Winter Palace.

ROMANCE

You can flirt with Blackwall early, from the moment he is recruited. All you have to do is pick the options with the romance icons. Blackwall will flirt back initially, thinking the flirts harmless.

Speak to Blackwall after the destruction of Haven. Here, when you express fondness for him, he pulls back. He realizes that the relationship might be progressing, and though he is attracted to you, he thinks indulging his feelings is inappropriate. You can try to persuade him, but he will leave, telling you that the dalliance shouldn't continue. To continue the romance, you must maintain a positive approval with Blackwall and complete his quests.

To obtain Blackwall's gift plot, speak to him in the stables at Skyhold once you've obtained adequate positive approval. Here he reveals he has something to show you in the Storm Coast, unlocking Explanations. Go with him to the Storm Coast and recover a badge. from his previous life.

Just when the relationship seems to be progressing well, Blackwall leaves Skyhold and the party, triggering the start of his personal plot, Revelations. Clues point you to Val Royeaux. Once in Val Royeaux, you're shown a scene with Blackwall. After the scene, you can go to the prison to speak with him and decide how to resolve the situation. Allowing Blackwall back into the Inquisition requires doing a mission on the war table and judging Blackwall. For the romance to continue, you must either send Blackwall to the Grey Wardens or tell him he is free to choose his own path. With Blackwall back in the Inquisition, you can culminate the romance by speaking to him at the stables in Skyhold, leading to a scene in your quarters.

THE IRON BULL

Inner Circle Quests:
- The Captain of the Chargers (Acquisition)
- Demands of the Qun (Personal Plot)
- Tough Love (Romance Plot)

Romance: Inquisitor can be any gender or race.

Qunari are known across Thedas as the brutal horned giants who descended from the north to nearly conquer the continent. These ruthless followers of a harsh philosophy enforce their will through the Ben-Hassrath: their spies and secret police. One brilliant agent did it all, hunting spies, rebels, and deserters until the day he finally broke. To preserve a valuable asset, his superiors sent him to Orlais to observe and report—and the Iron Bull was born.

Today, Bull's Chargers are famous mercenaries, fiercely loyal to the huge Qunari warrior who leads them into battles and taverns with equal enthusiasm. The Iron Bull still sends the Ben-Hassrath reports, but years of living outside Qunari rules have him wondering which identity is really him. Whoever he is, he's more than happy to join the Inquisition and get paid to kill demons.

SPECIALIZATION

Reaver: The Iron Bull's combat style has honed his aggression and anger to a killing edge. He has learned to turn his own pain into a fury that makes him even deadlier when the fight gets bloody.

FIRST ENCOUNTER

After addressing the clerics in Val Royeaux, speak to Krem standing outside the Chantry in Haven. He invites you to come to the Storm Coast and meet his commander, Iron Bull—this unlocks the quest The Captain of the Chargers. Before you can go to the Storm Coast, you must first scout it on the war table. Once at the Storm Coast, help Iron Bull and his Chargers eliminate a group of Tevinter mercenaries. Afterward, Iron Bull offers his group's services to the Inquisition. But he makes one thing clear: He is an agent of the Ben-Hassrath and will be reporting on the Inquisition's activities. If you're comfortable with having a Ben-Hassrath spy in your midst, welcome Iron Bull and his Chargers to the Inquisition.

APPROVAL

Iron Bull enjoys being brought along on missions and fighting good fights against tough enemies. He is fairly easy to win over, as he is inclined to support you and the Inquisition regardless of most of your choices. You can impress him (or at least entertain him) by fighting Venatori forces, and he will be incredibly grateful if you kill a dragon with him in the party. You have many chances to flirt with Bull, and in almost every case, Bull appears to completely miss the fact that you are flirting with him. Stay strong!

Approval Gained

- At Redcliffe Castle, make the rebel mages surrender and serve the Inquisition.
- At Therinfal Redoubt, accept the templars as allies.
- Allow the Grey Wardens to join the Inquisition after securing Adamant.
- Support Gaspard or Celene at the Winter Palace.
- Gain enough court approval (85+) to have Florianne arrested at the Winter Palace.
- Allow Empress Celene to be assassinated at the Winter Palace.
- Skip the rituals at the Temple of Mythal.
- Drink from the Well of Sorrows at the Temple of Mythal.

Approval Lost

- At Redcliffe Castle, accept the rebel mages as allies.
- At Therinfal Redoubt, disband the Templar Order.
- Exile the Wardens after securing Adamant.
- Allow Morrigan to drink from the Well of Sorrows at the Temple of Mythal.

ROMANCE

You can talk with Bull about his past, and once your approval is high enough, you can learn about his work in Seheron. This soon opens up his plot, Demands of the Qun, which offers a chance for an alliance with the Ben-Hassrath against the Venatori by taking out a Venatori smuggling ship. The plot offers a major choice that affects Bull's character, but neither option causes him to disapprove of you or ends a romance.

Once Bull's plot is complete and you have won Bull's approval, you get a scene reacting to the events of the plot, with Bull either reminiscing about the Chargers or dealing with Ben-Hassrath assassins. After this conversation is complete, if you have flirted with Bull on previous occasions, then the next time you speak with Bull, he will show up in your room to talk with you. If you are interested, confirm that you want to have sex. When that scene is done, speak with Bull again and ask to talk about what happened, and Bull will discuss the rules of your relationship, if you choose to pursue one. If you're interested, you can now begin a relationship with him.

Once you have begun your relationship, you can talk with Bull about the ramifications. If you wish to make things more serious, Bull talks about a special Qunari item—a necklace made from a dragon's tooth. Find a dragon, kill it, and visit the requisitions table to make its tooth into a necklace. Speak with Bull and choose to give him the gift. You'll be jumped to a scene where your relationship with Bull becomes public, and you have the chance to declare that it was just a fling (and end the romance) or to commit to it and give Bull his gift. After that, you and Bull are officially together for all the world to see, and you can later spend time with him if you wish for a final private moment.

DORIAN

Inner Circle Quests:

- One Less Venatori (Approval)
- Last Resort of Good Men (Personal Plot)
- The Magister's Birthright (Romance Plot)

Romance: Inquisitor must be male of any race.

Being from a proud bloodline of the Tevinter Imperium has its advantages: Dorian was born with a flair for magic that made him the envy of his peers. He is charming and confident, his wit as sharp as any blade, and if some suggest his manner cocky, it could be attributed to being a powerful mage in a land where mages rule. Indeed, Dorian would be the pride of his family—if he didn't oppose everything his homeland has come to stand for. He wears the labels of "pariah" and "outcast" proudly, knowing that views of the Imperium are unlikely to change until and unless someone of his ability stands up to make a difference.

> SPECIALIZATION

Necromancer: Dorian is well-versed in spells that bind and manipulate Fade spirits, a practice that does not have the same stigma in the Tevinter Imperium as it does elsewhere in Thedas.

> FIRST ENCOUNTER

Your first encounter with Dorian differs based on whether you chose to ally with the rebel mages or templars. If you chose In Hushed Whispers, Dorian is first encountered inside Redcliffe village's chantry after you've met Alexius. Here Dorian informs you of Alexius's devious plan and offers to help stop him. After your time-bending adventure through Redcliffe Castle, Dorian offers to stay and help the Inquisition. If you chose to pursue the templars in Champions of the Just, Dorian isn't encountered until you return to Haven after defeating the envy demon in Therinfal Redoubt. Dorian is the one who arrives at Haven's main gate to warn you of Corypheus's attack. Later, at Skyhold, you can speak to Dorian in the library and ask him to join the Inquisition.

> APPROVAL

Dorian is the ultimate rebel and nonconformist. He has embraced his "deviant" status by leaving home and actively working to reform the Imperium, even if that means he must do it from outside. Dorian approves of witty retorts and clever decision-making—especially when these decisions support mages and his efforts to reform Tevinter. While critical of the Imperium himself, Dorian takes exception when others disparage Tevinter. Blunt and aggressive responses also annoy him. Having seen firsthand what became of his mentor, Alexius, Dorian is wary of blood magic and any other forbidden uses of magic.

Approval Gained

- Ally with the rebel mages at Redcliffe.
- Say "Corypheus must be stopped" when made Inquisitor.
- Allow the Grey Wardens to join the Inquisition after securing Adamant.
- Gain enough court approval (85+) to have Florianne arrested at the Winter Palace.
- Reunite Celene and Briala at the Winter Palace.
- Allow Celene to be assassinated at the Winter Palace.
- Ally with Abelas at the Temple of Mythal.
- Defeat Calpernia without fighting at the Temple of Mythal.
- Allow Morrigan to drink from the Well of Sorrows at the Temple of Mythal (major approval if Dorian is in a romance with the Inquisitor)

Approval Lost

- Conscript the mages at Redcliffe.
- Disband or ally with the templars at Therinfal Redoubt.
- Make Alexius tranquil in his judgment.
- Say you'll "do it for my own power" when made Inquisitor.
- Exile the Grey Wardens after securing Adamant.
- Kill Ponchard during Dorian's romance gift plot.
- Choose Gaspard as the next emperor of Orlais.
- Refuse an alliance with Abelas at the Temple of Mythal.
- Drink from the Well of Sorrows at the Temple of Mythal (increased disapproval if Dorian is in a romance with the Inquisitor)

> ROMANCE

Dorian is a natural flirt in his conversations with women. But he maintains a respectful distance from men, fully aware that not every man will reciprocate his interest. However, if playing as a male Inquisitor you can fire back with your own flirts to indicate you're interested in being more than just friends.

The romance doesn't officially begin until after you've completed Dorian's personal plot, Last Resort of Good Men. Indicate your intentions to Dorian at the end of this quest or during a conversation at Skyhold. Once the romance has begun, you receive a message from Leliana, initiating Dorian's romance plot, The Magister's Birthright. But be careful when completing this quest; killing Ponchard ends not only the quest but also your romance with Dorian.

If the romance is still active following The Magister's Birthright, speak to Dorian in Skyhold. When Dorian suggests returning to your quarters, do so to culminate the romance. Your romance with Dorian is not popular with the Chantry, and Dorian feels you may be putting your personal interests ahead of the Inquisition's. You can call off the relationship at any point.

COLE

Inner Circle Quests:

- The Forgotten Boy (Acquisition)
- Subjected to His Will (Personal Plot)

Romance: Not available.

He is a ghost in the shadows, walking unnoticed through crowds. He can slit an enemy's throat before they even realize he's there, then slip away, never to be seen again. Those few who do notice him soon forget he ever existed...and Cole isn't certain that he does exist. He is a spirit, impossibly caught between the immaterial realm of the Fade and the confusing realities of our physical world, but does that make him real? Does it make him human or a demonic pretender, as some believe?

All Cole knows for certain is that the world is full of pain and he must find his place within it. Those who wish to restore order and help the helpless will find him a strange but unwavering ally. Those who use their power for selfish reasons may never see Cole again—if they remember that he was there to begin with.

SPECIALIZATION

Assassin: As a spirit dedicated to mercy, Cole is oddly suited to killing enemies with speed and precision. He can eliminate targets too dangerous to face directly with strikes they never even notice.

FIRST ENCOUNTER

Like Dorian, Cole can be encountered in a couple of different ways. If you chose to pursue an alliance with the templars, in Champions of the Just, Cole appears in the nightmare world, helping you escape and defeat the envy demon. After you return to Haven, Cole appears in the war room, giving you the opportunity to recruit him. If you chose to ally with the rebel mages, you don't encounter Cole until Haven is attacked by Corypheus—it's Cole who arrives at Haven's gate to warn you of the incoming attack. When the Inquisition regroups at Skyhold, look for Cole in the courtyard and give him the chance to join the Inquisition.

APPROVAL

Created from compassion, sensitive to the pain of others, Cole is a raw nerve, trying to help people in a world he does not fully understand. He is unsure about his past, knowing only that he wants to stay and help people. Cole is appreciative when you go out of your way to help those in need. These tasks may not advance the cause of the Inquisition, but they're met with Cole's approval.

Because he's a spirit, you gain approval from Cole for helping the helpless even if he's not present or even recruited. Completing quests to help people before recruiting Cole provides a large starting bonus to Cole's approval once he joins the Inquisition. Completing quests after recruiting Cole, but without Cole present, provides a normal approval bonus.

Also, during judgments, be wary of locking up prisoners. Events during *Dragon Age: Asunder* have led Cole to think of dungeons as a fate worse than death, and his approval drops accordingly.

Approval Gained

- At Redcliffe Castle, ally with the mages.
- At Therinfal Redoubt, disband the Templar Order.
- Exile the Grey Wardens after securing Adamant.
- Support Briala at the Winter Palace.
- Reunite Celene and Briala at the Winter Palace.
- Everyone lives at the Winter Palace.
- Gain enough court approval (85+) to have Florianne arrested at the Winter Palace.
- Ally with Abelas at the Temple of Mythal.
- The Inquisitor or Morrigan drinks from the Well of Sorrows at the Temple of Mythal.

Approval Lost

- At Redcliffe Castle, conscript the mages.
- At Therinfal Redoubt, ally with the templars.
- Allow the Grey Wardens to join the Inquisition after securing Adamant.
- Support Gaspard at the Winter Palace.
- Allow Empress Celene to be assassinated at the Winter Palace.
- Refuse alliance with Abelas at the Temple of Mythal.

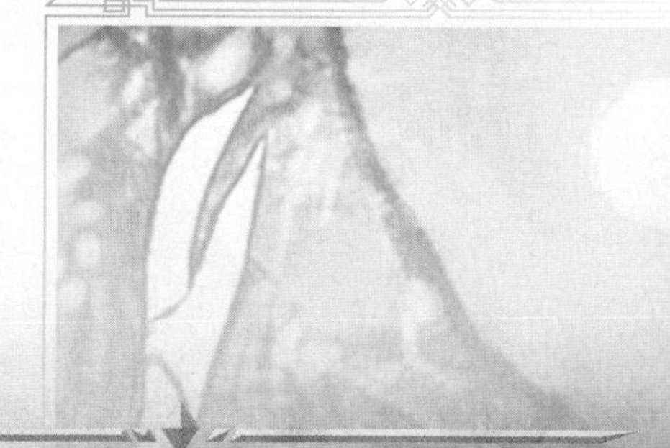

THE WAR COUNCIL

In the Inquisition, the war council is the governing body responsible for making the tough decisions necessary to restore order. The war council consists of Cassandra, Cullen, Leliana, Josephine, and you, the Inquisitor. Whether in Haven or Skyhold, the war council meets in a dedicated chamber, gathering around the war table. It is within this chamber that key decisions are made, operations are assigned, and Inquisition perks are allocated. However, the war council is not a democracy. As Inquisitor, it's up to you to determine how the Inquisition utilizes its power and influence.

IMPORTANT NOTE Please refer to the eGuide for detailed information about war table operations.

The eGuide access code is included on a page in the Standard Edition guide, on the back sheet of the Collector's Edition guide, and on a card in the Inquisitor's Edition guide.

ADVISORS

Cullen, Leliana, and Josephine are indispensable advisors to the Inquisition, relying on their experience and connections to provide insight on a variety of topics. But these three rarely see eye to eye, often arguing over the best course of action. As Inquisitor, it's your job to take the advice from these advisors and make the decision you feel is best. In addition to providing intelligence and advice, the advisors are tasked with fulfilling the orders of the Inquisitor. Even if they don't always agree with your decisions, the advisors are loyal and will do their best to make your will a reality.

CULLEN

Inner Circle Quests:

- Perseverance (Personal Plot)
- Happier Times (Gift Plot)
- Before the Dawn (Samson nemesis quest)

Romance: Inquisitor must be female human or elf.

Cullen has seen the worst that magic and corruption can do to innocent people. Trained from a young age, he has devoted more than half his life in service to the Templar Order. He saw the Ferelden Circle fall during the Blight and was witness to the mage-templar conflict that tore Kirkwall apart. In the aftermath, it was Cullen who rallied what remained of Kirkwall's templars to restore order to the devastated city. His leadership and integrity caught the attention of Cassandra Pentaghast, who recognized in him a vital component in forming the Inquisition. Now the world is falling into chaos. Cullen is through waiting for others to act, and he's determined that the Inquisition will make a difference for the people of Thedas.

Romance

If playing as a female elf or human, you can initiate a romantic relationship with Cullen. Take every opportunity to flirt with Cullen during conversations to progress the romance. However, these conversation options will not arise if you're currently in a relationship with someone else. If you want to pursue Cullen, call off any other relationships first.

Because he's a templar, lyrium is a very sensitive subject for Cullen. If you want to keep the possibility of a romance open, never order Cullen to take lyrium. If you persist in ordering Cullen to take lyrium, change your mind in the follow-up or tell him he can find a better way after the war. If you order Cullen to take lyrium, he will break up with you, or if the relationship hasn't started, it will now be impossible.

If you want to end the relationship with Cullen, you can do so by speaking to him in Skyhold (choose "We need to end this.") You can also break up with him during a heightened moment during his romance arc.

NOTE Unlike party members, advisors are not affected by the approval system—you cannot gain or lose approval with them. So you don't need to warm up to them in the same way before pursuing a romance. Instead, focus on flirtatious conversation options to advance the relationship.

LELIANA

Inner Circle Quests:

- The Left Hand of the Divine (Personal Plot)
- Under Her Skin (Calpernia nemesis quest)

Romance: Not Available.

She has many names. Most know her as "Sister Nightingale" or "the Left Hand of the Divine." To the rare friend, she is Leliana. They say she found faith amid darkness, and that her devotion to the Maker is matched only by her devotion to Divine Justinia V, a woman who is both mentor and savior. Those who have earned her loyalty know her as a steadfast ally. But enemies of the Divine know to fear her, for she is the shadow behind the Sunburst Throne—the one who watches and waits, who strikes when her mark is most vulnerable and least suspecting.

JOSEPHINE

Inner Circle Quests:

- Of Somewhat Fallen Fortune (Personal Plot)
- Heraldry From a Herald (Gift Plot)
- An Unexpected Engagement (Romance Plot)

Romance: Inquisitor can be any race or gender.

The Inquisition's power is not absolute: It must earn its place among the forces in conflict. Sister Leliana understands this well and has called on an old friend, Lady Josephine Montilyet, to be the Inquisition's ambassador in the halls of the influential. The eldest daughter of a noble Antivan family, Josephine is a rising star among diplomats, skilled at forging alliances with tact, grace, and carefully cultivated favors. She is a consummate planner who understands that resurrecting the Inquisition will require support and goodwill from Thedas's movers and shakers. Fortunately, the ambassador enjoys a challenge, and she sincerely believes that the Inquisition is the best way to halt the chaos sweeping Thedas.

Romance

Josephine can enter a romance with an Inquisitor of any race or gender. Talk to Josephine in Skyhold, and when romance options come up, take them. At some point Josephine will tell you Leliana wanted to speak with you—go to Leliana after that, and she'll ask you about your romantic intentions toward Josephine. Return to Josephine after that talk with Leliana, and that will trigger the conversations where you can choose to start the romance. You will now see a few new conversation options with Josephine. Taking them and coming back to speak with her advances the plot of the romance.

If you want to end the relationship with Josephine, speak to her at her desk in Skyhold. Choose "Let's talk about us" and then tell her you want to end things to permanently call off the romance. You can also break up with her during a crucial moment in her romance plot. Both these options have a broken-heart icon to indicate this will break off your romantic relationship with Josephine.

MORRIGAN: LIAISON TO THE INQUISITION

Whether the dark-haired sorceress seeks to influence the Imperial throne or harbors more sinister motives, no one knows for certain. This Witch of the Wilds arrived in Orlais rather suddenly three years ago as the newly appointed "arcane advisor" to Empress Celene. In this role, Morrigan presents a source of information unfiltered by religious dogma, and she satisfies Celene's lifelong curiosity about magic. However, whispers carry concern of Morrigan having Celene wrapped around her finger and teaching the empress forbidden, dark arts in secret.

Following events at the Winter Palace in Halamshiral, Morrigan is assigned as an Imperial liaison to the Inquisition. While not a party member or advisor, Morrigan plays a key role as the Inquisition ventures into the Arbor Wilds.

THE WAR TABLE

When the war council convenes, its members gather around the war table, displaying a massive map of southern Thedas. This is where the Inquisition can apply its power across Orlais and Ferelden by conducting operations. You can assign the three advisors to perform operations anywhere there's a marker on the map. Highlight the various markers to browse the available operations. Initially, there are only a handful of operations on the map, but as your Inquisition grows, more operations are unlocked, requiring you to carefully consider the allocation of your advisors. There are two types of operations available on the war table: scouting operations and missions.

SCOUTING OPERATIONS

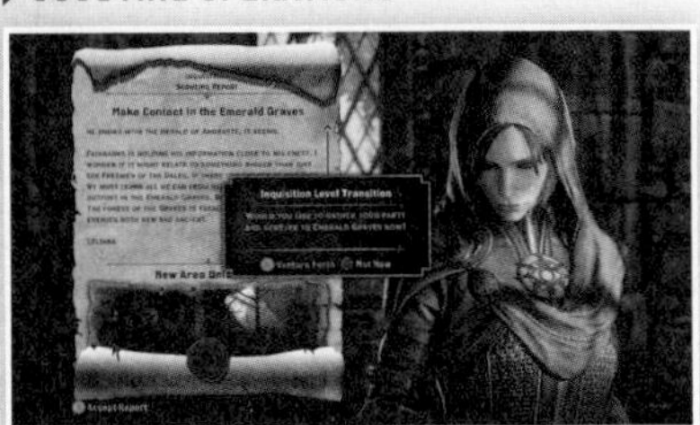

Completing scouting operations unlocks new locales to explore. But you'll need power. All scouting operations have a cost associated with them, requiring a specific amount of power. Power is obtained by completing critical path plots, establishing camps, closing Fade rifts, capturing keeps, finding all landmarks in a locale, or by defeating high dragons. Once you have acquired some power, select a scouting operation on the war table, often marked by a dagger. Here you'll see the cost associated with the scouting operation and choose an advisor to oversee it. Unlike missions, scouting operations do not occupy an advisor's time—they're completed instantaneously. Even if an advisor is already busy conducting a mission, he or she can still perform a scouting operation without interruption.

IMPORTANT NOTE Please refer to the eGuide for detailed information about war table operations.

The eGuide access code is included on a page in the Standard Edition guide, on the back sheet of the Collector's Edition guide, and on a card in the Inquisitor's Edition guide.

MISSIONS

Running the Inquisition becomes increasingly complex as the organization grows. As Inquisitor, you can't be everywhere at once. Fortunately, the advisors (and their agents) are available to conduct missions on their own—you just have to assign them. Missions expand the story of the Inquisition's adventures and earn rewards. Take time to read the details of each available mission and determine the best advisor for the job. Josephine is a diplomat and relies on connections and influence to complete her tasks. Leliana is a spymaster and utilizes her network of agents to collect information. Cullen, a former templar, leads the Inquisition's army and relies on displays of force. Each mission shows how much time it takes for an advisor to complete the task. Some missions take only a few minutes, while others take hours. The advisor who can complete the mission quickest is usually the best suited for the job.

TIP Missions are completed in real time. So if you encounter a mission that will take several hours to complete, consider assigning it before ending your gameplay session. When you come back and restart the game, the mission will probably be complete, assuming enough time has elapsed.

Mission Reports and Rewards

When a mission is complete a notification appears on-screen. Return to the war table and select the mission marker on the map to receive a report—the marker flashes when a report is available. The report details the outcome of the mission and lists any rewards received. Rewards can include gold, influence, equipment, or even approval for certain party members. And the reward you receive may differ depending on the advisor you assigned. You must collect reports from the war table in order for the associated rewards to be applied. Sometimes completing missions unlocks new, follow-up missions on the war table. Like rewards, these follow-up missions won't appear until the previous report is collected. So scan the war table regularly to ensure you're not missing any reports.

INQUISITION RANK

As your Inquisition grows in size and stature, so does its influence and rank. Similar to XP, influence is earned by completing most quests. But instead of leveling up your character, influence levels up the Inquisition. New Inquisition ranks are granted at regular intervals. And with each rank acquired, your Inquisition gains one perk point.

> PERKS

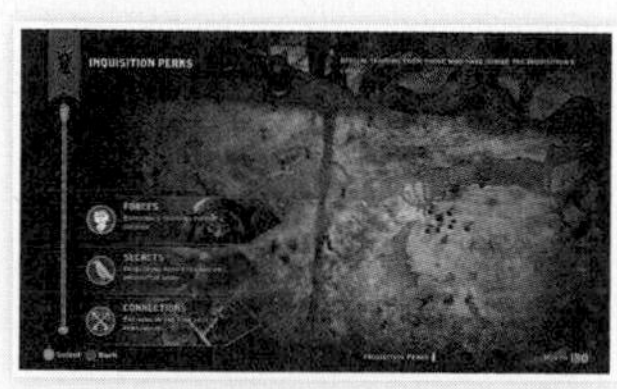

Perk points can be spent to acquire valuable perks, enhancing the Inquisition in specific ways. There are four categories to choose from: Forces, Secrets, Connections, and Inquisition. Within each category are various perks, each with a unique benefit. Some perks directly impact your party in the field, allowing you to carry more healing potions or increasing your party's inventory. Other perks offer more indirect benefits, like those that offer discounts or enhanced inventory from merchants. But not all perks are available to newcomers—some require dedicated investment in the category before they're unlocked. These advanced perks often provide greater benefit, making the investment worthwhile. However, choose your perks carefully—you won't be able to afford them all. In a standard game, you're likely to earn 10 or fewer perk points, and each perk (except for agent perks) costs one point. So consider your options carefully and formulate a long-term game plan to acquire the perks you desire. Study the following tables to view all available perks, including those provided by agents.

Inquisition Ranks

Rank	Equivalent Player Level	Influence Required
1	1-3	0
2	4-6	1,000
3	7-8	3,000
4	9-10	6,000
5	11-12	10,000
6	13-14	15,000
7	15-16	21,000
8	17-18	28,000
9	19-20	36,000
10	20-21	45,000
11	22-23	55,000

NOTE Agent-based perks do not cost perk points but count toward the total points required to unlock advanced perks—so recruit agents to acquire those advanced perks sooner. See the Agents section for more information.

Forces Perks (Cullen)

Name	Description	Prerequisite
Underworld Knowledge	Detailed study of underworld customs and their brutal but practical applications. Opens up new dialogue options related to criminal activities and grants +50% XP for each codex entry unlocked.	—
Massache's Method	A methodology developed by an Orlesian blademaster and used by chevaliers to analyze their own performance in combat. Grants a 5% increase in XP earned from killing foes.	—
Rider's Posture	Training in proper weight distribution during hard riding significantly increases resistance to being unseated.	Invest 2 points in Forces category.
Antivan-Stitched Saddle	Proper tack of fine Antivan leather, custom-fitted to both horse and rider, significantly increases resistance to being unseated.	Rider's Posture
Advanced Focus	Increase maximum focus from 100 to 200. Second-tier focus effect for abilities can now be triggered.	Invest 5 points in Forces category.
Master Focus	Increase maximum focus for all party members from 200 to 300. Third-tier focus effect for abilities can now be triggered.	Advanced Focus
True Grit	Harsh environment training can be dangerous but will harden anyone into a survivor. All party members gain a 10% increase to all defenses.	Capture any keep.
More Healing Potions	Increase the maximum number of potions the party can carry by four.	Invest 3 points in Forces category.
Mage Schematics	Many mages from all over Thedas have joined the Inquisition, hoping for some degree of order and protection. Reverse engineering their robes and staves will provide new, rare schematics.	Invest 4 points in Forces category.
Rogue Schematics	Many of Leliana's new agents bring gear from their previous employers. Gathering their collective gains will provide new, rare schematics.	Invest 4 points in Forces category.
Warrior Schematics	Sellswords, templars, chevaliers: The Inquisition's forces come from wide-ranging backgrounds. Scour the troops' arms and armors for new, rare schematics.	Invest 4 points in Forces category.
Lord Berand (Agent)	Lord Berand of Ferelden has pledged his sword, and those of his forces, to the Inquisition. The addition of those soldiers bolsters the Inquisition's forces. Reduces by 5% the time it takes for Cullen to complete operations.	Recruit Berand.
Clemence, the Tranquil (Agent)	Mage Clemence from Redcliffe is now using his knowledge of minor enchanting to reinforce the Inquisition's defenses. Reduces by 5% the time it takes for Cullen to complete operations.	Recruit Clemence.
The Blades of Hessarian (Agent)	The Blades are unquestioningly loyal and relentless in battle. The group's addition to the Inquisition lends significantly to its forces' strength. Reduces by 5% the time it takes for Cullen to complete operations.	Kill their leader, then recruit the Blades of Hessarian.
Vale's Irregulars (Agent)	Corporal Vale has founded Vale's Irregulars, a company of refugees willing and able to take up arms against the chaos. Reduces by 5% the time it takes Cullen to complete operations.	Recruit Corporal Vale.
Loranil (Agent)	Loranil's involvement with the Inquisition cements an alliance with his clan. The perspective of a Dalish elf also gives the Inquisition's forces an added advantage. Reduces by 5% the time it takes Cullen to complete operations.	Recruit Loranil.

Forces Perks (Cullen) continued

Name	Description	Prerequisite
Michel de Chevin (Agent)	Michel de Chevin, Empress Celene's former champion, brings to the Inquisition his considerable experience as a chevalier. Reduces by 5% the time it takes Cullen to complete operations.	Recruit Michel de Chevin.
Ser Barris (Agent)	Ser Barris's skill and leadership abilities make him indispensable to Cullen. With his understanding of the red templars, he is also well suited to preparing the Inquisition's soldiers for what they will face. Reduces by 5% the time it takes Cullen to complete operations.	Recruit Ser Barris (must survive Therinfal Redoubt)

TIP In the Forces category, consider selecting the More Healing Potions perk to increase the maximum number of healing potions your party can carry from 8 to 12—this can be a lifesaver during tough battles. Advanced Focus and Master Focus are also worth considering, allowing you to gain access to tier 2 and tier 3 focus abilities.

Secrets Perks (Leliana)

Name	Description	Prerequisite
Arcane Knowledge	A detailed study of magic and the places and creatures that interact with it. Opens up new dialogue options related to the Fade or arcane studies. Grants +50% XP for each codex entry unlocked.	—
Optimal Cutting	Detailed studies show how to get the maximum usable harvest from each plant. Grants a 10% chance to receive herbs with each harvest.	—
Eagle-Eyed	Training in spotting where the pattern breaks, in nature or civilization. Grants a significant increase to the discovery range of the searching action.	—
Enhanced Studies	Bolster the number of researchers working to study those who stand against the Inquisition. Grants an additional +50% XP for each foe studied, including those already completed (applied retroactively).	Invest 2 points in Secrets category.
Deft Hands, Fine Tools	The training, gear, and experience working with master locksmiths needed to tackle the toughest and most ingenious locking mechanisms. Allows all rogues in the party to open masterwork locks.	Invest 4 points in Secrets category.
Forward Scouts	With access to a forward training camp, the Inquisition's scouts can receive training to cover a wider area and identify items of interest to the Inquisitor. Reveals additional landmarks and points of interest on the maps of every area.	Capture any keep.
Trainee Herbalists	Gain a collection of tier 1 herbs.	—
Veteran Herbalists	Survival and harsh environment training will push Inquisition herbalists to gather more exotic and rare plants. As part of the training push, a large collection of uncommon herbs will be delivered for personal use.	Trainee Herbalists
Master Herbalists	Combat training, top-line equipment, and experience in both allow Inquisition herbalists to find the rarest of specimens. A large collection of rare herbs will be delivered for personal use.	Veteran Herbalists
Smuggler Tanner (Agent)	Tanner's contacts in the underworld supply the Inquisition with both rare goods and vital information that cannot be obtained elsewhere. Reduces by 5% the time it takes for Leliana to complete operations.	Recruit Tanner.
Witty Ritts (Agent)	Scout Ritts is now under Leliana's commend and has proven herself adept at intelligence-gathering, employing her wit and charm to coax secrets from her targets. Reduces by 5% the time it takes for Leliana to complete operations.	Recruit Ritts.
Servis (Agent)	Servis now aids the Inquisition as an informant. Intelligence from this contacts in the Tevinter Imperium will keep the Inquisition advised of Venatori movement. Reduces by 5% the time it takes for Leliana to complete operations.	Capture and judge Servis.
Frederic of Serault (Agent)	Frederic's extensive research into dragons intrigues scholars all over Thedas and draws them to the Inquisition, which benefits from shard knowledge. Reduces by 5% the time it takes for Leliana to complete operations.	Recruit Frederic.
Speaker Anais (Agent)	Speaker Anais has instructed her followers to spread out and gather information for the Inquisition. Their reports have been extremely useful. Reduces by 5% the time it takes for Leliana to complete operations.	Recruit Anais.
The Eager Recruit (Agent)	The young elven woman from Crestwood has joined the Inquisition. Her enthusiasm and dedication have set her apart from other recruits, and she has found a mentor in one of Leliana's best agents. Reduces by 5% the time it takes for Leliana to complete operations.	Recruit Jana.
A Magister in Disgrace (Agent)	Former Magister Alexius has been pressed into service for the Inquisition, improving its understanding of the arcane with his experience in pushing the boundaries of magic. Reduces by 5% the time it takes for Leliana to complete operations.	Judge and recruit Alexius.

TIP Have you found a door even your rogues can't open? Acquire the Deft Hands, Fine Tools perk to access these restricted areas.

Connections Perks (Josephine)

Name	Description	Prerequisite
Nobility Knowledge	Detailed study of politics, rhetoric, and those who wield them to best effect. Opens up new dialogue options related to nobles and politics. Grants +50% XP for each codex entry unlocked.	—
Sterling Reputation	Thanks to a few well-placed acquaintances and a carefully crafted reputation, merchants will pay the Inquisition 10% more for items sold to them.	—
A Favor for a Favor	From an expanding network of contacts among artisans, suppliers, and noble patrons, merchants will offer the Inquisition a 10% discount on their goods.	—
Elite Clientele	All merchants want to say they once did business with the Inquisition. Shops offer to buy and sell for 15% better prices.	Sterling Reputation
The Rare Stocks	Inquisition procurers can leverage the organization's reputation to purchase a shipment of rare and valuable raw materials for crafting.	—
Exacting Buyers	A little shrewd negotiation will allow Inquisition procurers to buy a shipment of high-quality materials for their craftspeople.	The Rare Stocks
Only the Finest	A word to the right people, and our Inquisition procurers can bid at auction on the very highest-quality, rare materials for their craftspeople.	Exacting Buyers
The Short List	Merchants eager to win favor from the Inquisition will give access to special offers for rare inventory.	Invest 5 points in Connections category.
Friends in High Places	Where the Inquisition deigns to spend its coin, people take notice. Merchants will send messengers when they have sales at their stores, in hopes the Inquisitor will put in an appearance.	Capture any keep.
Barter by Belle (Agent)	Belle's trading connections all over Thedas give the Inquisition access to valuable commodities and increase its influence with several merchant cartels. Reduces by 5% the time it takes for Josephine to complete operations.	Recruit Belle.
Speaker Anais (Agent)	Speaker Anais has spoken of the Inquisition to her followers. They in turn spread the word of the Inquisition and its mission. Reduces by 5% the time it takes for Josephine to complete operations.	Recruit Anais.
Enchanter Ellendra (Agent)	Enchanter Ellendra was persuaded to use her impressive knowledge of healing and protection spells to aid the Inquisition. Reduces by 5% the time it takes for Josephine to complete operations.	Recruit Enchanter Ellendra.
Fairbanks (Agent)	The rebel Fairbanks's close ties with the commoners in the Dales and his familiarity with the Emerald Graves will contribute significantly to the Inquisition's efforts to gain influence. Reduces by 5% the time it takes for Josephine to complete operations.	Recruit Fairbanks.
Lord Berand (Agent)	Lord Berand of Ferelden has returned to the Bannorn, bearing news of the Inquisition. His voice has turned many to the Inquisition's cause. Reduces by 5% the time it takes for Josephine to complete operations.	Recruit Lord Berand.
Sky Watcher (Agent)	Convinced that the Herald of Andraste was sent by the Lady of the Skies, a shaman of the Avvar tribes has sworn himself to the Inquisition's cause. Reduces by 5% the time it takes for Josephine to complete operations.	Recruit Sky Watcher.
The Noble Cadaver (Agent)	The Grand Duchess Florianne in a pine box is now among the Inquisition's assets. Florianne would be gratified to know that she is as formidable in death as in life (if only because of her odor). Reduces by 5% the time it takes for Josephine to complete operations.	Judge and order Florianne's remains to perform community service.

Inquisition Perks

Name	Description	Prerequisite
History Knowledge	Detailed study of Thedas's past. Opens up new dialogue options related to history and the Chantry. Grants an additional +50% XP for each codex entry found.	—
Antivan Tailoring	Antivan tailors are famed for their ability to hide pockets seamlessly in garments. A few words to the Inquisition's friends to the north, and its forces can carry more items in the field. Increases inventory capacity by 15.	—
Imperial Court Tailoring	The best tailors of Val Royeaux, experienced in the intricacies of the Grand Game, can add hidden compartments to armor and clothing, allowing even more items to be carried at once. Increases inventory capacity by 15.	Antivan Tailoring
Tempered Glass Flasks	Better techniques in glass-working make more durable flasks, allowing more potions to be carried safely at one time. Adds one more potion slot for all party members.	—
Exclusive Training	Gain 1 combat talent point, for the Inquisitor only.	Invest 5 points in Inquisition category.
Deeds Renown	A better network of bards and criers makes every Inquisition deed garner more power across Thedas.	Invest 4 points in Inquisition category.
Horsemaster Dennet (Agent)	Dennet lends his considerable experience with the training and handling of various steeds for the Inquisition.	Recruit Horsemaster Dennet.

TIP If you're constantly running low on inventory space and forced to sell (or destroy) items you'd otherwise keep, consider the Antivan Tailoring and Imperial Court Tailoring perks. Together these perks will boost your inventory capacity by 30.

DEVELOPER TIP

As the player gains enough influence to receive new perks, I always make sure to unlock the first perk in each category as fast as possible. These open up new and interesting dialogue options that can alter the flow of conversations in ways that may not be expected.

— Leo Potvin, QA Tester, Testing and QA II

AGENTS

During your journeys through Ferelden and Orlais, look for opportunities to recruit agents for the Inquisition. Sometimes you must complete certain quests before an agent can be recruited. Other times you must simply talk to them—sometimes it takes convincing from a specific party member to close the deal. Once recruited, agents are assigned to Cullen, Leliana, or Josephine, reducing the amount of time it takes each advisor to complete missions on the war table. Agents also count as a perk point, reducing the threshold necessary to unlock advanced perks within a particular category.

BARTER BY BELLE

Locale: Val Royeaux

Affiliated Quest: The Threat Remains

Inquisition Perk: Barter by Belle (Connections)

After addressing the clerics, speak with Belle, a merchant in Val Royeaux. Frustrated by the lack of action taken by the templars and the Chantry, Belle wishes to join the Inquisition. Accepting Belle into the Inquisition unlocks the Barter by Belle perk, reducing the time it takes Josephine to complete missions by 5 percent.

ENCHANTER ELLENDRA

Locale: The Hinterlands

Affiliated Quest: My Lover's Phylactery

Inquisition Perk: Enchanter Ellendra (Connections)

Ellendra can be convinced to join the Inquisition by Vivienne, following the sad news of her templar lover's passing. Alternatively, you can convince her to join if you're playing as a mage, have sided with the mages/templars, or have the arcane persuade conversation option.

HORSEMASTER DENNET

Locale: The Hinterlands

Affiliated Quest: Horses for the Inquisition

Inquisition Perk: Horsemaster Dennet (Inquisition)

Horsemaster Dennet admits his temptation to leave his lands and wife behind to join the Inquisition, but he is initially unwilling to make the commitment. However, Cassandra or Vivienne can convince him that the cause is righteous enough to join.

LORD BERAND

Locale: The Hinterlands

Affiliated Quest: Love Waits

Inquisition Perk: Lord Berand (Forces or Connections)

When you return to Lord Berand at the end of the Love Waits quest, he can be persuaded to either join the Inquisition personally as a soldier or go home and use his influence to help the Inquisition. The Lord Berand perk reduces the amount of time it takes Cullen or Josephine to complete an operation by 5 percent.

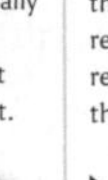

RITTS

Locale: The Hinterlands

Affiliated Quest: Strange Bedfellows

Inquisition Perk: Witty Ritts (Secrets)

As part of the Strange Bedfellows quest, Varric or a dwarven Inquisitor is able to convince Ritts that her unique talents are useful, enough that she will become one of Leliana's agents. This perk reduces the time it takes for Leliana to complete a war table operation by 5 percent.

CLEMENCE

Locale: The Hinterlands

Affiliated Quest: In Hushed Whispers

Inquisition Perk: Clemence, the Tranquil (Forces)

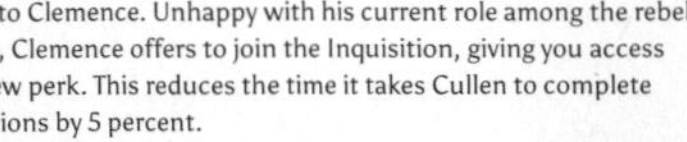

After meeting Alexius in the Gull & Lantern tavern in Redcliffe, speak to Clemence. Unhappy with his current role among the rebel mages, Clemence offers to join the Inquisition, giving you access to a new perk. This reduces the time it takes Cullen to complete operations by 5 percent.

SPEAKER ANAIS

Locale: The Hinterlands

Affiliated Quest: Praise the Herald of Andraste

Inquisition Perk: Speaker Anais (Secrets or Connections)

After closing the rift during the Praise the Herald of Andraste quest, ask Speaker Anais to "spread word of an Inquisition" to recruit an agent for Josephine (Connections). Or ask her to "listen and gather information" to make her an agent for Leliana (Secrets).

TANNER

Locale: The Hinterlands

Affiliated Quest: Business Arrangements

Inquisition Perk: Smuggler Tanner (Secrets)

A letter found on a dead templar suggests that Tanner is secretly doing business with the templars. Confront Tanner in Redcliffe, near the Chantry. Have Cassandra coerce Tanner into joining the Inquisition to unlock the Smuggler Tanner perk. This reduces the amount of time it takes for Leliana to complete operations by 5 percent.

CORPORAL VALE

Locale: The Hinterlands

Affiliated Quest: Various Hinterlands Quests

Inquisition Perk: Vale's Irregulars (Forces)

After helping refugees at the Crossroads with a series of small quests, speak to Corporal Vale to receive one of three possible rewards as well as a perk. If you ask Corporal Vale to recruit skilled refugees, you'll gain one power. If you ask that the refugees work for the Inquisition, you'll earn gold. Or ask to grow the Inquisition's reputation to make him an agent.

SKY WATCHER

Locale: The Fallow Mire

Affiliated Quest: Rifts in the Mire

Inquisition Perk: Sky Watcher (Connections)

You encounter the Avvar named Sky Watcher; he is staring at a partially closed Fade rift in the Fallow Mire. Opening the Fade rift, killing the demons it spawns, and then properly sealing it with your mark will convince Sky Watcher that there is something to the Herald of Andraste. By doing this, you have a chance to recruit him, after rescuing the soldiers from Hargrave Keep. Be warned that once you exit the area, he'll leave for good, so don't forget to speak to him.

> THE BLADES OF HESSARIAN

Locale: The Storm Coast

Affiliated Quest: Cleaning House

Inquisition Perk: The Blades of Hessarian (Forces)

Craft and equip the Mercy's Crest amulet before approaching the bandit camp—the guards will allow you to enter to challenge their leader. After defeating the Hessarian leader in combat, speak to one of the bandits. The Blades of Hessarian pledge their support to the Inquisition, becoming agents reporting directly to Cullen.

> JANA

Locale: Crestwood

Affiliated Quest: None

Inquisition Perk: The Eager Recruit (Secrets)

After encountering the Grey Wardens on the road outside the north gate camp, enter the nearby house to speak with Jana—she's excited the Grey Wardens saved her from the undead and wants to become a Warden herself. Convince her not to join the Grey Wardens. If Solas is in your party he can convince her to join the Inquisition instead.

> FREDERIC

Locale: The Western Approach

Affiliated Quest: The Abyssal High Dragon

Inquisition Perk: Frederic of Serault (Secrets)

Frederic's unique skills as an Orlesian draconologist come to the Inquisition only after a lengthy series of quests, culminating in the slaying of the Abyssal High Dragon. Afterward, he offers to join the Inquisition as a dragon expert. All you need to do is accept.

> LORANIL

Locale: The Exalted Plains

Affiliated Quest: By the Grace of the Dalish

Inquisition Perk: Loranil (Forces)

To be able to recruit Loranil, you must first earn favor with Keeper Hawen at the Dalish camp. Do this by completing requests of all the Dalish in the camp, and Hawen will admit that he sees your cause in a good enough light that he will allow one of his people to leave the camp. Loranil reduces Cullen's operation times by 5 percent.

> FAIRBANKS

Locale: Emerald Graves

Affiliated Quest: Noble Deeds, Noble Heart

Inquisition Perk: Fairbanks (Connections)

After an extensive series of quests, you have the ability to decide where the man who calls himself Fairbanks ends up: as an agent for the Inquisition or a noble for Orlais, trying to do right for the Dales.

> SER BARRIS

Locale: Therinfal Redoubt

Affiliated Quest: Champions of the Just

Inquisition Perk: Ser Barris (Forces)

If choose to ally with the templars and complete Champions of the Just, Ser Barris joins the Inquisition. He serves under Commander Cullen, reducing the time it takes to complete Cullen's missions by 5 percent.

> MICHEL DE CHEVIN

Locale: Emprise du Lion

Affiliated Quest: Call Me Imshael

Inquisition Perk: Michel de Chevin (Forces)

Speak to Michel outside the village to learn of Imshael. Defeat Imshael at Suledin Keep and then return to Michel, recruiting him as an agent of the Inquisition, serving under Cullen. If you encounter and defeat Imshael before speaking to Michel, he won't join the Inquisition.

> ALEXIUS

Locale: Skyhold

Affiliated Quest: Sit in Judgment

Inquisition Perk: A Magister in Disgrace (Secrets)

If you took Alexius alive following the events at Redcliffe Castle, you can judge him at Skyhold. Sentence him to research magic for the Inquisition to make him an agent serving under Leliana.

> SERVIS

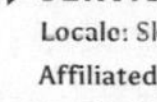

Locale: Skyhold

Affiliated Quest: Sit in Judgment

Inquisition Perk: Servis (Secrets)

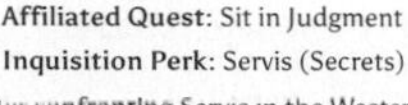

After confronting Servis in the Western Approach, return to Skyhold to judge him. Servis can be conscripted as an informant, supplying useful information to Leliana.

> FLORIANNE

Locale: Skyhold

Affiliated Quest: Sit in Judgment

Inquisition Perk: The Noble Cadaver (Connections)

If Florianne was killed at Halamshiral, you have the opportunity to judge her remains at Skyhold. Sentence her to community service to give Josephine another agent.

CRAFTING

As you travel through Thedas, you will find many materials that you can use for crafting. Divided across five categories, crafting materials are used for three major aspects of your survival: weapons, armor, and potions. Using recipes and schematics found in shops, learned from glyphs illuminated by veilfire, or on scrolls found in treasure caches, you can create powerful and necessary upgrades for your party. With the right materials, you can make weapons and armor that eclipse even some of the rare pieces of gear you discover in the field!

CRAFTING WEAPONS AND ARMOR

When you start the Inquisition, your blacksmith has the ability to craft weapons and armor. Additionally, the smith can craft upgrades that fit into the appropriate slots on a weapon or piece of armor. It is not until the Inquisition moves to Skyhold that you can recruit Dagna, a dwarven arcanist whose skills allow her to make runes that add elemental damage types to various weapons.

Schematics for equipment fit into one of three tiers. Tier 1 schematics yield tier 1 gear, and so on. The higher the tier, the more powerful the item can potentially be, but that also means you will need to spend more crafting material per slot on the schematic to make the item. Tier 1 weapon and armor schematics typically have two slots for crafting materials, while tier 3 schematics have four slots for materials, allowing you to heavily customize the final product but generally costing more materials per slot. The exceptions to this are helmets and upgrades, which do not gain more slots on their schematics, just increased material requirements.

WEAPON AND ARMOR CRAFTING MATERIAL SLOTS

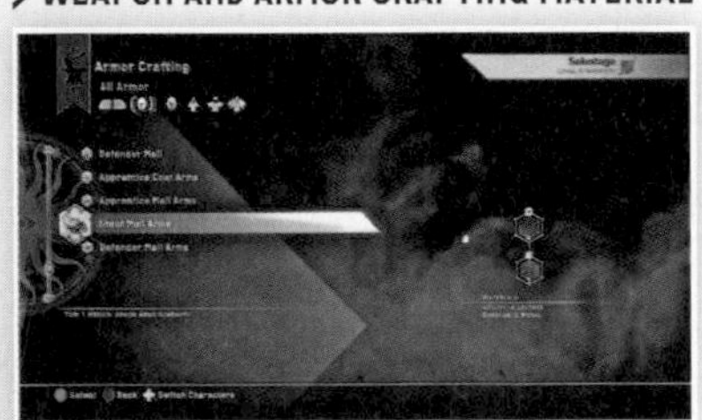

Most crafting materials used for weapons and armor have stats of their own that help determine the overall quality of the gear. These stats determine what that material will do for a given crafting slot on a schematic.

Primary Slot

This slot determines the base armor or attack value of crafted armor or weapons, and it can also determine the elemental damage of a staff. Materials can be rated as follows: low, medium, high, and very high armor/damage rating.

Utility Slot

This slot determines any core attribute upgrades to Strength, Dexterity, Magic, Cunning, Willpower, or Constitution. The higher the tier of a material, the higher each individual piece of the material can boost an attribute. For example, if a material provides two points of Strength and you use 20 of that item across multiple utility slots on a schematic, you'll have 40 Strength added to your core attribute!

Offense Slot

Special offense-based effects are granted by crafting materials placed in this slot. You can give your weapons increased damage against barriers or guard, impart the ability to ignore a percentage of the enemy's armor, cause bleeding effects, or have a chance to heal characters if they score a killing blow! When crafting any weapon, you can greatly increase its effectiveness if you stack the right offense slot effect across multiple schematic slots.

Defense Slot

Defense slot boosts include elemental and damage-type resistances. You can even cause enemies to start bleeding if they hit you with melee attacks! If you're willing to make the effort, you can create specific armor sets that heavily mitigate a certain element, which is a good idea for high dragon hunts if their breath attacks are proving too much to handle.

UPGRADE CRAFTING

Weapons and armor can have upgrade slots, and there are specific crafting schematics that allow you to make the upgrades that fit in these slots. Armor can have up to two upgrade slots. Weapons can have up to three. As with other forms of crafting, the materials used can greatly affect the quality of armor and weapon upgrades. The only exceptions to this are runes.

Rune Crafting

Unlike armor and weapon crafting, rune-crafting schematics are very straightforward. The quality of the materials does not affect the quality produced by a specific rune schematic. If you want a superb corrupting rune, you need the specific materials the schematic calls for.

MASTERWORK CRAFTING

Higher-tier weapon and armor schematics have a masterwork slot that can be filled by an optional masterwork crafting material. These materials provide special effects that no other crafting material can provide in any other slot. These can include a variety of chance-on-hit damage effects or chances to gain special buffs upon taking any damage. Additionally, there are special masterwork crafting materials that give you a 20–40 percent chance for critical crafting. Weapons and armor with critical crafting receive a 10 percent increase to all stats. Masterwork crafting allows you to make weapons and armor that give your parties a decisive advantage, so don't neglect it!

POTION CRAFT

Potions are your lifeblood in a protracted fight. They can heal you immediately or over a period of time. They can help you resist powerful elemental attacks, or they can act as another way to keep the enemy off balance with extra debilitating effects on top of all the damage you're already doing.

There are three types of potions in *Dragon Age: Inquisition*: potions (health recovery and magic boost), tonics (enhanced resistances and combat), and grenades (throwable area-damage weapons that cause a variety of effects). Each potion within these categories can be upgraded multiple times to increase its efficacy, at the cost of many, many herbs.

POTIONS

Healing Potion

Instantly restores 385 health.

Available Upgrades

- **Increase Healing I**: Increases healing amount by 50.
- **Increase Healing II**: Increases healing amount by 67.

Regeneration Potion

Restores 26 health every two seconds for 60 seconds.

Available Upgrades

- **Increase Duration I**: Increases duration by eight seconds.
- **Increase Duration II**: Increases duration by 10 seconds.
- **Increase Healing I**: Increases healing amount by three per second.
- **Increase Healing II**: Increases healing amount by four per second.
- **Lifeward**: Doubles the healing amount if the user is below 25 percent health.
- **Proximity Heal**: Heals nearby allies for the same amount.

Lyrium Potion

Increases Magic by 30 for 20 seconds.

Available Upgrades

- **Increase Maximum Mana**: Increases maximum mana by 25.
- **Increase Maximum Mana Bonus**: Increases the mana bonus by 25.
- **Increase Duration**: Increases duration by 20 seconds.
- **Increase Magic Bonus**: Increases the Magic bonus by 30.

TONICS

Fire Resistance Tonic

Grants a 40 percent resistance against fire damage for 120 seconds.

Available Upgrades

- **Increase Duration I**: Increases duration by 30 seconds.
- **Increase Duration II**: Increases duration by 30 seconds.
- **Increase Potency I**: Increases resistance by 10 percent.
- **Increase Potency II**: Increases resistance by 10 percent.
- **Proximity Resistance**: Apply resistance to all party members within two meters when the tonic is consumed.

Cold Resistance Tonic

Grants a 40 percent resistance against cold damage for 120 seconds.

Available Upgrades

- **Increase Duration I**: Increases duration by 30 seconds.
- **Increase Duration II**: Increases duration by 30 seconds.
- **Increase Potency I**: Increases resistance by 10 percent.
- **Increase Potency II**: Increases resistance by 10 percent.
- **Proximity Resistance**: Apply resistance to all party members within two meters when the tonic is consumed.

Electrical Resistance Tonic

Grants a 40 percent resistance against electrical damage for 120 seconds.

Available Upgrades

- **Increase Duration I**: Increases duration by 30 seconds.
- **Increase Duration II**: Increases duration by 30 seconds.
- **Increase Potency I**: Increases resistance by 10 percent.
- **Increase Potency II**: Increases resistance by 10 percent.
- **Proximity Resistance**: Apply resistance to all party members within two meters when the tonic is consumed.

Spirit Resistance Tonic

Grants a 40 percent resistance against spirit damage for 120 seconds.

Available Upgrades

- **Increase Duration I**: Increases duration by 30 seconds.
- **Increase Duration II**: Increases duration by 30 seconds.
- **Increase Potency I**: Increases resistance by 10 percent.
- **Increase Potency II**: Increases resistance by 10 percent.
- **Proximity Resistance**: Apply resistance to all party members within two meters when the tonic is consumed.

Mighty Offense Tonic

Applies a +13 damage bonus for 20 seconds.

Available Upgrades

- **Increase Damage I:** Increases damage bonus by 26.
- **Increase Damage II:** Increases damage bonus by 19.
- **Damage Bonus vs. Guard:** Grants a 50 percent damage bonus against enemies with Guard active.
- **Damage Bonus vs. Barrier:** Grants a 50 percent damage bonus against enemies with Barrier active.
- **Critical Damage Bonus:** Grants a 100 percent damage bonus on critical hits.

Rock Armor Tonic

Grants a +12 bonus to armor rating for 30 seconds.

Available Upgrades

- **Improved Duration I:** Increases duration by 30 seconds.
- **Improved Duration II:** Increases duration by 30 seconds.
- **Improved Potency I:** Improves armor rating bonus by 11.
- **Improved Potency II:** Improves armor rating bonus by 12.
- **Stun Enemies:** Any enemy that hits the user has a 50 percent chance to be stunned.

Tears of the Dead

The next three hits inflict poison on the target, causing 44 damage per second for 15 seconds. The poison remains on the weapon for 10 seconds before expiring.

Available Upgrades

- **Increase Duration I:** Increases poison duration on the target by five seconds.
- **Increase Duration II:** Increases poison duration on the target by five seconds.
- **Increase Damage I:** Increases damage by 37 per second.
- **Increase Damage II:** Increases damage by 67 per second.
- **Enhanced Potency:** Grants two extra hits and five extra seconds before the poison wears off.

GRENADES

Pitch Grenade

Coats the target location with pitch, which remains for 60 seconds, slowing any enemies that enter it.

Available Upgrades

- **Increase Duration I:** Increases duration by 30 seconds.
- **Increase Duration II:** Increases duration by 30 seconds.
- **Debilitate I:** Enemies caught in the pitch suffer 25 percent extra damage from all sources and inflict 25 percent less damage.
- **Debilitate II:** Increases the damage bonus against enemies by 25 percent and the damage penalty of enemies by 25 percent.
- **Immobilize:** Targets at the initial explosion location are stunned for 10 seconds.

Confusion Grenade

Enemies within the area of effect will attack other enemies for 20 seconds.

Available Upgrades

- **Increase Duration I:** Increases duration by 10 seconds.
- **Increase Duration II:** Increases duration by 10 seconds.
- **Rage I:** Confused targets now deal 25 percent extra damage.
- **Rage II:** The damage bonus while confused is increased by 25 percent.
- **Mind Wreck:** All targets suffer 635 spirit damage when the effect wears off.

Antivan Fire

Spreads sticky fire at the target location, causing 23 burning damage every second to enemies inside the fire. The fire remains for 30 seconds.

Available Upgrades

- **Increase Damage I:** Increases damage by 21 per second.
- **Increase Damage II:** Increases damage by 38 per second.
- **Increase Duration I:** Increases duration by 30 seconds.
- **Increase Duration II:** Increases duration by 30 seconds.
- **Shockwave:** Targets at the initial explosion location are stunned for five seconds.

Healing Mist

Creates a small healing mist in the target area, instantly healing allies within for 289 health.

Available Upgrades

- **Increase Healing I:** Increases healing amount by 38.
- **Increase Healing II:** Increases healing amount by 50.
- **Healing Mist:** Healing Mist can restore unconscious party members as well as heal them.

Jar of Bees

Summons a swarm of bees at the target location for 30 seconds. The swarm attacks the first enemy that comes near it, for 163 damage per second for 15 seconds. A target affected by the swarm has a 10 percent chance every second to become panicked.

Available Upgrades

- **Increase Panic Chance I:** Increases panic chance by 10 percent.
- **Increase Panic Chance II:** Increases panic chance by 10 percent.
- **Increase Duration I:** Increases the swarm's attack duration by five seconds.
- **Increase Duration II:** Increases the swarm's attack duration by five seconds.
- **And Some Wasps:** The swarm of bees splits off to attack the first enemy that comes near the original target, and both targets suffer the full effect of the swarm.

CRAFTING MATERIALS

These charts show you the crafting materials found in the five major categories: cloth, leather, metal, runes, and herbs.

> CLOTH

Cloth

Crafting Material Name	Tier	Primary Slot	Utility Slot	Offense Slot	Defense Slot
Cotton	1 (Common)	Low armor rating	+1 Willpower	+1.5% chance to heal on kill	+2% healing bonus from all sources
Crimson Color Pack	—	—	—	—	—
Dales Loden Wool	3 (Rare)	High armor rating	1.75 Magic	3% barrier damage bonus	1.75% magic defense
Darkened Samite	2 (Common)	Medium armor rating	1.5 Willpower	1.75% chance to heal on kill	3% spirit damage resistance
Dragon Webbing	4 (Rare)	Very high armor rating	1 Willpower/1 Magic	3.5% critical damage	4% fire damage resistance
Everknit Wool	2 (Common)	Medium armor rating	1.5 Magic	2.5% barrier damage bonus	1.5% magic defense
Highever Weave	2 (Common)	Medium armor rating	1 Magic/0.5 Willpower	1.5% attack	3% electric damage resistance
Imperial Vestment Cotton	3 (Common)	High armor rating	1.75 Willpower	2% chance to heal on kill	3% healing from all sources
Infused Vyrantium Samite	3 (Common)	High armor rating	1.75 Willpower	2% chance to heal on kill	3.5% spirit damage resistance
King's Willow Weave	3 (Common)	High armor rating	1 Magic/.75 Willpower	1.75% attack	3.5% electric damage resistance
Lambswool	1 (Common)	Low armor rating	1 Magic	2% barrier damage bonus	1% magic defense
Lustrous Cotton	2 (Common)	Medium armor rating	1.5 Willpower	1.75% chance to heal on kill	2.5% healing from all sources
Plaideweave	1 (Common)	Low armor rating	1 Magic	1% attack	2.5% electric damage resistance
Plush Fustian Velvet	3 (Common)	High armor rating	1 Magic/.75 Willpower	1.75% attack	3.5% electric damage resistance
Redcliffe Color	—	—	—	—	—
Ring Velvet	2 (Common)	Medium armor rating	1 Magic/0.5 Willpower	1.5% attack	3% electric damage resistance
Royale Sea Silk	3 (Common)	High armor rating	1.75 Magic	3% barrier damage bonus	1.75% magic defense
Samite	1 (Common)	Low armor rating	1 Willpower	1.5% chance to heal on kill	2.5% spirit damage resistance
Silk	1 (Common)	Low armor rating	1 Magic	2% barrier damage bonus	1% magic defense
Silk Brocade	2 (Common)	Medium armor rating	1.5 Magic	2.5% barrier damage bonus	1.5% magic defense
Velveteen	1 (Common)	Low armor rating	1 Magic	1% attack	2.5% electric damage resistance
Venatori Color Pack	—	—	—	—	—

> CLOTH MASTERWORK

Cloth Masterwork

Masterwork Crafting Material Name	Tier	Applied Effect
Fade-Touched Cotton	1	On dying: 5% chance to heal for half health
Fade-Touched Cotton	1	10% chance to apply Walking Bomb for 5 seconds, with detonation of 50% weapon damage
Fade-Touched Dales Loden Wool	3	30% focus gain
Fade-Touched Dales Loden Wool	3	10% chance to drop Caltrops on a hit, doing 70% weapon damage per second
Fade-Touched Darkened Samite	2	7.5% extra focus for each enemy within 8 meters
Fade-Touched Darkened Samite	2	5% chance to cast Mind Blast on a hit
Fade-Touched Everknit Wool	2	7.5% extra focus for each enemy within 8 meters
Fade-Touched Everknit Wool	2	10% chance to drop Caltrops on a hit, doing 50% weapon damage per second
Fade-Touched Highever Weave	2	On kill: +20 to magic for 10 seconds
Fade-Touched Imperial Vestment Cotton	3	On dying: 15% chance to heal for half health

Masterwork Crafting Material Name	Tier	Applied Effect
Fade-Touched Imperial Vestment Cotton	3	10% chance to apply Walking Bomb for 5 seconds, with detonation of 100% weapon damage
Fade-Touched Infused Vyrantium Samite	3	10% extra focus for each enemy with 8 meters
Fade-Touched Infused Vyrantium Samite	3	10% chance to cast Mind Blast on a hit
Fade-Touched King's Willow Weave	3	On kill: +30 to magic for 10 seconds
Fade-Touched Lambswool	1	On hit: gain 2 guard
Fade-Touched Lambswool	1	10% chance to drop Caltrops on a hit, doing 30% weapon damage per second
Fade-Touched Lustrous Cotton	2	10% chance to apply Walking Bomb for 5 seconds, with detonation of 75% weapon damage
Fade-Touched Lustrous Cotton	2	On dying: 10% chance to heal for half health
Fade-Touched Plaideweave	1	On kill: +10 to magic for 10 seconds
Fade-Touched Plush Fustian Velvet	3	7.5% extra focus for each enemy within 8 meters

Dragon Age Inquisition

Cloth Masterwork continued

Masterwork Crafting Material Name	Tier	Applied Effect
Fade-Touched Plush Fustian Velvet	3	10% chance to use Hidden Blades on a hit, with 5 added hits
Fade-Touched Ring Velvet	2	Abilities cost 7.5% less mana/stamina
Fade-Touched Ring Velvet	2	10% chance to use Hidden Blades on a hit, with 4 added hits
Fade-Touched Royale Sea Silk	3	Abilities cost 20% less mana/stamina if not being hit for 5 seconds.
Fade-Touched Royale Sea Silk	3	10% chance to cast Fade Cloak on a hit
Fade-Touched Samite	1	5% extra focus for each enemy within 8 meters
Fade-Touched Samite	1	2% chance to cast Mind Blast on a hit
Fade-Touched Silk	1	Abilities cost 10% less mana/stamina if not being hit for 5 seconds.
Fade-Touched Silk	1	2% chance to cast Fade Cloak on a hit
Fade-Touched Silk Brocade	2	5% chance to cast Fade Cloak on a hit
Fade-Touched Silk Brocade	2	Abilities cost 15% less mana/stamina if not being hit for 5 seconds.
Fade-Touched Velveteen	1	Abilities cost 5% less mana/stamina.
Fade-Touched Velveteen	1	10% chance to use Hidden Blades on a hit, with 3 added hits
Masterwork Cotton	1	Critical crafting chance 20%
Master Dales Loden Wool	1	Critical crafting chance 20%

Masterwork Crafting Material Name	Tier	Applied Effect
Masterwork Darkened Samite	1	Critical crafting chance 20%
Masterwork Everknit Wool	1	Critical crafting chance 20%
Masterwork Highever Weave	1	Critical crafting chance 20%
Masterwork Imperial Vestment Cotton	1	Critical crafting chance 20%
Masterwork Infused Vyrantium Samite	1	Critical crafting chance 20%
Masterwork King's Willow Weave	1	Critical crafting chance 20%
Masterwork Lambswool	1	Critical crafting chance 20%
Masterwork Lustrous Cotton	1	Critical crafting chance 20%
Masterwork Plaideweave	1	Critical crafting chance 20%
Masterwork Plush Fustian Velvet	1	Critical crafting chance 20%
Masterwork Ring Velvet	1	Critical crafting chance 20%
Masterwork Royale Sea Silk	1	Critical crafting chance 20%
Masterwork Samite	1	Critical crafting chance 20%
Masterwork Silk	1	Critical crafting chance 20%
Masterwork Silk Brocade	1	Critical crafting chance 20%
Masterwork Velveteen	1	Critical crafting chance 20%

LEATHER

Leather

Crafting Material Name	Tier	Primary Slot	Utility Slot	Offense Slot	Defense Slot
August Ram Leather	2 (Common)	Medium armor rating	1.5 Dexterity	2.5% flanking damage bonus	3% cold damage resistance
Bear Hide	2 (Common)	Medium armor rating	1.5 Dexterity	1.5% critical chance	3% cold damage resistance
Bronto Hide	1 (Common)	Low armor rating	1 Cunning	2% critical damage	1% ranged defense
Canine Leather	1 (Common)	Low armor rating	1 Dexterity	2% flanking damage bonus	2.5% cold damage resistance
Craggy Skin	3 (Common)	High armor rating	1.75 Cunning	3% critical damage	1.75% ranged defense
Deepstalker Hide	1 (Common)	Low armor rating	1 Dexterity	1% chance to bleed target on hit	1% chance to bleed attacker on being hit
Dragon Scales	4 (Rare)	Very high armor rating	1 Cunning/1 Dexterity	3.5% armor penetration	4% fire damage resistance
Dragonling Scales	1 (Common)	Low armor rating	1 Dexterity	1% chance to bleed target on hit	2.5% fire damage resistance
Druffalo Hide	1 (Common)	Low armor rating	1 Dexterity	1% critical chance	2.5% cold damage resistance
Fennec Fur	1 (Common)	Low armor rating	1 Dexterity	1% critical chance	2.5% cold damage resistance
Great Bear Hide	3 (Common)	High armor rating	1.75 dexterity	1.75% critical strike	3.5% cold damage resistance
Gurgut Webbing	2 (Common)	Medium armor rating	1 Dexterity/0.5 Cunning	1.5% chance to bleed target on hit	3% fire damage resistance
Halla Leather	2 (Common)	Medium armor rating	1.5 Dexterity	2.5% flanking damage bonus	3% cold damage resistance
Hardened Gurn Hide	3 (Common)	High armor rating	1 Dexterity/0.75 Cunning	1.75% chance to bleed on target	1.75% chance to bleed attacker on being hit
Lurker Scales	3 (Common)	High armor rating	1.75 Cunning	3% critical damage	1.75% ranged defense
Nugskin	1 (Common)	Low armor rating	1 Cunning	2% critical damage	1% ranged defense
Phoenix Scales	2 (Common)	Medium armor rating	1 Dexterity/0.5 Cunning	1.5% chance to bleed target on hit	1.5% chance to bleed attacker on being hit
Quillback Leather	2 (Common)	Medium armor rating	1.5 Cunning	2.5% critical damage	1.5% ranged defense
Ram Leather	1 (Common)	Low armor rating	1 Dexterity	2% flanking damage bonus	2.5% cold damage resistance
Red Hart Leather	3 (Rare)	High armor rating	1.75 Dexterity	3% flanking damage bonus	3.5% cold damage resistance
Rough Hide	2 (Common)	Medium armor rating	1.5 Cunning	2.5% critical damage	1.5% ranged defense
Snoufleur Skin	3 (Rare)	High armor rating	1.75 Dexterity	3% flanking damage bonus	3.5% cold damage resistance
Varghest Scales	2 (Common)	Medium armor rating	1 Dexterity/0.5 Cunning	1.5% chance to bleed target on hit	1.5% chance to bleed attacker on being hit
Wyvern Scales	3 (Common)	High armor rating	1 Dexterity/0.75 Cunning	1.75% chance to bleed on target on hit	3.5% fire damage resistance

> LEATHER MASTERWORK

Masterwork Crafting Material Name	Tier	Applied Effect
Fade-Touched August Ram Fur	1	Abilities cost 7.5% less mana/ stamina.
Fade-Touched August Ram Fur	1	10% chance to grant 8 seconds of Horn of Valor
Fade-Touched Bear Hide	2	Increase maximum stamina by 15
Fade-Touched Bear Hide	2	On kill: grants 35 stamina
Fade-Touched Bronto Hide	1	Increase maximum stamina by 10
Fade-Touched Bronto Hide	1	On kill: grants 20 stamina
Fade-Touched Canine Leather	1	10% damage bonus if not being hit for 5 seconds
Fade-Touched Craggy Skin	3	75% faster movement speed when in stealth
Fade-Touched Craggy Skin	3	10% chance to cast Veilstrike on a hit
Fade-Touched Deepstalker Hide	1	2% chance to cast Fear on a hit
Fade-Touched Deepstalker Hide	1	On hit: 5% chance to apply poison
Fade-Touched Dragonling Scales	1	Berserk: +10% damage bonus +100% damage from all sources
Fade-Touched Dragonling Scales	1	10% chance to inflict immolate damage at 50% weapon power
Fade-Touched Druffalo Hide	1	Increase maximum stamina by 10
Fade-Touched Fennec Fur	1	+25% faster movement speed when in stealth
Fade-Touched Great Bear Hide	3	Increase maximum stamina by 20
Fade-Touched Great Bear Hide	3	On kill: grants 50 stamina
Fade-Touched Gurgut Skin	2	+50% faster movement speed when in stealth
Fade-Touched Gurn Hide	2	Take only 1 damage from all attacks, but health lowered to 12
Fade-Touched Halla Leather	2	Enter stealth when not attacking during combat
Fade-Touched Lurker Scales	3	+75% faster movement speed when in stealth
Fade-Touched Lurker Scales	3	10% chance to cast Veilstrike on a hit
Fade-Touched Nugskin	1	+75% faster movement speed when in stealth
Fade-Touched Nugskin	1	2% chance to cast Veilstrike on a hit
Fade-Touched Phoenix Scales	2	10% chance to inflict immolate damage at 75% weapon power
Fade-Touched Phoenix Scales	2	+20 damage bonus if not being hit for 5 seconds
Fade-Touched Quillback Leather	2	Take only 1 damage from all attacks, but health lowered to 12
Fade-Touched Ram Leather	1	Abilities cost 5% less mana/ stamina
Fade-Touched Ram Leather	1	10% chance to grant 5 seconds of Horn of Valor
Fade-Touched Rough Hide	2	On hit: 10% chance to apply poison
Fade-Touched Rough Hide	2	5% chance to cast Veilstrike on a hit
Fade-Touched Snoufleur Skin	3	On hit: heal 1% of maximum health
Fade-Touched Snoufleur Skin	3	10% chance to grant 12 seconds of Horn of Valor
Fade-Touched Varghest Scales	3	+30% damage bonus if not being hit for 5 seconds
Fade-Touched Varghest Scales	3	10% chance to inflict immolate damage at 100% weapon power
Fade-Touched Varghest Scales	3	20% damage if not being hit for 5 seconds
Fade-Touched Varghest Scales	3	10% chance to inflict immolate damage at 75% weapon power
Fade-Touched Wyvern Scales	3	On hit: 15% chance to apply poison
Fade-Touched Wyvern Scales	3	10% chance to cast fear on a hit
Golden Halla Hide	2	Enter stealth when not attacking during combat
Masterwork Augusta Ram Fur	1	Critical crafting chance 20%
Masterwork Bear Hide	1	Critical crafting chance 20%
Masterwork Bronto Hide	1	Critical crafting chance 20%
Masterwork Canine Leather	1	Critical crafting chance 20%
Masterwork Craggy Skin	1	Critical crafting chance 20%
Masterwork Deepstalker Hide	1	Critical crafting chance 20%
Masterwork Dragonling Scales	1	Berserk: +10% damage bonus, 100% damage taken from all sources
Masterwork Druffalo Hide	1	Critical crafting chance 20%
Masterwork Fennec Fur	1	Critical crafting chance 20%
Masterwork Great Bear Hide	1	Critical crafting chance 20%
Masterwork Gurgut Skin	1	Critical crafting chance 20%
Masterwork Gurgut Webbing	—	—
Masterwork Gurn Hide	1	Critical crafting chance 20%
Masterwork Halla Leather	1	Critical crafting chance 20%
Masterwork Lurker Scales	1	Critical crafting chance 20%
Masterwork Nugskin	1	Critical crafting chance 20%
Masterwork Phoenix Scales	1	Critical crafting chance 20%
Masterwork Quillback Leather	1	Critical crafting chance 20%
Masterwork Ram Leather	1	Critical crafting chance 20%
Masterwork Red Hart Leather	1	Critical crafting chance 20%
Masterwork Rough Hide	1	Critical crafting chance 20%
Masterwork Varghest Scales	1	Critical crafting chance 20%
Masterwork Wyvern Scales	1	Critical crafting chance 20%

> METAL

Crafting Material Name	Tier	Primary Slot	Utility Slot	Offense Slot	Defense Slot
Bloodstone	2 (Common)	Medium armor rating/damage (staff damage type: fire)	1.5 Constitution	2.5% armor penetration	13 health
Blue Vitriol	1 (Common)	Low armor rating/damage (staff damage type: cold)	1 Strength	1% chance on stagger target on hit	1% chance to stagger attacker on being hit
Dawnstone	3 (Common)	High armor rating/damage (staff damage type: fire)	1.75 Constitution	3% armor penetration	15 health
Dragon Bone	4 (Rare)	Very high armor rating/damage (staff damage type: fire)	1 Constitution / 1 Strength	2% chance to bleed target on hit	4% fire damage resistance
Drakestone	1 (Common)	Low armor rating/damage (staff damage type: fire)	1 Constitution	2% armor penetration	10 health
Everite	3 (Common)	High armor rating/damage (staff damage type: electricity)	1.75 Strength	1.75% attack	1.75% melee defense
Iron	1 (Common)	Low armor rating/damage (staff damage type: electricity)	1 Strength	1% attack	1% melee defense
Lazurite	2 (Common)	Medium armor rating/damage (staff damage type: cold)	1 Strength / 0.5 Constitution	1.5% chance to stagger on hit	1.5% chance to stagger attacker on being hit
Nevarrite	3 (Common)	High armor rating/damage (staff damage type: cold)	1 Strength / 0.75 Constitution	1.75% chance to stagger target on hit	1.75% chance to stagger attacker on being hit
Obsidian	2 (Common)	Medium armor rating/damage (staff damage type: cold)	1 Strength / 0.5 Constitution	1.5% chance to stagger target on hit	1.5% chance to stagger attacker on being hit
Onyx	1 (Common)	Low armor rating/damage (staff damage type: cold)	1 Strength	1% chance on stagger target on hit	1% chance to stagger attacker on being hit
Paragon's Luster	2 (Common)	Medium armor rating/damage (staff damage type: electricity)	1.5 Strength	1.5% attack	1.5% melee defense
Pyrophite	2 (Common)	Medium armor rating/damage (staff damage type: fire)	1.5 Consititution	2.5% damage to guard	13 health
Serault Infused Glass	2 (Common)	Medium armor rating/damage (staff damage type: electricity)	1.5 Strength	1.5% attack	1.5% melee defense
Serpentstone	1 (Common)	Low armor rating/damage (staff damage type: electricity)	1 Strength	1% attack	1% melee defense
Silverite	3 (Rare)	High armor rating/damage (staff damage type: cold)	1 Strength / 0.75 Constitution	1.75% chance to stagger target on hit	1.75% chance to stagger attacker on being hit
Stormheart	3 (Common)	High armor rating/damage (staff damage type: electricity)	1.75 Strength	1.75% attack	1.75% melee defense
Summer Stone	1 (Common)	Low armor rating/damage (staff damage type: fire)	1 Constitution	2% damage to guard	10 health
Veridium	2 (Common)	Medium armor rating/damage (staff damage type: electricity)	1.5 Strength	1.5% attack	1.5% melee defense
Volcanic Aurum	3 (Common)	High armor rating/damage (staff damage type: fire)	1.75 Constitution	3% damage to guard	15 health

> METAL MASTERWORK

Masterwork Crafting Material Name	Tier	Applied Effect
Fade-Touched Bloodstone	2	7.5% extra damage for each enemy within 8 meters
Fade-Touched Bloodstone	2	5% chance to use Unbowed on a hit
Fade-Touched Blue Vitriol	1	Increase maximum stamina by 10
Fade-Touched Dawnstone	3	Heal 25% of damage taken over 10 seconds
Fade-Touched Dawnstone	3	10% chance to grant 3 seconds of Walking Fortress
Fade-Touched Drakestone	1	Increase maximum stamina by 10
Fade-Touched Drakestone	1	Increase maximum stamina by 10
Fade-Touched Everite	3	Heal 25% of damage taken over 10 seconds
Fade-Touched Everite	3	10% chance to grant 3 seconds of Walking Fortress
Fade-Touched Iron	1	Heal 15% of damage taken over 10 seconds
Fade-Touched Iron	1	2% chance to use Unbowed on a hit
Fade-Touched Lazurite	2	Increase maximum stamina by 15
Fade-Touched Nevarrite	3	On kill: target explodes for 75% weapon damage
Fade-Touched Nevarrite	3	Chance to cast Pull of the Abyss on a hit
Fade-Touched Obsidian	2	On hit: gain 3 guard
Fade-Touched Obsidian	2	10% chance to inflict Chain Lightning damage at 75% weapon power
Fade-Touched Onyx	1	On hit: gain 2 guard
Fade-Touched Onyx	1	10% chance to inflict Chain Lightning damage at 50% weapon power
Fade-Touched Paragon's Luster	2	Heal 20% of damage taken over 10 seconds
Fade-Touched Paragon's Luster	2	10% chance to grant 3 seconds of Walking Fortress

Metal Masterwork continued

Masterwork Crafting Material Name	Tier	Applied Effect
Fade-Touched Pyrophite	2	7.5% extra damage for each enemy within 8 meters
Fade-Touched Pyrophite	2	5% chance to use Unbowed on a hit
Fade-Touched Serpentstone	1	2% chance to use Shield Bash on a hit
Fade-Touched Serpentstone	1	Berserk: +10% damage bonus, 100% damage from all sources
Fade-Touched Silverite	3	On hit: gain 5 guard
Fade-Touched Silverite	3	10% chance to inflict Chain Lightning damage at 100% weapon power
Fade-Touched Stormheart	3	Berserk: 30% damage bonus, 300% damage from all sources
Fade-Touched Stormheart	3	10% chance to use Shield Bash on a hit
Fade-Touched Summer Stone	1	5% extra damage for each enemy within 8 meters
Fade-Touched Summer Stone	1	2% chance to use Unbowed on a hit
Fade-Touched Veridium	2	Berserk: 20% damage bonus, 200% damage from all sources
Fade-Touched Veridium	2	5% chance to use Shield Bash on a hit
Fade-Touched Volcanic Aurum	3	10% extra focus for each enemy within 8 meters
Fade-Touched Volcanic Aurum	3	10% chance to use Unbowed on a hit

Masterwork Crafting Material Name	Tier	Applied Effect
Masterwork Bloodstone	1	Critical crafting chance 20%
Masterwork Blue Vitriol	1	Critical crafting chance 20%
Masterwork Dawnstone	1	Critical crafting chance 20%
Masterwork Drakestone	1	Critical crafting chance 20%
Masterwork Everite	1	Critical crafting chance 20%
Masterwork Iron	1	Critical crafting chance 20%
Masterwork Lazurite	1	Critical crafting chance 20%
Masterwork Nevarrite	1	Critical crafting chance 20%
Masterwork Obsidian	1	Critical crafting chance 20%
Masterwork Onyx	1	Critical crafting chance 20%
Masterwork Paragon's Luster	1	Critical crafting chance 20%
Masterwork Pyrophite	1	Critical crafting chance 20%
Masterwork Serpentstone	1	Critical crafting chance 20%
Masterwork Silverite	1	Critical crafting chance 20%
Masterwork Stormheart	1	Critical crafting chance 20%
Masterwork Summer Stone	1	Critical crafting chance 20%
Masterwork Veridium	1	Critical crafting chance 20%
Masterwork Volcanic Aurum	1	Critical crafting chance 20%
Serault Infused Glass	1 (common)	On kill: target explodes for 75% weapon damage

RUNES

Runes

Material Name	Description
Superb Cleansing Rune	Inflicts bonus damage against red templars and darkspawn on each weapon strike.
Superb Corrupting Rune	Inflicts bonus damage against humanoids, beasts, and animals on each weapon strike.
Superb Demon-Slaying Rune	Inflicts bonus damage against demons and undead for each weapon strike.
Superb Dragon-Slaying Rune	Inflicts bonus damage against dragons on each weapon strike.
Superb Fire Rune	Adds fire damage to each weapon strike.
Superb Frost Rune	Adds cold damage to each weapon strike.
Superb Lightning Rune	Adds electricity damage to each weapon strike.
Superb Spirit Rune	Adds spirit damage to each weapon strike.
Master Cleansing Rune	Inflicts bonus damage against red templars and darkspawn on each weapon strike.
Master Corrupting Rune	Inflicts bonus damage against humanoids, beasts, and animals on each weapon strike.
Master Demon-Slaying Rune	Inflicts bonus damage against demons and undead for each weapon strike.
Master Dragon-Slaying Rune	Inflicts bonus damage against dragons on each weapon strike.
Master Fire Rune	Adds fire damage to each weapon strike.
Master Frost Rune	Adds cold damage to each weapon strike.
Master Lightning Rune	Adds electricity damage to each weapon strike.
Master Spirit Rune	Adds spirit damage to each weapon strike.
Cleansing Rune	Inflicts bonus damage against red templars and darkspawn on each weapon strike.
Corrupting Rune	Inflicts bonus damage against humanoids, beasts, and animals on each weapon strike.
Demon-Slaying Rune	Inflicts bonus damage against demons and undead for each weapon strike.
Dragon-Slaying Rune	Inflicts bonus damage against dragons on each weapon strike.
Fire Rune	Adds fire damage to each weapon strike.
Frost Rune	Adds cold damage to each weapon strike.
Lightning Rune	Adds electricity damage to each weapon strike.
Spirit Rune	Adds spirit damage to each weapon strike.

HERBS

Herbs

Material Name	Tier
Amrita Vein	3 (R)
Arbor Blessing	3 (C)
Black Lotus	1 (R)
Blood Lotus	1 (C)
Crystal Grace	1 (R)
Dawn Lotus	1 (R)
Deathroot	2 (C)
Deep Mushroom	3 (C)
Dragonthorn	1 (R)
Elfroot	1 (C)
Embrium	2 (C)
Felandaris	3 (R)
Ghoul's Beard	2 (R)
Prophet's Laurel	2 (R)
Rashvine	2 (C)
Rashvine Nettle	2 (R)
Royal Elfroot	1 (R)
Spindleweed	1 (C)
Vandal Aria	3 (C)
Witherstalk	1 (C)

(C) = Common, (R) = Rare

EXPLORATION

EXPLORATION

The path to saving Thedas from the machinations of those who caused the Breach will send you all across a land in turmoil. The average citizen has been greatly affected by the ongoing mage-templar war. Bandits run wild murdering the innocent and taking their goods. Fade rifts have appeared in nearly every locale, sending forth a host of demons to ravage the countryside. There's a seemingly overwhelming number of tasks and favors for the Inquisition to accomplish. The Explorations and Side Quests chapter of this guide is here to help you with all of that.

SIDE QUESTS

Any quest that does not fall into the Inquisitor's Path quest lines is an optional side quest. *Dragon Age: Inquisition* contains a massive amount of side content, much of which can be done in any order you see fit. When you pass by a potential quest, be it a person in a village or a note in the hands of a dead body in a ditch on the side of a road, your maps will be marked with an exclamation point. Many quests are simple: Go here, kill that, go back and report. Or sometimes they are a simple delivery job. However, some quests get slightly more elaborate, requiring you to travel across entire locales, or multiple locales, before the job is done.

Why do side quests at all? For power, experience, influence, loot, and the approval of your fellow party members. Additionally, you can find a lot of interesting codex entries while traveling on these assignments, while other codex entries are granted as rewards for completing a quest.

One of the most important resources earned through side quests is power. You need power to unlock new locales on the war table at Haven or Skyhold, or to accomplish certain tasks during side quests.

Experience means going up in levels, and you always want to do as much of that as you can. Later missions on the critical path can get very challenging if you haven't been doing a lot of fighting or questing.

Lastly, influence is a measure of the Inquisition's political and social strength across Thedas. It is tracked the same as your character levels are, and when you go up an influence level you can select an Inquisition perk.

Treasure Maps

There is a certain group of side quests that start when you find a sketch or crude map of a location where treasure has apparently been hidden. You must then follow the clues on the maps to find the location of this treasure, and then use your Search ability to scan the area until you uncover the treasure. We've marked not only the start for these quests on our maps, but the locations of the treasure themselves. You'll thank us later for this, trust us.

Fade Rifts

Fade rifts are places where the Veil was so weakened by the creation of the Breach that demons from the Fade tore their way into our world. Those tears, or rifts, in the Veil allow demons to pass through unhindered, and left unchecked they will eventually overwhelm Thedas. Fortunately, the Inquisitor has the means to close Fade rifts.

Closing a Fade rift is the same no matter where you go: approach the rift, slay the demons guarding it, kill the reinforcements that spill from the rift, and then seal it with the mark on the Inquisitor's hand. The major differences come from the types of demons you face at each rift. The further into the game you go, the more powerful the demons become, and that's matched by the increasingly more exotic demons that make up the forces you face.

Requisitions

Requisitions are quests offered by Inquisition scouts found at camps you establish throughout a locale. These quests are about delivering a list of items to the requisition table and then crafting the desired item. These quests are constantly offered, allowing you to gain power so long as you're able to deliver the goods.

AGENTS

Agents of the Inquisition can be recruited during special quests or conversations held with NPCs throughout the world. They count as points on your Inquisition perk trees and provide bonuses to how fast an advisor can complete a war table operation. This guide points out where any potential agents are and how they can be recruited for the Inquisition.

COLLECTIONS

Astrariums

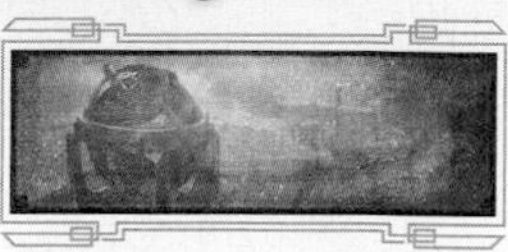

Astrariums are strange Tevinter devices strewn about in threes around different locales across Thedas. Solving the three astrarium puzzles within a locale grants you access to a special vault containing rare pieces of gear.

Bottles on the Wall

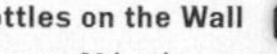

There are 29 bottles on the wall hidden throughout Thedas, typically found by searching areas where your mini-map starts pinging at you.

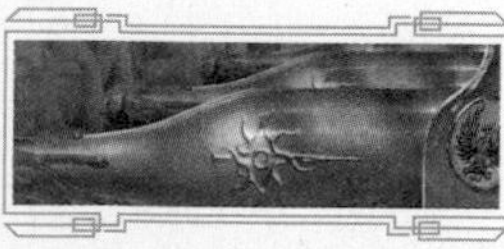

High Dragons

Ten high dragons have been spotted in Ferelden and Orlais. The largest and most dangerous predators in the wilds, high dragons are a menace to any settlement they decide is too close to their own territory. Hunting them down is a dangerous proposition, but the rewards are worth it. The rarest crafting materials come from high dragons, and you can find powerful weapons and equipment on their corpses. Each locale that has a high dragon has a special section dedicated to defeating her, and there's a special quest for taking down all 10 high dragons.

Inquisition Camps

Every locale has a number of camps you can establish in the name of the Inquisition. Not only do you get power, experience, and influence from doing this, but you gain new points you can fast travel between.

Regions

Every locale has a number of regions to discover. Regions are added to your list simply by walking or riding your horse into them.

Landmarks

There are certain monuments and locations that can be claimed by planting an Inquisition flag next to them. Unlike regions, landmarks will show up on your map if you get close enough to them.

Mosaic Pieces

There are five sets of mosaic pieces located throughout Thedas: Sacrifice, Invasion, The Fall, Archdemon, and Freed Are Slaves. Each set has been broken up into 12 pieces.

Oculara and Shards

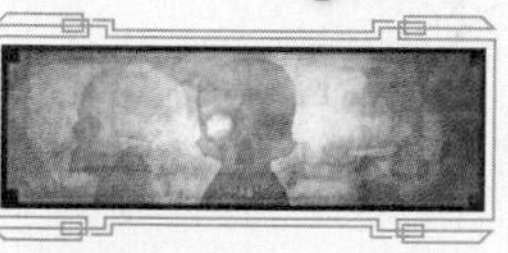

Oculara are strange, skull-tipped monuments found throughout Thedas. Going up to them allows you to search the area they are facing and discover hidden shards. Highlighting the shards with a ocularum reveals them on your map. From there on, the challenge is just to reach and collect them.

Glyphs

Occasionally, you will find yourself in places that can be illuminated by veilfire torches lit by mages. Veilfire can also reveal hidden glyphs and runes on the walls. Some of these glyphs are just for codex entries. Some contain special recipes for potions or schematics for runes you can enchant weapons with.

Song Lyrics

In between rounds of slaughtering wildlife in your quest to save the world, you can listen to bards singing tales. You can also find some songs by uncovering landmarks or finding lyrics written on a parchment. In total, there are 21 songs to collect for true patrons of the arts.

> A WORD ON LOOT

Loot is everywhere. Be it the ancient vases of a dead empire or a chest found in an abandoned cottage, loot is guaranteed to be found wherever you go. However, what you find isn't necessarily set in stone, and in fact most loot stashes are random in nature. You can't guarantee that you will get the same items that someone else playing the game was lucky to receive. Still, it's worth the effort to search for any loot chests or containers throughout the world. At the very least, you can sell what you don't need for cash, and occasionally you might find crafting recipes that are not available in any shops.

HAVEN

Haven once offered respite for pilgrims traveling to the Temple of Sacred Ashes farther into the Frostback Mountains. In the wake of the temple's destruction, the storied village—which was also home to a dragon-worshiping cult during the Fifth Blight—now serves as a makeshift camp for those working to pick up the pieces.

LOCALE SUMMARY

Scouting Cost: 0

Nestled in the Frostback Mountains, Haven is the Inquisition's modest first home. As a makeshift headquarters of the fledgling organization, Haven offers the most basic amenities, run by a dedicated staff of the faithful. Harritt, the blacksmith, does his best to keep the Inquisition armed and protected, while Adan, the alchemist, tinkers with herbs to create health-replenishing potions. Everyone in Haven does their part to make the Inquisition run as smoothly as possible. With the exception of a few tutorial-style quests, Haven serves primarily as a central hub of operations. It's often necessary to return to Haven to discuss the Inquisition's next move with the war council—an improvised war room has been established within the village's chantry. Outside the walls of Haven, rudimentary crafting materials can be found to create basic potions, weapons, and armor—some of these materials can also be used to complete requisitions. When you're not convening the war council or scouring the snow-covered terrain for crafting materials, engage your followers in conversation. They usually have something to say about the current state of affairs. They may also have some favors to ask of you, unlocking inner circle quests.

> CRAFTING MATERIALS

Common Materials:

- Elfroot
- Iron
- Fennec Fur
- Ram Leather

Rare Materials: None

Unique Materials: None

> COLLECTIONS

- Astrariums: 0
- Bottles of Thedas: 0
- High Dragons: 0
- Landmarks: 0
- Mosaic Pieces: 0
- Glyphs: 0
- Shards: 0
- Treasure Maps: 0
- Logging Stands: 1
- Quarries: 0

> INQUISITION PERSONNEL

Party Members

- Cassandra
- Varric
- Solas

LOCALE/COLLECTIONS MAP

MERCHANTS

Seggrit's Shop

Item	Cost
Upgrades (Highlights)	
Sturdy Bianca Grip	28
Aiming Module I	28
Bianca Arms I	19
Weapon Schematics	
Bianca Arms I	20
Bianca Aiming I	20
Sturdy Bianca Grip	20

Harritt's Shop

Item	Cost
The Tactician's Renewal	Special

NOTE The Tactician's Renewal is a unique single-use amulet that allows you to re-spec the abilities of any character who wears it. The initial cost of these amulets is low, but after your first purchase the price shoots up and stays up.

NOTE Once Dennet, the horsemaster, has joined the Inquisition, you can visit him at the stables to acquire more mounts. The mounts available at Dennet's store differ based on your progress. Initially you can purchase only the Taslin Strider, but more mounts are available later. For more information on mounts and their availability, reference the Skyhold section.

REQUISITIONS

Requisition Quests

Requisition	Materials
Requisition for Weapons	5 Iron, 1 Logging Stand
Lotus and Root*	4 Blood Lotus, 5 Elfroot

* Acquired from Mother Giselle

PARTY MEMBERS

> CASSANDRA

Affiliated Quest: The Wrath of Heaven

Initially, you're Cassandra's prisoner, held in a cell beneath the chantry following the tragedy at the Temple of Sacred Ashes. But she automatically becomes a member of your party as you begin the trek to the first Fade rift.

> VARRIC

Affiliated Quest: The Wrath of Heaven

Varric is first encountered at the first Fade rift, battling demons alongside Solas. Following this encounter, Varric automatically becomes a member of your party, joining you during the journey to the Breach.

> SOLAS

Affiliated Quest: The Wrath of Heaven

Solas shows you how to use the mark to close the first Fade rift in the Stormback Mountains. Following this encounter, Solas joins your party, alongside Cassandra and Varric.

SIDE QUESTS (RECOMMENDED LEVEL 1-4)

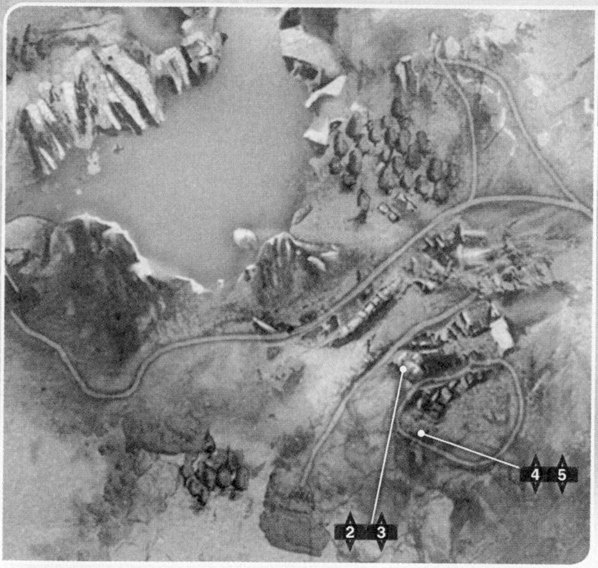

LEGEND

Level 1-4

1: Haven's Best and Brightest
2: The Right Armor
3: Piece by Piece
4: Passing Notes
5: Mixing Potions
6: Know Thy Enemy

1: HAVEN'S BEST AND BRIGHTEST

Quest Giver: N/A

Description: Even in these trying times, good help is not so hard to find. Explore Haven and meet some of the Inquisition's crafting masters.

Requirements: Available after meeting the war council

Reward: 50 XP

Objectives:

- Speak with the smith.
- Speak with the researcher.
- Speak with the quartermaster.
- Speak with the apothecary.

This quest is available immediately after leaving the game's opening cinematic. Start by speaking to the blacksmith, Harritt. He's located outside Haven's main gate. Harritt is the one who crafted the new armor you're currently wearing. Here you can craft new weapons and armor as well as modify existing equipment. Question Harritt about different aspects of his job to unlock two more quests: The Right Armor and Piece by Piece. These two quests can be completed here.

Adan, the apothecary, is on the west side of Haven, not far from Solas. He had a hand in your recovery following the incident at the temple. Adan is responsible with supplying the Inquisition with potions. You can come here to craft new potions using recipes and herbs. You can get the Passing Notes and Mixing Potions quests by speaking to Adan.

Next, speak to Threnn, the Quartermaster, near the tent outside the chantry. She's responsible for fulfilling requisitions. She has prepared a list of items the Inquisition needs—find some iron and a logging site to complete the Requisition for Weapons quest. Return to the table next to Threnn to complete requisitions.

Finally, talk to Minaeve, the researcher, in the chantry within Josephine's office. Some enemies drop unique collectibles. Return them to the researcher to learn more about your foes and earn combat bonuses against them. Interact with the table next to Minaeve to deposit some items, completing the Know Thy Enemy quest.

2: THE RIGHT ARMOR

Quest Giver: Harritt in Haven

Description: With the right materials, Haven's blacksmith can craft some pretty decent armor.

Requirements: Available after completing Haven's Best and Brightest

Reward: New armor

Objectives:

- Have some armor made.

Before you can craft some armor, you need to gather raw materials. Usually these items can be found in the wild during your journey. Fortunately, Harritt has a stash of materials nearby. Loot the crate next to the Craft Armor table—this will give you enough material to create some armor. Next, interact with the Craft Armor table. Armor is crafted using a schematic and raw materials. The schematic determines the appearance and potential power of the crafted armor, and the materials determine the specific stats and powers of the armor. Using the provided schematic and materials, craft a new piece of armor to complete the quest. Don't forget to equip the new armor.

3: PIECE BY PIECE

Quest Giver: Harritt in Haven

Description: The blacksmith can also improve existing armor.

Requirements: Available after completing Haven's Best and Brightest

Reward: Modified armor

Recommended Level: 2

Objectives:

- Modify some armor.

While you're still at the blacksmith's, take a moment to complete this simple quest. Start by looting the crate next to the Craft Weapons table. Inside is an armor upgrade. Next, go to the Modify Armor table. Upgrading armor adds the upgrade's stats to the armor's stats while also altering the armor's appearance. Choose the armor you wish to upgrade, preferably the armor you just crafted. Each piece of armor has two upgrade slots: arms and legs. Apply the upgrade you just retrieved from the crate, then select Confirm Changes to complete the process. Upgrades aren't permanent. They can be removed and applied to other armor. So before selling armor (or weapons), make sure you've removed any upgrades you wish to keep.

4: PASSING NOTES

Quest Giver: Adan in Haven

Description: Some technical notes were found while exploring Haven. They look like someone named Taigen put a lot of work into them.

Requirements: Available after scouting the Hinterlands

Reward: 100 XP, regeneration potion recipe

Objectives:

- Find Taigen's notes.
- Return the notes to Adan.

This quest is available after choosing the "Need any help?" conversation option while speaking to Adan—you can do this while completing the Haven's Best and Brightest quest. Adan needs some help finding Master Taigen's notes. Apparently Taigen was working on something special before he died at the Conclave. After speaking with Adan and selecting the quest, go to the purple mark on the quest map. As you near this area, a pulsing blue ring appears around the compass, indicating the presence of a hidden object. Press the button/key shown on-screen to begin searching. Once you initiate a search, a gold ring-like radius emanates from your character's feet. But the ring isn't uniform—it glows brighter along one edge, indicating the direction of the hidden object. Continue searching, using this indicator to move closer and closer to the hidden object. When you initiate a search next to the object, it finally appears on the ground, allowing you to retrieve it. Take Taigen's notes to Adan. In return he gives you access to a new potion recipe. You can now complete the Mixing Potions quest.

5: MIXING POTIONS

Quest Giver: Adan in Haven

Description: A recovered recipe can be used to mix a potion at a loadout station. There, the potion can also be equipped or replenished. Potion loadout stations are found in the Inquisition's base of operations or at any claimed camp.

Requirements: Available after completing Passing Notes

Reward: 50 XP

Objectives:

- Visit a potion loadout station.

Immediately after completing the Passing Notes quest, interact with the Equip Potions table next to Adan. This gives you access to your Potion Belt menu. Here you can assign or replenish potions for different party members. Healing potions, at the top of the radial, are replenished for free automatically, but all other potions require herbs to replenish them. Select the empty potion slot on the radial and assign the regeneration potion to it. It requires one elfroot to create each regeneration potion—replenish this potion to craft it from existing elfroot. If you don't have any elfroot, it can be acquired outside of Haven—it's by far the most common herb in the game and easy to find in multiple locales. Exit the Potion Belt menu to complete the quest.

6: KNOW THY ENEMY

Quest Giver: N/A

Description: Some items recovered in battle may later be worth studying.

Requirements: Available after scouting the Hinterlands

Reward: 50 XP

Objectives:

- Give Minaeve an item to research.

Chances are you completed this quest during Haven's Best and Brightest. Interact with the table next to Minaeve to deposit a research item. Research items can be looted from some fallen enemies following a battle. If you didn't retrieve any research items during your advance to the Temple of Sacred Ashes, you'll need to come back later and complete this quest.

THE HINTERLANDS

Nestled in the heart of Ferelden are the old forests and farmsteads of the Hinterlands. This rocky, rolling gateway to Redcliffe has now fallen into chaos. The conflict between mages and templars forced many off their lands, demons stalk the hills, and reports of strange magic abound near Redcliffe.

LOCALE SUMMARY

Scouting Cost: 1 Power

The first locale visited by the fledgling Inquisition, and one of the most expansive, the Hinterlands may seem intimidating at first. There's a lot of work to be done in order to secure power and influence throughout Thedas, and it's the Hinterlands where a lot of that work can be done. Inquisitors willing to spend time and effort in fully exploring this locale in the early part of the game can give themselves a lot of power to work with, allowing you to unlock other locales and potential party members. Major regions within the Hinterlands include the Crossroads, Redcliffe Farms, and the town of Redcliffe itself. The dungeon of Valammar awaits Inquisitors who take on a specific side quest.

Be careful where you wander early on. A few regions in the Hinterlands are far more dangerous than any demon, apostate, or enraged templar. Dragons have made the valley southwest of Redcliffe their home.

> CRAFTING MATERIALS

Common Materials:

- Elfroot
- Spindleweed
- Embrium
- Iron
- Canine Leather
- Fennec Fur
- Nugskin

Rare Materials:

- Royal Elfroot
- Deep Mushroom
- Obsidian

Unique Materials:

- Crystal Grace
- Drakestone
- Onyx
- Bear Hide
- Ram Leather

> COLLECTIONS

- Astrariums: 3
- Bottles of Thedas: 4
- High Dragons: 1
- Landmarks: 19
- Mosaic Pieces: 12
- Glyphs: 2
- Shards: 22
- Treasure Maps: 3
- Logging Stands: 2
- Quarries: 0

> INQUISITION PERSONNEL

Party Members

- Blackwall

Agents

- Clemence
- Enchanter Ellendra
- Horsemaster Dennet
- Lord Berand
- Ritts
- Speaker Anais
- Tanner
- Corporal Vale

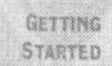

LOCALE MAP

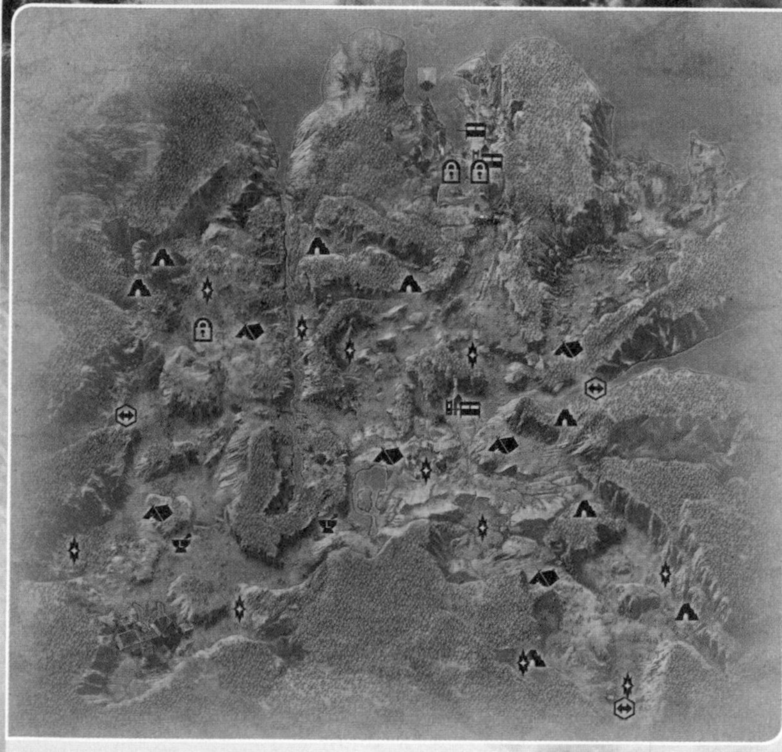

Legend

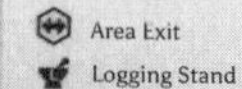

- Area Exit
- Logging Stand
- Quarry
- Cave/Dungeon
- Fade Rift
- Merchant
- Settlement
- Locked Door

Inquisition Camps

- Redcliffe Farms Camp
- Forest Camp
- Upper Lake Camp
- Dusklight Camp
- Outskirts Camp
- Dwarfson's Pass Camp

COLLECTIONS

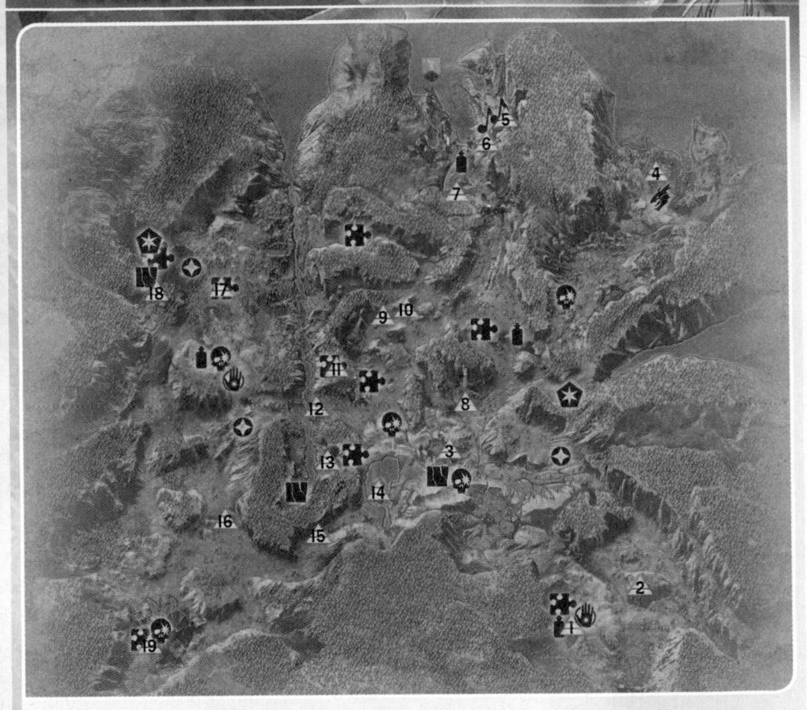

LEGEND

Astrariums

- Constellation: Judex
- Constellation: Draconis
- Constellation: Peraquialis

Bottles of Thedas

High Dragon

- Ferelden Frostback

Landmarks/Points of Interest

1. Lornan's Exile
2. The Tempter Burns
3. Thelm Gold-Handed, the Dreamer
4. Dragon Nest
5. The Gull and Lantern
6. The Hero of Ferelden
7. Redcliffe Windmill
8. The Departure of Her Lover
9. Hendir, Dwarf-Prince, Friend to Tyrdda
10. The Burial of the Beast
11. Fort Connor
12. Broken Bridge
13. Templar Camp
14. Tyrdda Bright-Axe, Avvar Mother
15. Thelm Gold-Handed, the Tempter
16. Tyrdda Flying to Her Lover
17. Tyrdda's Lover
18. Maferath Repentant
19. Grand Forest Villa

Mosaic Pieces

Oculara and Shards

Ocularum 1: The Outskirts

- Ocularum +4 Shards

Ocularum 2: Lake Luthias

- Ocularum +4 Shards

Ocularum 3: Redcliffe Farms

- Ocularum +5 Shards

Ocularum 4: Grand Forest Villa*

- Ocularum +5 Shards

Ocularum 5: Lady Shayna's Valley**

- Ocularum +4 Shards

Solas Artifacts

Glyphs

Song Lyrics

- Bards in Redcliffe sing multiple songs. You have to stick around and listen to collect them all.

Treasure Maps

- Map to a Waterfall
- Sketch of Calenhad's Foothold
- Map of a Farmland Cave

* You will need to clear out a part of the Grand Forest Villa of mercenaries in order to safely reach the ocularum.

** You will need to defeat the Ferelden Frostback High Dragon to safely reach the ocularum, much less collect all of the shards it reveals.

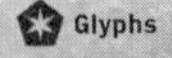

ASTRARIUM SOLUTIONS

Astrarium: Judex

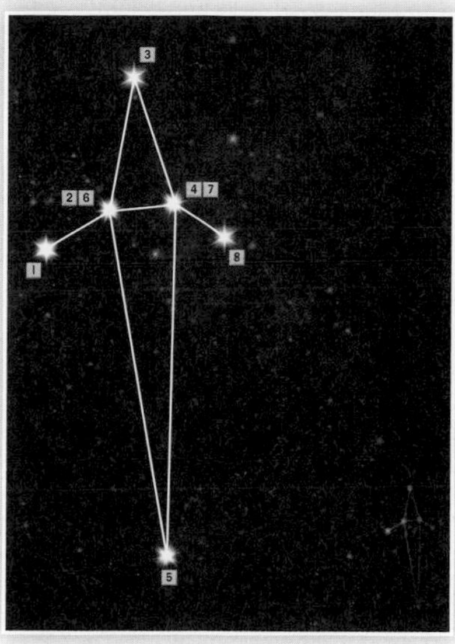

Astrarium: Draconis

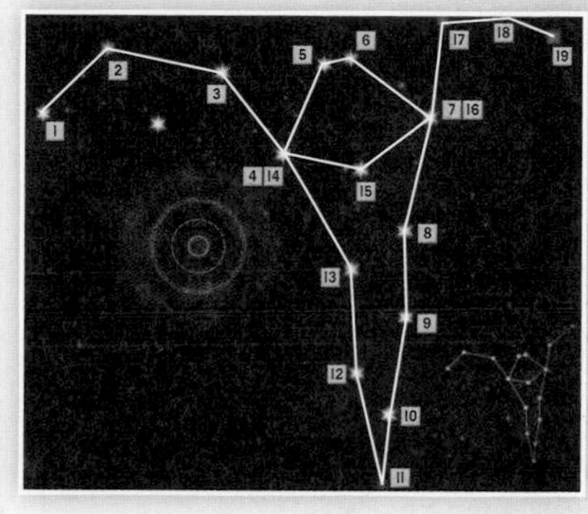

Astrarium: Peraquialis

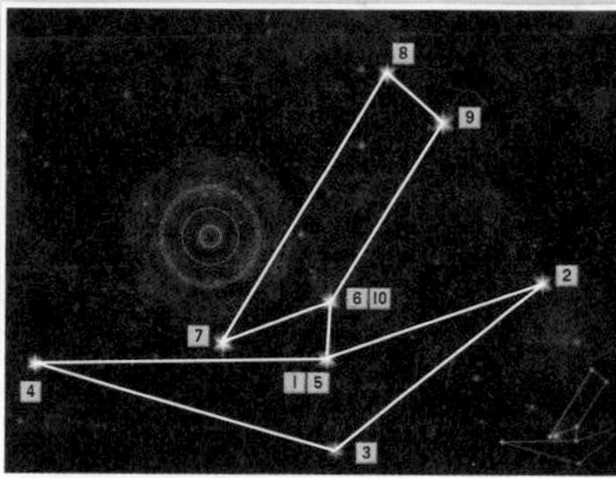

Astrarium Vault

After you solve all three astrariums in the Hinterlands, the door to the treasure chamber they locked will open. Its location is within the final cave you enter as part of the Apostates in the Witchwood side quest, and it will be marked on your quest map. See the information on that quest for further details on how to reach this cave.

FADE RIFTS

The first locale you visit is filled with Fade rifts to close. Expect the basic types of demons to oppose you at every one of these rifts: wraiths and shades, with terrors being among the greatest threat. You might occasionally see rage demons and despair demons appear during the later waves at some of these rifts, so be careful.

FADE RIFT DETAILS

QUEST	RIFTS	TOTAL POWER
Rifts on the Outskirts	2	2
Rifts at the Farm	2	2
Rifts at Dwarfson's Pass	3	3
Rifts at the Foothold	2	2
Rifts in the Woods	2	2

MERCHANTS

Crossroads Merchant

Item	Cost
Weapons (Highlights)	
Stormbreak	439
Mercenary Lord Blade	78
Upgrades (Highlights)	
Sturdy Bianca Grip	28
Aiming Module I	28
Bianca Arms I	19
Crafting Materials	
Spindleweed	20
Ram Leather	20
Nugskin	20
Fennec Fur	20
Elfroot	20
Druffalo Hide	20
Dragonling Scales	20
Canine Leather	20
Bronto Hide	20
Blood Lotus	20
Recipes	
Antivan Fire Grenade Recipe	53

Redcliffe Weapons Merchant

Item	Cost
Weapons (Highlights)	
Dagger of Faith	78
Upgrades (Highlights)	
Masterwork Firm Dagger Grip	70
Masterwork Hilted One-Handed Haft	70

Redcliffe Armor Merchant

Item	Cost
Armor (Highlights)	
Masterwork Battlemaster Mail	14,212
Masterwork Scout Armor	1,161
Superior Vanguard Coat	298
Superior Hunter Coat	298
Upgrades (Highlights)	
Superior Vanguard Coat Legs	70
Superior Vanguard Coat Arms	70
Superior Hunter Coat Legs	70
Superior Hunter Coat Arms	70

Redcliffe Schematics Merchant

Item	Cost
Weapon Schematics	
Templar Greatsword	129
Pointed Maul	129
Keeper Staff	129
Double-Bearded Axe	129
Raider Hatchet	64
Kite Shield	64
Thick Greatsword Grip	20
Rugged Two-Handed Haft	20
Rugged Bow Grip	20
Pointed Dagger Grip	20
Jeweled Staff Blade	20
Hilted One-Handed Haft	20
Dense Two-Handed Haft	20
Curved Staff Grip	20
Curved Longsword Grip	20
Bulky One-Handed Haft	20
Blunt Pommel	20
Balanced Dagger Grip	20
Army Longsword Grip	20
Acolyte Staff Blade	20
Armor Schematics	
Medium Adventurer Armor	176
Light Adventurer Armor	176
Heavy Adventurer Armor	176
Sturdy Scout Coat	159
Sturdy Scout Armor	159
Sturdy Defender Coat	159
Sturdy Defender Armor	159
Sturdy Apprentice Armor	159
Templar Helmet	28
Templar Scribe Cowl	20
Scout Hat	20
Scout Coat Legs	20
Scout Armor Legs	20
Scout Armor Arms	20
Defender Coat Legs	20
Defender Armor Legs	20
Apprentice Coat Legs	20
Apprentice Coat Arms	20
Apprentice Armor Arms	20
Apprentice Armor Legs	20

REQUISITIONS

Requisition Quests

Requisition	Materials
Hinterlands Drakestone Survey	2 Onyx, 5 Drakestone
Hinterlands Tapestry Requisition	5 Velveteen, 4 Decorative Gems
Hinterlands Cage Requisition	5 Fereldan Locks, 10 Iron

PARTY MEMBERS

BLACKWALL

Affiliated Quest: The Lone Warden

The Lone Warden quest is available immediately after returning from Val Royeaux. Search the western shore of Lake Luthias to find Blackwall busy training some Grey Warden recruits. After you help him fend off an attack from bandits, Blackwall offers his services to the Inquisition.

AGENTS

CLEMENCE

Affiliated Quest: In Hushed Whispers

Inquisition Perk: Clemence, the Tranquil (Forces)

After meeting Alexius in the Gull & Lantern tavern in Redcliffe, speak to Clemence. Unhappy with his current role among the rebel mages, Clemence offers to join the Inquisition, giving you access to a new perk. This reduces the time it takes Cullen to complete operations by 5 percent.

ENCHANTER ELLENDRA

Affiliated Quest: My Lover's Phylactery

Inquisition Perk: Enchanter Ellendra (Connections)

Ellendra can be convinced to join the Inquisition by Vivienne, following the sad news of her templar lover's passing. Alternatively, you can convince her to join if you're playing as a mage, have sided with the mages/templars, or have the arcane persuade conversation option.

HORSEMASTER DENNET

Affiliated Quest: Horses for the Inquisition

Inquisition Perk: Horsemaster Dennet (Inquisition)

Horsemaster Dennet admits his temptation to leave his lands and wife behind to join the Inquisition but is initially unwilling to make the commitment. However, Cassandra or Vivienne can convince him that the cause is righteous enough to join.

LORD BERAND

Affiliated Quest: Love Waits

Inquisition Perk: Lord Berand (Forces or Connections)

When you return to Lord Berand at the end of the Love Waits quest, he can be persuaded to either join the Inquisition personally as soldier or go home and use his influence to help the Inquisition. The Lord Berand perk reduces the amount of time it takes Cullen or Josephine to complete an operation by 5 percent.

RITTS

Affiliated Quest: Strange Bedfellows

Inquisition Perk: Witty Ritts (Secrets)

As part of the Strange Bedfellows quest, Varric or a dwarven Inquisitor is able to convince Ritts that her unique talents are useful, enough that she will become one of Leliana's agents, reducing the time it takes for her to complete a war table operation by 5 percent.

SPEAKER ANAIS

Affiliated Quest: Praise the Herald of Andraste

Inquisition Perk: Speaker Anais (Secrets or Connections)

After closing the rift during the Praise the Herald of Andraste quest, ask Speaker Anais to "spread word of an Inquisition" to recruit an agent for Josephine (Connections). Or ask her to "listen and gather information" to make her an agent for Leliana (Secrets).

TANNER

Affiliated Quest: Business Arrangements

Inquisition Perk: Smuggler Tanner (Secrets)

A letter found on a dead templar suggests that Tanner is secretly doing business with the templars. Confront Tanner in Redcliffe, near the chantry. Have Cassandra coerce Tanner into joining the Inquisition to unlock the Smuggler Tanner perk. This reduces the amount of time it takes for Leliana to complete operations by 5 percent.

CORPORAL VALE

Locale: The Hinterlands

Affiliated Quest: Various Hinterlands Quests

Inquisition Perk: Vale's Irregulars (Forces)

After helping refugees at the Crossroads with a series of small quests, speak to Corporal Vale to receive one of three possible rewards as well as a perk. If you ask Corporal Vale to recruit skilled refugees, you'll gain one power. If you ask that the refugees work for the Inquisition, you'll earn gold. Or ask to grow the Inquisition's reputation to make him an agent.

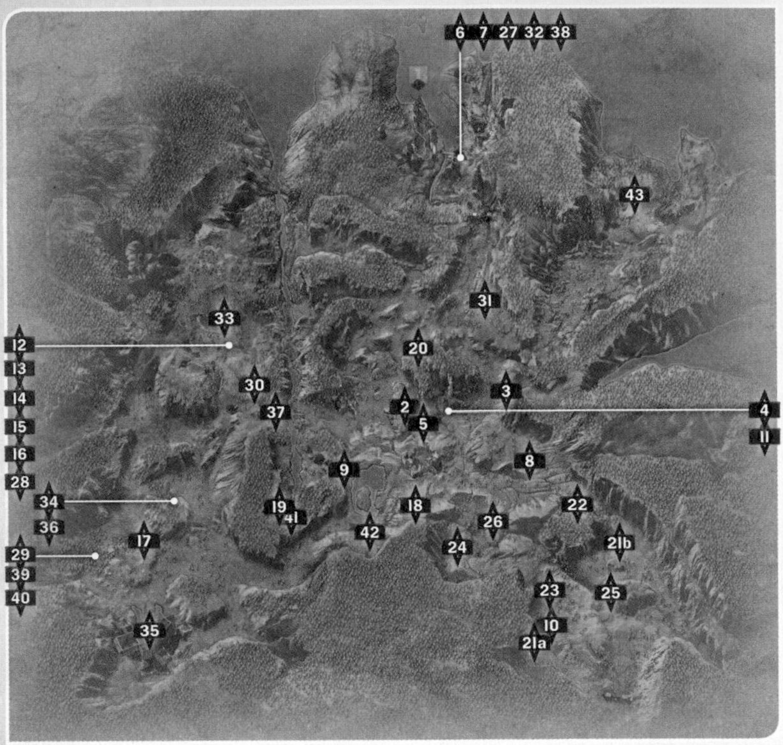

SIDE QUESTS (RECOMMENDED LEVEL 4-7, 8-11, AND 12+)

« LEGEND »

Level 4-7

1: Holding the Hinterlands
2: In the Elements
3: East Road Bandits
4: Hunger Pangs
5: A Healing Hand, A Common Treatment
6: An Advanced Treatment
7: A Rare Treatment
8: Apostates in the Witchwood
9: Templars to the West
10: Praise the Herald of Andraste
11: Shallow Breaths
12: In the Saddle
13: Master of Horses
14: Horses for the Inquisition
15: Farmland Security
16: Trouble with Wolves
17: Sketch of Calenhad's Foothold
18: Map to a Waterfall
19: Blood Brothers
20: Stone Dreams
21: Love Waits
22: Open a Vein
23: My Lover's Phylactery
24: Agrarian Apostate
25: Conscientious Objector
26: Strange Bedfellows
27: A Spirit in the Lake
28: Safeguards Against Looters
29: Letter from a Lover
30: Failure to Deliver
31: Business Arrangements
32: The Ballad of Lord Woolsley
33: Where the Druffalo Roam
34: Playing with Fire

Level 8-11

35: The Mercenary Fortress
36: Map of a Farmland Cave
37: Return Policy
38: Flowers for Senna
39: Bergrit's Claws
40: Hinterlands Who's Who
41: Deep Trouble
42: Dungeon: Valammar

Level 12+

43: High Dragon: The Fereldan Frostback

I: HOLDING THE HINTERLANDS

Quest Giver: Scout Harding

Description: Establish camps to hold the Hinterlands and support Inquisition activity in the region.

Requirements: Started as soon as you arrive in the Hinterlands

Reward: 50 Influence and 1 Power per camp, except for the starting camp

Objectives:

- Establish six camps.

There are six campsites clearly marked on your Hinterlands map while you have this quest actively tracked, and the first of these is set up as soon as you arrive in this locale. Establishing a camp provides experience, influence, power, and additional fast travel points, so there's no reason why you shouldn't make every effort to establish camps as early as possible. The primary challenge of the camp quests is simply reaching each location, and you'll find that every major wilderness locale has multiple camps to establish. At first, you may not be able to reach every site, because of either terrain or dangerous enemies.

2: IN THE ELEMENTS

Quest Giver: Recruit Whittle

Description: Apostate mages have supply caches hidden in the area. The supplies could help protect refugees from the elements.

Requirements: Speak with the recruit to the west of the Crossroads after securing it from the templar-mage fighting, or explore the southeast of the Hinterlands. Finding and claiming a cache will prompt small talk among your party that the supplies could benefit the Crossroads, and you will be given a waypoint that directs you to speak with the recruit.

Reward: 177 XP, 80 Influence, 1 Power

Objectives:

- Report the cache locations to Whittle.

This quest is a simple matter of going to the supply cache locations and claiming them. However, they are a fair ways south from the Crossroads. Thankfully, most of the caches are not particularly well hidden, and the quest map waypoints do a good job of putting you on the right path to each cache. However, one of the caches requires you to defeat a magical ice barrier. Be sure to take Solas (or any other mage) with you, assuming you're not a mage yourself. A mage can defeat the barrier faster with a powerful fire staff. Once you find and claim all five caches, return to Whittle to report their locations and complete the quest.

3: EAST ROAD BANDITS

Quest Giver: Recruit Bellette

Description: Bandits are attacking refugees along the King's Highway to the east of the Crossroads.

Requirements: Available as soon as you enter the Hinterlands

Reward: 177 XP, 80 Influence, 1 Power

Objectives:

- Dispense with the bandits on the road to the east.

Bellette is guarding a stone arch east of the Crossroads, warning travelers of the bandits on the road farther east. However, when you press for more information, it seems that there might be more to these bandits than meets the eye.

Follow the trails to the east to the first waypoint to encounter your first bandit ambush: two footmen, two archers. The archers can pick apart lighter-armored classes with ease, so consider wiping them out first. They don't have the health or armor to survive intense focus for long. The footmen can be occupied by someone tankier, like Cassandra.

The second group of outlaws is farther east, near a stone spire close to the edge of the Hinterlands. One of them attempts to retreat to the north toward more of his "bandit" brethren.

As you head north to the third waypoint, you enter Rebel Queen's Ravine, where the final confrontation with the bandits will commence. This can be a rough fight, with up to five archers to contend with, along with an outlaw enforcer, also known as a bruiser. The bruiser is the real threat, a mountain of a man armed with a two-handed axe that can flatten anyone who strays too close. Additionally, he resists many forms of crowd control, so you'll want to dedicate a tank to keeping him well away from softer party members.

Take out the archers first. Have one member of the party try to lock down the bruiser's attention, while the other three party members focus on one archer at a time, until the bruiser is left alone. Be prepared to quickly heal anyone who gets caught by the bruiser's vicious attacks!

After the bandits have been dealt with, loot their bodies to find a mysterious letter. It sheds no light on who started this little operation, but it does suggest a level of organization beyond mere opportunistic bandits. You can also set up a camp in this location, though we don't recommend you explore farther north until you are at least level 12 and sufficiently geared to fight the dragons in them thar hills.

4: HUNGER PANGS

Quest Giver: Refugee hunter, Crossroads

Description: Wild rams live in the hills near the Crossroads. Their meat could mean the difference between comfort and starvation for the refugees.

Requirements: Available after securing the Crossroads

Reward: 177 XP, 80 Influence, 1 Power

Objectives:

- Deliver 10 pieces of ram meat.

Behind a house across the road from Corporal Vale's position is a refugee hunter who worries for the starving refugees. He can't leave the village for fear of bandits, apostates, or templars, but asks that you hunt the rams down in his stead. A location where rams roam will be marked on your map. They are easy prey for any member of the Inquisition, but they can and will run away when they see danger approach. Fortunately, it doesn't take much to bring down a ram, and you should be able to deliver the 10 pieces of ram meat in short order. Speed this quest up by using fast travel to quickly bounce between the camp closest to the rams and the Crossroads.

5: A HEALING HAND

Quest Giver: Corporal Vale

Description: The refugees at the Crossroads would benefit from the services of an experienced healer.

Requirements: Available at the Crossroads after securing it from the templars and mages

Reward: 177 XP, 80 Influence, 1 Power

Objectives:

- Convince a healer to help the Crossroads refugees.

In the aftermath of the fighting around the Crossroads, speak to Corporal Vale about the troubles the villagers are facing. One of them is the lack of an experienced healer. He's heard of one in the village of Redcliffe to the north. Unfortunately, you can't reach the healer because the gate to Redcliffe is barred until you address the Chantry in Val Royeaux.

After the events in Val Royeaux, you can enter Redcliffe proper and speak with the medic, starting this quest. You learn that she has misgivings about going to the Crossroads because she's an elf, and she has dealt with racist attitudes from the humans there. You can convince her to help by various means. If you're an elf, you can can easily convince her by yourself. If that's not an option, Cassandra or Solas would be able to encourage her to go to the Crossroads. Or if you've invested in the Nobility Knowledge or History Knowledge Inquisition perks, you gain special dialogue options that can help convince her to move to the Crossroads.

NOTE If you convince her to go to the Crossroads, you can accomplish A Common Treatment, An Advanced Treatment, and A Rare Treatment at the Crossroads. If she stays at Redcliffe, you can do those quests at Redcliffe.

5: A COMMON TREATMENT

Quest Giver: Corporal Vale, the Crossroads

Description: The healer needs certain herbs to treat the injured patients.

Requirements: Available after addressing the Chantry at Val Royeaux

Reward: 44 XP, 40 Influence

Objectives:

- Convince the healer to help the Crossroads refugees.
- Find four elfroots and two spindleweeds.
- Bring the herbs to the healer.

When speaking with Corporal Vale, you can ask him multiple questions about the state of the refugees, and he will eventually pass word of a healer in Redcliffe. However, the village gate is closed until after you address the Chantry's grievances in Val Royeaux. After this, you can return to Redcliffe, but as you approach the gate, a Fade rift opens and forces you and the local guard contingent into battle!

After gaining access to the village, you can finally speak with this healer, who is reluctant to help the refugees initially, but with the right speech choices you can convince the elf of the necessity of their assistance. Solas or Cassandra can also do the same if one of them is with you. The healer will tell you to gather the herbs on the lists she places on a nearby countertop. Elfroot is practically everywhere, and spindleweed can be found growing near the lakes, ponds, and rivers of the Hinterlands.

6: AN ADVANCED TREATMENT

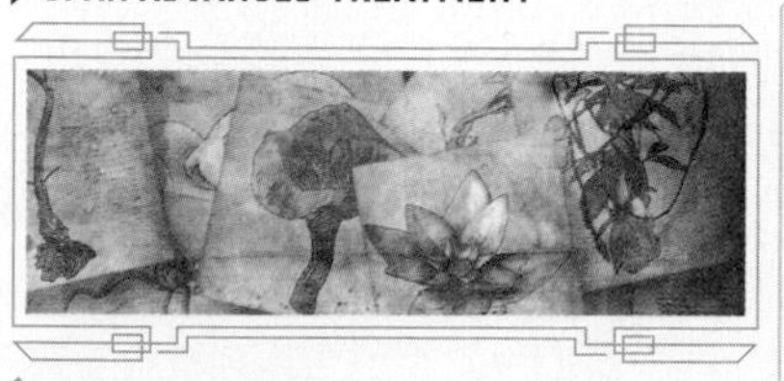

Quest Giver: Healer, Redcliffe

Description: The healer needs certain herbs to treat the injured patients.

Requirements: Complete A Common Treatment.

Reward: 44 XP, 40 Influence

Objectives:

- Find six elfroots and one royal elfroot.
- Bring the herbs to the healer.

The second list the healer provides is not much harder to fulfill. Royal elfroot grows on the small farm plot near the starting Hinterlands camp, where you also begin the Blood Brothers quest.

7: A RARE TREATMENT

Quest Giver: Healer, Redcliffe

Description: The healer needs certain herbs to treat the injured patients.

Requirements: Complete An Advanced Treatment.

Reward: 44 XP, 40 Influence

Objectives:

- Find five spindleweeds and two bunches of crystal grace.
- Bring the herbs to the healer.

The final list requires crystal grace. This herb grows more commonly in the southwestern region of the Hinterlands, but the enemies here are a definite step above most of what you'll find throughout the rest of this locale. Don't go flower picking in this neck of the woods if you're not ready to hunt bears or heavily armed mercenaries.

8: APOSTATES IN THE WITCHWOOD

Quest Giver: The dead body of an apostate to the southeast of the Outskirts camp. Can also be started by finding a note in a house on the road to Redcliffe from the Crossroads, or in one of the caves on the edge of the Witchwood.

Description: Fighting between apostate mages and rogue templars has driven refugees from their homes and endangered everyone in the area.

Requirements: Available as soon as you enter the Hinterlands

Reward: 354 XP, 200 Influence, 2 Power

Objectives:

- Search the Witchwood for the apostate stronghold.
- Deal with the apostates.

Just southeast of the first camp established by the Inquisition, a battle between apostates and Inquisition scouts is unfolding. You can intervene as soon as Scout Harding finishes briefing you on the situation, though you may find these apostates to be a bit tougher than what you've faced up to that point. After your party and the scouts wipe out the initial group of attackers, some will flee farther east. Among the dead will be a letter that can be looted, hinting at a larger apostate stronghold in the Witchwood, north of the Crossroads.

West of the Crossroads is a tunnel that takes you to the northern section of the Hinterlands, where a large-scale battle is raging between templars and mages. All will consider your party hostile, so try not to tick off too many groups of enemies all at once! Rogues will find that Stealth from the Subterfuge tree allows them to easily walk up behind a target and single them out for elimination—or break contact should they attract too much attention. There's also no shame in letting the enemy factions soften each other up before you dive in to present your independent third-party solution to their little spat.

TIP Be sure to explore and loot the battlefield as thoroughly as possible after every fight. There are landmarks to claim, not to mention the supplies left behind by fallen combatants. If you've used the ocularum overlooking the area, you'll also be able to recover a number of shards.

The first waypoint provided on the map encompasses the West Road region. There's a claimable landmark inside the battered Fort Connor just to the north of where you enter the West Road. Deeper inside of the keep is a mosaic piece belonging to the set The Fall.

A second mosaic piece is inside one of the burning huts in the field just south of Fort Connor. Avoid sticking around in the flames for too long, and use a rogue to pick the door lock to be able to get inside and retrieve the mosaic piece.

There are multiple battles to resolve before you reach your ultimate destination, marked by waypoints leading farther north from the initial fighting. Each battle you must contend with several footmen, templar and mage aligned. The real threats are guardsmen and mages. The mages can deal serious damage with their spells, and the guardsmen can charge and knock over anyone unlucky enough to be in the way of their big shields. Despite this, it's recommended you thin out the numbers of hostiles first by wiping out the basic footmen.

TIP This quest takes you close to some landmarks as you fight toward the final cave. Don't miss out on claiming these!

The fighting eventually takes you to a camp just outside a cave, guarded by a pair of mages and some more footmen. There are some interesting formations of ice springing out from the ground, products of the mages showing off their powers. You can use these to break line of sight with the enemy, which is one way you can limit the effectiveness of the mages.

After defeating this apostate camp, you now have to break into the cave itself. It is blocked off by a weak fire. Once you get past the barrier, you can enter the cave and deal with one last contingent of apostates. Again, handle the lesser footmen before focusing on the mages. The quest is complete once you eliminate this final group of apostates, but remember to loot the cave thoroughly for more supplies.

9: TEMPLARS TO THE WEST

Quest Giver: Letter on the corpse of a templar. You can also start this quest by finding a letter in Fort Connor or at a camp just outside along the road.

Description: Fighting between apostate mages and rogue templars has driven refugees from their homes and endangered everyone in the area.

Requirements: Kill the templars holding onto the Dalish ring for the Agrarian Apostate quest; you will find the letter on one of their corpses.

Reward: 354 XP, 200 Influence, 2 Power

Objectives:

- Locate the templar camp along the western road.
- Deal with the templars.

TIP We recommend you grab this quest before you travel to Redcliffe Farms to deal with the Inquisition's horse problem, just so it can be done along the way. Opening up the Upper Lake camp is also a good idea, as it can be useful should you need to resupply on potions. This is a combat intensive mission!

The letter from the templars in the southeastern side of the Hinterlands reveals the rough location of a templar encampment that blocks the western road that passes between the Crossroads and Redcliffe Farms. Simply follow the road to the west, and you will start to run into smaller camps filled with supplies you can loot.

The templars might take issue with you along the way. The first group you encounter along the road to the west consists of a templar defender and three templar knights. Ideally, you should have a tank (Cassandra, for example) start this fight to hold the attention of these dangerous fighters. The rest of the party should focus on burning down the knights before you go to work on the defender. Loot the small camp they were guarding after you finish them off.

As you travel forward, you'll come across the broken bridge that spans the river. Claim this landmark, then turn your gaze to the south. On the eastern side of the river, you should see a small side path leading up the cliffs to that side of the river.

Your next fight is a pair of templar defenders. This can be a challenging fight, as the Defenders are quite tough and can interrupt physical and magical attacks with their shields. Any abilities that can knock them down work wonders here! Check their camp for more loot after they have been killed, then continue along the path to the south. You will discover the Templar Encampment region and more templars to slay.

The entrance to the camp is guarded by a templar archer. However, once you make contact with him, four more templars rush to his aid. Players using a rogue can set up a very swift kill on this archer with the Stealth ability, or a ranged class can try to pull the archer out of the camp.

Two more archers deeper into the camp rush to join the fight, along with a templar knight. There are four other enemies in the camp at this point—if you're lucky they will not see fit to come aid their friends. If the whole camp gets alerted, be ready to burn through potions to stay standing, and use any means at your disposal to keep the mob off your weaker party members.

The remaining enemies in the camp are three templar knights, and one last defender. Fortunately, they aren't close to each other, so it is possible to pull the knights into combat separately from the defender, a more manageable fight than having to deal with all four together. Once you've cleared out the camp, the quest is complete, and you can freely partake in all of the treasure chests the templars left behind.

10: PRAISE THE HERALD OF ANDRASTE

Quest Giver: Speaker Anais

Description: Cultists are looking for a sign that the rifts in the Veil can be controlled.

Requirements: Available as soon as you enter the Hinterlands. Simply approach Speaker Anais in front of the gates to the Lornan's Exile enclave.

Reward: 177 XP, 80 Influence, 1 Power

Objectives:

- Seal the Fade rift.
- Speak with Anais.

Speaker Anais halts you as you approach Lornan's Exile. She doubts your capacity to seal the Fade rifts, as well as your title as Herald of Andraste, and will not sway from her position until she has proof the rifts are controllable. That's where you come in.

Approach the rift at the back of the enclave to trigger an ambush. Like any Fade rift you've encountered, this rift consists of multiple waves of enemies and generally starts off with a weaker enemy set before ramping things up in the second wave. Don't forget that it is possible to disrupt the rift while you are fighting the demons in order to stun them, a good tactic if you are feeling overwhelmed.

After sealing the Fade rift, go back to Speaker Anais to deliver the good news. She declares her loyalty to you and offers the services of her cult to the Inquisition. You can either have the cult help the refugees in the Hinterlands, spread word of the Inquisition across the continent, or act as informants and spies for your cause.

11: SHALLOW BREATHS

Quest Giver: Refugee, Crossroads

Description: A refugee at the Crossroads is having trouble breathing. Without a specific potion, she is likely to die.

Requirements: Secure the Crossroads from templar and apostate aggression and you will be able to talk to the frantic elf.

Reward: 44 XP, 40 Influence

Objectives:

- Get the potion from the refugee's son.
- Bring the potion to the refugee's husband.

If you approach a villager next to the Crossroads' claimable landmark, he will flag you down and request that you speak with his son Hyndel, who hides in a cult enclave far south of the Crossroads. Hyndel can make a potion that allows his mother to breath, and she needs it right now. You only need to speak with Hyndel to get the potion, and he's easily found near the enclave's central fountain. After delivering the potion back to the Crossroads, if Solas is in your party you can speak with Hyndel once more and convince him to return to the Crossroads in order to provide comfort to his family.

> 12: IN THE SADDLE

Quest Giver: Seanna, Redcliffe Farms

Description: A wealthy young landowner's daughter, Seanna, has built a course for racing horses.

Requirements: Available after earning a horse from Horsemaster Dennet

Reward: Gold

Objectives:

- Complete Seanna's first race.
- Complete Seanna's second race.
- Complete Seanna's final race.

Seanna has used the Redcliffe Farms trails to create race tracks for you to ride through on your new mount. To succeed, you need to race between the wooden posts that appear on the track, next to the conveniently lit torches that indicate where you need to go. The races increase in length and difficulty as you complete them, and the time limits get tighter. Complete all three to earn some extra gold for your trouble.

> 13: MASTER OF HORSES

Quest Giver: Scout Harding

Description: Horsemaster Dennet may be able to provide horses for the Inquisition. He just needs to be convinced.

Requirements: Enter the Hinterlands for the first time.

Reward: 177 XP, 80 Influence, 1 Power

Objectives:

- Speak with Dennet.
- Mount the horse at the stables.

Scout Harding has tried to get to Redcliffe Farms to requisition horses, but he has not been able to break through the fighting.

Your questing takes you through heavily contested territory to reach the farms, but when you speak with Dennet, he informs you that he simply can't give you the horses—at least, not until he has a guarantee they won't be stolen by bandits while traveling toward Haven. He asks that you speak with his wife and one of his servants to see to the tasks they provide.

On the plus side, Dennet does offer you a horse of your own. Go down to the stables, where his daughter Seanna also resides, and claim your new ride!

> **TIP**
> One of the bottles of Thedas, Carnal, 8:69 Blessed, can be found inside Dennet's home. Search the ground floor to find it!

> 14: HORSES FOR THE INQUISITION

Quest Giver: Dennet

Description: Convince Horsemaster Dennet to leave behind the farm and join the ranks of the Inquisition.

Requirements: Complete the quests The Trouble with Wolves and Farmland Security.

Reward: Horsemaster Dennet joins the Inquisition. 177 XP, 80 Influence, 1 Power

Objectives:

- Speak with Dennet.

After you complete the prerequisite quests, Dennet will provide horses for your cause. You are also able to converse with Dennet about becoming horsemaster for the Inquisition. Cassandra is capable of rousing the man to action, but Inquisitors of specific races and backgrounds might also be able to sway Dennet.

> 15: FARMLAND SECURITY

Quest Giver: Bron, Redcliffe Farms

Description: Bron believes building a series of watchtowers in the area would warn farmers and refugees of incoming attacks.

Requirements: Speak with Horsemaster Dennet.

Reward: 177 XP, 80 Influence, 1 Power

Objectives:

- Speak with Bron.
- Mark three watchtower locations.
- Complete the Watchtowers in the Farms operation at the war table.
- Inform Bron that the watchtowers have been built.

While this is not a difficult task, it is time consuming. First, you must ride out to the three locations marked on your quest map and claim them. They are not difficult to reach, but they are spread out enough that you may appreciate your new horse that much more.

When all three tower locations are claimed, return to Haven's war table to handle the special Watchtowers in the Farms mission. It requires two power and can take up to three hours to accomplish. Josephine will require the whole three hours, but Cullen's forces can get it done in less time. Once the towers are confirmed to be complete, speak with Bron.

16: TROUBLE WITH WOLVES

Quest Giver: Elaina, Redcliffe Farms

Description: Elaina has agreed to bring the farmers back once the area has been rid of wolves.

Requirements: Speak with the master of Redcliffe Farms to be directed to Elaina on how to solve some of the problems the farmers face.

Reward: 177 XP, 80 Influence, 1 Power

Objectives:

- Ask Elaina how to make the farmers safe again.
- Deal with the wolves.
- Tell Elaina the wolves are no longer a problem.

Elaina doesn't mince words: The farmers already have enough to deal with as it is, and the local wolf population trying to eat them doesn't make them inclined to remain farmers. She wants you to travel to the east to deal with the wolves and doesn't care how it gets done so long as the farmers are safe.

The first wolves you encounter are aggressive, attacking your party as you close in on their den. After putting them down, enter Wolf Hollow, the home they gave their lives to defend.

Wolf Hollow is, as you would imagine, populated by more black wolves. Their aggressive nature and the fairly tight spaces of the hollow make combat a challenge, as you don't have room to work. One "wolf" towers above the rest. Killing this terror is the primary goal of the quest, as it is the dark influence behind the crazed wolfpack. Looting the Token of the Packmaster from its corpse and equipping it on an active party member will turn all wolves friendly to your party. This works for all wolf packs in the world. You can even occasionally receive help from wolves that are nearby if you're in battle while wearing the token.

TIP Dark as this may sound, it's not a bad idea to purge the entire hollow of all wolves. The pelts can go toward armor for your party. The Inquisition requisition mission never ends!

NOTE The Safeguards Against Looters quest also sends you to Wolf Hollow, and there's no reason why you can't handle both quests in one go.

17: SKETCH OF CALENHAD'S FOOTHOLD

Quest Giver: A corpse near the starting camp in the Hinterlands

Description: This sketch of a castle on a rocky ridge marks a spot along a broken wall.

Requirements: Available as soon as you enter the Hinterlands for the first time

Reward: 44 XP, 40 Influence, rock armor schematic

Objectives:

- Find the spot marked on the sketch.

After recovering the sketch from the body just south of the starting Hinterlands camp, travel west from the camp, up the mountain path toward the castle ruins. There's a Fade rift near the ruins, part of the Rifts at the Foothold side quest, and there's a good chance you'll trigger the combat against the demons surrounding the rift as you approach Calenhad's Foothold.

To reach the point indicated, you must find a way to climb the broken-down wall that leads to the upper levels of a tower in the northwest corner of the ruins. The ground entrance is blocked off by rubble, unfortunately.

Use the pictured smaller pile of rubble near the collapsed section of wall. You'll have to jump repeatedly to make this climb, but if you can pull it off, you can walk along the wall until you reach the tower, then use a ladder to climb down into the blocked-off antechamber. Open the chest inside to retrieve an armor enhancement schematic!

NOTE Don't forget to explore Calenhad's Foothold thoroughly. You can claim a landmark here and scavenge potion materials and treasures.

> 18: MAP TO A WATERFALL

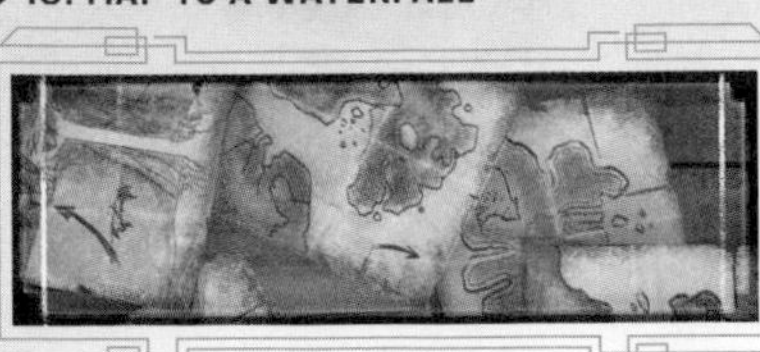

Quest Giver: A scroll west of the Upper Lake camp

Description: This map depicts a bridge with four pillars and a waterfall under a tree.

Requirements: Arrive in the Hinterlands for the first time

Reward: 44 XP, 40 Influence

Objectives:

- Find the spot marked on the map.

This is one of the easier treasures to reach. The river to the west of the templar camp you clear out in Templars to the West can be followed farther south, so follow the river from the broken bridge for a straight shot at the treasure. The treasure location is behind the waterfall, among the various iron nodes you can mine.

> 19: BLOOD BROTHERS

Quest Giver: A note in a hut just to the south of the Outskirts camp

Requirements: When you arrive in the Hinterlands for the first time, this quest can be started up immediately.

Reward: Mercenary lord blade, 44 XP, 40 Influence

Description: A templar has left a note for his apostate brother, challenging him to a fight.

Objectives:

- Go to the location mentioned in the letter.
- Loot the body.

You pass the hut containing the note that starts this quest on your way to the Crossroads from the Outskirts camp, and there's no harm in starting it up as soon as possible. The note itself describes a bitter fight in the making between two brothers, one an apostate, the other a templar. The templar has challenged his wayward brother to a battle to settle differences, and a waypoint is marked on your quest map. When you arrive, you'll find a corpse next to a locked hut. Inspect the corpse to recover the templar's sword and complete the quest.

TIP The hut near the templar is locked and requires a key. However, a rogue can easily pick the lock and ignore the key requirement.

Inside, you can search for one of the 29 collectible bottles of Thedas, Butterbile 7:84. There's also a treasure chest nearby for your trouble!

> 20: STONE DREAMS

Quest Giver: Note found inside an abandoned home north of the Crossroads

Description: A diary has been found, describing a man's troubling dreams and his plans to find peace in a cave in the hills.

Requirements: Arrive in the Hinterlands for the first time

Reward: 44 XP, 40 Influence

Objectives:

- Search the cave in the hills.
- Kill the apostate.

When you find the disturbed apostate's cave at the Ash Warrior's Refuge, he's hostile and attacks without provocation. Unfortunately for him, he's alone and up against a party led by the Herald of Andraste. Put the man out of his misery and search the cave for any goods he might have been storing.

> 21: LOVE WAITS

Quest Giver: Letter on a corpse to the east of Dwarfson's Pass, near the templars holding a ring for the Agrarian Apostate quest; or, speak with Lord Berand inside the enclave at Dwarfson's Pass. It is possible to start the quest from either location.

Description: A young noble named Berand joined the cult in the hills. He is worried that his lover, Vellina, has not yet arrived to join him.

Requirements: Available as soon as you arrive in the Hinterlands

Reward: 177 XP, 80 Influence, 1 Power

Objectives:

- Inform Berand of Vellina's death.
- Alternative: Find Vellina (only appears if you speak with Berand to start the quest).
- Offer Berand guidance (only appears if you inform Berand of Vellina's death but do not invite him to the Inquisition or send him home).

The enclave at the landmark of Lornan's Exile has several quests that deal with these cultists: Shallow Breaths, Praise the Herald of Andraste, and Love Waits. Should you visit this enclave first, you'll need to first get past the cultist leader in front of the gates by initiating the Praise the Herald quest. If you explore the dining hall on the right side of the enclave on the way to the Fade rift, you'll be flagged down by a nervous man on the second floor. He awaits word that his love has safely arrived at the enclave. If you speak with him, you will be given a waypoint on the map showing where to search for his now-dead lover, and you can then pass the news on to him

It's faster to get the letter first. You can find the corpse with the note near the templars that must be killed for the Agrarian Apostate side quest. Regardless of how you choose to accomplish this quest, you can then send the man home with a harsh rebuke, or you can invite him into the Inquisition. If you invite him, he will bring a small contingent of troops to further bolster your army, becoming an agent under Cullen's command and counting as one of his Inquisition perks.

TIP One of the 29 bottles of Thedas, Vint-9 Rowan's Rose, can be found by searching the tables near the cultist you deliver the letter to.

> 22: OPEN A VEIN

Quest Giver: A note found next to an apostate cache (see In the Elements for more details)

Description: A letter found on a dwarven corpse suggests that a cave in the hills has a valuable vein of lyrium waiting to be mined.

Requirements: Arrive in the Hinterlands for the first time, then locate the note.

Reward: 44 XP, 40 Influence

Objectives:

- Locate the vein of lyrium.

The body containing the letter that starts this quest is found in a cave to the southeast of the starting Outskirts camp. You'll know you're headed in the right direction if you find an astrarium along the way. Coincidentally, you find an apostate supply cache that you can claim as part of the In the Elements side quest started in the Crossroads.

After recovering the letter, you'll be provided a waypoint deeper south in the Hinterlands, where the lyrium vein waits inside a cave protected by a nearby apostate camp. Bring a mage armed with a fire-damage staff to make busting through the ice barrier blocking the mine entrance that much easier. If you don't have one handy, check the nearby chests to locate one.

TIP Try to start up the In the Elements quest before tackling this quest. The cave sealed by the ice barrier contains not just the lyrium vein you're looking for, but also a supply stash for In the Elements. Two birds with one stone!

> 23: MY LOVER'S PHYLACTERY

Quest Giver: A fallen templar in the Winterwatch Tower region.

Description: A phylactery found on a dead templar belongs to his mage lover, Ellendra. The phylactery could point other templars to Ellendra, and she may welcome its safe return, along with news of her lover.

Requirements: Available as soon as you enter the Hinterlands

Reward: 44 XP, 40 Influence

Objectives:

- Return the phylactery to Ellendra.

After recovering the phylactery, you can fast travel back to the Crossroads to find Ellendra in the northern part of the settlement, hiding in a cave well away from other civilians. Your conversation with Ellendra is short and to the point, though she's clearly upset by the fate of her lover despite her freedom from the templars. You can offer her a place in the Inquisition, but only Cassandra can truly convince Ellendra that it is better than the fools among the templars and mages who began this war.

> 24: AGRARIAN APOSTATE

Quest Giver: Widow Maura, or the ring on a templar you kill

Description: Templars killed an elven farmer, suspecting he was an apostate, and took his wedding ring as a prize. The farmer's widow wants them killed and the ring returned.

Requirements: Available as soon as you enter the Hinterlands

Reward: 44 XP, 40 Influence

Objectives:

- Recover the farmer's ring from the templars.
- Return the ring to the elven widow.

This quest can be started into two ways. One would be to visit the widow's humble home in the southern part of the hinterlands, to the southwest of the starting Inquisition camp. The other way would be to kill the templars holding her husband's ring and loot it from their corpses. The offending templars are to the east of Dwarfson's Pass and are not a particularly dangerous pair to handle with your party. Regardless of how you start the quest, your primary goal is to return the ring to the widow.

> 25: CONSCIENTIOUS OBJECTOR

Quest Giver: Dead corpse in the southeast of the Hinterlands

Description: A cabin in Witchwood is locked.

Requirements: Available as soon as you arrive in the Hinterlands

Reward: 44 XP, 40 Influence

Objectives:

- Find a key to the cabin.
- Go to the cabin in the highlands.

You will find a cabin key on a corpse next to the landmark that grants you the fourth stanza of the Saga of Tyrdda Bright-Ax, Avvar-Mother. The corpse also contains a letter that explains that this dead apostate was originally a proper circle mage, but he wished no part in the current schism. He wanted to retreat to an old cabin northwest of the Crossroads. The cabin's rough location will be marked on your quest map, and you can travel to the Witchwood to unlock it.

Alternatively, you can discover the locked cabin first. You're given a large search location in the southeast of the Hinterlands. Fast travel to the Dwarfson's Pass camp to get closer to your objective.

However you manage to start this quest, you can enter the cabin with the key. Once you enter, a terror demon attacks the party. Put it down, then loot the chest inside for some extra supplies and equipment.

> 26: STRANGE BEDFELLOWS

Quest Giver: Inquisition scout, just north of White Pass camp

Description: A scout on duty is worried something's happened to a fellow scout named Ritts, who was tasked with investigating apostates in the area.

Requirements: Available just after arriving in the Hinterlands

Reward: 177 XP, 80 Influence, 1 Power

Objectives:

- Search for the missing Inquisition scout.
- Update the worried scout on the status of Ritts.

If you're following the main road south, toward the White Pass Camp, you will encounter a worried Inquisition scout. He sent Scout Ritts farther south to investigate apostates in the area, and her general location will be marked on your map.

Ritts is at the top of a hill, under attack by some angry templars. She's a tough scout, more than able to hold her own against the enemy as you close in to assist, and the added bonus is that because the enemy is completely ignorant to your presence, you can score some hits before they turn their attention to your party. Rogues and mages can shut down at least one threat very quickly in situations like this. Work fast to save Ritts: The templars can kill her.

After saving Ritts, you can investigate the area near her using your Search ability. This points you to the corpse of a mage lying atop a picnic spread. Further investigation of the dead woman prompts Ritts to reveal the sordid truth of why she was attacked. Depending on your responses, you can either support Ritts's actions or viciously condemn them. If Varric is with you, you can also defer to him to provide advice on what Ritts should do next. Afterward, return to her friend to the north to deliver word of her condition. However, if Ritts is dead, all you can do is report the bad news to her scout friend, and you can't turn her into an agent.

NOTE If Varric convinces Ritts to use her talents for the Inquisition, she will become one of Leliana's best agents, listed under the Secrets Inquisition perks.

> 27: A SPIRIT IN THE LAKE

Quest Giver: Storyteller near the fast travel stone in Redcliffe

Description: A storyteller mentioned a spirit in a nearby lake. If offered a blood lotus, the spirit apparently gives a favor in return.

Requirements: Gain access to Redcliffe Village during In Hushed Whispers.

Reward: 44 XP, 40 Influence warlord greatsword

Objectives:

- Take a blood lotus to the lake.

A storyteller in Redcliffe village relays a tale regarding a spirit inhabiting a lake that is not sated by daisies brought to it by village girls, but by blood lotus. Take one to Lake Luthias, just south of the Upper Lake camp. Blood lotuses are more common in the Fallow Mire, but you can occasionally find some in item caches hidden throughout Redcliffe.

Placing a blood lotus in the offering bowl on one of the lake docks causes a sword to rise up from the waters, completing the quest and earning you a new weapon for warriors.

> 28: SAFEGUARDS AGAINST LOOTERS

Quest Giver: A letter on a farmer's corpse in the Redcliffe Farms region

Description: A man named Hessle fled the fighting to a cave in the northern hills with a secret project in tow.

Requirements: Available as soon as you enter the Hinterlands

Reward: 128 XP, 80 Influence

Objectives:

- Search the northern hills.

NOTE Search the northern hills. This quest takes you to the Wolf Hollow, where The Trouble with Wolves sends you. Try to do both at the same time!

Inside Wolf Hollow, one of Redcliffe's farmers managed to hide a container full of goods. Perhaps they believed the wolves would dissuade any looters. After clearing the cave of the wolf threat, take your time picking through the area, "recovering" the farmer's goods in the process.

> 29: LETTER FROM A LOVER

Quest Giver: A letter found in an abandoned campsite in Dead Ram Gorge

Description: You found a letter at an abandoned campsite. It instructs a young man to bring felandaris to a tree where a stone lady stands.

Requirements: Available as soon as you enter the Hinterlands

Reward: 44 XP, 40 Influence

Objectives:

- Bring felandaris to the tree on the hill.

Felandaris is a rare plant, not native to the Hinterlands. You may be able to find some in a loot stash somewhere in this locale. If you're not lucky, you may have to wait awhile to complete this quest; felandaris is most common in Emprise du Lion, which will not be accessible until near the end of the game.

Once you have the herb, go to the hill marked on your quest map and place the herbs on the altar. However, although the quest is complete, you still have to contend with an angry wraith that appears as soon as you set the herbs down.

> 30: FAILURE TO DELIVER

Quest Giver: Note lying next to a corpse and overturned cart

Description: A letter found on a dwarven corpse speaks of a package lost somewhere near the river north of the farms.

Requirements: Available after securing the Crossroads

Reward: Carta coat, 44 XP, 40 Influence

Objectives:

- Search the river for the package.

This is as simple as a quest can get! After you retrieve the note, a waypoint is provided on your quest map. You can easily find the package if you travel to the waypoint and begin using your Search ability. If you're close enough to the package, you'll be shown the direction it is relative to you. The package itself is a crate bundled in canvas lying on the shore next to the river. Search it to be able to loot the Carta coat and the gold found inside. The coat is limited to dwarf rogues, which makes it a great fit for Varric if you're not also playing a dwarf rogue yourself.

> 31: BUSINESS ARRANGEMENTS

Quest Giver: A note on a dead body north of the Crossroads, next to Old Fennick's place

Description: A letter found on a templar corpse suggests that someone named Tanner is secretly doing business with templars.

Requirements: Available as soon as you enter the Hinterlands. You cannot access Redcliffe village until after In Hushed Whispers.

Reward: 44 XP, 40 Influence, 0 Power

Objectives:

- Confront Tanner in Redcliffe village.

NOTE If you have not addressed the Chantry in Val Royeaux, you can't enter Redcliffe village to get to work on completing this side quest. There's no harm in picking up the quest early and coming back around when you have visited Val Royeaux.

If you've taken on the Blood Brothers quest, you'll be traveling to Old Fennick's place. Just north of the hut, a dead templar is guarded by an apostate and his sellsword guard. Eliminate them, then inspect the bodies to recover the note that begins the quest.

After gaining access to Redcliffe, you can find Tanner near the far rear of the village. This lady of the Chantry will try to play innocent, but you can confront her on her duplicity. However, if you're feeling forgiving and shrewd, you don't have to condemn Tanner entirely.

Invite this smuggler to the Inquisition and make use of her talents! Varric and Cassandra are able to speak on your behalf to sell this idea to her, but it is possible to convince her yourself if you have unlocked certain Inquisition perks.

TIP You can find Grey Whiskey/Ritewine/Conscription Ale in the locked house near the southern end of Redcliffe Village. However, the door barring the way requires the Deft Hands, Fine Tools Inquisition perk. Without that perk, you'll never be able to reach it.

32: THE BALLAD OF LORD WOOLSLEY

Quest Giver: One-Eyed Jimmy, Redcliffe

Description: A young man is distraught that his family's special ram, Lord Woolsley, has wandered off. He is offering a reward for the ram's return.

Requirements: Address the Chantry in Val Royeaux, then gain access to Redcliffe by sealing the Fade rift that opens before its front gates.

Reward: 177 XP, 80 Influence, 1 Power

Objectives:

- Locate Lord Woolsley and send him home.
- Return to Woolsley's owner for a reward.

One-Eyed Jimmy is convinced that his pet ram, Lord Woolsley, is responsible for his family's good fortune. He also is convinced Woolsley speaks. Question not what he believes, and just travel to the waypoint near Lake Luthias.

Once at the lake, you should be able to find a VERY distinctly colored ram. This is Lord Woolsley. If you approach him, your character will call out to the ram, and he will grunt in acknowledgement and return home. Simple job! Return to One-Eyed Jimmy for your reward.

CAUTION If you attack Lord Woolsley, he will become a rage demon and fight back! You will not be able to start or complete this quest if you harm or kill Lord Woolsley at any point in time.

33: WHERE THE DRUFFALO ROAM

Quest Giver: Notice Board, Redcliffe Farms

Description: A farmer's druffalo ran off, spooked by demons, and was last seen in the ravine.

Requirements: Available as soon as you enter the Hinterlands

Reward: 44 XP, 40 Influence

Objectives:

- Rescue the farmer's druffalo.
- Lead the druffalo back to the pasture.
- Tell the farmer that his druffalo is safe.

The druffalo in question is in a ravine to the west of Redcliffe Farms, just past the river (and an active Fade rift, if you haven't taken care of it yet). When you reach the druffalo, a pack of wolves is attacking it. Kill the wolves while avoiding causing harm to the druffalo. After you save it, it will follow you as you return to Redcliffe Farms. Once you get close enough, the druffalo happily returns to its field, and you can speak with a nearby farmer to complete the quest.

34: PLAYING WITH FIRE

Quest Giver: Letter on a corpse, Avvar Blade Valley

Description: A letter found on a corpse said: "Three times around the crowned statue, right hand close enough to brush the stone itself, and the spirits will listen." Doing so will apparently bring back someone's grandfather. The letter writer must really miss him.

Requirements: Available as soon as you enter the Hinterlands

Reward: 44 XP, 40 Influence master demon-slaying rune

Objectives:

- Bring the grandfather back.
- Defeat the demon.

You find this letter near a landmark containing the third stanza of the Saga of Tyrdda Bright-Ax. Walk around the statue in the manner the letter suggested to summon a demon that will possess a corpse. Destroy this unholy resurrection to complete the quest. The rune you can loot from the corpse can help the chosen weapon rip apart demons. It's worth holding on to until you find a powerful weapon that can accept it.

35: THE MERCENARY FORTRESS

Quest Giver: Orders found on or near mercenaries in Hafter's Woods or Avvar Blade Valley

Description: Mercenaries are stirring unrest in the Hinterlands. They have occupied an old fort in the woods.

Requirements: Available as soon as you enter the Hinterlands. Travel to Avvar Blade Valley and find the note.

Reward: 128 XP, 80 Influence

Objectives:

- Find the mercenary fortress.
- Defeat the mercenary leader.

Fighting through Avvar Blade Valley or Hafter's Woods, you may encounter groups of mercenaries, much like those fought during the East Road Bandits quest. Sometimes, you'll find a camp that is guarded by multiple mercs. You might find orders at the camps, or on the mercs themselves, that reveal their base of operations: the Grand Forest Villa.

The bridge to the villa is protected by several mercs, but the real challenge begins when you enter the villa's courtyard and are forced to face off against a pair of brutes! Ranged attacks from rogues and mages are the way to go here—just make sure your warrior tank is given a chance to grab their attention.

As you explore the villa, you'll find a ladder in a guard tower on the eastern side, taking you to a bridge that is guarded by another brute. The bridge is narrow, which can make things tough thanks to the confined space. Afterward, push across the bridge into a final confrontation with the mercenary leader and his remaining men. Your tank should try to keep the leader away from the rest of the party, while you eliminate his allies first. He's a tough brute himself, but by himself, he's still just one man. Clearing the Grand Forest Villa of all mercenaries will complete this quest.

NOTE You can find the key to Valammar inside the Grand Forest Villa, on the balcony the mercenary leader was protecting.

TIP There is a taller guard tower on the western side of the villa. If you make the climb to its roof, you can find a mosaic piece in the set The Fall.

36: MAP OF A FARMLAND CAVE

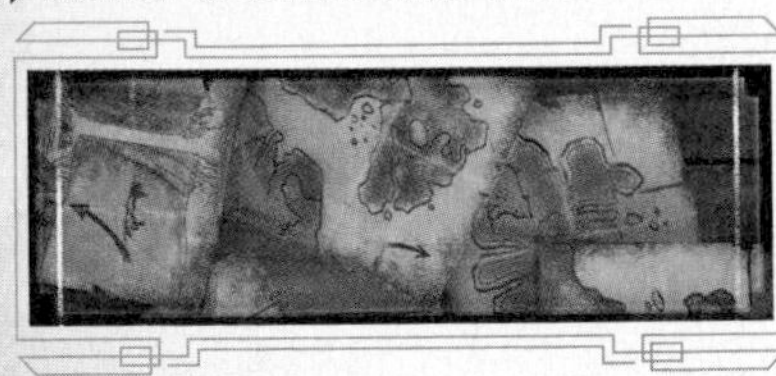

Quest Giver: Map found in Hafter's Woods, east of the mercenary fortress

Description: This map depicts a farmhouse near a cave.

Requirements: Available as soon as you enter the Hinterlands

Reward: 128 XP, 80 Influence

Objectives:

- Find the spot marked on the map.

The cave on the map is northeast of Dennet's home on Redcliffe Farms. Another landmark would be the astrarium east of the cave. The map depicts a winding route uphill behind Dennet's home, but it can be tough to see. We recommend navigating from the astrarium first, heading west until you reveal the presence of the cave on your quest map. Use the Search ability inside until you reveal the hidden treasure.

37: RETURN POLICY

Quest Giver: Note found on a corpse just west of the Broken Bridge

Description: A thief stole something important from a fortress to the west. A threatening note found on the thief's body suggests that whoever he stole it from very much wants it back.

Requirements: Available as soon as you enter the Hinterlands

Reward: 128 XP, 80 Influence

Objectives:

- Return the stolen treasure to the western fortress.

You can find this dead thief with the undelivered treasure early on, but actually getting to the drop-off point means fighting through the southwestern portion of the Hinterlands, where enemies level 8 and higher lurk and can make very short work of a weak party. Worse still, you will have to contend with the highly equipped mercenaries occupying the Grand Forest Villa, if you haven't already.

Across the bridge to the villa, the path of the hill branches in two directions. One to the left takes you into the villa itself. The path to the right takes you under another wooden bridge, up a trail on the western side of the villa, and eventually into a field where an altar awaits the return of the treasure.

As soon as you complete the ritual, a rage demon flashes into existence before your party! Unfortunately for it, the odds are in your favor. Don't get careless around its vicious fire attacks.

38: FLOWERS FOR SENNA

Quest Giver: Widower in Redcliffe

Description: An elderly widower visits his wife's shrine each year, but the fighting between the mages and templars has prevented him from making the trip.

Requirements: Gain access to Redcliffe after addressing the Chantry in Val Royeaux.

Reward: 128 XP, 80 Influence

Objectives:

- Take flowers to Senna's shrine.
- Return to the widower.

This can be a very easy quest to finish if you've established the Forest camp in Hafter's Woods. After hearing the aged elf's story, say that you can help him deliver the flowers to Senna's grave, and then fast travel to the Forest camp south of Redcliffe Farms. The gravesite is a short hike from the camp, but it should be safe. Watch for bears or mabari hounds, just to be safe.

After you've placed the flowers on the grave, return to the old elf to report the good deed.

39: BERGRIT'S CLAWS

Quest Giver: Note found on a corpse, Dead Ram Gorge

Description: A hunter named Bergrit was out looking for large bears to collect their claws, which appear to be of considerable value. It may be wise to pick up where he left off.

Requirements: Available as soon as you enter the Hinterlands

Reward: 3 Great bear claws 128 XP, 80 Influence

Objectives:

- Find three great bear claws

The bears in question are in the southwestern portion of the Hinterlands, near the Forest camp. Bears can be rough customers, and they resist many forms of crowd control, but a full party around level 7 or 8 should be able to smother each bear it encounters before things get dicey. The great bear claws you harvest can go toward improving your chances at masterwork crafting.

40: HINTERLANDS WHO'S WHO

Quest Giver: Letter found on a corpse, Old Simeon's Cave

Description: A hunter appears to have been mauled by a bear and died in its cave. According to his letter, he was trying to get enough of something to help. He must have been desperate.

Requirements: Available as soon as you enter the Hinterlands

Reward: 128 XP, 80 Influence

Objectives:

- Take the hunter's letter back to his family.

The hardest part of this quest is getting through bear country just to find the cave where the unfortunate hunter met his grisly end. Once you recover the letter, travel back to Redcliffe Farms. The mailbox where you can deliver the letter is marked clearly on your quest map.

NOTE

If you have not already done so, the house where you deliver the letter can be unlocked by a rogue. One of the mosaic pieces for The Fall is hidden inside the abandoned home.

41: DEEP TROUBLE

Quest Giver: Investigate the hidden alcove behind the waterfall south of Lake Luthias and eliminate the men guarding it. Inspecting the door prompts you to find a key and begins the quest. Alternatively, attack the mercenary fortress in the southwest of the Hinterlands and locate the key to Valammar.

Description: The Carta are setting up a red lyrium mining operation in the Hinterlands with the help of local mercenaries.

Requirements: Available as of your first visit to the Hinterlands

Reward: 1,025 XP, 400 Influence, 3 Power

Objectives:

- Find a key to the door.
- Seek out and eliminate the Carta leader in Valammar.

This quest can be divided into two distinct parts, and there are two ways that you can start it. The first, and easiest, is to investigate the waterfall south of Lake Luthias. A small path takes you behind the waterfall, where a locked door is guarded by some Carta thugs. Being level 6 to 8 should help you be prepared for the fight they'll put up; these dwarves are a step above the enemies you've fought in the northern Hinterlands. After clearing out the guards, you can try to open the door, but it's locked and requires a specific key.

Getting this key requires traveling to the mercenary fortress, far to the west of Lake Luthias. Traveling through the wilderness from Lake Luthias is a serious challenge if you're not around level 7 or 8, or are poorly geared. In addition to bears and wild packs of mabari war hounds, you encounter a large camp of very well-equipped, highly skilled mercenaries.

The fortress itself is filled with more of these mercenaries. However, once you reach the top of the fortress and defeat the mercenary leader, you can pick up the key to Valammar. You'll also receive a codex entry that shows a note from the Carta, saying that they hired these mercenaries to keep things in Valammar tightly secured from outside eyes. Your new objective is to return to Valammar and eliminate the Carta leader running the entire operation.

The other method for starting this quest is to find the key after eliminating all of the mercs as part of The Mercenary Fortress side quest. You'll be given the quest and be shown the entrance to Valammar on your map.

> 42: DUNGEON: VALAMMAR

Valammar is an old dwarven outpost, a crumbling ruin that reaches deep into the earth and must be reached from a passageway found in the Hinterlands. Within this dungeon lie many treasures that require a touch only a rogue can provide to reach, so bring Varric or Sera if your Inquisitor has chosen a different path. Come prepared with full inventories of potions and the best gear you can muster if you're coming in around level 7 or 8; the Carta will not give up this place without a fight, and if you go deep enough, you'll find that there are worse things than the Carta waiting for you.

VALAMMAR

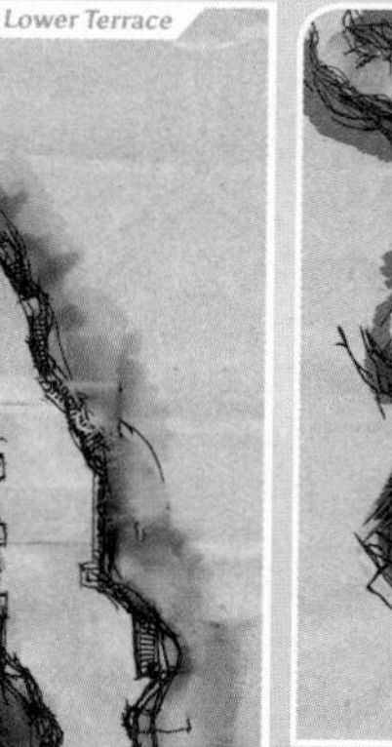

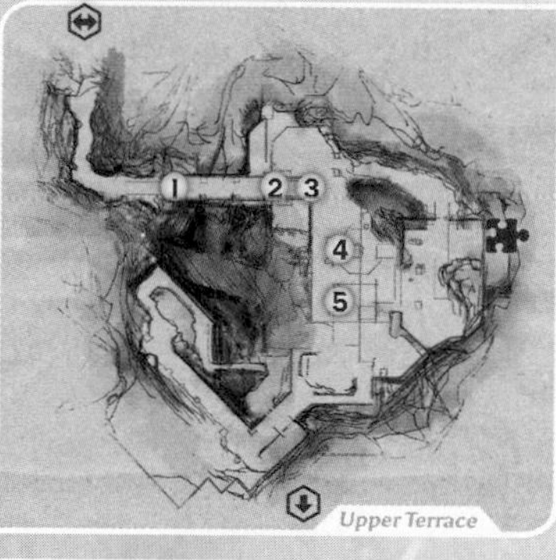

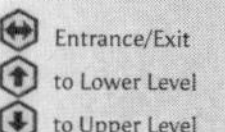

- Entrance/Exit
- to Lower Level
- to Upper Level
- Mosaic Piece

1. The bridge just past the entrance to Valammar is seemingly guarded by a lone Carta bowman. However, a Carta assassin is hiding in stealth somewhere on the bridge and will strike in the middle of your battle.

2. A nearby camp on the other side of the bridge also contains another bowman and a Carta grunt; they rush to aid their bridge comrades.

3. Two more bowmen command the stairs leading up from the bridge to the upper terrace.

4. This room contains a wall you can bash through with a warrior, which gains access to a small treasure room.

5. This door requires a rogue to unlock it. Beyond it is the Trading Post, containing more loot to pillage, along with some interesting Carta notes for your codex.

6. Continuing along the upper terrace and taking the next set of stairs down, you encounter two Carta bowmen engaging darkspawn hurlock on the bridge near your objective. Help both sides kill each other, then get ready for a rough fight against the Carta leader and their personal guards.

7. The vat room is where you'll find the Carta leader, a pair of bowmen, a grunt, and an enforcer. Not exactly a simple fight! Rip up the lighter targets first—and this includes the leader! The enforcer can survive a good beating while the rest of his allies go nuts, so take them out of the equation first, then put down the enforcer.

8. The quest is complete as soon as you kill off all the Carta in the Vat Room. Loot the place for all it's worth, and check out some of the notes and journals the Carta left behind. Among the spoils is a dwarven gear; looting it starts the Vault of Valammar side quest.

The Vault of Valammar

Quest Giver: Investigate the sealed vault door in the vat room inside Valammar.

Description: These gears should fit the lock on a large door clearly made to keep out thieves.

Requirements: Available after completing the Deep Trouble quest

Reward: 512 XP, 80 Influence, 2 Power

Objectives:

- Find two gears.
- Use the gears to open the vault.

9. The first gear, found near the Carta leader, can be placed right away on one of the two slots flanking the vault door. However, what's inside will remain locked away until you find the second gear. Go back to the bridge outside of the vat room [6] and cross it.

10. You discover the Halls of the Elders upon crossing the bridge, along with another hurlock. There's also a door you must unlock with a rogue.

11. Inside the treasure room is a mosaic piece for The Fall, as well as numerous treasure chests to loot. The biggest of these contains the second dwarven gear, meaning you can return to the vault door and unlock it!

12. If you continue past the treasure room, fighting through more hurlocks, you will find stairs leading down to the lower terrace. Your party starts discussing the massive hole in the stone that the darkspawn seem to be appearing from. If you have a mage in your party, you can energize the debris in the area to reseal that hole and prevent more darkspawn from invading Valammar.

13. Returning to the vault door, spin both gears until they stop to unseal the vault and complete the quest! You'll also discover The Vaults region as soon as you enter.

14. But you're not done fighting yet, not by a long shot. The vault has already been invaded by hurlocks, led by a monstrous hurlock alpha. The alpha fights like the bruiser enemy type, and his two-handed mace can knock out your less armored party members in a few swings. The three hurlocks accompanying him are all dangerous in their own right, as they can deal very heavy damage from afar or up close. Have your tank keep the big guy busy, while the rest of the party hunts down the other hurlocks.

15. The vault contains a lot of treasures for all the effort you just put out. Among them is another mosaic piece for The Fall.

43: HIGH DRAGON: THE FERELDEN FROSTBACK

Recommended Level: 12+

Recommended Party Composition: One warrior (sword and shield), one rogue, two mages (armed with frost damage staves)

Alternative Party Composition: Two warriors (sword and shield, two-handed weapon), two mages (armed with frost damage staves)

Initial contact with the Ferelden Frostback begins as you enter Lady Shayna's Valley. Her dragonlings populate the valley and attempt to slow you down while the Frostback takes flight and begins strafing the valley with her fiery breath. You can choose to kill the dragonlings as you head toward the Blood Cliffs farther north, but you will have to deal with the Frostback constantly strafing your party. Her flames can outright kill any party member in seconds if you are poorly equipped, so bring any form of fire resistance that you can.

If you choose to flee north, try to reach the Blood Cliffs as soon as possible. The Ferelden Frostback will land in the valley at the center of the Blood Cliffs region as you approach it and wait for you to come into range to begin the fight. Use this respite to eliminate any dragonlings that have followed you. You can return to the nearest camp, replenish your potion supplies, and then trek back to the Frostback: she'll wait warmly for you.

Be sure to bring frost staves for any mages in your party, and equip them before beginning the fight. If you can enchant melee weapons with frost runes, that can also be a big help.

The Frostback engages melee attackers with her legs in brutally powerful strikes. However, these attacks are highly telegraphed, allowing warriors to block the attacks and allowing rogues to clear out when they see the legs raised to strike. She will also bite at attackers and even swipe her tail to hit anyone behind her.

The Frostback will use her flame breath throughout the fight. She does so seemingly at random, but this brutal area-of-effect attack will also be used to flush out any rogues she sees drop into stealth. While she does announce this attack by rearing back, with flames dancing in her mouth, you may not be able to escape if you are already in range. Expect pain and casualties among party members lacking fire resistance. If you see any ranged attackers in danger of being caught in the fire blast, switch to them manually and quickly guide them out of the flames.

To further frustrate attackers, the Frostback will flap her wings, causing a wind pressure effect that will blow back any melee fighters that are close to it, and can deflect any ranged attacks from staves and bows. Additionally, the Frostback can roar so loud that it stuns the entire party. This can be a devastating moment during the fight, particularly if your party is stuck fighting any dragonlings that join the fray.

There is another challenging phase to this battle: The Frostback will leap onto one of two ledges and summon dragonlings to fight at her side. The dragonlings individually aren't dangerous if you're tough enough to be fighting the Frostback, but they have a tendency to go after ranged mages or bow-wielding rogues. They've got to be taken down fast before they overwhelm your party. Lastly, the Frostback will take flight and strafe part of the arena with flames, targeting as many party members as possible in a single pass. She will sometimes do this while you are desperately trying to clear out dragonlings. Pay attention for this!

The most important bit of advice is to remember that this high dragon battle, like all others, is a test of endurance as much as it is a test of your skill and your preparedness. Use any potions to enhance resistances or your offenses if you can, but save your health potions for dire emergencies. It might help to give your party members regeneration potions, to help keep them healthy as the fight progresses, and to conserve health potions for as long as possible.

Winning this fight demands that you manage to control the beast as best as possible. A sword-and-shield-bearing warrior can tank the Frostback with clever use of taunts and blocking abilities to build massive amounts of guard. Pay attention to where your other party members are standing, and get them out of harm's way if the need arises. Keep your other attackers on the flanks to avoid frustrating fire breath deaths.

It helps if at least one mage in the party has the Heal Focus ability on their command bar. This is your "uh-oh" button, and it can turn the fight around in a desperate moment by bringing the whole party back up to full health. You'll likely get only one use of this ability during the fight, so make it count.

Taking down the Ferelden Frostback will award you various rare dragon parts to use for crafting, as well as special equipment. Further exploration of this valley will reveal various bits of loot to collect and chests to open. You may need multiple trips to collect everything!

VAL ROYEAUX

The capital of Orlais has endured the ages to become a beacon of civilization, its citizens the measure of modernity. Just ask them. Val Royeaux is in every way a world leader—in commerce, culture, and its own exaggerated beauty.

LOCALE SUMMARY — Scouting Cost: 0

The Inquisition first travels to Val Royeaux during the critical path quest The Threat Remains. Here the Herald of Andraste attempts to calm the concerns of Mother Hevara and the Chantry. But things don't go according to plan. Beyond the brief meeting with Mother Hevara, Val Royeaux is a locale worth exploring. This is where the Inquisition can recruit Sera and Vivienne. Merchants scattered about the main level sell wares ranging from weapons and armor to furniture, windows, and drapery for Skyhold.

> Crafting Materials

Common Materials:

- Velveteen
- Silk
- Cotton

Rare Materials: None

Unique Materials: None

> Collections

- Astrariums: 0
- Bottles of Thedas: 0
- High Dragons: 0
- Landmarks: 0
- Mosaic Pieces: 0
- Glyphs: 0
- Shards: 0
- Treasure Maps: 0
- Logging Stands: 0
- Quarries: 0

> Inquisition Personnel

Party Members

- Sera
- Vivienne

Agents

- Barter by Belle

LOCALE/COLLECTIONS MAP

LEGEND

Area Exit · Merchant · Song Lyrics

MERCHANTS

Barnabus's Shop

Item	Cost
Accessories (Highlights)	
Enhanced Ring of Life-Drain	379

Havel's Shop

Item	Cost
Weapons (Highlights)	
Bloodied Wings	5,598
Punisher	1,371
Lifetaker Staff	3,428
Seeker Shield	528
Armor (Highlights)	
Masterwork Scout Coat	2,320
Superior Vanguard Armor	1,714
Superior Hunter Armor	1,714
Superior Enchanter Armor	1,714
Intense Elfsnake Vitaar	343
Upgrades (Highlights)	
Sten Sword Grip	738
Narrow Greatsword Grip	738
Masterwork Wrapped One-Handed Haft	738
Masterwork Engraved Two-Handed Haft	738
Masterwork Battlemage Staff Grip	738
Masterwork Battlemage Staff Blade	738
Superior Enchanter Staff Blade	211
Masterwork Spiked Pommel	211
Masterwork Bound Dagger Grip	211
Balanced Two-Handed Grip	211
Crafting Materials	
Blank Runestone	71

Pierre-Marie's Shop

Item	Cost
Weapons (Highlights)	
Fadewalker Staff	154
Dreamweaver Staff	154
Armor (Highlights)	
Intense Deathroot Vitaar	39
Superior Enchanter Coat	298

Crafting/Furniture Shop

Item	Cost
Crafting Materials	
Velveteen	20
Silk	20
Cotton	20
Skyhold Furniture	
Qunari Glass	1,568
Orlesian Glass	1,568
Fereldan Glass	1,568
Dwarven Glass	1,568
Dalish Glass	1,568
Andrastian Glass	1,568
Orlesian Bed II	713
Orlesian Bed I	713
Free Marches Bed II	713
Dwarven Bed	713
Tevinter Drapery	356
Templar Drapery	356
Qunari Drapery	356
Orlesian Drapery	356
Mage Circle Drapery	356
Inquisition Drapery	356
Grey Warden Drapery	356
Free Marches Drapery	356
Fereldan Drapery	356
Elven Drapery	356
Dwarven Drapery	356
Dalish Drapery	356
Chasind Drapery	356
Chantry Drapery	356

Willvan's Recipe Shop

Item	Cost
Recipes	
Spirit Resistance Tonic Recipe	53
Lightning Resistance Tonic Recipe	53
Fire Resistance Tonic Recipe	53
Cold Resistance Tonic Recipe	53

Schematic Shop

Item	Cost
Weapon Schematics	
Dwarven Maul	755
Thrusting Longsword	380
Ornate Pommel	223
Firm Pommel	223
Notched Two-Handed Haft	223
Armor Schematics	
Superior Hunter Coat	2,288
Orlesian Army Warrior Armor	3,075
Orlesian Army Scout Armor	3,075
Orlesian Army Battlemage Armor	3,075
Vanguard Coat	945
Enchanter Coat	945
Hunter Coat	945
Vanguard Coat Arms	223
Hunter Coat Arms	223
Elven Cowl	223

Saphi's Shop

Item	Cost
Armor (Highlights)	
Superior Battlemage Mail	3,691
Intense Felandaris Vitaar	2,953
Intense Elfsnake Vitaar	343
Upgrades (Highlights)	
Superior Prowler Mail Arms	738
Superior Prowler Coat Legs	738
Superior Battlemaster Mail Legs	738
Superior Battlemaster Mail Arms	738
Superior Battlemage Mail Legs	738
Superior Battlemage Mail Arms	738

Deraboam Shop (Upper Level)

Item	Cost
Golden Nug Statue	10,000

TIP Don't forget to visit Deraboam, the merchant on the top tier of the market, accessible through fast travel. He has one item that is available only after you've acquired a horse from Dennet, the horsemaster in the Hinterlands. The Golden Nug Statue costs 10,000 gold. Interacting with the statue unlocks The Big One operation on the war table. This two-hour operation unlocks all five greater mountain nuggalope mounts.

NOTE After the attack on Haven, you can purchase codex entries from a book merchant in Val Royeaux. He sells codex entries to locations you can no longer access.

PARTY MEMBERS

SERA

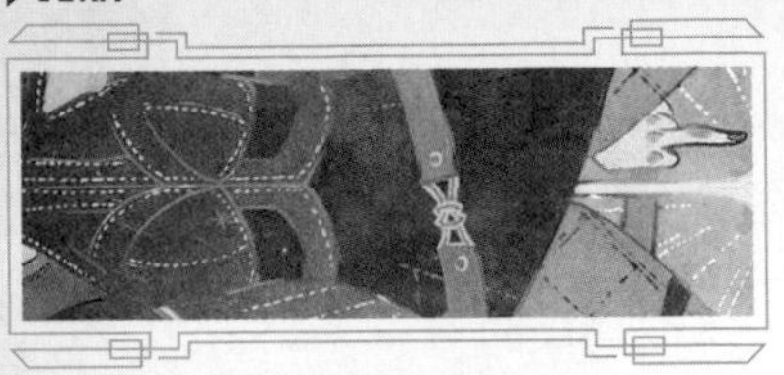

Affiliated Quest: A Friend of Red Jenny

After the meeting with Mother Hevara, listen for the sound of an arrow striking nearby. Interact with the arrow to begin A Friend of Red Jenny. After helping Sera dispatch some enemies, you have the opportunity to recruit her.

VIVIENNE

Affiliated Quest: The Imperial Enchanter

Look for a messenger in Val Royeaux extending an invitation to the Ghyslain Estate. Travel there on the world map to meet Vivienne. After a brief conversation you can invite her to the Inquisition.

AGENTS

BARTER BY BELLE

Affiliated Quest: The Threat Remains **Inquisition Perk:** Barter by Belle (Connections)

After addressing the clerics, speak with Belle, a merchant in Val Royeaux. Frustrated by the lack of action taken by the templars and the Chantry, Belle wishes to join the Inquisition. Accepting Belle into the Inquisition unlocks the Barter by Belle perk, reducing the time it takes Josephine to complete missions by 5 percent.

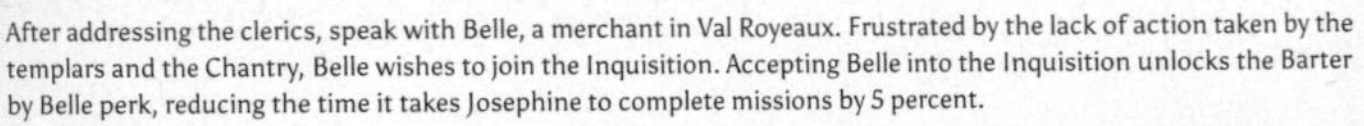

SIDE QUESTS (RECOMMENDED LEVEL 4-6)

LEGEND

Level 4-6

1: A Friend of Red Jenny 2: The Imperial Enchanter

> 1: A FRIEND OF RED JENNY

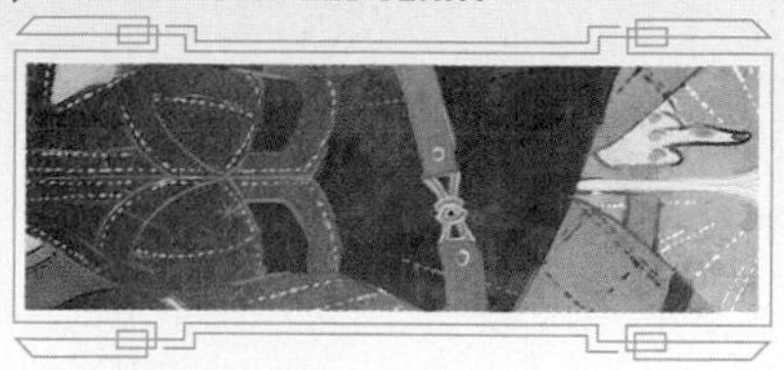

Quest Giver: Arrow in the Market

Description: The strange message, delivered via arrow, said there is an enemy of the Inquisition waiting to strike Val Royeaux. It said to search the market, café, and docks for things that are red.

Requirements: Available after addressing the clerics

Reward: Sera

Objectives:

- Examine the message.
- Search by the dock.
- Search in the café.
- Search the upper market.
- Fend off the guards.

Immediately following the conversation with Mother Hevara and the templars, a mysterious arrow lands nearby. This is the start of a small quest, requiring you to search for red satchels by the dock, café, and upper market. Go to each location marked on the compass and conduct searches to find and retrieve the three satchels. To reach the upper market, enter the blue doors on the southwest side of the market—this gives you access to the balcony above.

Once you've found all three red satchels, a secluded courtyard appears on the world map—travel there. This takes you to small courtyard occupied by hostile reach guards and freeman spotters. Eliminate the first group of enemies, then open the door to the west. Here you encounter a noble, unfriendly to the Inquisition. But he's soon killed by a potential ally, Sera, an elven rogue archer. Sera is the one who led you here. Help Sera fend off the remaining guards before resuming your conversation. Sera is part of a band of criminals, thieves, and vandals called the Friends of Red Jenny. Accept her offer to join the Inquisition.

> 2: THE IMPERIAL ENCHANTER

Quest Giver: Circle mage messenger in the market

Description: Vivienne de Fer, the First Enchanter of Montsimmard, has extended an invitation to her salon at the chateau of Duke Bastien de Ghyslain.

Requirements: Available after addressing the clerics

Reward: Vivienne

Objectives:

- Attend the salon.

Speak to the messenger in Val Royeaux's market to receive an invitation from Vivienne de Fer, a well-connected mage in Orlais. The invitation adds the Ghyslain Estate to the world map—travel there. Upon entering the chateau, you're rudely greeted by a marquis who has nothing kind to say about the Inquisition. But he's soon set straight by Vivienne—she even allows you to choose the marquis's fate. After introducing herself, Vivienne gets to the point. As the leader of the last loyal mages of Thedas, she feels compelled to join the Inquisition. Feel free to ask Vivienne more questions, but at the end of the conversation, welcome her aboard—she is a powerful ally, both on and off the battlefield.

THE FALLOW MIRE

South of the Hinterlands, the land is wet and miserable, subject to seemingly endless storms. Villagers have tried to carve out a meager existence in the Fallow Mire, but their lives are under constant threat by a tidal wave of undead rising from the murky waters flooding much of this region. The Avvars, a nomadic mountain people of strength and stature, have claimed a once abandoned keep and captured a small cadre of Inquisition scouts. From this makeshift fortress, the Avvar leader has issued a challenge to the Inquisition: He wants to meet with their leader, for aggressive negotiation.

LOCALE SUMMARY

Scouting Cost: 8 Power

The Fallow Mire is a dark and threatening locale, haunted by spirits and demons, subject to swarms of undead that rise when the water is disturbed by unassuming travelers. Your initial visit to this place will likely have you focused on surviving the trip through the marsh on your way to rescuing the Inquisition soldiers. While there are not many quests to accomplish here, it would not be good to abandon Inquisition soldiers to the Avvars, and nearly everything there is to do in the mire is more or less along the way to rescuing your people. The marshes and empty homes scattered throughout also hold resources you can use to better equip your party, and the constant presence of the undead gives early-level parties something to chew on while they train themselves for the battles to come.

> CRAFTING MATERIALS

Common Materials:

- Blood Lotus
- Blue Vitriol
- Summer Stone

Rare Materials: None

Unique Materials:

- Dawn Lotus

> COLLECTIONS

- Astrariums: 0
- Bottles of Thedas: 2
- High Dragons: 0
- Landmarks: 4
- Mosaic Pieces: 1
- Glyphs: 4
- Shards: 0
- Treasure Maps: 0
- Logging Stands: 0
- Quarries: 0

> INQUISITION PERSONNEL

Agents

- Sky Watcher

LOCALE MAP

Legend

- Area Exit
- Fade Rift
- Settlement
- Locked Door

Inquisition Camps

- Fisher's End Camp
- Old Thoroughfare Camp

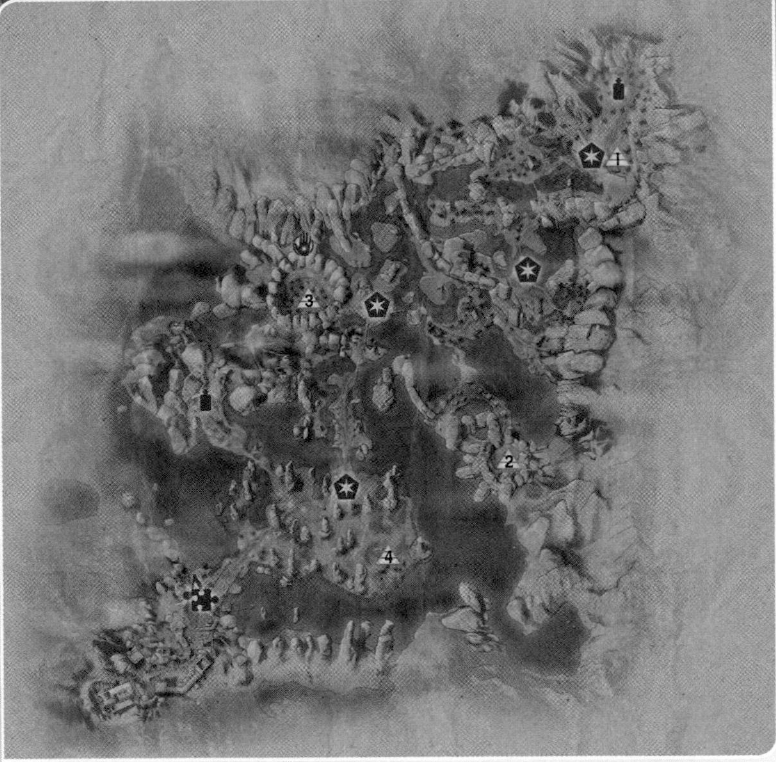

Legend

Bottles of Thedas

- Garbolg's Backcountry Reserve
- Dragon Piss

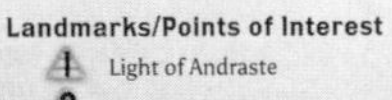

Landmarks/Points of Interest

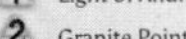
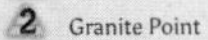

1. Light of Andraste
2. Granite Point

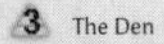

3. The Den

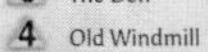

4. Old Windmill

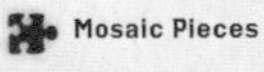

Mosaic Pieces

Song Lyrics

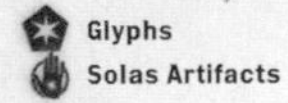

Glyphs

Solas Artifacts

FADE RIFTS

There are only two rifts to seal in the Fallow Mire, but they are tougher than the average rifts initially encountered in the Hinterlands, producing greater numbers of terrors than you may have seen before if you chose to come to the mire early in your travels. Sealing one of these rifts will earn you a new agent for the Inquisition, so it is worth seeking them out.

Fade Rift Details

Quest	Rifts	Total Power
Rifts in the Mire	2	4

REQUISITIONS

Requisition Quests

Requisition	Materials
Blue Vitriol Survey in the Mire	20 Blue Vitriol, 10 Summer Stones
Elixir Requisition in the Mire	5 Elfroots, 5 Diseased Tissues

AGENTS

> SKY WATCHER

Affiliated Quest: Rifts in the Mire

Inquisition Perk: Sky Watcher (Connections)

In a strange twist, you encounter the Avvar named Sky Watcher, staring at a partially closed Fade rift in the Fallow Mire. He is not openly hostile to you, and is in fact uninterested in the challenge the Avvar chieftain's son has issued to you. Opening the Fade rift, killing the demons it spawns, and then properly sealing it with your mark will convince Sky Watcher that there is something to the Herald of Andraste. If you've done this, after you rescue the Inquisition soldiers Sky Watcher will appear at the entrance to Hargrave Keep. Talk to him to recruit him. Be warned that once you exit the area, he'll leave for good.

SIDE QUESTS (RECOMMENDED LEVEL 8-10 AND 12-15)

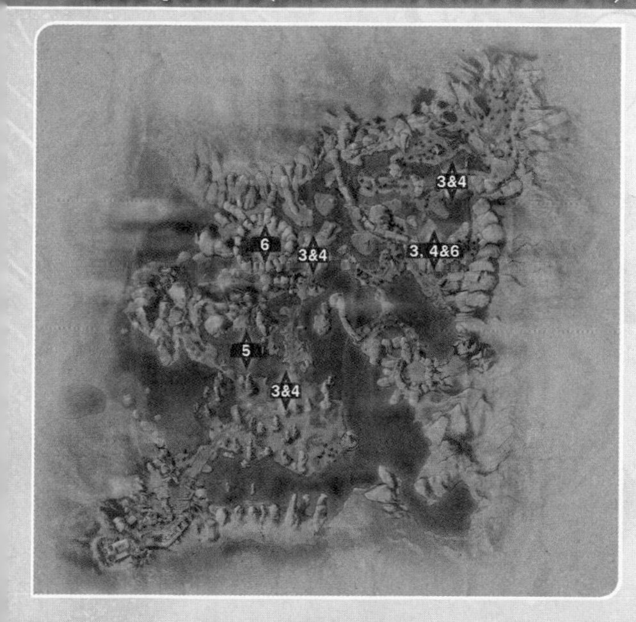

« Legend »

Level 8-10

1: Holding the Mire
2: Lost Souls
3: Beacons in the Dark
4: Beneath the Mire
5: Cabin Fever

Level 12-15

6: These Demons Are Clever

I: HOLDING THE MIRE

Description: Establish camps to hold the Fallow Mire and support Inquisition activity in the region.

Quest Giver: Scout Harding

Requirements: Started as soon as you arrive in the Fallow Mire

Reward: 50 Influence and 1 Power per camp, except for the starting camp

Objectives:

- Establish two camps.

There are only two camps to establish in the Mire, and one of those you start with right away. You'll likely take care of this objective after taking care of the the second monument on the Beacons in the Dark side quest. Head for the second camp as early as you can, so you can set up a forward base much closer to your final objective.

> **TIP**
>
> 
>
> The house close to the first camp contains one of the bottles of Thedas: Garbolg's Backcountry Reserve. Don't miss it!

2: LOST SOULS

Quest Giver: War table

Description: Inquisition soldiers are missing in the uncharted marshes of southern Ferelden.

Requirements: You will hear about soldiers gone missing in the Fallow Mire when you return to Haven after your first expedition to the Hinterlands. Investigate the mire from the war table by expending eight power to unlock the Fallow Mire for exploration, and you will be able to personally see to the rescue of the soldiers.

Reward: 3 Power, 1,025 XP, 400 Influence

Objectives:

- Go to the war table to locate the soldiers.
- Travel to the Fallow Mire.
- Locate the Avvar outpost.
- Open the gates.
- Defeat the Avvar leader.
- Release the Inquisition hostages.

The path to the Avvar outpost is fraught with danger and holds a number of side quests. So long as you follow the main road south, through all the veilfire beacons, you'll easily make your way to the castle outpost while accomplishing nearly every major side quest in the Mire.

Things get very exciting as you approach the castle far to the south of the first Inquisition camp. You encounter a horde of undead near the front gates, and more keep coming once you start fighting them. Listen to your party members when they tell you to run: The undead will not stop coming until you enter the dilapidated castle.

As you enter Hargrave Keep, the Avvars shout that the Herald has arrived, and the fight for the Inquisition soldiers begins, with an Avvar defender and bowman as your first obstacles. Take out all the Avvars beyond the front gate, then climb up the wooden ramps to the castle walls so you can use a switch to open the gate to the next section of the keep. Beyond the newly opened gate is another group of Avvar warriors. They are the last line of defense between you and the Avvar leader.

> **TIP**
>
> There is a door near the gate lever that requires the Deft Hands, Fine Tools Inquisition perk to open. Beyond it are many treasures to loot and a mosaic piece. You'll also come back to that room later to handle a quest for Blackwall, so don't forget it!

The Avvar leader announces himself as the Hand of Korth as soon as you climb up the final staircase into the Avvar base camp. The Hand fights like the enforcers you may have faced in the Hinterlands, and his massive axe hits for very high damage. Get a warrior to keep his attention while the rest of the party silences the Avvar defender and two bowmen that support their leader in this fight. Killing the Hand earns you his axe: the Gift of the Mountain Father. After you have negotiated the Avvar's permanent leave of this world, release the hostages from their prison cell. Your work in Fallow Mire is complete.

3: BEACONS IN THE DARK

Quest Giver: Approach a beacon in the Fallow Mire

Description: The Fallow Mire is plagued with demons. Lighting veilfire beacons should draw them out. Defeat the demons to make the area safer.

Requirements: Available as soon as you enter the Fallow Mire

Reward: 967 XP, 200 Influence, 2 Power

Objectives:

- Clear four beacons.
- Light the beacons and defeat the demons.

There are four stone beacons placed around the Fallow Mire, and their locations are revealed on the quest map when you approach one of them. Have a mage in your party light the veilfire torches mounted to the beacons. This triggers an ambush of undead, led by demonic terrors. Killing the terrors at each beacon will cause the undead to die along with them, so if you want to end these fights quickly, focus your party on the demons!

The beacons become more challenging to clear the farther you progress toward the fortress where the Inquisition soldiers are being held, with more undead coming out to try to distract you from the demons. Focus on the terrors to put an end to the fights as quickly as possible.

NOTE You can fast-travel to the stone beacons, making it easy to get around the Fallow Mire quickly.

4: BENEATH THE MIRE

Quest Giver: A rune planted on the stone beacons scattered in the mire

Description: Mysterious veilfire runes are inscribed on rocks and ruins in the mire. Perhaps they can be deciphered.

Requirements: Available as soon as you enter the Fallow Mire

Reward: 2 Power, 512 XP, 200 Influence

Objectives:

- Find all four veilfire runes.
- Recover the apostate's journal.

This quest is taken on simultaneously with the Beacons in the Dark side quest. Using a veilfire torch from one of the beacons, look for the runes on the beacons themselves. The first one you inspect begins the side quest. Each rune you light up with the veilfire will reveal more lore about the Fallow Mire. Finding all four runes will grant you a recipe that allows you to make the Tears of the Dead tonic.

NOTE The second beacon with one of the veilfire runes has a journal left behind by an apostate named Widris. She is clearly not in a positive mental state. The journal begins These Demons Are Clever.

5: CABIN FEVER

Quest Giver: A lost cabin key buried in the marsh

Description: Explore the Fallow Mire to find a way inside the locked cabin.

Requirements: Available as soon as you enter the Fallow Mire

Reward: 128 XP, 80 Influence

Objectives:

- Unlock the cabin door.

As you travel down the road from the third beacon on your way to the fourth, your Search ability will begin pinging at a point to the west of the path. This search takes you through deep water, so be sure to deal with the undead threat as you look for the hidden item. It turns out to be a cabin key, and it's very close to a cabin that conveniently can only be unlocked with that key.

6: THESE DEMONS ARE CLEVER

Quest Giver: A journal left on the ground near one of the veilfire beacons

Description: A journal recovered in the mire suggests a rather unstable apostate is roaming about somewhere. The apostate, apparently named Widris, seems to be mixed up with some demons and could be dangerous.

Requirements: Available as soon as you enter the Fallow Mire

Reward: 967 XP, 200 Influence, 2 Power

Objectives:

- Find Widris.
- Kill Widris.

After you recover Widris's journal, a search area is revealed on your quest map, to the west of the veilfire beacon at Misty Grove. Enter the circular stone formation where the Granite Point landmark waits to be claimed; you can close down one of the Fade rifts in the mire on your way to Widris. Be sure to search the area around Granite Point thoroughly for resources.

NOTE Taking out this Fade rift counts toward the Rifts in the Mire side quest.

On the west side of the Granite Point clearing, a passage leads out into a side area that will take you through water toward another clearing where the hidden apostate's camp awaits. As at all other bodies of deep water in the Fallow Mire, undead will attack when you disturb it. Make sure you clear the undead as best you can before proceeding to the camp. Widris awaits, and she's not friendly.

Apostate Widris can be a bit of a shock for players entering the mire early in the game. She's level 15, well above the average threat in the Fallow Mire, and she's got the support of a pack of wraiths, also level 15. Poorly prepared parties can find themselves dead very fast. Remember; the wraiths don't have much in the way of health or defenses, so you can destroy them pretty quickly if you're well geared, making it easier to focus on taking down Widris. Her campsite is very well stocked with loot, an additional reward for the trouble.

TIP

One of the elven artifacts that Solas has a keen interest in can be found near Widris's camp. If he's in your party, you can gain some approval from Solas when you activate it.

THE STORM COAST

The Storm Coast is adequately named. A nearly permanent overcast sky constantly rains down on the world, and winds kick up a sea that demands the sacrifice of sailors brave enough to face the weather. The Storm Coast is far enough out of the way that the Inquisition does not normally have much interest here, something that its enemies are counting on.

The Grey Wardens had a presence here, though they recently appear to have vanished. They are why the Inquisition has sent scouts here: If there's any hope of restoring order to Thedas, the Grey Wardens must come to its aid. Unfortunately, Inquisition scouts are being stymied by a group of bandits that know the area well.

More worrying, darkspawn ghouls have been sighted in the area, and in growing numbers. That would explain the Grey Wardens having been here, but it doesn't necessarily explain why they have vanished.

LOCALE SUMMARY

Scouting Cost: 8 Power

Like the Fallow Mire, the Storm Coast is light on quests compared to the Hinterlands. However, many quests do not appear until later in the game, and only after certain missions on the war table are dealt with. Some inner circle quests, such as Varric's Seeing Red and Blackwall's Memories of the Grey, require you to return to the Storm Coast. Explore the locale thoroughly for the 13 shards it provides; you need them for the temple in the Forbidden Oasis.

A Vinsomer high dragon controls the Storm Coast from its roost on Dragon Island. However, you can't reach that place until you get access to a secret port in the southwest, and you don't want any of that business until you're the right level to face it.

> CRAFTING MATERIALS

Common Materials:

- Spindleweed, Blood Lotus, Serpentstone, Summer Stone, Iron, Deep Mushroom

Rare Materials:

- Black Lotus, Prophet's Laurel

Unique Materials: None

> INQUISITION PERSONNEL

Party Members

- Iron Bull

Agents

- The Blades of Hessarian

> COLLECTIONS

- Astrariums: 3
- Bottles of Thedas: 2
- High Dragons: 1
- Landmarks: 5
- Mosaic Pieces: 0
- Glyphs: 1
- Shards: 13
- Treasure Maps: 0
- Logging Stands: 2
- Quarries: 1

LOCALE MAP

Legend

Area Exit

Cave/Dungeon

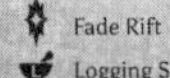
Fade Rift

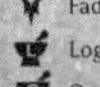
Logging Stand

Quarry

Inquisition Camps

- Storm's Solitude Camp
- Small Grove Camp
- Driftwood Margin Camp

COLLECTIONS

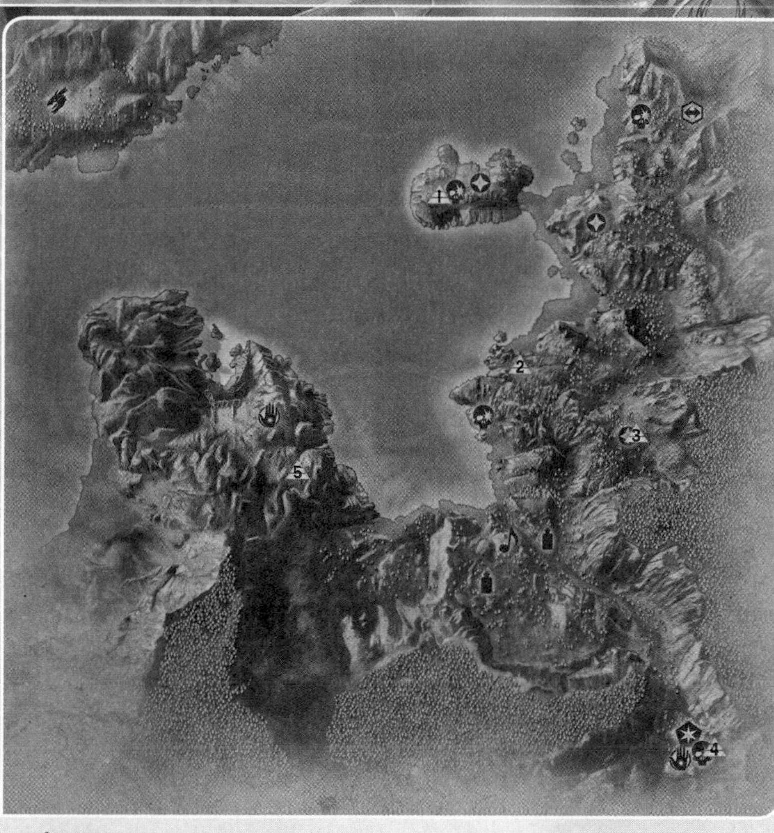

Legend

Astrariums

- Constellation: Servani
- Constellation: Fervenial
- Constellation: Bellitanus

Bottles of Thedas

High Dragon

- Vinsomer

Solas Artifacts

Landmarks/Points of Interest

1. Morrin's Outlook
2. Morrin's Steps
3. The Stone Tree
4. Lyrium Falls
5. Daerwin's Mouth

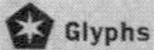

Glyphs

Oculara and Shards

Ocularum I: Storm's Solitude

- Ocularum +3 Shards

Ocularum 2: Morrin's Outlook

- Ocularum +3 Shards

Ocularum 3: Waterfall Cave

- Ocularum +3 Shards

Ocularum 4: Driftwood Margin

- Ocularum +4 Shards

Song Lyrics

ASTRARIUM SOLUTIONS

Astrarium: Servani

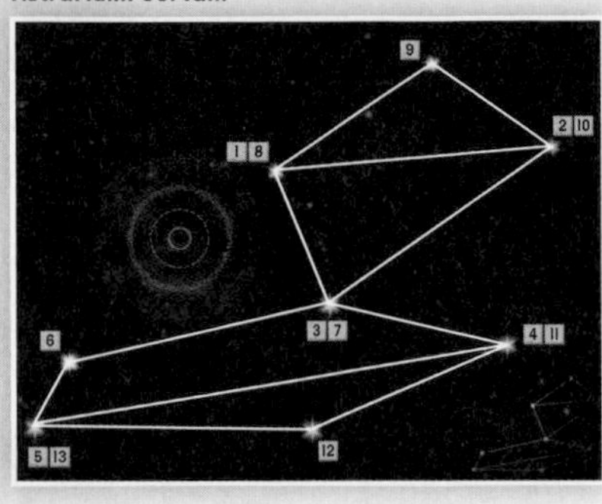

Astrarium: Fervenial

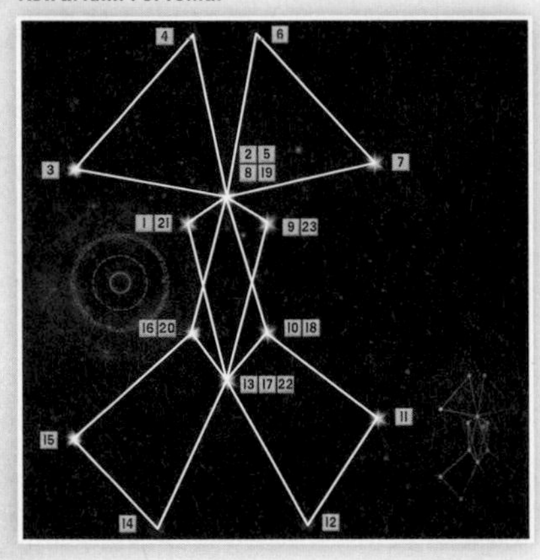

Astrarium: Bellitanus

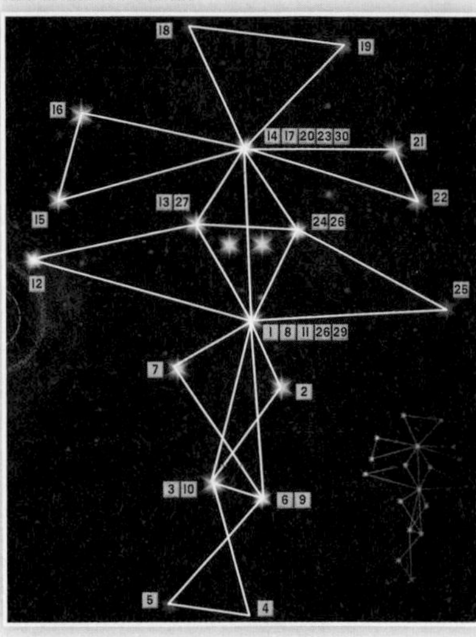

Astrarium Vault

This vault is deep inland, built into a stony hill that would be easy to simply walk past and not notice. Fortunately, the quest map directs you pretty close to where the vault is. The terrain itself is your worst enemy, making it tricky to navigate to the vault itself.

FADE RIFTS

The rifts of the Storm Coast are similar to those found in the Fallow Mire, but the enemies coming through the rifts here are stronger. Expect to see tougher variants of demons you've seen before.

FADE RIFT DETAILS

QUEST	RIFTS	TOTAL POWER
Rifts on the Coast	2	2
Rift at the Falls	1	1

CAUTION The lone rift at the falls takes you deep inland, through a small cave network infested by giant spiders. These eight-legged freaks are a bit roughhouse compared to the wildlife elsewhere on the island. Be prepared for some fighting before you even reach the rift. The rift itself provides level 9 demons to fight, which can be a tough battle to take on after plowing through the spider-infested cave.

Beware approaching the rift farther south along the coast in the Rifts on the Coast side quest. A giant tangles with a Vinsomer high dragon on the beach, but after a short scuffle the dragon leaves the area. If the giant sees you, he will come after you. Be prepared for a hard fight, even if you're at the same level. If you're not, find a way around the giant so you can approach the rift to deal with the demons.

PARTY MEMBERS

IRON BULL

Affiliated Quest: Captain of the Chargers

Recruiting Iron Bull is as simple as meeting with the man and taking his offer at face value: Although he is a spy for the Qunari, observing the Inquisition for his leaders back home and possibly providing information on the vulnerability of Thedas, he brings resources the Inquisition can use. He's willing to provide intelligence on his own organization, the Ben-Hassrath, and his mercenary band will be yours. Most importantly, you get Iron Bull himself, another extremely skilled warrior to fight alongside of.

REQUISITIONS

Requisition Quests

Requisition	Materials
Salvage Requisition on the Coast	5 Cotton, 5 Deepstalker Hides
Onyx Survey on the Coast	5 Serpentstones, 2 Summer Stones

AGENTS

THE BLADES OF HESSARIAN

Affiliated Quest: Cleaning House

Inquisition Perk: The Blades of Hessarian (Forces)

Craft and equip the Mercy's Crest amulet before approaching the bandit camp—the guards will allow you to enter to challenge their leader. After defeating the Hessarian leader in combat, speak to one of the bandits. The Blades of Hessarian pledge their support to the Inquisition, becoming agents reporting directly to Cullen.

SIDE QUESTS (RECOMMENDED LEVEL 7-11 AND 13-15+)

Legend

Level 7-11

1: Holding the Storm Coast
2: Cleaning House
3: Wardens of the Coast
4: Keeping the Darkspawn Down

Level 13-15+

5: Red Water
6: High Dragon: The Vinsomer

1: HOLDING THE STORM COAST

Description: Establish camps to hold the Storm Coast and support Inquisition activity in the region.

Quest Giver: Scout Harding

Requirements: Started as soon as you arrive in the Storm Coast

Reward: 50 Influence and 1 Power per camp, except for the starting camp

Objectives:

- Establish three camps.

The camps of the Storm Coast are not too close to each other, but they are close to key objectives that take you all across the region. Establish the camps as early as you can—it'll make taking care of quests like Keeping the Darkspawn Down and Wardens of the Coast much easier to handle.

2: CLEANING HOUSE

Quest Giver: Scout Harding

Description: Inquisition soldiers were dispatched to meet with a group of bandits operating on the Storm Coast. The Inquisition lost contact with its soldiers before their planned rendezvous with the bandits.

Requirements: Unlock the Storm Coast via the war table using eight power. Arrive at the Storm Coast for the first time.

Reward: 177 XP, 80 Influence, 1 Power

Objectives:

- Advance to the rendezvous point.
- Find the bandits and deal with them.

After you learn about the situation from Scout Harding, the rendezvous point is marked on your quest map. Follow the winding, mountainous path until you reach the ramshackle homes at the center of the search area. Bandits are already there, and they attack as soon as they catch sight of you. Unfortunately, the Inquisition soldiers are already dead.

Searching the houses, you can find some loot, as well as a map showing the location of the bandit hideout. More importantly, there's a message from the killers. They are no ordinary bandits, but rather they are the Blades of Hessarian. They wanted to test the mettle of the Herald (the soldiers were of no consequence to them). They were merely following a code of conduct.

An optional objective is offered here: Go directly to the Hessarian hideout and eliminate them immediately, or craft the Mercy's Crest at the requisition table of any camp in the region and challenge their leader. This requires one deepstalker hide and two serpentstones. It's possible to gather these materials in the Storm Coast, if you're lacking.

With or without the Mercy's Crest (it must be equipped by someone in your party), go to the Hessarian hideout farther south from the rendezvous point and kill every bandit that stands in your way. After the guards at the gate are killed, more bandits rush out to challenge you. They include guardsmen and archers in their ranks and are clearly better equipped than mere bandits.

If you have the crest equipped, the massive Hessarian leader, along with two of his equally massive Hessarian hounds, will challenge your party to battle. Hold nothing back, and eliminate the leader and his hounds to put an end to the Hessarian threat to the Inquisition. This also allows them to join your forces as agents, providing an additional Inquisition perk.

3: WARDENS OF THE COAST

Quest Giver: War table in Haven

Description: There are signs that several Grey Wardens passed through the area, but scouts have been unable to track them with all the bandits around.

Requirements: This quest opens up after you arrive at the Storm Coast.

Reward: 177 XP, 80 Influence, 1 Power

Objectives:

- Find four signs of the Wardens.

If you have recruited Blackwall, you learn some unfortunate news: All across Thedas, the Grey Wardens are vanishing, and he does not know why. The reason scouts traveled to the Storm Coast was to seek out the Wardens and hope to make use of them against the Breach. Use the war table to scout out the Storm Coast, and then travel there to carry out your own investigation. All four possible search locations are marked on your quest map as soon as you arrive.

Two of the locations are close to the Small Grove camp, nearly the middle of the coastline. Head east inland from the camp, entering the marked locations. Your Search ability pings as you close in on the abandoned Grey Warden camps. The notes and letters you find reveal more about why the Wardens passed through this region. They are apparently in search of someone, and even the darkspawn are secondary to this mission.

The second set of Warden signs is farther south, close to the Driftwood Margin camp, near the Westridge region. One of the Warden signs you uncover inside an abandoned shack is next to a hidden bottle of Thedas, so be sure to search thoroughly.

Once you recover all four signs of the Wardens, the quest is complete. The Wardens have moved on from the Storm Coast.

4: KEEPING THE DARKSPAWN DOWN

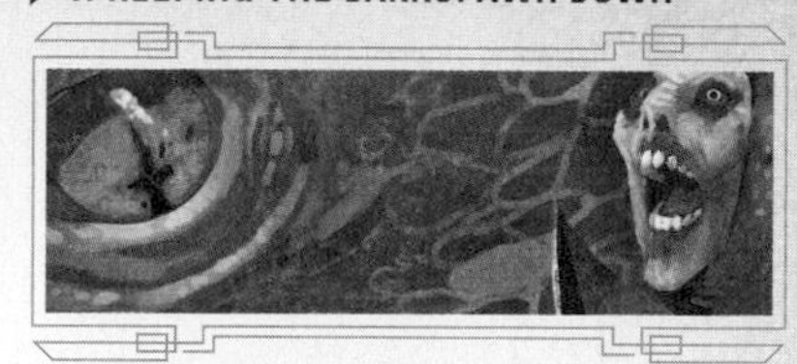

Quest Giver: War table at Skyhold

Description: Darkspawn are surfacing on the Storm Coast, and it's up to the Inquisition to put them down. They appear to be surfacing through tunnels. If these tunnels are sealed, it should keep the darkspawn underground where they belong.

Requirements: Available in Skyhold

Reward: 512 XP, 200 Influence, 2 Power

Objectives:

- Seal four tunnels.

After you reestablish the Inquisition at Skyhold, reports start coming in from all corners of Thedas. Among them is a report of darkspawn at the Storm Coast. A war table operation opens up, allowing you to scout out the locations of the darkspawn tunnels so that you can seal them yourself, as well as kill all the darkspawn in their vicinity. If you send Leliana, you will be given precise locations for the tunnels.

CAUTION Do not attempt this without a mage. You need at least one in the party to seal the tunnels when you reach them, otherwise you will have wasted your time.

One of the tunnels is east of the Driftwood Margin camp, a little ways inland from the beach. Several hurlocks and a hurlock alpha stand guard near the tunnel they used to reach the surface.

Another tunnel can be found inside the Waterfall Cave. The hurlocks and hurlock alpha here have more than you to contend with: The giant spiders of the cave are fighting anything entering their territory. Purge the area clean of all these monsters and seal the tunnel.

Inside the small cave system near the Great Cove region is a darkspawn tunnel. Be careful, as the caves are very dark, save for a few torches, and the darkspawn hurlocks can join forces with the local spider population to hunt you down.

One of the easier tunnels to reach is next to the Storm's Solitude camp. Head down to the beach from the camp and travel north. You'll eventually encounter another dark cave system filled with more spiders and more hurlocks.

5: RED WATER

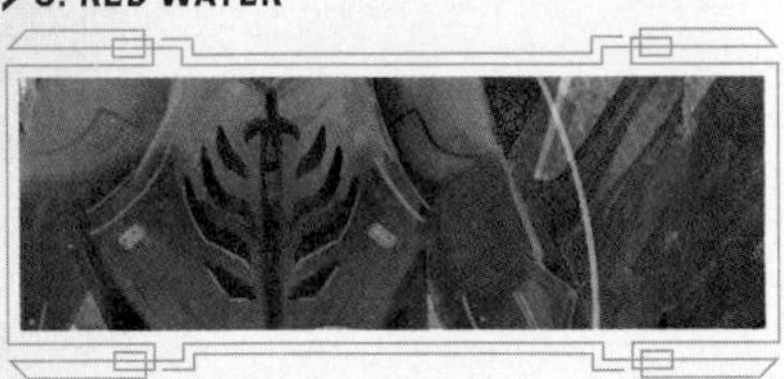

Quest Giver: War table at Skyhold

Description: Inquisition soldiers were dispatched to investigate a dwarven port on the Storm Coast that is currently being held by red templars. The port gives the red templars a foothold in the region. The soldiers have cleared the way to storm the port.

Requirements: Complete the Red Templars on the Storm Coast mission at the war table to start this side quest.

Reward: 512 XP, 200 Influence, 2 Power

Objectives:

- Storm the red templar stronghold.

You may have noticed the sealed dwarven cave entrance near the Driftwood Margin camp in the Storm Coast but have wondered how you can get inside. This quest is where it happens! After sending scouts out to the Storm Coast to unlock the stronghold the red templars have established, travel to the Driftwood Margin camp in the region and be prepared for war.

NOTE Bring Varric with you for this side quest. If you're trying to build approval with him, every successful fight against the red templars earns you approval. Additionally, his Seeing Red quest can be helped along during this operation: The caves have a number of primeval red lyrium nodes that you can destroy.

Pass through the unlocked entrance, now under Inquisition protection, and you'll enter the Daerwin's Mouth region. Push up the beach until you enter a large cave.

Immediately, you'll discover the presence of red lyrium lining the cavern walls, and not long after that you encounter your first red templar knights. To the right of them is a smaller cave that takes you deeper into the fortress.

Push past those knights to claim the Daerwin's Mouth landmark.

Climbing up the small passage way takes you to a stone walkway, connected to a bridge that crosses over a lower area. On the other side of the bridge are more red templars. If you haven't been unlucky enough to see them before now, this will be your first encounter with a red templar shadow. These horrific husks of once-men use their red lyrium blade-arms to great effect on your party. They fight similarly to other rogue-classed enemies but are clearly more horrific to look at on top of being very dangerous. Kill them first!

From the bridge crossing, you can go left and head down a staircase to explore the lower area. You might encounter a door that requires a key, but one of the red templars guarding this area will have it. Push past the locked door to find more loot, more deep mushrooms, another primeval red lyrium node, and an elven arcane device that can be activated for Solas's approval, if he's in the party. The way forward from all these goodies is cut off by a collapsed bridge, so go back up to the bridge crossing.

Going right from the bridge crossing, you can enter a treasure chamber on the upper level. Beyond it is another tunnel, then a wooden bridge to cross that leads to an even larger treasure room. Whatever the enemy is planning, they certainly appear to be stocking up for it.

From the second treasure room a stairwell leads down to a red templar ambush. Your chief concern is the presence of the red templar behemoth. Focus your party's efforts on bringing it down as quickly as possible, before it overpowers your team with its brutal attacks. After the fight, go left from the staircase to find another primal red lyrium node.

To the right of the behemoth's position is another passage that leads to the secret docks of Daerwin's Mouth. One last pair of red templar knights, backed up by a shadow, stand near a final primal red lyrium node. Eliminate them to break the red templars' control of this vital dock! You discover a seaworthy boat that the last templars were guarding, and it can take you to Dragon Island.

If you're prepared.

6: HIGH DRAGON: THE VINSOMER

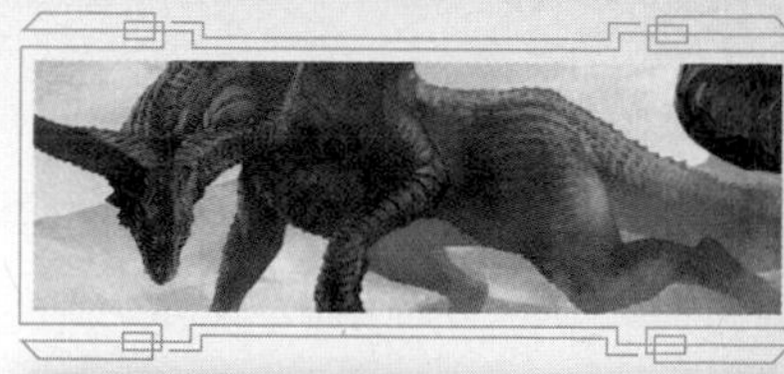

Recommended Level: 15+

Recommended Party Composition: One warrior (sword and shield), one rogue, two mages (armed with staves that do extra spirit damage)

Alternative Party Composition: Two warriors (sword and shield, two-handed weapon), two mages (armed with staves that do extra spirit damage)

Dragon Island itself is home to the Vinsomer high dragon that rules the Storm Coast, and it can be reached by taking the boat from Daerwin's Mouth. You may have spied the Vinsomer battling a giant, much earlier in the game. Now it's time to hunt her down and pry some of the great treasures from her fallen corpse—if you can survive the battle, that is!

The Vinsomer is electric by nature, meaning you should take any form of electric resistance you can muster to make life easier. Mages should not use any form of magic of that element, and their staves should also not be electric. The Vinsomer is vulnerable to spirit damage, but it isn't easy to come by without rune enchantments. It's worth it so your mages can bring the hurt that much faster. At level 16, the Vinsomer can flatten unprepared or underleveled parties in a hurry, so don't slack on gearing up for the fight.

Ideally, you should come to the fight with full focus bars, so you can unleash the power of the Anchor on the high dragon for heavy damage, as well as use your mages' Heal focus ability to fully restore the party in a pinch.

Watch out for dragonlings. Kill them as quickly as possible to avoid spending potions on healing. You want to save as many of your resources as you can for the big battle.

The Vinsomer possesses many of the same physical attacks that the Ferelden Frostback used, complete with the same tells. Attacks with her limbs or tail are preceded by a very clear raising of the implement she wants to inflict pain with. The Vinsomer is also very active, leaping or hovering across parts of the arena often, making life difficult for warriors trying to tank her. This is also a threat to ranged classes that rely on distance to stay alive. She gains a full bar of guard to further stymie any attacks striking her. The Vinsomer calls in dragonlings to assist and can stun the whole party with an inescapable roar.

Watch the Vinsomer's neck if you're standing in front of the dragon. As the fight goes on, you will see it crackle with lightning. This electric storm will continue to intensify until the Vinsomer unleashes her electric breath onto the field. This devastating attack covers a larger area as the dragon sweeps it across the area in front of her head, and it can fry weaker characters in seconds. Your best hope for escaping the breath is simply to not be where it is when the attack begins.

The Vinsomer is a tough fight, as one would expect of any high dragon, but so long as you stay on top of your game, avoid taking needless blows from the limbs or tail, and avoid the electric breath, you can grind her down even if you're a couple levels lower than she is. If you're a warrior, pay attention to attacks you can block to build up for guard. Melee rogues should *always* remember to get out of the way of a limb that is raised to strike. Ranged attackers need to be aware of Vinsomer's lightning breath by paying attention to where the Vinsomer's head is pointed when the lightning storm around her neck reaches its peak.

FORBIDDEN OASIS

The Forbidden Oasis lies in the northern stretches of the Western Approach. A mining company from Val Firmin once set up shop in the region but moved on when profits dried up. A mysterious temple lies at the heart of the oasis, but no one has managed to enter it.

LOCALE SUMMARY

Scouting Cost: 4 Power

The Forbidden Oasis will prove to be a significant location in your quest to save Thedas from the forces of chaos, one that you will return to every so often throughout the game. There aren't too many quests in this locale, but four of them center around locating all of the shards hidden across all of Thedas and delving deeper into the temple at the center of oasis. If you unlock the Forbidden Oasis as early as possible, you will not be able to open all the doors in the temple until much later, but you can still open some of the doors and enjoy the treasures they guard. Be wary when exploring the tunnel networks throughout the oasis. Giant spiders have made their home here and rank among some of the most dangerous wildlife in the area.

Make sure you have at least one warrior and mage in your party at all times while exploring the oasis. There are walls a warrior can smash through, veilfire torches for mages to light, and bridges a mage can reconstruct. This is a great place to find some shards quickly.

CRAFTING MATERIALS

Common Materials:

- Elfroot
- Spindleweed
- Blood Lotus
- Deep Mushroom
- Serpentstone

Rare Materials:

- Dragonthorn
- Wither Stalk
- Paragon's Luster

COLLECTIONS

- Astrariums: 0
- Bottles of Thedas: 1
- High Dragons: 0
- Landmarks: 8
- Mosaic Pieces: 1
- Glyphs: 2
- Shards: 15
- Treasure Maps: 0
- Logging Stands: 0
- Quarries: 0

DEVELOPER TIP

Open the big, scary door in the Forbidden Oasis as early as possible.

— Ben Gelinas, Editor

LOCALE MAP

LEGEND

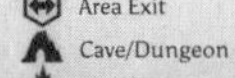

- Area Exit
- Cave/Dungeon
- Fade Rift

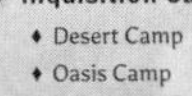

Inquisition Camps

- Desert Camp
- Oasis Camp

COLLECTIONS

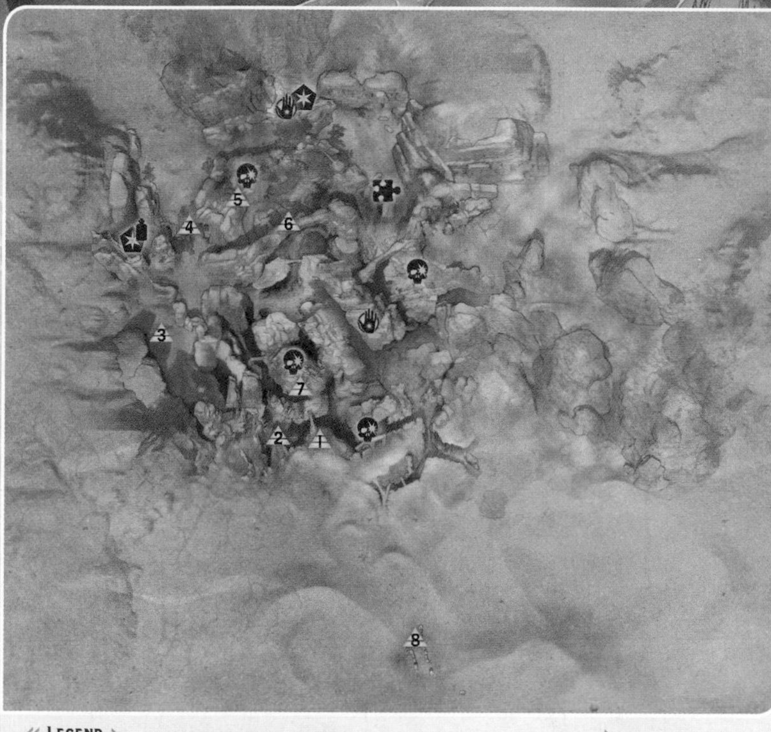

Legend

- **Bottles of Thedas**
- **Landmarks/Points of Interest**
  1. Wooden Bridge
  2. The Weight of War
  3. Spiral Mine
  4. Envers Mining Company
  5. Upper Walkways
  6. Intrinsic Pool
  7. Worn Pillars
  8. The Marker
- **Mosaic Pieces**
- **Oculara and Shards**
  - **Ocularum I: Desert Edge**
    - Ocularum +5 Shards
  - **Ocularum 2: Aires Peak**
    - Ocularum +5 Shards
  - **Ocularum 3: Solasan**
    - Ocularum +2 Shards
  - **Ocularum 4: Upper Walkway**
    - Ocularum +3 Shards
- **Glyphs**
- **Solas Artifacts**

NOTE The shards of the oasis are placed in such a way that it can be difficult to collect multiple shards at once, as they all take you on routes far off the beaten path. Make sure you have a mage to recreate bridges and a warrior to kick down barriers, as this can make things easier.

FADE RIFTS

The Forbidden Oasis is complex to navigate, enough so that going after the rifts will take you out of the way of most points of interest in the oasis itself. The average strength of the demons pouring out of the rifts here is level 9, so prepare accordingly. Rage and despair demons are becoming a more common occurrence, so be ready to handle the heavy fire and frost damage they can respectively dish out.

TIP The Fade rift at the Spiral Mine has a bottle of Thedas collectible very close to its location.

Fade Rift Details

Quest	Rifts	Total Power
Rifts in the Oasis	3	6
Rifts High and Low	2	4

REQUISITIONS

Requisition Quests

Requisition	Materials
Mining Requisition in the Oasis	5 Iron, 5 Nugskins
Serpentstone Survey in the Oasis	10 Serpentstones, 2 Paragon's Luster

SIDE QUESTS (RECOMMENDED LEVEL 8-12, 5-15, AND 18-20)

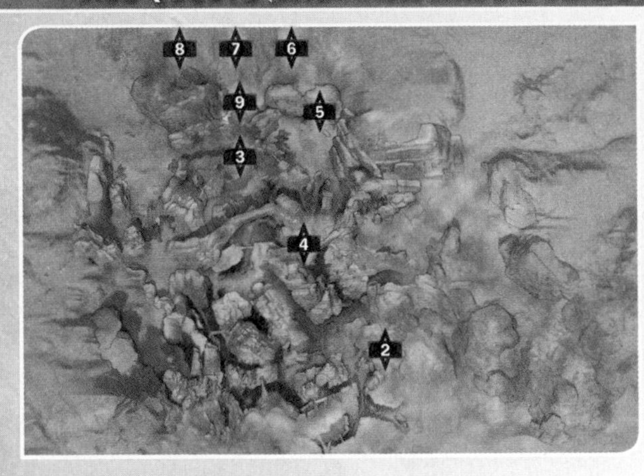

« LEGEND »

Level 8-12

1: Shard Collector

2: Holding the Oasis

3: The Temple of Pride

Level 12-15

4: What It's Worth

5: The Door in Par'as Cavern

Level 5-15

6: The Fire Captured

7: The Spirit Calmed

8: The Cold Endured

Level 18-20

9: A Prideful Place

1: SHARD COLLECTOR

Quest Giver: Collect a shard from any locale in Thedas to start this quest.

Description: A strange shard has been discovered. It appears to be of ancient origin and may be part of a larger set. Further study could reveal more.

Requirements: Collect a shard to unlock this quest, then spend four power at the war table to research the shards. This war table mission needs to be completed in order to access the Forbidden Oasis.

Reward: Open the Forbidden Oasis.

Objectives:

- Investigate shards at the war table (four power required).
- Travel to the Forbidden Oasis.

2: HOLDING THE OASIS

Description: Establish camps to hold the Forbidden Oasis and support Inquisition activity in the region.

Quest Giver: Scout Harding

Requirements: Started as soon as you arrive in Forbidden Oasis

Reward: 50 Influence and 1 Power per camp, except for the starting camp

Objectives:

- Establish two camps.

With only two camps in the area, including the one you start with, traveling around the Forbidden Oasis requires you to get familiar with the winding pathways and interconnected tunnels. Reaching the camp down in the oasis itself can be somewhat challenging, but as long as you follow any ramps that take you to the canyons (and avoid detours), you can make a pretty straight shot at the second camp.

3: THE TEMPLE OF PRIDE

Quest Giver: Scout Harding

Description: The entrance to a mysterious temple the ancient elves called Solasan stands tall, foreboding, and sealed in the middle of the Forbidden Oasis. It seems to have some connection to strange shards scattered across Thedas.

Requirements: Unlock the Forbidden Oasis via the war table using four power after finding your first shards and completing the research war table missions. Arrive at Forbidden Oasis for the first time to begin this quest.

Reward: 354 XP, 200 Influence, 2 Power

Objectives:

- Find the door to Solasan.

After you find your first shards and complete the necessary research that leads the Inquisition to the Forbidden Oasis, your first major side quest is simply to reach the front entrance of the temple. From the oasis camp, travel north to the Intrinsic Pool and make a right. A small mine shaft is blocked off by wooden barriers that a warrior can kick through. Follow this tunnel up and make a left at the T junction to arrive directly at the front door to the temple.

Alternatively, you can reach the temple from a desert entrance on the eastern side of the canyon. This takes you right past an ocularum, which can be used as a landmark for you to help find this passage, which is the same tunnel that the oasis mine shaft leads to.

TIP

A mosaic piece for the Freed Are Slaves collection can be found at this tunnel junction.

The door to the temple is sealed and will not budge unless you have acquired six shards. If you haven't already found six shards, there are oculara in the oasis that can let you get enough shards to unseal the temple. Opening the door completes the quest.

TIP

A rune can be found inside the temple, on the wall to the right of the Fire Captured path's first door. A veilfire torch on the opposite side of the room can help reveal it. Additionally, an elven device sits on a pedestal across from the first Cold Endured door. Activating it while Solas is in the party garners his approval.

4: WHAT IT'S WORTH

Quest Giver: A miner wandering the canyons in the oasis

Description: A former miner is salvaging valuables in the Forbidden Oasis. She mentioned an old wedding ring, but the cave where she once stored supplies has been overrun with spiders.

Requirements: Available upon arrival in the Forbidden Oasis

Reward: 242 XP, 80 Influence

Objectives:

- Retrieve the ring.
- Return the ring to the miner.

Wandering the canyons is a former miner, in search of old equipment that can be salvaged from the oasis. Speak with her to learn that she's looking for a wedding ring she left behind for reasons she's not willing to divulge. Whatever they are, she wants the ring back regardless. Unfortunately, the cave in question is infested with giant spiders, and she can't deal with so many by herself.

NOTE Finding the miner to speak to can be a pain: She's constantly walking through the canyons, meaning you can't guarantee she'll be in a convenient spot to chat with. Thankfully, when you get close enough to her, an exclamation point appears on your map, so you can at least point yourself in her direction. Afterward, any objectives that point you back to the miner will have her marked on your maps.

Par'as Cavern, where the miner claims she stored the ring, is in the Stratos region, on the eastern side of the Forbidden Oasis. A note found outside the cavern claims a torch will either scatter or draw in the spiders. Not exactly reassuring.

Across the room from the cavern entrance sits a locked door that requires a key. Do not run haphazardly across the room to that door unless you can handle a swarm of level 12-15 spiders! Instead, work your way around the room, lighting the torches. This makes the spider threat somewhat manageable. Push your way into the spider holes on the east and west sides of the room, exterminating the eight-legged freaks to reach the treasures they guard. Among the chests they protected will be the wedding ring. Return it to the owner to complete the quest.

5: THE DOOR IN PAR'AS CAVERN

Quest Giver: The miner wandering the canyons. Alternatively, inspect the locked door in Par'as Cavern to start the quest.

Description: There is a locked door in Par'as Cavern.

Requirements: You must complete What It's Worth to gain the key for the door in Par'as Cavern.

Reward: 44 XP, 40 Influence

Objectives:

- Find a key to the door.
- Open the door.

Grateful for your return of her ring, the miner hands over her key to the locked door inside Par'as Cavern. Return to the cavern and unlock the door to complete this quest and gain access to the treasures it protected.

> 6: THE FIRE CAPTURED

Quest Giver: Fire door inside Solasan

Description: An eerie heat emanates from a locked door within the temple.

Requirements: Gain access to Solasan as part of the Temple of Pride side quest.

Reward: 1,656 XP, 480 Influence, 5 Power

Objectives:

- Gather 6 shards.
- Open the first door.
- Gather 12 shards.
- Open the second door.
- Gather 18 shards.
- Open the final door.

The three elemental doors inside Solasan lead to chambers filled with monsters, gold, and a coffin filled with treasure, as well as magic that enhances your natural resistance toward a type of elemental damage. Each coffin you open boosts that elemental resistance by 4, 6, and 10 points, respectively. As you might guess, going down the fire path will help boost your fire resistance, the frost path builds up your frost resistance, and the spirit path enhances that resistance.

Each path has three doors to unlock, and the monsters behind each door become progressively more challenging. Additionally, elemental glyphs mark the floors of the treasure chambers, acting like land mines that deal damage based on the theme of the elemental path.

The first door offers monsters around level 7 and 8.

The second door reveals a room with monsters at level 9 and 10...

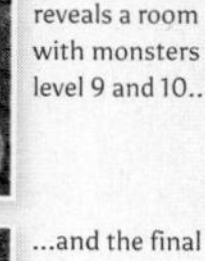

...and the final door stands between you and a chamber filled with level 12 to 15 demons, including a rage demon in the fire route.

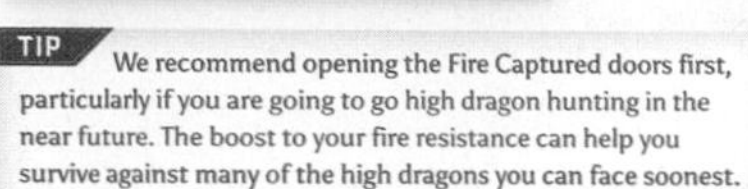

TIP

We recommend opening the Fire Captured doors first, particularly if you are going to go high dragon hunting in the near future. The boost to your fire resistance can help you survive against many of the high dragons you can face soonest.

> 7: THE SPIRIT CALMED

Quest Giver: Spirit door inside Solasan

Description: An earthy smell emanates from a locked door within the temple.

Requirements: Gain access to Solasan as part of the Temple of Pride side quest.

Reward: 1,656 XP, 480 Influence, 5 Power

Objectives:

- Gather 6 shards.
- Open the first door.
- Gather 12 shards.
- Open the second door.
- Gather 18 shards.
- Open the final door.

Like the Fire Captured doors, the Spirit Calmed doors follow the same shard requirements and have the same setup for monsters and traps you'll face inside each treasure chamber. The demon in control of the final room is an arcane horror, so be prepared to deal with its lethal ranged magic blasts.

> 8: THE COLD ENDURED

Quest Giver: Frost door inside Solasan

Description: An unnatural cold emanates from a locked door within the temple.

Requirements: Gain access to Solasan as part of the Temple of Pride side quest.

Reward: 1,656 XP, 480 Influence, 5 Power

Objectives:

- Gather 6 shards.
- Open the first door.
- Gather 12 shards.
- Open the second door.
- Gather 18 shards.
- Open the final door.

The Cold Endured doors again follow the same setup seen in the other two elemental paths. Your final threat in the third treasure chamber is a horde of undead, led by a dreadfully powerful revenant. Bring mages with powerful fire staves to quickly put down this monster before it becomes a problem.

> 9: A PRIDEFUL PLACE

Quest Giver: Open all fire, spirit, and frost doors in Solasan to be given this quest automatically.

Description: The door at the heart of the temple has opened.

Requirements: All nine doors in the first three elemental paths must be opened.

Reward: 5,076 XP, 600 Influence, 2 Power

Objectives:

- Discover what lies within.

You may have noticed on repeat visits to the temple that a door in the front chamber has had a series of lights appearing in an arch over it, corresponding with the number of doors you have opened in other paths. Once all nine are open, this final door opens, revealing the final challenge of Solasan.

Entering the final chamber, you will encounter a pride demon and four skeleton archers, all standing strong at level 19. Surrounding them all is a set of lightning glyphs, which make approaching the enemy a challenge. The glyphs appear in random patterns, designed to scatter your party. Rip apart the archers as fast as you can, then focus on the pride demon.

The final coffin opened in the temple provides your Inquisitor with 20 additional lightning resistance. With this, the temple of Solasan has been fully cleared!

SKYHOLD

Following the destruction of Haven, an abandoned castle in the Dales known as Skyhold now houses the only thing keeping Thedas from its darkest hour. Skyhold is larger and significantly more defensible. It should serve the Inquisition well.

LOCALE SUMMARY

Scouting Cost: 0

The Inquisition comes to Skyhold during the From the Ashes quest, following the attack on Haven. Upon their arrival, Skyhold is in great disrepair, crumbling due to years of abandonment and neglect. Little by little, the Inquisition fortifies the walls and applies regal decor, fitting of the up-and-coming organization. As the castle takes shape, you have the option of customizing Skyhold, choosing everything from drapery and heraldry to thrones and beds. Once established, Skyhold functions much like Haven. Come here to meet with the war council to discuss the Inquisition's plans. The Inquisitor can also judge prisoners of the Inquisition, determining their fate in the throne room. Skyhold is home to merchants, party members, and various support staff. So take the time to visit with your people to stay apprised of what's happening. Your party members always have interesting things to say and may even ask for help in completing inner circle quests.

> CRAFTING MATERIALS

Common Materials:

- Blank Runestone
- Serault Infused Glass

Rare Materials: None

Unique Materials: None

> COLLECTIONS

- Astrariums: 0
- Bottles of Thedas: 0
- High Dragons: 0
- Landmarks: 0
- Mosaic Pieces: 0
- Glyphs: 0
- Shards: 0
- Treasure Maps: 0
- Logging Stands: 0
- Quarries: 0

LOCALE/COLLECTIONS MAP

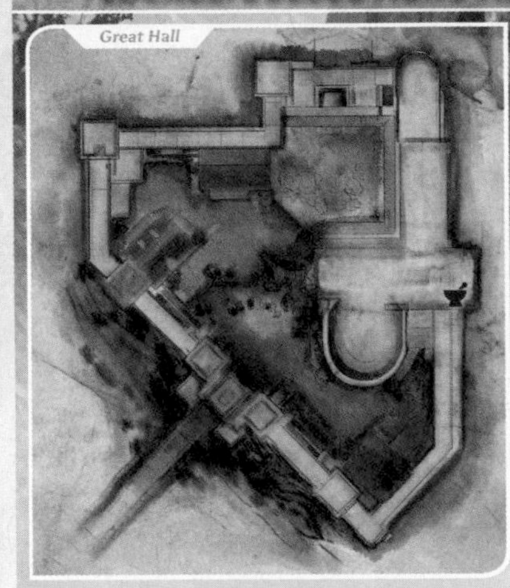

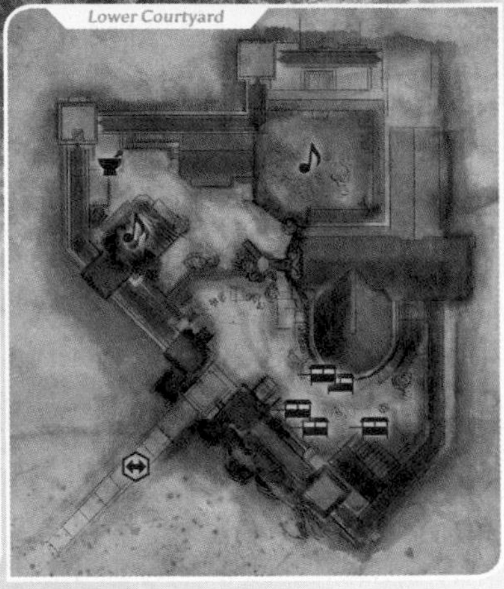

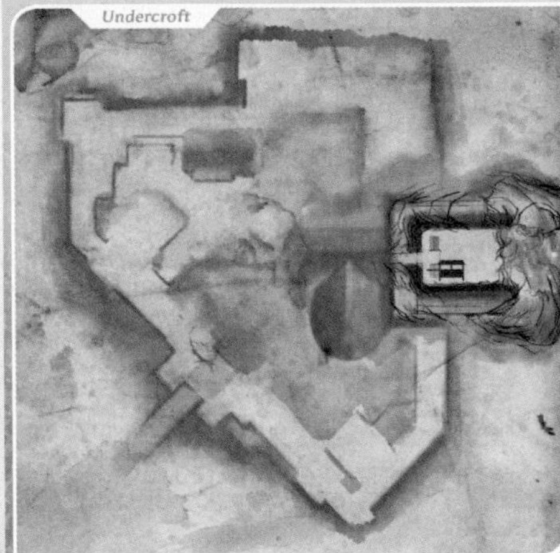

LEGEND

- Area Exit
- Crafting Station
- Merchant

Song Lyrics

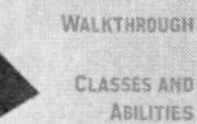

MERCHANTS

Bonny Sims's Shop

Item	Cost
Weapons (Highlights)	
Axe of the Dragon Hunter	11,540
Magehunter	7,629
Grunsmann's Bow	4,082
Upgrades (Highlights)	
Firm Bianca Grip	738
Ornate Bianca Grip	211
Aiming Module I	211
Aiming Module II	211
Aiming Module III	738
Bianca Arms II	28
Bianca Arms III	70
Bianca Arms IV	175
Bianca Arms V	474
Crafting Materials	
Blank Runestone	71
Serault Infused Glass	42
Fusing Agent	214
Weapon Schematics	
Super Corrupting Rune	7,294
Firm Bianca Grip	934
Bianca Arms III	934
Bianca Aiming III	934
Dragon-Slaying Rune	182
Bianca Arms II	89
Bianca Aiming II	89
Ornate Bianca Grip	20
Bianca Arms I	20
Bianca Aiming I	20
Recipes	
Lyrium Potion Recipe	53

Seggrit's Shop

Item	Cost
Weapons (Highlights)	
Siege's End	21,433
Tenasarin	11,110
Upgrades (Highlights)	
Sturdy Bianca Grip	28
Aiming Module I	28
Bianca Arms I	19
Weapon Schematics	
Bianca Arms I	20
Bianca Aiming I	20

Farris the Representative

Item	Cost
Influence Boosters*	
Protocols of Passage: Free Maches (limit: 10)	6,886
Perendale Entente Cordiale (limit: 10)	6,886
Favors of Marque and Reprisal (limit: 10)	6,886
Estwatch Alliance of Names (limit: 10)	6,886
A Pact of Certain Favors (limit: 10)	6,886
Western Orlais Independent Compact (limit: 10)	1,690
Southern Nevarra Independent Compact (limit: 10)	1,690
Southern Ferelden Independent Compact (limit: 10)	1,690
Northern Ferelden Independent Compact (limit: 10)	1,690
Coastal Antiva Independent Compact (limit: 10)	1,690
Montsimmard Accord (limit: 10)	490
Mont-de-Glace Accord (limit: 10)	490
Highever Accord (limit: 10)	490
Hasmal Accord (limit: 10)	490
Arlesans Accord (limit: 10)	490
Private Trade Agreement: Seleny (limit: 10)	167
Private Trade Agreement: Hunter Fell (limit: 10)	167
Private Trade Agreement: Dales End (limit: 10)	167
Private Trade Agreement: Churneau (limit: 10)	167
Private Trade Agreement: Ayesleigh (limit: 10)	167

NOTE Influence boosters are available in limited quantities and can be quite expensive to buy. However, if you need an influence boost to reach another Inquisition perk, and you have money to spare, this vendor can be a great help.

The Stables: Horsemaster Store

Item	Cost	Availability
Horses		
Taslin Strider	0	After Dennet joins
Green Dales Feral	200	After Haven
Dalish All-Bred	200	After Haven
Orlesian Courser	285	After Haven
Amaranthine Charger	627	After Halamshiral
Free Marches Ranger	627	After Halamshiral
Anderfel Courser	1,200	After Adamant
Imperial Warmblood	1,200	After Adamant
Dracolisks		
Hunter Shade Dracolisk	0	After killing one high dragon and completing the Hunter Shade Dracolisk operation
Abyssal Hang-Tooth	385	After obtaining Hunter Shade Dracolisk and capturing keep in Crestwood
Basking Longma	812	After obtaining Hunter Shade Dracolisk and capturing keep in Emprise du Lion
Blue River Bane	812	After obtaining Hunter Shade Dracolisk and acquiring Inquisition rank 9
Desert Lightning	1,800	After obtaining Hunter Shade Dracolisk and capturing keep in Western Approach
Sharp-Tail	4,400	After obtaining Hunter Shade Dracolisk and acquiring Inquisition rank 9
Harts		
Brecilian Sure-Foot	450	After acquiring Inquisition rank 5
Tirashan Swiftwind	641	After scouting Emerald Graves
Pride of Arlathan	1,400	After scouting Emprise du Lion
Wild Hart	2,300	After scouting the Exalted Plains

Undercroft Shop

Item	Cost
Accessories	
The Tactician's Renewal	Special

NOTE The Tactician's Renewal is a unique single-use amulet that allows you to re-spec the abilities of any character who wears it. The initial cost of these amulets is low, but after your first purchase the price shoots up and stays up.

AGENTS

ALEXIUS

Affiliated Quest: Sit in Judgment

Inquisition Perk: A Magister in Disgrace (Secrets)

If you took Alexius alive following the events at Redcliffe Castle, you can judge him at Skyhold. Sentence him to research magic for the Inquisition.

SERVIS

Affiliated Quest: Sit in Judgment

Inquisition Perk: Servis (Secrets)

After confronting Servis in the Western Approach, return to Skyhold to judge him. Servis can be conscripted as an informant, supplying useful information to Leliana.

FLORIANNE

Affiliated Quest: Sit in Judgment

Inquisition Perk: The Noble Cadaver (Connections)

If Florianne was killed at Halamshiral, you have the opportunity to judge her remains at Skyhold. Sentence her remains to community service to give Josephine another agent.

SIDE QUESTS (RECOMMENDED LEVEL 10-12)

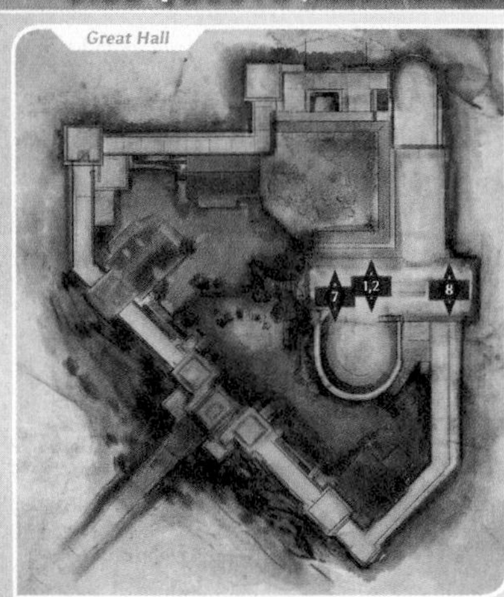

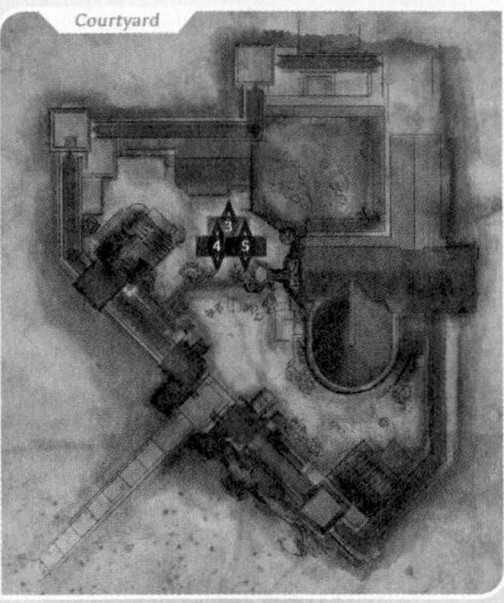

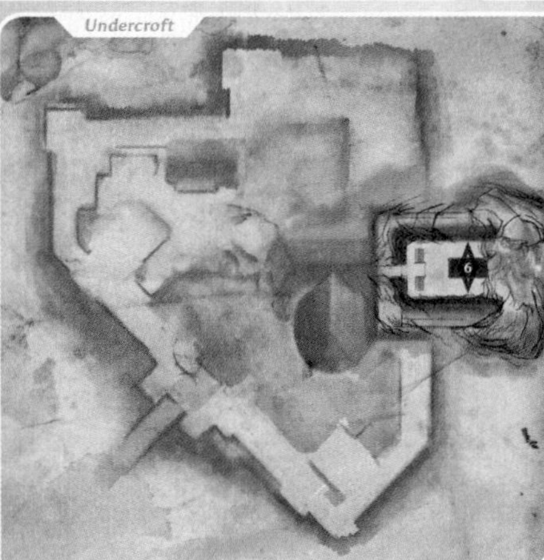

Legend

Level 10-12

1: Welcome to Skyhold
2: Inquisition Trappings
3: A Greener Garden
4: A Better Courtyard
5: A Superior Tower
6: Rune Crafting
7: Scattered in Skyhold
8: Sit in Judgment

> 1: WELCOME TO SKYHOLD

Quest Giver: N/A

Description: This new home for the Inquisition has a lot to offer. Take a look around.

Requirements: Available after entering Skyhold

Reward: 50 XP

Objectives:

- Find the war room.
- Find the blacksmith.

The new war room is down the hall from Josephine's office in the antechamber. If you haven't already, visit the war room and assign advisors to new missions. Remember to collect rewards from any complete missions as well.

Harritt has set up shop in the undercroft—enter the door directly south of the throne. This area contains all the blacksmith stations you became familiar with in Haven. It also contains tables where you can equip and craft potions. Use this opportunity to craft new armor, weapons, and upgrades.

> 2: INQUISITION TRAPPINGS

Quest Giver: N/A

Description: Skyhold can be customized in a variety of ways to best reflect the style and priorities of the Inquisition.

Requirements: Available after entering Skyhold.

Reward: Skyhold appearance customization

Objectives:

- Go to the undercroft.
- Customize Skyhold.

While you're in the undercroft, approach the Skyhold customization bench to plan out the design of the castle. From this menu you can select custom banners, beds, drapery, heraldry, decor, thrones, and windows. You'll notice that some of these customization options are locked. You must acquire new items through exploration—some objects can also be purchased from merchants in Val Royeaux. These options affect merely the aesthetics of Skyhold and do not impact gameplay.

> 3: A GREENER GARDEN

Quest Giver: N/A

Description: With the right materials, improvements can be made to Skyhold's garden.

Requirements: Available after Skyhold construction is complete

Reward: Garden in Skyhold

Objectives:

- Upgrade Skyhold's garden.
- Obtain 30 spindleweeds, 30 elfroots, 30 blood lotuses, and one logging stand.

The Skyhold garden is a surprisingly useful for cultivating additional resources. Look into making this upgrade as soon as possible, so you can get the most out of the garden for the duration of your quest.

4: A BETTER COURTYARD

Quest Giver: N/A

Description: With the right materials, improvements can be made to Skyhold's courtyard.

Requirements: Available after Skyhold construction is complete

Reward: Improved courtyard in Skyhold

Objectives:

- Upgrade Skyhold's tower.
- Obtain 30 elfroots, two quarries, and two logging stands.

The courtyard and tower upgrades allow you to choose how you want Skyhold to be perceived and how it services the members of the Inquisition. For the courtyard, you can leave it as a medical triage station, or you can turn it into a training ground for the Inquisition troops.

5: A SUPERIOR TOWER

Quest Giver: N/A

Description: With the right materials, improvements can be made to Skyhold's tower.

Requirements: Available after Skyhold construction is complete

Reward: New tower for Skyhold

Objectives:

- Upgrade Skyhold's tower.
- Obtain 10 spirit essences, three quarries, and three logging stands.

The main tower of Skyhold can be converted into a proper mage tower or into an improved guard tower.

6: RUNE CRAFTING

Quest Giver: N/A

Description: Recruiting an arcanist will allow the Inquisition to craft runes to enhance weapons and armor.

Requirements: Dagna must be recruited via a war table operation.

Reward: Rune crafting is now available.

Objectives:

- Recruit an arcanist at the war table.
- Craft a rune in the undercroft.

The arcanist in question is a dwarf named Dagna. Despite her quirky personality, she's good at her work, and that's enchanting weapons. Her runes will provide distinct advantages in future battles, so be ready to visit her often. You recruit her by completing a war table mission.

This quest acts as a tutorial for rune crafting. Simply speak with Dagna and follow her instructions to craft your first rune!

7: SCATTERED IN SKYHOLD

Quest Giver: N/A

Description: Varric's writing is more popular than he lets on. Find all 48 copies of *Hard in Hightown* in Skyhold.

Requirements: Available after Skyhold construction is complete

Reward: 200 Influence for each book found

Objectives:

- Find all 48 copies of *Hard in Hightown*.

If you speak with one of the librarians in the Skyhold library, you'll hear about how 48 copies of *Hard in Hightown* are missing from the shelves, checked out by residents of the castle. You can find copies sitting alone, or in stacks of two or three. Stacks reappear between visits to Skyhold, so if you remember where you found a number of books, you can always recollect them to count toward your total.

8: SIT IN JUDGMENT

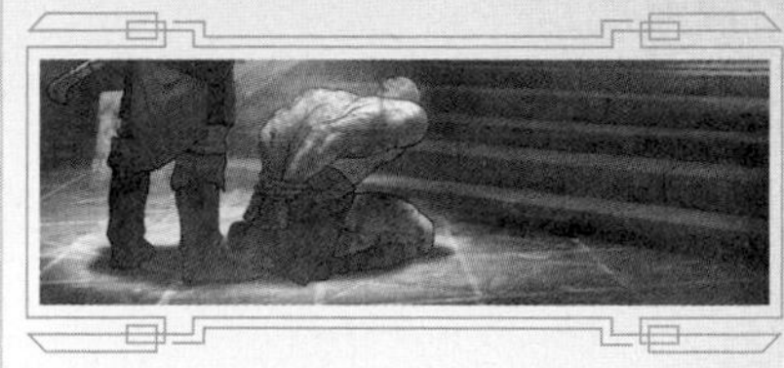

Quest Giver: Josephine

Description: Someone being held in Skyhold awaits judgment.

Requirements: Available anytime a prisoner is taken into the Inquisition's custody

Reward: Varies

Objectives:

- Judge the prisoner.

When the quest is available, interact with the throne to get an introduction to the process from Josephine. After this conversation, all future interactions with the throne will initiate a judgment. The number of judgments you can perform depends on how many enemies you've captured alive. Reference the following table for a listing of all possible judgments. Some of the prisoners can be conscripted into the Inquisition and serve as agents. Completing judgments unlocks new thrones.

Judgments

Prisoner	Capture Locale	Unlock	Details
Avaar Tribesman	The Fallow Mire	Chasind Throne	In this lighthearted judgment, choose what to do with the Avaar tribesman captured in the Fallow Mire following the Lost Souls quest.
Alexius	Redcliffe Castle	—	If you took Alexius into custody at Redcliffe Castle, order him to research magic to make him an agent.
Knight-Captain Denam	Therinfal Redoubt	—	Following events at Therinfal Redoubt, you have the opportunity to judge Knight-Captain Denam. You can sentence him to death, imprison him, or turn him over to the uncorrupted templars.
Servis	Western Approach	—	Servis is always taken as a prisoner following the fight in the Western Approach. Recruit him as an informant to make him an Inquisition agent, serving under Leliana.
Mayor Dedrick	Crestwood	Ferelden Throne	After Still Waters in Crestwood, complete the Find Crestwood's Mayor operation on the war table to track down Dedrick and bring him to justice. He had a good reason for flooding the old village, but were his actions justified? You can have him executed, imprisoned, or exiled.
Erimond	Adamant	—	After Adamant, choose what to do with Erimond. You can imprison him, kill him, or make him tranquil.
Ser Ruth	Adamant	—	This Warden was under the spell of Corypheus and killed other Wardens at Adamant during a binding ritual. She requests the death sentence, but you can be more lenient. Consider turning her over to the Wardens to please Blackwall.
Grand Duchess Florianne (alive)	Halamshiral	—	If you took Florianne alive at Halamshiral, she's brought back to Skyhold for judgment. You can't have her executed, but there are other fitting punishments.
Grand Duchess Florianne (dead)	Halamshiral	—	If Florianne was killed at Halamshiral, you can judge her remains, contained within a wooden box. Sentence Florianne's remains to community service to make her an agent working under Josephine. Politics—it's complicated.
Thom Rainier	Val Royeaux	—	During the Blackwall's Revelations inner circle quest, you can bring Thom Rainier back to Skyhold and judge him for his past crimes.
Mistress Poulin	Emprise du Lion	Orlesian Throne	Mistress Poulin must account for her business dealings with the red templars. There are numerous punishments, including death. But perhaps it would be most constructive if you ordered her to rebuild the town—Sera approves of this.
Samson	The Arbor Wilds	—	If you defeat Samson at the Temple of Mythal, he is brought back to Skyhold for judgment. If you avoid a conflict at the Temple of Mythal, you can track down Samson through an operation on the war table and take him into custody for judgment.

SPECIALIZATIONS

Once you've settled in Skyhold, visit the war room and select the Specializations for the Inquisitor mission on the war table. This mission costs no power and takes no time to complete. Upon completion, three trainers arrive in Skyhold—each trainer is capable of unlocking a new ability tree. But before an ability tree is unlocked, you must complete a quest offered by each trainer. These quests function like requisitions, requiring you to collect items scattered across multiple locales. Once a quest is complete, you have the opportunity to choose the associated specialization. But you can only choose one out of the three specializations, even if you complete all three quests. So put some thought into this—reference the Classes and Abilities chapter to preview the different specialization ability trees before making your decision.

Inquisitor Specializations

Discipline	Name	Trainer	Quest	Description
Rogue				
	Artificer	Three-Eyes	Way of the Artificer	These specialists control the battlefield with deadly traps. Neither they nor their explosive mines are ever where the enemy expects them to be.
	Assassin	Heir	Way of the Assassin	Any rogue can kill a target, but assassins make death into an art form. They specialize in quick, deadly kills that let them slide back into shadows undetected, or indirect kills that eliminate targets while the assassin is safely away.
	Tempest	Kihm	Way of the Tempest	These unpredictable experts specialize in using alchemical mixtures that wreathe them in frost or flame. Fast, chaotic, and possibly mad, they wade into the fight and dare enemies to face the storm.
Warrior				
	Champion	Lord Chancellor de Lion	Way of the Champion	These powerful defenders protect their allies from harm, standing strong against devastating blows with expert training and fierce determination. Enemies can't kill them—and usually can't survive them.
	Reaver	Breaker Thram	Way of the Reaver	As the battle gets bloodier, these vicious and deadly warriors get even more brutal. Hurting them just makes them mad, a mistake most enemies don't live to repeat.
	Templar	Ser	Way of the Templar	These unrelenting warriors specialize in fighting mages and demons. No enemy's magic can withstand them, and they inspire and protect their allies with their righteous power.
Mage				
	Knight-Enchanter	Commander Helaine	Way of the Knight-Enchanter	These rare mages received special dispensation from the Chantry to serve in battle. They summon blades from the Fade and are experts in protection and defense.
	Necromancer	Viuus Anaxas	Way of the Necromancer	These mages specialize in binding the spirits that are drawn to death. They can put the fear of death into enemies, bring spirits to fight on their behalf, and even cause devastating explosions when their enemies die.
	Rift Mage	Your Trainer	Way of the Rift Mage	These mages draw upon the force of the Fade, either pulling matter from the Fade to attack or twisting the Veil itself into a weapon to stagger or crush their enemies.

PARTY MEMBER SPECIALIZATIONS

As soon as the Inquisition arrives in Skyhold, all party members automatically unlock a unique specialization—no quests must be completed. So as these characters level up, remember to browse the new abilities in these trees.

Character Specializations

Character	Discipline	Name	Description
Blackwall		Champion	Blackwall has sworn to give his life to protect his friends and allies. He puts himself between them and danger, and his experience and resolve let him stand against attacks that would fell weaker warriors.
Cassandra		Templar	Long ago, the Seekers of Truth founded the Templar Order and taught the templars how to deal with hostile mages and their spells. Cassandra thus possesses all of a templar's abilities, without the risk of lyrium addiction.
Cole		Assassin	As a spirit dedicated to mercy, Cole is oddly suited to killing enemies with speed and precision. He can eliminate targets too dangerous to face directly with strikes they never even notice.
Dorian		Necromancer	Dorian is well-versed in spells that bind and manipulate Fade spirits, a practice that does not have the same stigma in the Tevinter Imperium as it does elsewhere in Thedas.
The Iron Bull		Reaver	The Iron Bull's combat style has honed his aggression and anger to a killing edge. He has learned to turn his own pain into a fury that makes him even deadlier when the fight gets bloody.
Sera		Tempest	With a satchel of dirty tricks, Sera takes the fight to her opponents before they know they're in it, committing fast and hard—and if covered in alchemical fire, all the better.
Solas		Rift Mage	Years spent studying the Fade have given Solas the ability to manipulate its energies in unpredictable ways. He can pull matter from the Fade and even twist the veil into a weapon to hammer his opponents.
Varric		Artificer	After years of experience with the merchants guild and the publishing world, Varric has become an expert at handling deadly traps and convoluted devices.
Vivienne		Knight-Enchanter	Whether it's high fashion or the battlefield, Vivienne prefers to be at the forefront and in control of everything around her. She will personally see order restored—by the blade, if necessary.

SKYHOLD CUSTOMIZATION

Visit Skyhold's undercroft to interact with the Skyhold Customization table. Here you can plan out the design of the castle, selecting from a variety of themes. Some of the items are available automatically when you acquire Skyhold, but some items must be unlocked by completing specific tasks or by simply buying them—Val Royeaux sells a wide variety of beds, drapery, and windows. Here's a complete listing of the customization options, revealing how each item is unlocked.

Customization Options

Theme	Unlock
Banners	
Andrastian Chantry	Automatically unlocked
Dalish	Automatically unlocked
Dwarven	Automatically unlocked
Ferelden	Automatically unlocked
Free Marches	Automatically unlocked
Inquisition	Default
Circle of Magi	Automatically unlocked
Orlais	Automatically unlocked
Templar	Automatically unlocked
Tevinter Imperium	Automatically unlocked
Grey Warden	Automatically unlocked
Banner Toppers	
Chantry Topper	Unlock the chantry garden
Circle of Magi Topper	Unlock the mage tower
Dalish Topper	Exalted Plains
Dwarven Topper	Storm Coast
Ferelden Topper	Crestwood
Free Marches Topper	Storm Coast
Inquisition Topper	Capture all keeps (3)
Orlesian Topper	Villa Maurel
Templar Topper	Unlock templar tower
Tevinter Imperium Topper	Hissing Wastes
Grey Warden Topper	The Forbidden Oasis
Bed	
Orlais	For sale in Val Royeaux (713 gold)
Free Marches	Default
Free Marches II	For sale in Val Royeaux (713 gold)
Orlais II	For sale in Val Royeaux (713 gold)
Orlais III	For sale in Val Royeaux (713 gold)
Dwarven	For sale in Val Royeaux (713 gold)
Drapery	
Basic	Default
Ferelden	For sale in Val Royeaux (356 gold)
Orlais	For sale in Val Royeaux (356 gold)
Andrastian Chantry	For sale in Val Royeaux (356 gold)
Dalish	For sale in Val Royeaux (356 gold)
Dalish II	For sale in Val Royeaux (356 gold)
Dwarven	For sale in Val Royeaux (356 gold)
Free Marches	For sale in Val Royeaux (356 gold)
Inquisition	For sale in Val Royeaux (356 gold)
Templar	For sale in Val Royeaux (356 gold)
Tevinter Imperium	For sale in Val Royeaux (356 gold)
Grey Warden	For sale in Val Royeaux (356 gold)

Theme	Unlock
Circle of Magi	For sale in Val Royeaux (356 gold)
Chasind	For sale in Val Royeaux (356 gold)
Qunari	For sale in Val Royeaux (356 gold)
Heraldry	
Basic	Default
Ferelden	Automatically unlocked
Orlais	Automatically unlocked
Andrastian Chantry	Automatically unlocked
Dalish	Automatically unlocked
Dwarven	Automatically unlocked
Free Marches	Automatically unlocked
Inquisition	Automatically unlocked
Templar	Automatically unlocked
Tevinter Imperium	Automatically unlocked
Grey Warden	Automatically unlocked
Circle of Magi	Automatically unlocked
Chasind	Automatically unlocked
Qunari	Automatically unlocked
Decor	
Basic	Default
Ferelden	Automatically unlocked
Orlais	Automatically unlocked
Andrastian Chantry	Automatically unlocked
Free Marches	Automatically unlocked
Tevinter Imperium	Automatically unlocked
Throne	
Andrastian Chantry	Complete Cassandra's inner circle quests
Chasind	Complete judgment of Avvar Tribesman
Mage	Complete Vivienne's inner circle quests
Ferelden	Complete judgment of Mayor Dedrick
Inquisition	Default
Orlais	Complete judgment of Mistress Poulin
Qunari	Complete Iron Bull's inner circle quests
Windows	
Andrastian Chantry	For sale in Val Royeaux (1,568 gold)
Dalish	For sale in Val Royeaux (1,568 gold)
Dwarven	For sale in Val Royeaux (1,568 gold)
Ferelden	For sale in Val Royeaux (1,568 gold)
Inquisition	Default
Orlais	For sale in Val Royeaux (1,568 gold)
Qunari	For sale in Val Royeaux (1,568 gold)
Boon of the Serault Glassworks	Complete the Serault Operations with Cullen

CRESTWOOD

Gloomier than the Storm Coast, Crestwood clings to life in the aftermath of a great tragedy, but a new tragedy is forming in the dark waters of the neighboring lake. When the darkspawn struck all of Ferelden during the last Blight 10 years ago, the village took in refugees from fallen territories. Unfortunately, the darkspawn took control of the local dam, flooding Old Crestwood and killing the refugees and many of the town's citizens. Since then the village has tried to eke out a meager existence further uphill from the flooded ruins, but the glow of a Fade rift from under the lake has caused the dead to rise, and demons lead them in a charge on the weary survivors. It is clear that Crestwood will not last long without help, and yet even the Grey Wardens are unable to spare a single man.

The Inquisition has its own purpose here in Crestwood. It seeks a rogue Grey Warden by the name of Stroud, who claims he has information regarding the disappearance of the Wardens all across Thedas. The Inquisition may also be the only force that can save the beleaguered town in time. Doing so, however, will mean unearthing an old secret deep beneath the lake...

LOCALE SUMMARY

Scouting Cost: 8 Power

Crestwood is where a great many things about Corypheus and his influence on world events begin to reveal their true extent. It is possible to continue forward with the story and ignore Crestwood's plight after you've met Stroud. However, there are many benefits to exploring this locale. Cave systems filled with treasure and resources await the hardy and brave adventurer. For the strongest men and women on Thedas, a high dragon, the Northern Hunter, claims this land as her own. This is an excellent place for the Inquisitor to build skills in preparation for the battles that lie ahead. All of the major side quests in this locale are best experienced around level 10 through 12. The high dragon, however, should be challenged by a party of level 13 or higher.

Crafting Materials

Common Materials:

- Elfroot
- Spindleweed
- Blood Lotus
- Deep Mushroom
- Embrium
- Iron
- Drakestone
- Onyx

Rare Materials:

- Royal Elfroot
- Obsidian
- Everite

Unique Materials: None

Collections

- Astrariums: 3
- Bottles of Thedas: 4
- High Dragons: 1
- Landmarks: 10
- Mosaic Pieces: 5
- Glyphs: 1
- Shards: 0
- Treasure Maps: 0
- Logging Stands: 1
- Quarries: 1

Inquisition Personnel

Agents

- Jana

LOCALE MAP

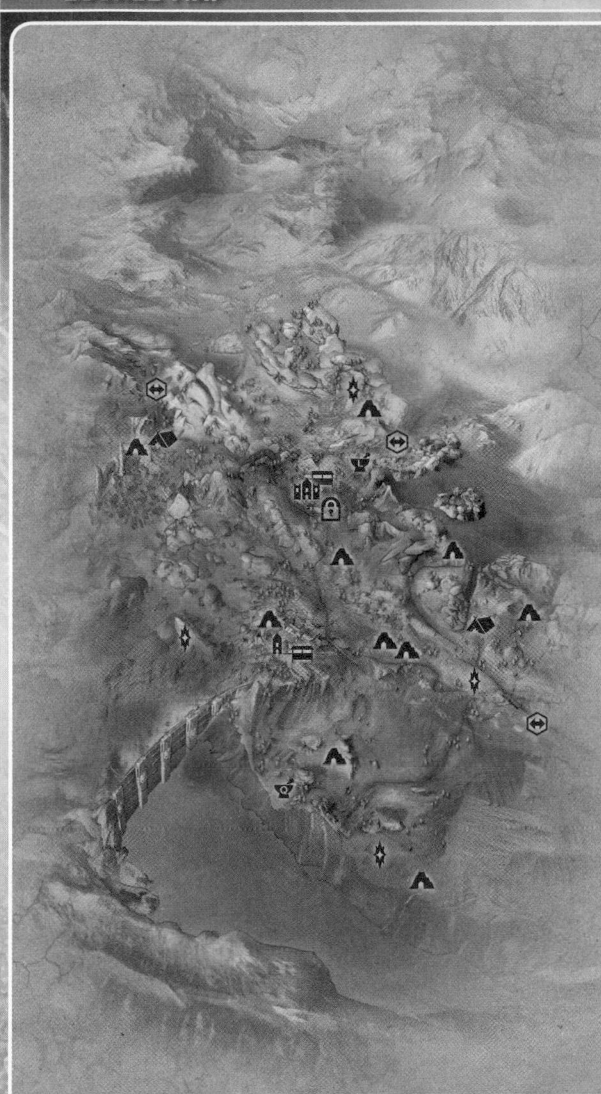

« LEGEND

- Area Exit
- Cave/Dungeon
- Fade Rift
- Keep
- Merchant
- Settlement
- Logging Stand
- Quarry

Inquisition Camps

- North Gate Camp
- Three Trout Farm Camp

NOTE This map changes once you drain the floodwaters from the dam. Doing that grants access to a pair of new regions: Old Crestwood and the Flats.

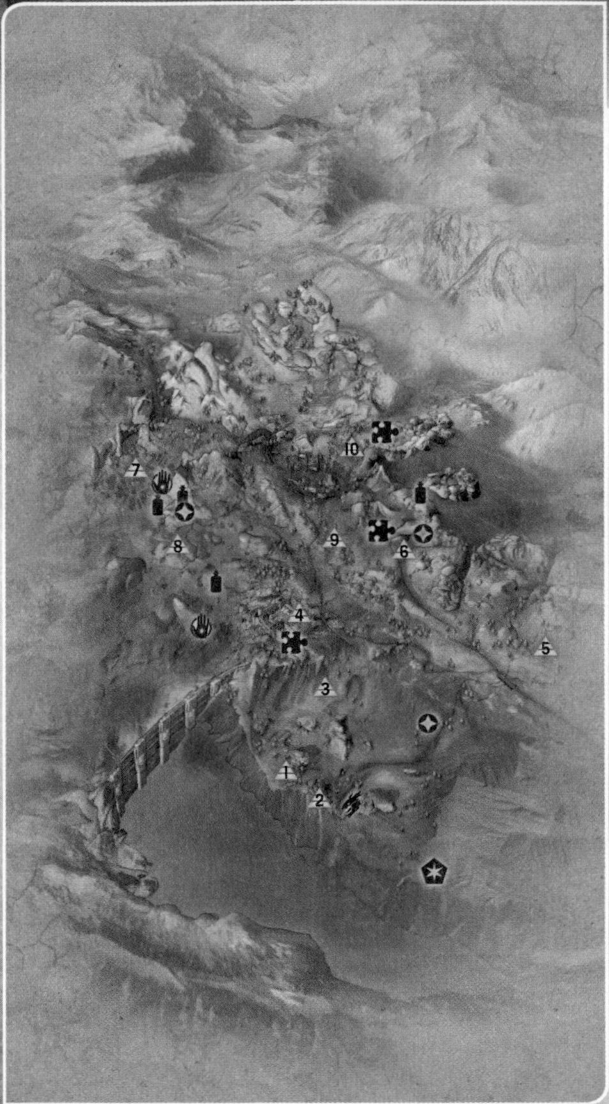

COLLECTIONS

Legend

Astrariums

- Constellation: Tenebrium
- Constellation: Kios
- Constellation: Silentir

Bottles of Thedas

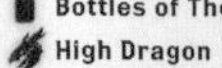

High Dragon

- Northern Hunter

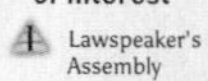

Landmarks/Points of Interest

1. Lawspeaker's Assembly
2. Ferelden Wyvern Statues
3. Wyvern's Watch
4. The Gallows of Caer Bronach
5. The Pit in the Pond
6. Guide of Falon'Din
7. Mayor's Old Home
8. Fisherman's Hut
9. Hidden Cave*
10. The Memorial

NOTE The Hidden Cave landmark is important to find: It holds loot, some refugees, and a mosaic piece for the Freed Are Slaves collection.

Mosaic Pieces

Glyphs

Solas Artifacts

ASTRARIUM SOLUTIONS

Astrarium: Tenebrium

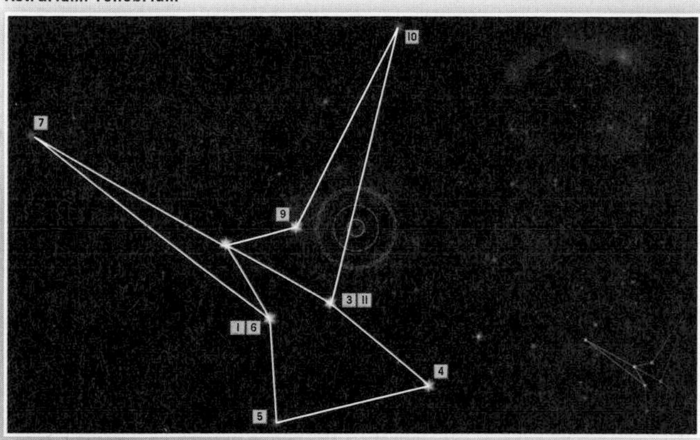

Astrarium: Kios

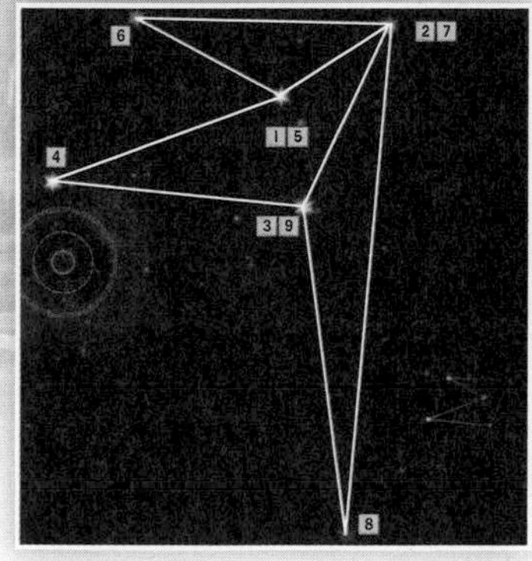

Astrarium: Silentir

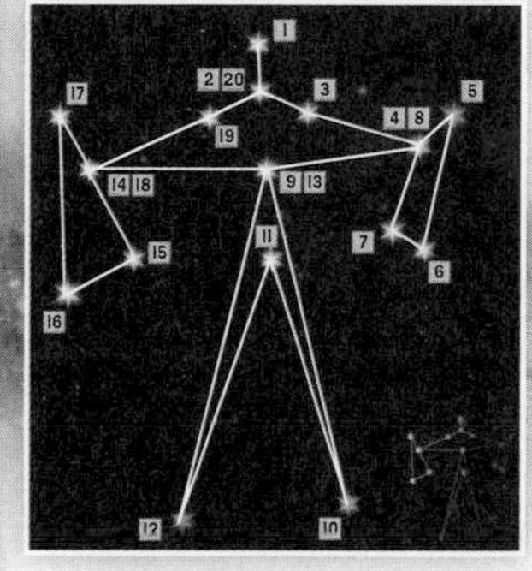

Astrarium Vault

You may have ridden through Dead Man's Pass without even seeing this astrarium vault's door. After solving all three astrarium puzzles, return to the pass to enter the vault and claim your riches.

FADE RIFTS

Stronger demons are beginning to spill forth from the rifts: Greater terrors can be seen on occasion, while despair and rage demons are starting to become common threats. Bringing two mages in the party in order to use Dispel on the demons before they fully manifest can help your party manage things.

Fade Rift Details

Quest	Rifts	Total Power
Rift near the North Gate	1	2
Rifts at the Farm	2	4
Rift at Caer Bronach	1	2

MERCHANTS

New Crestwood Merchant

Item	Cost
Weapons (Highlights)	
The Dueling Blade	941
Firm Tevinter Mace	409
Seeker Shield	211
Upgrades (Highlights)	
Masterwork Spiked Pommel	211
Balanced Two-Handed Grip	211
Crafting Materials	
Blank Runestone	71
Rashvine	42
Embrium	42
Deep Mushroom	42
Deathroot	42

Caer Bronach Merchant

Item	Cost
Weapons (Highlights)	
Thunderstrike	8572
Silkdart	472
Accessories (Highlights)	
Enchanted Amulet of Willpower	801
Enchanted Amulet of Strength	801
Enchanted Amulet of Magic	801
Enchanted Amulet of Dexterirty	801
Enchanted Amulet of Cunning	801
Enchanted Amulet of Constitution	801
Crafting Materials	
Blank Runestone	71
Spindleweed	20
Elfroot	20
Blood Lotus	20
Weapon Schematics	
Master Demon-Slaying Rune	1844

REQUISITIONS

Requisition Quests

Requisition	Materials
Caravan Requisition in Crestwood	5 Plaideweave, 10 Iron
Iron Survey in Crestwood	20 Iron, 10 Obsidian

AGENTS

> JANA

Affiliated Quest: None

Inquisition Perk: The Eager Recruit (Secrets)

After encountering the Grey Wardens on the road outside the North Gate camp, enter the nearby house to speak with Jana—she's excited the Grey Wardens saved her from the undead and wants to become a Warden herself. Convince her not to join the Grey Wardens. If Solas is in your group he can convince her to join the Inquisition instead.

SIDE QUESTS (RECOMMENDED LEVEL 10-12 AND 13+)

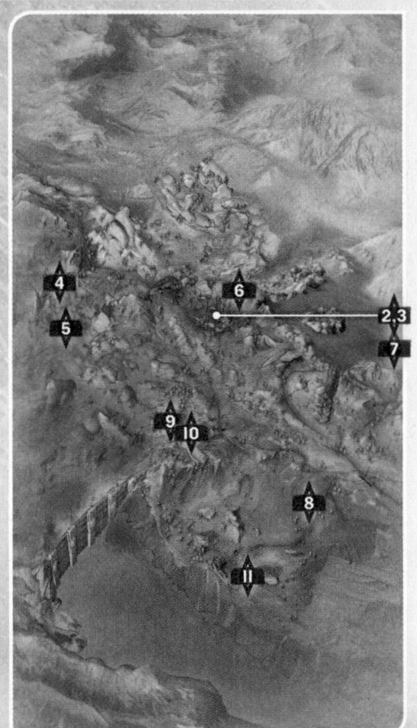

Legend

Level 10-12

1: Holding Crestwood
2: Still Waters
3: Capturing Caer Bronach
4: Dungeon: The Flooded Caves
5: Burdens of Command
6: Homecoming
7: Naturalist
8: Wyrm Hole
9: High Stakes
10: Weeding Out Bandits

Level 13+

11: High Dragon: The Northern Hunter

I: HOLDING CRESTWOOD

Description: Establish camps to hold Crestwood and support Inquisition activity in the region.

Quest Giver: Scout Harding

Requirements: Started as soon as you arrive in Crestwood

Reward: 100 Influence and 1 Power per camp, except for the starting camp

Objectives:

- Establish two camps.

As with the Forbidden Oasis, a mere two camps can be set up by the Inquisition here in Crestwood. However, the terrain here isn't nearly as complicated to navigate. Both camps are in good spots, placing you near areas where multiple quests overlap. It's worth establishing the second camp as early as possible to cut down on your travel times across the whole locale.

2: STILL WATERS

Quest Giver: Scout Harding

Description: Undead have terrorized Crestwood since a Fade rift appeared in the lake. There must be a way to close it.

Requirements: Using eight power, unlock Crestwood via the war table once you've spoken to Hawke in Skyhold. Arrive at Crestwood for the first time to begin this quest.

Reward: 1,934 XP, 400 Influence, 3 Power

Objectives:

- Help Crestwood fight back the undead.
- Speak to Crestwood's mayor.
- Claim the keep to reach the dam.
- Enter the building on the dam.
- Unlock the door to reach the controls and drain the lake.
- Find an entrance to the Flooded Caves.
- Enter the Flooded Caves under Old Crestwood.
- Close the Fade rift.
- Inform the mayor that the rift is closed.

Your ultimate goal during Still Waters is to somehow reach the Fade rift in the lake near the new Crestwood and seal it. Prepare yourself—this is a long side quest. By its very nature, it will take you throughout Crestwood, and during it you can start, and complete, other side quests: Burdens of Command, Homecoming, High Stakes, and Capturing Caer Bronach. All of these quests will at some point be encountered during and overlap with Still Waters.

After leaving the starting camp, head toward the town of Crestwood following the main road. You encounter a pair of Grey Wardens defending a elven woman from the undead. Help put an end to the battle. The grateful woman runs off, while the Wardens plead for the Inquisition to help Crestwood. They're here looking for Stroud, the Warden that Hawke spoke of back at Skyhold, and their orders do not allow them to stay in the area.

NOTE You can speak to this elven woman in a house on the outskirts of Crestwood, in the East Side Hills region. She expresses a strong desire to join the Grey Wardens after being rescued by them. However, she instantly recognizes the Inquisitor. You can encourage her to join them, or encourage her to not join the Wardens.

Continue heading toward the town, fighting off the undead as you encounter them. You'll reach the gates of the town, currently being held by a few defenders while undead and demons try to break through. After saving the gate guards, you're invited into town to go speak with the mayor.

Mayor Dedrick is initially glad for the help, but when the Inquisitor mentions draining the lake by opening the dam to reach the Fade rift, he becomes very nervous about what it may unleash. Even so, he says that the only way to get the dam open requires going through the old fort of Caer Bronach. After further conversation, he offers a key that will let you reach the gate controls, assuming you can get past the bandits in the fort. This starts the Capturing Caer Bronach side quest. You must take the keep before you can drain the lake, so get your party geared up for a fight and then go start one with the bandits of the keep. This can be a grueling series of battles, so don't hesitate to fall back to a camp to restock potions if necessary.

TIP While in Crestwood, look for the villagers who can start the Naturalist and Homecoming side quests. Simply following through with the Still Waters quest will help you take care of Homecoming, and Naturalist can be completed while you deal with other quests on the eastern side of Crestwood.

There's a door that requires the Deft Hands, Fine Tools perk for a rogue to unlock, but it's currently barred by wooden planks that can't be removed. Check back after you complete this quest.

3: CAPTURING CAER BRONACH

Quest Giver: Mayor of Crestwood

Description: Bandits known as the highwaymen have occupied Caer Bronach. Without the fortifications of this legendary keep for protection, the villagers of Crestwood and the surrounding area are left exposed to undead plaguing the region.

Requirements: Speak to Mayor Dedrick as part of the Still Waters side quest.

Reward: Caer Bronach falls under Inquisition control.

Objectives:

- Take back Caer Bronach.

The fight for Caer Bronach begins by shattering the front door. This alerts every bandit in the courtyard that you have arrived for their heads, so make sure you don't even begin your siege until you are fully stocked with potions and have your party set up the way you are most comfortable with.

As you enter the courtyard, mabari hounds rush the party, while archers try to shoot you from a rooftop ledge facing the front door. If you have a melee rogue in the party, get them up there to assassinate these shooters, while the rest of the party handles the hounds. Alternatively, a warrior with the Grappling Chain ability can bring them down to your level.

From the stairwells to the left and right of the archers' position, more bandits rush after you as soon as the first group is defeated. Take them out, then advance up the stairs and enter the next courtyard.

A highway guardsman holds the ground level of the second courtyard, while more archers fire from the upper level and the stairwell leading up to it. Don't let your party get torn up by those archers—try to bring the fight to them. The guardsman will follow. Also, be on the alert for highwaymen prowlers! Their acrobatics, combined with stealth and the ability to take an unassuming mage or rogue out of the fight in mere seconds, cannot be underestimated!

From the upper level, you'll pass through another courtyard that is surprisingly empty. Keep pushing forward until you reach another set of stairs, leading to another open area and another ambush led by highwaymen lieutenants. Don't let them distract you too long from the archers supporting them from afar!

Killing off this group prompts the leader of the bandits to rush down a final set of stairs, along with his most trusted men. The leader is an Avvar with incredible strength and stamina. If you can, blast him with Mark of the Rift, and if you're a melee fighter, try not to fight him on the narrow walkway he and his lieutenants run down to greet you. The narrow confines mean that his broad melee strikes can easily hit multiple party members.

With the bandits completely routed, go up the stairs the leader charged down and set the Inquisition banner on the flagpole to make the keep yours, completing this quest. Inquisition forces move in to the keep in short order, setting up useful facilities for you. Additionally, one of Leliana's scouts, a man named Charter, has moved into the area and has some important work for you to do. Most important of all, now that the keep is in your hands, you can use the key given to you by the mayor to reach the controls to the dam and drain the water of the lake to gain access to the Fade rift.

NOTE A Word on Keeps

Keeps are essentially super-camps. Not only can you use them for fast travel, restoring your potion inventory, and changing your party members, but they open up new war table operations and allow you to create weapons and equipment and modify them. Additionally, merchants can set up shop inside a keep, selling rare items, equipment, and schematics for you to use. They are a Skyhold away from Skyhold for all practical purposes, and there's no reason to not capture every keep you come across.

TIP Check a storage room that is just behind where your party appears in the keep after the cinematic showing the Inquisition flag being raised. A mosaic piece for the Freed Are Slaves collection can be found.

NOTE Behind Caer Bronach, on the cliffs facing the lake, is a rear entrance to the keep behind a rusted gate. A whole host of poison spiders, including the level 11 elite named Snowball, guard this entrance. Do not take these monsters lightly! Snowball provides the recipe for the healing mist grenade, a very useful tool to have in the pouch!

> STILL WATERS CONTINUED...

After you deal with the bandits in Caer Bronach, a door leading to the keep's rear exit will be marked on your map. Go through until you are back outside the keep, and follow the winding path to the west until you reach the dam itself. Cross over the dam until you reach The Rusted Horn, then enter the tavern.

Inside the tavern, you encounter a couple trying to spend some private time together. Obviously, this is not a very happening place if they can get away with that. Depending on your answers during this short conversation, you might get Cassandra's approval for reporting this dalliance or her disapproval of keeping it a secret. After looting the tavern of any goods you find, head over to the controls for the dam and drain the lake. Travel back to North Gate camp to load up on supplies, then head into Old Crestwood. With the water drained, you can now look for an entrance to the Flooded Caves, where the Fade rift awaits.

Old Crestwood's buildings remain in surprisingly good shape for having been covered by floodwaters for 10 years. Spirits haunt this place, along with other, more dangerous demons. Search the homes for any supplies as you seek the Flooded Caves. You can even enter the mayor's old home and find an interesting piece of reading. Going back to speak with the mayor after either draining the lake or finding his home will open up a judgment later in Skyhold.

NOTE With Old Crestwood no longer submerged, you can continue the Homecoming side quest offered by Sister Vaughn in Crestwood. Additionally, a spirit in this dead village isn't hostile per se, but she is very demanding. Catering to her whims starts you on the Burdens of Command side quest.

TIP Search Old Crestwood thoroughly to find two of the bottles of Thedas: Hirol's Lava Burst and a Conscription Ale, Vintage: Warden Gibbins somehow managed to survive the flood.

The entrance to the Flooded Caves is on the northern side of Old Crestwood, in an abandoned mine entrance. Replenish your potions before diving in—demons infest this place.

4: DUNGEON: THE FLOODED CAVES

The Flooded Caves are filled with spirits attracted to the death and destruction caused by the floods a decade before. Many are harmless, wandering about and reliving the terror of the flood victims. However, through the Fade rift traveled more hostile demons, and the corpses of the dead rise up under the influence of the Fade. The caves give way to an ancient dwarven ruin, filled with secret treasures to tempt the bold. Explore carefully and thoroughly if you intend to see all there is in this place.

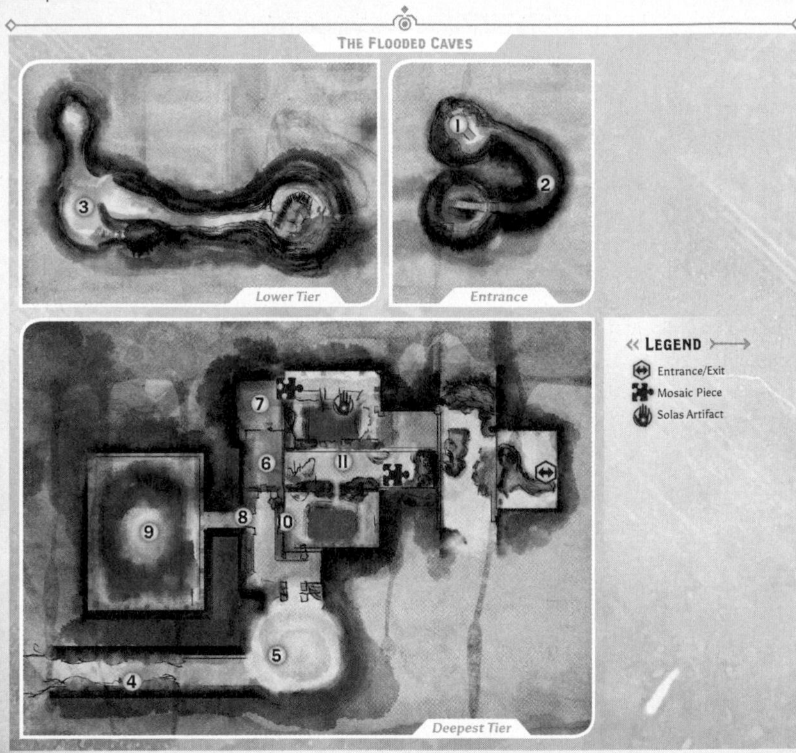

1. The first floor of the caves is straightforward. Proceed down the dark cave, lighting torches as you go, until you reach a large chasm, lit by the moon through the cracks in the ceiling. A wooden walkway takes you down to the lower tier of the caves.

2. Reaching the lower tier, travel down the eastern corridor until you encounter a strange sight: undead corpses kneeling in supplication before a despair demon. Destroy them all, then explore the area to uncover some more hidden treasure. After you're done looting, proceed down another wooden walkway to reach the dwarven ruins at the bottom of the caves.

3. As you move into the ruins, look for a door on the right. It requires the Deft Hands, Fine Tools perk to unlock. Inside the room, you find some interesting codex entries on the dwarven society, along with a treasure chest.

4. A rage demon patrols the first large chamber of the dwarven ruins. This is the rage demon the wraith in Old Crestwood spoke of. Banish it from this world and return to the surface once you've sealed the Fade rift to complete the Burdens of Command side quest.

5. A warrior can kick down this weakened wall, allowing your party to explore a tomb.

6. This tomb contains some treasure chests and a mosaic piece for the Freed Are Slaves collection.

7. The entrance to the chamber containing the Fade rift has a crate full of potions. Restore your stocks before taking on the demonic threat!

8. Unlike many other Fade rifts you've come across up to this point, this one is very resilient. Four waves of demons will assault your party. Expect wraiths, shades, terrors, rage demons, and despair demons! Here is where having a mage or two to dispel the demonspawn before they can manifest can come in handy. If you're lucky, you might even be able to dispel two demons with one spellcast! Additionally, the area the demons appear in is relatively small, so a well-placed Mark of the Rift can wreck an entire wave in short order. Once you seal the rift, you can return to Crestwood and inform the mayor of the good news. But don't leave the caves until you're certain you've looted as many valuables as you can carry.

9. The door across from the passage leading to the Fade rift room leads to another section of the dwarven ruins. On an altar in the west side of this chamber is another mosaic piece for the Freed Are Slaves collection.

10. After making another sweep of this last chamber, head out through another door on the west side of the room. After a couple more chambers, you'll eventually reach a ladder that acts as an alternative exit to the Flooded Caves. Faster than going all the way back to the first floor entrance!

NOTE One of the veil measurement devices that Solas is interested in can be found in this part of the dwarven ruins.

The alternative exit leads to another ladder to climb and a locked door that can be opened with a lever. Don't leave too hastily, as there's more loot to grab and yet another mosaic piece for the Freed Are Slaves collection.

The exit takes you to a cave in the East Side Hills, not far from the new Crestwood. The sun has come out, with only a light rain shower as opposed to the oppressive darkness and thunderstorm that blanketed the place before. Head down to Crestwood to deliver the good news to the mayor...except that the man is long gone, leaving only a letter of confession in his home, a full disclosure of the truth behind the events of 10 years ago. Your quest is complete, but justice is not yet served. If you spoke to the mayor after finding his house or draining the lake, you can return to Skyhold and use a war table quest to hunt down the mayor, then judge him before the Inquisition.

NOTE **The Flats**

Now that you've drained the floodwaters and solved the problems of Crestwood, save for the errant mayor, you can now explore the region covered by the waters known as the Flats. There's lots of good loot hidden throughout this area, including another bottle of Thedas hidden in a ruined home. Additionally, you can finally reach and seal the rift at Caer Bronach.

5: BURDENS OF COMMAND

Quest Giver: A wraith in Old Crestwood

Description: A spirit in Old Crestwood has a task for you.

Requirements: You must drain the lake before you can reach Old Crestwood, where this spirit haunts.

Reward: 512 XP, 200 Influence, 2 Power

Objectives:

- Destroy the rage demon in the Flooded Caves.
- Inform the spirit in Old Crestwood of the demon's demise.

A wraith in Old Crestwood shouts commands at you as you pass by the home it has taken residence in. If you take the time to speak with it, you learn that it despises demons, or "those who would suck this world dry." It claims that it is the concept of leadership and command personified, and it will not leave this world until something in it obeys its instructions. If you've talked to it to learn all you can from it, you can offer to follow its commands, beginning this side quest.

The wraith demands vengeance: A rage demon chased it across the lake, and incensed by this the wraith orders you to destroy it. This requires delving into the Flooded Caves. You can take on this side quest while also dealing with the Still Waters quest. See the section for Still Waters for a map of the Flooded Caves and more details on how to reach this rage demon. After you report successful mission completion to your "commander," the wraith is satisfied and rewards you for your actions.

6: HOMECOMING

Quest Giver: Sister Vaughn, Crestwood

Description: Sister Vaughn wants to cremate the bodies of people lost in a flood 10 years ago.

Requirements: Available after speaking with the mayor of Crestwood

Reward: 512 XP, 200 Influence, 2 Power

Objectives:

- Find three piles of bodies.
- Return the remains to Sister Vaughn.

Sister Vaughn has wanted to retrieve the bodies of the dead from Old Crestwood so that she may give them a proper funeral pyre as per the Chant. However, this would require draining the lake, an act the mayor has been reluctant to commit to. Fortunately, that happens to be in the cards for Inquisitors looking to seal the Fade rift in the lake depths.

After draining the waters of the lake, you're able to enter Old Crestwood and see the aftermath of the flood for yourself. Be mindful of the demons and the undead lurking throughout the ruined village, and search for piles of bodies that the sister can reclaim for the funeral pyre. After finding all three groups of bodies, inform the sister to complete the quest.

7: THE NATURALIST

Quest Giver: Gauld, a villager in Crestwood

Description: A man in Crestwood is concerned that a friend of his, Judith, isn't safe living outside of town. He'd appreciate someone checking up on her.

Requirements: Available upon arrival in Crestwood

Reward: 128 XP, 80 Influence

Objectives:

- Check up on Judith.

Given the weather and constant attacks by demons and the undead, Gauld's concerns for Judith are well founded. However, when you do reach the woman at Forester's Homestead, she's in perfect health, and even chides you for the visit while citing the dangers you were sent to secure her from. She does appreciate Gauld's gesture and provides you with plenty of good information about the surrounding area, including the presence of a lethal wyvern that has gotten more territorial in recent days, and of a roaming high dragon.

You can also ask her the most important question: "Seriously, why does anyone live out here?" There's no good answer to that. Quest completed anyway!

8: WYRM HOLE

Quest Giver: Judith, hermit of the homestead

Description: An aggressive wyvern is harassing Crestwood's villagers. It lives in a cave up in the hills. A woman named Judith outside of town seems interested in the body if someone manages to kill it.

Requirements: Speak with Judith about the wyvern after completing Naturalist.

Reward: 242 XP, 80 Influence

Objectives:

- Kill the cave wyvern.
- Return to Judith.

Make a stop at the Three Trout Pond camp before heading up the rocky slope; you'll want to be well prepared for this fight, as well as the fights leading up to it! As you climb up the rocky slope, you encounter a hostile force dependent on the choice you made back in Redcliffe. Be they red templars or rebel mages, they are a step up from mere bandits wandering the roads and can surprise an ill-prepared party. After eliminating the threats outside of the cave they were guarding, loot their camp for all its worth, then enter the cave.

NOTE Antivan Sip-Sip, one of the 29 bottles of Thedas, can be found in the cave leading to the wyvern. Search thoroughly!

The wyvern Judith mentioned is not alone; it has two smaller wyverns at its side when you find it. It is *not* to be taken lightly. As a level 12 elite, this wyvern's bite can brutalize rogues or mages caught in its reach, and worse still, the bite is poisonous enough to finish off those it wounds. Its young are also elites, and even at level 11 they are more than capable of ruining your party if they should be allowed to run free. Fortunately, the monsters have a vulnerability to cold-based damage, so plan accordingly. Mages should bring cold-damage staves and spells to the fight and be prepared to shield any comrades in melee range.

Initiate the fight by sending a warrior tank in first, to get the attention of the beast and its young before the rest of the party attacks. Then direct any mages in the group to stand back and let the monster have it from afar, or force your rogues to flank the wyvern before they strike. Hold nothing back—use Mark of the Rift on the wyverns to help speed things along. The fight outside of the wyvern's cave should have built you enough focus to use even a tier 1 version of that spell.

After surviving this tough fight, return to Judith to inform her that the wyvern is dead by your hand. The quest is complete. For your trouble, Judith hands over an armor schematic.

9: HIGH STAKES

Quest Giver: Charter.

Description: Leliana's "eyes and ears" in the region, a spy named Charter, mentions that her man Butcher seems to be running a little behind.

Requirements: Capture Caer Bronach and speak with Charter.

Reward: 128 XP, 80 Influence

Objectives:

- Find Butcher.
- Inform Charter of Butcher's fate.

Head toward the Three Trout Farm camp and search to the southeast. Look for a set of stone spires rising from the ground. It's there that you'll find Butcher and learn of his fate. The enemies of the Inquisition reached him before he could reach Caer Bronach.

Just as you finish reading the notes on the body, red templars or mages attack your party. Eliminate them with all haste, then return to Caer Bronach to inform Charter of Butcher's death, and of the notes he carried. The quest is complete, though Charter is concerned that there's a traitor in the ranks of the Inquisition. This creates a mission that can be assigned on the war table to expose who this traitor is.

Dragon Age Inquisition

> 10: WEEDING OUT BANDITS

Quest Giver: An agent in the Caer Bronach keep

Description: A handful of highwaymen remain on watch at farms around Crestwood and should go the way of their brethren in the keep.

Requirements: Capture Caer Bronach

Reward: 128 XP, 80 Influence

Objectives:

- Kill all eight bandits.

A simple job. Find bandits, remove them, with all the prejudice worthy of an Inquisition. They tend to roam in groups, and occasionally you may find a prowler among them. Or rather, the prowler will suddenly find its daggers in the back of someone in your party; these things happen. Aside from that, you should be more than capable of handling these stragglers to complete this quest.

> 11: HIGH DRAGON: THE NORTHERN HUNTER

Recommended Level: 13+

Recommended Party Composition: Two warriors (sword and shield, two-handed weapon), two mages (armed with frost or fire damage staves, with spirit damage enchantments); rogue optional

Alternative Party Composition: Three warriors (sword and shield or two-handed weapon), one mage (armed with frost or fire damage staves, with spirit damage enchantments), rogue optional

The Northern Hunter uses powerful electrical breath, just like the Vinsomer on the Storm Coast. She is an untauntable, raging beast that will go after whoever is hitting her the hardest at a given time or whoever is generating the greatest threat. Bounding and charging around the castle ruins of the Black Fens, the Northern Hunter naturally stymies the efforts of rogues, who rely on positioning to deal the best damage.

Beyond this, the Northern Hunter fights similarly to other high dragons you encounter. As always, watch the limbs or tail to prepare yourself to avoid taking unnecessary damage, and watch the dragon's mouth to spot the electric breath and move yourself accordingly. The Inquisitor should try to come to the fight with some levels in focus built up to be able to drop Mark of the Rift right on the Northern Hunter for very heavy damage.

Warriors excel during this fight. They have the armor to survive heavy damage, and their ability to build guard allows them to stay safe even if the dragon should manage to get past their defensive abilities. A mage or two should be on hand to use the focus Heal ability should things go pear-shaped in the middle of the fight.

For mages you bring, try to ensure their staves can produce spirit damage. The Northern Hunter resists electricity and isn't too bothered by other elements. The extra spirit damage can help burn the beast down that much faster.

THE WESTERN APPROACH

The desolate badlands known as the Western Approach are as massive as they are barren. Bordered to the west by steppes and crawling with monsters, the Approach is a place most avoid and from which few explorers return. The Grey Warden fortress Adamant sits on the edge of a great chasm on the Approach's southern reaches, one of the few remaining signs that the greatest battles of the Second Blight were fought here.

LOCALE SUMMARY — Scouting Cost: 8 Power

The camp you arrive in at the Western Approach is somewhat misleading as to the size of this locale. A number of quests and one of the two dungeons in this locale are all in relatively close proximity. However, as you strike out to the west, the vastness of this desert soon becomes apparent. Extremely hostile creatures, including the Abyssal High Dragon, stalk these sands, and clouds of sulfur divide the western expanse. In addition to a keep to repossess from the Venatori, there's a lot of work to do in the Western Approach, and a lot of ground to cover while doing so.

Crafting Materials

Common Materials:

- Elfroot
- Spindleweed
- Blood Lotus
- Deathroot
- Deep Mushroom
- Serpentstone
- Paragon's Luster

Rare Materials:

- Dragonthorn
- Witherstalk
- Ghoul's Beard
- Lazurite
- Everite

Unique Materials:

- None

Collections

- Astrariums: 3
- Bottles of Thedas: 3
- High Dragons: 1
- Landmarks: 6
- Mosaic Pieces: 14
- Glyphs: 4
- Shards: 14
- Treasure Maps: 0
- Logging Stands: 2
- Quarries: 3

Inquisition Personnel

Agents

- Frederic

LOCALE MAP

Legend

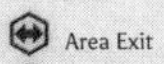
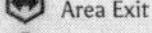
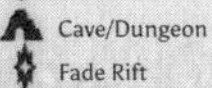

- Area Exit
- Cave/Dungeon
- Fade Rift
- Keep
- Merchant
- Logging Stand
- Quarry

Inquisition Camps

- Lost Spring Canyon Camp
- Craggy Ridge Camp
- Nazaire's Pass Camp
- Echo Back Canyon Camp

COLLECTIONS

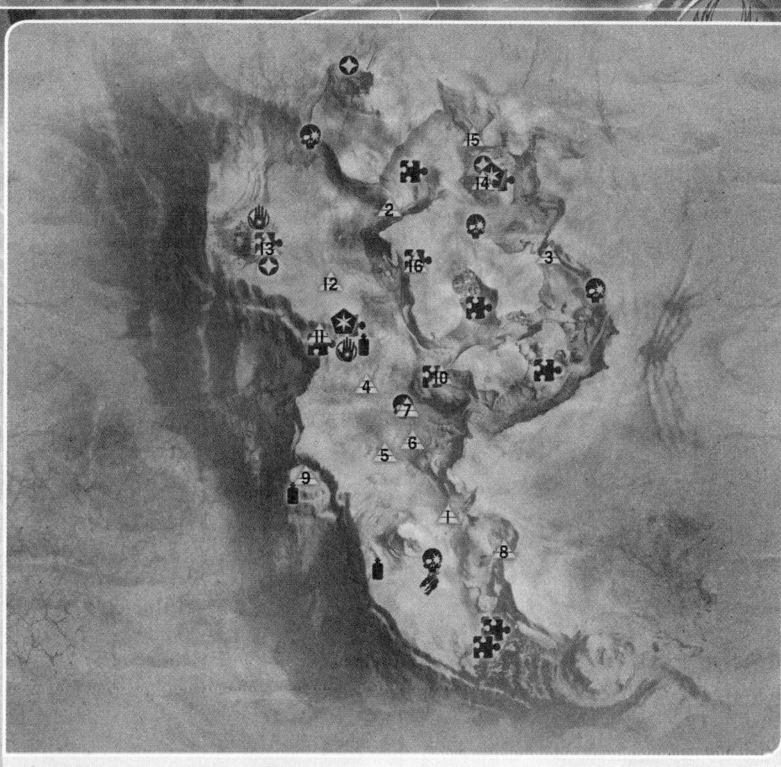

LEGEND

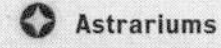

Astrariums
- Constellation: Toth
- Constellation: Fenrir
- Constellation: Satinalis

Bottles

High Dragon
- Abyssal High Dragon

Landmarks/Points of Interest
1. Griffon Wing Monument
2. Gates of Andoral
3. Gates of Toth
4. Zhores Tower
5. The Surveyor
6. Lamarr Tower
7. Shortcut
8. Shimmer Stone Mine
9. Ritual Tower
10. Lost Idol*
11. Hidden Stairway*
12. Tesoro Tower
13. The Old Well
14. Echoback Fort
15. The Last Step
16. The Thing in the Dark*

*An Archdemon mosaic piece is near this landmark.

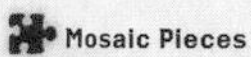

Mosaic Pieces

Oculara and Shards

Ocularum 1: Giant's Staircase
- Ocularum +3 Shards

Ocularum 2: Dustytop Fort
- Ocularum +3 Shards

Ocularum 3: The Canyons
- Ocularum +3 Shards

Ocularum 4: Echoback Canyon
- Ocularum +3 Shards

Ocularum 5: Old Prison Road
- Ocularum +2 Shards

Glyphs

Solas Artifacts

ASTRARIUM SOLUTIONS

Astrarium: Toth

Astrarium: Satinalis

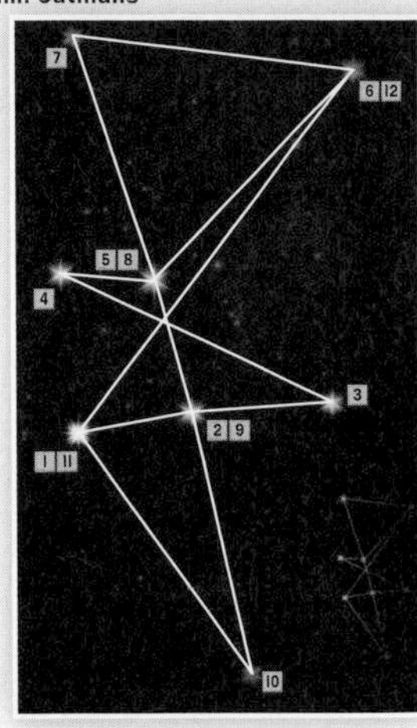

Astrarium: Fenrir

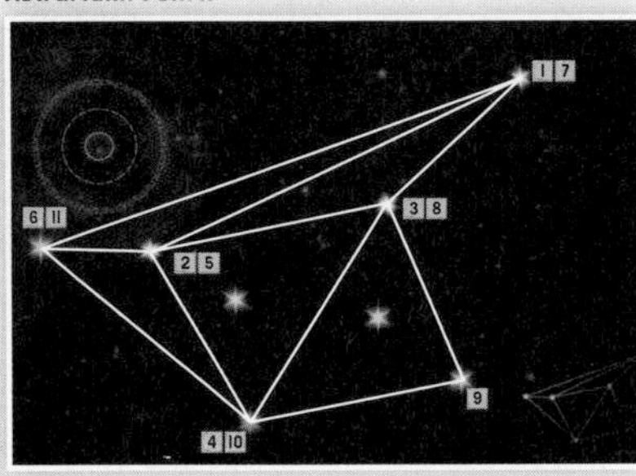

Astrarium Vault

The astrarium cave in the Western Approach is near a camp at Blight Overlook. Among the riches recovered from this vault is an Archdemon mosaic piece. Don't miss out on using a veilfire torch to uncover the master fire rune schematic at the back of the treasure chamber!

FADE RIFTS

Tougher and tougher still. Despair demons are becoming an unfortunate regular occurrence from these rifts, particularly in Echoback Canyon. Greater terrors are also starting to slip through the rifts, so be ready to focus everyone in the party on them to get them out of the fight before they take someone down.

Fade Rift Details

Quest	Rifts	Total Power
Rifts in Sand and Dust	2	4
Rifts in the Canyons	2	4
Rifts in Echoback	2	4
Rifts off the Pass*	2	4

NOTE *A wine bottle, Vintage: Warden Jairn, can be found in Dustytop Fort, near one of the rifts.

MERCHANTS

Griffon Wing Keep Merchant

Item	Cost
Weapons (Highlights)	
Lifetaker Staff	1371
Witch Fire Staff	703
Balanced Sniper Bow	456
Seeker Shield	211
Accessories (Highlights)	
Enhanced Tonics Belt	801
Enhanced Stamina Amulet	801
Enhanced Potions Belt	801
Enhanced Guard Belt	801
Enhanced Grenades Belt	801
Enhanced Belt of Focus	801
Enhanced Lifeward Amulet	226

Item	Cost
Upgrades (Highlights)	
Superior Enchanter Staff Blade	211
Masterwork Spiked Pommel	211
Balanced Two-Handed Grip	211
Crafting Material	
Blank Runestone	71

REQUISITIONS

Requisition Quests

Requisition	Materials
Code Requisition in the Approach	5 Message Fragments, 1 Venatori Cipher
Luster Survey in the Approach	20 Paragon's Luster, 10 Lazurite

AGENTS

FREDERIC

Affiliated Quest: The Abyssal High Dragon

Inquisition Perk: Frederic of Serault (Secrets)

Frederic's unique skills as an Orlesian draconologist come to the Inquisition only after a lengthy series of quests, culminating in the slaying of the Abyssal High Dragon. Afterward, he offers to join the Inquisition as a dragon expert. All you need to do is accept.

SIDE QUESTS (RECOMMENDED LEVEL 10-13 AND 14+)

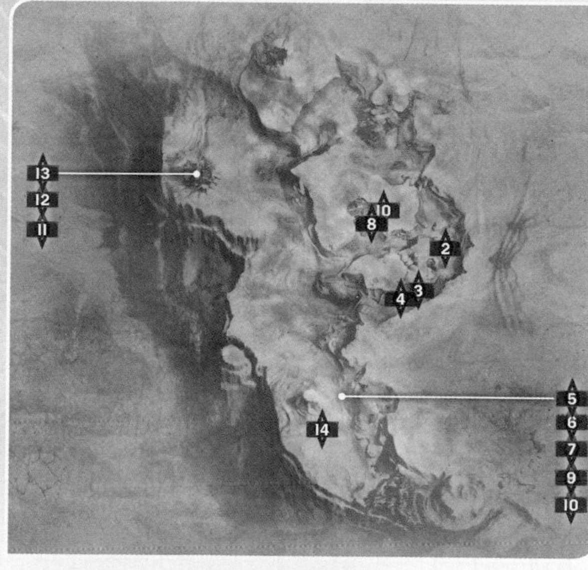

Legend

Level 10-13

1: Holding the Western Approach
2: The Venatori
3: Draconology
4: On the Chantry Trail
5: Frederic's Livelihood
6: How to Lure a Dragon
7: Hunting Patterns

Level 14+

8: Dungeon: Still Ruins (A Tevinter Relic Hunt, A Stranger Rift in the Ruins, The Heart of the Still Ruins, A Manuscript of Some Authority)
9: Sharper White Fangs
10: Assault on Griffon Wing Keep
11: This Water Tastes Funny
12: Fortress Squatters
13: The Trouble with Darkspawn
14: The Abyssal High Dragon

1: HOLDING THE WESTERN APPROACH

Description: Establish camps to hold the Western Approach and support Inquisition activity in the region.

Quest Giver: Scout Harding

Requirements: Starts as soon as you arrive in the Western Approach

Reward: 100 Influence and 1 Power per camp, except for the starting camp

Objectives:

- Establish four camps.

Reaching all four camps in the Western Approach is simply not possible right away. One of them sits next to the exit of Coracavus, a Tevinter ruin that you can explore. Unfortunately, getting there initially just isn't possible with the sulfur clouds steaming forth from portions of the desert to the northwest, while the Gates of Toth block entry to Echoback Ridge on the eastern side of the map.

2: THE VENATORI

Quest Giver: Scout Harding

Description: The Venatori seem to be busy in the Western Approach. A report from someone named Servis mentioned activity in a mine somewhere in the canyons.

Requirements: Quest is given to you after Harding's briefing on the Western Approach.

Reward: 128 XP, 80 Influence

Objectives:

- Search for the mine.
- Read the Venatori report.

Read the Venatori papers at your starting camp to learn more about their plot here in the Western Approach. It seems they've made an agreement with the local variety of scum, the White Claw bandits. From there head north, then follow the western route through the canyons to make your way toward the mine. You'll come across a Fade rift that's part of the Rifts in the Canyons assignment.

You'll also encounter an encampment of White Claw bandits on your way to the mine entrance if you take the route past the Fade rift. Remove the bandits, then loot the camp for all it is worth. Remember this place, as it is part of a quest later in your local exploration.

The mine entrance is across the canyon from the Still Ruins entrance, at the stop of a short climb uphill. Enter the mine (while stripping it clean of its delicious everite), fighting off the giant spiders that rush you. Look for an open book lying on one of the work tables in the mine. Reading it uncovers some potentially disturbing information about the Venatori connection with the mages or the templars, depending on whom you chose to support after your first visit to Val Royeaux. It seems that whatever operation was being set up here in the Western Approach has been hastily abandoned, in favor of another locale, Emprise du Lion.

NOTE This mine contains another red lyrium vein to destroy for the Varric's Seeing Red quest. If you continue on through this mine and have a mage energize through the barrier at the end, you can visit the Sand Rock Mine next to this mine and find another red lyrium vein to break, along with a mosaic piece for the Archdemon collection.

3: DRACONOLOGY

Quest Giver: Corpse next to a looted caravan. This quest can also be started by finding a missing supply package on any White Claw raider or in their camps.

Description: A shipment of goods, destined for a University of Orlais researcher named Frederic, appears to have been waylaid by bandits. The shipping label suggests his camp is somewhere in Nazaire's Pass.

Requirements: Available upon entering the Western Approach.

Reward: 128 XP, 80 Influence

Objectives:

- Find Frederic.

You can find this shipment just outside of the Sand Rock Mine entrance. A lone corpse stands out among cages that are covered with blood. The corpse contains a package that directs you to Frederic and Nazaire's Pass. It's a long walk through rough terrain and hazardous wildlife, but you'll find that Frederic is just fine, albeit calling more attention to himself than any draconologist should with such a gaudy set of armor. Speaking with him about the fate of his assistants completes the quest.

NOTE Frederic provides a number of quests that ultimately lead to a direct confrontation with the Abyssal High Dragon. If you want to hunt that beast, you'll need to accomplish tasks for Frederic. One of these quests takes you into the Still Ruins, one of two dungeons in the Western Approach.

4: ON THE CHANTRY TRAIL

Quest Giver: A stone marker in the canyons west of the Sand Rock Mine (or any stone marker on this trail)

Description: There are Chantry symbols out in the desert. They appear to lead somewhere.

Requirements: Available upon arrival at the Western Approach

Reward: 128 XP, 80 Influence

Objectives:

- Follow the trail.
- Find where the trail leads.

The first stone marker is to the west of the Sand Rock Mine. The trail sends you on a winding route through hostile territory, in the direction of Nazaire's Pass (where you can conveniently locate Frederic for the Draconology side quest and set up another camp). You will keep finding more Chantry symbols as you go. The second of these symbols is near another camp of White Claw bandits, for example.

NOTE The bandits' camp near the second Chantry symbol contains supplies for the Frederic's Livelihood side quest.

The third symbol is found near Death Drink Springs, presumably named for the cloud of sulfur hanging over everything in sight. Don't forget to claim this location to set up a war table mission for later that will help clear away this poisonous filth! From here, head south toward the fourth symbol. Here, more of the wildlife can be encountered. Expect phoenixes and quillbacks stalking the sands. Continue through the Giant's Staircase region on your way toward Nazaire's Pass. There is a Fade rift along the way, but if you're in a hurry you can easily run past it.

NOTE The war table mission you unlock at Death Drink Springs, called Crossing the Sulfur Pits, requires five power. Get this done as soon as possible, ideally after you unlock the camp at Nazaire's Pass, to enable swift travel to where you need to be. This also enables you to reach Griffon Wing Keep, part of another quest in the region.

TIP There's no harm in killing phoenixes or quillbacks as you follow the Chantry trail. You can get the necessary materials from them for the How to Lure a Dragon side quest!

Continue through Nazaire's Pass (stopping by to speak with Frederic to take care of any quests related to him along the way). The next Chantry symbol is just before you enter the Wastes, a massive region filled with ancient Tevinter ruins. Another symbol can be found in the Wastes—just be wary of the level 14 varghests stalking the sands here. You're close to the end of the trail!

The trail ends with a cave warded by a spirit barrier. Bust it down and then you can enter a cave containing treasures, some interesting codex entries, and a mosaic piece for the Archdemon collection.

5: FREDERIC'S LIVELIHOOD

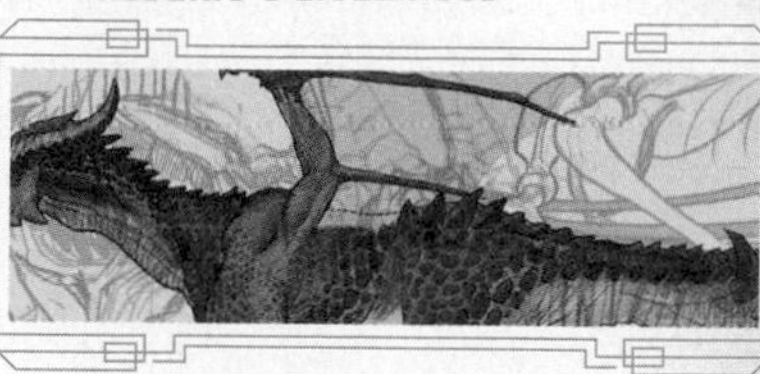

Quest Giver: Frederic

Description: White Claw raiders have made off with Frederic's supplies. Search areas where White Claw raiders ae active to recover the supplies.

Requirements: Speak with Frederic at his campsite, or recover the supplies first from packs of bandits around destroyed caravans around the Western Approach.

Reward: 128 XP, 80 Influence

Objectives:

- Return Frederic's supplies.

You can actually accomplish the tough part of this quest early on. When you first arrive at the Western Approach, the canyons you start in have supply caravans that have been ransacked by White Claw raiders, and they're still at those camps. You might fight your way through these camps and loot the supplies for yourself while in the midst of other quests. The supplies can be found on the raiders themselves or in bags scattered around the destroyed caravans. However, if you do not do this, Frederic himself will explain his predicament, and your quest map will show you generalized search locations to visit.

Don't take the bandits too lightly. They tend to have rogues of their own within the groups that stole the supplies, and they can be a nasty surprise if you're not paying attention!

6: HOW TO LURE A DRAGON

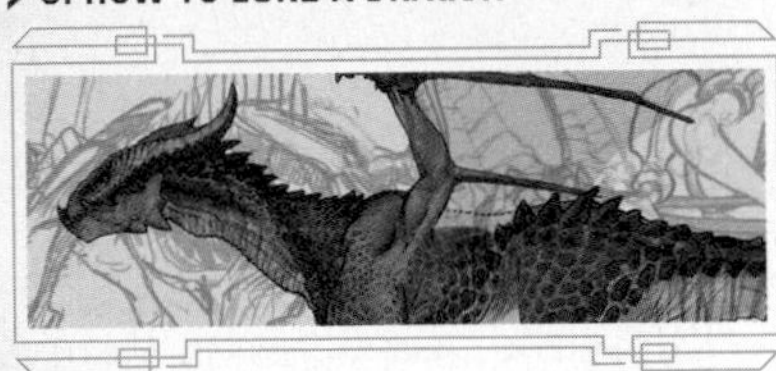

Quest Giver: Frederic

Description: Frederic wants to concoct dragon bait. He has almost everything he needs, save for two rather specific ingredients.

Requirements: Find the materials by killing phoenixes and quillbacks, or complete the Draconology side quest.

Reward: 512 XP, 200 Influence, 2 Power

Objectives:

- Gather quillback intestines.
- Gather phoenix tail feathers.
- Deliver the ingredients to Frederic.

This is a simple fetch quest that can be done while you complete the On the Chantry Trail quest, though you may also start it by speaking with Frederic first. Killing quillbacks and phoenixes should be easy for parties averaging around level 10 or 11, and there are plenty of both kinds of beast throughout the Giant's Staircase region. You only need one of each ingredient. Speak with Frederic to deliver the items and complete the quest.

7: HUNTING PATTERNS

Quest Giver: Frederic

Description: High dragon hunting patterns are largely undocumented. Frederic is interested in the location of any dead gurn showing signs it was killed by a dragon.

Requirements: Available after completing Draconology

Reward: 128 XP, 80 Influence

Objectives:

- Find four dragon signs.
- Return to Frederic with hunting locations.

The gurns Frederic wants you to investigate are scattered throughout the regions north of his camp. Use your search ability as you close in on the gurn corpses to fully investigate them, and return to Frederic as soon as you've found four. You will have to complete a war table operation to clear the sulfur from Death Drink Springs in order to reach some of the gurn corpses.

8: DUNGEON: STILL RUINS

When Frederic speaks of the ancient Tevinter studies on draconology, he laments that their ruins may have contained priceless documents, now likely lost to the sands of the Western Approach. This begins the side quest A Manuscript of Some Authority, which sends you directly to the Still Ruins in the Canyons region. However, approaching this place puts you in conflict with Venatori magisters who are combing their way through these ruins, in search of something that can aid their cause. And when you enter the actual ruins, things get weird.

NOTE This dungeon encompasses four separate side quests: A Tevinter Relic Hunt, A Manuscript of Some Authority, A Stranger Rift in the Ruins, and The Heart of the Still Ruins.

Beyond the barrier is a level 15 Venatori spellbinder, standing guard alone. Defeating him starts A Tevinter Relic Hunt, and you also get access to the ruins themselves. You should be at least level 13 before entering this dungeon. The enemies average around level 15, and they can pick apart the unprepared with surprising speed.

Gaining entry to the Still Ruins is easy enough. Fight your way through the contingent of Venatori warriors and mages protecting the front gates, then have a mage in your party to destroy the magical ice barrier barring entry to the ruins.

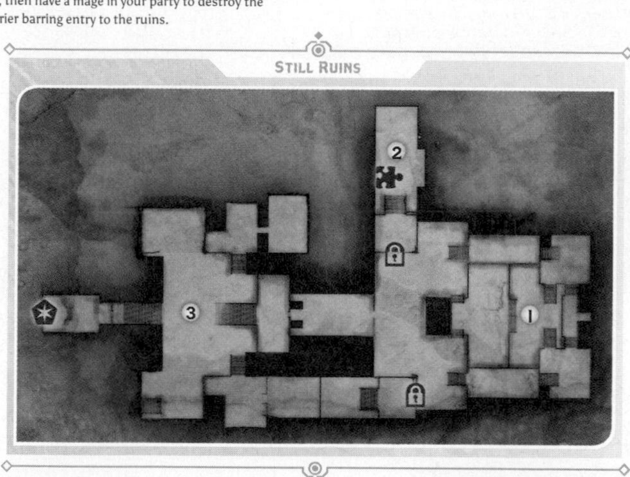

A Stranger Rift In the Ruins

Quest Giver: Fade rift inside the Still Ruins

Description: There's ancient magic at work in the Still Ruins that appears to be slowing time. A Fade rift appears frozen in place, and whatever's keeping the magic at work is preventing the rift from closing.

Requirements: Enter the Still Ruins and discover the frozen Fade rift.

Reward: 967 XP, 200 Influence, 2 Power

Objectives:

- Disable the time magic.
- Close the Fade rift.

1. As soon as you enter the ruins, you notice right away that something is up. A Fade rift, frozen in time, hovers above the great hall, with demons also frozen in place. However, not everyone or everything is frozen. Venatori patrol the chamber, attacking you on sight. Kill them, then try to inspect the rift. Yep, it's definitely frozen.

2. There's a door that requires the Deft Hands, Fine Tools perk to open on the northeastern corner of the room. Inside it is a mosaic piece for the Freed Are Slaves collection, along with some nice treasure and some interesting reading about the proper use of blood magic.

3. Continue pushing north beyond the rift room, through the Hall of Silence and into Viridis Walk. This is where you encounter Lucanus, leader of the Venatori forces in these ruins. He is a magister of considerable power and skill, and as a level 15 elite, he's more than capable of surviving a beating for quite some time. He is not alone! Watch out for his allies while fighting him, especially the Venatori marksmen. Killing Lucanus ends the Venatori presence in the Still Ruins.

A Tevinter Relic Hunt

Quest Giver: Killing the Venatori spellbinder in front of the Still Ruins entrance activates the quest.

Description: Venatori are raiding the Still Ruins under the Western Approach. Whatever lies inside was important enough to protect with a barrier.

Requirements: Available as soon as you defeat the spellbinder.

Reward: 1,934 XP, 400 Influence, 3 Power

Objectives:

- Stop the Venatori.

This quest is complete as soon as you defeat Lucanus in Viridis Walk. Loot his corpse to find a mysterious keystone.

A Manuscript of Some Authority

Quest Giver: Frederic

Description: The ancient Tevinter manuscript has some marvelous diagrams, but Frederic is unable to read the script.

Requirements: Speak with Frederic to begin this quest.

Reward: 242 XP, 80 Influence

Objectives:

- Find Tevinter writing on dragon luring.
- Deliver the manuscript to Frederic.
- Arrange for a translation at the war table (five power required).
- Return to Frederic.

4. In a small chamber in the southwest corner of Viridis Walk is a chamber containing a manuscript that is very much to Frederic's interests. In that same chamber, you can find some extra book reading.

TIP

In this room, there is a torch you can energize with veilfire. Take this veilfire to the inner sanctum during The Heart of the Still Ruins. Behind the staff floating at the center of the room is a rune that gives you a schematic to enchant staves with spirit runes.

Unfortunately, bringing the manuscript back to Frederic means nothing: He can't even decipher it. However, the Inquisition, more specifically Josephine, is able to get someone who can. Go back to Skyhold and use the war table to complete the Translate the Dragon Text mission. The results are instant! Return to Frederic with the good news. You're now another step closer to being able to track down the Abyssal High Dragon!

The Heart of the Still Ruins

Quest Giver: Stone recovered inside the Still Ruins

Description: Lucanus dropped a strange stone while searching the ruins. Its distinct pattern suggests it could be a keystone of some kind. Perhaps there are more.

Requirements: Pick up the stone Lucanus drops.

Reward: 242 XP, 80 Influence

Objectives:

- Collect all five keystones to open the sealed chamber.
- Enter the sealed chamber.

After killing Lucanus and taking his keystone, you must find four other keystones scattered throughout Viridis Walk. They look like shards found out in the world.

Shard 1

Shard 2

Shard 3

Shard 4

5. Once you locate the four shards inside Viridis Walk, take them to the door on the north side of the room to enter the inner sanctum and complete this quest. You'll find a strange-looking staff floating in the air, surrounded by blood flowing in a sphere around it. Not suspicious at all. Collect it anyway to make exciting things happen! The staff itself is called Tempest, a powerful cold damage weapon with some fancy modifications already in place.

TIP Don't miss the rune you can reveal behind the Tempest's altar! Use the veilfire from the room the manuscript was found in to earn a helpful schematic.

Completing A Stranger Rift in the Ruins

Recovering the Tempest causes time to begin flowing normally again, and you are immediately beset by a greater shade. This also means that the demons now move freely throughout the Still Ruins, and they will make you fight for every step you take back toward the Fade rift to seal it. Expect greater and lesser terrors, shades, and wraiths in Viridis Walk.

The Fade rift in the main chamber is a level 15 challenge, so expect really nasty stuff like a despair demon or greater terrors. Fortunately, the battle lasts for only two waves, and you can cut this short by using Dispel to catch multiple demons before they fully manifest, thanks to the confined space the rift summons them in.

With this, the Still Ruins are now truly still, for reasons other than ancient Tevinter blood magic.

9: SHARPER WHITE CLAWS

Quest Giver: Frederic

Description: The White Claws won't be happy that their traps were destroyed. Senior raiders will likely investigate, an ideal moment to take them out.

Requirements: Available after completing How to Lure a Dragon

Reward: 967 XP, 200 Influence, 2 Power

Objectives:

- Destroy all five traps.
- Kill the White Claws.
- Return to Frederic.

The traps are scattered throughout the Wastes region to the south of Frederic's camp. It's a wide search area, and the traps themselves can be tough to spot. Just work your way across the search area, and you'll find the traps. You will also find White Claw bandits camped out across this area, so be ready to remove them.

Sure enough, destroying the traps is the last straw for the White Claws, and they send a force out to meet and beat you. The greatest threats in this hostile force are the footpads. Stealthy and evasive, they can quickly put down lightly armored targets like rogues and mages. But don't ignore the archers among these bandits; they can be just as dangerous if left alone for too long!

NOTE Once you've destroyed the White Claw traps, you can return to Frederic to begin the final step in his quest line: actually calling forth the high dragon of the Western Approach. See page 236 for more details.

> 10: ASSAULT ON GRIFFON WING KEEP

Quest Giver: A note found outside of the Still Ruins, or Frederic

Description: Venatori occupied an isolated keep in the Western Approach, a key outpost on the treacherous trip to Adamant. It would be of great benefit to the Inquisition to capture it and drive the Venatori from the area.

Requirements: Available as soon as you enter the Western Approach.

Reward: Griffon Wing Keep falls under Inquisition control.

Objectives:

- Capture the keep.

Griffon Wing Keep is a vital location that the Venatori have occupied, which should be enough motivation for you to want to take it. It is seriously nice to have the ability to fully prepare your equipment outside of Skyhold, especially for when you want to take on the Abyssal High Dragon.

There are two ways to begin the assault on the keep. One is to crash through the front door, killing every Venatori enemy in sight. The front gates are protected by several foot soldiers and, more importantly, two marksmen on walls overlooking the main entrance. It helps to bring mages to pick them off.

If you're feeling sly, you can climb into the front courtyard by taking a cave entrance at the rear of the fortress's plateau. After you blast through the spirit barrier, the cave beyond takes you to the keep's well and a landmark you can claim. From there you can climb up into the courtyard. This lets you ambush the marksmen at the front walls.

However the assault begins, after clearing the front entrance explore the courtyard thoroughly for any useful goods, then continue up the stairs on the west side of the courtyard. More Venatori foes loudly challenge your presence. Once again, the ramparts are manned by Venatori marksmen and spellbinders, while foot soldiers and guardsmen try to occupy you. If you have a rogue in the group, it might not be a bad call to use Stealth to sneak up to these snipers to pick them off while the rest of the party handles the threats on the lower levels. Once this second battle is won, the final gate leading to the highest part of the keep opens.

Climb the last stairwell to meet the final line of defense for the Venatori. A magister named Macrinus, two footmen, and two marksmen stand between you and claiming this keep. Macrinus can be a serious pain if you allow him to start casting spells; mob him immediately with any stuns or knockdown abilities at your disposal. Direct a rogue or warrior to go after the marksmen, should you have one to spare, but otherwise try to keep the whole Venatori group focused on your tank.

Killing Macrinus and his men ends the Venatori hold on Griffon Wing Keep. Claim the place for the Inquisition, which rapidly makes it a home away from home. Speak with Knight-Captain Rylen after setup is complete. There are still issues in the keep that must be addressed.

NOTE The war table at Skyhold begins to fill with special missions throughout the second act, and it is particularly busy with the Western Approach. Be ready to make a few trips back home to get your advisors on important tasks.

I1: THIS WATER TASTES FUNNY

Quest Giver: Knight-Captain Rylen

Description: Griffon Wing's well has been tampered with and cannot support the keep. An alternative source of fresh water must be secured. A nearby oasis called Lost Wash Creek would do, if it weren't crawling with varghests.

Requirements: Capture Griffon Wing Keep and speak with Rhylen.

Reward: 128 XP, 80 Influence

Objectives:

- Clear out the varghests at Lost Wash Creek.

Once you learn of the keep's water woes, you can go to Skyhold's war table to try to find a fresh source of water. This takes time, so you can accomplish other quests. Afterward, you'll get another war table operation that lets you select how to deal with the varghests. Depending on your choices, you may have to go to the Lost Wash Creek yourself and handle the situation.

At level 15, the varghests of the creek can be quite dangerous, but seeing as how you can't start this quest without having captured Griffon Wing Keep, your party is likely over-prepared to handle one varghest at a time. Sweep through the designated area, kill the varghests, and return to the knight-captain with the good news!

I2: FORTRESS SQUATTERS

Quest Giver: Knight-Captain Rylen

Description: Bandits have occupied an old Warden fortress in the Western Approach and are raiding caravans that Griffon Wing Keep depends on for supplies.

Requirements: Capture Griffon Wing Keep, complete the Here Lies the Abyss event in the Western Approach, and then speak with the knight-captain.

Reward: 967 XP, 200 Influence, 2 Power

Objectives:

- Clear out the bandits.

The fortress itself should be familiar: You witnessed the Wardens do something incredibly rash at the ritual tower. Now it is home to a small group of bandits. Expect footpads among the bandits here. If your party includes one, have a rogue sneak up on and try to execute one of the footpads at the start of the fight, while the rest of the party goes all in on the remainder of the bandits. The quest is complete as soon as the last bandit falls.

> 13: THE TROUBLE WITH DARKSPAWN

Quest Giver: Knight-Captain Rylen

Description: There is increased darkspawn activity in the Western Approach.

Requirements: Capture Griffon Wing Keep and speak with the knight-captain.

Reward: 1,934 XP, 400 Influence, 3 Power

Objectives:

- Search for more signs of darkspawn.
- Find the source of the darkspawn (five power required).
- Access the Tevinter ruin.
- Investigate the area.
- Seal the hole. Locate those responsible for the excavation.
- Track down Servis in the Western Approach.

Exploring the desert to the north of Griffon Wing Keep, you'll discover that more sulfur clouds cover the terrain, making continued exploration impossible. Claim the land near a broken bridge, then return to Skyhold and head for the war table.

An operation, Find the Source of the Darkspawn, is now available, costing five power to smother the sulfur clouds and create a bridge that crosses the toxic land.

With the bridge made, cross it to reach the Old Prison Road, passing by an ocularum as you continue toward the Tevinter ruin. You'll encounter darkspawn ghouls and hurlocks in the canyons ahead, so be ready for a fight.

The canyon leads to a series of wooden ramps and ladders that take you to the ruins of an old prison, Coracavus. Venatori are guarding the entrance to the ruins, an enforcer standing tall among them. Take them out, then enter the dungeon.

Dungeon: Coracavus

The search for how the darkspawn have been able to appear in the Western Approach in ever-increasing numbers has taken you to the ancient Tevinter prison of Coracavus. The Venatori have been scouring the desert in search of artifacts and information to help their cause, but it's becoming clear that they uncovered something they did not want.

Coracavus is the second dungeon of the Western Approach, but unlike the Still Ruins, it acts as only one part of a quest. You cannot finish The Trouble with Darkspawn without coming through this ancient prison.

CORACAVUS

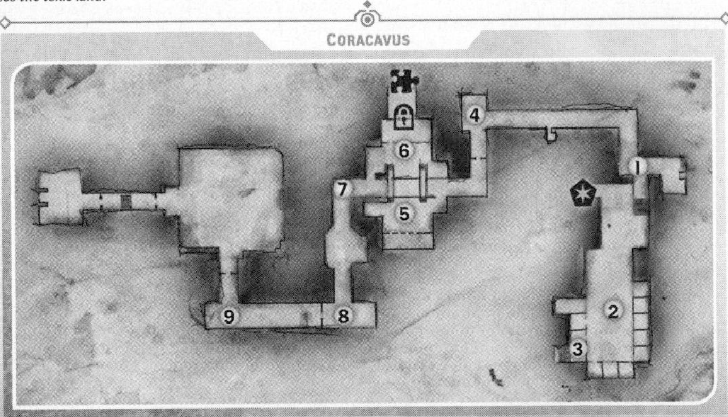

I. As you enter Coracavus, you'll have a choice of going left, into the holding cells, or continuing south down the guards' hall. Go into the holdings cells first.

2. The holding cells are a disaster area, filled with many recently departed Venatori slaves and a few ghouls. Explore this area carefully, as there's lots of loot to be had, and many of the valuables here are worth quite a bit to shop owners.

3. A veilfire torch can be found in this cell. Use it to reveal a rune on the floor of a torture chamber [4] in the southwestern corner of the holding cells. It's a schematic for the master spirit rune.

4. With things taken care of in that side area, move through the guards' hall, killing every Darkspawn in sight, until you finally reach the apparent source of this madness. The darkspawn tunnel can be blocked by a mage energizing some debris, but you'll have to clear the immediate area of all darkspawn to safely pull that off. With their tunnel sealed, you can now continue deeper into Coracavus in search of the Venatori responsible for this.

5. Entering the records room, check the eastern side of the room before crossing the walkways over to the west side. Snag treasure and do some light codex reading.

6. Crossing the walkway, you'll encounter a hurlock alpha and a number of hurlocks and ghouls. If you can bait them onto the bridge, you can catch the whole group in AoE spells with greater ease. These darkspawn were guarding a door that requires Deft Hands, Fine Tools. There's more loot, along with a mosaic piece for the Freed Are Slaves collection.

7. The front corridor contains more darkspawn, well within your ability to handle. More troubling is the roar heard from somewhere else in the ruins.

8. Investigate the corpse near this door to find a wrapped prison key. The wrap turns out to be a note that fingers exactly who is responsible for this: a magister named Servis. He remains in hiding somewhere in the Western Approach.

9. Continue down the corridor until you reach the south entrance, where the source of the roaring becomes apparent. A level 15 elite giant stalks the courtyard. As always, have your tank initiate this fight to keep the giant's attention, then move the rest of the party in for the kill. After slaying the giant, collect your loot, then take the doors on the south side of the room to leave this place. Servis is in the Echoback Canyon, just outside Coracavus's south entrance.

In Pursuit of Servis

Exiting Coracavus, set up the camp just outside the dungeon so you can restore your potion supplies. Servis is in Echoback Fort, a short ride by mount to the south of the camp.

As you have probably come to expect, Servis is not alone. The fort is occupied by a strong Venatori force: marksmen on the ramparts, footmen on the ground floor, including a dangerous Venatori brute. Servis himself can be very bothersome as a level 15 elite. Ideally, you assign a rogue to stun him to prevent his spells from causing problems to the party while they deal with his backup.

After defeating Servis and his men, this quest is complete at last. Servis is taken into custody and can be judged back at Skyhold—he can serve as an informant for Leliana if you choose. Search through the fort to find a mosaic in the Archdemon collection.

NOTE If Blackwall is with you, you can find one of the signs of Wardens for the Memories of the Grey side quest in Echoback Fort. Next to this is a veilfire torch you can use to find a rune in a nearby cave that leads up to an astrarium. The rune grants you the schematic for frost runes, which can be applied to your melee weapons.

14: HIGH DRAGON: THE ABYSSAL HIGH DRAGON

Recommended Level: 14+

Recommended Party Composition: one warrior (sword and shield), one rogue, two mages (armed with frost damage staves)

Alternative Party Composition: two warriors (sword and shield, two-handed weapon), two mages (armed with frost damage staves)

- Place five lures.
- Slay the Abyssal High Dragon.
- Report back to Frederic.

The Abyssal High Dragon is highly vulnerable to cold damage, so gear yourself accordingly. As with other high dragons, your tank will have to keep her attention by being the most intimidating and dangerous threat on the field, as the dragon ignores taunting. Try to keep any ranged party members at her flanks, to avoid getting caught in the fire breath. However, the Abyssal can fire longer-ranged fireballs at random targets for very heavy damage. Any fire resistance you can scrounge up could be very useful!

After completing all of Frederic's tasks, you are finally able to set lures to summon the Abyssal High Dragon. Go back south to the Wastes, fully stocked and with your best equipped party, and set down five lures. The White Claw bandit traps can now be set with your own specially made lures.

She uses the same arm and tail melee attacks as other high dragons, so melee players should keep that in mind. She can also produce a wind barrier with her wings to protect herself from ranged attacks, but in those instances those characters can move into close range to maintain the pressure. As always, try to come into this fight with full focus meters for your party, to take advantage of Mark of the Rift or any emergency heals from your mages.

After slaying the dragon and collecting your spoils, return to Frederic to report the news. While he is a little put out that you killed the beast before you could take some proper research notes, he's enthusiastic about the research conducted in the Western Approach and feels both you and he could benefit by his joining the Inquisition. There's no real benefit to refusing his offer, but whichever you choose, this quest is completed!

THE EXALTED PLAINS

The Exalted Plains are steeped in conflict. Centuries ago, the elves of the Dales made their last stand here. More recently, the plains played host to some of the most heated conflicts of the Orlesian Civil War. Somehow, despite ages of unrest, the lands the elves call "Dirthavaren" retain a fragile beauty.

LOCALE SUMMARY

Scouting Cost: 8 Power

A juxtaposition of civil war and ancient history, the Exalted Plains do not need to be visited as part of the Inquisition's journey to put an end to Corypheus, but the rewards for coming to this place are worth a visit or three. There is much to learn about the state of Orlais while traveling across these plains, and much in the way of resources to help prepare the Inquisition for the near future. The Exalted Plains are massive, in some places seemingly peaceful, but with devastation and demonic presence in others.

Of special note is an ancient underground temple, in the bog to the east of the front lines. Reaching it requires some extra work, but if the Inquisitor can solve the mystery of that ruin, something of worth may await.

> CRAFTING MATERIALS

Common Materials:
- Dragonthorn
- Witherstalk
- Ghoul's Beard
- Lazurite
- Everite

Rare Materials:
- Royal Elfroot
- Black Lotus
- Rashvine Nettle
- Obsidian

Unique Materials:
- None

> COLLECTIONS

- Astrariums: 0
- Bottles of Thedas: 4
- High Dragons: 1
- Landmarks: 17
- Mosaic Pieces: 7
- Glyphs: 0
- Shards: 16
- Treasure Maps: 3
- Logging Stands: 2
- Quarries: 1

> INQUISITION PERSONNEL

Agents
- Loranil

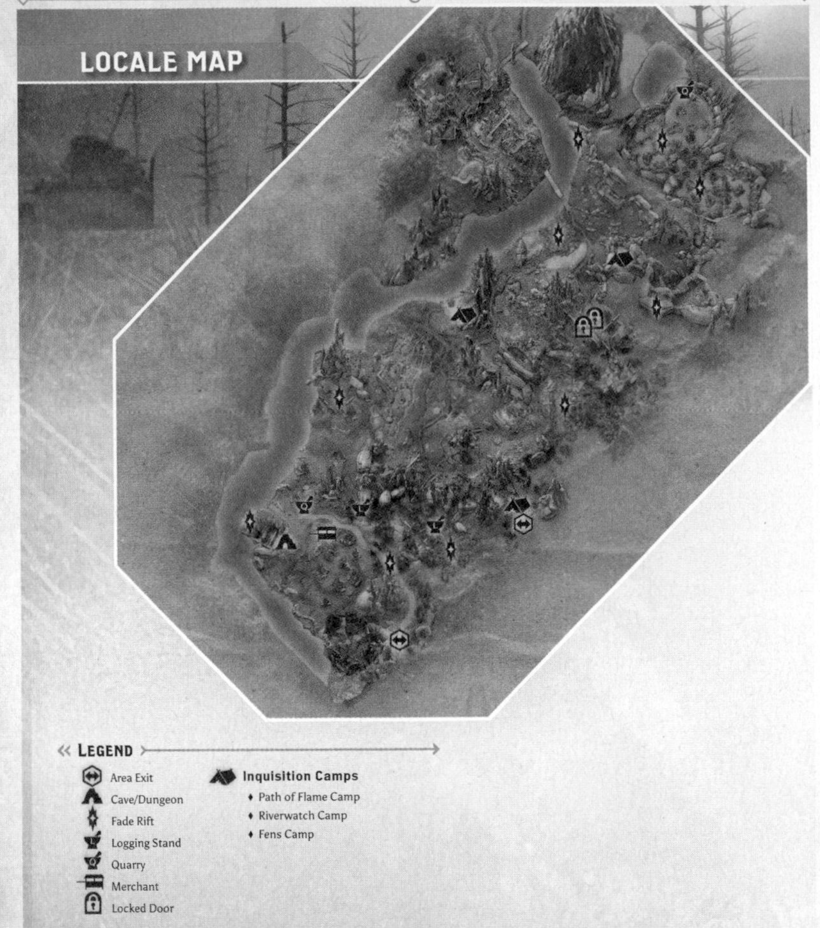

*A burning home in this region contains a bottle of Thedas called Vintage: Warden Tontiv.

**Near Ville Montevelan's well is a destroyed house containing a bottle of Thedas called Vintage: Warden Korenic.

COLLECTIONS

LEGEND

- **Bottles of Thedas**
- **High Dragon**
  - Gamordan Stormrider
- **Landmarks/Points of Interest**
  1. Guardians of the Path x 2
  2. The Path of Flame
  3. Var Bellanaris
  4. Ruined Arches
  5. Demetrius's End
  6. Lindiranae's Fall
  7. Andruil's Messenger
  8. Fort Revasan
  9. The Dead Hand**
  10. Broken Dog
  11. Offering to the Dread Wolf
  12. Riverside Garrison
  13. Triumph of the Light
  14. Ville Montevelan
  15. Pont Agur*
  16. The Raven
  17. Citadelle du Corbeau

*When you first encounter Pont Agur, the bridge is out. You need to claim a spot next to the gap in the bridge to set up a war table operation to repair it. You cannot complete For the Empire until that bridge is repaired.

**The Dead Hand landmark is a statue shaped like a hand, and in the palm is a mosaic piece for the Invasion set.

- **Mosaic Pieces**
- **Oculara and Shards**
  - **Ocularum I: Halin'Sulahn***
    - Ocularum +6 Shards
    - *Ocularum is near the Ruined Arches landmark.
  - **Ocularum 2: Eastern Ramparts**
    - Ocularum +5 Shards
  - **Ocularum 3: Riel**
    - Ocularum +5 Shards
- **Glyphs**
- **Song Lyrics**
- **Treasure Maps**
  - Sketch of Enavuris River
  - Map of Halin'Sulahn
  - Map of Enavuris
- **Solas Artifacts**

FADE RIFTS

Whatever lies beyond the Veil is apparently starting to take you seriously now. Arcane horrors and revenants have a chance to appear from Fade rifts all throughout the Exalted Plains. Revenants in particular should be a major cause for concern; their powerful sword strikes can down even the most heavily armored equal-level party member in short order. If you haven't been casting Dispel before the rifts summon follow-up waves of demons after the first, you should get into that habit now!

Fade Rift Details

Quest	Rifts	Total Power
Rifts in the Old Plains	4	8
Rifts on the Battlefield*	4	8
Rifts in the Fen	3	6

*One of the rifts on the battlefield is part of a side quest called No Word Back.

REQUISITIONS

Requisition Quests

Requisition	Materials
Armor Requisition on the Plains	4 Malachite, 20 Veridium

AGENTS

> LORANIL

Affiliated Quest: By the Grace of the Dalish

Inquisition Perk: Loranil (Forces)

To be able to recruit Loranil, you must first earn favor with Keeper Hawen at the Dalish Camp. Do this by completing requests of all the Dalish in the camp, and Hawen will admit that he sees your cause in a good enough light that he will allow one of his people to leave the camp. He reduces Cullen's operation times by 5 percent.

MERCHANTS

Dalish Camp

Item	Cost
Weapons (Highlights)	
Lifetaker Staff	1,371
Witch Fire Staff	703
Armor (Highlights)	
Robes of the High Keeper	14,212
Upgrades (Highlights)	
Superior Enchanter Staff Blade	211
Crafting Materials	
Blank Runestone	71
Quillback Leather	42
Phoenix Scales	42
Ram Leather	20
Weapon Schematics	
Witch Staff	533
Templar Shield	444
Dwarven Shield	444
Masterwork Jeweled Greatsword Grip	182
Ornate Staff Blade	89
Dwarven Longsword Grip	89
Dual-Crescent Greatsword Grip	89
Dense Longbow Grip	89
Chalice Dagger Grip	89
Adorned Staff Grip	89
Armor Schematics	
Warden Warrior Armor	985
Warden Battlemage Armor	985
Sturdy Hunter Armor	444
Sturdy Enchanter Armor	444
Vanguard Armor	378
Sturdy Vanguard Armor	378
Hunter Armor	378
Enchanter Armor	378
Superior Warden Helmet	182
Superior Adventurer Hat	182
Vanguard Armor Arms	89
Hunter Armor Legs	89
Hunter Armor Arms	89
Enchanter Armor Legs	89
Enchanter Armor Arms	89
Vanguard Armor Legs	9

SIDE QUESTS (RECOMMENDED LEVEL 10-13 AND 13-16)

Legend

Level 10-13

1: Holding the Exalted Plains (given when entering locale)
2: Undead Ramparts to the West
3: Lay Rest the Western Ramparts
4: Calming Victory Rise
5: From the Beyond
6: Scattered Glyphs
7: By the Grace of the Dalish
8: Golden Halla
9: Someone to Lose
10: Something to Prove
11: A Well-Stocked Camp
12: The Spoils of Desecration
13: A Father's Guidance
14: Another Side, Another Story

Level 13-16

15: Lay Rest the Eastern Ramparts
16: No Word Back
17: Left to Grieve
18: Ghilan'nain's Grove
19: Sketch of Enavuris River
20: Map of Enavuris
21: Map of Halin'sulahn
22: A Familiar Ring
23: For the Empire
24: Pressed for Cache
25: High Dragon: The Gamordan Stormrider
26: Dungeon: Lost Temple of Dirthamen

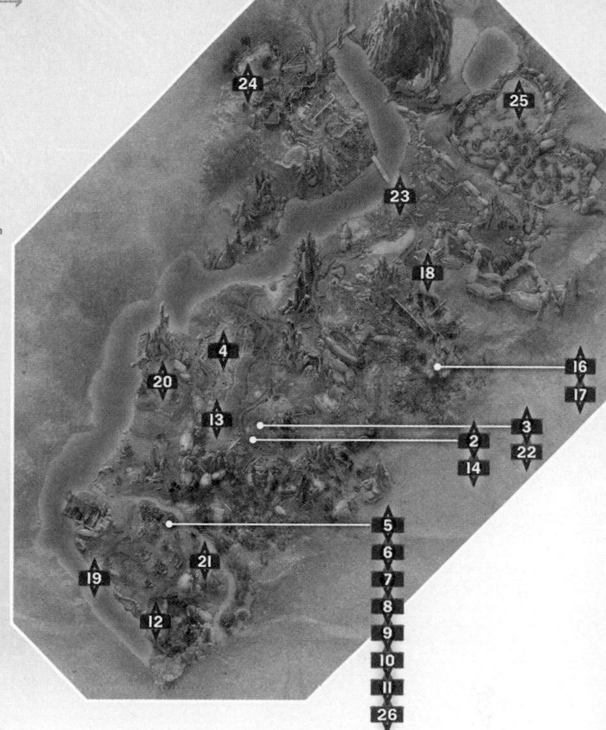

1: HOLDING THE EXALTED PLAINS

Description: Establish camps to hold the Exalted Plains and support Inquisition activity in the region.

Quest Giver: Scout Harding

Requirements: Started as soon as you arrive in the Exalted Plains

Reward: 100 Influence and 1 Power per camp, except for the starting camp

Objectives:

- Established three camps.

There are only three camps available throughout the Exalted Plains, so be prepared to be on a mount often. While the camps do place you near very important locations, the Exalted Plains are massive. Between the camps and your ability to fast-travel to the Dalish camp (and Fort Revasan and the Riverside Garrison once you have freed them from demonic assault), you can quickly cut your travel time.

One of the camps, Ghilan'nain's Grove, is not accessible right away, as it is blocked by collapsed stone. For that camp, you need to claim the blocked passage, then return to Skyhold and use the war table to get workers out to the Exalted Plains to clear your path. It'll cost you five power, but it is well spent.

2: UNDEAD RAMPARTS TO THE WEST

Quest Giver: Scout Harding

Description: Corporal Rosselin reports undead holding the Western Ramparts. They are rising from somewhere within the trenches. He believes it may have something to do with the group Freemen of the Dales.

Requirements: Arrive in the Exalted Plains for the first time

Reward: 128 XP, 80 Influence

Objectives:

- Investigate the Western Ramparts.

Leaving the starting camp, you encounter a group of Freemen of the Dales. These rebels immediately recognize your party and attack without mercy. After killing them, you can loot a letter from one of the dead, containing orders to deny the Inquisition access to the ramparts, but without mentioning why this is important.

Traveling out farther west, you can start to see the devastation the war has wrought, and you begin encountering demons. You'll also encounter Corporal Rosselin, attempting to fight off undead at the southern entrance to the Western Ramparts. Rescue him from his fate, and try to learn more about what is happening. It turns out that the Freemen used some form of magic in the ramparts, and now the dead are rising in ever increasing numbers.

3: LAY REST THE WESTERN RAMPARTS

Quest Giver: Corporal Rosselin

Description: Pits are piled with bodies, attracting spirits and causing the dead to rise. To make matters worse, the pits are protected by magical barriers, preventing anyone from reaching the dead to burn the remains. Once all the bodies are burned, a signaling horn will alert Gaspard's troops that the undead threat to the ramparts has been dealt with.

Requirements: Available immediately upon arriving at the Exalted Plains

Reward: 512 XP, 200 Influence, 2 Power

Objectives:

- Set fire to the south pit.
- Set fire to the north pit.
- Blow the signaling horn.
- Return to Corporal Rosselin.

Each of the pits is guarded by a magical barrier. Each of the pits is guarded by a magical barrier. The northern pit is protected by an ice barrier, while the southernmost pit is protected by a fire barrier. As long as the bodies remain unburned, undead will continue to rise from these pits. Further complicating things is the presence of an arcane horror at these pits.

Once you've burned both pits of corpses, go to the signaling horn to call Gaspard's troops back to the trenches. Your mission is complete! Go report to Corporal Rosselin to learn more.

> 4: CALMING VICTORY RISE

Quest Giver: Marshal Proulx

Description: Victory Rise is under siege just as the Western Ramparts were.

Requirements: Can be done immediately after arriving in the Exalted Plains.

Reward: 512 XP, 200 Influence, 2 Power

Objectives:

- Set fire to the west pit.
- Set fire to the east pit.
- Blow the signaling horn.

The Freemen assault has also affected Victory Rise, another defensive position to the west of the Western Ramparts. You'll have to dispel fire and ice elemental barriers to reach the pits as before, then contend with waves of undead and the arcane horrors commanding them. Once both pits of Victory Rise are set aflame, use the signaling horn to call for Gaspard's troops.

NOTE This quest can be tackled immediately after you arrive at the Exalted Plains, as Victory Rise is a short horse ride to the west of the Western Ramparts. Alternatively, you can hold off on doing anything about the situation with the undead until you speak with Marshal Proulx, stationed at Fort Revasan far to the northeast.

> 5: FROM THE BEYOND

Quest Giver: Keeper Hawen

Description: There's an old Dalish burial site in the plains known as Val Bellanaris. Spells protecting the dead there have been broken, attracting demons. Cleansing the grounds of the demons would gain favor from the Dalish.

Requirements: Encounter the Dalish at Halin'sulahn and offer your assistance.

Reward: 967 XP, 200 Influence, 2 Power

Objectives:

- Defeat the demons at Var Bellanaris.
- Speak with Keeper Hawen.

When you discover the Dalish elves camped out in Halin'sulahn, Keeper Hawen has little time or patience to deal with the likes of you. However, if you offer to help his people with the problems they face, you will earn his good graces. An immediate problem is that hostile spirits infest Var Bellanaris, and he needs them dealt with.

NOTE You can fast-travel to the Dalish camp after discovering it; take advantage of this very useful feature.

Wraiths and shades swarm throughout the burial ground and attack as soon as you approach. Keep yourself well away from the tombstones and wipe out the demons you see. As soon as that's done, return to Keeper Hawen to report that the task is complete. Out of thanks, he informs you of glyphs scattered throughout the Exalted Plains that could be of use to the Inquisition, starting another side quest if you have not already completed it.

CAUTION Going to Var Bellanaris is a delicate affair. Killing the demons is simple enough, but unless you want to tank your approval with the Dalish, do not go around breaking open the elven graves throughout these ruins! You'll also have to deal with the sudden appearance of more angry demons for having disturbed the graves!

> 6: SCATTERED GLYPHS

Quest Giver: A glyph found somewhere in Halin'sulahn or the Ancient Baths, or Keeper Hawen of the Dalish

Description: There are ancient elven glyphs scattered across the plains that appear to be pieces of a greater message.

Requirements: Available upon entering the Exalted Plains

Reward: 512 XP, 200 Influence, 2 Power

Objectives:

- Find four glyphs.
- Go to the war table to investigate the glyphs (five power required).

There are two ways to begin this quest. One is to speak with Keeper Hawen of the Dalish. He will assign you a side quest to earn his trust, and afterwards he will tell you of glyphs scattered across the plains.

Alternatively, as you explore parts of Halin'sulahn, the Shrine to Sylaise, or the ruins of the Ancient Baths, you may find a veilfire torch. Use these torches to find glyphs scattered throughout the southern half of the Exalted Plains. As soon as you find one, the quest map will show you general search areas to comb over. For reference, we have screenshots showing where exactly four glyphs can be found. The quest requires only four glyphs, but there are more than four hidden in this locale.

Ancient Baths

Halin'sulahn

Enavuris

Shrine to Sylaise

NOTE The Shrine to Sylaise contains one of the glyphs. It also contains a spirit barrier that, once broken, grants you access to a small shrine. Loot the corpse on the other side of the barrier to find Lindiranae's Talisman. This Dalish artifact is required for another side quest in the Halin'sulahn region, so don't discard it! We recommend making the shrine one of the four glyph locations you visit, so you can knock another side quest out of the way while you're in the area.

With four glyphs found, the Inquisitor decides to take the information back to Skyhold so researchers can try to decipher it. Using the Inquisition's connections (and five power), you reveal the location of an ancient temple meant to worship Dirthamen, elven god of secrets. Coverage for the Lost Temple of Dirthamen dungeon is at the end of the Exalted Plains quest walkthroughs.

> 7: BY THE GRACE OF THE DALISH

Quest Giver: Loranil

Description: Dalish would be skeptical of any force as powerful and connected as the Inquisition. It will take considerable effort to earn the favor of Hawen's clan.

Requirements: Available as soon as you enter the Exalted Plains

Reward: 512 XP, 200 Influence, 2 Power

Objectives:

- Earn enough favor to recruit Loranil.
- Speak to Loranil about joining the Inquisition.

Loranil recognizes the Inquisitor immediately and has much praise to shower. He wants to join the Inquisition, but Keeper Hawen is understandably suspicious of anything to do with the Chantry in any way. You can convince him of the righteousness of your cause to recruit Loranil by completing the requests the Dalish have for you.

CAUTION If you're going to recruit Loranil, and there's no reason not to, you probably should not complete the quest The Spoils of Desecration until that's taken care of. That side quest has you going to an elven burial ground and, you guessed it, desecrating the burial sites to find the key to a tomb. Doing so will cost you much, if not all, of the good will you earn completing the other quests around the Dalish camp and can make it impossible to recruit Loranil.

Of course, if you attempt that quest before you make contact with the Dalish, you may be able to get away with such a dishonorable act...

> 8: THE GOLDEN HALLA

Quest Giver: Ithiren

Description: A golden halla known as Hanal'ghilan is said to visit the Dalish in times of great need. A hunter named Ithiren believes the legendary halla now roams the Exalted Plains.

Requirements: Speak with Ithiren at the Dalish Camp.

Reward: 512 XP, 200 Influence, 2 Power

Objectives:

- Find the golden halla.
- Herd the halla to the Dalish.
- Return to Ithiren.

Ithiren of the Dalish would like for you to retrieve the golden halla, to ensure that the Orlesians in the Exalted Plains don't poach the majestic creature for its hide and horns.

The golden halla is fairly simple to find, grazing peacefully on the plains southwest of the Dalish camp. Herding it to the camp is a bit time consuming because of how fast it runs and how it doesn't always go exactly where you want it to. Just keep following it to try to "urge" it to go toward the camp. When you get close enough to Ithiren, the golden halla will go to the cage where the rest of the halla are being held on its own, and Ithiren will be most grateful.

This can go fairly smoothly if you're lucky. However, Freemen are also camped out in Halin'sulahn, and they will attempt to kill the beast. Don't let this happen; it will cost you favor with the Dalish. Aim for the marksmen among any Freemen groups, to prevent them from shooting at the golden halla. After you kill the Freemen, the halla will likely have fled somewhere safe. Approach it slowly and continue herding it toward the camp.

CAUTION The golden halla does not take to getting attacked by you very well and will try to fight back. This may prompt your other party members to intervene, and you'll have a very dead halla within seconds. Try not to let that happen.

> 9: SOMEONE TO LOSE

Quest Giver: Emalien

Description: A Dalish teenager named Valorin ran off after being passed over for the keeper's apprenticeship. He has yet to return, and his sister Emalien fears the worst.

Requirements: Complete From the Beyond to be able to speak with Emalien.

Reward: 128 XP, 80 Influence

Objectives:

- Find Valorin.
- Return Valorin's effects to Emalien.

After speaking to Emalien, head north from the Dalish camp, toward the Western Ramparts. In the remains of a house, you find a corpse, with evidence of blood magic having been used. The journal found on the body confirms that this is Valorin. The boy was attempting to use the blood magic to help him in recovering the Lindiranae's Talisman. It did not go well. You must now return to Emalien to deliver the sad news. You can either speak the truth, that he used blood magic, or refuse to sully her memories of a younger brother.

NOTE Depending on your answer to Emalien's questions of her brother's fate, you gain or lose approval among your party members. Dorian disapproves of your hiding the use of blood magic, regardless of how the girl feels. On the other hand, Cole appreciates it if you hide the truth and make Valorin's passing less difficult on Emalien.

Picking up Valorin's journal also begins the Something to Prove side quest.

10: SOMETHING TO PROVE

Quest Giver: Valorin's journal

Description: Valorin was searching for Lindiranae's Talisman, a lost Dalish artifact of particular importance to Hawen's clan. Valorin's journal mentions ruins on the plains where the talisman may be found.

Requirements: Available as soon as you enter the Exalted Plains; you can either find this journal first or speak with Emalien to begin Someone to Lose.

Reward: 128 XP, 80 Influence

Objectives:

- Find Lindiranae's Talisman.
- Return the talisman to Emalien.

Valorin died attempting to find Lindiranae's Talisman, an elven artifact of great value. Unfortunately, he was headed in the wrong direction. The Shrine to Sylaise, where the artifact rests, is far to the south of Halin'sulahn. Follow the river south until you reach a waterfall with a statue looking down from it. A little farther south, you'll find the shrine entrance.

A spirit barrier inside the shrine stands between you and the corpse of an unfortunate soul who tried to take the talisman. Retrieve the artifact, then return to the Dalish camp. Emalien, to whom you may have already delivered the bad news about Valorin, is somewhat comforted by the fact that you completed the task in his name, and the quest is complete.

11: A WELL-STOCKED CAMP

Quest Giver: Nissa

Description: With the war ongoing and demons preventing safe travel through much of the Dales, the Dalish in the plains have had trouble keeping supplies stocked. An elf named Nissa has made a list of what they need for their camp in her ledger.

Requirements: Available after earning favor with the Dalish Camp

Reward: 128 XP, 80 Influence

Objectives:

- Read Nissa's ledger.
- Find and deliver five bushels of spindleweed.
- Find and deliver ten bushels of elfroot.
- Find and deliver ten pieces of canine leather.
- Find and deliver five pieces of iron.
- Find and deliver three great bear pelts.

If you have been diligent in gathering materials throughout your quest to save Thedas, four of these deliveries should be a simple affair. You must first read the ledger, then drop off the items requested in her storage container. Then you can read the ledger again to see the next step in this quest.

The final item on her list, three great bear pelts, is a bit trickier. The bears in question are in the Emerald Graves, and they are dangerous, enormous, ferocious, and voracious creatures that care very little for what the Inquisitor or the Dalish want if it doesn't have anything to do with being the next meal. Once you complete this quest, you should have gained more than enough favor with the Dalish to allow Loranil to join the Inquisition, so the effort is worthwhile!

12: THE SPOILS OF DESECRATION

Quest Giver: The door to Unadin Grotto

Description: The entrance to Unadin Grotto is locked.

Requirements: Go to the Unadin Grotto and attempt to enter it.

Reward: 128 XP, 80 Influence

Objectives:

- Find the key to Unadin Grotto.
- Use the key to open the tomb door.

When going to Var Bellanaris for the From the Beyond side quest, you may be tempted to explore the area and may come across the entrance to Unadin Grotto. Unfortunately, the door is sealed tight and requires a key.

Unfortunately, this key is scattered into multiple pieces, and the pieces are within the burial mounds. You'll have to crack open the graves to search the corpses for the key pieces. Disturbing each grave causes demons to appear, and you'll also lose approval with the Dalish clan.

Once you have the key, you can enter the tomb, immediately completing the quest. Treasures to discover while inside the grotto include a mosaic piece for the Invasion set.

13: A FATHER'S GUIDANCE

Quest Giver: Letter in a ruined home, west of the Western Ramparts

Description: A farmer abandoned his home during the war, but he hid what valuables he could, afraid they might be stolen by bandits.

Requirements: Available upon arriving at the Exalted Plains

Reward: 128 XP, 80 Influence

Objectives:

- Locate the farmer's valuables.

After reading the letter, you'll have to travel to the Enavuris region. The valuables are hidden in a chest, next to a tree growing out of the ground at an odd angle, obscured by bushes.

14: ANOTHER SIDE, ANOTHER STORY

Quest Giver: Corporal Rosselin

Description: Now that the undead trouble has been dealt with at the Western Ramparts, it would be wise to meet with Gaspard's marshal, who is holding Fort Revasan in the name of the usurper.

Requirements: Complete Lay Rest to the Western Ramparts.

Reward: 967 XP, 200 Influence, 2 Power

Objectives:

- Enter Fort Revasan.
- Speak with Marshal Proulx.

After saving the Western Ramparts, you're told by Corporal Rosselin about the marshal in Fort Revasan. With the usurper's army in disarray following the sudden Freemen attacks and subsequent rise of the dead, it falls to you to travel far to the northeast to pass the word of the success in saving a key position. It's a long trip, and you can expect to run across demons or more Freemen along the way.

NOTE

Depending on how you travel to Fort Revasan, you might see these two guard towers near the main road to the fort. They require Deft Hands, Fine Tools to unlock, but there is some loot that could be of use inside them.

As you reach Fort Revasan, it's under siege by demons and the undead, and the front gate is threatening to fall. Assist the surviving soldiers until the enemy is vanquished, then enter the fort itself.

Inside the fort, you find Marshal Proulx, commander of the garrison. Despite the fanciful armor, the marshal is all business, with a touch of humor, as he relays one piece of bad news to after another. Fade rifts are producing demons throughout the entire battlefield. Another set of ramparts closer to Fort Revasan, the Eastern Ramparts, has fallen into the hands of the Freemen, and they are in the process of turning the dead and even more demons on the marshal's garrison. Messengers are failing to reach outposts to relay news. A frontline riverside outpost has been out of contact for long enough that it is assumed lost to demons. The Inquisition has its work cut out for it, to say the least.

15: LAY REST THE EASTERN RAMPARTS

Quest Giver: Marshal Proulx

Description: The Eastern Ramparts have been overwhelmed by the Freemen of the Dales, and now they raise an army of undead to continue their assault on the forces of both the empress and the usurper.

Requirements: Speak with Marshal Proulx.

Reward: 512 XP, 200 Influence, 2 Power

Objectives:

- Set fire to the body pit.

The Eastern Ramparts were the last line of defense before the enemy could reach Fort Revasan, and the Freemen of the Dales now have possession of it. Approaching the ramparts forces you to cross a wooden bridge protected by marksmen and a guardsman. Be prepared; these Freemen are a fair bit tougher than the random groups you've found in the field.

Climbing up the hill from the first ambush, you come across a second group of Freemen next to a large tree. This is a more dangerous encounter thanks to the Freemen infiltrator. Don't let one slip behind your party members—they can kill with frightening speed.

From the tree, take the path to the south so you can reach the body pit. You find it protected by three more Freemen, one of which is Gordian, a powerful mage. As a level 14 elite, he can take a huge amount of punishment despite his fanciful clothes, so it might be best to kill his allies before going to town on him. Be aware that he is immune to cold-related debuffs. He isn't immune to the various knockdowns caused by other elements, or by rogues and warriors.

With Gordian and his men dead, the body pit is protected only by a spirit barrier. Have a mage break this barrier, then set fire to the pit to put an end to this source of undead. With that, travel west from the body pit to reach the signaling horn, and the quest is complete.

NOTE

To the north of the Eastern Ramparts, there's a guard tower you can reach by going through the trenches. Inside it is a bottle of Thedas, Alvarado's Bathtub Boot Screech. There's also an ocularum close by, and one of the seven soldier letters you need to complete Left to Grieve is on a body next to it.

16: NO WORD BACK

Quest Giver: Marshal Proulx

Description: Marshal Proulx sent a patrol out in the hopes of reclaiming the Riverside Garrison. No word has been heard since.

Requirements: Speak with Marshal Proulx, or enter the riverside fort to seal the Fade rift. The quest begins automatically.

Reward: 128 XP, 80 Influence

Objectives:

- Investigate the Riverside Garrison.
- Close the rift.
- Blow the signaling horn.

The Riverside Garrison is a strategic location near Pont Agur, a broken bridge that leads to territory being held by Empress Celene's loyalists. It's no surprise that the marshal wants to have a way to control the most important bridge in all of the Exalted Plains.

The garrison was occupied by Proulx's men, but unfortunately for them, a Fade rift is in the depths of the fort. Clear out the surface to assist the survivors, then descend a stairwell into the underground section of the fort. You'll take ladders deeper into the depths.

Once you reach the bottom level of the garrison, you will find the Fade rift. Descending to the rift more or less commits your party to victory or death, so make sure you are fully stocked, just to avoid any problems.

TIP

Search the Fade rift chamber carefully. Another bottle of Thedas, Finale by Massaad, can be recovered here.

With the Fade rift closed and the demons dead, sound the horn back on the surface to invite friendly soldiers to restore their presence at the garrison. With this last deed, the fort is in the hands of Gaspard's men.

17: LEFT TO GRIEVE

Quest Giver: Sergeant Meursault

Description: Letters from soldiers who fell on the plains were left behind in the midst of battle. Sergeant Meursault wants to return them to the families of the dead.

Requirements: Available as soon as you complete Another Side, Another Story.

Reward: 128 XP, 80 Influence

Objectives:

- Find seven soldiers' letters.
- Deliver the letters to Sergeant Meursault.

Thankfully, when you accept this quest from the good sergeant, she provides the rough locations of the soldiers carrying letters. Use your Search ability to pick them out from debris and other forms of ground clutter when you reach the search areas. Once you have seven letters, return to the sergeant, and she will reward your kindness.

18: GHILAN'NAIN'S GROVE

Quest Giver: Automatic after completing a war table operation to gain access to the grove

Description: Inquisition laborers have opened a passage to Ghilan'nain's Grove.

Requirements: Find the blocked passage to the grove, then complete the war table operation to open the passage.

Reward: 242 XP, 80 Influence

Objectives:

- Investigate Ghilan'nain's Grove.
- Clear out the gurguts.

To complete the Holding the Exalted Plains side quest, first find the blocked passage to Ghilan'nain's Grove. After you claim it, return to Skyhold and complete the war table operation Gain Access to Ghilan'nain's Grove for five power. When you return to the Exalted Plains, the passage is open and under Inquisition guard.

Ghilan'nain's Grove is currently the home to a pack of gurguts, and they are very displeased at your sudden intrusion. However, they are also weak to electricity and cold damage abilities, which are things you can easily exploit with mages. Once the gurguts are wiped out, the quest is complete, and you can safely set up camp.

Exploring the Fens

With access to the far eastern portion of the Exalted Plains now established, you've got some exploring to do. There are rifts in the fens to be dealt with, landmarks to claim, and new regions to explore.

Of these, the most interesting is the Dead Hand, both the landmark and the underground temple. The temple is sealed by a fire barrier, and once you get past it, you are in a chamber that is actually a puzzle writ large. If you correctly light the globes at the center of the chamber, you gain access to another chamber deeper inside the temple. It holds a superior amulet of cunning, some extra loot, and a codex entry for Falon'Din. Just be ready to face an arcane horror and a swarm of undead for your trouble!

An alternative route from the Ghilan'nain's Grove camp takes you to the Crow Fens, where the High Dragon Gamordan Stormrider makes its home. Bring electricity protection if you intend to hunt this beast! Also be wary of the gurgut packs roaming the fens, as two of these monsters can suddenly become five or six when their friends come to play.

19: SKETCH OF ENAVURIS RIVER

Quest Giver: A scroll found southwest of Fort Revasan

Description: Someone died with this sketch of a river in his hands. A spot is marked on the water's edge.

Requirements: Arrive in the Exalted Plains for the first time.

Reward: 242 XP, 80 Influence

Objectives:

- Find the spot marked on the sketch.

The sketch is found in the hands of someone who decided to die inconveniently very far from where the actual treasure is hidden. Travel to the Halin'sulahn region and search the shores to the south of the Ancient Baths. Nestled behind some stones that block the view upriver is a pile of loose dirt containing the treasure.

20: MAP OF ENAVURIS

Quest Giver: A scroll to the south

Description: This map, found in a bunker of Celene's Victory Rise ramparts, depicts a spot visible through three tall windows.

Requirements: Arrive in the Exalted Plains for the first time.

Reward: 242 XP, 80 Influence

Objectives:

- Find the spot marked on the map.

The ruins of Enavuris south of Victory Rise have the windows in question, and they are pointing at a pair of stone spires found roughly halfway between the ruins and the rise.

> 21: MAP OF HALIN'SULAHN

Quest Giver: A scroll found in a small camp in the Crow Fens

Description: This map was in a hunter's shack in the fens. It appears to mark a spot on high ground in the Exalted Plains.

Requirements: Available after getting access to Ghilan'nain's Grove

Reward: 242 XP, 80 Influence

Objectives:

- Find the spot marked on the map.

After collecting the note, return to the Dalish camp in Halin'sulahn, then follow the river south toward the Shrine to Sylaise. On the western side of the river, just before the waterfall, is the vantage point described by the map. You'll have to do some tough climbing, but eventually your mini-map should start pinging that you're close to the treasure. The actual location has a direct view of the stone spire that the Dalish camp is located by.

> 22: A FAMILIAR RING

Quest Giver: A soldier locked away in a bunker at Victory Rise

Description: With her dying breath, a soldier fighting for Celene has asked that a ring be delivered to her commander in the citadel.

Requirements: Complete war table mission Repair Pont Agur, in order to reach the citadel where the commander is.

Reward: 128 XP, 80 Influence

Objectives:

- Give the ring to Commander Jehan.

The bunker the soldier is found in is locked, and you'll need a rogue to get to her. She'll hand over the ring just before expiring, wanting it delivered to Commander Jehan, the leader of Celene's forces at the Exalted Plains.

Commander Jehan is at the Citadelle du Corbeau, across the Pont Agur near the Riverside Garrison. However, you discover upon trying to cross the bridge that it needs to be repaired. Once it's repaired, you face another obstacle standing between you and the commander: a swarm of undead infesting the citadel.

> 23: FOR THE EMPIRE

Quest Giver: Available at the start of questing in the Exalted Plains

Description: The bridge to Citadelle du Corbeau has been repaired by the Inquisition. Celene's forces were stationed beyond the bridge and have not been seen since it was destroyed.

Requirements: Complete war table mission Repair Pont Agur.

Reward: 967 XP, 200 Influence, 2 Power

Objectives:

- Go to Citadelle du Corbeau.
- Burn two body pits.
- Reach the stranded troops.
- Disable the defenses.
- Rescue Celene's troops.

The usurper's forces are not the only ones affected by the sudden assaults by the Freemen of the Dales. Empress Celene's soldiers have been pushed back to a castle on the eastern side of the Enavuris River. Unfortunately, reaching them isn't immediately possible without first surveying the destroyed Pont Agur bridge, claiming it, and returning to Skyhold to complete a war table operation. With the bridge repaired, you can finally cross the river and see to relieving Celene's forces.

Crossing the bridge, you immediately encounter undead along the dirt roads heading up toward the Northern Ramparts. These defenses were once all that stood between the Usurper's forces and Citadelle du Corbeau. Now, demons and undead control the ramparts. As with the other positions you secured on the eastern side of the river, you must fight your way to the body pits and remove the defensive barriers before you can burn the pits.

Watch for hay bales as you fight your way to the body pits. You can set them on fire, a good way to hurt the undead as they swarm toward you. It also wouldn't hurt if you kept fire staves on hand. The undead and the arcane horrors protecting the body pits are especially vulnerable to fire, and you can break through the ice barriers protecting the body pits even faster.

As soon as you set fire to the second pit, a door leading deeper into the ramparts is kicked down by a revenant. Get your warrior tank on it right away, as a revenant can one-shot an equal-level mage or rogue if it blindsides them! Push past the revenant to enter Citadelle du Corbeau.

Right away, you know something is up when a beam of fire shines down from a castle tower, burning across the ground and through the undead swarming to greet you. The beam follows a specific pattern, so you can stay out of it while fighting the undead that manage to make it to you. Don't miss collecting the landmark in the courtyard, then push past it to find a locked gate. A wounded survivor explains that the castle defenses were uncontrollable, but that there may still be survivors. Open the gate and press forward.

The next corridor leads you past another section under guard by that magic weapon. Don't dally in that corridor for too long, lest the beam catch your party and the undead together. Fight through them as quickly as you can, and keep following the stairs up.

The upper level of the citadel is a disaster zone, totally ravaged by the tower's beam and the hordes of undead. It is possible to search the area for treasures, but it might be best to push toward the survivors' position. That way, you'll be able to shut down the magical defenses scouring the place and make your treasure hunting easier.

Eventually, you encounter a mass of corpses lying in front of a locked door. You've found the last place the holdouts could have run. Before you can greet the survivors, you must disable the castle defenses by working a rotating lever on one of the walls. Afterward, you can go down to the door where a survivor will, after some convincing, allow you inside, completing the quest.

NOTE Don't forget to speak with Commander Jehan. Deliver the soldier's ring to the commander to complete the side quest A Familiar Ring. She has some more work for you as well.

24: PRESSED FOR CACHE

Quest Giver: Commander Jehan

Description: Supply caches belonging to the Imperial Army have gone missing in Lake Town. Mark the crates so they can be collected.

Requirements: Complete the For the Empire quest.

Reward: 967 XP, 200 Influence, 2 Power

Objectives:

- Find 10 supply caches.

The few survivors in Citadelle du Corbeau have been scraping by on minimum supplies in the weeks following the cease-fire and the flood of undead storming the castle. Ten crates, scattered throughout the Exalted Plains, belong to the Imperial Army, and if they are marked for pickup, Celene's troops can get resupplied. Compared to what you just did to simply reach the troops, this is a walk in the park. Find all 10 caches to complete the quest.

25: HIGH DRAGON: THE GAMORDAN STORMRIDER

Recommended Level: 13+

Recommended Party Composition: One warrior (sword and shield), one rogue (set up for ranged combat), two mages (armed with non-electric damage staves)

Alternative Party Composition: Two warriors (sword and shield, two-handed weapon), two mages (armed with non-electric damage staves)

Initial contact with the Gamordan Stormrider occurs as soon as you enter the Crow Fens. She ignores you and travels north, to the place where you will battle her. An electric-type high dragon, the Stormrider fights as you'd expect most other high dragons to fight, in terms of melee abilities: tail swipes, claw strikes, and piercing roars that stun the party are all part of its arsenal. She will leap around the watery arena and lash out at seemingly random targets of her ire.

However, the real threat comes from her electric breath. When the Stormrider begins spitting lightning, that's your cue to get out of the water. After several seconds, any party member in the water will be stunned in place while taking damage!

This makes engaging the Stormrider a difficult task for melee characters, as they'll spend a good portion of the fight unable to do anything. Since the Stormrider can't be taunted, a stunned tank will not be able to grab her attention when she decides to go eat a mage or ranged rogue.

Bring electric resistance and any stun-reducing items if you can, especially for the Inquisitor. Have your mages ready with Heal to spend their focus on, and make sure they are standing on dry land as the fight progresses, so they can't get stunned by the electric breath. Mages should also have spirit damage runes on their chosen staves, to get that extra bit of damage rolling. Fortunately, when the Stormrider breathes lightning, she's also standing in place, allowing your ranged fighters to really go to work.

Ideally, your Inquisitor comes to the fight with a filled focus meter, so Mark of the Rift can be dropped on the high dragon if the party manages to knock her down. Other preparations should include jars of bees or other damaging concoctions to throw at the Stormrider throughout the fight.

Above all else, this is a fight that demands patience and finesse, especially if you're at or just under the Stormrider's level. You only have so much in the way of healing resources, so you really have to be on the ball when it comes to avoiding preventable damage and stuns—otherwise you'll be whittled down before long.

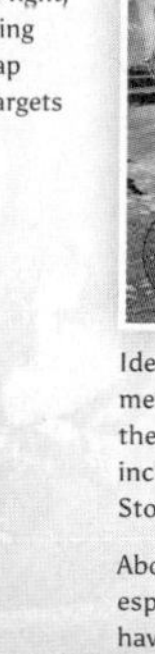

26: DUNGEON: LOST TEMPLE OF DIRTHAMEN

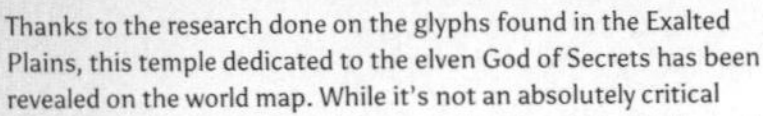

Thanks to the research done on the glyphs found in the Exalted Plains, this temple dedicated to the elven God of Secrets has been revealed on the world map. While it's not an absolutely critical location for the Inquisition, the secrets that lie within this long-abandoned shrine may provide an additional boost to the Inquisition's war effort. Bring a mage to make veilfire and a rogue to pick locks if you want to fully explore this place.

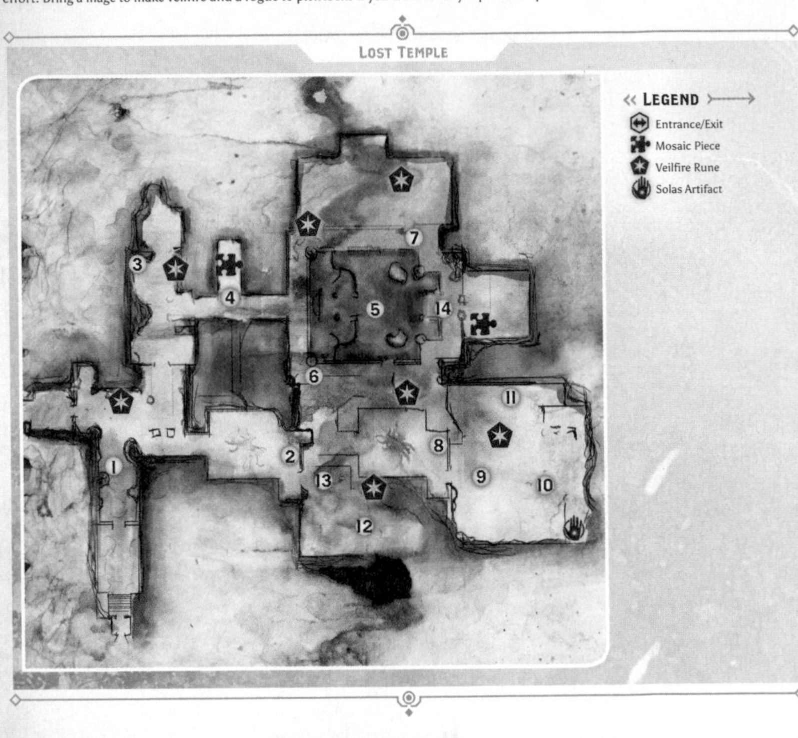

God of Secrets

Quest Giver: War table in Skyhold

Description: Cillian's reading of the glyphs has revealed the location of the Lost Temple of Dirthamen. Who knows what secrets this ancient eleven ruin may hold.

Requirements: You must complete the Scattered Glyphs quest.

Reward: 1,934 XP, 400 Influence, 3 Power

Objectives:

- Investigate the area.
- Recover six sets of remains.
- Summon the Highest One.
- Search the Chamber of the Oracle.

1. Arriving in the temple, you find it wet and dark, though you encounter a veilfire torch as you reach a T junction in the corridor. Hang a left to reach the Chamber of Misery. There's a statue inside that requires the veilfire torch to light the offering bowl in its hands. This causes an ambush of undead to appear in the room. Take them down, then continue down the main corridor in the opposite direction. Every time you pick up one of the remains, you are attacked by undead! Be sure to not only wipe them out but search the loot they drop.

2. There is a locked gate at this location, but you have to go through the rest of the temple to reach the mechanism that opens it from the other side.

3. Another chamber of remains is just past this waterfall, but you can't take the torch through the water without losing it. First use the lever to the left of the waterfall to shut off the water flow, allowing you to take a veilfire torch into the Chamber of Whispers. Once again, collecting the remains from the statues causes an undead ambush. This room also contains a rune for the Runes in the Lost Temple quest.

4. An ice barrier on the left side of this corridor can be taken down, leading to some loot and a mosaic piece in the Freed Are Slaves collection.

5. The sanctuary is the central area of the temple. It is where you will return to once you have all six remains.

6. The Chamber of Sorrow is in a room on the south side of the sanctuary as you enter it for the first time. Taking the remains from here will cause more undead to rise up and assault your party.

7. On the north side of the sanctuary is the Crypts of the Forgotten room. It has a door that a rogue needs to unlock. This lets you reach another of the six remains. More undead rise to take back what you've stolen. Make sure to loot their corpses for a key that will let you go farther into the temple. Also, thoroughly search the full extent of the Crypts of the Forgotten for another two veilfire runes.

8. Another locked door for a rogue is at the end of this corridor. To the left is another gate opened via level, allowing to make your way toward the Chamber of Unheeding.

9. A warrior can kick through a section of wall just past the gate. One of the runes is inside this secret room, along with more loot.

10. Across from the breakable wall is another winding corridor that takes you to another veilfire rune.

11. Taking the remains from the Altar of Unheeding causes an arcane horror and two undead to appear.

12. Going through the Path of Secrets, make sure you search for another veilfire rune to the left of the stairs as you're climbing up them.

13. The Chamber of Despondency takes you back to the gate you found near the start of this little jaunt, with the final piece of the remains. A lever near the offering statue allows you to open the gate and take another path back to the central sanctuary or the temple exit. Taking the remains here causes a trio of arcane horrors to appear in this room. Have your mage ready with fire spells to help take them down faster!

With all the remains recovered, return to the central sanctuary and place them on the altars at the center of the room to summon the Highest One. What appears is a level 15 elite despair demon. At random intervals, the Highest One will create an arcane barrier that should be dispelled by your mage as soon as possible. Meanwhile, throughout the fight, you will be forced to contend with undead constantly rising from the waters in the lower part of the room. Remember to use Mark of the Rift should you need the extra damage boost.

14. With the Highest One defeated, the door to the Chamber of the Oracle can be unlocked. Don't miss another Freed Are Slaves mosaic piece inside that chamber while you loot the room. Cleaning out the glowing chest at the back of the room completes this quest! To leave, head back to the entrance of the temple.

However, it appears that you're not the only ones who knew of this place. Depending on your choice of whom to side with, you will face mages or red templars as you reach the exit to the temple!

Runes in the Lost Temple

Quest Giver: Finding a veilfire rune

Description: Find all veilfire runes.

Requirements: You must complete the Scattered Glyphs quest.

Reward: 200 Influence

Objectives:

- Find seven veilfire runes.

Close to the veilfire torch in the starting corridor is a statue. Walk next to it with the torch in hand to reveal a veilfire rune. Seven are hidden throughout the temple, and it's worth your while to collect them all. You can reference their locations on the map.

EMERALD GRAVES

This forest in the Dales, once known as the Emerald March, is now the Emerald Graves. A tree grows here for every elven knight who died in the Dales while protecting the region from the humans during their Exalted March on the Dales.

LOCALE SUMMARY

Scouting Cost: 8 Power

The Freemen that are terrorizing this region are stronger and better equipped than their counterparts in the Exalted Plains. They have to be, being the muscle behind red lyrium shipments passing through the region. The local wildlife is also a bit nastier, with great bears the size of horse-drawn carts, horse included, stalking through the trees. Far to the north, giants have apparently made their home near elven ruins, while a group of lyrium smugglers attempts to clear them out. The verdant beauty of the Emerald Graves looks inviting, but the denizens are very dangerous.

> Crafting Materials

Common Materials:

- Elfroot
- Spindleweed
- Blood Lotus
- Deep Mushroom
- Rashvine
- Embrium
- Arbor Blessing
- Iron
- Bloodstone
- Pyrophite

Rare Materials:

- Royal Elfroot
- Black Lotus
- Prophet's Laurel
- Rashvine Nettle
- Felandris
- Obsidian
- Everite
- Stormheart
- Dawnstone

Unique Materials: None

> Collections

- Astrariums: 3
- Bottles of Thedas: 4
- High Dragons: 1
- Landmarks: 22
- Mosaic Pieces: 5
- Glyphs: 1
- Shards: 13
- Treasure Maps: 6 (Four are found inside Chateau d'Onterre.)
- Logging Stands: 1
- Quarries: 2

> Inquisition Personnel

Agents

- Fairbanks

LOCALE MAP

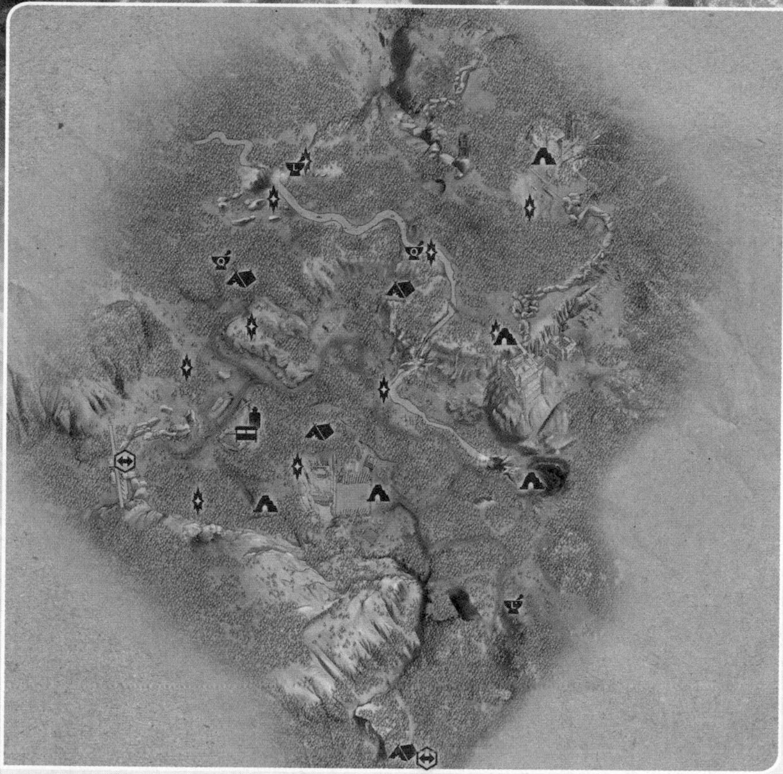

Legend

- Area Exit
- Cave/Dungeon
- Fade Rift
- Merchant
- Logging Stand
- Quarry

Inquisition Camps

- Hill Camp
- Briathos' Steps Camp
- Gracevine Camp
- Direstone Camp

COLLECTIONS

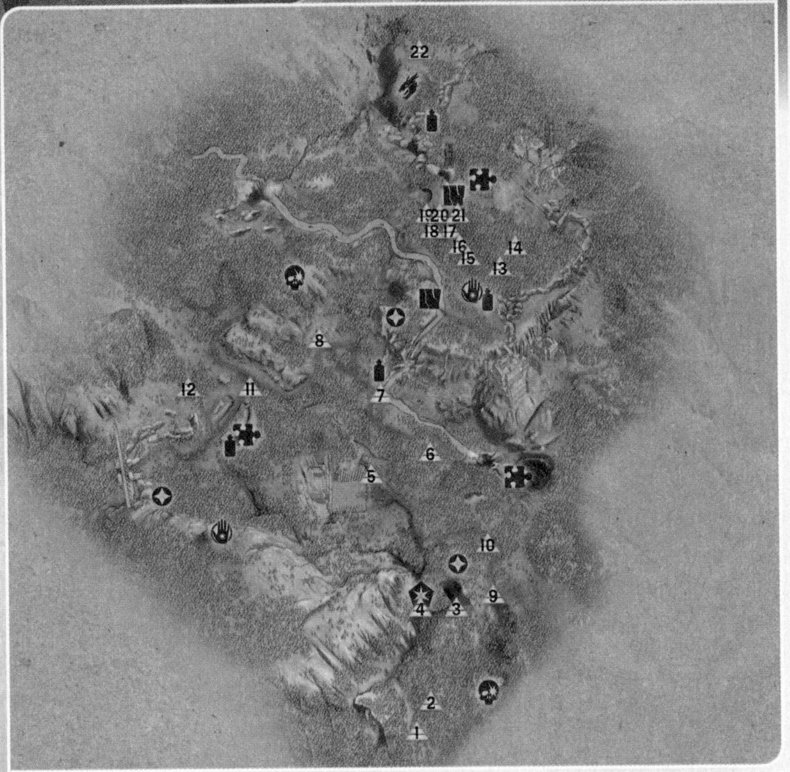

LEGEND

Astrariums

- Constellation: Solium
- Constellation: Equinor
- Constellation: Eluvia

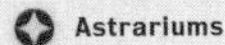

Bottles of Thedas

High Dragons

- The Greater Mistral

Landmarks/Points of Interest

1. Knight's Guardian
2. Andraste's Light
3. Wolf Falls
4. The Watcher
5. The Betrayer
6. Andraste's Mercy
7. Silver Falls*
8. The Lion's Pavilion
9. Andraste's Promise
10. The Guide
11. Andraste's Strength
12. Whiteshadow
13. Ralaferin's Tree
14. Calmar's Tree
15. Elnora's Tree
16. Lindiranae's Tree
17. Briathos' Tree
18. Vaharel's Tree
19. Mathalin's Tree
20. Tanaleth's Tree
21. Sulan's Tree
22. The Twisted Tree

*A bottle of Thedas, Sun Blonde Vint-1, is near the Silver Falls.

Mosaic Pieces

Ocularа and Shards

Ocularum 1: Great Bear Cove

- Ocularum +7 Shards

Ocularum 2: Gracevine

- Ocularum +6 Shards

Glyphs

Solas Artifacts

Treasure Maps

- Map of Watcher's Pass
- Map of Elgar'nan's Bastion

ASTRARIUM SOLUTIONS

Astrarium: Solium

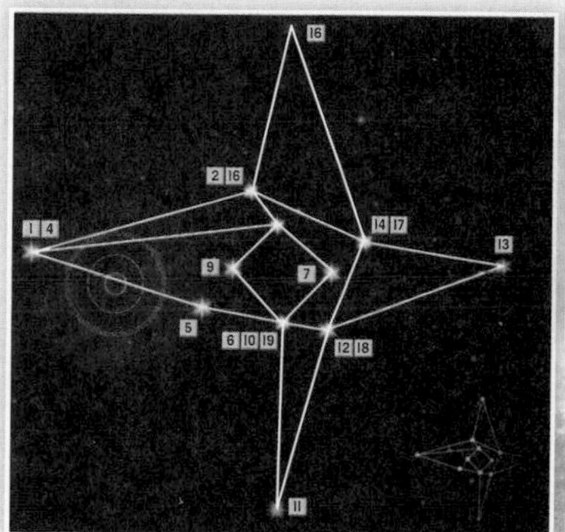

Astrarium: Eluvia

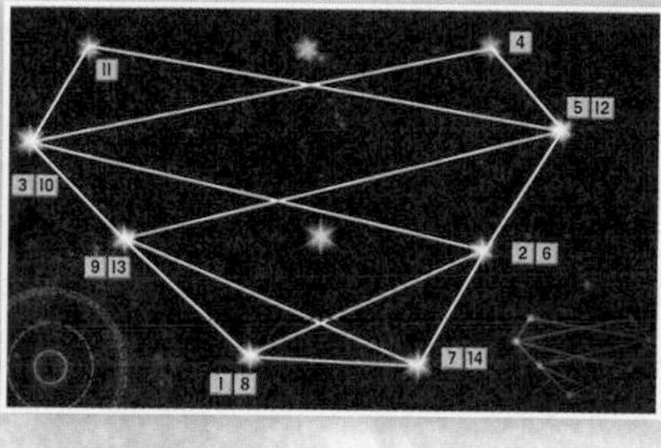

Astrarium: Equinor

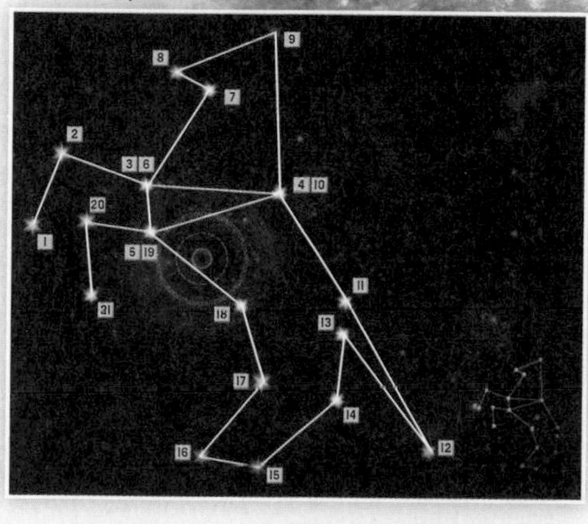

Astrarium Vault

Hidden in a ravine found between Briathos' Steps and the Harrow, this astrarium vault appears to have been warded at some point by cold magic, as parts of the storage here are encased by stalagmites made of ice.

FADE RIFTS

Rage demons, despair demons, and greater terrors are all far more common in the Emerald Graves, particularly as you travel farther north to deal with the rifts there. For parties struggling to deal with follow-up waves of demons after the first, it might be a good idea to take two mages so they can cast Dispel to eliminate more demons before they fully manifest.

Fade Rift Details

Quest	Rifts	Total Power
Rifts at the Cove	2	4
Rifts at the Pavilion	4	8
Rifts at the Reach	2	4
Rifts near the Sighs	3	6

MERCHANTS

Argon's Lodge Merchant

Item	Cost
Weapons (Highlights)	
Balanced Sniper Bow	456
Upgrades	
Masterwork Bound Dagger Grip	211
Crafting Materials	
Essence Containment Apparatus	20
Blank Runestone	71
Pyrophite	42
Paragon's Luster	42
Obsidian	42

REQUISITIONS

Requisition Quests

Requisition	Materials
Lure Requisition in the Graves	10 Deep Mushrooms, 3 Ring Velvet
Obsidian Survey in the Graves	5 Obsidian, 10 Bloodstones
Remedy Requisition in the Graves	10 Rashvine, 5 Nugskins

> FAIRBANKS

Affiliated Quest: Victims of War

Inquisition Perk: Fairbanks (Connections)

After an extensive series of quests, you have the ability to decide where the man who calls himself Fairbanks ends up: as an agent for the Inquisition or a noble for Orlais, trying to do right for the Dales.

SIDE QUESTS (RECOMMENDED LEVEL 14-16 AND 16-20)

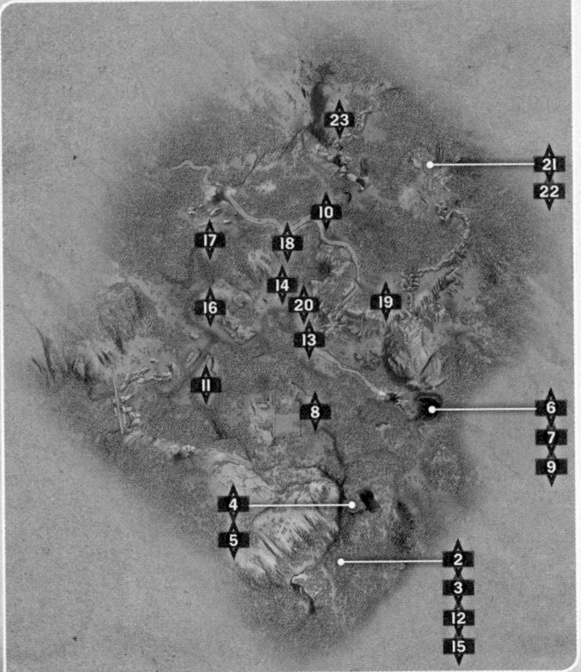

Legend

Level 14-16

1: Holding Emerald Graves (given when entering locale)
2: Devotion
3: Watcher's Reach Refugees
4: Map of Watcher's Pass
5: A Fallen Sister
6: Not Everyone's Free
7: A Vicious Thug
8: A Corrupt General
9: A Deluded Chevalier
10: Victims of War
11: Noble Deeds, Noble Heart
12: Fairbanks Patrol Under Attack
13: Motherly Encouragement
14: A Lover's Promise

Level 16-20

15: A Bear to Cross
16: Observing the Menace
17: Map of Elgar'nan's Bastion
18: Last Wishes
19: Dungeon: Chateau d'Onterre
20: A Puppet Master
21: The Knight's Tomb
22: Dungeon: Din'an Hanin
23: High Dragon: The Greater Mistral

> 1: HOLDING EMERALD GRAVES

Description: Establish camps to hold the Emerald Graves and support Inquisition activity in the region.

Quest Giver: Scout Harding

Requirements: Started as soon as you arrive in Emerald Graves

Reward: 100 Influence and 1 Power per camp, except for the starting camp

Objectives:

- Establish four camps.

There's a lot of ground to cover in the Emerald Graves, and the terrain is not the easiest to cross. You'll want access to all the camps as early as you can manage it. Fast travel makes many of the quests in this region a lot simpler to deal with, as the nature of the forest makes traveling on foot or by horseback difficult when seeking out particular objectives.

> 2: DEVOTION

Quest Giver: A letter found near the Andraste's Light landmark

Description: Dolores lights a candle for her son at the chantry each year on the anniversary of his death. She is unable to do so this year because of the war.

Requirements: Available as soon as you enter the Emerald Graves

Reward: 242 XP, 80 Influence

Objectives:

- Light a candle at the shrine.

It's a long walk through some dangerous territory from where you find the letter (close to the starting camp) to where the writer wants you to go to honor the dearly departed, the Lion's Pavilion. However, once you actually get to the shrine, there are surprisingly no major complications. Complete the requested ritual, and the quest is finished. While you can start this quest early, you might find that heading straight to the shrine would be going out of your way to avoid completing numerous other quests first. Save this for later.

> 3: WATCHER'S REACH REFUGEES

Quest Giver: Scout Harding

Description: Inquisition scouts have been approached by an Orlesian rebel named Fairbanks who requests protection. Fairbanks and his followers are being attacked by a suspicious group calling themselves the Freemen of the Dales.

Requirements: Travel to Emerald Graves for the first time.

Reward: 242 XP, 80 Influence

Objectives:

- Go to the Watcher's Reach camp.
- Speak with Fairbanks.
- Examine Fairbanks's documents.

After Scout Harding briefs you on the situation in the Emerald Graves, travel north toward the Watcher's Reach camp. You encounter a squad of Freemen trying to blockade the road. Explain to them with violence just how bad an idea this is, then continue toward the camp. Make your way through Watcher's Canyon until you reach the center of the camp, where Fairbanks is.

Fairbanks is honored to meet the Inquisitor in person, but he sets that aside and immediately gets to business. He has intel on your enemies and how they are colluding with the Freemen of the Dales. He believes that with that information, you can deal with his problems and yours simultaneously. Without help, it's apparent that his little settlement will eventually be overrun.

Inside a cave near Fairbanks is a table containing all of the intel. Read through it all to learn of Sister Costeau, an important name in the ranks of the Freemen.

> 4: MAP OF WATCHER'S PASS

Quest Giver: Map found in Watcher's Reach

Description: A massive figure with arm outstretched stands guard at the spot marked on this map.

Requirements: Enter the Watcher's Reach camp and speak with Fairbanks.

Reward: 242 XP, 80 Influence

Objectives:

- Find the spot marked on the map.

The map is inside the cave at Watcher's Reach. The actual treasure location is very far to the north, in the Rush of Sighs region, just northeast of the bridge crossing the river. You have to climb some rocks to reach it, and it can be amazingly easy to just ride past and not trigger your mini-map's Search ping. This is another quest you can start early in your exploration of Emerald Graves, but it might be best to hold off on getting it done until you actually are in the area and have more camps you can fast travel between.

> 5: A FALLEN SISTER

Quest Giver: Fairbanks's intel documents at Watcher's Reach

Description: Fairbanks's documents mention a Freemen target named Sister Costeau, who was last stationed at the veridium mine in the Emerald Graves.

Requirements: Read Fairbanks's documents to learn of this fallen sister.

Reward: 967 XP, 200 Influence, 2 Power

Objectives:

- Go to the veridium mine.
- Deal with Sister Costeau.

The main path away from Watcher's Reach to the veridium mine is guarded by patrols of Freemen. Always be on the lookout for any scouts among the groups when taking them on, so you don't suddenly take a knife to the back. On some of the corpses, you might find notes that give away just how much more desperate the Freemen's situation truly is. The front entrance of the mine itself is through another small ravine, protected by a trio of swordsmen and a guardsman.

Upon entering the mine, you'll have to contend with a swordsman and a pair of Freemen snipers using crates for cover.

With all of her men defeated, Sister Costeau kicks open the door from her private chambers to face you in combat, joined by two more swordsmen. The "good" sister packs a massive shield, making life difficult for melee attacks unless they manage to flank her. Her mace also packs a devastating punch, able to pound mages and rogues into paste in short order. Your tanks should make getting her attention a top priority.

Try to get your rogues and mages to stun or knock her down, to make taking her out easier. Killing her completes this quest, but you're not done in the veridium mines just yet. Search the area thoroughly for more items, and you will probably also hear prisoners from the nearby cells calling for help. Additionally, there are notes left behind by Sister Costeau, detailing her concerns with some of her less savory comrades.

NOTE The mine contains a mosaic piece for the Invasion set, sitting on some crates close to the cells. There's more primeval red lyrium to go toward the Varric's Seeing Red side quest.

> 6: NOT EVERYONE'S FREE

Quest Giver: A prisoner in the veridium mine

Description: The Freemen have taken residents of Watcher's Reach captive.

Requirements: Complete the quest A Fallen Sister.

Reward: 242 XP, 80 Influence

Objectives:

- Find the cage key.
- Free the captives.

If you approach the prison cell in the mine, a woman in the cell says that one of the guards had a key but apparently set it down somewhere. She gives you general directions on where to walk to find the key. Release the prisoners to complete the quest!

> 7: A VICIOUS THUG

Quest Giver: A note found in the veridium mine held by Sister Costeau

Description: Documents found in Costeau's camp mention a commander for the Freemen named Duhaime. He is among peers holding a deserted villa in the Emerald Graves.

Requirements: Locate the papers inside the veridium mine after defeating Sister Costeau.

Reward: 967 XP, 200 Influence, 2 Power

Objectives:

- Kill Duhaime.

Over in the Villa Maurel region is Duhaime, a cruel man who is in no small part related to the very negative reputation the Freemen of the Dales have earned among the civilians in the Emerald Graves. He leads a sizable gang of troops and is a vicious combatant himself. This mountain of muscle and his two-handed axe can be a problem, but not if he's left alone after you wipe out his buddies.

> 8: A CORRUPT GENERAL

Quest Giver: A key found on the corpse of Duhaime

Description: Documents on Duhaime's corpse detailed the whereabouts of the Freemen leader. The man, known as Maliphant, is likely somewhere inside a villa held by the Freemen in the Emerald Graves.

Requirements: Kill the bruiser in front of Villa Maurel to retrieve the key that grants access to the villa.

Reward: 967 XP, 200 Influence, 2 Power

Objectives:

- Enter Villa Maurel.
- Deal with Maliphant.

In front of Villa Maurel, you fought and killed Duhaime, a dangerous and power-mad thug using the Freemen's cause to murder innocents. On his corpse was a key to the villa itself, where a general of the Freemen awaits.

Safekeeping

Quest Giver: A piece of a runed key found in Villa Maurel

Description: There are fragments of a runed key scattered throughout Villa Maurel. If the fragments are reassembled, the key may unlock something of value.

Requirements: Find a runed key fragment in the villa.

Reward: 242 XP, 80 Influence

Objectives:

- Find three key fragments.
- Find a way to reassemble the runed key.
- Find a use for the runed key.

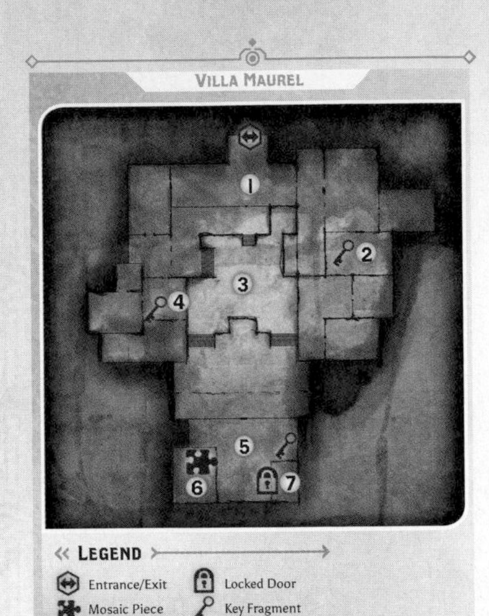

A mansion for a very rich and powerful man, Villa Maurel is now in the possession of the Freemen of the Dales, acting as the stronghold for Maliphant, the commanding general for these rebels. Apparently, a meeting of minds between Corypheus's own commanders and Maliphant himself is underway. It's your perfect chance to catch them all in one place.

1. In the dining hall, several Freemen discuss the current events befalling their organization. Relieve them of their worries as quickly and violently as possible, then rummage through the dining hall for useful goods.

2. The east hall contains a key fragment on a workbench; don't miss out on recovering it! You need it for the Safekeeping quest.

3. The courtyard contains a large gathering of Freemen, and once you begin the fight, more rush in from the other parts of the villa if you haven't cleared them. Maliphant, along with red templars and a pair of Freemen, also joins the fray. This can be a very intense battle for under-prepared parties. Maliphant is an Orlesian prowler, and a highly aggressive one at that. He can strike from stealth and wipe out a party member in seconds. You can track him via your mini-map, as he's counted as a moving quest objective. Always be on the look out for archers, as they tend to get lost in the chaos of battle. After Maliphant's death, survey and loot the courtyard. You'll find a note that once again ominously brings up Emprise du Lion.

4. The private chambers on the west side of the villa contain another key fragment, along with more possible encounters with Freemen troops if you have not already engaged the whole villa by going straight for the courtyard. Be sure to search the private chambers thoroughly for some interesting reading.

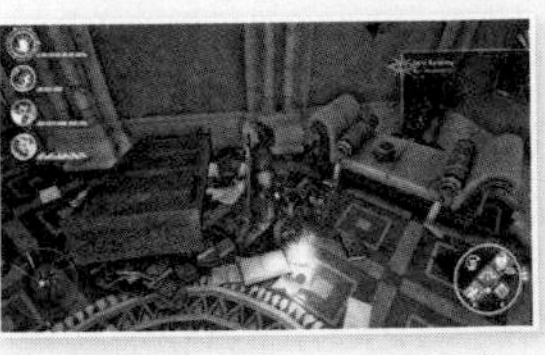

5. The study on the southern side of the villa contains a key fragment, along with plenty of interesting reading about Maliphant and his dealings with "C".

6. A warrior can kick down a wall in the study. The personal storeroom it hid contains a device that can be used to restore the three key pieces into one whole key—it just requires a mage to power it. There is also a mosaic piece for the Invasion set in this room.

7. The door across from the personal storeroom can be unlocked by the runed key, completing the Safekeeping quest and getting you access to some useful loot!

9: A DELUDED CHEVALIER

Quest Giver: A note found in the veridium mine held by Sister Costeau

Description: Documents found in Costeau's camp mention a chevalier named Auguste who is working for the Freemen. He was last seen at Argon's Lodge in the Emerald Graves.

Requirements: Locate the papers inside the veridium mine after defeating Sister Costeau.

Reward: 967 XP, 200 Influence, 2 Power

Objectives:

- Go to Argon's Lodge.
- Deal with Chevalier Auguste.

Approaching Argon's Lodge from the north, you will find a large contingent of Freemen barring entry to the small settlement. Begin the fight, clearing out as many of the troops as you can. As the fight progresses, reinforcements flood in from the north. With so many threats to deal with, including multiple archers and guardsmen, a well-timed Mark of the Rift may be a good idea.

Eventually Chevalier Auguste will step up to try to defeat you himself, joined by his personal guard, which includes more snipers and a bruiser. Get rid of the snipers quickly. If they target the same rogue or mage together, that character is probably going to die. Pop your mage's focus ability Heal if things get too hairy, and make sure the party is getting shielded while dealing with the bruiser. Survive this battle and the lodge will be secured.

NOTE The lodge contains a mosaic piece for the Invasion set, along with a bottle of Thedas: Absence. Don't miss out!

10: VICTIMS OF WAR

Quest Giver: Defeat Chevalier Auguste to start this quest.

Description: With all the Freemen leaders dead, Fairbanks and his people should feel a lot safer in the Emerald Graves.

Requirements: Complete A Fallen Sister, Not Everyone's Free, A Vicious Thug, A Corrupt General, and A Deluded Chevalier.

Reward: 242 XP, 80 Influence

Objectives:

- Speak with Fairbanks in Watcher's Reach.

After you've completed your task of ending the key threats from the Freemen of the Dales, you can return to Fairbanks in Watcher's Reach. With the Freemen effectively evicted from the Emerald Graves, he decides that the recently recovered Argon's Lodge would be a fine place to take his surviving band.

11: NOBLE DEEDS, NOBLE HEART

Quest Giver: Clara

Description: Clara heard a rumor that Fairbanks is of noble descent. She believes it and wants proof to show the Council of Heralds. If Fairbanks gains power, she hopes he can do more for the people of the Dales.

Requirements: Defeat Chevalier Auguste.

Reward: 1324 XP, 600 Influence, 2 Power

Objectives:

- Find three pieces of proof of Fairbanks's nobility.
- Present proof of Fairbanks's nobility to an interested party.

This side quest is only available after you complete A Fallen Sister, Not Everyone's Free, A Vicious Thug, A Corrupt General, and A Deluded Chevalier. In Argon's Lodge, a woman named Clara is obviously quite taken with Fairbanks, and she believes that proving his nobility could make things better for all people of the Dales. If you speak with Fairbanks himself before beginning the search for proof, he is less than amused at this prospect.

Just north of Argon's Lodge is a small wooden storage hut that can be broken into with Deft Hands, Fine Tools. Inside is one of the pieces of proof you're looking for.

Two bits of proof can be found in the storage houses just outside of Villa Maurel.

After gathering the proof, you're faced with a choice. Clara wants to use the proof right away to get Fairbanks properly recognized and empowered. If you speak with Fairbanks, he insists that he does not want these privileges, nor does he want to become entangled in the social politics that led to where he is today.

If you give the proof to Fairbanks, he will destroy it, and war table missions will become available to further reap the benefits of having defeated the Freemen. If you give it to Clara, she will persist in trying to get Fairbanks recognized as a noble, and you will receive a unique war table mission. The choice is yours.

12: FAIRBANKS PATROL UNDER ATTACK

Quest Giver: Witness a patrol under attack by the Freemen.

Description: One of Fairbanks's guards is under attack nearby.

Requirements: Occurs randomly throughout the Emerald Graves.

Reward: 242 XP, 80 Influence

Objectives:

- Protect the patrol.

On occasion, you will spot a patrol of Fairbanks's soldiers engaged in combat with the Freemen, which will automatically begin this quest. Defeating the Freemen attacking the patrol completes the quest. This can happen multiple times in your adventure throughout this locale.

13: MOTHERLY ENCOURAGEMENT

Quest Giver: Dead corpse at the Silver Falls

Description: A young woman fell from a cliff to her death under mysterious circumstances.

Requirements: Find the body in the river.

Reward: 242 XP, 80 Influence

Objectives:

- Investigate the fatal fall.

Reaching the place where the poor woman fell from takes some doing. You'll find evidence at Silverspray Perch overlooking the Silver Falls, with crystal grace growing perilously away from the ledge. A nearby journal reveals some interesting information about the woman and her family, as well as the cause of death. This case is closed.

14: A LOVER'S PROMISE

Quest Giver: Letter on a wall at the Lion's Pavilion.

Description: A man has asked his lover to meet him in Gracevine, so they can run away together.

Requirements: Reach the Lion's Pavilion.

Reward: 242 XP, 80 Influence

Objectives:

- Go to the Gracevine grove.

Just north of the camp you can set up in Gracevine is the promised place for this couple. However, you find the site devoid of anything until you inspect the picnic blanket. A level 15 elite giant spider takes offense and drops down from the trees to attack you! Couples have really got to stop trying to elope in the most dangerous places on Thedas.

> 15: A BEAR TO CROSS

Quest Giver: Johnson

Description: A large, territorial bear has been rampaging through the Inquisition camp, scaring people and destroying supplies.

Requirements: Complete Noble Deeds, Noble Heart.

Reward: 242 XP, 80 Influence

Objectives:

- Hunt down the problem bear.

Johnson doesn't exactly get across just how ridiculously big this bear he's talking about truly is. Old Scarred Paw is in the cave to the northeast from the Andruil's Wall camp. Dwarfing the two bear cubs, it charges out of the cave as soon as you get close, so make sure you allow a tank to open up the combat: Old Scarred Paw is more than capable of outright killing anyone less armored than a warrior with one solid attack. However, it is extremely vulnerable to fire, which can help even the odds. Killing the beast completes the quest.

> 16: OBSERVING THE MENACE

Quest Giver: A journal found south of the Gracevine camp

Description: Troilus Herbtubise is researching Fade rifts for what he calls his "Great Mission." He appears to have camped at a safe distance from each rift for a time, observing its behavior.

Requirements: Available as soon as you enter the Emerald Graves

Reward: 242 XP, 80 Influence

Objectives:

- Search for the river camp.
- Search for the second river camp.

CAUTION

As you travel farther north for some of the later quests in Emerald Graves, be on your guard. Red templar or mage camps are very common throughout the locale starting around the Rush of Sighs region, and their presence extends to the northernmost reaches of the Emerald Graves. These camps of enemies begin around level 15-16, but as you go north you may encounter red templars and mages reaching level 19 or 20!

After picking up the first journal left behind by Troilus, head north to the first campsite. It lies just out of reach of a Fade rift, so if you're looking to avoid taking on the demons, it is possible to skirt just far enough from it while reading Troilus's observations from the second journal. He mentions another camp, to the east, where he planned to seal a rift on his own.

As you might have already guessed, Troilus's attempted sealing of a rift went very badly. You find him lying dead at his last campsite, with no further observations save that the world is doomed. Perhaps he would have found comfort in knowing the Inquisition had taken up his Great Mission.

17: MAP OF ELGAR'NAN'S BASTION

Quest Giver: A scroll found near the Gracevine camp

Description: This map, found near an ancient elven ruin in Gracevine, marks a spot near a distinctive arch in the Emerald Graves.

Requirements: Available as early as you're willing to go to Gracevine and pick up the map.

Reward: 242 XP, 80 Influence

Objectives:

- Find the spot marked on the map.

West of Elgar'nan's Bastion is where you can find this treasure. The stone arches described in the map are still very prominent. A large tree growing just outside of the ruin faces this stone arch, and the treasure lies near it.

18: LAST WISHES

Quest Giver: A note found near an urn of ashes

Description: Robert Caron's last wish was to have his ashes scattered on the plateau overlooking the Greatwood. His wife was too frail to complete the task.

Requirements: Available upon entering the Emerald Graves

Reward: 242 XP, 80 Influence

Objectives:

- Scatter Robert's ashes.

You must travel to the northernmost reaches of the Emerald Graves to scatter Robert's ashes. Be wary of the red templar/mage camp set up at the Southfinger Watch. You can bypass it easily, but the prowler-class enemies at the camp may be patrolling out far enough that they will be the first to rush you if you get close enough.

TIP You can find a bottle of Thedas in this camp: Chasind Sack Mead.

Scattering the ashes from the cliff's edge in the far north of the Graves should prevent more ash wraiths from forming.

19: DUNGEON: CHATEAU D'ONTERRE

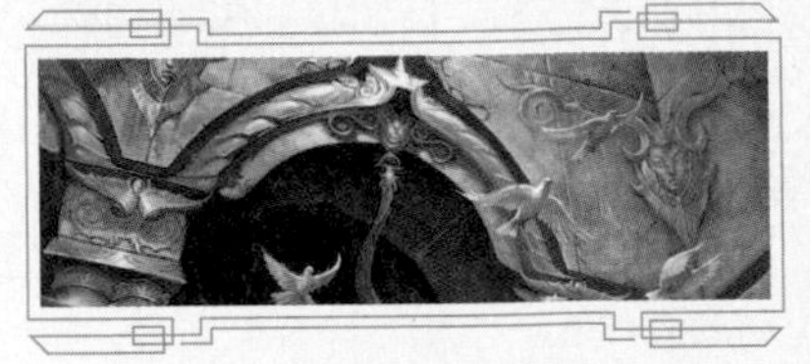

Quest Giver: The quest automatically begins when you enter the chateau.

Description: An ancient horror has awakened in the chateau courtyard.

Requirements: Enter the chateau.

Reward: 967 XP, 200 Influence, 2 Power

Objectives:

- Gain access to the grand balcony.
- Kill the arcane horror.

As soon as you enter Chateau d'Onterre, it is apparent that something is very wrong in this place. It's dark, yet as you move through this quiet mansion, torches light up as you approach them. Undead begin to rise and patrol the halls in ever-increasing numbers. Something happened in this place.

Chateau d'Onterre

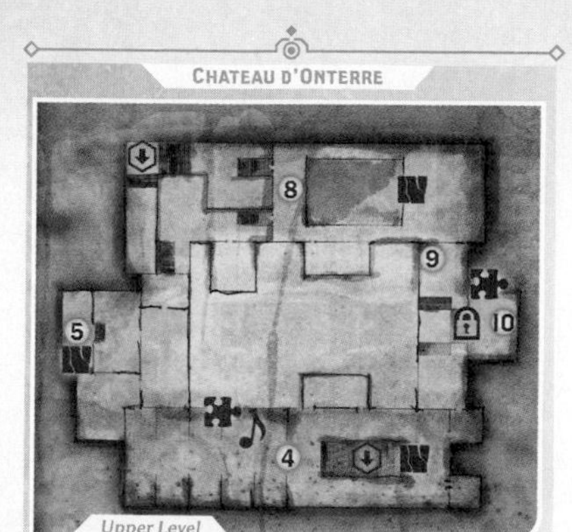

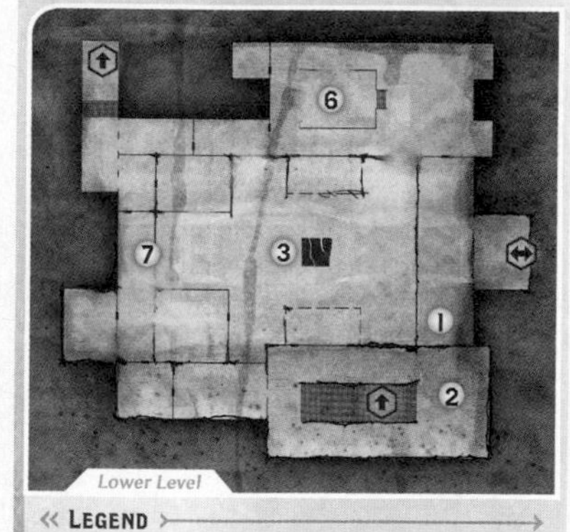

Legend

- Entrance/Exit
- Mosaic Piece
- Treasure Map
- Song Lyrics
- Locked Door
- to Upper Level
- to Lower Level

1. Look for notes and diary entries left around the mansion, like this one. It will help you understand the nature of the horror that struck down the chateau.

2. In the gallery, you find a large group of dead bodies. An unlucky group of looters met their end here. If you have a rogue, you can unlock a door on the north side of the gallery to enter the formal gardens at the center of the chateau. A stairway leads up the chateau's second floor.

3. In the formal gardens, you can find a note, the first of the set you need to collect before you can leave this place. This garden will become important later on in your investigation of the chateau.

4. The gallery stairs lead to the library. Another sketch is hidden underneath a decoration facing the stairs from the east side of the room. Another door on that side of the room leads to a side chamber with another door leading to the grand balcony, but you still need the balcony key to open it. The library itself is filled with interesting codex entries.

5. The bedchambers contain another sketch hidden behind a painting. This sketch shows a dragon and some sort of pendant.

6. The ballroom holds another diary note. Look up from the dance floor to see a very realistic looking high dragon staring down on you.

7. The servants' quarters hold the cook's diary, which can shed more light on the mystery of the mansion. Another stairwell leads to the second floor, to the antechamber, and another staircase there takes you to the upper floor of the ballroom.

8. While on the ballroom's upper level, go around to the high dragon's head and move the small box-like decoration in front of it. This moves the dragon's tail. Go to the tail to recover another chilling note along with a key: It is an explicit warning to not use the key to the balcony. Obviously, you must now do this!

9. With the balcony now opened, clear out the undead, then go to the mysterious, rapidly spinning cube on the balcony railing. Upon touching it, you gain a 10-point boost to Cunning. Also, an arcane horror manifests in the formal gardens.

10. Don't run off to fight the demon just yet. On the grand balcony is another door that requires Deft Hands, Fine Tools to unlock. Behind it is a mosaic piece for the Invasion set.

With the nature of the chateau's darkness finally unveiled, return to the formal gardens and slay the arcane horror. With that, the chateau falls silent, completing this side quest. You can freely explore the place for any loot you may have missed!

20: A PUPPET MASTER

Quest Giver: Leliana

Description: Inquisition agents have lured Carroll, the red templar responsible for manipulating the Freemen of the Dales, to the Lion's Pavilion in the Emerald Graves. It's time to finish this.

Requirements: Complete A Vicious Thug, A Fallen Sister, A Corrupt General, and A Deluded Chevalier.

Reward: 1,324 XP, 600 Influence, 2 Power

Objectives:

- Defeat Carroll.

With the Freemen leadership effectively destroyed in the Emerald Graves, some officers have managed to escape. However, Leliana uses her agents to call out the apparent ring leader behind the Freemen's sudden and violent rise to prominence in the Dales. They have promised to meet the Freemen in the Lion's Pavilion, in the Dales.

Among the forces gathered with Carroll, two red templar shadows are present. Don't let yourself get surprised by these monsters; ideally, a mage or a rogue class can set traps on the stairs of the pavilion to catch them as they come after you. Once you kill the enemy leader and wipe out all the other hostiles around Lion's Pavilion, the quest is complete.

21: THE KNIGHT'S TOMB

Quest Giver: Keeper Hawen (Exalted Plains). Alternatively, visit Elgar'nan's Bastion in the Emerald Graves.

Description: Elves are investigating a tomb somewhere in the Emerald Graves that may hold secrets of great historical significance to the Dalish.

Requirements: Complete the events at Halamshiral, then return to the Exalted Plains to speak with Keeper Hawen. Alternatively, simply travel to the Emerald Graves after Halamshiral and go to Din'an Hanin.

Reward: 967 XP, 200 Influence, 2 Power

Objectives:

- Find the tomb.
- Find nine emerald seal pieces.
- Enter Elandrin's chamber.
- Locate the artifact.
- Sell the histories to the Chantry or return the histories to the Dalish.

When you first go to Elgar'nan's Bastion in the Emerald Graves, you encounter a group of Dalish elves, members of the same group you met in the Exalted Plains. They're investigating a knight's tomb, Din'an Hanin, and while they are for the most part friendly or ambivalent to Inquisition presence, they are not willing to let you into the ruins while they explore it.

After the events of Halamshiral, you can send soldiers on a mission to these tombs via the war table. However, once you arrive, you find the tombs open and unguarded, and the Dalish and your soldiers are lying dead.

TIP

Bring a rogue, and try to have Deft Hands, Fine Tools as one of your Inquisition perks. You need both if you want to fully explore this place.

22: DUNGEON: DIN'AN HANIN

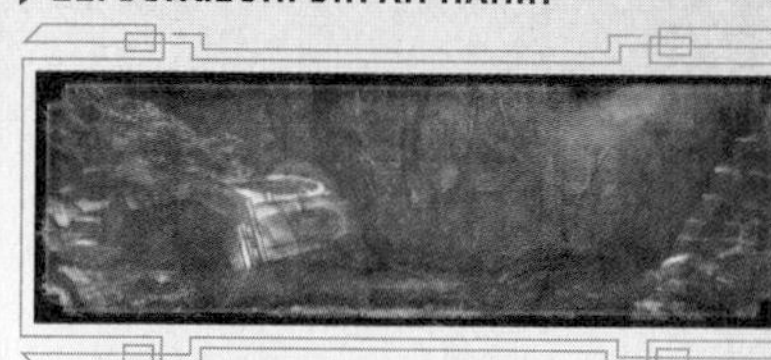

The Emerald Knights once marched in the halls of Din'an Hanin. Now it is nothing more than a tomb, a reminder of a time when the elves had a nation of their own, a reminder of the Exalted March that took everything from them. Some Dalish believed the truth of their fall could be found in Din'an Hanin. The Venatori, allied with Corypheus, also felt this place held something of value, and they will fight to keep it out of Inquisition hands.

DIN'AN HANIN

Lower Crypts

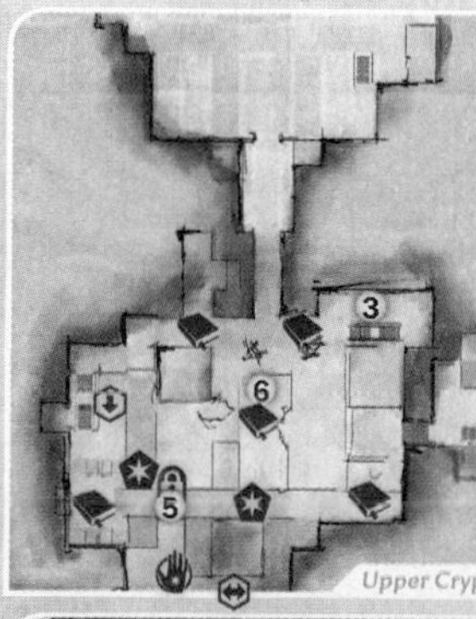

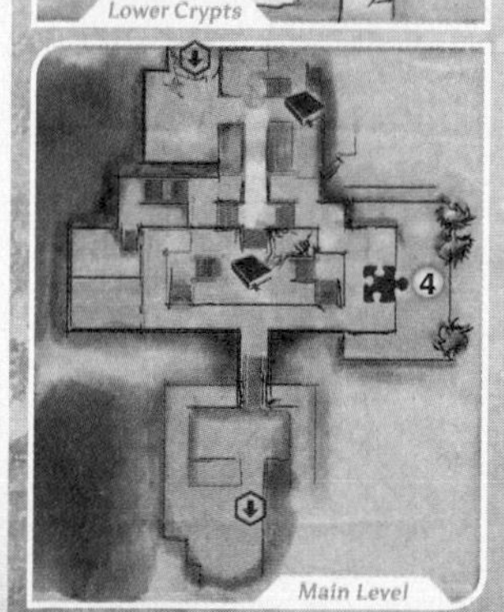

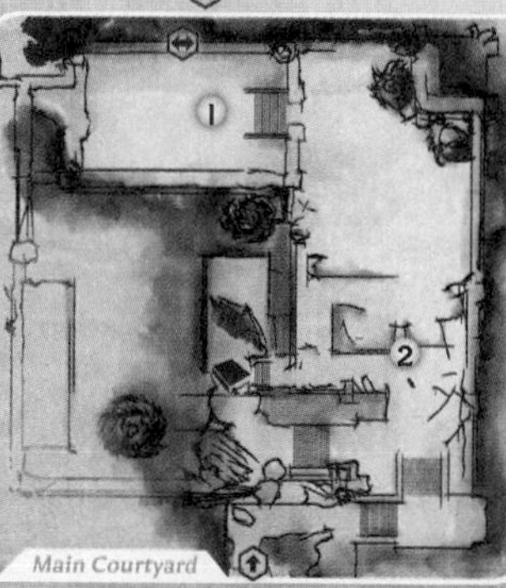

LEGEND

- Entrance/Exit
- to Upper Level
- to Lower Level
- Locked Door
- Mosaic Piece
- Emerald Seal
- Veilfire Rune
- Solas Artifact

1. As soon as you enter the ruins, you find more dead elves, joined by dead Inquisition soldiers. Not far from the entrance you encounter the cause: Tevinter forces, backed by Venatori mages.

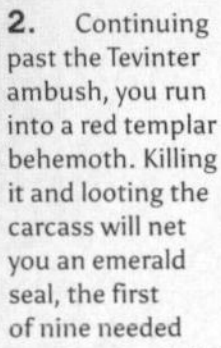

2. Continuing past the Tevinter ambush, you run into a red templar behemoth. Killing it and looting the carcass will net you an emerald seal, the first of nine needed to enter a sealed chamber inside of this place. Refer to our map for the general search locations of seal pieces not carried by your enemies.

3. The upper crypts contain more seals, as well as a squad of Venatori foes patrolling the area. Among the enemy a behemoth should be stomping about. Keep in mind that you'll have to use your Search ability to find the seals not carried by foes.

4. Don't miss out on the mosaic piece for the Invasion set.

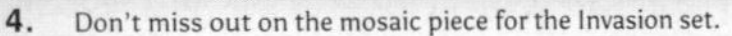

5. The lower crypts have a door needing Deft Hands, Fine Tools to unlock. No emerald seal pieces are behind it, but the treasures that lie beyond may be worth the effort.

6. The Venatori presence is heavier in the lower crypts, but there are lots of ways to thin out the odds from afar before you try to engage them on their level. Just beware their archers or mages.

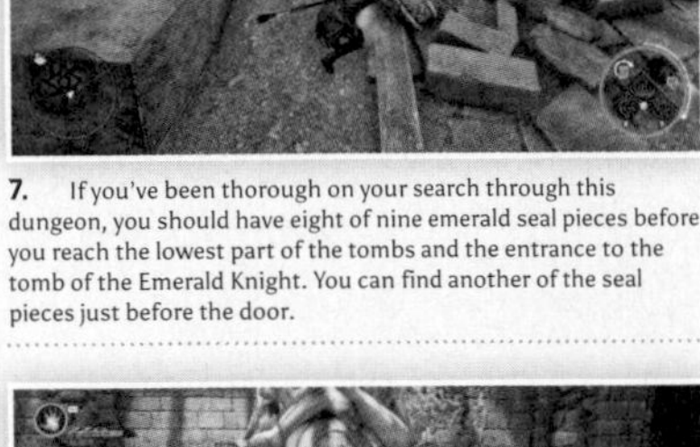

7. If you've been thorough on your search through this dungeon, you should have eight of nine emerald seal pieces before you reach the lowest part of the tombs and the entrance to the tomb of the Emerald Knight. You can find another of the seal pieces just before the door.

8. Now that you're inside the tomb, you can see the scroll the Dalish are interested in, suspended over a large pit that seems impassable. However, if you let a mage energize the veilfire torches on the four pillars surrounding the pit, you'll raise a platform that will let you reach the scroll! Be prepared to fight off the undead with every torch you light, and stay alert: The last torch you light brings a revenant out to play.

Once you collect the scroll, your time in Din'an Hanin is at an end. But you have one more thing to decide before this quest is complete: Do you travel to Val Royeaux and sell the scroll to the Chantry, denying the Dalish greater knowledge of the past, or do you give it to Keeper Hawen in the Exalted Plains, whose fallen Dalish sought it out to begin with?

TIP Choosing the Dalish opens a new war table mission, Bestowing Mourning Halla.

23: HIGH DRAGON: THE GREATER MISTRAL

Recommended Level: 17+

Recommended Party Composition: Two warriors (sword and shield, two-handed weapon), one rogue, one mage (armed with fire damage staff)

Alternative Party Composition: One warrior (sword and shield), one rogue, two mages (armed with fire damage staves)

Located in the northernmost region of the Emerald Graves is the Greater Mistral, an ice-type high dragon. Prepare your weapons, armor, and skills accordingly before the fight: This dragon is vulnerable to fire. The Mistral's ice breath can be devastating to be struck by, and the dragon is very proactive at singling out party members who are far from the rest of the group to spit ice balls at them.

The Greater Mistral regularly buffs herself with a full guard bar, which makes the process of taking her down slower if you don't have attacks that can quickly break through it. Another challenging aspect to the Mistral is when she begins flapping her wings. The resulting wind vortex damages anyone outside of the field that appears around the dragon while pulling them toward it. During this attack, the only "safe" spot is right next to the Mistral, which puts you in reach of her claws, jaw, or tail.

It is because of the wind vortex ability that it's recommended you take a warrior-heavy party. Mages and ranged rogues have survivability issues against the wind vortex because, unless you're willing to constantly babysit their position around the dragon, they'll take heavy damage before they're pulled into the safe zone. If their Barrier or Fade Step skills are on cooldown, they may not live long enough to even reach the center of the vortex. Meanwhile, warriors and melee rogues will be safe from the worst of the vortex, and both have their own means of negating or avoiding the Mistral's powerful melee attacks and the occasional ice breath.

Regardless of your chosen party, it should include at least one mage, for emergency revival of party members from afar, and for the use of the focus ability Heal to get everyone back up to full strength, should the situation call for it.

As the fight progresses, the Greater Mistral takes flight, firing aimed ice blasts at party members as she circles the battlefield. Fortunately, the Mistral does not call for the assistance of dragonlings, but she will use her roar to try to stun the party. Watch for her to try a roar stun, followed by a tailswipe.

Bring Antivan Fire, if you have that potion schematic. Every extra bit of damage your party can get going on the Mistral the better.

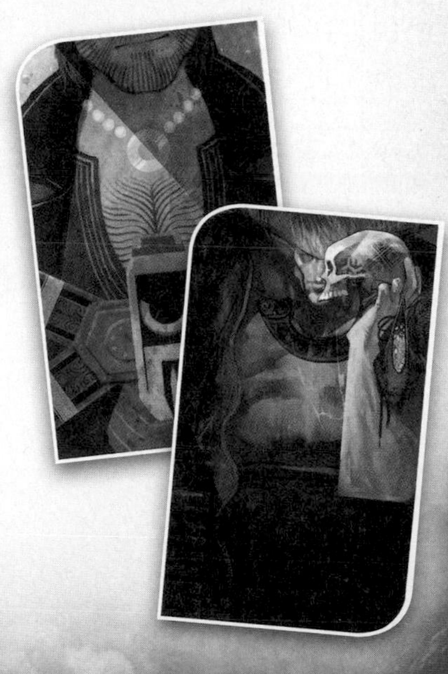

EMPRISE DU LION

An unexpected cold snap has frozen the Elfsblood River in Emprise du Lion, which has paralyzed the village of Sahrnia and made it nearly impossible for vital supplies to make it to the inhabitants. Demons have been flooding into the region in distressingly high numbers, some of the strongest the Inquisition has yet to face. Corypheus's forces have taken control of a vital fortress and a lyrium mine of great importance to his cause. As if that weren't enough, it appears that three high dragons have made their home in the ruins in the east.

LOCALE SUMMARY

Scouting Cost: 25 Power

Emprise du Lion's primary threat involves the staggering red lyrium production being handled by Corypheus's forces. Be they red templars or the mages you neglected from Redcliffe, expect some of the best men, women, and monsters they have at their disposal to try to stop your progress through the Lion.

Questing in Emprise du Lion can be divided into two very distinct groups: the fight to take control of Suledin Keep and everything else. A number of quests can be taken on and accomplished while you push toward the keep, while others have you stray from that path to take on objectives well away from the keep itself.

CRAFTING MATERIALS

Common Materials:

- Elfroot
- Rashvine
- Arbor Blessing
- Bloodstone

Rare Materials:

- Black Lotus
- Rashvine Nettle
- Felandris

Unique Materials:

- None

COLLECTIONS

- Astrariums: 0
- Bottles of Thedas: 2
- High Dragons: 3
- Landmarks: 11
- Mosaic Pieces: 1
- Glyphs: 2
- Shards: 13
- Treasure Maps: 0
- Logging Stands: 2
- Quarries: 0

INQUISITION PERSONNEL

Agents

- Michel de Chevin

LOCALE MAP

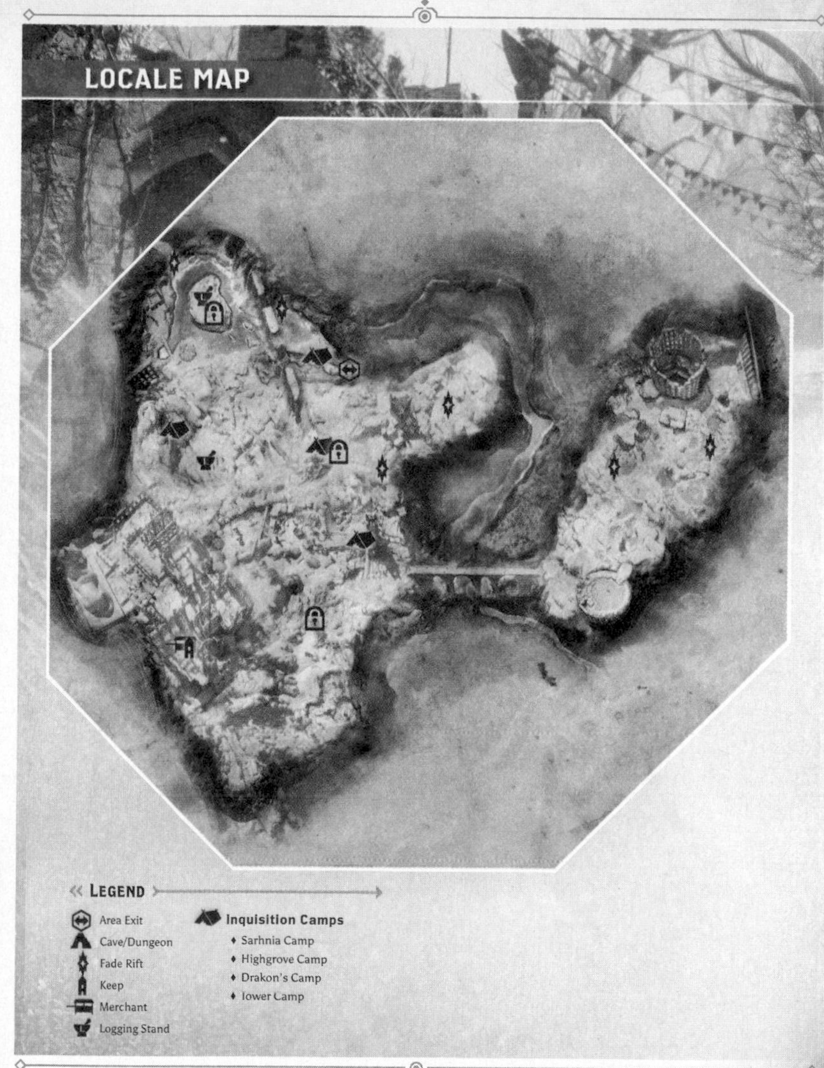
Legend
Area Exit
Cave/Dungeon
Fade Rift
Keep
Merchant
Logging Stand
Inquisition Camps
Sarhnia Camp
Highgrove Camp
Drakon's Camp
Tower Camp

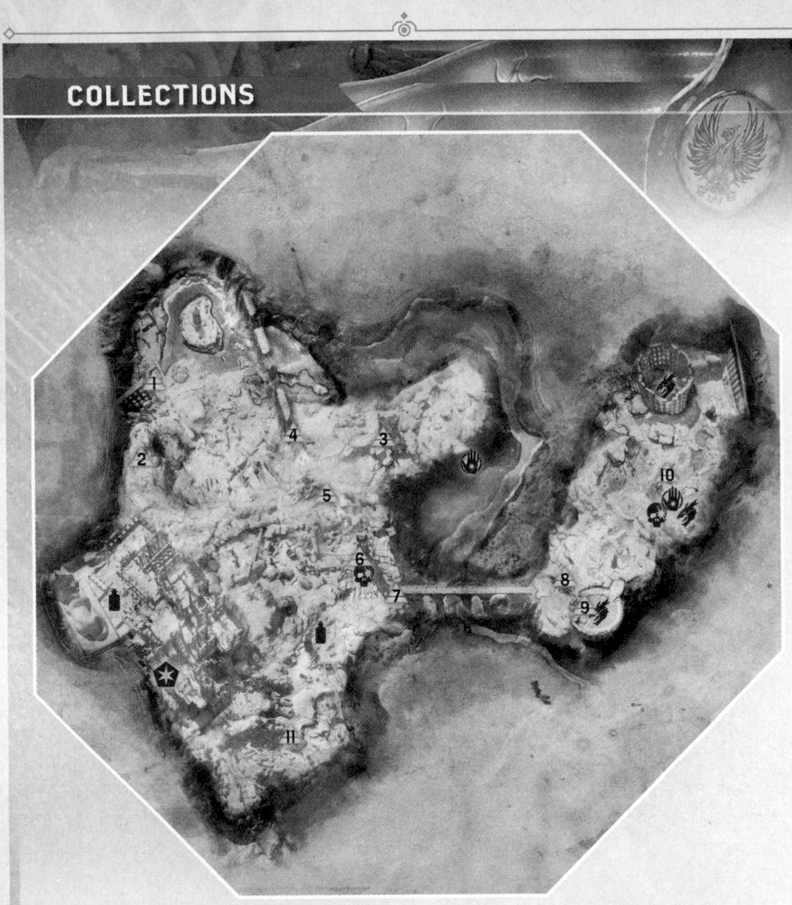

« Legend

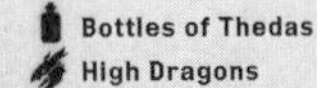

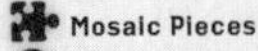

Bottles of Thedas

High Dragons

- Hivernal
- Kaltenzahn
- Highland Ravager

Landmarks/Points of Interest

1. Crystal Cascade, Frozen
2. Dalish Wolf Carving
3. Valeska's Watch
4. Ruined Highway
5. Deep Roads Entrance
6. Tower of Bone
7. Judicael's Crossing
8. Hector in His Time of Dying
9. Pools of the Sun
10. Leontine's Steward
11. Sahrnia Quarry

Mosaic Pieces

Oculara and Shards

Ocularum 1: Tower of Bone

- Ocularum +6 Shards

Ocularum 2: Judicael's Ring

- Ocularum +7 Shards

Glyphs

Solas Artifacts

FADE RIFTS

Pride demons, which you have not seen with regularity, become more commonplace at Emprise du Lion. In some ways, some Fade rifts can deal out a tougher battle than some of the major setpiece fights you face on the way to claiming Suledin Keep.

Fade Rift Details

Quest	Rifts	Total Power
Rifts on Frozen Water	1	2
Rifts at Elfsblood Tower	1	2
Rifts at Drakon's Cleft	2	4
Rifts in the Spring	2	4

REQUISITIONS

Requisition Quests

Requisition	Materials
Coat Requisition in the Emprise	5 Plush Fustian Velvet, 10 Snoufleur Skins
Shelter Requisition in the Emprise	1 Quarry Location, 1 Logging Stand
Bloodstone Survey in the Emprise	10 Bloodstones, 20 Dawnstones

AGENTS

MICHEL DE CHEVIN

Affiliated Quest: Call Me Imshael

Inquisition Perk: Michel de Chevin (Forces)

Speak to Michel outside the village to learn of Imshael. Defeat Imshael at Suledin Keep and then return to Michel, recruiting him as an agent of the Inquisition, serving under Cullen. If you encounter and defeat Imshael before speaking to Michel, he won't join the Inquisition.

MERCHANTS

Suledin Keep

Item	Cost
Weapons (Highlights)	
Knight-Commander Longbow	7383
Bloodied Wings	5598
Purity's Light	5167
Emperor Guard Blade	4306
Pirate Captain Cutlass	3691
Upgrades (Highlights)	
Sten Sword Grip	738
Narrow Greatsword Grip	738
Masterwork Wrapped One-Handed Haft	738
Masterwork Engraved Two-Handed Haft	738
Masterwork Battlemage Staff Grip	738
Masterwork Battlemage Staff Blade	738
Crafting Materials	
Blank Runestone	71

Item	Cost
Weapon Schematics	
Masterwork Skull Grip	2,238
Superb Cleansing Rune	7,294
Hossberg Twainer	6,545
First Enchanter Staff	6,545
Formation Shield	6,078
Dual-Curved Blade	3,273
Masterwork Ornate Two-Handed Haft	2,238
Templar Longbow	1,736
Inscribed Bearded Axe	1,537
Thick Longbow Grip	934
Tevinter Longsword Grip	934
Split Staff Grip	934
Solid Longbow Grip	934
Masterwork Ornate Dagger Grip	934
Inscribed Two-Handed Haft	934
Inscribed Staff Grip	934
Dense Dual-Blade Grip	934
Decorative Two-Handed Haft	934
Curved Greatsword Grip	934
Butterfly Greatsword Grip	934
Blunt Staff Edge	934
Battlemage Staff Blade	934
Balanced Longsword Grip	934
Armor Schematics	
Superior Inquisitor Hat	182

SIDE QUESTS (RECOMMENDED LEVEL 16-19 AND 19-22)

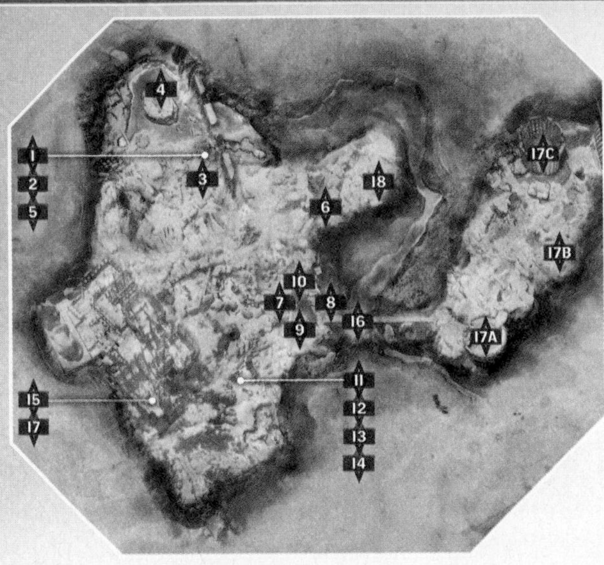

LEGEND

Level 16-19

1: The Corruption of Sahrnia
2: Mama's Ring
3: Call Me Imshael
4: Stalker
5: Take Back the Lion
6: Valeska's Watch
7: Capturing Suledin Keep
8: Sifting Through the Rubble
9: Turning the Tables
10: Rocky Rescue
11: Red Captors
12: Caged Confession
13: Words Not Hollow
14: Quarry Quandary

Level 19-22

15: They Shall Not Pass
16: Securing Safe Passage
17: Breeding Grounds
18: Dungeon: The Cradle of Sulevin

1: THE CORRUPTION OF SAHRNIA

Quest Giver: Scout Harding

Description: The people of Sahrnia are cornered by the elements and by the red templars/mages that have overtaken the region.

Requirements: Arrive in Emprise du Lion for the first time.

Reward: 331 XP, 150 Influence

Objectives:

- Speak with the townspeople about what can be done.

Throughout the battered town, there are a number of townsfolk to visit with and quests to start. However, one of the most important people to speak with is Mistress Poulin. She is the head of the town, and she's also partly reponsible for what has happened to it. She sold her quarry to your enemies out of desperation, and now they have gone back on their promises and are attacking the town to take more people. You have seen by now what the enemy is using red lyrium for. After you finish speaking with Mistress Poulin, you are given the side quest Take Back the Lion. It is an extensive, multi-part side quest that also encompasses other quests in this locale.

2: MAMA'S RING

Quest Giver: Granny Mae in Sarhnia

Description: An elderly woman left an heirloom ring behind when she was forced out of her home by the red templars/ mages.

Requirements: Enter Sarhnia for the first time.

Reward: 331 XP, 150 Influence

Objectives:

- Find the ring.
- Return the ring to its rightful owner.

An old woman in Sarhnia, clearly in a damaged mental state, laments the loss of a family keepsake ring. It's found in the ruins close to to the Tower of Bone, but you're not going to get there without heavy fighting at first. After claiming the tower, head east over a wooden bridge to enter the ruins where the ring was lost. After dealing with some of Corypheus's troops, you can freely search the area. When you do locate the ring, bring it back to the old woman to complete the quest.

3: CALL ME IMSHAEL

Quest Giver: Michel de Chevin

Description: Ser Michel spoke of a demon named Imshael that has taken up residence in Suledin Keep. Michel has made it his mission to track down and kill this demon.

Requirements: Speak with Ser Michel in Sahrnia.

Reward: 1,324 XP, 600 Influence, 2 Power

Objectives:

- Find Imshael.
- Inform Michel of Imshael's demise.

You find Ser Michel standing guard in front of Sarhnia, a passing swordsman with whom Vivienne is acquainted. He has decided to stand as one of Sarhnia's protectors. He seeks a demon that calls itself Imshael. However, there is no way for him to reach the demon, as Suledin Keep is the strongpoint for all of Corypheus's forces in Emprise du Lion.

NOTE It is possible to not speak with Ser Michel at Sarhnia. In that case, you will find him at the front gates of the long road leading to Suledin Keep, fighting the red templars alone.

When you first arrive at Emprise du Lion, there is simply no easy way to reach the keep to confront Imshael. You'd have to fight through extensive numbers of red templar just to get to the keep itself, and then you must confront the demon after all of that fighting. Simply put, it will not be easy to reach Imshael.

NOTE As the battle with Imshael takes place during a separate quest, any tips related to the actual combat can be found in the Capturing Suledin Keep quest section.

After you deal with Imshael, return to Sahrnia with the news. Michel is somewhat put off by your relatively effortless attempts to corner and defeat the demon after spending so much time on the hunt himself, but he is grateful regardless. You are then able to recruit Michel to be an agent of the Inquisition.

CAUTION If you made a deal with Imshael, Ser Michel pays the price for it. You will find him dead near Sarhnia, with a note left by Imshael. Imshael apparently decided to take care of loose ends first. You can't recruit a dead man into the Inquisition, so consider your choice carefully!

> 4: STALKER

Quest Giver: A journal found near Elfsblood Tower

Description: A hunter came through here, obsessively stalking some elusive prey.

Requirements: Available upon entering Emprise du Lion

Reward: 331 XP, 150 Influence

Objectives:

- Find the ruins mentioned in the hunter's note.

TIP The journal is found near Elfsblood Tower, and the tower can be unlocked by rogues enhanced with the Deft Hands, Fine Tools Inquisition perk. It's worth looking inside the tower for the weapon you discover at the top.

The hunter clearly has an issue with boundaries. If you travel north from his camp at Elfsblood Tower to the elven ruins, you will find his target's camp, long abandoned. She has left a note for the stalker, informing him that she's skipped the restraining order and gone straight to "Kill on sight." The quest is complete, but there's no other sign of the hunter or his prey...

> 5: TAKE BACK THE LION

Quest Giver: Mistress Poulin

Description: Mistress Poulin sold her quarry to the red templars/mages, who have now occupied much of the Emprise du Lion. Advance into the region's heart to learn why.

Requirements: Available after speaking with Mistress Poulin

Reward: 2,649 XP, 2,000 Influence, 3 Power

Objectives:

- Wipe out the red templars/mages at Highgrove.
- Claim Highgrove for the Inquisition.
- Wipe out the red templars/mages at Drakon's Rise.
- Claim Drakon's Rise for the Inquisition.
- Wipe out the red templars/mages at the Tower of Bone.
- Claim the Tower of Bone for the Inquisition.

This quest involves "leapfrogging" from one campsite to the next, taking on Corypheus's forces as you go. Expect to do a lot of fighting, so don't skimp on restoring your potion inventory at every camp you set up.

The first camp is not far from Sahrnia, and it should be a good indication of what to expect from the enemy. Expect all varieties of red templar/mage combatants throughout this side quest, but just because you start seeing more exotic threats on the field doesn't mean you should neglect killing archers or prowlers as quickly as you can. Send a rogue of your own after any marksmen, while the rest of the party deals with melee enemies.

TIP It may help to have a warrior set up to use a sword and shield be your tank for this mission, as the sheer number of enemies can quickly overwhelm the less armored classes.

After clearing an enemy position, you're prompted to set up camp. This will help you replenish supplies and switch your party around as needed.

After claiming Highgrove, leave the camp through Alphonse's Passage to the north, fighting your way past more enemies and claiming a landmark. Your next target is Drakon's Rise, another strongpoint that Corypheus's forces are trying to hold down against your onslaught. Their desperation should become apparent at this point, from both the numbers they are throwing at you and the notes you find in their camp once they have been defeated.

The Tower of Bone is your next target, but the hike to it is made more difficult by the presence of Fade rifts. They're part of the Rifts at Drakon's Cleft quest, and it's worth knocking these out of the way to avoid extra backtracking in the future.

NOTE A Detour

As you continue toward the Tower of Bone, you encounter an abandoned campsite that once belonged to Grey Wardens. They were apparently the guards of a nearby dwarven ruin. Locate the key at this camp to start the Valeska's Watch side quest.

6: VALESKA'S WATCH

Quest Giver: Find the key to enter the dwarven ruins.

Description: An old key, found in Emprise du Lion and shaped vaguely like a griffon, has the words "Valeska's Watch" scratched into its face.

Requirements: Locate the key to the ruins.

Reward: 331 XP, 150 Influence

Objectives:

- Enter Valeska's Watch.

It is a simple enough quest. Find the key on a corpse at the abandoned camp, unlock the door to the dwarven ruins, and the quest is automatically completed. However, for those willing to press forward through the darkspawn gathered in these ruins, there is useful treasure, along with plenty of experience for the hardy adventurer.

NOTE More of Blackwall's Memories of the Grey quest can be resolved by exploring Valeska's Watch.

The first chamber, just beyond the landmark, is filled with ghouls. Hurlocks are on the upper-level ledges surrounding the area, and they have clean lines of sight on anyone fighting in the center of the room. Charging in recklessly means you'll just get picked off with arrows from the hurlocks.

As you're fighting off the first wave, more ghouls and hurlocks come pouring in through a door on the west side of the room. They are led by a hurlock alpha. Now might be a good time to drop your Mark of the Rift if it's ready, along with any major focus abilities other party members might have!

After clearing out this first room, collect your spoils and loot any chests you find, then proceed deeper into the watch. Don't miss the locked door that a rogue can pick!

In the lowest parts of the watch is another hurlock alpha, flanked by two lesser hurlocks. As you fight them, ghouls stream up from the massive chasm at the center of this final chamber. Again, if Mark of the Rift is ready, this is an excellent opportunity to take pressure off your party! Once you kill the hurlock alpha, the reinforcements cease, and you can seal the chasm with a mage. Make a sweep of this last room to claim another landmark and some more loot before you leave this dreadful place behind.

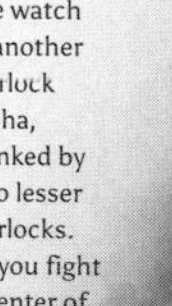

Take Back the Lion Continued...

The gate before you enter the Tower of Bone region is the first line of defense the enemy has set up. Breaking through them and continuing south, you'll come across a much larger second group at the base of the tower. There's enough clutter in the area that it can be easy to lose ranged attackers in the chaos, so keep an eye on your mini-map, lest you get sniped to oblivion.

With the base of the tower cleared, you'll have to climb up a set of wooden walkways to reach the campsite, which will have another set of defenders waiting for you. Winning this battle allows you to claim the Tower of Bone and complete this quest!

NOTE Search the newly established camp and the area surrounding the Tower of Bone. There are additional quests to unlock that can be done as you advance on Suledin Keep or are within the general vicinity of the keep.

7: CAPTURING SULEDIN KEEP

Quest Giver: Quest is given as soon as you claim the Tower of Bone.

Description: The red templars/mages have been pushed back to the long-abandoned Suledin Keep. If they lose this ancient elven fortress, their grip on the region will be severely weakened.

Requirements: Complete the quest Take Back the Lion.

Reward: Suledin Keep falls under Inquisition control.

Objectives:

- Travel to Suledin Keep.
- Claim the keep for the Inquisition.

Having lost every outpost from Highgrove up to the Tower of Bone, Corypheus's chosen army has effectively been pushed out of much of Emprise du Lion. Now it is time to go for the jugular! Make sure you are fully stocked with potions. The fighting along the winding paths to reach the top of the keep is going to test your ability to maintain your resources through many battles.

The approach to Suledin Keep begins by busting through a wooden gate. Of course, it is protected by a squad of red templar/mages. More enemies await inside the first courtyard. As the main route toward the top of the keep continues, you will pass cages filled with giants that have been experimented on with red lyrium. You can open these cages with a rogue to check for loot.

From the cages, keep winding south, batting aside any hostile groups as you meet them. Watch for your mini-map to start pinging. There's a bottle of Thedas, Abyssal Peach, hanging out on a wall in the snowy forest section. Reaching it takes some clever scaling of the nearby terrain.

Not far from the bottle is a large contingent of red templars/mages protecting a gap in the walls of the keep. Inside is an infected giant, much stronger than the ones found in Emerald Graves thanks to red lyrium experimentation. Try not to take all of these enemies on at once, if you can help it. Go for the standard troops first, then eliminate the infected giant.

Before you enter the paddock the giant was in, take the time to explore the paths leading away from its cage. You can find some extra loot in the side areas, and an alternative route that will take you closer to the heart of the keep. Or, you can skip that and keep following the stairs inside the giant paddock upward.

After several sets of stairs, there's another clearing where hostiles are gathered. Take the next set of stairs behind those goons to the south and pass through the doors. You arrive in another large courtyard with yet another group of enemies lying in wait.

If you've not strayed from your route, you will eventually encounter a potion supply cache. Take this time to save and take a breather: You're about to face Imshael, the demon that Michel de Chevin warned you about back in Sahrnia.

Imshael is a smooth talker. He attempts to negotiate with you with three offers: riches, power, or virgins. You can also end the conversation early by attacking him outright, before he even provides the options!

If you ask for virgins, Imshael complains that he can't find any. Lazy demon. If you ask for riches, he will bestow upon you expensive valuables that you can sell for a tidy profit. If you seek power, Imshael grants you an amulet of power, pure spirit essence, and a unique warrior shield: the March of the Everlasting. However, accepting this deal has consequences. Imshael runs free, and as he leaves Emprise du Lion, he will murder Ser Michel, making it impossible to recruit the brave soldier into the Inquisition.

When the fight begins, Imshael shifts into a demonic form, summoning fearlings and the assistance of nearby red templars/mages. As Imshael grows weaker, he will shift into different forms, such as that of a rage demon and finally a pride demon. While he's got a lot of health, and he starts with assistance, once you've got him alone, it's only a matter of time for a well-equipped party to put him down.

After killing Imshael, you are able to get through a magic barrier that had prevented you from claiming the keep. At the top of the final stairwell, a dying soldier greets you. If you speak to him in his final moments, you can learn more about the true madness behind Imshael's work with the red lyrium. Claim the keep for the inquisition to complete the quest complete.

8: SIFTING THROUGH THE RUBBLE

Quest Giver: A note found in the ruins east of the Tower of Bone

Description: A fisherman was near Judicael's Crossing when the red templars/mages brought the bridge down. He thought he saw something glimmering in the rubble but was too scared to investigate, worried the red templars/mages might spot him.

Requirements: Take Back the Lion completed

Reward: 331 XP, 150 Influence

Objectives:

- Find what was glimmering in the rubble.

To reach the treasure mentioned in the notes, you need to repair Judicael's Crossing. Return to Skyhold and complete the war table mission to repair the bridge and open a new part of Emprise du Lion. There are complications, however. Corypheus's forces have made the place unsafe to travel through. More worrying are the high dragons spotted flying over the Tevinter ruins.

Fortunately, you don't have to go dragon hunting just yet. Once the bridge is repaired, make your way across, then investigate the ground on the north side of the bridge, specifically a small pile of bricks in the snow. Take what you find in the rubble to complete the quest.

9: TURNING THE TABLES

Quest Giver: Diary found in the ruins east of the Tower of Bone

Description: A note at an abandoned camp, left by a huntress, suggests she is being tracked by a former lover and intends to turn the tables on him.

Requirements: Reach the note after claiming the Tower of Bone.

Reward: 331 XP, 150 Influence

Objectives:

- Learn her next move.

The huntress that was being stalked made camp within the Sahrnia Quarry region, hidden among the trees. Recover her journal at this camp to complete the quest.

10: ROCKY RESCUE

Quest Giver: Papers found at the Tower of Bone

Description: Mistress Poulin said the red templars/mages "took workers" from the town. They may be held captive somewhere in the quarry.

Requirements: Complete Take Back the Lion.

Reward: 1,324 XP, 600 Influence, 2 Power

Objectives:

- Search the quarry.
- Free seven villagers.

Rescuing the villagers is a simple matter of finding their cages and unlocking them. However, Corypheus's troops will put up a terrible resistance to deny you this. Make sure you enter the quarry fully stocked on supplies, since you will you be encountering resistance every step of the way.

TIP Check the guard towers near the quarry's main entrance. A rogue must unlock them, but they contain some goods and a bottle of Thedas: Legacy White Shear.

I1: RED CAPTORS

Quest Giver: Kill a red templar/mage lieutenant.

Description: The red templars/mages captured townspeople to mine the quarry in the heart of Emprise du Lion.

Requirements: Kill one of the designated enemy officers to start the quest.

Reward: 1,324 XP, 600 Influence, 2 Power

Objectives:

- Rid the quarry of five red templars/mages.

As you fight through the enemy forces guarding the quarry, you'll encounter particularly aggressive commanders among their number. Killing one starts you on the quest to hunt down all five lieutenants running the show here at the quarry.

I2: CAGED CONFESSION

Quest Giver: A note found within the quarry

Description: After Louis was captured by the red templars/mages, he wrote a note confessing to the murder of his wife's brother, Garde.

Requirements: Available at the start of Emprise du Lion

Reward: 331 XP, 150 Influence

Objectives:

- Return to Sahrnia with Louis's note.
- Give the confession to Louis to keep his secret.
- Give the confession to Linette to reveal what really happened to her brother.

When you return to Sahrnia to deliver the letter, you discover that Louis, author of this note, is alive and well, living with his wife in the ruins of the town. Linette's brother, Garde, has gone missing, and the letter Louis wrote contains the truth of his fate. She is unaware of this, and Louis would would prefer to keep it that way. You can either shatter her faith in Louis or allow the man to continue living his lie.

I3: WORDS NOT HOLLOW

Quest Giver: Dying woman in the Sahrnia quarry

Description: A woman, infected by red lyrium and unable to walk, has asked for a letter to her husband to be placed in a hollow tree by the river.

Requirements: Find the woman in Sahrnia Quarry.

Reward: 331 XP, 150 Influence

Objectives:

- Place the woman's letter in the hollow of a marked tree by the river.

You find the dying woman next to one of the cages filled with prisoners. She wants you to deliver a letter to a spot indicated on your quest map, quite close to the town of Sahrnia. Compared to everything else you've done in Emprise du Lion, this is refreshingly simple.

TIP

A master frost rune schematic can be found in the northern section of the Sahrnia quarry.

> 14: QUARRY QUANDARY

Quest Giver: Orders found in the quarry

Description: Mistress Poulin confessed to selling her family quarry to the red templars/mages. But what would they want with a quarry?

Requirements: Find the letter in the quarry.

Reward: 331 XP, 150 Influence

Objectives:

- Speak with Mistress Poulin.

According to documents found in the quarry, it's apparent that Mistress Poulin was collaborating with the enemy, providing villagers she picked herself for the red lyrium operation to keep moving forward. But when you confront her, she argues that had she not collaborated in some way, she would be dead, as would every villager. Regardless of how you respond, this quest is complete...but justice has not been served. You may preside over her fate at Skyhold after her fellow villagers turn her in to the Inquisition.

> 15: THEY SHALL NOT PASS

Quest Giver: Baron Edouard Desjardins

Description: Judicael's Crossing has been destroyed, presumably by the red templars, to restrict access into the region.

Requirements: Capture Suledin Keep.

Reward: 331 XP, 150 Influence

Objectives:

- Inspect the bridge to see if it can be repaired.

After capturing Suledin Keep, the Inquisition moves in with fresh troops, and administration of the keep itself is left to Baron Edouard Desjardins. He's got a lot on his mind, and one of those problems is the impassable bridge of Judicael's Crossing. If you haven't already repaired the bridge, you can speak with him and he will point you in its direction. Go there and claim the bridge, then return to Skyhold and use the war table to send people out to Emprise du Lion to fix the bridge. Once the bridge is complete, you can cross it to complete the quest.

> 16: SECURING SAFE PASSAGE

Quest Giver: Quest starts as soon as you repair Judicael's Crossing.

Description: Now that Judicael's Crossing is rebuilt, the road must be secured to allow free travel in and out of the area. There are abandoned towers along the road that, if secured, may be ideal for keeping watch.

Requirements: Repair Judicael's Crossing.

Reward: 5076 XP, 600 Influence, 2 Power

Objectives:

- Secure the first tower.
- Claim the first tower for the Inquisition.
- Secure the second tower.
- Claim the second tower for the Inquisition.
- Secure the third tower.
- Claim the third tower for the Inquisition.

There are three guard towers in the Pools of the Sun region that are currently occupied by Corypheus's troops. Simply wipe out these enemies, then claim the towers to turn them over to the Inquisition.

> 17: BREEDING GROUNDS

Quest Giver: Baron Edouard Desjardins

Description: As if the red templar/mage occupation isn't enough, dragons have moved into the region. So far, only a few high dragons have been spotted: a Hivernal, a Kaltenzahn, and a Highland Ravager. But if they breed, the presence of these unique and powerful beasts could prove an even greater threat to the local population than the templars/mages.

Requirements: Capture Suledin Keep and speak with the baron.

Reward: 1,324 XP, 600 Influence, 2 Power

Objectives:

- Slay the Highland Ravager.
- Slay the Kaltenzahn.
- Slay the Hivernal.

It's only three high dragons. What could possibly go wrong?!

If you've been hunting high dragons before coming to Emprise du Lion, you already have a fair idea of what to expect from these powerful creatures. However, each one of these dragons has some unique capabilities that you should be ready to deal with.

High Dragon: The Hivernal

Recommended Level: 19+

Recommended Party Composition: One warrior (sword and shield), one rogue, two mages (armed with fire damage staves)

Alternative Party Composition: Two warriors (sword and shield, two-handed weapon), two mages (armed with fire damage staves)

The first of two cold-typed high dragons in this locale, the Hivernal is the easiest target in relative terms. She will still destroy you if you don't prepare. Any cold protection you can bring is of high value. Ideally, your mages should have their most powerful fire staff equipped, with a full battery of fire spells for offense, while they maintain your emergency focus Heal and shielding spells.

In addition to all the usual high dragon melee attacks, the Hivernal uses her ice breath to devastating effect, singling out a party member for a high-damage puff that can also freeze them entirely, making a follow-up melee strike a day ruiner. The Hivernal can also produce a icy wind barrier that causes damage to party members within it and deflects any ranged attacks.

After sustaining a certain amount of damage, the Hivernal takes flight, sweeping around the arena and trying to pelt the party with ice blasts. She also occasionally swoops over the arena while breathing a trail of ice as it passes overhead. This can be highly lethal, so keep your eyes on the Hivernal and stay on the move.

As the fight progresses, the Hivernal can buff itself with a full guard bar. This can lengthen the fight considerably if you do not have abilities that can do additional damage to guard.

High Dragon: The Kaltenzahn

A major threat to your survival in this fight is the Kaltenzahn's ability to pull the entire party into melee range by flapping her wings. Ranged characters suffer the most from this, as anyone caught outside the "field" that appears around the dragon will take damage until they are inside the Kaltenzahn's melee range. Because of this we recommend a melee-heavy party, ideally with weapons enchanted with fire runes. One mage should be present, to shield and revive party members or provide an emergency focus ability Heal for the whole party.

Recommended Level: 21+

Recommended Party Composition: Two warriors (sword and shield), one rogue, one mage (armed with fire damage staff)

Alternative Party Composition: Three warriors (sword and shield, two-handed weapon), one mage (armed with fire damage staves)

The Kaltenzahn is larger and tougher than the Hivernal. She shares some similarities: untauntable, stunning roar, and the ability to buff herself with a full guard bar. Your preparations should be similar: cold protection, weapons that can cause fire damage, fire-based skills at the ready. Try to come with your Inquisitor's Mark of the Rift ready to be used.

At around half health, the Kaltenzahn begins roaring for help from dragonlings, which will start to put a serious amount of pressure on your party's survivability. The roars that summon the dragonlings also stun your party, so if you fail to clear out each wave before new ones arrive, you can quickly be overwhelmed. During this phase of the fight you want to have Mark of the Rift ready. If you can pull off a knockdown of the dragon, drop Mark of the Rift right on the center of her body to pile on the damage. This last phase of the fight is a sprint: If you can't kill her before you run out of extra healing potions, you'll either need to play almost flawlessly to avoid taking damage, or be prepared to try again.

The Kaltenzahn's cold breath works a bit differently, as it is a continuous stream that leaves formations of ice on the ground for a short amount of time, slowing characters caught in it, while still causing damage. The dragon can also spit ice balls at targets for heavy damage, and often tries to do this if all possible targets are outside of range for its attacks. She can also spit ice at you while she flies around the battlefield. The Kaltenzahn can also perch herself atop part of the ruins on the western side of the arena, shooting more ice blasts at the party.

High Dragon: The Highland Ravager

Recommended Level: 22+

Recommended Party Composition: One warrior (sword and shield), one rogue, two mages (armed with frost damage staves)

Alternative Party Composition: Two warriors (sword and shield, two-handed weapon), two mages (armed with frost damage staves)

The Highland Ravager begins this battle asleep, a good chance for you to get into position to start the attack. Unlike the last two high dragons you've fought here, this one is based around the fire element. Switch out your weapons to cause cold damage if you can, and get yourself some fire resistance! Because the Highland Ravager starts out asleep, it's a good plan for your Inquisitor to drop a Mark of the Rift right on top of Sleeping Beauty here. If you've leveled up your focus through the Forces Inquisition perks, you can easily take out almost a third of her life before the fight can really get going!

As the strongest of the three high dragons, the Ravager's melee attacks are the most dangerous. Rogues should be prepared to flee out of range at any time, and warriors may be better served using sword and shield to better protect themselves. Mages should stay far away and try to keep melee fighters shielded as often as possible.

Like the other two high dragons, the Ravager can use her wings to create a dangerous wind barrier. This one causes damage to anyone in close range to the dragon, which is why it isn't a bad idea to bring two mages to the fight. They can stay well outside of range of this ability, while still keeping the pressure on from afar with cold magic. You will have to babysit them a bit, because the Ravager likes to leap around the arena.

The Highland Ravager can breathe streams of fire at a swath of ground in front of her, and when she rears back with a shout, fire circles appear on the ground. When she slams her forelegs back down, the circles erupt into flames. Don't be in a circle when that happens.

Like the Kaltenzahn, the Highland Ravager calls in dragonlings at about the halfway point of her health. Try to bring down the dragonlings quickly, so you don't get overwhelmed should the Ravager use a stunning roar to freeze your party defenselessly in place.

It should be noted that the arena you fight the Highland Ravager in is the smallest of all three battle locations. This can make getting away from the fire breath or wind barrier difficult if it's in the center of the arena.

If you manage to defeat all three high dragons, the Breeding Grounds quest will be complete!

> 18: DUNGEON: THE CRADLE OF SULEVIN

An ancient temple that is said to hold the finest blade ever produced by elven hands, the Cradle of Sulevin is where the storied blade was apparently hidden away. Because it was relegated to myth and the story around the blade was corrupted and twisted over the centuries, modern elves scarcely believe the blade actually existed. However, some Dalish continue to pursue this weapon, in hopes of retaining yet another part of elven lore.

North of Drakon's Tower, you'll find a primeval red lyrium vein that can be destroyed for the Varric's Seeing Red quest. A short distance north from that vein is a camp near the cliff's edge. You find a journal on one of the elven corpses that contains information on the Cradle of Sulevin. This prompts you to return to Skyhold and use the war table to send out scouts to find the location of this temple. You can then select it as a location to visit on your world map.

Ruined Blade

Quest Giver: A journal found on dead elves in Emprise du Lion

Description: There is a legendary elven sword rumored to be found within an overgrown ruin on the edge of the Arbor Wilds.

Requirements: Available as soon as you reach the journal

Reward: 10,152 XP, 2,000 Influence, 3 Power

Objectives:

- Find the Cradle of Sulevin at the war table (10 power required).
- Collect the shattered pieces of the Sulevin Sword.
- Recover four sword pieces.
- Bring the pieces of the sword to someone who can repair it.

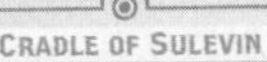

Stairlight Chambers

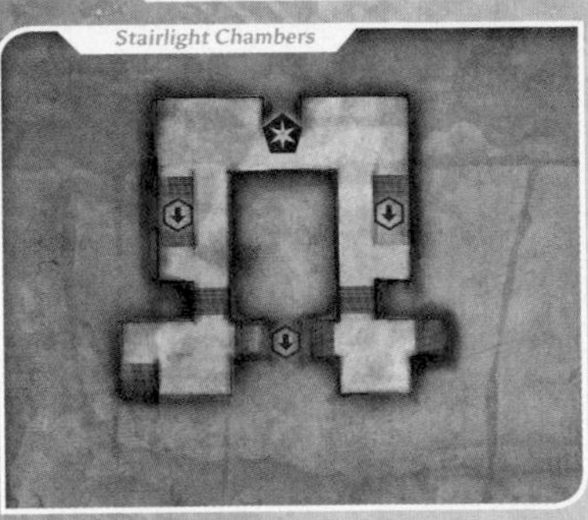

Hallowed Passageway

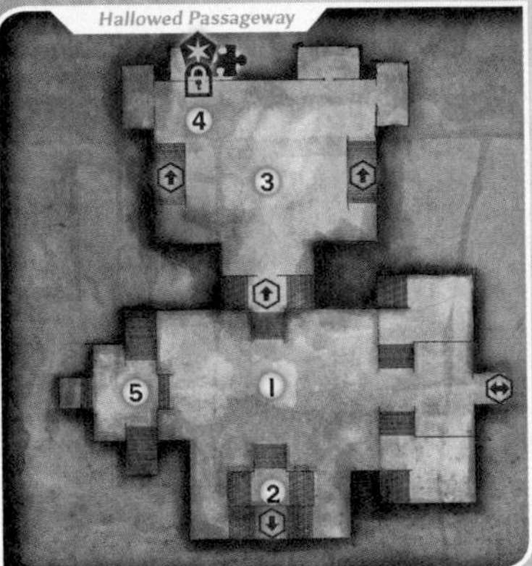

Sanctuary of the Dead

LEGEND

- Entrance/Exit
- Veilfire
- Locked Door
- Mosaic Piece
- to Upper Area
- to Lower Area

1. You begin in the Hallowed Passageway, a short distance away from one of the altars containing a sword piece. Grab a nearby veilfire torch and return to the altar. This causes a revenant to appear. After defeating it, you can loot one of the sword pieces from the remains.

2. To the left of the first altar is a stairwell that leads down to the Sanctuary of the Dead. Take the next stairwell that leads you deeper underground, light the up the area using a veilfire torch, and proceed toward the next altar. Bringing the torch to the altar calls out a second revenant and a swarm of undead. After clearing out the enemy and retrieving the sword piece, be sure to sweep the chamber to collect the piles of gold left lying around.

3. Lighting the altar in the Starlight Chambers brings out another revenant and even more undead.

4. There's lots of loot to find throughout the Cradle of Sulevin, and among it all is a locked door in the Starlight Chambers, on the northern wall of the first floor. You need Deft Hands, Fine Tools to open it. Inside you'll find a mosaic piece for the Freed Are Slaves set and a superb spirit rune schematic on one of the walls. Bring a veilfire torch!

5. At the western end of the Hallowed Passageway is a fourth altar, which summons a final revenant/undead group to put down. With all four sword pieces recovered, you can return to Skyhold to complete the quest, but make a thorough sweep of the temple grounds. There are a lot of chests to pick through and a lot of loot to grab!

With all four sword pieces in hand, go to Dagna at Skyhold. She will enthusiastically use those sword pieces to create a powerful two-handed sword, the Sulevin Blade. It requires the user to be at level 20, but rest assured the warrior using it will hit like a high dragon.

THE HISSING WASTES

The Hissing Wastes is a stretch of sandy desert north of the Western Approach, a lonely place where the wildlife is hungry and hostile. Among the hungriest and most hostile are the dragons that make their nests here. The rare person wandering into the wastes is either hunting prized beasts or hoping to uncover evidence of a long-vanished civilization in the dunes.

LOCALE SUMMARY

Scouting Cost: 20 Power

The Hissing Wastes are brutal, and the wildlife has no sympathy for anyone who is unprepared. The wastes are massive, easily the largest locale you've visited across all of Thedas. They are also home to dwarven ruins, filled with things that the Venatori and the red templars want. This means that the Inquisition wants them even more.

While there are few quests in the Hissing Wastes compared the neighboring Western Approach, the daunting size of the place makes getting around time-consuming, even on the fastest of mounts. Even then, expect to get unseated by the local wildlife, and expect to do a lot of fighting. Despite the looks, the wastes are a Venatori stronghold for all intents and purposes, and they are on the lookout for you specifically.

> CRAFTING MATERIALS

Common Materials:

- Elfroot
- Vandal Aria
- Serpentstone

Rare Materials:

- Amrita Vein
- Ghoul's Beard
- Zangolia
- Dragonthorn
- Witherstalk
- Lazurite
- Volcanic Aurum

Unique Materials:

- Nevarrite

> COLLECTIONS

- Astrariums: 0
- Bottles of Thedas: 3
- High Dragons: 1
- Landmarks: 9
- Mosaic Pieces: 12
- Glyphs: 1
- Shards: 8
- Treasure Maps: 6
- Logging Stands: 2
- Quarries: 2

LOCALE MAP

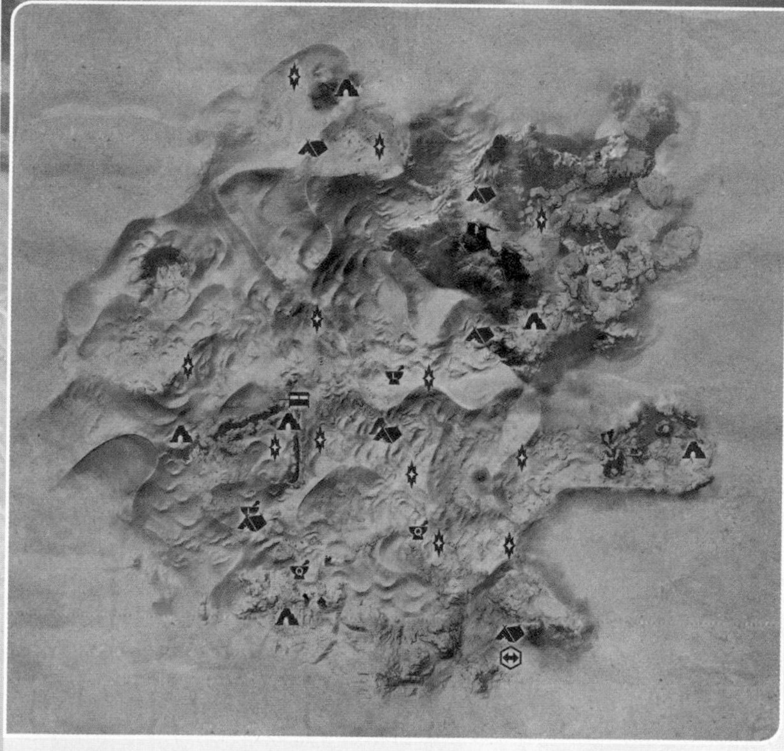

Legend

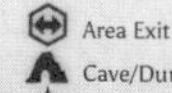

Area Exit

Cave/Dungeon

Fade Rift

Merchant

Logging Stand

Quarry

Inquisition Camps

- The Cove Camp
- Mountain Fortress Camp
- Sand Crags Camp
- Logging Camp
- The Canyon Camp
- Sunstop Mountain Camp
- Statue Camp

COLLECTIONS

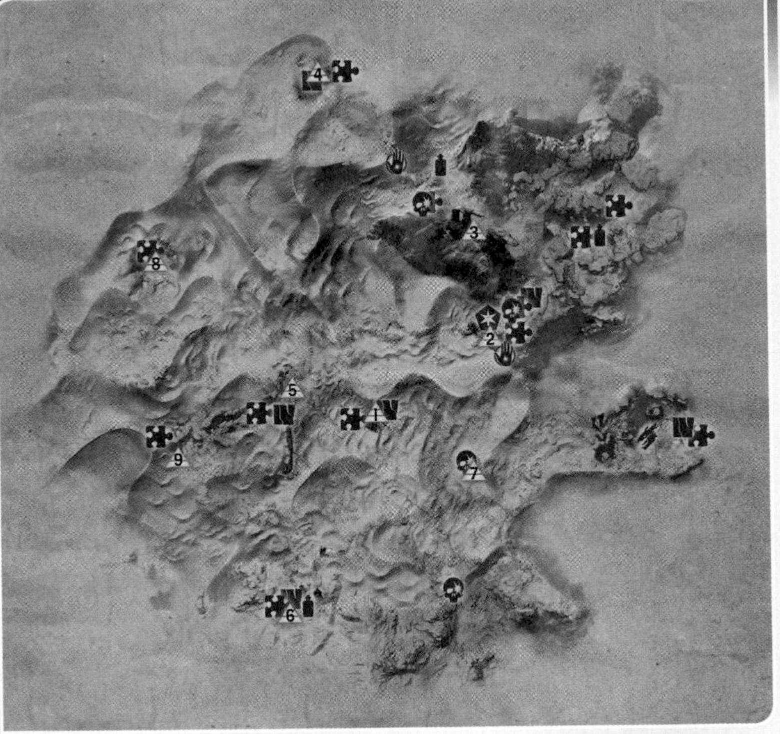

Legend

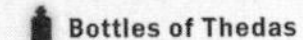

- **Bottles of Thedas**
- **High Dragon**
  - Sandy Howler
- **Landmarks/Points of Interest**
  1. The Four Pillars
  2. Blocked Doorway
  3. Stone Over Sky
  4. The Colossus of Orlais
  5. Canyon Overlook
  6. The Empty Square
  7. Lonely Light
  8. The Oasis
  9. Venatori Canyon Camp
- **Mosaic Pieces**
- **Oculara and Shards**
  - **Ocularum 1: Rock Top Ridge**
    - Ocularum +1 Shard
  - **Ocularum 2: Sunstop Mountains**
    - Ocularum +3 Shards
  - **Ocularum 3: The Sand Crags**
    - Ocularum +2 Shards
  - **Ocularum 4: The Cove**
    - Ocularum +2 Shards
- **Glyphs**
- **Treasure Maps**
- **Solas Artifacts**

FADE RIFTS

Greater terrors, pride demons, and despair demons are commonplace with every wave. Whatever's happening in the Fade to call out to demons, it is at its worst here. Bringing two mages in a party is not a bad idea at all, if only to dispel more demons before they can fully manifest.

Fade Rift Details

Quest	Rifts	Total Power
Rifts near the Cove	3	6
Rifts near the Sand Crags	3	6
Rifts at the Sunstop Mountains	3	6

MERCHANTS

Betyar's Canyon Market

Item	Cost
Armor (Highlights)	
Helm of the Drasca	6,103
Intense Felandaris Vitaar	2,953
Skirmisher Hat	1,291
Upgrades (Highlights)	
Superior Prowler Armor Legs	2,953
Superior Battlemaster Armor Legs	2,953
Superior Battlemage Armor Legs	2,953
Superior Prowler Mail Arms	738
Superior Prowler Coat Legs	738
Superior Battlemaster Mail Legs	738
Superior Battlemaster Mail Arms	738
Superior Battlemage Mail Legs	738
Superior Battlemage Mail Arms	738
Crafting Material	
Blank Runestone	71
Weapon Schematics	
Superb Demon-Slaying Rune	7,294

Item	Cost
Armor Schematics	
Superior Venatori Helmet	1,279
Templar Armor	9,044
Dalish Scout Armor	9,044
Sturdy Prowler Armor	8,183
Sturdy Battlemaster Armor	8,183
Sturdy Battlemage Armor	8,183
Prowler Armor	3,839
Battlemaster Armor	3,839
Battlemage Armor	3,839
Prowler Armor Legs	934
Prowler Armor Arms	934
Battlemaster Armor Legs	934
Battlemaster Armor Arms	934
Battlemage Armor Legs	934
Battlemage Armor Arms	934

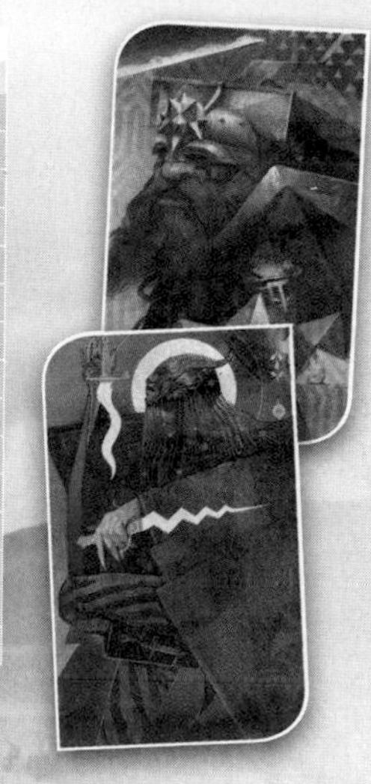

REQUISITIONS

Requisition Quests

Requisition	Materials
Artifact Requisition in the Wastes	1 Dwarven Toy Soldier, 1 Dwarven Dragon Statuette, 1 Dwarven Vase, 1 Dwarven Plate
Relief Requisition in the Wastes	20 Nevarrite, 10 Vandal Aria

SIDE QUESTS (RECOMMENDED LEVEL 19-23)

LEGEND

1: Holding the Hissing Wastes
2: Field of Bones
3: Let's Slay the Beast
4: Notes on the Wastes
5: Sand and Ruin
6: The Tomb of Fairel
7: High Dragon: The Sandy Howler

1: HOLDING THE HISSING WASTES

Quest Giver: Scout Harding

Description: Establish camps to hold the Hissing Wastes and support Inquisition activity in the region.

Requirements: Available when you arrive in the Hissing Wastes

Reward: 200 Influence and 1 Power per camp, except for the starting camp

Objectives:

- Establish seven camps.

Scout Harding says that the wastelands are vast, and she's not joking. A brief look at the map suggests that many of the camps are packed close together. The map doesn't quite convey the real size of this place. Expect to be on horseback often and for long periods of time, even with all the camps established. Having them taken care of early in your travels through the wastes can save you a lot of time.

2: FIELD OF BONES

Quest Giver: Journal found near the Four Pillars landmark

Description: A patrol has gone missing in the bone fields between the Canyon Camp and the Four Pillars.

Requirements: Available upon entering the Hissing Wastes

Reward: 331 XP, 150 Influence

Objectives:

- Locate the missing patrol.

Near the Four Pillars landmark, you set up one of the seven camps of the region and explore a sand-covered tomb. Near the camp, you can find a note that describes a missing Venatori patrol. It also warns of spiders in the region where they were assigned.

When you do reach the patrol's location, they are long dead, and the field is dominated by bones, corpses, and poison spiders. Always with the spiders!

Put them down, then search around the cage the soldiers had been guarding. It's empty, but you can find a chest next to it. Taking its contents completes the quest.

3: LET'S SLAY THE BEAST

Quest Giver: Hunter

Description: Hunting is a popular pastime in the often desolate Hissing Wastes. While varghests in particular are prized, there are rumors of a rarer breed out there, one legendary varghest known for its intimidating stature. Any hunter able to slay it would surely earn respect.

Requirements: Speak with the hunter to start the quest, or go to the Golden Oasis and slay the varghest.

Reward: 5,076 XP, 600 Influence, 2 Power

Objectives:

- Find and kill a legendary beast.

The friendly hunter met wandering the wastes has no real agenda but to pass advice to travelers and make money off valuable materials found while on the hunt. She does warn you about a beast stalking the Golden Oasis, to the far northwest of the Hissing Wastes.

The beast in question is a brightly colored varghest, among the young wyverns also infesting the place. By now, your party should be able to pick apart a lone varghest, regardless of its color. With the varghest slain, the quest is complete.

NOTE Check the Golden Oasis thoroughly. There's a landmark to claim, a journal to find for the Notes on the Wastes quest, and some valuable loot hidden away in chests and containers throughout the oasis.

4: NOTES ON THE WASTES

Quest Giver: A journal found in the wastes

Description: A page was recovered from a log book that was apparently kept by someone studying old dwarven ruins. Perhaps there are additional pages to be found deeper in the Hissing Wastes.

Requirements: Find one of the notes in the Hissing Wastes.

Reward: 1,269 XP, 150 Influence

Objectives:

- Find eight journal pages.

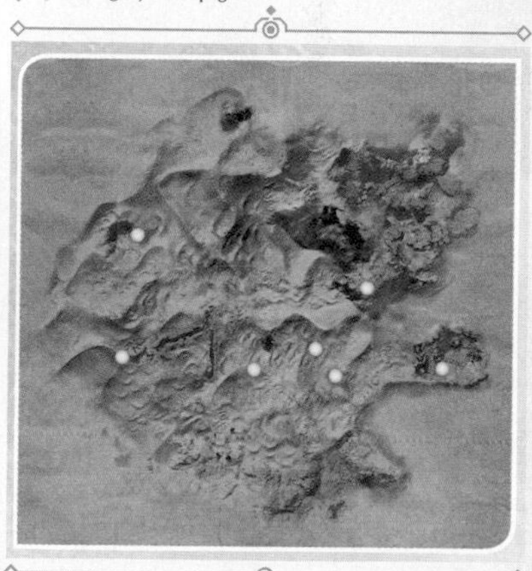

As you travel the wastes, you might start receiving pings on your mini-map. If you search about, you may discover you have randomly come across one of eight journal pages left behind by a dwarven explorer, who made interesting observations of the ruins in the wastes as well as the Venatori excavation efforts.

Searching for all eight journal pages without assistance can be difficult, as you're not even given general search locations for the pages, nor are any called out on your in-game maps by any special icons. However, you can reference the map we have provided, along with the images showing more exact locations.

Page 1

Page 2

Page 3

Page 4

Page 5

Page 6

Page 7

Page 8

> 5: SAND AND RUIN

Quest Giver: A sand-covered note

Description: There is a sizable Venatori presence in the Hissing Wastes. It is an odd place for them to be dispatched at all, let alone in such significant numbers.

Requirements: This war table mission is unlocked after establishing Skyhold.

Reward: 5,076 XP, 600 Influence, 2 Power

Objectives:

- Go to the war table to stop the Venatori advancing in the west (20 power required).
- Search the Venatori camp north of the cove.
- Search the Venatori camp near the canyon.
- Search the Venatori camp known as the Watchtower.
- Search the Venatori camp in the mountains.

As soon as you enter the Hissing Wastes and receive Scout Harding's briefing on the situation, you're told to start scouting out Venatori positions and establishing camps throughout the desert. You're given a location to start, but you can head to any one of the potential campsites. Among the closest to your starting camp is one near a landmark called the Four Pillars.

Expect the Venatori to be ready for a fight. They will defend their own camps vigorously and with plenty of numbers on their side.

Four Pillars Camp, North of the Cove

After defeating the Venatori force outside of the camp, establish your own Inquisition camp, then delve into the nearby ruins. You can find notes on the campgrounds that will help reveal more information about the Venatori operation throughout the Hissing Wastes, including a sketch of another tomb located somewhere in the wastes.

TIP The Four Pillars camp is right next to a dwarven tomb that contains a key fragment necessary for the Tomb of Fairel side quest. See the information for that quest to see the solution to the veilfire puzzle found within the tomb!

Venatori Camp near the Canyon

West of the canyon is a sizable Venatori campsite near another dwarven ruin. You can find another sketch that shows the location of a tomb inside the canyon, as well as a sketch of the burial grounds tomb, at the southern end of the wastes.

TIP The small ruin north of the main Venatori camp near the canyons has a Sacrifice mosaic piece to recover.

Venatori Watchtower Camp

After taking this camp from Venatori foes, you can read the books on a nearby workbench. One contains a sketch showing the way to enter the Colossus tomb. The other provides additional information about a large camp behind the Sunstop Mountains region.

TIP If you climb up the ladders near the Watchtower camp, you can get closer to the mountain summit. An ocularum and a mosaic piece in the Sacrifice set await you.

Sunstop Mountains Camp

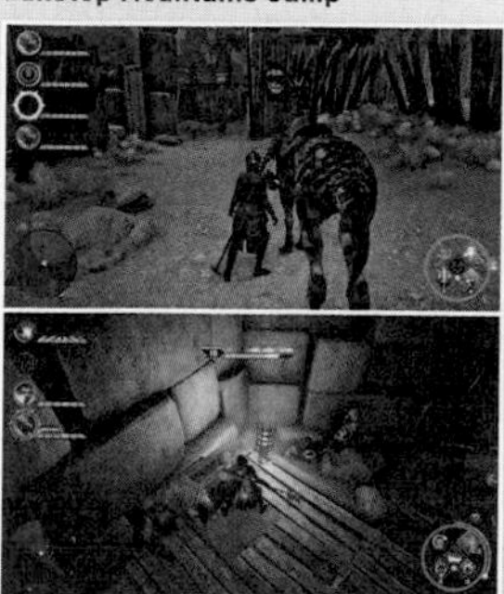

The largest Venatori camp in the wastes is not lacking in manpower! Try to take on small groups of enemies, as opposed to alerting the whole camp at once. While you sweep the camp for foes to put down, keep an eye out for the Overseer! This mage is the most powerful of all the Venatori enemies in the region, and he protects another missive that further details their purpose in the region.

> **TIP**
>
> 
>
> Another Sacrifice mosaic piece can be found near a campfire on the western side of the camp. It sits out in the open but also happens to be guarded by a pair of Venatori brutes. A little farther south, you can find a bottle of Silent Plains piquette to add to your wine collection.

Once you have found all the documents of value from the four designated camps, this quest is complete, and you should have a good idea of where many of Fairel's tombs are located all across the wastes.

6: THE TOMB OF FAIREL

Quest Giver: Quest starts as soon as you find a key fragment in a ruin somewhere in the Hissing Wastes.

Description: Rumors tell of a grand treasure buried in a tomb in the Hissing Wastes. Explore the wastes, using any available clues and maps to find it.

Requirements: Find a key fragment in one of the ruins in the Hissing Wastes.

Reward: 10,152 XP, 2,000 Influence, 3 Power

Objectives:

- Find five Tomb of Fairel key fragments.
- Follow the treasure map to the tomb.
- Find the statue tomb's treasure.
- Find the mountain fortress tomb's treasure.
- Find the graveyard tomb's treasure.
- Find the canyon tomb's treasure.
- Enter the tomb of Fairel and retrieve the dwarven relics.

The first order of business is to locate the five key fragments scattered across the Hissing Wastes. Even if you find the Tomb of Fairel immediately, you won't be able to open it without the five key fragments. And there is the issue of the Sandy Howler, a high dragon. It has taken up residence in the valley before the tomb. Recover the fragments first, so you can do everything in one trip.

> **NOTE**
>
> This quest is deeply connected with the Sand and Ruin side quest. The Venatori have set up many camps throughout the wastes, protected by powerful mages and red templars. The camps contain valuable intelligence on the Venatori operation, and they also provide map sketches on the whereabouts of tombs containing the key fragments you need.

You can find the key fragments in the following locations.

Four Pillars Camp Ruins

This key can be found in the Four Pillars tomb treasure room. There is a veilfire torch puzzle in these ruins. Should you light the pillars out of order, you will face demons, and any torches you did light in the correct order will be snuffed out. The correct order can be established by reading the passages on the pillars and lighting the torches in the order that allows the passages to be read in the correct order, as follows:

> This is the tale of Fairel, Paragon among Paragons, father of two sons,
>
> Who, against their father's wishes, fought from foolish words and foolish pride.
>
> For pride these halls were made—to honor a father's deed, and grieve his loss.
>
> And for loss these halls were made, to honor a brother mourned.

The Colossus of Orlais

The Colossus of Orlais is a massive stone monument in the northwest part of the wastes. Once you cut your way through the spiders nesting in the front hall, you'll encounter a another veilfire torch puzzle, similar to that found in the Four Pillars Camp ruins. Don't forget to loot the key fragment from the large chest inside the tomb's treasure room!

> Fairel, Paragon, fled from the strife his brilliance created,
>
> The strife that destroyed thaigs, sundered houses, from weapons that clan used against clan.
>
> His own clan and two sons followed Fairel to the pitiless surface,
>
> The surface where they would hide from the war that took their home.

> **TIP**
>
> Don't miss the Sacrifice mosaic piece found inside the Colossus treasure room after you solve the puzzle.

The Tomb in the Canyon

The canyon region contains one of the few vendors in the Hissing Wastes. It also contains another of the tombs with another veilfire puzzle to solve:

> After many years Fairel, greatest of Paragons, could not bear life's burden.
>
> And with the burden growing, he called his sons to his bedside.
>
> He bade each son swear he would take care of his brother,
>
> And the brothers swore, and mourned when their father returned to the Stone.

Burial Grounds Tomb

Nestled in the southwestern portion of the wastes, the burial grounds tomb is but a mere shadow of itself. Thankfully, the torch pillars, along with their passages, are still around. Use the veilfire near the sealed treasure chamber to make a torch, then light the torches in the correct order to undo the seal. The pillars are scattered around the burial grounds, so be sure to read the passages on them to ensure you're following the correct order.

> Fairel's sons built monuments to their father, locking away his great works,
>
> And worked together, for a time, side by side. Each ruled half the thaig,
>
> But each ruled differently. They argued, and heated words made the brothers duel,
>
> And where one brother fell, the other raised bloodied axe in hand, alone.

TIP A bottle of aqua magus can be found near a campfire somewhere on the burial grounds, just to the east of the Empty Square landmark. And when you unlock the tomb, you can find another mosaic piece behind the treasure chest.

The Mountain Fortress Tomb

This is the largest tomb you will explore in the Hissing Wastes. The Venatori have set up a presence to protect the tunnel their slaves dug at the top of the Sunstop Mountains, down into the heart of the tomb itself. Once you get past them, you can descend safely into the tomb.

TIP Don't miss searching for one of the note pages for Notes on the Wastes! It can be found on a table in the first chamber you visit inside this tomb.

As you keep going deeper in the tomb, keep the veilfire torch ready at all times. You can locate a superb fire rune schematic on the walls of the third floor.

The collectibles keep rolling in! Just as you reach the bottom of the tomb, in the room just before you enter the veilfire puzzle chamber, you can find a Sacrifice mosaic piece.

After reaching the bottom of the tomb, you have one last veilfire puzzle to solve. The correct order of the passage is as follows:

> The sun burned above oceans of sand,
>
> But in the sand was Stone, strong and true.
>
> Fairel hewed the stone, and built—as great as any thaig in the deep.
>
> And with his sons' help, he ensured the thaig prospered and grew.

Collect your final key fragment, and you are at last prepared to go to the Tomb of Fairel. Get healed, and get loaded up for a High Dragon; the last obstacle between you and the secret of the tomb is the Sandy Howler.

TIP Don't miss another mosaic piece inside the tomb's final chamber.

With all the key fragments yours, it's time to go to the Tomb of Fairel. It is not marked on your map, but it can be found by heading northeast from the starting camp, following the mountain until you encounter a pair of dwarven statues standing guard at a passage leading to the Tomb of Fairel...

...as well as a sleeping high dragon. It's possible to sneak past the Sandy Howler and go straight for the tomb entrance. With all five key fragments in your possession, you can avoid this fight, if you want to. But why would we want to do that?

7: HIGH DRAGON: THE SANDY HOWLER

Recommended Level: 20+

Recommended Party Composition: One warrior (sword and shield), one rogue, two mages (armed with frost-damage staves)

Alternative Party Composition: Two warriors (sword and shield, two-handed weapon), two mages (armed with frost-damage staves)

The Sandy Howler starts out at a big disadvantage. Asleep, the beast is defenseless, meaning you can start the fight by dropping Mark of the Rift right on her sleepy little head, as well as any cold-based magic spells from your mages. Any rogues or warriors brought to this fight can speed things along by having ice runes enchanted to their weapons.

Once the Sandy Howler's nap is rudely interrupted by your party, the fight's on! If you've been dilligent with your high dragon hunts, you should be more than prepared to handle the usual repertoire of physical attacks these beasts are capable of. She will buff herself with a full guard bar, so make sure your physical attackers have abilities that can break those defenses quickly and efficiently. She will use her wings to generate a powerful wind pressure field that hurts anyone in range of her, while deflecting ranged attacks. Any mages in the group should be made to shield the frontliners during the wind pressure so they can stay on the Howler's limbs, hopefully forcing a knockdown as soon as possible.

The Sandy Howler has an affinity to fire, appropriate for a desert dweller such as herself. Expect fire breath attacks in between leaps around the arena.

When the Sandy Howler's health drops to around 50 percent, she will start to use stunning roars that call in dragonlings to assist her. Cull these as quickly as you can before turning the party's attention back to the Sandy Howler.

With the Sandy Howler dead, or resting peacefully, enter the Tomb of Fairel with your assembled key fragments. After everything else you've gone though, the last part of this quest is refreshingly simple: Go to the treasure chest at the end of the tomb's hall and loot the whole thing. The Venatori have lost their chance at these relics, thanks to the Inquisition's efforts!

The Dalish shun the Arbor Wilds. When the people who would start a war over a single crumbling wall ignore a large elven ruin to the south, it bodes disaster. There is beauty and curiosity in the forest, such as trees that rise tall as towers, but those who travel too deep into them never return.

LOCALE SUMMARY

Scouting Cost: 50

Following the events at Adamant and Halamshiral, the Inquisition invades the Arbor Wilds in an effort to stop Corypheus from attaining ancient elven knowledge from the Temple of Mythal. Unlike other locales, the journey through the Arbor Wilds is fairly linear, as the Inquisitor, party members, and Morrigan battle Corypheus's army blocking the path to the temple. Be warned: Once you leave the Wilds you can't return, so pick up any loot you find when you can. There aren't many collectibles or crafting materials here, but be sure to look out for deposits of stormheart during your trek through the forest. The journey culminates with the party's arrival at the Temple of Mythal, an ancient elven ruin. Here the Inquisition faces some tough decisions. Should the party perform the rituals and enter the temple's inner sanctum? Will an alliance with Abelas and his guardians benefit the Inquisition? Who will drink from the Well of Sorrows? These dilemmas and a confrontation with the Inquisitor's nemesis (Samson or Calpernia) are just some of the challenges awaiting in the Arbor Wilds.

> Crafting Materials

Common Materials:

- Elfroot

Rare Materials:

- Arbor Blessing
- Stormheart
- Silverite

Unique Materials: None

> Collections

- Astrariums: 0
- Bottles of Thedas: 0
- High Dragons: 0
- Landmarks: 0
- Mosaic Pieces: 0
- Glyphs: 0
- Shards: 0
- Treasure Maps: 0
- Logging Stands: 0
- Quarries: 0

LOCALE MAP

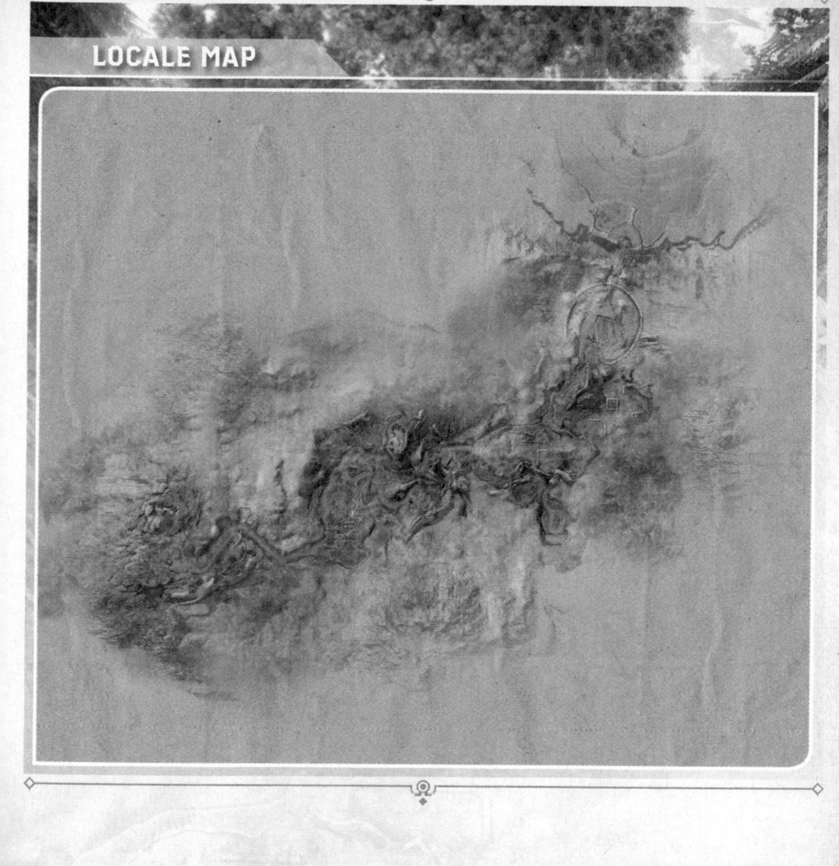

Dragon Age Inquisition

THE TEMPLE OF MYTHAL

The Temple of Mythal houses the Well of Sorrows, also known as the Vir'abelasan. The waters of this well contain the accumulated knowledge of all previous elven guardians. The race to reach and secure the well, before Corypheus does, is a critical objective in the What Pride Had Wrought quest.

The Temple of Mythal

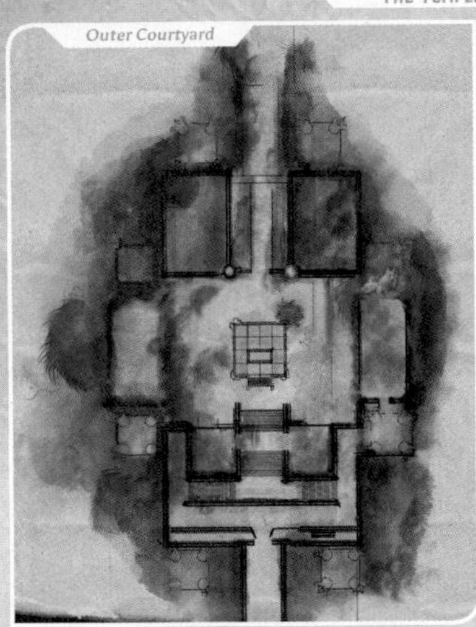

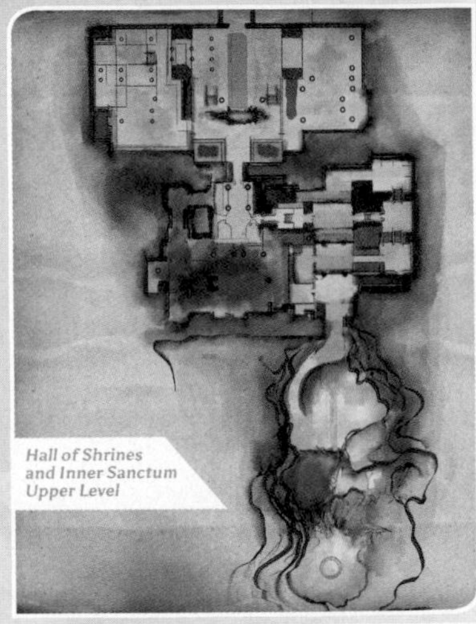

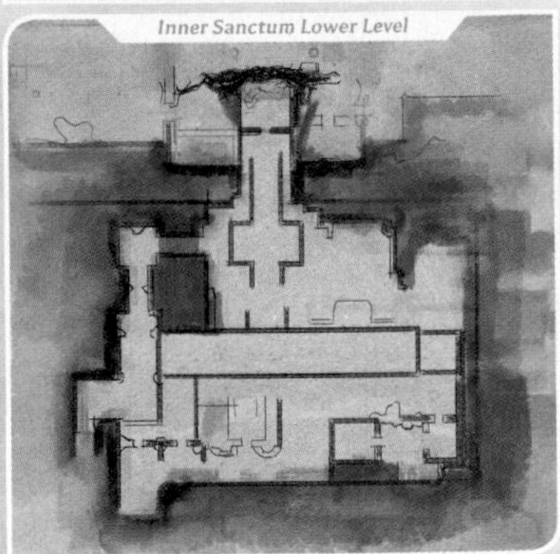

NOTE If you choose to ally with Abelas and his guardians, a guide will lead you through the inner sanctum. If you refuse an alliance, you must fight your way through.

> TEMPLE RITUALS

To enter the Temple of Mythal you must complete at least one ritual, located in the outer courtyard. But if you wish to enter the inner sanctum, you must complete three more rituals, located in the Hall of Shrines. Each ritual is a tile puzzle, requiring you to walk across a series of tiles. If you can't figure them out on your own, reference these diagrams to complete each ritual.

Outer Courtyard

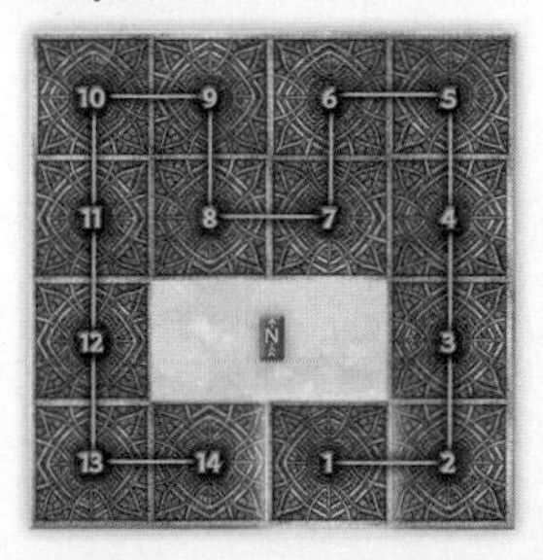

You must illuminate all of the tiles surrounding the altar, but you can't step on the same tile twice. Reference the accompanying diagram to solve it. Once all tiles are lighted, the door to the Hall of Shrines is unlocked. This is the only ritual you must complete to proceed—the other rituals are optional.

Hall of Shrines: Western Ritual

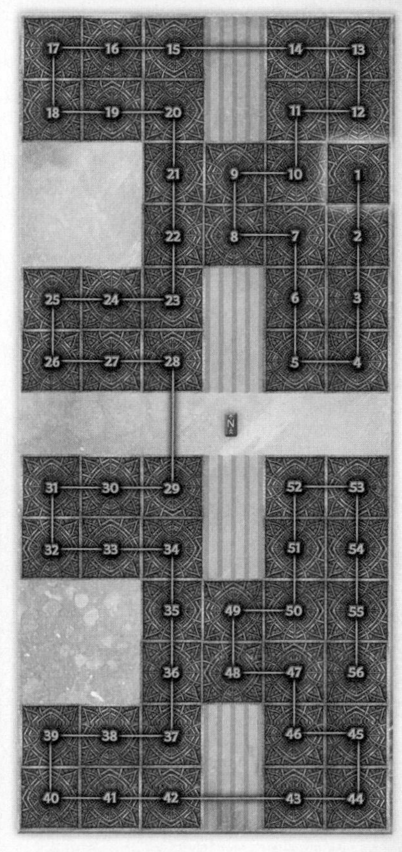

If you want to gain entry to the inner sanctum, you must complete all three rituals in the Hall of Shrines. This puzzle is divided into a northern section and southern section, but both puzzles must be solved to complete the ritual. Start by working on the northern section first, completing it near the divider on the south side, at tile 28. Once the northern side is complete, jump onto the divider and proceed to the southern section of the puzzle. The second half of the puzzle is solved using a movement pattern similar to the first one—reference the diagram to avoid making a misstep.

Hall of Shrines: Eastern Ritual

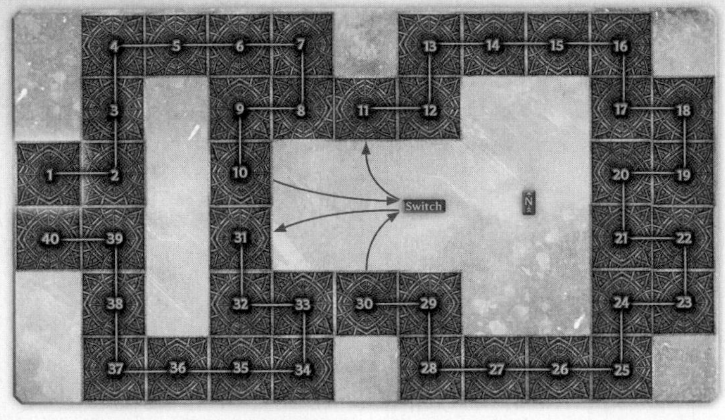

Although smaller, this puzzle is a bit trickier. Sections of this puzzle must be lowered and raised using a switch in the middle. Start by looping around the north side, then cross to the neutral platform after stepping on tile 10. On the platform, interact with the switch—this lowers tiles to the west and raises tiles to the east, allowing you to proceed. Step onto tile 11, to the north, and complete the eastern half of the ritual, as seen in the diagram. When you reach tile 30, step back onto the central platform and interact with the switch again, raising the tiles to the west. From the platform, step onto tile 31, to the west, and complete the ritual.

Hall of Shrines: Northeastern Ritual

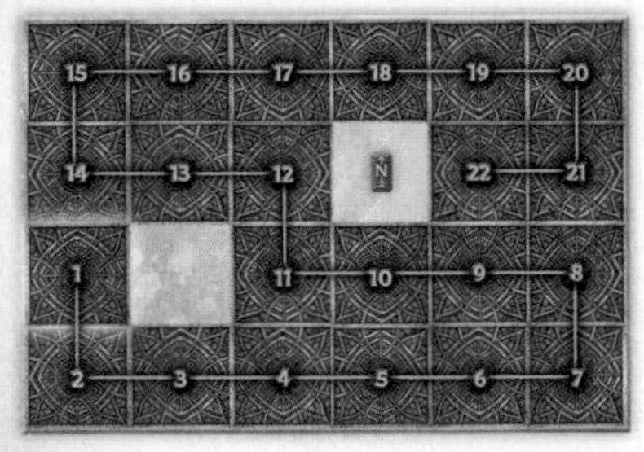

Don't let the small size of this ritual fool you—it can be tricky. As long as you follow the zigzag path shown on the diagram, you'll have no problem conquering this ritual. Like all the rituals, this puzzle can be solved in many ways. The three rituals can be completed in any order. Once all three Hall of Shrine rituals are complete, the door to the inner sanctum unlocks. Time to go see what's inside.

INNER CIRCLE QUESTS

The Inquisitor's inner circle comprises followers and advisors loyal to the Inquisition's ambitious cause. In some way, all members of the inner circle have distinguished themselves, either on the field of battle or in the equally treacherous arena of Orlesian politics. But like the people they have sworn to protect, the Inquisitor's inner circle members have needs, too. It is up to the Herald to assist these friends and allies, so that they can return the favor and hopefully pull the continent back from the brink of catastrophe.

Each follower and advisor has a set of inner circle quests, requiring you to fulfill a variety of tasks. Helping your inner circle is a good way to build approval and may also nurture a budding romance. Among these quests are the two nemesis quests, offered by Cullen and Leliana. If you sided with the mages, your nemesis is Samson, making Cullen's Before the Dawn quest available. Allying with the templars makes Calpernia your nemesis, and Leliana's Under Her Skin quest becomes available.

> UNFINISHED BUSINESS

Quest Giver: Cassandra

Description: Since the Seekers' strange absence, some of their high-profile cases have been left unchecked. Help Cassandra hunt the targets down.

Requirements: Available at Skyhold

Reward: 2,025 XP, 910 Influence, 2 Power

Objectives:

- Take down Ser Rebenger Torn in the Ferelden Hinterlands.
- Take down Leo of Lucien Bay in the Western Approach.
- Take down Ser Hildebrandt in the Exalted Plains.
- Take down Jepler the Unbound in the Emerald Graves.
- Take down Gordon the Frank in the Emprise du Lion.

After the setback that sends you to Skyhold, you can talk to Cassandra, and she will explain that the Seekers, no longer a presence in affairs across Thedas, have allowed some dangerous people to run free. The list of targets has them spread far and wide, and you may not be able to reach them all initially. The marks all increase in difficulty based on the locale they are found in.

Ser Torn is a rogue, and he can be rather evasive in combat. He does have an ally with him, but the pair shouldn't be hard to handle. You'll find him near the Forest Camp.

Leo is a mage of considerable skill with ice magic, and he's got three other mages at his side. Strike fast, strike hard—no mercy to any of these apostates. He waits in Echoback Canyon.

Hiding in the Crow Fens, Ser Hildebrandt is a guardsman of repute, and his shield makes frontal assaults a challenge. Also bothersome is the large group of archers tagging along with him.

Jepler has hidden himself in the Hopwood of the Emerald Graves, joining sides with the Freemen of the Dales. He has backup in the form of more mages.

Gordon is camped out near Elfsblood Tower. He is the most dangerous of all the targets, speaking strictly from individual strength. He has another rebellious mage at his side.

> PROMISE OF DESTRUCTION

Quest Giver: Cassandra

Description: Cassandra has reason to believe that Corypheus is behind the disappearance of the Seekers of Truth, but she requires help to prove it.

Requirements: Available at Skyhold

Reward: 1,025 XP, 400 Influence, 3 Power

Objectives:

- Investigate the disappearance of the Seekers.
- Travel to Caer Oswin.
- Explore the castle.
- Find Lord Seeker Lucius.

During a conversation with Cassandra she voices concern about the disappearance of the Seekers of Truth and asks for your help. Offer your support by completing the Locate the Missing Seekers operation on the war table. This unlocks the Castle of Caer Oswin on the world map—go there with your party.

Proceed along the outskirts of the castle until you come to a door leading to a dungeon. Fight your way past several foot soldiers, retrieving a dungeon key off one of their bodies. The key unlocks the nearby door, providing access to the castle's interior. Enter the castle courtyard from the elevated walkway on the west side, preferably using your ranged party members to fire down on the enemies below. Cassandra finds a note from Samson on one of their bodies. it appears the Seekers have been sold to the cultists.

After the discussion with Cassandra, climb the stairs to the north to enter a large chamber filled with more cultist enemies. Following the fight, continue advancing through the castle until you discover a wounded Seeker, Daniel—a former apprentice of Cassandra. Daniel reveals it was Lord Seeker Lucius who lied and sold out the Seekers to Corypheus. At Daniel's request, Cassandra ends his suffering. Cassandra is now determined to find Lucius.

Climb a series of stairs, entering another courtyard filled with more cultist enemies. Defeat the cultists and follow the path to a door—open it to confront Lucius. The Lord Seeker cannot be reasoned with, so prepare for a fight—Lucius is resistant to electricity and spirit-based attacks. Wait until Lucius and his soldiers are in a tight group, then use an AoE attack (like Mark of the Rift) to hit them all at once. Focus on eliminating Lucius's security detail first, then consolidate your offensive power on the Lord Seeker himself. After the battle, interact with the door to the west to return to Skyhold. Speak to Cassandra there to complete the quest.

> GUILTY PLEASURES

Quest Giver: Cassandra

Description: It seems Cassandra really likes Varric's book *Swords & Shields*. And she's caught up. And the book's unfinished. See Varric about getting the last chapter for Cassandra.

Requirements: Available at Skyhold

Reward: Cassandra's approval

Objectives:

- Talk to Varric about *Swords & Shields*.
- Give Cassandra the latest chapter of *Swords & Shields*.

If you speak with Cassandra at Skyhold, you might catch her reading *Swords & Shields*. In the amusing conversation that follows, she endures Dorian's mockery, and your own if you want to earn her disapproval. However, she does suggest that you could possibly order Varric to complete the series.

Varric is surprised that he has a reader in Cassandra. You can convince him to complete the book for her, but he will insist on being there for the fun. This is totally worth it and you should ensure maximum embarrassment for all parties involved. Once you get Varric to complete the book, go back to Cassandra and watch things unfold.

> THE IDEAL ROMANCE

Quest Giver: Cassandra

Description: When it comes to romance, Cassandra prefers the ideals. Someone who sweeps her off her feet with candles, poetry, and flowers. Track these things down for her.

Requirements: Finished Guilty Pleasures and on friendly terms with Cassandra. Male Inquisitor only.

Reward: 128 XP, 80 Influence

Objectives:

- Talk to a vendor in Redcliffe about poetry books.
- Find the dwarven bookseller's missing caravan.
- Talk to a gardener about flowers in Val Royeaux.
- Search the stores of Val Royeaux for some candles.
- Romance Cassandra with the candles, a poetry book, and flowers.

Poetry, candles, and flowers are all classic romantic gestures, so travel to Redcliffe to find a book of poetry to recite to Cassandra. The bookseller has unfortunately been robbed. Track down the thieves, defeat them, and pick up the book of poetry. The other two items can be found in Val Royeaux—speak with a gardener about purchasing some flowers, then search the other stores for some candles. Once you have all the items, return to Cassandra.

She will be impressed by the sincerity of your efforts, and you two share a tender, passionate moment together, becoming romantically involved from now on.

> MEASURING THE VEIL

Quest Giver: Solas

Description: Solas has learned of an artifact in the Hinterlands that he wishes to study.

Requirements: Available at Haven

Reward: Solas's approval

Objectives:

- Travel to the Hinterlands with Solas.
- Locate the artifact.
- Use the artifact.

Speaking with Solas in Haven, you can eventually earn his trust enough that he will ask for assistance with investigating a relic he's heard of in the Hinterlands. Take him in your active party and head toward the East Road, where the artifact is said to be.

As you approach the ruins, you'll find a warrior named Mihris in battle against multiple demons. Saving her from the demons prompts a chat. She's here for an artifact, much like Solas is. She claims it can measure the Veil, and possibly allow for predictions on where more Fade rifts will appear. You can tell her to leave, or you can allow her to stay while you push into the ruins. A veilfire torch can be lit near the entrance of the cave ruins—you'll need it later.

The cave is infested with more demons. Clearing them out, you find the artifact at the back the cave, and it measures the Veil, as was rumored. At this point, if Mihris is still present, she is happy to tell you that things have worked out, and now it is time to part ways. You can prompt Solas to convince Mihris to hand over an Amulet of Power she tried to slip out of the ruins with.

What Lies Dormant

The measuring devices are scattered across Ferelden and Orlais, and we've marked them on locale maps throughout the Exploration chapter. If Solas is in your party when you find and activate them, you gain approval. Should you find at least 10 of the devices, you can unlock a war table operation: Measure Veil Strength. Complete the operation, and you'll hear word from Solas about the location of a Fade rift that has yet to open. Go to the designated location in the Hinterlands behind the Redcliffe Farms, and prepare for a fight to seal the rift. This is a high-level fight, so be prepared for some very tough demons!

ALL NEW, FADED FOR HER

Quest Giver: Solas

Description: One of Solas's old friends, a spirit, has been summoned against its will, and needs his help.

Requirements: Available at Skyhold

Reward: 1,025 XP, 400 Influence, 3 Power

Objectives:

- Find the spirit with Solas in the Exalted Plains.
- Deal with the demon.
- Speak to Solas.

Solas's personal plot begins with a plea to help him assist his friend in the Exalted Plains. The spirit, summoned against its will, reached out to Solas for a brief moment in time. Take Solas with your active party to the Exalted Plains. The spirit itself is not far from the Dalish camp.

When you arrive at Enavuris in the plains, you find that the spirit has been turned into a pride demon. A mage runs up, begging for help, and Solas is furious. After a short conversation with the mage, a solution to the demon problem is brought up: disrupt the summoning circle.

The summoning circle consists of four summoning stones surrounding the pride demon. Destroy these as quickly as possible.

Afterward, the spirit, restored to a less monstrous form, exchanges a farewell with Solas before fading away. Solas then threatens to murder the mages who summoned the spirit, and it's here that you can choose to let him commit the crime or get him to stand down. Regardless of what you do, Solas leaves the party. You must then return to Skyhold and meet him at the front entrance. After one final conversation, Solas returns to your inner circle, with many questions still left unanswered.

SEEING RED

Quest Giver: Varric

Description: Varric saw enough red lyrium in Kirkwall for one lifetime. Now it's everywhere, and the worst of it "sings" like the shard that drove his brother mad. Varric would take no small pleasure in destroying those. Locate and destroy primeval red lyrium nodes.

Requirements: Available at Haven

Reward: 967 XP, 200 Influence, 2 Power

Objectives:

- Find 12 primeval red lyrium deposits.
- Destroy the primeval red lyrium deposits.

Varric has had some personal experience with red lyrium, so destroying any veins you can find will be something he can appreciate. Primeval red lyrium veins are scattered all over the world throughout different locales, all of which are marked on your quest map. Even after you destroy the 12 he asks for, you can destroy others you find for continued approval gains with Varric.

WELL, SHIT

Quest Giver: Varric

Description: Bianca was waiting in the Deep Roads. Travel underground to the center of the lyrium mining operation and shut it down.

Requirements: Available at Skyhold; complete Here Lies the Abyss.

Reward: 1,025 XP, 400 Influence, 3 Power

Objectives:

- Enter Valammar.
- Open the locked door.
- Find a key for the second floor.
- Speak with Varric about all this.

After dealing with the Grey Warden corruption in Adamant, return to Skyhold. If you speak with Varric, you find him involved in a conversation with a female dwarf. This is Bianca. After some conversation, you discover that she has information about a lyrium mining operation that appears to be benefiting Corypheus's forces.

It's in Valammar, an old dwarven trading post that leads to the Deep Roads. Depending on how you've explored up to this point, you may already be well acquainted with the place, especially if you've completed Deep Trouble. Bianca says she will wait for you and Varric, if you offer to help.

Make your way into Valammar, fighting past any Carta or darkspawn that may have repopulated the place. You need to make your way over to the Halls of the Elders. The smugglers responsible for mining the red lyrium have dug themselves into a room that only Bianca can open. Once inside, clear out all of the smugglers you find. You'll find the key to the lyrium at the end of the fighting.

Varric isn't stupid, and he suspects there is something Bianca isn't telling the group. It turns out that she not only discovered the red lyrium, but she handed the key to the doors that barred it over to the smugglers. She was hoping to make things right, but Varric is still upset. Surprisingly, Varric approves of you if you don't tear into her for lying, so if you want to keep on his good side, hold back on the anger.

After the events at Valammar, return to Skyhold and speak with Varric. He feels that he's entirely responsible for Bianca putting herself in danger, and he's not dealing with it well at all. Your responses here can earn his disapproval if they're full of snark. For once, he's not in the mood. Regardless, the situation is settled and the quest is complete.

A FRIEND OF RED JENNY

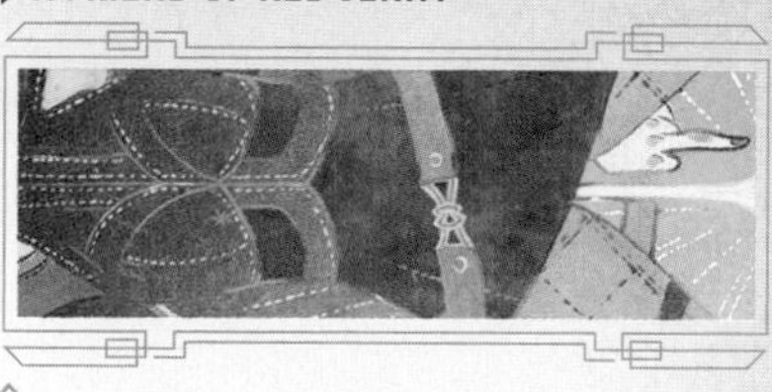

Description: The strange message, delivered via arrow, said there is an enemy of the Inquisition waiting to strike Val Royeaux. It said to search the market, cafe, and docks for things that are red.

Quest Giver: Arrow in the market

Requirements: Available after addressing the clerics in Val Royeaux

Reward: Sera joins the Inquisition.

Objectives:

- Examine the message.
- Search by the dock.
- Search in the cafe.
- Search the upper market.
- Fend off the guards.

Immediately following the conversation with Mother Hevara and the templars, a mysterious arrow lands nearby. This is the start of a small quest, requiring you to search for red satchels by the dock, cafe, and upper market. Go to each location marked on the compass and conduct searches to find and retrieve the three satchels. To reach the upper market, enter the blue doors on the southwest side of the market—this gives you access to the balcony above.

Once you found all three red handkerchiefs, a secluded courtyard appears on the world map—travel there. This takes you to a small courtyard occupied by hostile reach guards and Freemen spotters. Eliminate the first group of enemies, then open the door to the west. Here you encounter a noble, unfriendly to the Inquisition. But he's soon killed by a potential ally, Sera, an elven rogue archer. Sera is the one who led you here. Help Sera fend off the remaining guards before resuming your conversation. Sera is part of a band of mercenaries called the Friends of Red Jenny—accept her offer to join the Inquisition.

> THE VERCHIEL MARCH

Description: Sera says there's trouble in Verchiel. She's asked for an Inquisition presence—a few troops to march through town—to spook the nobles into pushing her people around there.

Quest Giver: Sera in Skyhold

Requirements: Speak with Sera in Skyhold.

Reward: 1,025 XP, 400 Influence, 3 Power

Objectives:

- Order a march through Verchiel.
- Return to the war table.
- Talk to Sera about the march.
- Travel to the stash location.

After speaking with Sera about the problems in Verchiel, send in the troops via the war table. When you receive the update on the situation, meet with Sera and travel to Verchiel.

Once at Verchiel, you encounter one of Sera's friends, who warns a group of nearby mercenaries of Sera's arrival. The ensuing fight begins after archers kill the informant. It's a mixed group of foot soldiers and archers, led by a mercenary enforcer. Not the worst odds you've faced during this adventure.

After the battle is over, Lord Pel Harmond steps out to explain the "misunderstanding." His quarrel is entirely with Red Jenny, meaning Sera and any of her "friends." You can try to learn more about what was going on in Verchiel, but as the conversation drags on, Sera gets progressively angrier. The major decision is whether or not you allow Sera to kill the noble, join forces with said scumbag, or allow him to go free. Working with him or letting him go earns serious disapproval from Sera.

If you've done anything other than let Sera have her way with Lord Harmond, your conversation at Skyhold will be your chance to patch things up with her. If you apologize outright, she's stunned, having expected you to do otherwise.

> A WOMAN WHO WANTS FOR NOTHING

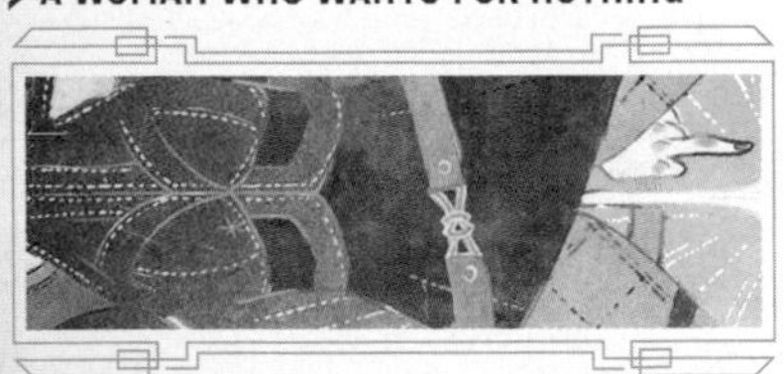

Quest Giver: Sera

Description: Sera has gotten you a gift. What could you give in return?

Requirements: Be in a romance with Sera, with all the requirements that entails.

Reward: Sera's approval

Objectives:

- Talk to everyone in your inner circle.
- Talk to Sera

After you've completed Sera's other quests and have begun a romance with her, she will surprise the Inquisitor with a gift, which makes you decide that a gift in return is the least you can do for her.

The problem is, you have no clue what to get Sera—she doesn't seem to have a thing she desires in particular, outside of your own company. And so it comes to asking the rest of your inner circle just what it is a woman like Sera could ever want as a gift. You get a lot of ideas, most of them not all that useful to your predicament. You can eventually return to Sera and admit that, despite asking for help from the rest of the group, you have nothing for her in exchange.

She thinks this is hilarious; as far as she's concerned the idea of you asking some of the more prudish members of the Inquisition for gift ideas is a gift in itself. With that, your gift exchange is complete.

> THE IMPERIAL ENCHANTER

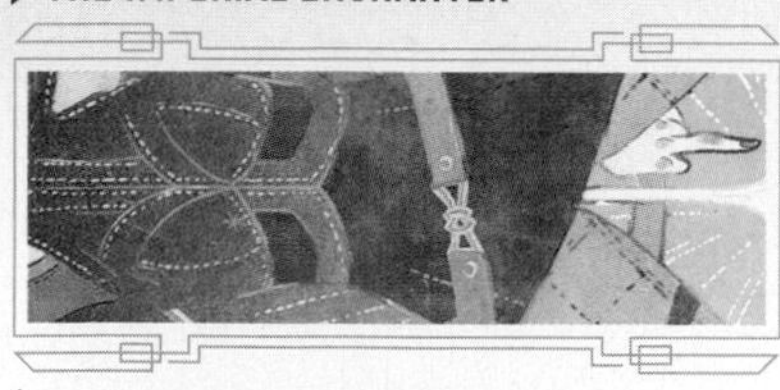

Description: Vivienne de Fer, the First Enchanter of Montsimmard, has extended an invitation to her salon at the chateau of Duke Bastien de Ghyslain.

Quest Giver: Circle Mage messenger in the market

Requirements: Available after addressing the clerics

Reward: Vivienne joins the Inquisition.

Objectives:

- Attend the salon.

Speak to the messenger in Val Royeaux's market to receive an invitation from Vivienne de Fer, a well-connected mage in Orlais. The invitation adds the Ghyslain Estate to the world map—travel there. Upon entering the chateau, you're rudely greeted by a marquis who has nothing kind to say about the Inquisition. But he's soon set straight by Vivienne—she even allows you to choose the marquis's fate. After introducing herself, Vivienne gets to the point. As the leader of the last loyal mages of Thedas, she feels compelled to join the Inquisition. Feel free to ask Vivienne more questions. But at the end of the conversation, welcome her aboard—she is a powerful ally, both on and off the battlefield.

> FAVORS THE FIRST ENCHANTER

Description: Vivienne wishes to undo the damage done to her beloved Circle of Magi and hopefully restore it to its former relevance. Recovering phylacteries and tomes lost with the fall of the circles will help.

Quest Giver: Vivienne

Requirements: Available at Skyhold

Reward: 286 XP, 120 Influence

Objectives:

- Find three Circle tomes.
- Find a Circle tome in the Hinterlands.
- Find a Circle tome in the Western Approach.
- Find a Circle tome in the Exalted Plains.

After reaching Skyhold, you can speak with Vivienne about matters regarding the future of the Circle. She will foist this task upon you. Every book you find gets you some approval with Vivienne if she's with you during the collection.

This tome is found on a rampart that sits just north of the Crossroads, on the main road headed toward the town of Redcliffe.

Circle tome, Western Approach

The Shimmer Stone Mine, near Nazaire's Pass, is where a tome has been hidden.

Circle tome, Exalted Plains

A burned out home in the Riel region contains this final tome.

BRING ME THE HEART OF SNOW WHITE

Quest Giver: Vivienne

Description: Vivienne requires the heart of a wyvern to complete an alchemical formula. Though all wyvern hearts look more or less the same, she specified that it needs to be from a rare beast known as the snowy wyvern.

Requirements: Available at Skyhold

Reward: 1,025 XP, 400 Influence, 3 Power

Objectives:

- Obtain the heart of a snowy wyvern from the Exalted Plains.
- Give Vivienne the heart of the snowy wyvern.

Vivienne is cagier than usual when you try to get her to explain why she needs the heart from a snowy wyvern. There's no harm in going out to get what she needs, save for the obvious dangers that wyvern hunting always has. Go to the Crow Fens in the Exalted Plains to find your target. A prepared party should be able to make short work of it.

After retrieving the heart, return to Vivienne. She is shocked that you've returned, more so if you offer the heart without conditions or snide refusal. In return, she not only provides payment but also offers to show you why she needed this heart so badly. Unfortunately, to her dismay, the man for whom she did all this fades away.

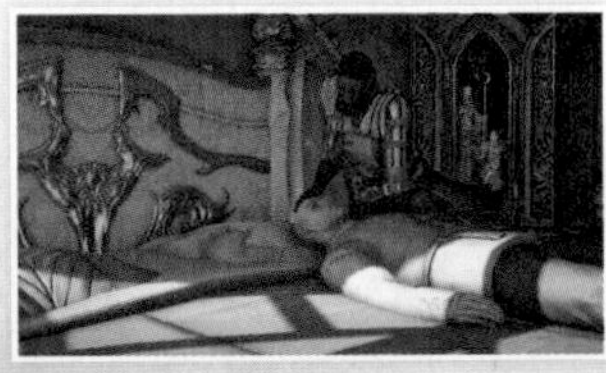

Return to Skyhold to speak with Vivienne. If you show concern, she approves of it greatly, and she can begin moving on from this chapter in her life.

THE LONE WARDEN

Description: One of Leliana's agents reported a man, calling himself Blackwall, dressed in full Grey Warden regalia and last seen traveling through the Ferelden Hinterlands. With so many Wardens disappearing in the wake of the Divine's death, this Blackwall should be questioned.

Quest Giver: Leliana in Haven

Requirements: Available after returning to Haven from Val Royeaux

Reward: Blackwall

Objectives:

- Search for Blackwall in the Hinterlands.

Blackwall's camp can be found on the western shore of Lake Luthias in the Hinterlands. He's busy training some recruits when you arrive. But just as you begin talking to Blackwall, his camp is attacked by a group of bandits. Help Blackwall and his recruits defeat the bandits. After the battle, question Blackwall about the disappearance of the Grey Wardens. Blackwall insists the Wardens had nothing to do with the death of the Divine and doesn't know why Wardens have disappeared—he works alone and rarely has contact with other Grey Wardens. As you're about to leave, Blackwall offers to join the Inquisition. Accept his offer and consider adding him to your current party.

> **NOTE** Blackwall must be recruited before going to Adamant. If you haven't recruited Blackwall by then, you can never get him.

MEMORIES OF THE GREY

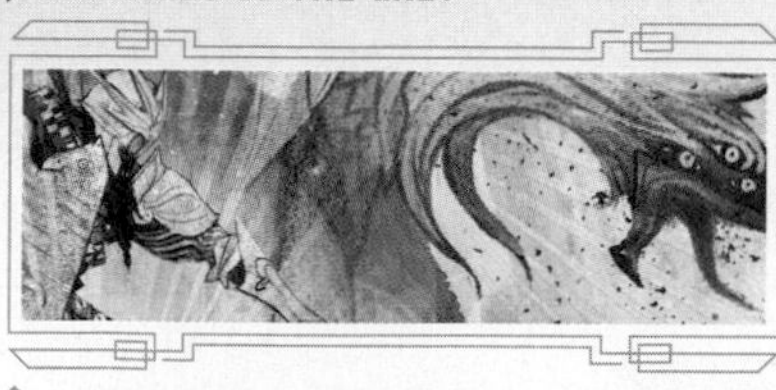

Description: Blackwall possesses maps that chart old Warden camps and outposts throughout Ferelden and Orlais. The Wardens who abandoned these camps may have left behind artifacts of interest to Blackwall.

Quest Giver: Leliana in Haven

Requirements: Available after returning to Haven from Val Royeaux; Blackwall must be recruited.

Reward: 503 XP, 270 Influence

Objectives:

- Find two Storm Coast artifacts.
- Find two Hinterlands artifacts.
- Find two Western Approach artifacts.
- Find two Fallow Mire artifacts.
- Find two Emprise du Lion artifacts.

When going after these artifacts, make sure you take Blackwall with you. Him being present for every artifact found will increase his approval toward you. The locations on your quest map are pretty exact, so it isn't too difficult to locate the artifacts. You'll know you're especially close when your mini-map begins pinging, which is your prompt to use Search until the artifacts are revealed.

NOTE Make sure you have Deft Hands, Fine Tools among your Inquisition perks. You need this skill to open the locked door in the Fallow Mire's Hargrave Keep, where one of the artifacts is hidden.

EXPLANATIONS

Quest Giver: Blackwall

Description: There's an old Warden outpost in the Storm Coast that Blackwall wants to visit. It seems important to him.

Requirements: Available at Skyhold, after Revelations, but only if you have flirted with Blackwall enough to have been rebuffed by him after Haven is destroyed

Reward: 128 XP, 80 Influence, 0 Power

Objectives:

- Travel to the Storm Coast with Blackwall.

If you've flirted enough with Blackwall, in the aftermath of Haven's destruction he will try to draw the line between you, the Inquisitor, and him, the Grey Warden. If you're not willing to leave your relationship at that, go to the stables in Skyhold and strike up a conversation. He feels he owes you an explanation for his actions and wants you to come with him to the Storm Coast—he wants to show you something.

Gather a party (with Blackwall) and travel to the Storm Coast, arriving at Small Grove camp. Upon your arrival at Small Grove camp, travel south and conduct a search on the nearby cliff. Here you find several skeletons and weapons on the ground. A search reveals a badge among the remains—interact with it. This was Blackwall's badge, and life, before he met you—"crumbling ruins, endless battles, death." Convince him he doesn't need to face these things on his own. This is all he needed to show you. He suggests talking to him at Skyhold. If you've maintained warm approval and have shown romantic interest, you can culminate the romance with Blackwall during your next conversation in Skyhold.

REVELATIONS

Following a particularly dark conversation with Blackwall in Skyhold's tavern, he goes missing.

Quest Giver: Blackwall

Description: Blackwall has left the Inquisition. It appears to have something to do with the impending execution of a man named Mornay, one of the soldiers responsible for the Callier massacre.

Requirements: Become Blackwall's friend by gaining his approval, complete the events at Adamant and Halamshiral, and then speak with Blackwall at Skyhold.

Reward: 1,934 XP, 400 Influence, 3 Power

Objectives:

- Attend Mornay's execution.
- Speak to "Rainier" in his cell.
- Discuss the situation with Cullen.
- Optional: Order the advisors to find a way to release Rainier from prison.
- Judge Rainier at Skyhold.

Speak to the Inquisition messenger in the stables to get a lead. A crumpled report handed over by the messenger suggests Blackwall is attending the execution of a man called Mornay in Val Royeaux—the man is accused of taking part in a massacre as ordered by his captain, Thom Rainier. Travel to Val Royeaux to see what's going on. Upon your arrival, Blackwall interrupts the execution, revealing he was the one who ordered Mornay. He is actually Thom Rainier. Following this revelation, Blackwall is arrested and escorted to Val Royeaux's prison.

Proceed to the prison and visit Blackwall in his cell to get more details. Thom Rainier was a respected Orlesian captain who ordered the death of Lord Callier and his entourage—Mornay was Rainier's second in command. When these events came to light, Rainier ran. While on the run, Rainier encountered a Grey Warden named Blackwall. Rainier served and learned the ways of the Wardens from Blackwall. When the original Blackwall died during a darkspawn ambush, Rainier carried on the name. But now that Mornay had been captured, Rainier couldn't let him take the fall for his crime. The man you knew as Blackwall is filled with guilt and ready to face his punishment at the gallows.

After getting information from Blackwall, speak to Cullen about what to do next.

He reveals that Thom Rainier was convinced to perform a political hit on one of Empress Celene's biggest supporters, Lord Callier. Most of Rainier's men took the fall for this massacre. But Rainier and Mornay managed to escape. Cullen suggests that the Inquisition can use its leverage to get Rainier released. You can then judge him yourself back at Skyhold. If you choose to leave him in prison in Val Royeaux, Blackwall is out of the Inquisition and no longer available as a party member. However, if you order Cullen to get Rainier out of prison, you'll get him back. But you'll need to go back to Skyhold to make these arrangements.

CAUTION If you do not complete the war table operation to rescue Rainier before you commit to the endgame, Blackwall will be gone from Skyhold for good. You will not be able to rescue him even during the post-game.

Back in Skyhold, visit the war room and choose the Thom Rainier's Fate operation from the war table, costing one power. Select Josephine to complete this operation to avoid any complications. Once Rainier has been transferred into Inquisition custody, head to the throne room and conduct a judgment. There are three options. You can set Rainier free, make him serve the Inquisition against his will, or turn him over to the Wardens once Corypheus is defeated. Blackwall greatly approves if you set him free (tell him he should be himself) or send him to the Wardens. After the judgment, the quest is complete.

> THE CAPTAIN OF THE CHARGERS

Description: A Qunari warrior known as the Iron Bull is offering aid for the Inquisition from his mercenary company, the Bull's Chargers.

Quest Giver: Krem in Haven

Requirements: Available after returning to Haven from Val Royeaux.

Reward: Iron Bull joins the Inquisition.

Objectives:

- Meet Iron Bull at the Storm Coast.

Before you can go to the Storm Coast, you must first scout it on the war table, costing five power. When you arrive at the Storm Coast, head northwest to find Iron Bull and his Chargers engaged in battle against several Tevinter zealots. Once your party arrives, the enemies are outnumbered—help Iron Bull and the Chargers mop up the rest. Following the battle, Iron Bull strikes up a conversation, offering his group's services to the Inquisition. But he also reveals he's working for the Ben-Hassrath, the Qunari secret police. As an agent of the Ben-Hassrath, Iron Bull is tasked with keeping an eye on the Inquisition—the Qunari have a vested interest in closing the Breach. In return, he offers to share Ben-Hassrath information with the Inquisition. If you agree with Iron Bull's terms, ask him to join the Inquisition.

> DEMANDS OF THE QUN

Quest Giver: Iron Bull

Description: The Ben-Hassrath have offered an alliance with the Inquisition. Accompany Iron Bull and his Chargers to meet with their contact in the Storm Coast.

Requirements: You must have high approval with Iron Bull, and you must have discussed Seheron with Iron Bull during conversation at Skyhold. You will know you have good approval with Bull after a few hard-core drinking sessions, possibly a few high dragon battles, and a group chat with the Chargers at Bull's behest.

Reward: 1,025 XP, 400 Influence, 3 Power

Objectives:

- Head for the Storm Coast with Bull.
- Speak with Bull to begin the assault.
- Clear out the Venatori.
- Signal the dreadnought.
- Check on Bull back at Skyhold.

Bull's extension of the Ben-Hassrath's offer is a surprise even to him, and you can voice your distrust of the Qunari to his disapproval. If you choose to go for it, head to the Storm Coast with Bull and two other bruisers. You'll have to crack some Venatori skulls before the day is up.

You meet Bull's contact, Gatt, at the Storm Coast, and he lays out the plan. A Qunari dreadnought intends to end a Venatori smuggling operation. Their cargo is red lyrium, and the Ben-Hassrath see this as a clear and present threat to Qunari ambitions. Once the briefing is over, speak with Bull to begin the assault.

The fighting begins in earnest, with Venatori troops trying to defend their positions on the nearby ridge from your relentless assault, while the rest of the Chargers attempt to hold a different position. You should be able to clear the area in minutes, and then you can signal the dreadnought.

However, it's apparent that the Venatori are well prepared, with a large number of mages on the beach marching in range of the dreadnought and the other Chargers. You are forced to make a major decision: Tell Bull to order his men to retreat, more or less betraying the Ben-Hassrath and becoming Ial-Vashoth, or allowing Bull to watch his men die. If the Chargers are sacrificed, the alliance with the Ben-Hassrath is secure. If they retreat, the mages destroy the dreadnought, and all hopes of an alliance will be crushed.

Regardless of how you choose, when you return to Skyhold, speak with Bull to help him get over the decision—though if his men are dead, there are not enough Qunari sayings or condolences you can pay to make him happy for their sacrifice.

> TOUGH LOVE

Quest Giver: Iron Bull

Description: According to the Qunari tradition, the gift of a dragon's tooth, broken in two, is symbolic of a deep, emotional connection. Also, Bull really likes dragons. A dragon tooth might be the perfect gift for him.

Requirements: Iron Bull must have high approval of you. You must have completed all of his side quest and have chosen to flirt during your conversations with him. Any gender or race is accepted.

Reward: 128 XP, 80 Influence

Objectives:

- Slay a dragon and collect a tooth.
- Obtain one piece of obsidian.
- Requisition the Necklace of Kadan.
- Give Iron Bull the necklace.

After enough flirting and fighting, Iron Bull gets the hint. When you next speak with Bull at the Skyhold tavern, you trigger a scene of your Inquisitor wandering to their room, distracted by paperwork. Waiting there, in bed, is the Iron Bull, and he's very frank about what he believes you want to do. You can rebuff his advances, rejecting a relationship, or accept them.

After your exhausting fade to black, go speak with Bull at the Skyhold tavern. You can choose to end things there or ask for another go. Iron Bull takes this second sexual encounter much more seriously. He says he will never hurt you (without permission), he will provide what you need, and you only need to speak one word to end the relationship. If you intend to pursue the relationship, have another tryst with Bull.

Return to the Skyhold tavern to speak with Iron Bull once more. You can ask him if what you're having with him is serious. It's now that you learn of a gift that Qunari share with a lover, if that relationship is meant to be more than a passing dalliance. You gain a requisition recipe to craft the Necklace of Kadan.

After crafting the necklace at a requisition table (one helpfully located very close to the tavern), speak with Bull again and give him his gift, leading to another intimate encounter that is interrupted by Cullen, Josephine, and Cassandra (in that order). Here, you can declare that the relationship is more than a mere fling: Iron Bull belongs to you, and you to him.

> THE FORGOTTEN BOY

Quest Giver: Cole

Description: After the dust settled, Cole was nowhere to be found. It's hard to believe he isn't hanging around somewhere in Skyhold.

Requirements: Establish Skyhold.

Reward: Cole

Objectives:

- Look for Cole.

You find Cole the center of a debate between Solas, Vivienne, and Cassandra. Solas feels that Cole is not to be feared despite his nature as spirit. Vivienne and Cassandra are not convinced, and your own input on the matter can gain you the approval of one side of the argument.

Speaking with Cole himself, you can learn more about his nature as a spirit. He feels he can help people, help them through suffering, such as the wounded in the courtyard of Skyhold. You can accept his help or send him away. Cole is an effective melee rogue, a good addition to the team. Solas will greatly approve of Cole; Vivienne will disapprove of his recruitment.

> SUBJECTED TO HIS WILL

Quest Giver: Cole

Description: Solas says that finding an Amulet of the Unbound will prevent Venatori mages from binding Cole.

Requirements: Complete Here Lies the Abyss, then talk to Cole in Skyhold.

Reward: 1,934 XP, 400 Influence, 3 Power

Objectives:

- Send scouts to investigate possible amulet locations.
- Give the amulet to Cole.

Cole is badly shaken by the events at Adamant, and he wishes for Solas to bind him, so that less savory mages do not. Solas is insistent on refusing to bind Cole but suggests that the Inquisition could seek out an Amulet of the Unbound. This would make Cole immune to blood magic. Go to the war table and send an advisor to complete the new operation that has opened up.

When the amulet is obtained, seek out Cole at the Skyhold tavern. You catch up to him trying to "help" a mourning woman, and you can actually interrupt his usual tricks of making people forget him, if you desire. Afterward, give him the amulet so Solas can try to save him from future blood mages.

Unfortunately, it does not work. Varric steps in to provide his own two cents, suggesting that the amulet does not work because Cole is not just a spirit or a demon. After a debate, Varric suggests that Cole work with Cullen to find the source of what is going "wrong" with the enchantment.

You're then taken to Redcliffe. Cole immediately spies the problem and seeks to end it. A man that Varric suspects is a former templar is nearly killed on the spot. It turns out that Cole created himself in memory of an apostate who died after being locked up by that templar. Cole stalks after the man after he escapes, leaving Varric and Solas to debate what Cole is and how he should handle this. Varric insists that Cole is no mere spirit, and that he must learn to work through this anger as a person would. Solas believes that Cole must forgive the man and avoid compromising his nature as a spirit.

What you choose determines Cole's future development. Bear this in mind.

> LAST RESORT OF GOOD MEN

Quest Giver: Dorian

Description: Mother Giselle passed along the letter written by Dorian's father. Dorian may wish to read it, but it may be best just to take him to the tavern to sort this out in person.

Requirements: Available after establishing Skyhold

Reward: 1,025 XP, 400 Influence, 3 Power

Objectives:

- Bring Dorian to the Gull & Lantern.
- Optional: Speak to Dorian about the letter.

Dorian's issues with his father are deep seated, and it's possible to convince him to not even bother going to visit the inn, assuming you bother telling him about the letter to begin with. If you choose to not tell him, and just travel to Redcliffe on your own, he does not appreciate the surprise. Over the course of an intense conversation between Dorian and his father, you learn much about the man and what drove him to leave Tevinter. You can encourage Dorian to hold on to his anger and leave without reconciliation, or you can help him finally speak with his father. This act ultimately makes him loyal to the Inquisitor, and if you're playing a male, this can lead toward romance.

> ONE LESS VENATORI

Description: They may come from the same place, but there's a world of difference between the Venatori and most people from Tevinter. Dorian wants a particular group of Venatori mages dead.

Quest Giver: Dorian

Requirements: Available after establishing Skyhold

Reward: Dorian's approval.

Objectives:

- Kill three groups of Venatori with Dorian.

After the events in Redcliffe, Dorian is eager to prove his loyalty to the Inquisition and get some payback on the Venatori. Dorian would be very happy to join you in hunting down three groups of Venatori hiding around Thedas. Killing them in his presence earns his approval.

> THE MAGISTER'S BIRTHRIGHT

Quest Giver: Dorian

Description: When Dorian went south, he did so with little in the way of coin and sold an amulet that proves his connection to House Pavus. A merchant from Val Royeaux named Ponchard de Lieux now has the amulet and apparently refuses to give it back to Dorian.

Requirements: Be a male Inquisitor, complete Dorian's two inner circle quests, and have high approval.

Reward: Romance with Dorian

Objectives:

- Pay Ponchard a visit.
- Make the necessary arrangements at the war table.
- Return to the war table.
- Give the amulet to Dorian.
- Speak with Dorian.

Dorian's flirtatious nature seems directed at women, but if you've led Dorian to meet with his father, you will have learned that he prefers the company of men. If you're a male Inquisitor and have made clear to Dorian that your concern for him extends beyond friendship, your romance can begin. Through conversation with Dorian, you can learn that he was forced to sell a keepsake that proved his true birthright.

Later, you receive word from Leliana about this matter. The amulet is in the possession of Ponchard, a merchant of Val Royeaux. When you visit the merchant, he refuses to return the amulet. You can kill him for it, an act that Dorian greatly disapproves of, bringing an end to your relationship. If you're a rogue, you can intimidate Ponchard. Your other alternative is to give Ponchard what he wants: membership in the League de Celestine.

If intimidation isn't an option, go to the war table and make the arrangements for Ponchard. The amulet is delivered as promised. A grateful Dorian offers to meet you in your room in private for a physical culmination of the romance.

Romancing Dorian can be challenging, as it is something the Chantry approves of, and even Dorian himself fears that you may be putting personal interests before those of the Inquisition. You can break off the relationship at any time.

> OF SOMEWHAT FALLEN FORTUNE

Quest Giver: Josephine

Description: Josephine attempted to reinstate her family as a trading power in Orlais, which triggered an assassination contract taken out more than 100 years ago by a family known as the Du Paraquettes. Despite the contract's age and the fact that the Du Paraquettes are no longer nobility, the contract is still binding. A group of assassins honoring the contract, called the House of Repose, won't rest until Josephine is dead.

Requirements: Available at Skyhold

Reward: 1,025 XP, 400 Influence, 3 Power

Objectives:

- Meet with Josephine in Val Royeaux.
- Return to Skyhold and speak with Josephine.
- Speak with Josephine about the next move.
- Go to the war table and find a sponsor for the Du Paraquettes.
- Speak with Countess Dionne in Val Royeaux.
- Return to Skyhold and speak with Josephine.
- Arrange a favor for Judge Auld at the war table.
- Speak with Josephine.
- Go to the war table and find a way to meet Bellise.
- Optional: Dispatch Leliana's assassins.
- Go to the marquis's party.
- Speak with Josephine.
- Meet Josephine in Val Royeaux.

After you speak enough to Josephine, you'll learn that she's been trying to reestablish her family in Val Royeaux, only to have her messengers murdered. She wants to meet you at the city while she meets with someone who claims to know why her messengers are dead. Go to Val Royeaux to meet with Josephine, and tell her you're ready to see Comte Boisvert.

The conversation with the comte does not go as planned. The comte has been replaced by an assassin from the House of Repose. The Du Paraquettes, a now dead noble lineage, signed a contract to eliminate anyone attempting to restore the Montilyets to Val Royeaux. A hundred and nine years ago. You can learn more from the assassin before he decides to leave. You also have the choice to kill him if you feel that he's earned it. Return to Skyhold.

Josephine says that if the Du Paraquettes can be restored as nobles, they can annul the contract. This requires time, many favors that you must attend to personally by completing operations on the war table, and meeting people of import. Alternatively, you can send Leliana's agents into the House of Repose vaults to destroy the original contract, but it is not the option that Josephine will be happiest with.

First, you must arrange a meeting with Countess Dionne in Val Royeaux, to confirm the well being of her lover in the war engulfing Orlais. After returning to Skyhold to plan your next move, you find that assassins made an attempt on Josephine. You're once again tempted to send Inquisition agents to the House of Repose.

Next, you're to set up a favor for Judge Auld. You need to send a complement of soldiers via a war table operation to accompany the judge on his latest hunt. It will take some time before the operation completes, but once it's done you can move on to the next step: a meeting with Minister Bellise. Set up yet another war table operation to arrange the meeting.

Bellise is supremely arrogant, and she's fishing for you to make an offer she won't outright refuse. Offer whatever you like—a favor from the Inquisition is tempting enough she agrees to help you.

With all the favors complete, or if you dispatched Leliana's agents to deal with the problem, meet with Josephine in Skyhold to confirm the good news regarding the Du Paraquettes. Afterward, return to Val Royeaux to speak with her once again after she completes the final negotiations. During this last conversation, you can learn more about your ambassador's past. If you're looking to romance Josephine, there is a dialogue option to set that up as well.

> HERALDRY FROM A HERALD

Quest Giver: Josephine

Description: Josephine has long wished to see an example of her family's ancestral crest, which has been impossible to come by since the Montilyets' exile from Orlais.

Requirements: Available at Skyhold; complete Of Somewhat Fallen Fortune.

Reward: Josephine's approval

Objectives:

- Go to the war table to find Josephine's family crest.
- Return to the war table.
- Search Val Royeaux's shops for a Montilyet family crest.
- Present the crest to Josephine in Skyhold.

If you've been taking romance options with Josephine and have completed Josephine's personal quest, you can start a romance with her. If you're in a romance, go to her office and ask her if her ancestors were Orlesian. Josephine confirms it and mentions a desire to see her family's lost ancestral crest. This prompts a war table operation to hunt down this crest. After it's located, go to Val Royeaux to purchase it from one of the vendors, and then return to Skyhold with Josephine's present. She is overjoyed to receive such a thoughtful gift.

> AN UNEXPECTED ENGAGEMENT

Quest Giver: Josephine

Description: Josephine's parents have arranged for her to marry Lord Adorno Ciel Otranto of Antiva. Given the circumstances, she does not wish to honor the betrothal.

Requirements: Available at Skyhold

Reward: Romance with Josephine

Objectives:

- Go to the war table to challenge Otranto to a duel.
- Wait for a response.
- Speak with the messenger in Skyhold.
- Go to Val Royeaux to duel Otranto.

After you begin your romance with Josephine, yet another possible complication arrives at your doorstep: the arranged marriage to a man with more names than is reasonable. Josephine is distraught and wants to put your relationship with her on hold while she tries to diplomatically work her way out of this situation. You can try to fish for more details on how to handle this, but the most important clue is that she lets slip that you can challenge this nobleman to an honorable duel. To the war table!

If you have the Underworld Knowledge perk, you can be a jerk and try to discredit Otranto before the duel begins, sending Leliana's spies out to dig up dirt on the man.

Your message to Otranto is answered quickly via a messenger you may meet at the front gate to Skyhold. Otranto accepts your duel and will meet you in Val Royeaux.

In the central pavilion, Otranto greets you in an aggressively polite fashion, tossing you a rapier. You can try to bring your own weapons into the fight, but it will not look honorable to the rapidly gathering crowd.

As the duel of weapons and words claws towards its climax, Josephine herself interferes with the duel, upset that you are putting your life and reputation on the line for her. This is your last chance to break off the romance or confirm it. In light of the latter, Otranto withdraws coolly from the battlefield, knowing love when he sees it.

> PERSEVERANCE

Quest Giver: Cullen

Description: Cullen is suffering the effects of lyrium withdrawal. Cassandra wonders if now is the best time for Cullen to stop taking it.

Requirements: Available at Skyhold. You must have spoken with Cullen about his lyrium woes and have spent time playing chess against him before this quest becomes available.

Reward: 1,025 XP, 400 Influence, 3 Power

Objectives:

- See why Cullen and Cassandra are meeting.
- Speak with Cullen.

Cullen tries to keep fighting his lyrium addiction, but you soon learn he's not handling it well. An aide in his office informs you that Cullen is currently meeting with Cassandra about an important issue. When you go to meet them near the Skyhold blacksmith, you discover that Cullen is questioning his ability to perform as one of your advisors and is asking for Cassandra to name a replacement. Knowing that you have a good relationship with Cullen, she defers to you on how to help him through the withdrawals.

Go to Cullen's office to speak with him. The withdrawals are so painful he's frustrated and on the verge of giving up. Do what you can to talk him down, but there is a major decision to make here. You can encourage him either to keep fighting the addiction or to give in. If you told him to take lyrium again, then when you go speak with him at the Skyhold blacksmith later, you have one more chance to confirm your decision to force him back on lyrium or turn him back toward recovery.

> HAPPIER TIMES

Quest Giver: Cullen

Description: Cullen wants to have a private talk with you somewhere less hectic than Skyhold.

Requirements: Available at Skyhold after Perseverance is done, if you are in a romance with Cullen

Reward: Romance with Cullen

Objectives:

- Agree to travel with Cullen to Ferelden.

After you've completed Perseverance and are in a romance with Cullen, he will ask you if you'd like to accompany him to Ferelden, as he has business there. You can go right away or take him up on his offer later. Once you agree to travel with Cullen, you will be taken to a small lake in rural Ferelden. Cullen reminisces about growing up in this area, then presents you with a gift and a kiss. After that, you're taken back to Skyhold.

> THE LEFT HAND OF THE DIVINE

Quest Giver: Leliana

Description: A letter, written by Divine Justinia and posthumously delivered to Leliana, directed Leliana to visit Valence, a small village on the Waking Sea. The Divine left something in the chantry that Leliana must see.

Requirements: Available at Skyhold

Reward: 1,025 XP, 400 Influence, 3 Power

Objectives:

- Join Leliana at the chantry in Valence.

During a conversation with Leliana at Skyhold, she asks you to meet her at a chantry in Valence. She has just received an unexpected letter from Divine Justinia directing her to visit this specific chantry. After receiving this request form Leliana, access the world map and choose the Valence Cloister as your destination.

Upon your arrival at the chantry, the Inquisitor and Leliana are greeted by a Sister Natalie, a chantry cleric. But something isn't right. While Natalie and Leliana continue their conversation, begin looking around. There are three hidden mechanisms in the chantry—use the Search feature to find them all. Once you interact with all three hidden mechanisms, a secret door is unlocked, to the north. Search at this point and then interact with the door to reveal a hidden chamber containing a small, ornate box.

Suddenly, Leliana turns on Natalie, holding a dagger to her throat— she knows Natalie has been lying all this time and is working for Grand Cleric Victoire, who seeks to make an enemy of the Inquisition. You can convince her to spare Natalie if you've softened Leliana by telling her to not kill the traitor agent named Butler during an early conversation at Haven, and supported her decision to pull back her agents just before Corypheus attacked Haven. If you have not done these things, Leliana will kill Natalie regardless of what you say. Alternatively, if you've softened Leliana, you can push her to kill Natalie to her dismay, but she is understanding that she must do what is necessary for the Inquisition.

After dealing with Natalie, Leliana turns to the secret chamber. But the box inside is empty. Still, there's an inscription on the box: "The Left Hand should lay down her burden." How Leliana reacts to your dialogue choices here also depends on how you've influenced her.

Either way, it seems to clear her head—she requests to see you at Skyhold. Leave the chantry and return to Skyhold; upon your arrival, speak to Leliana to conclude the quest.

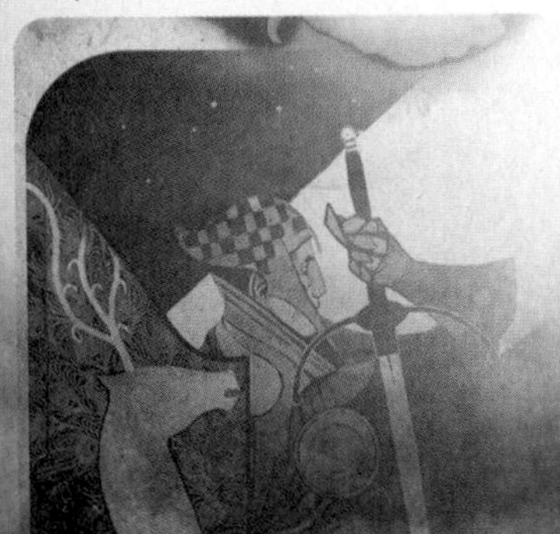

> UNDER HER SKIN (NEMESIS QUEST)

Quest Giver: Leliana

Description: Much like the Inquisition, Corypheus has invested great time and effort building a trusted inner circle. Calpernia leads the Venatori—and it seems she's been busy. In the search for a particular set of elven ruins, she and her army of Tevinter extremists have taken a keen interest in a merchant named Vicinius. Perhaps finding him would shed more light on Calpernia and her motivations.

Requirements: Available at Skyhold; Inquisitor must have allied with the templars (completed Champions of the Just).

Reward: 1,025 XP, 400 Influence, 3 Power

Objectives:

- Find Vicinius in Val Royeaux.
- Find three crystal pieces.
- Acquire the services of an arcanist.
- Speak to Dagna about the crystal pieces.
- Arrange for a spy to plant the recording crystal in Calpernia's camp.
- Listen to the receiving crystal with Leliana.
- Have Leliana locate the Shrine of Dumat.
- Explore the Shrine of Dumat.
- Speak to Leliana about the fate of Magister Erasthenes.

Speak to Leliana in Skyhold to learn more of Calpernia, leader of the Venatori and a Corypheus acolyte. But Leliana wants to gather more information on Calpernia. She has a lead—a merchant named Vicinius in Val Royeaux. Travel there and track down this merchant. But upon your arrival, Vicinius's home has been ransacked. Defeat the Venatori found upstairs and interact with what's left of Vicinius—search the room for three pieces of a shattered memory crystal. Once you have all three pieces, return to Skyhold and speak with Leliana.

Leliana reveals that Calpernia was a slave before becoming leader of the Venatori. It appears Corypheus freed her and now she serves him. Leliana tells you to take the crystal pieces to Dagna. In the undercroft, Dagna manages to restore the three pieces, forming a memory crystal. This crystal has recorded a conversation between Calpernia and Corypheus—he wants Calpernia to become "the vessel." But it appears Calpernia isn't quite enthusiastic about Corypheus's plan. Leliana has an idea—she suggests hiding half of the crystal among Calpernia's belongings while keeping the other half in Skyhold, allowing Leliana to listen in.

Go to the war room and choose the Investigate the Elven Ruins operation on the war table, located in eastern Orlais. This operation costs four power, but it allows one of Leliana's agents to plant half of the crystal into Calpernia's camp. Once the operation is complete, collect the report and go back to Leliana.

As hoped, the crystal has recorded another conversation between Calpernia and Corypheus. In order to become the vessel, Calpernia wants to train at the Shrine of Dumat. But the recording ends shortly after Calpernia discovers the crystal and smashes it—she knows the Inquisition has been listening to her. Leliana is curious to know what Calpernia's next move will be. In the meantime, it's a good idea to check out that shrine. Go to the war table and select the operation The Shrine of Dumat, in northern Orlais. This costs one power, but it unlocks the Shrine of Dumat on the world map. Gather your party and travel to the shrine.

Shrine of Dumat

Enter the shrine and fight your way through a variety of demons, including a massive pride demon. After defeating the pride demon, enter the chamber marked on the compass to find a man trapped beneath a blue, dome-shaped magical barrier—this is Magister Erasthenes. Once a Tevinter scholar, this man is now bound to Corypheus. Erasthenes reveals that Calpernia will be bound by Corypheus if she becomes the vessel. At the end of the conversation you get to choose Erasthenes' fate: You can kill him, let him live, or make him tranquil.

CORYPHEUS'S MEMORIES

Before leaving the shrine, track down six memory crystals to complete the Corypheus's Memories side quest. There are three crystals in the upstairs chamber and three in the downstairs chamber—but watch out for more demons when you head downstairs. Each time you collect a crystal, a different recording from Corypheus can be heard discussing a variety of topics. When you've gathered all six crystals, return to Skyhold.

Conclusion

Speak to Leliana back at Skyhold. Now that you know Calpernia will be bound by Corypheus when she becomes the vessel, you have some valuable information to use against her—surely Calpernia doesn't want to lose her free will and become a slave again. Later on, at the Temple of Mythal, you can confront Calpernia with this evidence and make her turn away from the Well of Sorrows, avoiding a conflict. Complete the conversation with Leliana to complete the quest.

BEFORE THE DAWN (NEMESIS QUEST)

Quest Giver: Cullen

Description: Much like the Inquisition, Corypheus has invested great time and effort building a trusted inner circle. Samson is a former templar, a lyrium addict, and now the leader of the red templars. Cullen knows Samson well, and he believes intercepting caravans smuggling red lyrium in the Emerald Graves could get the Inquisition closer to taking him down.

Requirements: Available at Skyhold; the Inquisitor must have allied with the mages (completed In Hushed Whispers) and completed the side quest Red Water.

Reward: 1,025 XP, 400 Influence, 3 Power

Objectives:

- Find three smuggler letters.
- Take the smuggler letters to Cullen.
- Raid Sahrnia Quarry.
- Return to Cullen with the information found at the quarry
- Acquire the services of an arcanist.
- Speak with Dagna about Samson's armor.
- Go to the war table to find Samson's weakness.
- Speak to Cullen about what Dagna discovered.
- Dispatch agents to locate Maddox.
- Speak to Cullen about raiding Samson's camp.
- Travel to Samson's camp at the Shrine of Dumat.
- Find Maddox.
- Search the camp to find clues about Samson's armor.
- Meet Cullen at Skyhold to discuss Maddox's tools with Dagna.

After becoming established at Skyhold, take time to speak with Cullen to handle some of his problems. Chief among them is a former templar named Samson, who has become a chief lieutenant for Corypheus. Cullen has no leads, but he has leads on how you can get those leads. It's to the Emerald Graves with you, your task being to intercept smugglers trafficking red lyrium. Be sure to loot the cargo the smugglers were protecting; there are red lyrium shards you can use for powerful runes for your weapons.

The three smuggler letters you find must be taken back to Cullen. He determines your next destination: Sahrnia Quarry, in the Emprise du Lion. Red templars will have taken control of it, as well as most of the whole locale, so reaching the quarry itself requires a lot of fighting if you haven't already secured the area.

Once you get there, you're looking for documents left by Samson himself, detailing the horrific process of growing red lyrium. They also mention hints about an armor he now wears that he swore was like drowning in fire when he first donned it, and by enduring it he has become fit to be "The Vessel." This is not at all ominous; report back to Cullen as soon as possible.

When you meet with Cullen he is incensed by what you have learned, but there's a solution to be found in your own camp if you've already recruited the dwarven arcanist, Dagna, Cullen points you in her direction. If there's anyone who can figure out a solution, it is her.

NOTE It is possible to start this quest without having hired Dagna in to the Inquisition. In that case, you'll be prompted by Cullen to use the war table to hire Dagna.

Dagna's suggestions lead you back to the war table to the Find Samson's Weakness operation. After the agents return with word on Samson's armor, speak with Cullen once again. A tranquil mage named Maddox, another acquaintance of Cullen's, is apparently working with Samson, being responsible for maintaining the armor he wears. Another trip to the war table is necessary, in order to pinpoint the exact location of Samson and Maddox. This leads the Inquisition to the Shrine of Dumat.

After the shrine is discovered, you can gather a party and travel to the shrine from Cullen's office. There, you can expect the best of the best from the red templars, their full ranks on display, averaging around level 19. Cullen will join your party to add a fifth man running around and crushing the enemy. Fight your way through the shrine until you reach the laboratory where Maddox is located. Samson and the armor are long gone.

Maddox himself isn't long for this world, having consumed a bottle of poison so that he can maintain the secrets of the armor. Maddox's loyalty is indeed admirable, but drinking poison isn't enough to keep the armor safe from you. Search his labs for implements you can bring back to Dagna in Skyhold for analysis.

One final conversation with Cullen ties the loose ends together. Dagna's analysis of Maddox's tools has revealed a possible method for destroying Samson's armor, and she's crafted a special rune just for that purpose. When you run into Samson in the future, he won't have a clue what hit him. With this, the quest is complete.

BESTIARY

Even before demons started pouring from Fade rifts, southern Thedas had seen more than its fair share of turmoil and bloodshed. The mage rebellion has caused great instability in Ferelden, prompting refugees to flee their homes as they attempt to escape the war between the mages and templars. A civil war has been equally destructive in Orlais, as Empress Celene clings to power, challenged by her own cousin, Grand Duke Gaspard.

Now an unknown threat has torn a hole in the sky, allowing demons to cross over from the Fade. But instead of putting their differences aside and focusing on the Breach, a threat to the whole world, the warring parties are more concerned with winning their relatively petty conflicts. It is only the Inquisition who stands as a stabilizing force in southern Thedas, determined to close the Breach and restore order. But the world is not a safe one—dangers lurk in every wilderness, be it from creatures, demons, or humans. Travel forth with great caution and careful preparation.

NOTE When discussing immunities in this chapter, the Physical Effects category includes stun, knockdown, interrupt, and knockback. Also, a creature's health modifier is relative to the global health amount for that particular level. Foot soldiers are always 1x, so this can be explained relative to their health. For example, a bruiser has 1.75x a foot soldier's health at equal level.

WILDLIFE

Ferelden and Orlais are both teeming with wildlife. Most of these creatures are docile and nonconfrontational—they're likely to scatter as you and your party approach. These passive animals appear as blue dots on the compass. But some creatures are hostile and will attack when you intrude on their territory—they appear as red dots on the compass. Whether passive or aggressive, all creatures are integral parts of the crafting system. When you slay one of these creatures, it will usually drop at least one piece of crafting material, appearing on the ground as loot. The furs and hides supplied by these creatures allow you to craft better equipment for yourself and party members.

> ARMORED MABARI

LOCALE: Crestwood, Storm Coast
LEVEL RANGE: 4-11
HEALTH MODIFIER: 1.5
ARMOR: High
RESISTANCES:
- Cold

VULNERABILITIES:
- Fire

IMMUNITIES:
- Physical Effects

CRAFTING MATERIAL:
- Canine Leather

"The mabari are an essential part of Fereldan military strategy. Trained hounds can easily pull knights from horseback or break lines of pikemen, and the sight and sound of a wave of wardogs, howling and snarling, has been known to cause panic among even the most hardened infantry soldiers."

— From *Ferelden: Folklore and History*, by Sister Petrine, Chantry scholar

> AUGUST RAM

LOCALE: Hissing Wastes, Emerald Graves, Emprise du Lion
LEVEL RANGE: 12-15
HEALTH MODIFIER: 0.25
ARMOR: Very Low
RESISTANCES:
- Cold

VULNERABILITIES: None
IMMUNITIES: None
CRAFTING MATERIAL:
- August Ram Leather

"The slender and sleek hide gives the animal the grace of a hart halla. Its curved horns spiral back over delicate ears twitching at the slightest rustle of grass. When startled, speed is the august ram's only defense against the hunter. It is difficult to sneak up on these shy and wary creatures."

— An excerpt from the diary of Tillendall Lemallen, noted painter of wildlife and portraits to the Orlesian Court

> BEAR

LOCALE: Emerald Graves, The Hinterlands, Storm Coast
LEVEL RANGE: 8-12
HEALTH MODIFIER: 3
ARMOR: High
RESISTANCES:
- Cold

VULNERABILITIES:
- Fire

IMMUNITIES:
- Physical Effects
- Paralyze
- Freeze

CRAFTING MATERIAL:
- Bear Hide

"I would've liked to watch the little family playing in the stream all day, but the wind changed and the mama bear caught our scent, even with Eldwin working his magic. She leapt in our direction, stopped when she couldn't see anything, then rose up on her hind legs and roared. What a sight that was! I estimate she was half again as tall as I. Quick as anything, she charged toward us, snapping branches as she went. I dove out of the way, but Eldwin, bless his heart, was too slow. A massive paw caught him right in the chest and he went down. Poor Eldwin. Nature is ruthless but magnificent."

— An excerpt from the *Wilds of Thedas: Volume Two*, by Stephan D'Eroin

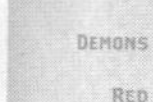

> BLACK WOLF

LOCALE: Crestwood, Hinterlands, Emerald Graves, Emprise du Lion, Exalted Plains
LEVEL RANGE: 4-19
HEALTH MODIFIER: 1.5
ARMOR: Low
RESISTANCES:
- Cold

VULNERABILITIES:
- Fire

IMMUNITIES: None
CRAFTING MATERIAL:
- Canine Leather

"The scouts report activity uncharacteristic of lupine behavior. The Breach and resulting rifts have caused unprecedented disruptions in the Veil. Such alterations to the environment may account for the unnatural aggression. If this is indeed the case, I cannot yet say how widespread the impact. How many wolves does this environmental imbalance influence? What threat do they pose to resistant members of the pack? The local population? This warrants further investigation."

— Report submitted to Seeker Pentaghast by Minaeve, mage apprentice and Inquisition researcher

> BRONTO

LOCALE: Crestwood, Emerald Graves
LEVEL RANGE: 16-19
HEALTH MODIFIER: 2
ARMOR: Very High
RESISTANCES:
- Cold

VULNERABILITIES:
- Fire

IMMUNITIES:
- Physical Effects
- Paralyze
- Freeze

CRAFTING MATERIAL:
- Bronto Hide

"The dwarven Shaperate originally bred this hulking beast as a beast of burden and food source, the rough equivalent of surface oxen and cows. Some versions of the bronto have even been developed as dwarven mounts, valued more for sure-footedness and stamina than speed. While present in Orzammar in large numbers, some brontos still exist in packs in the Deep Roads, having returned to a wild state after the fall of the dwarven kingdoms. They require remarkably little sustenance, absorbing nutrients from water, fungus, and even rocks (hence the "rock-licker" appellation many dwarves use to describe brontos), and exist primarily in a dormant state until provoked. An angry, charging bronto is considered a rather dangerous opponent."

— From *Tales from Beneath the Earth*, by Brother Genitivi

> DEEPSTALKER

LOCALE: Crestwood, Storm Coast
LEVEL RANGE: 8-15
HEALTH MODIFIER: 0.5
ARMOR: Very Low
RESISTANCES: None
VULNERABILITIES:
- Electricity

IMMUNITIES: None
CRAFTING MATERIAL:
- Deepstalker Hide

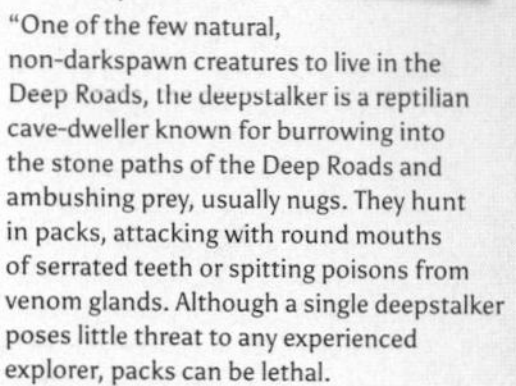

"One of the few natural, non-darkspawn creatures to live in the Deep Roads, the deepstalker is a reptilian cave-dweller known for burrowing into the stone paths of the Deep Roads and ambushing prey, usually nugs. They hunt in packs, attacking with round mouths of serrated teeth or spitting poisons from venom glands. Although a single deepstalker poses little threat to any experienced explorer, packs can be lethal.

— From *Tales from Beneath the Earth*, by Brother Genitivi

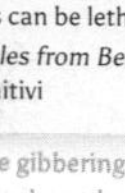

NOTE The gibbering horror, found in the Fade, looks and performs much like a deepstalker, albeit with slightly more health.

> DRAGONLINGS

LOCALE: Emprise du Lion, Hissing Wastes, Storm Coast
LEVEL RANGE: 8-21
HEALTH MODIFIER: 1
ARMOR: Low
RESISTANCES:
- Fire

VULNERABILITIES:
- Electricity

IMMUNITIES:
- Physical Effects

CRAFTING MATERIAL:
- Dragon Blood
- Dragon's Tooth
- Dragonling Scales

Newly hatched dragons are roughly the size of a deer and voraciously hungry. They live for a short time in their mother's lair before venturing out on their own. The slender, wingless creatures are born in vast numbers, as only a few survive to adulthood.

> DRUFFALO

LOCALE: Crestwood, Frostback Mountains, The Hinterlands
LEVEL RANGE: 1-11
HEALTH MODIFIER: 2
ARMOR: Very High
RESISTANCES:
- Cold

VULNERABILITIES:
- Fire

IMMUNITIES:
- Physical Effects
- Paralyze
- Freeze

CRAFTING MATERIAL:
- Druffalo Hide

"As I searched for my courage, I heard a crashing through the undergrowth. Bandits, I thought. Or a bear. But instead it was a giant beast, with pelt of blue-gray and gleaming black horns. And riding its muscled back was my Guy. The druffalo was enormous but gentle as a doe. The children called her Bluebell."

— From a diary found in a refugee tent in the Hinterlands

> FENNEC

LOCALE: Crestwood, Hissing Wastes, Hinterlands, Forbidden Oasis, Western Approach
LEVEL RANGE: 1-15
HEALTH MODIFIER: 0.15
ARMOR: Very Low
RESISTANCES: None
VULNERABILITIES: None
IMMUNITIES: None
CRAFTING MATERIAL:
- Fennec Fur

"I want a fennec. Please, please, please get one for me. I saw a picture in a book that Brigid was carrying for Master Fergal, and it is the fluffiest and most delightful creature I have ever seen. The book says they live in the mountains and eat voles and repulsive things like that."

— A note from Habren Bryland to her father, Leonas Bryland, arl of South Reach, written in 9:31 Dragon

> GIANT

LOCALE: Emerald Graves, Emprise du Lion, Forbidden Oasis, Storm Coast, Western Approach
LEVEL RANGE: 8-19
HEALTH MODIFIER: 3
ARMOR: Very High
RESISTANCES: None
VULNERABILITIES:
- Electricity

IMMUNITIES:
- Physical Effects
- Fear
- Paralyze
- Freeze
- Sleep
- Weakness
- Snare

CRAFTING MATERIAL: None

"I followed one specimen from the north, where they are somewhat more common (Tevinter breeding grounds? Warmth of the seasons? Corruption of Silent Plains?). It followed waterways, preferring to float its bulk, but never did I see any sense in its eye, and never did it appear to plan beyond its immediate surroundings. But I remain intrigued, for they wave hands, and that means potential to raise them in praise. Throughout creation, upright beings with hands have been a sign of greater purpose. What lesson, Maker, in these strange children? I will approach tomorrow, in your name."

— Last entry in *The Letters of Brother Estomahr*

> GIANT SPIDER

LOCALE: Crestwood, Emerald Graves, Hissing Wastes, Hinterlands, Forbidden Oasis, Revenant Church, Storm Coast, Western Approach
LEVEL RANGE: 8-19
HEALTH MODIFIER: 1
ARMOR: Very Low
RESISTANCES:
- Electricity

VULNERABILITIES: None
IMMUNITIES: None
CRAFTING MATERIAL:
- Giant Spider Glands

"Maybe it's meant to be that size, and the regular ones are miniatures. I mean, a just and caring Maker would create them big to start. Then they can't hide. That's what bothers you, isn't it? The hiding? A big one like that, a good 12-footer, sure, it's all fangs and such, but you know where it is: dark places where the Veil is weak. You're never surprised by a giant one because you had to go to their "house." They're not on your face at night or in your boot in the morning..."

— From records of a Redcliffe guard, 14 Guardian 9:39

> GREAT BEAR

LOCALE: Emerald Graves, Emprise du Lion
LEVEL RANGE: 11-19
HEALTH MODIFIER: 3
ARMOR: High
RESISTANCES:
- Cold

VULNERABILITIES:
- Fire

IMMUNITIES:
- Physical Effects
- Paralyze
- Freeze

CRAFTING MATERIAL:
- Great Bear Hide

"The Orlesian great bear is so named because it is very large. Very large, indeed. Other names for it include the colorful "Old Man of the Forest" and the less-charming, but more clearly descriptive, "Woodsman Death." I am told that not even the nobility is willing to hunt for them, which makes them unique among the rare, giant, deadly, exotic fauna of Thedas: the only thing the Orlesians are truly afraid of."

— From *In Pursuit of Knowledge: Travels of a Chantry Scholar*, by Brother Genitivi

> GURGUT

LOCALE: Exalted Plains
LEVEL RANGE: 12-15
HEALTH MODIFIER: 3
ARMOR: Low
RESISTANCES:
- Fire

VULNERABILITIES:
- Electricity

IMMUNITIES:
- Physical Effects

CRAFTING MATERIAL:
- Craggy Skin

"I have seen the gurgut basking in a slanted shaft of sunlight in the penumbral canyon, its putrescent tongue scenting the rancid air of the nameless and unnameable swamp, swishing the uncaring grass of the plains with its passage. It is some cousin of the wyvern, but bereft of the savage ferocity for which the latter is praised and hunted by Orlesian nobles. Its thick-lidded eyes stare witlessly, and its jaw hangs agape; it is not befuddled or frustrated by its want of reason, but perfectly content, a drooling idiot. Its pallid belly stretches and distends, disdaining all reason, when it gorges itself upon its prey. I have seen such a lowly beast swallow a chevalier whole, the great and shining warrior taken by surprise in the tall grass, his silverite armor gleaming as the gurgut unhinged its jaw to draw the chevalier in. Across its belly, I saw the kicks and struggles grow frenzied and then still, and the idiot beast settled into a happy torpor. The ruined armor of the noble chevalier lay among the gurgut's spoor several days later."

— An excerpt from *An Anatomie of Various Terrible Beasts*, by Baron Havard-Pierre d'Amortisan

> GURN

LOCALE: Hissing Wastes, Western Approach
LEVEL RANGE: 8-19
HEALTH MODIFIER: 2
ARMOR: Very High
RESISTANCES:
- Cold

VULNERABILITIES:
- Fire

IMMUNITIES:
- Physical Effects
- Paralyze
- Freeze

CRAFTING MATERIAL:
- Gurn Hide
- Hardened Gurn Hide (Hardened Gurn)

"We woke to a herd from nowhere, just standing around the camp. And it wasn't the first time. Getting water at an oasis, humming to myself, poof, there's one behind me. Talk to another rider for a few minutes, and there's two, just staring. I think they think talking is weird. Harmless, so long as you don't treat them like cattle. Maybe farm-raised, but not wild. One time, we figured we'd saddle one. Maybe break it like a horse? Because that hump would bounce arrows real nice. Bad idea. Did not end well for Five-Toe. We used to call him Six-Toe, but not because of his feet. He got the horn something fierce."

— *Excerpts on the Gurn, Voices of Working Caravans*, collected by Philliam, a bard

> HALLA

LOCALE: The Exalted Plains
LEVEL RANGE: 8-19
HEALTH MODIFIER: 0.25
ARMOR: Very Low
RESISTANCES: None
VULNERABILITIES: None
IMMUNITIES: None
CRAFTING MATERIAL:
- Halla Leather

"The first thing you must understand about the halla is that they are not our servants. They are not our pets. They are our brothers and sisters. Remember that Ghilan'nain, the first halla and mother of them all, was once a huntress of the people. Without the halla, there would be no Dalish. The second thing you must understand about the halla is that you cannot force a halla to do something against her will. I have heard tales of shemlen who come across herds and attempt to capture the halla, using ropes and bridles. Many shemlen have died impaled on horns as a result of this foolishness. Never forget that the halla once bore our knights into battle. The fierce blood of a warrior still runs through her veins and she would sooner fight to the death than demean herself. Like the Dalish, the halla are proud. A halla knows who she is, and will tolerate no being that tells her that she is less."

— Adara, halla-tender of the Ralaferin clan, to her apprentice

HIGH DRAGON

LOCALE: Crestwood, Emerald Graves, Emprise du Lion, Exalted Plains, Hissing Wastes, Hinterlands, Storm Coast, Western Approach
LEVEL RANGE: 13-23
HEALTH MODIFIER: 36
ARMOR: Average
RESISTANCES: Varies (see table)
VULNERABILITIES: Varies (see table)

IMMUNITIES:
- Physical Effects
- Fear
- Paralyze
- Freeze
- Sleep
- Snare
- Confuse

CRAFTING MATERIAL:
- Intense Dragon Blood
- Dragon's Tooth
- Dragon Webbing
- Dragon Scales
- Dragon Bone

A fully mature adult female dragon is a high dragon: the great monster of legend, the rarest of all dragonkind. These dragons hollow out massive lairs for themselves, for they need the space to house their harem of drakes as well as their eggs and dragonlings. High dragons are seldom seen. They spend most of their time sleeping and mating, living off prey their drakes bring back. But once every hundred years or so, the high dragon prepares for clutching by emerging from the lair and taking wing. She will fly far and wide, eating hundreds of animals—most often livestock—over the course of a few weeks, leaving smoldering devastation in her wake. She then returns to her lair to lay her eggs and will not again appear in the skies for another century.

Abilities

ARMORED: Allows a dragon to generate guard.
BERSERK: A devastating 40-meter area-of-effect attack utilizing the dragon's elemental ability.
COLD: The dragon inflicts cold elemental damage; it can be countered by fire.
ELECTRICITY: The dragon inflicts electrical elemental damage; it can be countered by spirit.
FIRE: The dragon inflicts fire elemental damage; it can be countered by cold.
MATRIARCH: The dragon summons dragonlings to join the fight.
RED LYRIUM: The dragon utilizes red lyrium-based attacks.

High Dragon Attributes

Dragon	Locale	Resistance	Vulnerability	Abilities
Ferelden Frostback	The Hinterlands	Fire	Cold	Matriarch and Fire
Vinsomer	Storm Coast	Electricity	Spirit	Armored, Berserk, and Electricity
Northern Hunter	Crestwood	Electricity	Spirit	Berserk and Electricity
The Abyssal High Dragon	Western Approach	Fire	Cold	Armored and Fire
Gamoran Stormrider	The Exalted Plains	Electricity	Spirit	Electricity
Greater Mistral	Emerald Graves	Cold	Fire	Armored and Cold
Hivernal	Emprise du Lion	Cold	Fire	Berserk and Cold
Kaltenzahn	Emprise du Lion	Cold	Fire	Armored, Matriarch, and Cold
Highland Ravager	Emprise du Lion	Fire	Cold	Armored, Berserk, Matriarch, and Fire
Sandy Howler	Hissing Wastes	Fire	Cold	Armored, Matriarch, and Fire
Ancient Dragon	Arbor Wilds	Fire	Cold	Fire
Archdemon (Corypheus Dragon)	Finale	—	—	Armored and Red Lyrium

NOTE For more details on fighting each dragon, reference the Exploration chapter.

DEVELOPER TIP

High Dragons

- Dragons have big tells on their attacks—you can use the tactical camera to simultaneously move your party members out of danger.
- Shield warriors can use Shield Wall to block projectiles and melee attacks, at the cost of stamina.
- Make sure you have your focus bar full before engaging a dragon; these abilities can be key to your success.
- Damaging the limbs of a dragon so that she is severely bleeding will prevent the dragon from performing swipes with that limb, making life easier for melee characters.
- Damaging a pair of limbs will cause the dragon to fall down to that side, opening her up for increased damage and preventing her from attacking for a duration.
- Determine the element of the dragon, then craft and equip gear with resistance against that element to greatly increase your chance to survive the encounter. The elemental resistance potions really help out for this.
- Dragons are fearsome creatures and are immune to almost all status effects; however, they can still be taunted. Use that to your advantage to try to control whom the dragon is attacking.
- If a dragon leaps away and starts flying, take that time to pick up your party members and take a breather.
- Dragons spit projectiles that leave devastation on the ground. Make sure to move out of these areas and try to avoid the projectile in general.
- Dragons with the Matriarch ability can summon dragonlings to help them in their fight. This is telegraphed by an area-of-effect stun before the creatures come out. To make life easier, have an ability equipped that will let you escape stuns.
- Some dragons have the Berserk ability. This is telegraphed by their neck flaring up with the color of their element. This causes a 40-meter AoE around the dragon that will apply damage and an effect specific to her element.
- Dragons with the Armored ability are defensive, and they'll generate guard. Make sure to bring guard-breaking abilities. The warrior's Shield Bash and mage's Spirit Blade can damage guard. You can also craft weapons that do damage against guard.
- When dragons flap their wings they'll start sucking prey toward them to make it easier to attack. They also deflect all projectiles while they're flapping.
- You can craft magic resistance onto your gear, which will vastly increase your survivability against a dragon's breath attacks and projectiles.
- Equip your mage with Resurgence for emergencies—the AI is very efficient at casting it should you fall.
- Adjusting AI ability tactics can help your party members cast the correct spells for the dragon. For example, this allows your mage to set cold abilities as "Preferred Abilities" vs. a fire dragon while disabling fire abilities, since they do reduced damage.
- Try not to let your ranged party members stray too far away from the dragon. The dragon has a powerful vortex she can create that damages them and pulls them towards her.
- Some AoE spells and weapons can deal damage to all the dragon's limbs, if properly placed.
- Focusing on one leg can cause the dragon to fall, allowing you some time to do some damage.

> HYENA

LOCALE: Forbidden Oasis, Western Approach
LEVEL RANGE: 8-11
HEALTH MODIFIER: 2
ARMOR: Low
RESISTANCES:
- Cold

VULNERABILITIES:
- Fire

IMMUNITIES: None
CRAFTING MATERIAL:
- Canine Leather

"The common hyena is a remarkable predator, flourishing in the harshest of conditions. Packs working in concert have sometimes taken down prey as formidable as a great bear. It's an incredible sight, but you should keep your distance because one of those beauties took down my bronto in under a minute."

— From *The Wilds of Thedas: Volume Two*, by Stephan d'Eroin

> LURKER

LOCALE: Hissing Wastes
LEVEL RANGE: 16-19
HEALTH MODIFIER: 1
ARMOR: High
RESISTANCES: None
VULNERABILITIES:
- Electricity

IMMUNITIES: None
CRAFTING MATERIAL:
- Craggy Skin

"You want to hunt lurkers? All right, then there's a few things you should know. First, they don't just live in caves. Some of the locals call them 'cave lurkers,' but I've seen them in the wastelands, in the marshes...really anywhere you think creatures shouldn't be able to live. Why? Because they eat almost anything and they eat rarely. When they're not hunting, they curl up in a sort of hibernation to conserve energy. If you can catch them in that state, consider yourself lucky. If not, you'll need to be on your toes. They're quiet when they want to be, you see. Hence the 'lurk' part of their name. They hunt in packs. They spit poison. In fact, I've lost more than one fellow because a group of lurkers descended upon him while he took a piss in the bushes. They surround him, paralyze him, and then tear him to pieces—all without the rest of the camp knowing a single thing was going on, not 20 feet away."

— From *The Most Dangerous Things to Eat*, by Pol Ageire Phridee

> MABARI

LOCALE: Hissing Wastes, Hinterlands, Storm Coast
LEVEL RANGE: 8-11
HEALTH MODIFIER: 1
ARMOR: Low
RESISTANCES:
- Cold

VULNERABILITIES:
- Fire

IMMUNITIES: None
CRAFTING MATERIAL:
- Canine Leather

"Dogs are an essential part of Fereldan culture, and no dog is more prized than the mabari. The breed is as old as myth, said to have been bred from the wolves who served Dane. Prized for their intelligence and loyalty, these dogs are more than mere weapons or status symbols: The hounds choose their masters, pairing with them for life. To be the master of a mabari anywhere in Ferelden is to be recognized instantly as a person of worth."

— From *Ferelden: Folklore and History*, by Sister Petrine, Chantry Scholar

> NUG

LOCALE: Crestwood, Emerald Graves, Emprise du Lion, Exalted Plains, Frostback Mountains, Hinterlands, Forbidden Oasis, Storm Coast
LEVEL RANGE: 1-15
HEALTH MODIFIER: 0.05
ARMOR: Very Low
RESISTANCES: None
VULNERABILITIES: None
IMMUNITIES: None
CRAFTING MATERIAL:
- Nugskin

"I was sure before the Blight they were a whole lot more rare. Should ask a Warden about that, if killing archdemons leaves nugs all over. And the poor things don't seem built for anywhere. I mean, they feed on anything, but they blister in the desert and freeze in the snow, and they're easier to track than your own arse. Everything eats them (except me, the hands put me off), yet they thrive. Randy bastards outpace every tooth and claw."

— Excerpt from the private letters of "Captain" Byrne, lap-nug dealer

> PHOENIX

LOCALE: The Western Approach
LEVEL RANGE: 8-11
HEALTH MODIFIER: 1.5
ARMOR: Average
RESISTANCES:
- Fire

VULNERABILITIES:
- Electricity

IMMUNITIES: None
CRAFTING MATERIAL:
- Phoenix Scales

"Orlesians believe the phoenix to be a herald of woe, perhaps because the creatures frequent inhospitable places where sane travelers fear to tread. It may also be because they belch a sort of sulfurous gas that reeks of rotten eggs and ancient peat bog, and flocks of the beasts have a pervasive odor of death about them. Orlesians are not always so metaphorical as they like us to believe."

— From *In Pursuit of Knowledge: Travels of a Chantry Scholar*, by Brother Genitivi

> POISON SPIDER

LOCALE: Crestwood, Hissing Wastes, Revenant Church, Western Approach
LEVEL RANGE: 8-19
HEALTH MODIFIER: 1
ARMOR: Very Low
RESISTANCES:
- Electricity

VULNERABILITIES: None
IMMUNITIES:
- Poison

CRAFTING MATERIAL:
- Unknown

"A sound from above, then legs, fangs, and poison. I do not know the number—less than my nightmares bear, but still too many. Only quick fires from our Circle apprentice allowed us to retreat. But not all. Several of our numbers were paralyzed in the instant, as must have been the case for many before. When I close my eyes, I see them—new recruits to that silent army, frozen in "praise" of a moving ceiling, waiting to be hollowed."

— Excepted from *We Need Not Demons: Our Dangerous World, A Collection of Natural Horrors and Wonders*, edited by Philliam, a bard

> QUILLBACK

LOCALE: Western Approach
LEVEL RANGE: 8-11
HEALTH MODIFIER: 3
ARMOR: High
RESISTANCES:
- Cold

VULNERABILITIES:
- Fire

IMMUNITIES:
- Physical Effects
- Paralyze
- Freeze

CRAFTING MATERIAL:
- Unknown

"Its hooked beak describes a smile that makes mock of the laws of man and Maker, and in the sagging folds of its rough and squamous hide lies no elegant simplicity. But look upon its dorsal ridge for the proof, if logic be your refuge, for in the ebon spines that jut uncaringly from its back, no man of learning can fail to see the cold and twisted spires of the Black City itself. What Maker would give mock to our ebullient transgressions by marking his domicile into the flesh of this repugnant eater of flesh, this scavenger of wastes and deserts?"

— From *An Anatomie of Various Terrible Beasts*, by Baron Havard-Pierre D'Amortisan

> RAM

LOCALE: Crestwood, Frostback Mountains, Hinterlands, Skyhold, Storm Coast
LEVEL RANGE: 1-7
HEALTH MODIFIER: 0.25
ARMOR: Very Low
RESISTANCES: None
VULNERABILITIES: None
IMMUNITIES: None
CRAFTING MATERIAL:
- Ram Leather

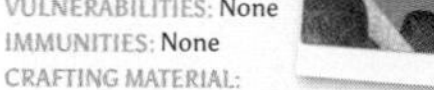

"The ram is a marvelous creature. Its wool makes the best lining for winter coats this side of the mountains. The horns and bones can be crushed into powder and mixed with the soil for a healthy crop, or charred and ground into ink powder. The hide makes good cover in a window against the winds. You can burn the dung in a pinch. Melt down its fat for candles. I haven't even mentioned the meat! With a full-grown ram, you could make stew big enough for a village and have enough left over for a week."

— Letter from a Fereldan farmer to his son

> SNOUFLEUR

LOCALE: Emprise du Lion, Exalted Plains
LEVEL RANGE: 8-15
HEALTH MODIFIER: 0.05
ARMOR: Very Low
RESISTANCES: None
VULNERABILITIES: None
IMMUNITIES: None
CRAFTING MATERIAL:
- Snoufleur Fur

"And then going through the Dales, we see one of those long-nosed pigs with the stump legs. It's just crossing the highway, dragging its stupid belly along the ground, as they do. Bless the Maker and all, but He was deep in His holy golden cups the day He made that thing. Anyway, I turn to Lockey, and I say, "Hey, it's one of them snufflers." Marchand starts in with his giggle. Lockey and me, we look at him. "Snuffler!" he says, like he just caught me naked with his lady mother. "Non—tu dois dire 'snoufleur.'" Because "snuffler" just isn't fancy enough for Orlee. So I say it like he does: snoooou-fleeeeur. Can't keep a straight face. Marchand goes red like a virgin with skirts blown up. And good old Lockey, he just shoots the thing with an arrow while it's snuffling its way across the road. "Now it's dead, and we call it dead," he says. That was that.

— From the hunting log of Kerr of West Hill, dated 17 Solace

> TUSKET

LOCALE: Forbidden Oasis, Storm Coast
LEVEL RANGE: 12-15
HEALTH MODIFIER: 0.05
ARMOR: Very Low
RESISTANCES: None
VULNERABILITIES: None
IMMUNITIES: None
CRAFTING MATERIAL:
- Unknown

"The curving tusks protruding from the snout are present in both males and females of the species. Rarely used in combat, the upper tusks play an important part in mate selection. It's believed that tuskets choose prospective mates based not only on the size, but also on the curve and even slight color variation found in another's tusks. Considering tuskets bond for life, careful mate selection is crucial to the continued success of the herd. Bonded tuskets have been seen gently clicking their tusks together as a sign of affection. The role of the tusket's signature ornamentation in the mating process led to an unfortunate rumor that their tusks could increase virility in other species. Although usually docile, tuskets will defend themselves if cornered (or if someone attempts to saw off part of their anatomy). It's said Baron Vandermine lost three servants this way."

— From *Observed Behaviors in the Common Tusket*, by Tilda Adere

> VARGHEST

LOCALE: The Western Approach
LEVEL RANGE: 12-15
HEALTH MODIFIER: 3
ARMOR: Low
RESISTANCES:
- Fire

VULNERABILITIES:
- Electricity

IMMUNITIES:
- Physical Effects

CRAFTING MATERIAL:
- Varghest Scales

"The varghest is now known to be a distant relative of wyverns and dragons, but in ancient times, it was believed to be a spirit manifest in the world. Ciriane legend says that the varghest hunts those who have committed great wrongs against their own kin, and when the creature finds its quarry, it drags the guilty party to the Gods for judgment. This is perhaps due to the beasts' hunting habit: Varghests prefer to bring prey still living to their nests to feed their young."

— From *A Study of the Southern Draconoids*, by Frederic of Serault, published by the University of Orlais

> WYVERN

LOCALE: Crestwood, Hissing Wastes
LEVEL RANGE: 8-19
HEALTH MODIFIER: 3
ARMOR: Low
RESISTANCES:
- Fire

VULNERABILITIES:
- Electricity

IMMUNITIES:
- Physical Effects

CRAFTING MATERIAL:
- Wyvern Scales

The wyvern—like its relative the dragon—has nearly been hunted to extinction. Wealthy Orlesians are particularly fond of the wyvern chase, although their servants and dogs take the risks while the noblemen merely accept the praise. It is the venom that makes the creature so valuable. It's used in potion-making, alchemy, and the production of a rare and potent liquor called aquae lucidius. The minuscule quantity of the venom remaining in the aquae after distillation leads to a unique hallucinatory effect.

COMMON FOES

Whether confronting bandits, mercenaries, or soldiers affiliated with a hostile army, you're likely to face these common units in combat. While their allegiances may differ, their basic combat doctrine and stats remain the same. But don't become complacent. Level ranges differ greatly depending on the locale your party is exploring—for example, an archer you face in the Hinterlands will be at a lower level than one you face in the Hissing Wastes. Higher-level enemies perform the same but are much tougher to kill and inflict more damage with each successful strike. Proceed with caution.

> ARCHER

LOCALE: Various
LEVEL RANGE: 4-30
HEALTH MODIFIER: 0.75
ARMOR: Low
RESISTANCES: None
VULNERABILITIES: None
IMMUNITIES: None

"Few soldiers have the skill or strength to make good use of a longbow. Respect those who do. Against such an enemy, cover is the only defense. Move quickly across his field of vision, forcing him to compensate for movement. Do not charge directly unless your allies can distract him. A fully drawn longbow can drive an arrow through a chevalier's plate at a hundred yards. A fight between an archer and a chevalier is a test of cunning versus patience. We are too often patient—heavily armored as we are—and faced with lightly armored foes who would harass us. While archers frustrate me as they do most chevaliers, it is good that we fight them, so we remember how to be cunning, how to break an opponent's patience."

—An excerpt from *A Meditation Upon the Use of Blades,* by Swordmaster Massache de Jean-Mien, required reading at the Academie des Chevaliers

TIP Archers can be deadly if not dealt with quickly. Make it the priority of your ranged party members to take out these enemies at the beginning of a battle. If you don't deal with archers soon, they'll slowly drain the health of your party members, one arrow at a time.

> BRUISER

LOCALE: Various
LEVEL RANGE: 8-30
HEALTH MODIFIER: 1.75
ARMOR: Very High
RESISTANCES: None
VULNERABILITIES:
- Electricity

IMMUNITIES:
- Physical Effects
- Fear*
- Paralyze*
- Freeze*
- Sleep*
- Taunt*
- Snare*

* Only when enraged

"You must watch the weapon, but only to gauge its length. Otherwise, as in all fights, the opponent's hips and shoulders will tell his intent. The great weapons are dangerous only when moving or poised overhead to strike down. You must give ground, but only against the true threat. If he advances but is not truly prepared to strike, you must rush in, cut him, and withdraw to your guard before his blow is ready. It may take 10 cuts to kill him. Even after the ninth, he may cleave your head from your body if you do not respect the distance he can cover."

—An excerpt from *A Meditation Upon the Use of Blades,* by Swordmaster Massache de Jean-Mien, required reading at the Academie des Chevaliers

TIP Use warrior abilities like Shield Bash and Break Their Spirit (War Horn) to break through a bruiser's guard.

> FOOT SOLDIER

LOCALE: Various
LEVEL RANGE: 4-30
HEALTH MODIFIER: 1
ARMOR: Average
RESISTANCES: None
VULNERABILITIES: None
IMMUNITIES: None

"When engaging with such an opponent, respect his speed. His hands and feet will move a great deal; ignore them. Watch his hips and shoulders instead. First deny what advantage he has in his allies or environment, unless you have trained equally in such matters. Once you control his weapon, overwhelm him. He has no shield, and you need not fear a second blade."

—An excerpt from *A Meditation Upon the Use of Blades,* by Swordmaster Massache de Jean-Mien, required reading at the Academie des Chevaliers

> GUARDSMAN

LOCALE: Various
LEVEL RANGE: 4-30
HEALTH MODIFIER: 1.25
ARMOR: High
RESISTANCES: None
VULNERABILITIES:
- Electricity

IMMUNITIES: None

"Your goal is not the shield, but the man behind it. Circling or locking shields may gain you an advantageous position. Failing that, rain blows upon his defenses until he tires and his guard grows sloppy. If you are neither skilled enough to slip past him nor fit enough to wear him down, you will most likely die."

—An excerpt from *A Meditation Upon the Use of Blades,* by Swordmaster Massache de Jean-Mien, required reading at the Academie des Chevaliers

TIP Flanking is essential when dealing with these shield-bearing enemies. Use a warrior to taunt while the rest of your party flanks, striking the guardsman from the sides or rear.

> MAGE

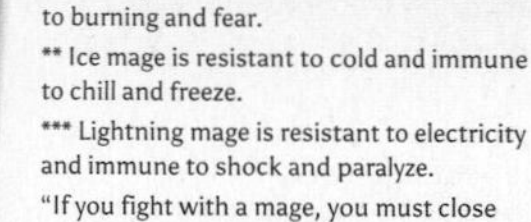

LOCALE: Various
LEVEL RANGE: 8-30
HEALTH MODIFIER: 1
ARMOR: Low
RESISTANCES: None
VULNERABILITIES:
- Fire*
- Cold**
- Electricity***

IMMUNITIES:
- Sleep
- Fear*
- Paralyze***
- Freeze**
- Burning*
- Shocked***
- Chill**

ELEMENTAL ATTACK:
- Cold, Fire, or Electricity

* Fire mage is resistant to fire and immune to burning and fear.

** Ice mage is resistant to cold and immune to chill and freeze.

*** Lightning mage is resistant to electricity and immune to shock and paralyze.

"If you fight with a mage, you must close with him, regardless of the danger, or risk being overwhelmed. A mage's strike rarely hits with the force of a trained chevalier's blade, but it often carries unnatural energies: fire that boils a man inside his armor, lightning that steals the strength from his limbs, and so forth. To hold back is to give him time to alter the battlefield to his advantage in some fashion, whether he summons a wall of ice, a demonic ally, or magical flames that strengthen the blades of his guards. We know that the warrior who controls the battlefield is most often the victor. You must keep him reacting to you and continue your attack."

—An excerpt from *A Meditation Upon the Use of Blades*, by Swordmaster Massache de Jean-Mien, required reading at the Academie des Chevaliers

TIP

Mages are most vulnerable to physical attacks. Rush them with your warriors and dual-wield rogues to deal heavy damage. Just watch out for any glyphs on the ground around the enemy mage.

> PROWLER

LOCALE: Various
LEVEL RANGE: 4-30
HEALTH MODIFIER: 1
ARMOR: Average
RESISTANCES: None
VULNERABILITIES: None
IMMUNITIES:
- Fear
- Sleep
- Snare

"A skirmisher will strike by surprise, relying upon allies to draw your attention. In a great battle with many troops on each side, you must assume that the enemy has such skirmishers within its ranks. Once you know such an enemy opposes you, be vigilant and remember that you wear more armor than he does. He will hide; do not enter the shadows, where he is strongest, to pursue him. He will harass you at range; do not take the bait he offers. A chevalier deserves a better death than a poisoned dagger in his unprotected armpit, and such is the death of those who grow impatient while chasing enemies they deem beneath their honor. Be calm, be methodical, and wait for your opponent to yield to fear of your blade and shield. When he does, he will convince himself that he can attack you directly, that his blades are fast enough to slip past your shield. Then he will move, and then you may kill him."

—An excerpt from *A Meditation Upon the Use of Blades*, by Swordmaster Massache de Jean-Mien, required reading at the Academie des Chevaliers

TIP

Prowlers rely on the Stealth ability to sneak up on their opponents. Once they're identified, deal with these pesky enemies as soon as possible. Otherwise their devastating flanking attacks will take a serious toll.

> SPELLBINDER

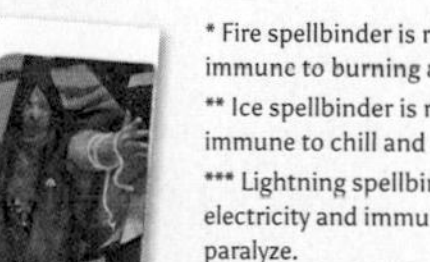

LOCALE: Various
LEVEL RANGE: 4-30
HEALTH MODIFIER: 1
ARMOR: Very Low
RESISTANCES:
- Fire*
- Cold**
- Electricity***

VULNERABILITIES: None
IMMUNITIES:
- Sleep
- Fear*
- Paralyze***
- Freeze**
- Burning*
- Shock***
- Chill**

ELEMENTAL ATTACK:
- Cold, Fire, or Electricity

* Fire spellbinder is resistant to fire and immune to burning and fear.

** Ice spellbinder is resistant to cold and immune to chill and freeze.

*** Lightning spellbinder is resistant to electricity and immune to shock and paralyze.

"These 'spellbinders,' as they call themselves, bind many simple spirits, usually to books or other easily compartmentalized objects set with runes, and they have stripped the interaction with spirits of its importance, reducing it to a mere mechanical exercise. That such magic is useful to the spellbinder, I do not argue. Although the power contained in these objects is difficult to focus, the diffused magic can easily distribute energy across a broad area, augmenting the mage's allies. The spellbinders insist that no individual spirit is capable of breaking their bindings, and that the spirits cannot cooperate well enough to escape together. Furthermore, they maintain that because the bindings are all tied to the spellbinder personally, there is no risk of these enchanted books falling into the wrong hands. Still, the books are in their hands, and I am concerned."

—An excerpt from *Life Among the Dead*, by Enchanter Rodomonte Van Heigl, senior member of the Mortalitasi

TIP

Spellbinders can teleport from one location to another. To reduce their mobility, hit them with ranged attacks that knock them off their feet—this allows your warriors to close in and land heavy blows.

DEMONS

Following the tragic events at the Temple of Sacred Ashes, demons have invaded Thedas, emerging from Fade rifts scattered throughout Ferelden and Orlais. Most demons linger around Fade rifts, attacking anyone who approaches. The demons encountered at each Fade rift vary based on locale. Early on, you're most likely to encounter wraiths, shades, and terrors. But as your adventures continue, expect to confront more powerful demons, including despair demons, rage demons, and massive pride demons. Therefore, exercise extreme caution when approaching Fade rifts—and don't be afraid to retreat if you get in over your head. Demons are bound to the rift and will not travel great distances to pursue you and your party.

> DESPAIR DEMON

LOCALE: Various
LEVEL RANGE: 12-30
HEALTH MODIFIER: 1
ARMOR: Very Low
RESISTANCES:
- Cold

VULNERABILITIES:
- Fire

IMMUNITIES:
- Freeze
- Sleep
- Chill

ELEMENTAL ATTACK:
- Cold

"Once upon a time, we classified these as demons of sloth, but we learned that despair demons are something quite different. They are not the antithesis of justice or valor, but rather hope. They form nightmares tearing away the foundations of self and purpose. When brought into the world, they are most attracted to places the downtrodden populate: alienages, slums, prisons, and the like. The miasma they spread can lead to extreme behavior. We look for a rash of unexplained suicides, men and women so filled with grief they lash out. The most intelligent of these creatures are to be feared, for they not only feed on despair, they understand its causes...and seek to bring it about. From the shadows they ruin lives, drinking the tears of those who have no idea the cause of their misery is not random chance."

— From a lecture by renowned hunter Ser Hayward, of the Templar Order

> FEAR DEMON

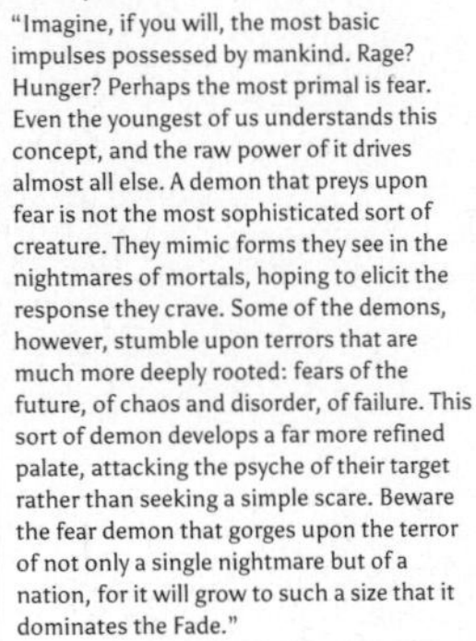

LOCALE: Various
LEVEL RANGE: 12-30
HEALTH MODIFIER: 1.75
ARMOR: Average
RESISTANCES: None
VULNERABILITIES:
- Electricity
- Spirit

IMMUNITIES:
- Fear
- Freeze
- Sleep
- Weaken

ELEMENTAL ATTACK:
- Spirit

"Imagine, if you will, the most basic impulses possessed by mankind. Rage? Hunger? Perhaps the most primal is fear. Even the youngest of us understands this concept, and the raw power of it drives almost all else. A demon that preys upon fear is not the most sophisticated sort of creature. They mimic forms they see in the nightmares of mortals, hoping to elicit the response they crave. Some of the demons, however, stumble upon terrors that are much more deeply rooted: fears of the future, of chaos and disorder, of failure. This sort of demon develops a far more refined palate, attacking the psyche of their target rather than seeking a simple scare. Beware the fear demon that gorges upon the terror of not only a single nightmare but of a nation, for it will grow to such a size that it dominates the Fade."

— From a lecture by renowned templar Ser Hayward

> PRIDE DEMON

LOCALE: Various
LEVEL RANGE: 12-30
HEALTH MODIFIER: 2
ARMOR: Very High
RESISTANCES:
- Electricity

VULNERABILITIES: None
IMMUNITIES:
- Physical Effects
- Freeze
- Sleep
- Paralyze
- Shock

ELEMENTAL ATTACK:
- Electricity

"The most powerful demons yet encountered are the pride demons, perhaps because they, among all their kind, most resemble men; as clever and manipulative as the desire demon, with a penchant for cruel irony that is almost human. While the demons of desire largely engage in the bribery of mortals, pride will use mortals' own best nature against them. Clever men outwit themselves. Strong men crush themselves. Humble men forget themselves. Jealous men fear themselves. They turn corruption and ruin into an art."

— From *Beyond the Veil: Spirits and Demons*, by Enchanter Mirdromel

TIP While attempting to close Fade rifts, the mage's Dispel ability is useful for preventing more demons from emerging. After eliminating the first wave of demons, target one of the green glowing areas on the ground. This will prevent a demon from spawning at the targeted location.

> RAGE DEMON

LOCALE: Various
LEVEL RANGE: 8-30
HEALTH MODIFIER: 1.5
ARMOR: High
RESISTANCES:
- Fire

VULNERABILITIES:
- Cold

IMMUNITIES:
- Burning
- Physical Effects*
- Fear*
- Paralyze*
- Sleep*
- Taunt*

ELEMENTAL ATTACK:
- Fire

* Only when enraged

"Encountered in the Fade, the true form of a rage demon is a frightening sight: a creature of pure fire, seemingly made of amorphous lava, its eyes pinpricks of baleful light radiating from its core. The abilities of such a demon center on the fire it generates. It burns those who come near, and the most powerful are able to lash out with bolts of fire and even firestorms affecting entire areas. Fortunately, even powerful rage demons are less intelligent than other varieties. Their tactics are simple: Attack enemies on sight with as much force as possible until they perish. Some rage demons carry their heat-based abilities into possessed hosts; otherwise one rarely sees their true form outside the Fade unless mages specifically summon one to do their bidding."

— Transcript of a lecture given by Vheren, Templar-Commander of Tantervale, 6:86 Steel

TIP Cold-based attacks are most effective against rage demons. Use Winter's Grasp to freeze this demon, then pour on more attacks while it's frozen and incapable of retaliating with its devastating, fiery attacks.

> SHADE

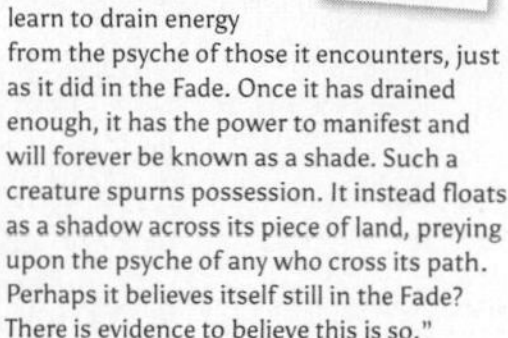

LOCALE: Various
LEVEL RANGE: 1-30
HEALTH MODIFIER: 1.1
ARMOR: Low
RESISTANCES: None
VULNERABILITIES: None
IMMUNITIES: None

"These demons watch. They lurk. They envy. In time, such a demon will learn to drain energy from the psyche of those it encounters, just as it did in the Fade. Once it has drained enough, it has the power to manifest and will forever be known as a shade. Such a creature spurns possession. It instead floats as a shadow across its piece of land, preying upon the psyche of any who cross its path. Perhaps it believes itself still in the Fade? There is evidence to believe this is so."

— From *Beyond the Veil: Spirits and Demons*, by Enchanter Mirdromel

> TERROR

LOCALE: Various
LEVEL RANGE: 1-30
HEALTH MODIFIER: 1.5
ARMOR: Low
RESISTANCES: None
VULNERABILITIES:
- Spirit

IMMUNITIES:
- Fear

"But we all heard something different, you see? One of the others said he'd run into darkspawn at Ostagar, and the scream he heard was from something called a 'shriek.' Another said it was a dragon roar, just like the beast that burned his family. That's when I knew what was out there was a demon. Something that wasn't just looking to make us afraid—it wanted us gibbering in terror. It wanted us running for our lives. And we did. I couldn't rightly tell you what it even looked like. There was something in the shadows, and even though we were ready when it let out that howl, I turned and ran. I couldn't even control myself. My bowels turned to water, I dropped my sword, and I took off. It was only later when I realized I was separated from the others, and that there were more of those demons out there, hungry for more of my panicked tears."

— From a report given by Haren, soldier of the Ferelden Army, 9:15 Dragon

TIP Terrors pose a serious threat to novice explorers, because they are capable of disappearing and then reappearing in a new location—they often use this escape technique to target your most vulnerable party members, namely mages and archers. Utilize abilities that knock them off their feet, then pummel them while they're flat on their back.

> WRAITH

LOCALE: Various
LEVEL RANGE: 1-30
HEALTH MODIFIER: 0.35
ARMOR: Very Low
RESISTANCES:
- Fire*
- Cold*
- Electricity*

VULNERABILITIES: None
IMMUNITIES:
- Physical Effects
- Poison
- Weaken*
- Burning*
- Shock*
- Chill*

ELEMENTAL ATTACK:
- Spirit**

* Gains special attributes depending on which demon is nearby:
- Weaken Immunity: Fear Demon
- Burn Immunity and Fire Resistance: Rage Demon
- Chill Immunity and Cold Resistance: Despair Demon
- Shock Immunity and Electricity Resistance: Pride Demon

** Wraiths take on the elemental attack of nearby demons. Otherwise they default to spirit.

"Like wisps, wraiths are sometimes thought to be the remains of spirits or demons that have been destroyed. They cannot shape the Fade around themselves, nor are they capable of mimicking forms they see in the minds of dreamers as many weaker spirits do. Instead, they are the scavengers of the Fade, dwelling in the shadows of stronger beings, feeding on scraps of thought and emotion."

— From *Beyond the Veil: Spirits and Demons*, by Enchanter Mirdromel

TIP Like archers, wraiths are evasive and use ranged attacks to slowly whittle away at their victims' health. Use your ranged party members to take them out as quickly as possible. Fortunately, they have very low health. But some wraiths are capable of casting a Barrier, effectively extending their lifespan.

RED TEMPLARS

The consumption of red lyrium has transformed these misguided templars into something sinister and grotesque. Early initiates benefit from super-human strength, making them extremely deadly in combat. But as the toxic lyrium takes root within their bodies, these templars undergo a physical transformation beyond their control, turning them into rage-filled beasts. Needless to say, encounters with red templars are extremely dangerous. Before engaging in combat, activate the tactical camera and scout the different types of enemies to devise a plan of attack. Be on the watch for archers and shadows—consider making these your primary targets.

> BEHEMOTH

LOCALE: Various
LEVEL RANGE: 12-30
HEALTH MODIFIER: 1.5
ARMOR: Very High
RESISTANCES:
- Fire

VULNERABILITIES:
- Cold

IMMUNITIES:
- Physical Effects
- Fear
- Paralyze
- Sleep
- Weaken
- Burning

"We could have held off a battering ram, but the behemoth? It took the gate off at the hinges. Then it screamed. Not a roar or growl—a scream, all rage and pain. As I drew my blade, all I could think was: 'There's a templar in there.' Somewhere in that thing was a brother or sister of the Order; every fiber of my soul was crying out to them. But whoever it might have been, whoever's son or daughter, they were lost to us, swallowed by corruption and lies. I held the only way I could, the only way any of us can. We must end their suffering. And, Maker willing, we must try to remember them as they were."

— From the reports of Knight-Captain Veddir, *Tactical Considerations for the Inquisition*

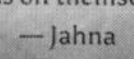

> HORROR

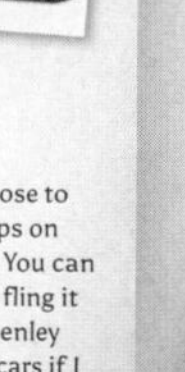

LOCALE: Various
LEVEL RANGE: 4-30
HEALTH MODIFIER: 1
ARMOR: High
RESISTANCES:
- Electricity

VULNERABILITIES:
- Spirit

IMMUNITIES:
- Fear*
- Paralyze*
- Freeze*
- Sleep*
- Shock

* Only when enraged

"Whatever you do, don't get too close to those red templars with giant lumps on their backs. They can 'spit' lyrium! You can actually see it growing before they fling it at you from their palms. One hit Henley in the face. (He'd have a mass of scars if I hadn't been there to heal the wounds as we plucked the stuff out.) We started to beat it down with some spells, and the air went sour. I felt sick, like you do when you've been around too much raw lyrium. Lyra almost passed out. I grabbed her and ran. With luck, the thing found better prey than us. I never loved the templars, but seeing them mutilated with lyrium doesn't give me cheer. I don't understand why they'd inflict this on themselves."

— Jahna

> RED TEMPLAR ARCHER

LOCALE: Various
LEVEL RANGE: 4-30
HEALTH MODIFIER: 0.75
ARMOR: Low
RESISTANCES: None
VULNERABILITIES: None
IMMUNITIES: None

"Take aim. Red lyrium isn't the weak stuff they fed you all your life. The song is deeper. It's got a will of its own. Tame it, and it will do things the Chantry's instructions never dreamed of. Listen. Focus on the arrow in your hand. Pour power into it when it leaves the bow. That strength can fly across a battlefield and punch a hole through the thickest armor. Soon you won't need to stop to hear it. Practice, and the song will always be in your blood. And fire."

— Red templar archer, instructing new recruits starting to take red lyrium

> RED TEMPLAR GUARDSMAN

LOCALE: Various
LEVEL RANGE: 8-30
HEALTH MODIFIER: 1.25
ARMOR: High
RESISTANCES: None
VULNERABILITIES:

- Electricity

IMMUNITIES: None

"When I saw the templars marching up the road, my heart was glad. I asked if they'd come to stop the rebel mages who burned down the farms, but one growled it was none of our business. That's when I noticed his eyes were red. Not like he'd had a long night at the inn, but really truly red. Vernie announced that these were the bann's lands, and it was his business who was in them. The templar bastard cut him down without a word! A dozen of us against three of them, and we never got a strike past their shields. They're stronger than any man I've known. The templars swung full tower shields of metal like they weighed nothing."

— An excerpt from a letter from a guardsman employed by Bann Harkwold

> RED TEMPLAR KNIGHT

LOCALE: Various
LEVEL RANGE: 8-30
HEALTH MODIFIER: 1.25
ARMOR: Very High
RESISTANCES:

- Cold

VULNERABILITIES:

- Fire

IMMUNITIES:

- Physical Effects
- Paralyze
- Freeze
- Chill

"More and more my fellow templars stop talking when I walk into rooms. There is little talk of continuing our hunt for the rebel mages. There is little talk of anything at all. I see the red vials they wear openly around their necks, no longer hidden. They are stronger than the rest of us, and it suddenly seems as if proper blue lyrium has become rare. 'Shortages,' they tell me. I saw Ser Randall the morning, and his eyes were red. For the first time, I am wondering if I should abandon my post and flee the Order for good."

— Excerpt from the journal of Ser Caitlin of the Order of Templars, 9:41 Dragon

> RED TEMPLAR FOOT SOLDIER

LOCALE: Various
LEVEL RANGE: 4-30
HEALTH MODIFIER: 1
ARMOR: Average
RESISTANCES: None
VULNERABILITIES: None
IMMUNITIES: None

"The soldiers looked like normal men and women, but they rained down blows so hard it numbed my arm through my shield. It took three minutes to kill just one, and he only stopped when I cut off his head! That's when I saw their leader: a huge misshapen knight. He made a gesture and a streak of light streamed from him into one of the soldiers. Red lyrium bursts through the soldier's back; he changed into some kind of thing that made all the mages sick. I still don't know how we survived. These mages are children and frightened scholars, hiding from the war after their Circle fell. Still, if one of them wasn't a healer, I'd have lost my sword arm."

— An excerpt from a letter from a templar knight who left the Order, to her husband

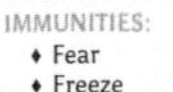

> SHADOW

LOCALE: Various
LEVEL RANGE: 12-30
HEALTH MODIFIER: 1.2
ARMOR: Average
RESISTANCES: None
VULNERABILITIES: None
IMMUNITIES:

- Fear
- Freeze
- Sleep
- Snare

"The specimen was fresh, killed only a few hours ago by a troop of chevaliers patrolling outside the city. Their captain told me, in a strained and sickly voice, that a group of red templars had descended on his men and massacred them. I gave him my condolences, but he seemed not to hear me. The one on my slab was fast, the captain muttered, much nimbler than its bulk suggested. Imagine my nausea when I opened up the creature and saw that red lyrium had fused to the bones, overgrown its lungs, and spread like a fungus into the brain. As I watched, the red crystal pulsed and spread the smallest fraction of an inch deeper into the flesh of the corpse. Blood drained out of the surrounding tissue, as if the lyrium itself were feeding on it."

— An excerpt from the diary of Professor Auffret, a naturalist studying at the University of Val Royeaux

UNDEAD

While there's no solid evidence, there appears to be a connection between the appearance of the Breach and a resurgence of undead activity in Ferelden and Orlais. Locales like the Fallow Mire and Crestwood have seen a disturbing rise in attacks by the undead. Unlike living foes, undead enemies are immune to a variety of effects—they can't be poisoned, put to sleep, or demoralized in any way. But they are vulnerable to fire- and spirit-based attacks. And when elemental magic isn't available, physical attacks will suffice, granting them a permanent death.

> ARCANE HORROR

LOCALE: Various
LEVEL RANGE: 8-30
HEALTH MODIFIER: 5
ARMOR: Low
RESISTANCES:

- Cold

VULNERABILITIES:

- Fire
- Spirit

ELEMENTAL ATTACK:

- Spirit

IMMUNITIES:

- Physical Effects
- Fear
- Paralyze
- Sleep
- Chill
- Poison

"Upon ascending to the second floor of the tower, a gruesome sight greeted us: a ragged collection of bones wearing robes of one of the senior enchanters. I had known her for years, watched her raise countless apprentices, and now she was a mere puppet of some demon."

— Transcribed from a tale told by a templar in Antiva City, 7:13 Storm

> CORPSE

LOCALE: Various
LEVEL RANGE: 4-30
HEALTH MODIFIER: 0.7
ARMOR: Very Low
RESISTANCES:
- Cold

VULNERABILITIES:
- Fire
- Spirit

IMMUNITIES:
- Fear
- Sleep
- Chill
- Poison

"In most corners of Thedas, funeral rites include burning or dismembering the dead to prevent them from becoming host to demons. But not everyone gets a proper burial. It is not unheard of for the dead to be thrown into mass graves in the aftermath of a battle or execution, almost asking some demon to claim the corpses."

— From *Beyond the Veil: Spirits and Demons*, by Enchanter Mirdromel

> REVENANT

LOCALE: Various
LEVEL RANGE: 12-30
HEALTH MODIFIER: 6
ARMOR: Very High
RESISTANCES:
- Cold

VULNERABILITIES:
- Fire
- Spirit

IMMUNITIES:
- Physical Effects
- Fear
- Freeze
- Sleep
- Chill
- Poison

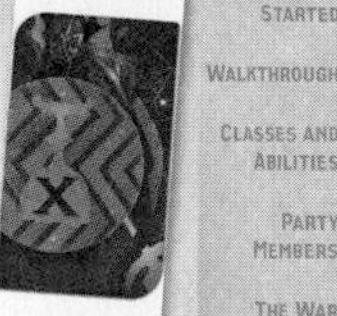

"It appears to be no simple skeleton. The descriptions of the creature's abilities were eerily similar to those our brothers at Marnas Pell encountered almost an age ago: men pulled through the air to skewer themselves on the creature's blade, and attacks so quick that it was able to assault multiple opponents at once. No, Your Perfection, what we have here is indeed a revenant and nothing less."

— From a letter to Divine Amara III, 5:71 Exalted

DARKSPAWN

While reports of darkspawn activity are rare, any sighting is a serious concern. Once thought to be suppressed following the previous Blight, darkspawn have been spotted in several locales across Thedas, with a troubling number reported in the Western Approach. Perhaps the recent absence of the Grey Wardens has allowed darkspawn to gain a new foothold? Whatever the reason, take these threats seriously and work to end their expansion. With demons emerging from the Fade, the last thing Thedas needs now is another Blight.

> GHOUL

LOCALE: Emprise du Lion, Storm Coast, Western Approach
LEVEL RANGE: 4-19
HEALTH MODIFIER: 0.5
ARMOR: Average
RESISTANCES: None
VULNERABILITIES: None
IMMUNITIES: None

"Among the saddest legacies of the Fifth Blight are those poor souls who survived the darkspawn attacks across Ferelden only to succumb to the corruption of the Blight itself. We have seen animals—birds, wolves, and even bears—corrupted into mindless ruinations of their former selves, but humans are by no means immune. Those unfortunate victims not killed quickly by contact with darkspawn blood or disease become mad with fever. Their bodies lose their hair and become misshapen with sores; in their last lucid thoughts, many speak of hearing whispered words, or a song that no one else can catch. It is vital that once victims begin hearing such things, they are put out of their misery quickly and mercifully. There are stories across Ferelden of these ghouls, maddened by the corruption of the Blight, attacking their friends and spreading the corruption further. While it is likely that the sickness will eventually kill a ghoul, the dying strength of these poor creatures makes them nearly as great a danger as the darkspawn themselves. They are no longer our friends, our family, or our countrymen. They are victims of the Blight, and must be given the same mercy Hessarian showed Andraste: a swift sword."

— An excerpt from *Marks of the Blight*, by Sister Dorcas Guerrin

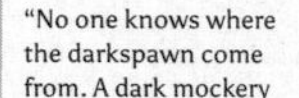

> HURLOCK

LOCALE: Emprise du Lion, Deep Roads, Storm Coast, Western Approach
LEVEL RANGE: 8-19
HEALTH MODIFIER: 1.25
ARMOR: High
RESISTANCES: None
VULNERABILITIES: None
IMMUNITIES: None

"No one knows where the darkspawn come from. A dark mockery of men: In the darkest places they thrive, growing in numbers as a plague of locusts will. In raids, they will often take captives, dragging their victims alive into the Deep Roads; most evidence suggests these are eaten. Like spiders, it seems darkspawn prefer their food still breathing. Perhaps they are spawned by the darkness. Certainly, evil has no trouble perpetuating itself. The last Blight was in the Age of Towers, striking once again at the heart of Tevinter, spreading south into Orlais and east into the Free Marches. The plagues spread as far as Ferelden, but the withering and twisting of the land stopped well beyond our borders. Here, darkspawn have never been more than the stuff of legends. In the northern lands, however, particularly Tevinter and the Anderfels, darkspawn haunt the hinterlands, preying on outlying farmers and isolated villages, a constant threat."

— From *Ferelden: Folklore and History*, by Sister Petrine, Chantry scholar

> HURLOCK ALPHA

LOCALE: Emprise du Lion, Storm Coast, Western Approach
LEVEL RANGE: 8-19
HEALTH MODIFIER: 1.75
ARMOR: Very High
RESISTANCES: None
VULNERABILITIES:
- Electricity

IMMUNITIES:
- Physical Effects
- Fear*
- Paralyze*
- Freeze*
- Sleep*
- Taunt*
- Snare*

* Only when enraged

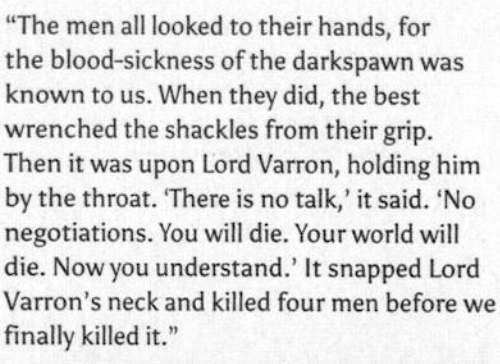

"The men all looked to their hands, for the blood-sickness of the darkspawn was known to us. When they did, the best wrenched the shackles from their grip. Then it was upon Lord Varron, holding him by the throat. 'There is no talk,' it said. 'No negotiations. You will die. Your world will die. Now you understand.' It snapped Lord Varron's neck and killed four men before we finally killed it."

— An excerpt from *The Blighted Codex*, a classified collection of studies on the darkspawn

Dragon Age Inquisition

MULTIPLAYER

While the Herald of Andraste and the inner circle of heroes gallivant across Thedas in their quest to defeat Corypheus, the Inquisition itself gathers conscripts from all over the continent. These men and women do not possess the mark that the Herald does, they are not as infamous as Leliana and Varric, and they do not have the connections of Vivienne. Compared to the inner circle, the regulars of the Inquisition rely on numbers and luck.

Among these regulars are specialists, sent on the toughest assignments, ones that the average soldier cannot handle. With the odds stacked heavily against them, even these specialists cannot hope to succeed alone. But with allies, they may stand a chance to survive their missions, grow stronger, and serve the Inquisition against threats the Herald cannot personally see to.

INTRODUCTION TO MULTIPLAYER: WHAT IS DIFFERENT?

Inquisition multiplayer will place you and three allies against very long odds, with minimal chance of success. Fortunately, you won't have to learn how to control your character all over again, as the basics learned in single-player mode apply to multiplayer. But there are some key differences between a party member in single player and a party member in multiplayer, such as in how weapons, equipment, and potions are earned and in how crafting materials are gathered.

You can have only *four* active abilities: This is arguably the greatest change to gameplay in multiplayer. Having only half the slots available for active skills in this game mode changes how you want to level your characters and how you want to set them up for combat. You can't be nearly as much of a generalist with any of the classes, since you can't necessarily take everything with you that you want to use.

Abilities cannot be changed in the field: If you feel you made a mistake with your current setup, you're stuck with it until the mission is complete or the party falls.

Equipment cannot be changed in the field: This is a major challenge. You go into missions not knowing initially who you are up against, so you can't equip weapons that you know will be effective against specific types of enemies. Bring your hardest-hitting gear and the best armor you own. It will be up to your skills to make up for any deficiencies in your setup.

Four types of potions can be carried right away: You start with only health potions, but using the store to buy loot can give you a wide variety of potions, and you can equip up to four types. Granted, you won't be able to carry as many of each as the Inquisitor could...

Crafting supplies are heavily limited: You can't just farm iron from every location you fight through. Crafting supplies come only from breaking down old equipment, and you only get equipment from looting chests while on a mission or purchasing chests at the store.

Experience is awarded *after* a mission succeeds or fails: This is another big change from single player. Normally, you would gain experience and could even level up in the middle of combat. Now, you're stuck at the level you entered the mission on until you complete it or die. This means that your first attempts with a fresh party can go very poorly near the end, and even coordinated teams of players will be forced to play it very safe, or they will fall.

You get three falls only: Running out of health in combat is not the end. Your character will be forced to crawl around, looking for allies to help them to their feet. However, on the third defeat, you immediately fall into the Fade, where you are forced to view the action as a wraith while the rest of your party struggles against a foe that has just gained a significant boost in power, a reward for killing an agent of the Inquisition!

THE CHARACTER CLASSES

As in the single-player game, there are three basic classes that all 12 characters fall into: warrior, mage, and rogue. A balanced party will have at least one of each category in their ranks, with the fourth party member falling into whichever preference the group may have. You start multiplayer with the Legionnaire, the Keeper, and the Archer all unlocked and ready to use. Classes generally fall into distinct roles:

Warriors: The frontliners, these characters act as tanks, shielding the party from physical violence while dishing out some of their own.

Mages: The lightly armored magic users combine support skills with powerful elemental magics meant to control and crush the enemy.

Rogues: These characters inflict high damage, mixed with some battlefield control utility. These scouts can kill the enemy quickly from up close or afar, but they won't survive long if they catch too much attention.

To fully clear a mission, you need one of each class at the very least, not just to handle combat better, but to be able to bypass barriers that stand between you and alternative paths through a level or treasure. Warriors can kick down weakened walls, mages can dispel magical barriers, and rogues can pick locked doors.

WARRIORS

You can't survive these missions without a proper warrior leading the team, making first contact with enemies, and holding their attention while the cloth- and leather-wearers ply their trade safe from aggression. Warriors must make themselves the loudest, most obvious threats the enemy sees, even if in reality they are the distraction. Without a warrior's ability to tank, a party will find itself in serious jeopardy.

There are two kinds of warrior you can play as in multiplayer: sword-and-shield warriors and two-handed weapon warriors. The former rely heavily on a shield to mitigate the worst the enemy throws at them, allowing them to withstand the hate of the enemy and return as much of it as they receive. Two-handed weapon warriors rely heavily on the support of mages to keep them protected, in turn allowing the warriors to tear through the hordes with their massive weapons, keeping their attention with pure violence.

DEVELOPER TIP

If you plan to have multiple warriors in your party, pick their skills and equipment to complement each other. Multiple warriors using AoE taunts make a combat harder to control, not easier.

— Matthew Fisher, Senior Level Designer

> LEGIONNAIRE

A walking fortress of dwarven steel

The Legion of the Dead is Orzammar's most famous and dedicated troop of warriors. These dwarves declare themselves dead and venture into the Deep Roads to join the endless fight against the darkspawn pushing toward the gates of their city. Korbin is one of them. A highly decorated warrior from Orzammar, he volunteered for the Legion. As a result of an alliance between the dwarven king and the Inquisition, Korbin now fights on the surface against Thedas's greatest threat.

Ability Trees: Guardian and Combined Arms

The Legionnaire is the warrior you start multiplayer with, and this is where players will either learn how to tank or die trying to learn. The Legionnaire is a sword-and-shield warrior, sturdy and strong, but not particularly agile unless you purchase Combat Roll. He begins with a powerful damage-dealing ability, Payback Strike, but that requires him to have taken or have successfully blocked some form of damage with Shield Wall. Build guard with Shield Wall, hold your ground, and make sure enemies must first get past you before they can reach the others. Early on, you lack the ability to taunt enemies off your allies, so it is imperative that once you have the attention of the enemy, you are the first thing they can see and harm.

> TEMPLAR

A soldier of faith who will step between allies and the strongest magic and demons

Belinda is a noble from Starkhaven and a recent initiate into the templars, taking her vows just months before the Order split from the Chantry. Horrified to see the Order she loved turn against the Chantry she believed in, she left the templars and remained loyal to the Divine. When Justinia was killed, Belinda remained with the newly formed Inquisition, hoping to make things right.

Ability Trees: Divine and Sentinel

The Templar differs from the Legionnaire right out of the gate by starting with a group buff, as opposed to a powerful attack. This should clue you into what the Templar is: a supporter. She starts out able to constantly buff the group's damage with Blessed Blades, which means that everyone on the front line of a fight will be able to kill that much faster. Many of the Templar's unique passive and active abilities are built around improving the damage output or survivability of the group in one way or another. A party with the Templar and the Keeper working together can theoretically be extremely hard to break, but unfortunately the Templar herself isn't quite the damage dealer found in other warrior classes.

> KATARI

A Qunari giant who brings death and destruction

"Katari" means "one who brings death" in Qunlat. The Katari is a Tal-Vashoth mercenary who left the Qun to forge his own path. However, choosing one's own way after being raised to follow orders is difficult. For the moment, the Katari makes his living as a sellsword, paid to fight for the Inquisition. His name is a description of what he does—though he has left the Qun, certain habits are hard to break.

Ability Trees: Onslaught and Tactics

Of the two-handed weapon warriors, Katari is weaker in terms of sheer potential damage output. Unlike the Reaver, the Katari's strength does not have to come at the same grievous cost. The Katari can be set up to reward a finesse player. He's able to set up improvements to his defenses, including guard increases, sooner than the Reaver, while still being more than capable of meting out heavy damage to groups of foes. Earthshaking Strike is one of the Katari's most devastating abilities; it can ruin large groups of foes trying to push past a chokepoint.

> REAVER

A formidable warrior who draws strength from a dark ritual

Tamar is a fearsome warrior who developed her abilities by consuming dragon blood. One of the cultists who lived in Haven during the Fifth Blight, she escaped the Chantry by fleeing into the mountains. Tamar was later captured by Inquisition agents and given the choice to serve or die. Execution in captivity would have been shameful; Tamar wishes to die in battle, the blood of her enemies on her sword and a war cry on her lips.

Ability Trees: Bloodlust and Assault

The Reaver is almost less of a tank and more of a somewhat-better-protected rogue who carries a big two-handed weapon. Correctly specced, the Reaver can help a team quickly devastate groups of enemies surrounding her, and with a good weapon and the right abilities she can hit so hard that she should rarely have difficulty grabbing attention. Tamar is at her best when she's nearly dead: Ring of Pain combined with Devour is more powerful when she's hurting. Getting to that state, particularly on higher difficulties, is risky. Her best friend is an attentive Keeper constantly providing help via the Barrier ability.

MAGES

Mages are highly valued in a balanced party, but they are also the most fragile of all party members. Marksmen can snipe mages from across a hall, possibly killing them outright. Terrible foes like the red templar shadow can slip past a mage's party members in stealth and murder them before they even have a chance to react. They rely on warriors and rogues to prevent the enemy from attacking them. Without the use of the Barrier ability, mages will die in short order.

Despite these seemingly crippling weaknesses, a mage is one of the most valuable party members on a squad. Able to readily exploit the elemental weaknesses of a foe with a stave or spell, enhance the defenses of comrades, or assist in controlling or corralling the enemy into choke points, a mage on a team can mean the difference between success or death.

DEVELOPER TIP

When leveling up and equipping your mages, don't put all your eggs in one basket: Avoid using a staff that has the same damage type as your main offensive spells, or you could be in serious trouble if you encounter tough enemies who are immune to that damage type.

— Matthew Fisher, Senior Level Designer

> KEEPER

A proud elven apprentice who wields Dalish magic to protect or destroy

The Ralaferin clan is renowned throughout Thedas for former Keeper Gisharel's willingness to share Dalish lore with non-elven scholars. Neria was born into the Ralaferin clan and was chosen as Keeper Elindra's apprentice. Trained from youth to defend and serve her people, she takes great pride in her magic and her role as Elindra's First. Now with the Inquisition as a Dalish emissary, Neria does all she can to see that the interests of the Dalish elves are not forgotten amidst the chaos.

Ability Trees: Protection and Primal Spirit

The Keeper is the first, and possibly the most important, mage to have on a squad. Her Barrier ability is available from the outset, and among all mages in multiplayer, her Barrier ability is the strongest. That alone should make her a vital member of any starting group, but her utility extends far into the higher difficulties, where her barriers may be all that stand between the group and a swift death. Her Protection ability tree is worth heavy investment if you intend to focus on being strong support for the team, but her Primal Spirit tree allows you to bring some hefty lightning-based offense to the fight.

DEVELOPER TIP

In multiplayer the Keeper can make the difference between a successful mission or death. Practice good battlefield awareness, cast barriers where they are most needed, stun groups of enemies to give allies a chance to recover, and always know where your party members are and what they are doing.

— Stefan Bekolay, Quality Assurance

> ELEMENTALIST

An explosive personality who controls primal forces

Rion was one of the first mages in the Ostwick Tower to take up the flag of rebellion. Horrified by abuses he saw in Kirkwall, Rion embraced the cause with fervent idealism...and very little sense of its practical costs. His ardor dampened as he saw the rebellion's price measured in lives lost, mage and non-mage alike. Now supporting the call for peace, he went to Haven to await the Divine Conclave's outcome; when the temple was destroyed, his hope for a resolution was lost. Rion signed up with the Inquisition, seeing it as the mages' last chance for peace.

Ability Trees: Destruction and Control

The Elementalist is geared heavily toward offense, as his ability trees show right away. Destruction favors fire, while Control contains many ice- and lightning-based spells, with defensive staples such as Barrier located so far down the Control tree that you would sacrifice much to reach it early on, and even then it is not anywhere close to as powerful as the Keeper's Barrier. Thus, most users of the Elementalist will find themselves standing and delivering from afar, attempting to live up to the old adage: The best defense is to light them on fire, freeze them, or electrocute them before they can get close enough to hurt you.

> NECROMANCER

A cold mistress of magic with terrifying power

Raised in secret in Nevarra by a Mortalitasi mage, Sidony was brought up to revel in her magical abilities. She feels no kinship with mages who do not share her pride and has little but disdain for most other people. Sidony's only goal is to uncover her full potential as a mage, so she hungers for magical knowledge. When news of the Breach reached her, she headed directly to see it for herself, hoping that whatever secrets it held would be the key to her own advancement.

Ability Trees: Gravelord and Permafrost

The Necromancer specializes in spirit- and frost-dealing spells, and she has absolutely no spells that provide special protection to her allies, as befits her personality. Her Gravelord tree contains passive and active abilities that enhance the effects of horror on the enemy, opening them up to extra damage from the rest of the party. Her Permafrost tree contains valuable spells, including a powerful and useful AoE spell, Blizzard. The Necromancer is highly focused on the destruction of the enemy, so parties taking her along for the ride should be prepared to handle the fact that she does not cast Barrier.

> ARCANE WARRIOR

A mage with blades dedicated to an ancient elven art

Like Neria, Cillian was born to the Ralaferin clan. In his youth, he lived apart from his people in order to resurrect a lost elven art: that of the Arcane Warrior. Although he was originally driven by the need to seek glory for his people, Cillian's years of meditation and solitude gave him wisdom and respect for all life. When the Breach opened, he knew his duty was to stand against it, fighting to save all he knows and loves.

Ability Trees: Mentalism and Elemental

The Arcane Warrior is an interesting type of mage, starting off with the powerful Spirit Blade ability, meant to rip through enemy defenses like hot butter. When upgraded it can even deflect ranged attacks! Many of his passive abilities are meant to allow the Arcane Warrior to fight and survive through close combat with the enemy, while dealing heavy damage with the Spirit Blade or the upgraded Fade Cloak. Although he's incapable of casting protective barriers on his allies, one of the Arcane Warrior's Elemental passive abilities, Rejuvenating Barrier, allows any party members with an active barrier to regenerate mana or stamina 35 percent faster! This makes the Arcane Warrior an excellent second mage to bring to the fight alongside the Keeper.

ROGUES

Rogues are problem solvers. If a problem exists, they can solve it, with arrows to the neck or daggers to the spine. If a door needs to be unlocked, they can defeat it. If you need someone somewhere they are not meant to be, a rogue can be that someone. Two varieties of rogue are playable, one specializing in ranged combat and one in up-close-and-personal knife-fighting. The ranged rogues bring a form of control to a fight, as they can set traps and help hold down choke points. The dagger-wielding rogues bring high-damage, single-target focus to a team. Both types of rogue can be set up to quickly put down a target of choice, which makes them excellent at counter-rogue assignments. If the enemy brings scouts or shadows to the field, a rogue can be there, waiting for them to reveal themselves before springing into action.

ARCHER

An expert marksman and sniper

Hall is a survivor from the Wilds, a woodsman and archer. A Dalish hunter rescued him from a bandit raid when he was a child and taught him her skills. But he was human, and not welcome in her clan; once he could fend for himself, he was turned out. Hall wandered for years, never quite finding his place. When a beam of light tore the sky, he was drawn toward it, knowing that it spelled disaster and—for once—understanding that he was needed.

Ability Trees: Marksman and Evasion

Specialized in the bow, the archer named Hall is your first rogue. Capable of singling out and picking off lone targets from afar, the Archer can provide heavy damage that does not fall into particular elemental archetypes. He possesses skills that allow him to stay away from the enemy in a pinch. Additionally, the Archer starts off with the Caltrops ability, which by itself may not seem impressive, but it allows Hall to help the party lock down choke points because the spikes slow and hurt enemies that try to run over them. That very basic starting ability can serve a group well even on Perilous-level missions!

HUNTER

A grizzled trapper and master of the bow

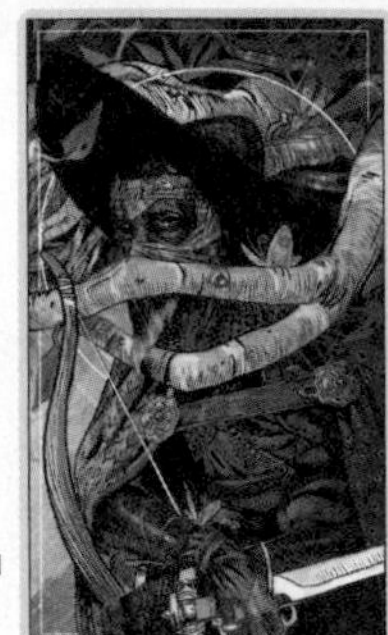

Thornton is a veteran ranger. An experienced soldier, he has served different masters, lived through several wars, and always lived to tell the tale. What the Inquisition faces now, however, is altogether different and far more terrifying, and it will take everything he's ever learned to get through it. But he will get through it—because Thornton always does.

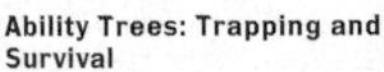

Ability Trees: Trapping and Survival

The Hunter uses unique traps to foul up enemy charges, while also capable of high damage output from afar, like the Archer. Thornton's survivability starts off much greater than the Archer's, with Fallback Plan as one of his two default abilities. The Hunter can also spec into Stealth, and when that's combined with abilities like Full Draw, the Hunter can put down an unsuspecting target very early into a fight, a perfect way to deal with major threats.

ALCHEMIST

An eccentric dwarf with an assortment of strange brews and explosives

Luka remembers the prison in the Vimmark Mountains: She was nobody, clearing out tunnels for the Carta, not important enough to know the truth about why they were there. She watched as the Carta descended into madness, never learning who pulled the strings. When Hawke destroyed the prison, she was trapped, alone and forgotten. It took years, but she got out, using salvaged treasures to blast her own exit to freedom. Then the Inquisition came calling, because they also remembered the prison—and what was held there.

Ability Trees: Alchemy and Cunning

The Alchemist could be considered the brawler of the two dagger rogues, specializing in poisons and explosives meant to bring harm to as many targets at once as possible. With Stealth available at the outset, the Alchemist makes an excellent scout, able to lead the team into dangerous territory and pick out the greatest threats before the fighting begins. A good way to leverage the poison talents available to the Alchemist is to craft a pair of dual-blade daggers for her. She can poison groups of enemies while pounding them with a relentless slashing whirlwind, tossing bombs to cause further chaos.

ASSASSIN

A knife from the shadows.

Argent was named the old Orlesian word for "quicksilver." She is swift, strong, and deadly—trained from birth to be a weapon. Argent has served many masters, sometimes as a bodyguard, often as an assassin. Passed from noble to noble, she was bought and sold like a prized sword, a fact that does not bother her. A weapon has no loyalty—it serves whoever wields it. Now, the Inquisition wields Argent.

Ability Trees: Assassination and Stalker

The Assassin is exactly what her title describes. From the outset, Argent is prepared to come from the shadows and give one unfortunate victim a proper lesson in violence. Early in the Assassination tree, you can pick up Hidden Blades, a powerful skill that when upgraded can hit one target six times, at 300 percent weapon damage a strike.

Much of the Assassin's best work comes in the moment just after she breaks Stealth, and many of her early available skills are meant to enhance that initial brutal burst of damage. Players using the Assassin are well suited to picking off the odd red templar shadow that tried to sneak through the party or hunting down the highly annoying marksmen fielded by the templars or the Venatori. They can also be saviors, able to put down a foe that is on the verge of killing a wounded party member.

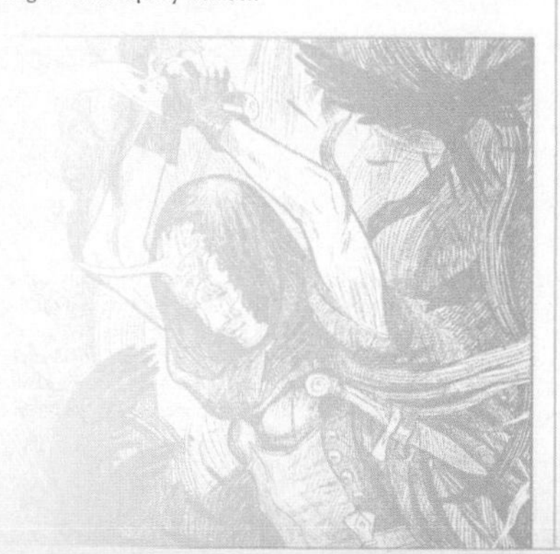

LEVELING YOUR CHARACTERS

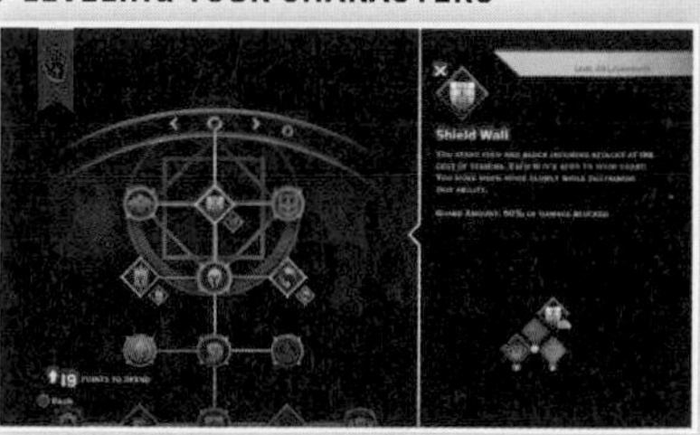

Experience is distributed to the party after a mission succeeds or fails. You gain bonus experience from kill streaks, completing in-mission events, and from completing challenges. Gaining a level earns you one ability point, regardless of race or class, and the maximum level in multiplayer is 20. Because you have only 19 ability points to work with, you really need to think about where you want those points to go, to maximize your character stats while also getting the active abilities you want! You can't get all of the abilities, but you can get some active and passive abilities that really complement how you want to play your character.

A Note on Respeccing

There's a reason why the game makes you confirm whether or not you want to spend an ability point! However, mistakes can be made, and unfortunately there is only one way to undo them: by purchasing loot chests and lucking into getting a character respec in your loot. This will free up your points so you can try to spend them correctly! Just don't mess up twice in a row—you cannot count on respecs always being available.

CHARACTER PROMOTION

At level 20, there is no more you can do for your character in terms of experience. You can choose to keep playing at that level, improving their equipment every chance you get, or you can promote your character.

Promoting characters resets them to level 1. However, depending on the class of the promoted character, you'll receive a bonus point to one of three stats, across *all* of your currently unlocked characters.

Promoting a Warrior: +1 Constitution
Promoting a Mage: +1 Willpower
Promoting a Rogue: +1 Cunning

Don't be afraid to promote characters! You can still use old gear provided it doesn't have a level requirement, which can make reaching level 20 again that much easier!

PREPARING FOR BATTLE

Proper preparation and prudent planning prevents pretty poor performance.

Inquisition multiplayer is not going to hold your hand through battle. If you don't keep up with your weapons and equipment, if you're forgetting to equip potions (and forgetting to restock them), and if you're not setting up your abilities as you unlock them, your experience in the field will be sad and short lived. However, if you take the time to make sure you're ready, you and your allies will eventually be ready to fight through even Perilous-level missions!

> WEAPONS AND EQUIPMENT

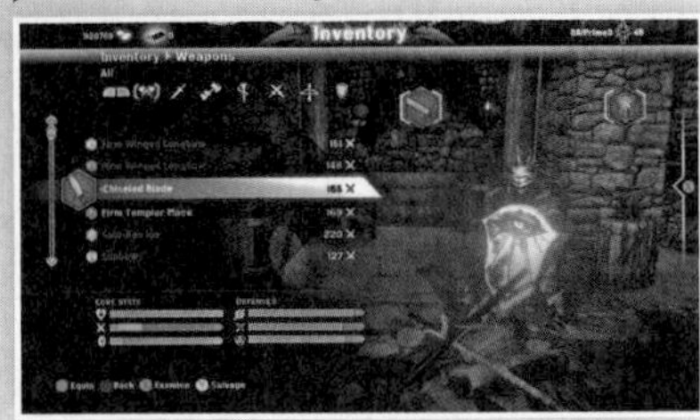

Weapons and equipment work as they do in single-player mode, but there are some slight differences. For one, there is no helmet slot to worry about. Another major difference is that characters in multiplayer stick to only one weapon type. For example, even though Katari is part of the warrior class, he cannot use a sword and shield. He must use two-handed weapons.

Upgrading armor or weapons works similarly as well, but fortunately you don't need to go to a specific menu to attach armor upgrades or runes. Simply go to the upgrade or rune you want to use in the Inventory menu, then select it to go to your Upgrade menu.

A key difference with upgrades in multiplayer is that, unlike in single player, armor upgrades cannot be removed from the armor: They can only be overwritten by a new upgrade. Make sure you're using the upgrade you want on the right piece of gear!

Another function of the Inventory menu is the ability to salvage almost every piece of gear you earn, save for the starting weapons and armor. This is more than just freeing up space: You need to do this to get crafting material.

> CRAFTING

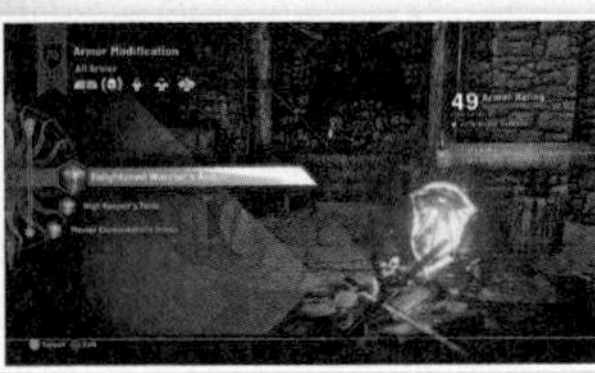

Crafting weapons and armor is one of the most important things you can do to ensure your survival. You start off with schematics that cover the spectrum of armor and weapons you can use across all 12 characters, as well as upgrades for them all. What you don't start with is crafting material. That is earned by salvaging other pieces of equipment you earn while on a mission, or you can purchase loot chests at the store.

Crafting's other major function is to help unlock new characters. As you play the game and complete missions, you earn gold that you can use at the store. The chests purchased at the store have a chance to come with an armor schematic for a new character. If you then craft that character's armor, he or she will become playable. You start out with the Legionnaire, the Archer, and the Keeper, but all others must be unlocked via crafting.

> SETTING SKILLS

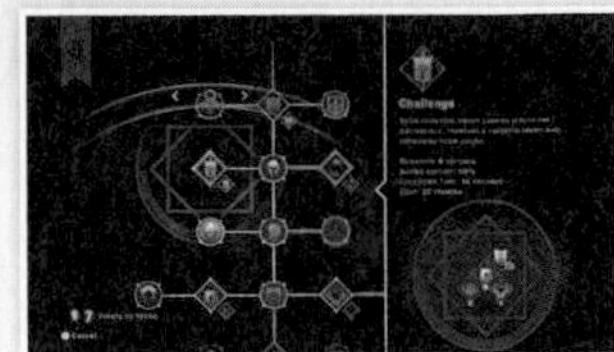

With only four slots available for active abilities, you will not be as versatile as a character can be in single-player mode. You need to pick passive abilities that best serve the active abilities you're going to use, and since you have at most 19 ability points to work with by level 20, you can't just pick your upgrades haphazardly.

> POTIONS

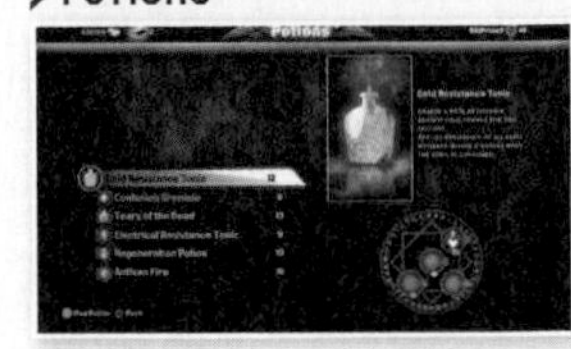

The other four slots on your action bar are used for potions of all kinds. You start multiplayer with two health potions in your inventory, and that's also the maximum of that kind you can carry. A potion can only go into one slot, so you can't just fill out your inventory with nothing but health potions and face-roll through battles. It's typically best to go with a generalist loadout. Specialized potions that increase specific resistances are great, but you can't guarantee what forces you'll run up against, and that means you might have wasted a potion slot on something you can't use. A safe loadout would include health potions and healing mist potions to help allies in need. Jar of bees is a useful AoE attack anyone can carry, and it's especially good at revealing shadows or scouts trying to sneak past a choke point with Stealth.

> THE STORE

The store is where you can spend the gold earned during missions on loot chests and potion chests. When you first start playing multiplayer, the game awards you a starter's chest that contains a variety of potions, and possibly some gear, to help you get settled in for your first mission. Everything else after that must be purchased with your hard-earned cash.

Chests

Chests provide loot and potions. You can't tell what's in them until you open them!

Small Chest: 270 Gold

Contains one random loot item and two potions.

Medium Chest: 725 Gold

Contains three random loot items and three potions.

Large Chests: 1,200 Gold

Contains five random loot items and five potions.

Potions

Potions play a big role in your survival, so you may want to spend money on potion chests specifically to try to build up your inventory.

Healing Potion Crate: 250 Gold

A container of five healing potions. Perfect for restoring your supply.

Mixed Potion Crate: 250 Gold

A container of five random potions for an extra advantage on your operation.

TO THE FIELD

When you're finally ready to go on a mission, select Quick Match to join a game or Create Match to set up a game based on your exact preferences. Quick Match allows you to select your preferred difficulty and destination. Create Match lets you be the leader of a given team, and also allows you to determine difficulty, destination, and whether or not the game is public or friends-only.

Difficulty

There are three difficulty settings, catering to characters of specific levels and strength.

Routine

Routine operations are recommended for beginner players, levels 1-8.

Threatening

Threatening operations are recommended for experienced players, levels 8-16.

Perilous

Perilous operations are recommended for expert players, levels 16+.

> DESTINATIONS

Three destinations are available to players at launch: Elven Ruins, Orlesian Chateau, and Tevinter Ruins. These destinations do not have a set map to follow, because the maps are created by drawing from a series of randomized "rooms" that you fight through. Familiar settings may have passages blocked off that previously were not. Doors that are sealed permanently shut may be unlocked by a rogue during a later run. A solid wall during one visit may be kicked down by a warrior during the next. You might realize, halfway through one area, that you once entered this place from the exit you're now heading toward. There's no way to know for certain what the map will be like until you actually get there, and even the time of day can change. You may arrive late at night to a destination shrouded by darkness, lit by precious few torches, or you could start the operation in the middle of the day.

Elven Ruins

The Elven Ruins are a good location to cut your teeth for the Inquisition. Many of the possible locations you visit throughout the ruins are set up to allow a group to properly funnel the enemy through choke points. The ruins extend above and below ground, and it is below ground where things can get dicier. Tighter spaces to work with, mixed with low lighting, can get a team turned around or, worse yet, flanked with surprising ease.

Orlesian Chateau

Narrow alleys and gaudy hallways make up the majority of the Orlesian Chateau. There's not much space to work with, particularly if your paths take you to the outside of the chateau, where enemies have begun sacking the place, making the alleys treacherous to pass, particularly if there are enemies capable of their own area-of-effect spells. Beware of enemy scouts in Stealth in the chateau; the visibility may be low enough inside that you miss them sneaking toward you.

Tevinter Ruins

The snow-covered Tevinter Ruins are similar to the Elven Ruins in that you'll find yourself passing above and below ground, making your way through the winding tunnels and courtyards. Some sections are open enough that trying to fight off enemies when they have so many ways to approach you is not wise, and on higher difficulty levels you may find your team forced back far from when you made initial contact with a hostile force, seeking a more easily controlled choke point.

> THE ENEMY FACTIONS

Randomly chosen once an operation begins, there are three potential forces your party can come across: red templars, Venatori mages, and demons. All three forces have their own unique enemy types, and they'll force you to change your tactics on the fly. Since you do not get to choose what you're up against, your best bet is to set up your characters to be able to fight all three forces adequately.

> **NOTE** Your first clue about the enemies you're fighting in an operation comes when the camera pans across the start area. For the red templars, you'll see veins of red lyrium. The Venatori have crates of supplies. The demons will have set up strange monuments covered in skulls.

Red Templars

Infused with red lyrium to the point where they barely resemble the men and women they once were, the red templars act as Corypheus's vanguard. Well armed and armored, the templars are an especially fearsome foe to face in melee combat. At range, their threat is mainly provided by red templar marksmen and red templar horrors. The marksmen in particular should be feared, as they can quickly overwhelm a single target if they're allowed to draw a bead on them.

The red templar shadow is one of the most feared melee combat units to run across, both in terms of their strength and their appearance. If you don't spot one before they stealth up, your first evidence of a problem might be when the shadow reappears behind one of your teammates as they fall to the ground dying.

Venatori Mages

Tevinter magisters who feel that the Imperium should return to prominence in Thedas once more have formed an extremist faction known as the Venatori, and they have allied themselves with Corypheus. The Venatori mages themselves bring powerful magicks to bear on unsuspecting parties, while their foot soldiers and marksmen provide the bulk of their muscle.

Like the red templars, the Venatori employ assassins of their own, in the form of the scout. They are just as lethal as the red templar shadow. Now imagine being surprised by a Venatori scout that suddenly gains a shield from a mage comrade...things get very interesting.

Demons

Spreading across Thedas due to the Breach and the many Fade rifts appearing across the continent, the demonic menace is entirely different from the human and once-human forces met among the templars or Venatori. Terrors rip across the ground through portals they form at their feet. Rage and pride demons burn and electrocute unfortunate victims. Coming up against the demons is facing a flood head on; they rush as a horde, trying to overwhelm careless parties quickly, while wraiths support from afar.

THE OPERATIONS

The operations you are deployed on are divided into four phases, culminating in the boss phase, where the enemy commander attempts to put an end to your little band personally. Getting through a phase takes you to a room where you can use a recovery font that heals the entire party, and then you can keep pushing onward.

Phases I and 3

These phases have you attempting to fight your way through the zone you've entered. You face multiple groups of enemies, and there are plenty of side areas you can take the time to explore, if you have the right party members to get through the locked doors, magic barriers, and weakened walls strewn throughout.

Exploration of side areas is important, as you can locate treasure chests filled with gold or equipment. Sometimes, these chests are traps, and you must fend off an undead ambush, possibly lead by an arcane horror. If you're especially unlucky, a revenant could be summoned, and unless your warrior tank is on their game, this can be the end of your little band.

Phases 2 and 4

These two phases can also be called "event phases." A member of the Inquisition war council narrates the nature of the surprise objective. It can be the escort of another Inquisition agent who was stranded in the zone, or it can be recovering weapons or artifacts that the enemy is attempting to destroy. The escort missions are complicated, as the agent will attempt to "help" you during a fight, putting them in the line of fire. The item recovery missions demand that you move quickly: A timer appears on the upper right corner of the screen, telling you how close you are to failing the objective.

Failing these events does not end your mission entirely, but you lose out on bonus gold and experience, so it is worth doing your best to get these events done.

Boss Phase

The last phase of an operation places you against a powerful boss enemy, along with a massive number of reinforcements. A party member must first plant the Inquisition flag at a designated location, triggering this final battle. Each enemy faction has a unique boss, and the battles themselves act as a sort of test of the party's ability. Warrior tanks must tank the boss, and rogues and mages must kill the reinforcements as quickly as possible while supporting the tank fighting the boss as much as possible.

> ENDING AN OPERATION

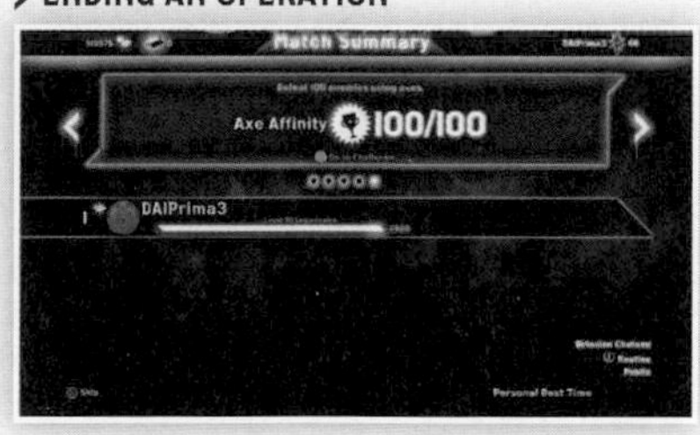

Regardless of whether or not you complete or fail an operation, you earn gold and experience based on how far you manage to go, how many enemies you've slain, and how much treasure you've recovered. The end-of-match screen shows you how much you've earned in all these categories. Additionally, you'll be shown all of the challenges you've made progress on. There are hundreds of challenges, and they all have multiple levels of completion. You'll be busy for quite some time trying to finish them all!

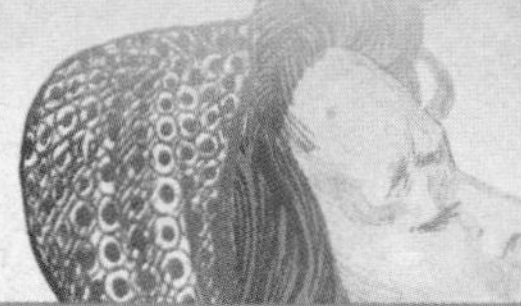

COMBAT TIPS

Here is some general advice that can help you at nearly every skill level.

Prepare to die a lot: You're going to lose. There's no helping this, especially early on. Getting hit by enemies at your level is a painful mistake that you cannot easily recover from. Getting hit on Perilous-level missions can mean an instantly downed mage or rogue.

Bring a defensive ability: If you're a warrior, you should have some skill that can help you build guard. If you're a rogue, an evasive technique will keep you alive should the enemy get too close. Mages should have either one of the teleport abilities or a Barrier skill to protect themselves and their allies.

Communicate: Don't be shy! Battlefield awareness relies on more than just looking at your mini-map for enemy locations. Call out important threats. Designate what needs to die first.

Have patience: Don't rush at the enemy blindly! You need to pull groups into areas that force them through traps you've set, into tight spaces where you can catch multiple enemies in AoE attacks, into areas that force marksmen to come to you rather than shoot you easily from afar.

Use choke points: Every area has them, and you should use them. You simply can't expect to survive by standing in the open and taking attacks from all directions. Get to a place that forces enemies to funnel past a warrior in a confined space where the party can drop AoE attacks and debuffs.

Rogues solve problems: Rogues can put down a single target very quickly, and so they should spec themselves accordingly. Prime targets for a rogue are marksmen, red templar shadows, and Venatori scouts, and these problems should be "solved" very quickly.

Keepers keep parties keepin' on: Early on, the Keeper is the only mage you have, and her Barrier skill is incredibly important. The Keeper is still valued as a party member later in the game, able to keep the group standing in the worst fights imaginable. Get acquainted with this valuable member of the team.

Four Keepers? It'll never work: Building a balanced party is the difference between victory and defeat. While it is possible to succeed with gimmick groups, like four assassins, that depends heavily on player skill and a lot of luck. A balanced group that has at least one warrior, mage, and rogue, with the fourth character doubling up on one of those classes, is the best. Plus, you need at least one of each class to get past the various "class doors" you'll encounter during an operation.

COMPENDIUM

Achievements and Trophies

Icon	Name	Description	Gamerscore	Trophy
	The Wrath of Heaven	Finish the prologue.	20	Bronze (15)
	Opposition in All Things	Close the Breach.	20	Bronze (15)
	In Your Heart Shall Burn	Survive an attack on the Inquisition.	20	Bronze (15)
	Wicked Eyes and Wicked Hearts	Make an impression on the Orlesian Court.	20	Bronze (15)
	Here Lies the Abyss	Face your fears in the Fade.	20	Bronze (15)
	What Pride Had Wrought	Reach an ancient ruin before your enemies.	20	Bronze (15)
	On Burning Wings	Recruit a powerful ally to even the score.	20	Bronze (15)
	Doom Upon All the World	End the threat once and for all.	20	Bronze (15)
	The Brightest of Their Age	Recruit all possible companions in a single playthrough.	20	Bronze (15)
	Beloved and Precious	Commit to a romantic relationship	20	Bronze (15)
	They Who Stand	Recruit a new companion.	20	Bronze (15)
	Speak Only the Word	Gain access to a major city for the Inquisition.	20	Bronze (15)
	Saddled Up	Purchase or secure five different mounts of any kind.	20	Bronze (15)
	Well-Prepared	Craft a weapon or piece of armor in single-player mode.	20	Bronze (15)
	Customized	Enchant or upgrade a piece of equipment in single-player mode.	20	Bronze (15)
	Commander	Complete a timed mission on the war table.	20	Bronze (15)
	Trailblazer	Discover a campsite and establish an Inquisition camp in any wilderness area.	20	Bronze (15)
	Sharp-Eyed	Find and recover a shard identified by an ocularum.	20	Bronze (15)
	Well-Read	Recover a veilfire rune.	20	Bronze (15)
	Skilled	Upgrade any ability once in single-player mode.	20	Bronze (15)
	Specialized	Choose a specialization class.	20	Bronze (15)
	Cavalier	Secure a mount.	20	Bronze (15)
	Synergized	Trigger a cross-class combat with a character you control in single-player mode.	20	Bronze (15)
	Botanist	Harvest 50 herbs from Skyhold's garden in a single playthrough.	20	Bronze (15)
	Wyrmslayer	Kill a high dragon in single-player mode.	20	Bronze (15)

Icon	Name	Description	Gamerscore	Trophy
	Decorator	Purchase any new decoration element for Skyhold.	20	Bronze (15)
	Belle of the Ball	Gain the full approval of the Orlesian court.	20	Bronze (15)
	Hard Hitter	Land a single blow in excess of 1,000 damage in single-player mode.	20	Bronze (15)
	Master Builder	Craft an item from tier 3 materials in single-player mode.	20	Bronze (15)
	Master Alchemist	Upgrade your alchemic potions, grenades, or tonics 30 times in a single playthrough.	20	Bronze (15)
	Dragon's Bane	Slay 10 high dragons in single-player mode.	20	Bronze (15)
	Herald	Finish the single-player campaign on at least Hard without lowering the difficulty.	20	Bronze (15)
	Inquisitor	Finish the single-player campaign on Nightmare without lowering the difficulty.	20	Bronze (15)
	Stargazer	Unlock five astrariums in a single playthrough.	20	Bronze (15)
	Focused	Spend 10 points in a single talent tree with any one single-player character.	20	Bronze (15)
	Well-Funded	Earn 50,000 or more gold across all single-player playthroughs.	20	Bronze (15)
	Keymaster	Enter the heart of the Solasan temple.	20	Bronze (15)
	Pathfinder	Claim an Inquisition camp in every location.	20	Bronze (15)
	Liberator	Liberate three keeps in a single playthrough.	20	Bronze (15)
	High Commander	Complete 50 operations in a single playthrough.	20	Bronze (15)
	Regal	Completely upgrade one throne.	20	Bronze (15)
	Persuasive	Acquire 10 Inquisition agents in a single playthrough.	20	Silver (30)
	Veteran	Reach level 20.	20	Silver (30)
	Peerless	Level up the Inquisition to rank 10.	20	Silver (30)
	People Person	Become friends with at least three of your inner circle in one playthrough.	20	Silver (30)
	Loremaster	Collect 250 codex entries in a single playthrough.	20	Silver (30)
	Demonslayer	Defeat 1,000 demons in single-player mode.	20	Gold (90)
	Invincible	Defeat 2,500 enemies in single-player mode.	20	Gold (90)
	Quartermaster	Complete 20 requisition requests in a single playthrough.	20	Gold (90)
	Marked for Greatness	Seal 75 rifts in a single playthrough.	20	Bronze (15)
	Platinum (PS only)	Earn all 50 trophies.	—	Platinum

QUEST INDEX

NOTE Quests in **bold** are critical path quests.

BIOWARE

Aaron Dibbs
Aaryn Flynn
Adam Philp
Adriana Lopez
Aedan Burnett
Aidan Scanlan
AJ Sharp
Alain Baxter
Alan Hildebrandt
Alec Antrim
Alex Lucas
Alex Scott
Alexander Djuric
Alistair McNally
Allan Schumacher
Allan Smith
Amanda Klesko
Amanda Ruddock
Amanda Tuckey
Amelia Von Haden
Amy Fraser
Amy Walker
András Babós
Andre Santos
Andreas Papathanasis
Andres Rutnik
Andrew Butcher
Andrew Cooke
Andrew Farrell
Andrew Gauthier
Andrew Leung
Andy Kempling
Andy W. Desplenter
Angela Penner
Angela White
Ann Lemay
Anthony Sparapani
Arne Schober
Aron Bend
Arone Le Bray
Ash Matheson
Barbara Klimek
Barrett Rodych
Bastiaan Frank
Ben Carriere
Ben Gelinas
Ben McGrath
Benjamin Blanchard
Benoit Houle
Bill Campbell
Billy Buskell
Bjorn Taylor
Blair Brown
Blake Grant
Boldwin Li
Boyd McKenzie
Brad Paras
Bradley McLeod
Bradley Share
Brandon Dolinski
Brandon Matheson
Brenden Frank
Brenon Holmes
Brent Scriver
Brett Tollefson
Brian Almquist
Brian Mills
Brianne Battye
Bruce McLavy
Bruce Venne
Bryan Derksen
Bryan Johnson
Bryce D'Andrea
Byron Proulx
Caleb Caswell
Cameron Harris
Cameron Lee
Carlo Lynch
Carlos Arancibia
Caroline Livingstone
Carson Fee
Carson McConnell
Casper Konefal
Cassandra Weir
Catherine Lundgren
Celia Arevalo
Charlene Czirfusz
Charles Looker
Chester Szeto
Chris Bain
Chris Buzon
Chris Christou
Chris Cook
Chris Corfe
Chris Hoban
Chris Johnson
Chris Nickerson
Chris Orthner
Chris Priestly
Chris Schanche
Christina McSherry
Christine Mikhaiel
Christopher Kerr
Christopher Pangrass
Christopher Pickford
Christopher Ryzebol
Christopher Smith
Ciaran Begley
Clayton Campbell
Clayton Vaught
Cody Behiel
Cody Paulson
Cody Watts
Colin Jansen
Colin Walmsley
Colleen Perman
Conal Pierse
Cori May
Cory Whyte
Costa Zervos
Craig Graff
Craig Moroney
Cristian Encisco
Curtis Onuczko
Curtis Toye
Dan Fessenden
Dan Plunkett
Daniel Busse
Daniel Carrier
Daniel De Freitas
Daniel Kading
Daniel Leon
Daniel Martin
Daniel Mellar
Daniel Sperry
Daniel Torres
Daniel Trottier
Danielle Butkovic
Darin Casier
Darren Clark
Darren Wong
Dave Gerhart
Dave McGruther
Dave Schaefer
Dave Stenton
David Chung
David Crooks
David Doucet
David Falkner
David Gaider
David Lam
David Mergele
David Murphy
David Robillard
David Robinson
David Rybie
Dean Andersen
Dean Crowell
Dean Roskell
Deann Cable
Deanna Dombroski
Derek Beland
Derek French
Derek Hollan
Devin Doucette
Devon Gardner
Dieter Goetzinger
Dimitar Tzvetanov
Dmitri Prykhodko
Domini Gee
Dominic Belanger
Dominic Lavallee
Dominic Mathieu
Don Nicholas
Dorian Kieken
Duane Webb
Duncan Grimshaw
Dusty Everman
Edward Bassett
Elliot Christian
Elliot Mestas
Emilie Garnier
Eric Isberg
Eric Vervaet
Eric Welwood
Eric Wong
Erin McIntyre
Etienne Chenard
Evan McKnight
Fabien Houlmann
Fabrice Condominas
Fei Wang
Félix Langelier
Fernando Melo
Fernando Secco
Ferret Baudoin
Flor Garcia Ruiz
Francis Lacuna
Francis Thibodeau
Francois Bedard
François Chaput
Frank Gordon
Frank Oracheski
Frank Petreikis
Frederic Macre
Gabriel Moreno Fortuny
Galen Scorer
Gary Ian Stewart
Gavin Burt
Gavin Vankosky
Geordie Moffatt
George Coomber
Graeme Armstrong
Graham Kelly
Graham Scott
Grant Mackay
Guilherme Ramos
Guillaume Anctil
Harold Chaput
Hayden Duvall
Heather Rabatich
Herbert Lowis
Hilary Shapiro
Holly Rees
Hunter Corey Eastman
Ian Bowes
Ian Mitchell
Igor Pereira Machado
Jacky Xuan
Jacques Lebrun
Jae Keum
James Farnel
James Goldman
James Jahraus
James Leung
James Li
James Redford
Jamie Schuit
Janice Thoms
Jarrett Fellows
Jarrett Lee
Jason Barlow
Jason Baxter
Jason Hill
Jason Knipe
Jason Leong
Jason Phillips
Jason Turner
Jay Zhou
JC Delannoy
Jean-Francois Bertrand
Jean-Francois Tremblay
Jean-Remi Desjardins
Jeff Marvin
Jeff Rousell
Jeff Ryan
Jeff Skelton
Jeff Theriault
Jeff Vanelle
Jennifer Chan
Jennifer Cheverie
Jennifer Hepler
Jenny McKearney
Jeremie Voillot
Jeremy Smereka
Jeremy Stemo
Jerome Lee
Jesse Reid
Jessica Hara Campbell
Jessica Merizan
Jessica Potter
Joanna Berry
Joce Legault
Joe Hegarty
Joel Beach
Joel Green
John Boos
John Campbell
John Ebenger
John Epler
John Fedorkiw
John McDonnell
John Santos
Jon Cooper
Jon Galbraith
Jon San Agustin
Jon Thompson
Jonathan Epp
Jonathan Fuller
Jonathan Kha
Jonathan Perry
Jordan Ivey
Jordan Soch
Jordon Davis
Jos Hendriks
Joseph Botardo
Josh Dean
Joshua Langley
Joshua Stiksma
Joshua Wilson
Julien Deschamps
Julien Gagnon
Julio Alas
Julio Juarez
Jun Liu
Justin Edmond
Justin Yong
Kaelin Lavallee
Karin Weekes
Karl Davis
Keith Hayward
Keith Warner
Keith Yerex
Kelly Wambold
Kevin Ng
Kirk McKenzie
Kris Schoneberg
Krista-Leah Goguen

Kristin Warren
Kristina Drozdiak
Kyle Hubbard
Kyle Navarro
Kyle Scott
Laila Aslund
Leah Shinkewski
Leanne Korotash
Lee Evanochko
Lee Kaburis
Lee Scheinbeim
Leo Lucien-Bay
Leo Potvin
Leroy Chen
Liz Lehtonen
Louis Auger
Louis-Philippe Thibodeau
Lukas Kristjanson
Luke Barrett
Mandy Jacek
Marc-Andre Loyer
Marcel Silva
Maren Wilson
Mark Darrah
Mark Kluchky
Mark Ramsden
Mark Wilson
Mary Kirby
Masah Kalugin
Matt Berner
Matt Besler
Matt Komsthoeft
Matt Peters
Matt Rhodes
Matt Servold
Matthew Church
Matthew Fisher
Matthew Goldman
Melanie Faulknor
Melanie Fleming
Michael Burden
Michael Johnson
Michael Kent
Michael Liaw
Michael Webb
Michelle Zupet
Mickael Zerihoun
Mika Uusnakki
Mike Laidlaw
Mike Plouffe
Mike Thistle
Mike Wellman
Mimi YuFan You
Muhammad Ashfaq
Nadia Phillipchuk
Nathan Brierley
Nathan Frederick
Nathan Kozlowski
Nathan Matichuk
Nathan Zufelt
Nathaniel LaMartina
Neil Flynn
Neil Thompson
Neil Valeriano
Nelson Housden
Nicholas Lachapelle
Nick Sadler
Nick Thornborrow
Nicolas Desjardins
Nicolas Latour-Saicans
Nicolas NgManSun
Noel Borstad
Nolan Cunningham
Owen Borstad
Pat LaBine
Patrick Biason
Patrick Chan
Patrick Demkiw
Patrick Irwin
Patrick Michalak
Patrick Weekes
Patrik Karlsson
Paul Dutton
Paul Roffel
Paul Schultz
Peng Zhang
Peter Woytiuk
Phil Shen
Pierre-Luc Loyer
Pierre-Vincent Belisle
Ramil Sunga
Randy Hildebrand
Ray Lim
Ray Sormaz
Raylene Deck
Reid Buckmaster
Renata Cronin
Rhys Twelves
Richard Boisvert
Richard Boylan
Richard Iwaniuk
Rion Swanson
Rob Bartel
Rob Krajcarski
Robert deMontarnal
Robert Freeling
Robert Girardin
Robert McKenna
Robyn Theberge
Rohan Knuckey
Ryan Desaulnier
Ryan Ebenger
Ryan Hoyle
Ryan Love
Ryan Rosanky
Ryan Treadwell
Ryan Warden
Ryan Willcott
Sam Decker
Sandy Thomson
Sarah Demone
Sarah Hayward
Scott Horner
Scott Nye
Scylla Costa
Sean Obrigewitch
Sebastian Hanlon
Shanda Wood
Shane Gaudry
Shane Hawco
Shauna Perry
Shawn Kassian
Sheila Nash
Sherban Gaciu
Sherwin Tam
Sheryl Chee
Simon Jubinville
Simon Lieutaud
Skyler Dawson
Sonia Budac
Sören Hesse
Spencer Koenig
Stefan Bekolay
Stefan Lipsius
Stefano Marchesini
Stephane Levesque
Stephanie Volpi
Stephanie Wong
Stephen Jahns
Steve Klit
Steve Lam
Steve Middleton
Steve Runham
Steven Bigras
Steven Deleeuw
Steven Gilmour
Steven Maschmeyer
Suhas Holla
Suhwan Pak
Susanne Hunka
Sydney Tang
Sylvain Martel
Sylvain Vignaud
Sylvia Feketekuty
Tania Poulter
Tanner Bachnick
Tanner Boyajian
Teresa Meester
Teri Drummond
Terry Fairfield
Thomas Desplenter
Thomas Roy
Thomas Zaplachinski
Tim Golem
Tim Griffith
Tim Saumer
Tim Smith
Tim Song
Tom Perlinski
Tom Rhodes
Tonia Laird
Tony Jung
Trevor Gilday
Tulay Tetiker McNally
Tyler Lee
U Ri So
Vanessa Alvarado
Vanessa Potter
Varden Bates
Vince Waldon
Warren Heise
Wayne Mah
Wen Hua Fan
Will Kuhn
William Brewer
William Kwan
Yanick Roy
Yaron Jakobs
Yuri Leontiev
Yuting Cai
Zousar Shaker

DRAGON AGE™ INQUISITION

Prima Official Game Guide

Written By
David Knight and Alexander Musa

Senior Licensing Manager: Aaron Lockhart
Product Managers: Paul Giacomotto & Shaida Boroumand
Design & Layout: In Color Design
Copy Editor: Deana Shields
Technical Editor: Dan Herrera
Map Editor: Loren Gilliland
Digital Design: Christina LaRoche

SPECIAL THANKS

The following individuals provided legendary efforts to support this guide...specifically Blair Brown, the super ninja dragon-slaying champion of all champions.

Alexander Lee
Alexander Musa
Barbara Klimek
Blair Brown
Bastiaan Frank
Brandon Olafsson
Bryan Johnson
Catalyst Marketing Inc.
Chris Bain
Chris Corfe
Dan Herrera
Daniel Kading
David Knight
Deana Shields
Gianna Giacomotto
Jennifer Cheverie
Karin Weekes
Keith Warner
Loren Gilliland
Luke Barrett
Mark Bernard
Melanie Fleming
Patrick Weekes
Reid Buckmaster
Rick Wong
Rob deMontarnal
Targa Funk
Thomas Perlinski
Tyler Lee
Yaron Jakobs

Prima Games
An Imprint of Penguin Random House, LLC 3000
Lava Ridge Court, Suite 100 Roseville, CA 95661
PrimaGames.com/DAI and Primagames.com

BIOWARE™ 

AU wholesale distributor: Bluemouth Interactive Pty Ltd, Suite 1502, 9 Yarra Street, South Yarra, Victoria, 3141. (+613 9646 4011)

EMAIL: support@bluemouth.com.au

ISBN: 978-0-804-16294-4 / 978-0-804-16297-5 / 978-1-101-89827-7 Printed in the United States of America